Judith M. Anderson

January 1987

MODERN PORTFOLIO THEORY
The Principles of
Investment Management

Modern Portfolio Theory

The Principles of
Investment Management

ANDREW RUDD

&

HENRY K. CLASING, JR.

Foreword by Barr Rosenberg

DOW JONES-IRWIN
Homewood, Illinois 60430

ISBN 0-87094-191-7

Library of Congress Catalog Card No. 81–71910

Printed in the United States of America

1 2 3 4 5 6 7 8 9 0 D 9 8 7 6 5 4 3 2

Foreword

by Barr Rosenberg

Modern Portfolio Theory is the keystone of a disciplined approach to investment. It is concerned with the construction of portfolios and the analysis of their performance.

The past decade has seen rapid growth in the use of portfolio technology, especially among institutional investors—those investors who are responsible for the management of large sums of money. This growth stems from the confluence of several factors. Perhaps the most critical factor has been the accumulation of experience in MPT applications, through the happy cooperation of portfolio theoreticians and practitioners. This book may be said to have originated in one such exchange, for the authors were respectively consultant and client, academician and practitioner, when they met and planned this book.

The materials included in this text therefore reflect investment procedures that are actively used. Indeed, many of the materials were developed by associates at BARRA, a consulting firm whose clients include many of the larger institutional investors and owners of funds and other investment consultants throughout the country. The work was made possible by the support and encouragement of professional investors, and their suggestions and criticisms have contributed greatly to its effectiveness.

This book is a very valuable compendium of modern practice in portfolio construction and portfolio analysis. The methods which are described are complementary to investment research, and play a part in the management of hundreds of billions of dollars worth of securities. The theory underlying the applications is a natural extension of the pioneering work of Markowitz, Sharpe, Lintner, Mossin, and others. Although termed *modern,* the developments of the past decade have been in the nature of refinements of their earlier work, so that in the rapidly changing world of investments the subject has already ripened to middle age. On the other hand, the careful exposition of implementation is truly modern for it reflects practice which is current.

There have been rapid strides in the practice of portfolio theory, and widely increased acceptance of its relevance in recent years. This book is unique in reflecting the current state of the art, and is therefore an especially relevant guide for the investor. The authors have done us all a signal service in their imaginative synthesis and clear presentation of the subject.

Preface

Our aim in this book is to describe portfolio theory and its implications for investment management. The challenge we faced was to tie together in one source and in readable form the basic assumptions and many of the practical applications of the body of knowledge which has become known as *modern portfolio theory*. Many of the important ideas in finance and investment are contained in a large collection of separate, highly technical reports, and since these ideas are heavily based on mathematical statistics, a new student of the topic who reads these reports could easily become inundated in detail. Fortunately, complicated as the mathematics may appear, the foundations of modern portfolio theory rest on a set of assumptions that lead to some very clear conclusions, all of which can be plainly stated in English.

Each chapter of this text is presented with a minimum of mathematics. Graphic presentations are used as a substitute for equations where possible, and case studies are presented to offer practical examples. For those desiring a more rigorous presentation, supplements included after each chapter derive and explain the important results. Beyond this, the book is heavily referenced, so that an avid student is presented with enough material to thoroughly cover the subject matter.

This book has been designed for a variety of readers. We hope that its organization will make it accessible to investment practitioners who have a desire to discover the message of modern portfolio theory without wading through lengthy mathematical treatises. We also hope that MBA and Ph.D. students will be encouraged to develop their own ideas by our descriptions of the investment processes and by the models sketched in the supplements. The book is not designed to be an encyclopedic manual of financial techniques. Nor is it meant to be a mathematical text. Rather, it presents the important investment concepts by way of simple paradigms. These paradigms also serve to introduce various subtleties of investment management which must be faced by financial organizations.

Chapter 1 and Supplement 1 present the foundations on which the remainder of the book rests. Chapter 1 reviews the essentials of portfolio theory with a heavy emphasis on graphic description. For those who would like a review of applied statistics, Supplement 1 covers the essentials. We stress that Chapter 1 and Supplement 1 are merely a review, and we encourage readers who wish to gain a broader perspective or other viewpoints to study some of the referenced articles.

Chapter 2 examines risk and reward and covers the basic elements of these two important concepts. This leads to a discussion of both active and passive strategies. Chapter 3 expands the coverage of risk measurement and introduces the concept of using fundamental measures to aid in the prediction of risk. The next logical step is the estimation of reward, which is covered in Chapter 4. A discussion of the nature of efficient markets introduces several approaches to estimating abnormal returns, including a complete description of a dividend discount model. The application of the preceding topics is the design of portfolios, which is briefly introduced in Supplement 4 by an analysis of three different styles of portfolio management. Supplement 4 also gives an analysis of the value-added in the research process.

Chapter 5 presents portfolio management strategies, including several portfolio optimization techniques. Supplement 5 offers a case study of a yield-biased passive portfolio (a recent innovation) from an optimization perspective. At this point, the basic theory has been covered and several examples of practical applications have been provided.

In Chapter 6 we emphasize a major organizational problem of asset management, namely the multiple management of portfolios. We firmly believe that the organization of multiple portfolio managers is one of the most important problems faced by plan sponsors today. It is also, perhaps, the least understood problem. Chapter 7 covers another important application of modern portfolio theory, performance attribution and measurement.

The final chapter offers an overview of the current state of the art and an analysis of the current trends and some likely future directions. Although widely acknowledged only recently, MPT is an important force for change in today's investment community. If this work communicates the reasons for that fact and helps introduce many of today's investment practitioners to this growing field, the authors will feel that their efforts have been well spent.

As usual with a book covering a complex subject, the authors owe many debts for friendly and informative help that they received along the way. Without doubt, our greatest debt is to Barr Rosenberg, whose influence was felt throughout the writing of the book. William Sharpe and Mark Rubinstein read the entire manuscript and provided detailed criticisms and suggestions for improvement; the book is considerably better for their comments.

Hal Arbit, at the American National Bank in Chicago, read part of an early draft of the manuscript and provided useful comments. David Tierney, at the Standard Oil Company (Indiana), and Roger Sayler, at the Morgan Guaranty Trust Company, generously prepared reviews of individual chapters. Arnie Wood of Batterymarch, Ron Lanstein of BARRA, and John Nagorniak of State Street Bank offered many helpful ideas. Several practitioners, particularly Phil Binzel, David Shaw, and George Williams, generously imparted their views of the state of the art. At the Harris Bank, Richard Caldwell, John Kirscher, and Tom Richards took part in many helpful discussions. In the area of practical application of forecasting and measurement techniques, Steve Einhorn and Arnold Moskowitz deserve thanks.

The exposition was greatly improved by comments received during a lecture series based on the book that one of the authors gave at the Bankers Trust Company. Our thanks go to Allan Martin, who arranged the series, and to the portfolio managers and security analysts who took part in many excellent debates. Several other audiences unknowingly provided a fertile proving ground for parts of the material. In contrast, the students of Investment Management at the Graduate School of Business and Public Administration at Cornell University may have been only too well aware that they were being cast in the role of guinea pigs. We hope that acknowledgment of their help is sufficient recompense.

This book formed the basis for a one-semester course on Investment Management for second-year MBA students specializing in Finance at Cornell University. In addition, Professor Barr Rosenberg at the University of California at Berkeley and Professor William Sharpe at Stanford University also pretested the book in the classroom. We are grateful for their comments and for the comments of students in their courses.

Our thanks also go to Gloria Mark, Irene Silverman, and Jill Welch, who at various times provided editorial assistance, and to Karen Carleson, Barb Drake, and Peggy Rose, who typed the manuscript through seemingly interminable revisions.

Andrew Rudd
Henry K. Clasing, Jr.

Contents

About the Notation in this Book

We have tried to use notation consistently throughout the book, and we include here a list of all the symbols used, with a description of their meaning. There are three subsections. The first describes our conventions for matrix notation; the second describes the meaning of special subscripts, superscripts, and other symbols; and the third is an alphabetical list of the variables used in the text. Occasionally the same symbol is used in different places to denote different things. Where this happens, we indicate the location of the particular usage.

Matrix Notation

Matrix notation is designed to simplify the burden of explaining mathematical derivations when working in several dimensions or with many variables. It has its own set of rules, which are actually very straightforward and can be found in most statistics and econometrics texts. For readers wishing to learn more about this valuable language, we suggest:

Johnson, J. *Econometric Methods*. New York: McGraw-Hill, 1972. Chapter 4.

Theil, H. *Principles of Econometrics*. New York: John Wiley & Sons, 1971. Chapter 1.

Briefly, a vector is a one-dimensional set of elements, which by convention is written as a column. For instance, the investment holdings in a two-security portfolio may be written:

1

$$\begin{bmatrix} h_1 \\ h_2 \end{bmatrix}.$$

To indicate the transpose of column vector to row vector, we use a prime (');
that is, the portfolio holdings may also by written as $[h_1\ h_2]'$.

A matrix is a two-dimensional set of elements. For instance, the covariance
matrix between the returns on the two assets can be written as:

$$\begin{bmatrix} V_{11} & V_{12} \\ V_{21} & V_{22} \end{bmatrix},$$

and its transpose as:

$$\begin{bmatrix} V_{11} & V_{21} \\ V_{12} & V_{22} \end{bmatrix}',$$

where V_{jk} is the covariance between assets j and k (j, $k = 1$, 2) and by convention the first subscript (j) refers to the row and the second subscript (k) refers
to the column.

Vectors and matrices are indicated by symbols printed in boldface. A lowercase symbol represents a vector, while an uppercase character represents a
matrix. For instance, the holding vector could be denoted by:

$$\boldsymbol{h} = \begin{bmatrix} h_1 \\ h_2 \end{bmatrix},$$

and the covariance matrix could be denoted by:

$$\boldsymbol{V} = \begin{bmatrix} V_{11} & V_{12} \\ V_{21} & V_{22} \end{bmatrix}.$$

Subscripts and Special Symbols

1. Uppercase subscripts generally (but not always) denote categories of assets.

A	Aggregate portfolio
F	Risk-free asset
M	Market portfolio
N	Normal portfolio
P	Portfolio in question
R	Residual component
S	Systematic component
T	Target value of an attribute

Occasionally two subscripts are used; e.g., *PR* is used to denote the residual component of a particular portfolio attribute.

2. Lowercase subscripts generally refer to particular assets, particular managers, or the timing of events; e.g.:

j, k, l, n	Individual assets or managers
t	Time index
min, max	Minimum, maximum

Sometimes two subscripts are used (for instance, r_{nt}) to denote some attribute of a particular security in a particular time period (excess return of stock *n* at time *t*).

3. Only one superscript, namely *R*, is used frequently; the others are used only locally.

R	Required return
A	Active
c	Cumulative
min	Risk minimizing
0	Original (or prerevision) value
opt	Optimal
*	Logarithm

4. Special symbols:

'	Prime to denote vector or matrix transposition
^	Hat to denote an estimate
—	Overscore to denote average value
$(\cdot)^+$	Maximum of · and zero
E[ ]	Expectation operator
Var[ ]	Variance operator
Cov[,]	Covariance operator
Log( )	Logarithm function
exp( )	Exponential function

Alphabetical List of Symbols and Their Description

a_j, a_A, a_M, a_M^R	Abnormal return on asset (category) *j*, *A* or *M*
$\hat{a}$	Estimate of intercept in regression equation

A	Matrix of constraint coefficients (Supplement 5)
A	Variance matrix of abnormal market returns; explained variance matrix (Chapter 6)
α_j, α_P, α_j^R, α_P^R	Alpha, or expected abnormal return
b_j, b_{jk}, b_{Pj}	Factor loadings (Supplement 3)
b_j	Dependence-adjustment factor (Chapter 6)
b_i, $\hat{b}_i$	Estimate of coefficient on an independent variable in a regression
b	Vector of right-hand-side values in portfolio optimization
β_j, $\hat{\beta}_j$, β_P, β_T	Beta, or exposure to the market
c	Continuously compounded rate of return (Supplement 1)
c	Coefficients in a regression equation (Chapter 3)
c	Covariance between forecasts of abnormal return by two managers (Supplement 6)
C, C_S	Certainty equivalent rate of return
C_t	Coupon payment at time t (Chapter 8)
C	Covariance matrix
γ_{Pj}	The discrepancy between the jth factor loading on the portfolio and the equal-beta levered market portfolio
γ_P	The vector of discrepant factor loadings
d_j	The slope of the risk bowl in the direction of asset j or the partial derivative of portfolio residual standard deviation with respect to the holding in asset j (Chapter 3)
d_t	Discount factor to be applied to a payment at time t (Chapter 8)
d_{kj}	The kth descriptor value for asset j
D_t	Dividend payment at time t
δ_j, δ_{Pj}	The active holding in a portfolio
Δ	A small increment (as in ΔE or ΔV)
e and ε	Error term in a regression
E_i, E_M, E_P	The expected rate of return
f_j	Rate of return on a factor

f_j	Feasibility adjustment (Supplement 5)
F_{jl}	Covariance between factors j and l
F	Principal or par value of a bond (Chapter 8)
F	The factor covariance matrix
g	The geometric mean return
$h_j,\ h_{Pj},\ h_{Mj}$	Holding of the jth asset in a portfolio; when there may be some confusion as to which portfolio, another subscript is used
$H\beta,\ H\hat{\beta}$	Historical beta
$i_j,\ i_F,\ i_P,\ i_M$	The rate of return on asset (category) j, F, P, or M
J	The total number of descriptors or the total number of managers
κ	The relative aversion between residual and systematic risk
λ	Aversion to risk (as measured by variance)
λ_s	Aversion to risk (as measured by standard deviation)
Λ_β	Disutility from deviating from the beta target
Λ_ω	Disutility from residual risk
Λ_Y	Coefficient of (linear) yield in utility function
Λ_C	Disutility from deviating from yield target
Λ_T	Amortization factor for transactions costs
M	The mean-square-error matrix
$v,\ \bar{v}$	Mean absolute residual return (Supplement 3)
N	The number of assets or the number of periods
p_i	Probability of an event (Supplement 1)
p_k	Purchase variable derived in portfolio optimization (Supplement 5)
P	Price of a security
π_{ij}	Correlation between predictions from managers i and j
q_j	Probability of an event (Supplement 1)
q_l	Sale variable derived in portfolio optimization (Supplement 5)
q_j	The covariance between the market forecast for manager j and the realized unexpected return (Chapter 6)

r_j, r_P, r_M	The random excess return
$r_{t,t+1}$	Forward rate of interest over the interval between t and $t + 1$ (Chapter 8)
R_t	Spot rate of interest over the interval between now and time t (Chapter 8)
R	Residual variance matrix (Chapter 6)
ρ_{jk}	The correlation coefficient between assets j and k
ρ_j	The correlation between manager j's forecast and the realization (Supplement 6)
$\hat{s}(\,\cdot\,)$	Standard error of $(\,\cdot\,)$ (Supplement 1)
s_j	Coefficients in a regression model (Supplement 3)
s	Slack variables (Supplement 5 and Chapter 6)
S_j, S_P, S_M	The standard deviation of asset (category) j, P, or M
σ_j	The specific standard deviation of asset j
$\sigma_j^2, \overline{\sigma}_j^2$	The specific variance of asset j
θ	The mean/variance ratio
$u, \hat{u}$	The residual return
U, U_P, U_{PS}, U_{PR}	Utility
V_{jk}	The covariance between assets j and k
V	Covariance matrix
V_P, V_M	The total variance of category P or M
w_j	The investment proportion of manager j in the total portfolio
$\omega_P (\omega_P^2)$	The residual standard deviation (variance)
x_i	Bond characteristic (Chapter 8)
x_{Nk}, x_{Ak}, x_{jk}	The normal value of the portfolio exposure to the kth element of risk (Chapter 6)
y_j, y_P, y_M, y_T	The cash yield
Y	Yield to maturity on a bond (Chapter 8)
$Z_j, Z_P, \overline{Z}$	The ratio of expected return to standard deviation, or information ratio
$Z_j^2, Z_P^2, Z_{PS}^2, Z_{PR}^2$	The Sharpe ratio, or the square of the information ratio

Chapter 1

Introduction to Portfolio Theory

Modern portfolio theory (MPT) is the scientific approach to investment. It deals with the selection of portfolios by investors who wish to maximize the expected reward consistent with their individual willingness to bear risk. The two major building blocks of the theory are Dr. Harry M. Markowitz's pioneering work *Portfolio Selection: Efficient Diversification of Investment,*[1] which began as a doctoral dissertation in 1950–51, and much of the research—conducted originally by Professors Cootner[2] and Fama[3]—concerning the random character of stock prices.

Markowitz's early work was an attempt to rigorously apply probability theory to portfolio selection with the aim of integrating the degree to which certain securities did or did not move in unison. His major contribution was the con-

---

[1]Harry M. Markowitz, *Portfolio Selection: Efficient Diversification of Investment* (New York: John Wiley & Sons, 1959).

[2]Paul Cootner, *The Random Character of Stock Market Prices* (Cambridge, Mass.: MIT Press, 1964).

[3]Eugene F. Fama, "The Behavior of Stock Market Prices," *Journal of Business,* January 1965, pp. 34–105.

cept of an efficient, or optimal, portfolio that would provide the greatest expected return for the level of risk an investor was willing to assume. Unfortunately, the Markowitz approach was beyond the capacity of most 1950-vintage computers and the scope of the vast majority of the investment practitioners of the time.

The concept of an efficient market is the result of empirical research into the behavior of security prices. Initially, the focus of market efficiency was aimed at what is commonly called the random walk hypothesis. Under this hypothesis, stock price changes between successive intervals of time are unrelated, so that future stock price changes are random and thus unpredictable. A more useful definition of an efficient market is one in which a security's price is a fair estimate of its true value. In other words, the price of a security reflects the consensus of all market participants as to its correct value. It would be naive to believe that market inefficiencies can be consistently and systematically exploited in highly competitive and developed capital markets. By implication, the opportunities to earn abnormal profits cannot be common.

During the three decades since the appearance of Markowitz's original work, much effort has been expended to make this approach to investment management more susceptible to measurement and therefore more applicable. Perhaps the greatest credit for the early work along these lines should go to Professor William F. Sharpe of Stanford University for his many articles and books dedicated to the application of Markowitz's early concepts.[4] In recent years, major refinements in the measurement process have been developed by Barr Rosenberg, professor of business administration at the University of California at Berkeley, and his associates at BARRA.[5] As a result of this constant inquiry and research, MPT has evolved into a practical tool which has achieved respectability both from its theoretical foundations and its successful implementation.

The key to understanding the importance of MPT lies in one concept—measurement. The world of investment, so dependent on the vagaries of human behavior and judgment, has been able to exist for centuries with customs that were almost beyond question. The advent of better measurement is bringing this to an end. The age of the computer, systematic analysis, and rational decision making based on economic theory has dawned.

Risk and Reward

But what are the basic precepts of MPT, and how are they being applied? Perhaps the most important precept is that all investment decisions, as well as the behavior of the investment vehicles or securities, exist in a world of uncertainty. This implies that decisions must be made only after explicitly acknowl-

---

[4]William F. Sharpe, *Portfolio Theory and Capital Markets* (New York: McGraw-Hill, 1970); and William F. Sharpe, *Investments* (Englewood Cliffs, N.J.: Prentice-Hall, 1978).

[5]A financial consulting partnership founded by Barr Rosenberg and based in Orinda, California.

edging the impact of risk, which, in turn, requires the application of statistics and probability theory.[6] Each security, or each portfolio of securities, offers a potential reward if the purchase and subsequent sale result in a profit. This profit from price appreciation, when combined with any dividends received during the holding period, defines what is known as a total return, or *return*. When an attempt is made to predict returns, each return estimate is multiplied by its probability of occurrence, and these products are then summed to form the result, which is termed the *expected return*.

The annual return on a security or a portfolio will be a number, such as 0.8 or 1.1. These numbers indicate that the value of the investment (including any dividends received) at the end of the year is 80 percent or 110 percent of the value at the beginning of the year. We will also use the term *rate of return* to describe the rate of appreciation or depreciation of the investment over the holding period. A rate of return with a magnitude of -0.1 or 0.2 would indicate that the investment has declined by 10 percent or increased by 20 percent. Clearly, the rate of return is equal to the total return minus one.

The *expected return* informs the investor of the average reward that may be anticipated from investing in the security over the holding period. It is a measure that has meaning at the beginning of the period; at the end of the period, the actual realized return may be quite different from the return that was anticipated. This difference—the uncertainty in the security return—is a result of changes in the economy that were not expected at the beginning of the period.

The characterization of investment uncertainty is more complicated than defining the expected return. It is an attempt to measure the variability, or *risk*, in the return on the security or portfolio over the holding period. A measure of this uncertainty termed the *standard deviation* tries to account for both the probability and the magnitude of a loss or gain. Therefore, the expected return (reward) is the average total return anticipated over a specific holding period, while the risk indicates the potential variation around that expected return and is characterized by the standard deviation, which captures the degree of dispersion (or spread) of a probability distribution about its expected value.

A simple example of the standard deviation as a measure of dispersion is the familiar bell-shaped curve, which most people are first exposed to in college when a professor grades the results of a test on a scale designed to group a percentage of the class within certain bands. The statistical term for this bell-shaped curve is the *normal probability distribution*. The range from plus one standard deviation to minus one standard deviation encompasses roughly 68 percent of the values under the curve; the range from plus two to minus two standard deviations encompasses 95 percent; and the range from plus three to minus three standard deviations includes 99.5 percent of all values.[7] In order to distribute grades on the basis of relative performance rather than the actual

---

[6]Since an understanding of elementary statistics is fundamental to the application of MPT, we include a brief review of the important concepts in the supplement to this chapter.

[7]The exact values are: one standard deviation, 68.26 percent; two standard deviations, 95.46 percent; and three standard deviations, 99.74 percent.

test scores, a professor assigns a grade according to the percentile of the normal distribution in which the score falls. This makes it possible to control the proportion of students in certain grade ranges, for instance to ensure that two thirds of students have grades in the range from B + to D −.

The application to investment management is straightforward. In specifying an annual standard deviation of 40 percent (a typical value for a common stock), we are making a statement about the likely range of outcomes at the end of the year. We are stating that there is a two-thirds probability of the return lying in the range of 40 percent on either side of the expected value and that there is a 95 percent chance of the return lying in the range from the expected value less 80 percent to the expected value plus 80 percent. Clearly, the larger the range of dispersion, the larger the standard deviation. Since security prices fluctuate over time and can be characterized by probability distributions, the standard deviation as a measure of risk seems both valid and applicable.

Another precept of MPT is that efforts to attain a greater expected return generally entail a greater degree of risk. This practical observation of reality has engendered, as a benchmark for measuring performance, a concept termed the *risk-free rate of return*. While there is some disagreement among practitioners on what best reflects this concept, the most widely accepted instrument is the 90-day Treasury bill, which is as close to riskless as can be practically achieved.[8] This concept can best be described by a diagram, as shown in Figure 1.1.

The point A, intersecting the vertical axis of the diagram at 6 percent, represents the risk-free rate of return. The point B can represent the complete investment of all available funds in a portfolio of securities not including the risk-free security. The set of portfolios obtained by mixing the risk-free security and portfolio B lie along the straight line between A and B. If one wanted to borrow funds (or purchase securities on margin) based on the equity of the invested portfolio, one could purchase additional amounts of risky investments (portfolio B) which would offer a greater expected return commensurate with the greater degree of risk assumed. Such a *levered portfolio* can be represented by point C. If further borrowing is desired in order to produce an even greater expected return, a portfolio such as that represented by point D could be constructed.[9] The important concept is that, depending upon the relative holdings of risk-free, low-risk, and high-risk securities, a whole series of portfolios with varying degrees of expected reward and risk can be formed.

---

[8] In nominal terms, that is. The impact of uncertain inflation causes even Treasury bills to become risky in real terms. One caveat is that Treasury bills have a particular advantage (satisfaction of reserve requirements) for one class of investors who may consequently bid up their price. This "clientele effect" may effectively reduce Treasury bill yields for investors who cannot take advantage of this characteristic.

[9] The truth of the proposition that portfolios A, B, C, and D lie along a straight line is shown in the supplement to Chapter 2.

Figure 1.1
Risk and Return Combinations for a Risky Portfolio and Risk-Free Security

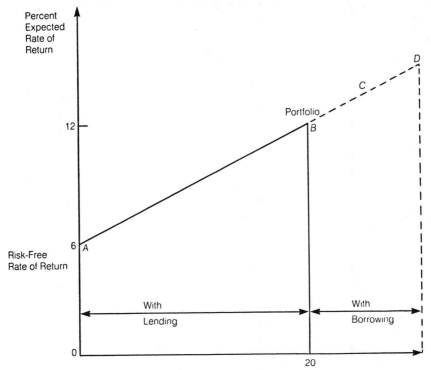

Our explanations of MPT to this point have introduced the idea that a reward is to be gained from investing in a security or portfolio and that a certain degree of risk is encountered in attempting to achieve that reward. The expected return is the average reward which is anticipated from holding a particular portfolio. The risk, or uncertainty, of this expected return is measured by the standard deviation of the return. This leads us to an important assumption, namely that *an investor is willing to choose among portfolios based entirely on the two measures of expected return and standard deviation of return.*

Investor Preferences

The next requirements to enhance the applicability of the theory are rules an investor would use for selecting an optimal portfolio. Figure 1.2 shows four portfolios. The expected rate of return is measured along the vertical axis, and the standard deviation of return is measured along the horizontal axis.

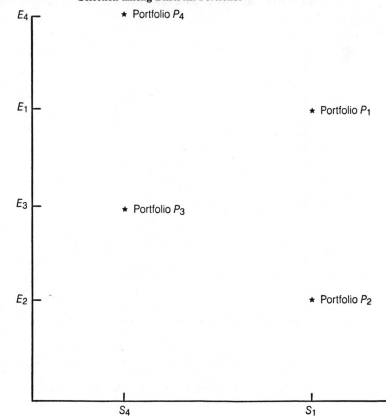

Figure 1.2
Selection among Different Portfolios

Percent Expected Rate of Return

E_4 — ★ Portfolio P_4

E_1 — ★ Portfolio P_1

E_3 — ★ Portfolio P_3

E_2 — ★ Portfolio P_2

S_4 S_1

Percent Risk (standard deviation of return)

Portfolios P_1 and P_2 have the same standard deviation, but the expected rate of return is higher for portfolio P_1. Portfolios P_3 and P_4 also have identical standard deviations, which are less than the standard deviations of portfolios P_1 and P_2; but again, the expected rates of return differ, with portfolio P_4 having a greater expected rate of return than portfolio P_3.

Which portfolio will investors choose? If two portfolios offer the same reward, but at different levels of risk, then the rational investor will choose the portfolio with the lower risk. Similarly, if two portfolios have the same risk, but different levels of reward, then the rational investor will choose the portfolio with the greater reward. The rules are: expected return is "good," with more being better than less, all other things being equal; risk is "bad," with less being better than more, all other things being equal. If these two rules are applied to the examples of Figure 1.2, portfolio P_1 is preferred to portfolio P_2, since it offers a higher expected return for the same amount of risk, and portfolio P_4 is preferred to portfolio P_3 for the same reason. Among all four portfolios, portfolio P_4 is the most preferred because it offers the greatest expected return for the smallest degree of risk.

In the above example, the preference of any rational investor is clear. But what would the investor's preference be if the choice were between portfolios P_1 and P_3. Unfortunately, portfolio P_1 has greater reward and greater risk than portfolio P_3, a situation not covered by our rules. In order to choose between these two portfolios, and indeed between other portfolios with different rewards and risks, we need a much more general method of analyzing investor preferences.

This general method is provided by the use of *indifference curves,* a concept which originated in the field of economics. As the term suggests, investors have the same preference for all portfolios that lie along the same indifference curve. Since all portfolios on the same indifference curve are equally preferred, investors are indifferent to which one they hold. Figure 1.3 offers two extreme cases. Case A is a family of curves (straight lines) that reflect investors' willingness to accept any degree of risk in order to achieve a given expected return. Along the horizontal indifference curve I_3, any portfolio offering the expected rate of return of 10 percent is indistinguishable from any other portfolio offering the same return, without regard for the amount of risk taken. Common sense would suggest that this is not a very practical approach.

The other extreme case, shown as case B, is the total risk averter who will not tolerate any additional risk in order to achieve a greater expected return. In other words, the investor is indifferent to all portfolios that have the same risk level no matter what expected return is promised. Again, experience indicates that while such rewards are ideal, they are seldom, if ever, to be found in real life. One usually must take greater risks in order to realize greater rewards.

In actuality, indifference curves lie somewhere in the middle of the two extreme cases just given. As Figure 1.4 indicates, the steep upward-sloping curves of case A approach the vertical indifference curves of Figure 1.3 but are obviously less extreme. The flatter curves of case B indicate an investor who is willing to take a greater degree of risk in order to achieve the same degree of expected return as that achieved by the cautious investor in case A. Indifference curves indicate portfolios for which the investor is indifferent; in other words, the level of satisfaction, or *utility,* is constant along an indifference curve where the utility is evaluated from a function which combines the reward and risk preferences of an investor into a simple relation.

The indifference curves in both cases are upward sloping, indicating that all risk-averse investors will demand greater expected return for bearing additional risk. The slope at each point along the curve measures the degree of risk aversion (the "risk/reward trade-off"). For instance, the curves in case B are less steep at all points than those in case A, implying that investor B demands less compensation for risk than investor A or that investor B is willing to be more

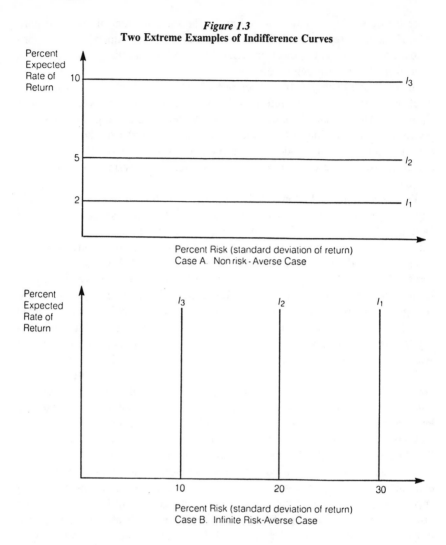

Figure 1.3
Two Extreme Examples of Indifference Curves

aggressive in search of additional expected return compared to investor A. In short, investor A is more risk-averse than investor B.

From the indifference curves in Figure 1.4, we learn not only the risk/reward trade-off but also the relative ranking of different investment opportunities. Because the investor is indifferent to all portfolios that plot along a single indifference curve, we can find the equivalent risk-free return for those portfolios by looking at the point where the curve cuts the expected return (vertical) axis. It follows from the definition of the indifference curve that all portfolios on, for example, the indifference curve I_3 provide the same level of utility to the investor. A risk-free rate of return of C_3, which lies on this curve, is as beneficial to the investor as any of the portfolios with greater risk on I_3.

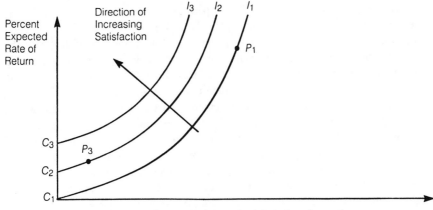

Figure 1.4
Two Cases of Families of Indifference Curves

Percent Risk (standard deviation of return)
Case A. Steep Upward-Sloping Curves of Highly
Risk-Averse Investor

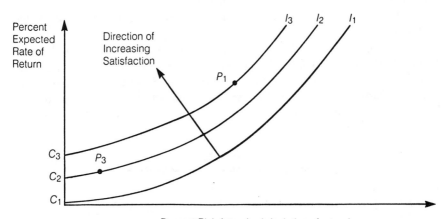

Percent Risk (standard deviation of return)
Case B. Less Steep Upward-Sloping Curves of
Average or Below-Average Risk Averter

Along the vertical axis, all portfolios provide certain rates of return, shown as C_1, C_2, and C_3. Since C_3 is greater than both C_1 and C_2, all portfolios plotting along I_3 are preferred over those plotting along I_2, which, in turn, are preferred over those plotting along I_1. (This ranking also holds for the curves shown in Figure 1.3.) We can now infer that portfolio P_3 is preferred to portfolio P_1 by investor A even though portfolio P_1 has the greater expected return. This is true because P_1 has so much more risk than P_3 that the additional reward is not sufficient compensation for the increased risk. Of course, there will be other (less risk-averse) investors who will prefer P_1 to P_3. One such investor is investor B, shown in the bottom panel of Figure 1.4.

Portfolio Formation

The concept of indifference curves permits a structured framework for selecting the investor's optimal portfolio. However, prior to portfolio selection lies the task of portfolio formation, that is, constructing a portfolio from the list of approved securities. We can show this step diagrammatically by drawing the region in the risk/reward plane that includes all the portfolios attainable from a given list of securities at a given point in time. This region, the *attainable set*, shows all the possible expected return and risk combinations that correspond to portfolios constructed from the securities.

In Figure 1.5 there are three securities with standard deviations S_1, S_2, and S_3, respectively. Notice that some portfolios are more desirable than others; for instance, at risk level S_2 portfolio P_2 has the greatest expected return. At every risk level we can single out a portfolio that has the greatest expected return; the set of all these portfolios is an important construct, the *efficient frontier*. The efficient frontier is the set of portfolios which has the greatest expected return for each given level of risk, or equivalently, the smallest risk for each given level of expected return. It is clear than every rational investor would prefer a portfolio lying on the frontier over the portfolios lying in the interior of the region.

One property of the efficient frontier is evident from the figure. By forming portfolios from securities 1, 2, and 3, it may be possible to obtain a greater expected return than that offered by the individual securities at the same level of risk. How can this be? The answer has to do with the particular manner in which securities are grouped together to form a portfolio. The reward aspect is

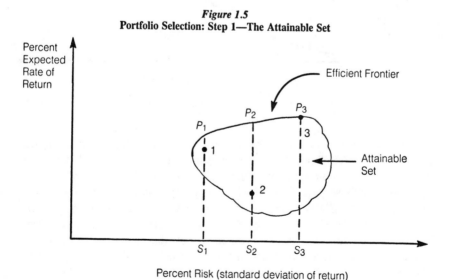

Figure 1.5
Portfolio Selection: Step 1—The Attainable Set

Percent Risk (standard deviation of return)

straightforward because the expected return of a portfolio is the sum of the expected return of each individual security multiplied by its weight in the portfolio. Thus, the portfolio expected return is simply the weighted average of the expected returns of the component securities. The risk side is mainly complicated by the fact that securities tend to move together, or "covary." The nature of the comovement, statistically termed *covariance*, was one of the basic foundations of Markowitz's original model. The existence of covariance between securities is crucial, as the proper grouping of securities into a portfolio produces an insurance effect known as the *diversification of risk*. We can illustrate this effect with the help of Figure 1.6.

Figure 1.6 shows two stylized versions of the rates of return on two securities. Case *A* illustrates the situation in which the rates of return tend to move together over time. In this case, the two securities are said to be *positively*

Figure 1.6
Covariance and Portfolio Risk

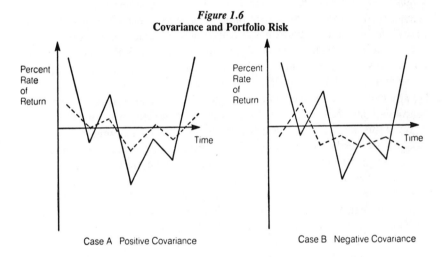

Case A   Positive Covariance

Case B   Negative Covariance

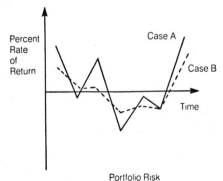

Portfolio Risk

correlated since they tend to move in the same direction. When two positively correlated securities are combined into a portfolio, the fluctuation in the portfolio rate of return tends to mirror the fluctuations in the component securities, as shown in the lower diagram. Thus, the formation of a portfolio of such securities simply causes portfolio risk to be the average of the risks of the individual securities. Case *B* illustrates a situation in which the rates of return move in opposite directions over time. Here the securities are said to be *negatively correlated*. Now when these securities are combined into a portfolio, the resulting portfolio rate of return displays considerably less fluctuation than does either of the two component securities. This is again shown in the lower diagram.

Figure 1.6 demonstrates a simple implication of covariance. When the covariance between two securities is small (i.e., the rates of return tend to be unrelated), the risk of a portfolio constructed from them can be less than the average risk of either security. The effect of investing in more than one security is to diversify away part of their individual risks. This effect is particularly evident in institutional portfolios because the covariance among the stocks in such portfolios is typically small. Returning to Figure 1.5, diversification is the reason why portfolios can be formed which plot on a risk/reward diagram above and to the left of the straight line between any two securities. Therefore, the efficient frontier of the attainable region follows a smooth curve dominating securities 1 and 2.[10]

From this analysis, it is clear that much of the attainable region is unimportant. All we need to know is the efficient frontier, since each rational investor will choose a portfolio lying on the frontier rather than in the interior, because then the investor is guaranteed a maximum expected return per unit of risk. But which portfolio along the frontier will be chosen?

The optimal portfolio has, by definition, the greatest level of utility for the investor and therefore lies on the highest indifference curve. It can be found by placing a set of indifference curves on the risk/reward region to determine the intersection with the efficient frontier, as shown in Figure 1.7. The investor's optimal portfolio is located where the indifference curve just touches ("is tangent to") the efficient frontier. For highly risk-averse investor *A*, the optimal portfolio *A* occurs at a low risk/reward point on the efficient frontier compared to that of the optimal portfolio of investor *B*, who achieves a greater expected rate of return by being willing to bear greater risk.

Up to this point we have only selected a portfolio from a universe of risky securities. Let us now extend the analysis to include the risk-free security; in other words, let us permit the investor to borrow or lend funds at the risk-free rate of interest. The analysis for borrowing funds (i.e., levering up) is not of great interest to institutional investors because of legal constraints which typi-

---

[10]The worst case is for the frontier to pass through 1 and 3 but to dominate 2. In the real world this worst case is rarely encountered, so that the figure is accurate. The correlation coefficient between the rates of return on two common stocks usually lies in the range of 0.2 to 0.3.

Figure 1.7
**Portfolio Selection: Step 2—Intersecting the Efficient Frontier with Various
Indifference Curves**

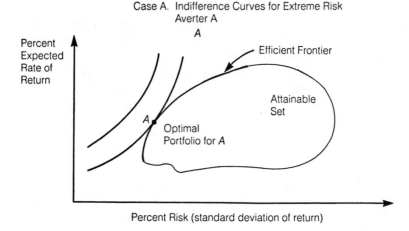

Case A. Indifference Curves for Extreme Risk
Averter A

Percent Expected Rate of Return

Percent Risk (standard deviation of return)

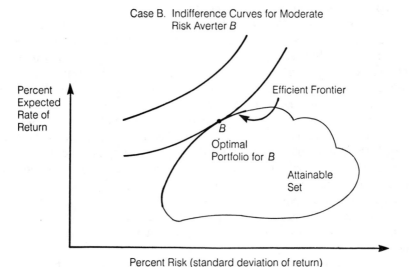

Case B. Indifference Curves for Moderate
Risk Averter *B*

Percent Expected Rate of Return

Percent Risk (standard deviation of return)

cally prevent them from pursuing this strategy. The situation where funds are lent is more important since it is the simplest version of *asset allocation,* which, as the name suggests, is the process of determining the mix of funds allocated between various security categories (e.g., stocks and bonds).

Recall from Figure 1.1 that a risky portfolio and a risk-free security can be mixed to form a whole series of portfolios which plot along the straight line between them in the risk/reward diagram. This is shown in greater detail in

Figure 1.8. In the upper panel, the curved line *LMN* describes the efficient frontier composed only of risky assets (i.e., it is similar to the efficient frontier shown in Figure 1.7); *A* represents the risk-free rate of interest; and portfolio *K* represents any interior, inefficient portfolio. If an investor chose to mix the risky portfolio *K* with the risk-free security *A*, any of the portfolios along *AK* could be formed (portfolios between *A* and *K* would have positive holdings in both the risk-free security and the risky portfolio *K*).

Are these portfolios along *AK* the best that the investor can achieve? Clearly not, since all the risky portfolios along the frontier above *AK* are better than those in the interior along *AK*. Because we know that the combination of the risk-free security and a risky portfolio plots along the straight line running through them, it follows that the portfolios which offer the greatest satisfaction are to be found by rotating the ray from *A* counterclockwise as much as possible. This is shown in the upper panel of Figure 1.8. The efficient frontier with a risk-free security is now given by *AMB*, where *M* is the tangency point between *AB* and the risky frontier *LMN*. Portfolios along *AMB*, and indeed along any other ray from *A* through the attainable set above *K*, certainly dominate those along *AK*. Portfolio *M* is the best risky portfolio to combine with the risk-free security; for this reason portfolio *M* is sometimes referred to as the *optimal combination of risky securities*.

The straight line *AMB* in Figure 1.8 represents the efficient frontier, which, by definition, is the set of optimal portfolios. Hence an investor will choose a portfolio somewhere along *AMB*. Where? To locate the optimal portfolio for a given investor, indifference curves are superimposed on the diagram, as shown in the lower panel. The diagram shows the optimal portfolios to be P_1 for an extreme risk averter and P_2 for a more moderate risk averter.

So far, we have covered tha basic precepts and some of the structural framework of MPT, but how is the analysis carried out, and what are the major steps? Three basic phases are required to obtain the optimal portfolio.[11] The first phase is the analysis of the securities that make up the portfolio. This entails the estimation of the potential rewards, the riskiness of each security encountered in attempting to achieve those rewards, and the degree of comovement of individual securities in the marketplace. In other words, we need a complete description of each security, both individually and relative to each other.

The second phase is portfolio formation, which involves constructing portfolios that optimally reflect the security descriptions of phase 1, and computing the expected return and risk for each constructed portfolio. The output from this phase is the efficient frontier, which is the input for the third and ultimate step, portfolio selection. As we have just seen, this involves defining the investor's risk/reward trade-off, then locating the particular intersection of indifference curve with the efficient frontier which defines the optimal portfolio. From

---

[11]This description is highly stylized in order to give an overview of the tasks involved.

Figure 1.8
Introduction of Risk-Free Asset

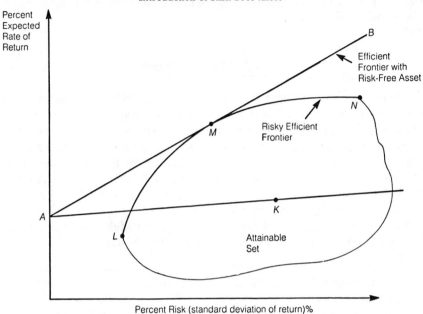

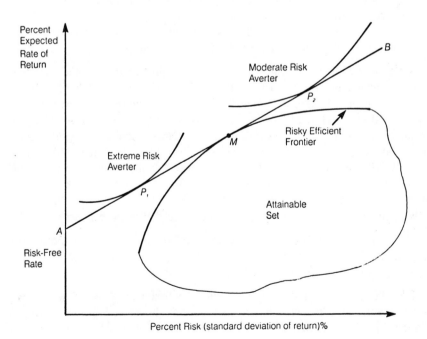

this description it is obvious that the stability of the structure rests very heavily on the accuracy of the initial inputs (security analysis) and the representation of the investor's preferences.

Capital Market Theory

Up to this point we have been concerned exclusively with a normative or decision-making theory, that is, how to choose an optimal portfolio for a particular rational investor. Since an individual investor is only a small part of the entire market and is, in some sense, competing against all other investors, it would be useful to discover the financial implications for the market if every investor acted rationally. Capital market theory describes the effects on the market of portfolio decisions made by rational investors, in particular, the relationship between security expected return and risk.

In order to aggregate individual decisions meaningfully, we need to make some basic assumptions about the investment environment.

1. Each investor makes decisions on the basis of expected rates of return, standard deviations of return, and the covariance of return among the securities. In addition, all investors have the same predictions.
2. Each investor constructs an optimal portfolio based on the steps outlined in the previous section.
3. Each investor can borrow or lend to any degree desired at the risk-free rate of interest. All investors are equal in this regard.
4. The market is "perfect," so that there are no barriers or impediments that would prevent an investor from holding an optimal portfolio.

Notice that while all investors are assumed to agree on their predictions, the investors would obviously differ in their willingness to bear risk. The main concern of capital market theory is equilibrium conditions in the marketplace regarding the portfolio holdings and prices of securities. The concept of equilibrium is important, for once equilibrium is obtained, there are no pressures to change away from it, provided that no new information enters the marketplace and investors have not revised their predictions. Admittedly, equilibrium is an ideal state, but because it is ideal, it will be the state in which we are most likely to derive the most powerful relationships. This turns out to be the case, as we will now describe. The major questions the theory answers are:

1. What is the relationship between expected return and risk for portfolios and securities?
2. What is the appropriate measure of portfolio risk?

Each investor has predictions regarding the future behavior of securities, which enables an efficient frontier, such as that shown in Figure 1.8, to be formed. The next step, as has been described, is to determine the correct mix between the risky and riskless securities, i.e., the location of the optimal port-folio along *AMB*. Before proceeding, however, notice that under our assump-tions all investors face the same diagram so that all investors will locate their optimal portfolio, which is a mixture of portfolio *M* and the risk-free security, somewhere along *AMB*. Exactly where they position themselves will depend on their particular risk/reward trade-off, but they will form their optimal port-folio from only two components: first, the risk-free security, and second, port-folio *M*. In this world the only investment decisions are the asset allocation decision (i.e., the mix between the risk-free asset and portfolio *M*), and the determination of the asset holdings in portfolio *M*.

In theory, however, there is only one decision since the determination of portfolio *M* is trivial.[12] The optimal portfolio of the risky securities, *M*, in-cludes all securities in proportion to the overall holdings of those securities in the marketplace. This proportional weighting in line with the actual structure of the marketplace follows from the fact that all investors purchase only port-folio *M* as their representative risky "security." Accordingly, the optimal risky portfolio is the *market portfolio,* which is defined as the unique portfolio com-prised of all securities weighted by their capitalization.

To see this, suppose that portfolio *M* does not contain the stock of company XYZ. Therefore, no investor would purchase stock in XYZ, so the price would fall to zero and XYZ would cease to exist. Is it possible that company ABC, which constitutes 5 percent of the total market value of all risky securities, would only comprise 2 percent of portfolio *M*? No, since all investors will place 2 percent of their funds at risk in ABC, and thus ABC will constitute 2 percent of all funds invested in risky assets. It is impossible for ABC to be 2 percent and 5 percent of the same total.

The important point to be derived from Figure 1.8 is that at equilibrium all optimal portfolios lie along the line *AMB*, with adjustments for individual pref-erences made by varying the proportions of the risk-free asset and the market portfolio. Since this line has such importance, it is termed the *capital market line* (CML).

The vertical intercept for the diagram in Figure 1.8 is the pure interest rate. It reflects the cost of immediate consumption of one's wealth, or, alternatively, it is the reward available for forgoing current consumption. The slope of the CML measures the trade-off between the expected portfolio return and the risk encountered to achieve that return. The slope relates how much additional ex-pected return can be achieved for a given increase in risk. Or, alternatively, it measures how much expected return must be forgone in order to achieve a certain reduction in risk. Conceptually, the slope can be thought of as the cost (in forgone expected return) of risk reduction.

The CML is shown in Figure 1.9. If the coordinates of the market portfolio

---

[12]Practical difficulties cause complications in the determination of portfolio *M*. We will con-sider this point in Chapter 5.

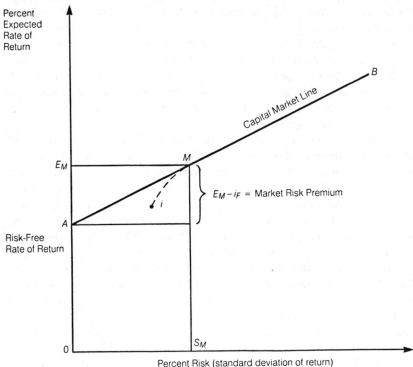

Figure 1.9
Constructing a Portfolio Composed of an Individual Security and the Market Portfolio

M are given by E_M (Expected rate of return) and S_M (Standard Deviation of return), then the additional return provided by the market over the risk-free rate (i_F), called the *market risk premium*, is given by $E_M - i_F$. Further, the slope of the CML is given by $(E_M - i_F)/S_M$. With this framework, we can answer part of the question, which we posed earlier, as to the relationship between risk and reward for portfolios. If the portfolio is an efficient portfolio lying on the CML, then the equation of a straight line gives the result:

$$E_P - i_F = S_P(E_M - i_F.)/S_M,$$

where E_P and S_P are the expectation and standard deviation of an efficient portfolio P. The extension to inefficient portfolios and individual assets is a little more complex. One of the easiest ways to understand the effect of a single security is to analyze a portfolio composed of an individual risky security and the market portfolio M.

Figure 1.9 offers a pictorial presentation of this exercise. The point marked i represents a total investment in one risky security, while the point marked M represents a total investment in the market portfolio. To be consistent with the concept that at equilibrium all optimal portfolios lie along the CML, the dashed line indicates that as a portfolio composed of M and i in varying porportions approaches a total investment in the market portfolio, the slope of the two lines will be equal.[13] This is important because the slope of the CML is a measure of the cost of reducing risk.

The figure shows that the marginal impact of purchasing more of security i is to move down the CML from M toward A. But what is this impact in terms of reward and risk? The change in expected return is simply the difference between the expected returns on the security and the expected returns on the market portfolio. The change in risk depends upon the diversification effect of security i. For instance, if security i were a low-risk security which was negatively correlated with portfolio M, then the risk reduction would be much greater than if security i were very risky and positively correlated with portfolio M. In short, the marginal impact in the risk dimension depends upon the covariance between security i and the market portfolio M, so that the horizontal distance moved (marginal change in risk) is related to the covariance of the security with the market portfolio.

Hence, in equilibrium the effect of increasing the holding in security i is the "benefit" of the reduction of portfolio risk in an amount dependent upon the covariance of the security with the market portfolio at a "cost" of reduced reward, which is the difference between the expected returns on the security and the expected returns on the market portfolio. Now recall that security i was arbitrary. We could have used any security, and the effect would still have been to move away from M toward A along the CML. Thus, for every security the cost divided by the benefit is a constant, namely the slope of the CML. Without mathematics the relationhip is: The stock's expected return less the risk-free rate equals a constant times the manner in which the stock return covaries with the market portfolio return.[14] This relationship between the covariance of the individual stock return and the market portfolio return leads to the creation of another construct, the *security market line* (SML), shown in Figure 1.10.

The importance of the SML is that every portfolio and every security will lie at some point along it, as opposed to the CML, on which only efficient portfolios lie. This is true because in equilibrium all assets will be priced according to their contribution to the risk of the market portfolio, or covariance, rather than their total risk. As can be seen in Figure 1.10, the market portfolio lies along the SML, together with the three securities 1, 2, and 3. Any combination of 1 and 2, 1 and 3, 2 and 3, or 1, 2, and 3 would also lie along the line.

The difference between the CML and the SML is that for the former risk is

---

[13] If this were not the case, then it would be possible to construct a portfolio that would lie above the CML, which results in a contradiction. This point is explained in more detail by Professor Sharpe, who originally presented this argument in his paper "Capital Asset Prices: A Theory of Market Equilibrium under Conditions of Risk," *Journal of Finance*, September 1964, pp. 425–42.

[14] The mathematics for this relationship are derived in the supplement to Chapter 2.

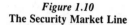

Figure 1.10
The Security Market Line

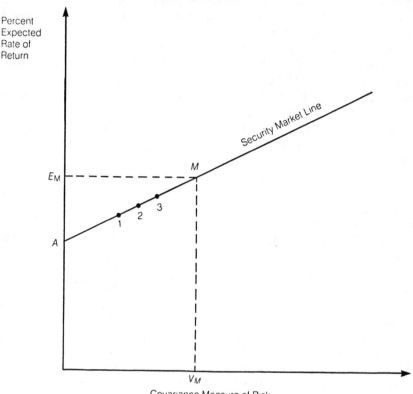

Covariance Measure of Risk

Note: V_M = Variance of the market portfolio return = S_M^2.

measured as the standard deviation of the return, while for the latter it is measured by the covariance of the security return with the market portfolio return. Why should covariance rather than the standard deviation be the important measure of risk? The answer to this question, as to so many other questions in finance, is diversification. Since the optimal risky portfolio is the market portfolio, the compensation that is provided for holding a security is not related to its total risk, much of which can be diversified away when it is combined with other risky securities, but to its contribution to the risk of the market portfolio. Recall that covariance measures the degree to which one variable changes when another variable changes. Hence, the component of a security's risk that arises from covariance with the market portfolio cannot be diversified away and so must be compensated. The market only pays an investor for bearing that part of risk which is inescapable—and in general only a fraction of the total risk of a security cannot be diversified away.

Another frequently used measure of risk, which is a simple transformation of covariance, is the security's *beta*, or systematic risk coefficient. Beta is a standardized measure of covariance obtained by dividing covariance by the market variance, and like covariance, it describes the relationship between the change in a security's rate of return and changes in overall market performance.[15] One way of graphically describing this measurement is to hypothesize a linear relationship between the random excess rate of return (over the risk-free rate) on an individual security and on the market portfolio, as shown in Figure 1.11.

The graph indicates the relationship between these two excess rates of return by the line passing through the point connecting the random excess rate of

Figure 1.11
The Security Characteristic Line

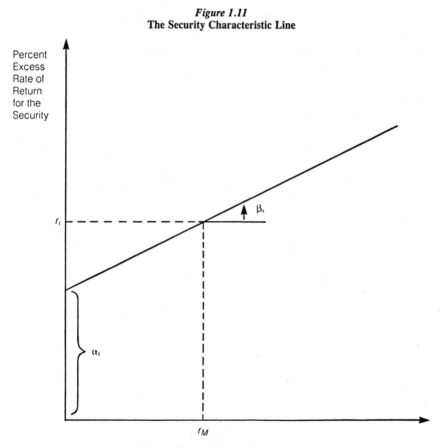

Percent Excess Rate of Return for the Market

---

[15]The covariance of a variable with itself is equal to the variance of the variable. *Variance* is the statistical term which is defined as the standard deviation squared. See the supplement to this chapter for more discussion of these terms.

return for the market, denoted as r_M, with the random excess rate of return for the stock, denoted as r_i. The only factors missing, which would precisely define the security characteristic line, are the slope and intercept on the vertical axis.[16] The equation of any straight line on this diagram has the form:

$$r_i = \alpha_i + \beta_i r_M, \tag{1-1}$$

Where

r_i = the excess rate of return for security i;

α_i = the intersection (intercept) of the straight line with the vertical axis;

β_i = the slope of straight line, or the length of "rise" compared with the length of "run" in the diagram; and

r_M = the excess rate of return for the market portfolio.

Thus, in trying to find the relationship between the security and the market, we are looking for β_i, the symbol for the slope. It can be shown mathematically (as is done in the supplement to Chapter 2) that the security's beta does relate the return on the security with the return on the market portfolio. Therefore, the security's beta, represented by β_i, is the measure of the characteristic line slope shown in Figure 1.11.

If there is no change at all in the price of security i for any change in the value of the market portfolio, the change in stock i versus the change in the market is obviously zero. This case is represented in Figure 1.12 as the horizontal line labeled "$\beta_i = 0$." If the change in security i correlates perfectly and moves in the same direction with the same percent change as the market, the security sensitivity to the market is 1.0 and is represented by the upward-sloping line labeled "$\beta_i = 1.0$." A security that moves completely contrary to the market but with the same percentage change as that of the market would have "$\beta_i = -1.0$" and is so labeled on the graph.

Figure 1.13 shows this relationship for Digital Equipment Corporation (DEC) and International Business Machines (IBM) using the 60 monthly excess rates of return up to December 1978, and the S&P 500 as a proxy for the market portfolio.[17] These two diagrams show that the observed relationship between the realized market excess returns and the security excess returns tend to form a cluster of points around the characteristic line rather than being exactly linear. Thus, rather than hypothesizing that equation (1-1) is the natural representation of the security characteristic line, it is more realistic to hypothesize:

$$r_i = \alpha_i + \beta_i r_M + \varepsilon_i, \tag{1-2}$$

---

[16]The term *characteristic line* was first used in Jack Treynor, "How to Rate Management of Investment Funds," *Harvard Business Review*, January–February 1965, pp. 63–75.

[17]Notice that the returns for IBM are more tightly bunched than those for DEC. This is even more noticeable when it is realized that the two vertical scales are slightly different. For a statistical analysis of these two stocks, see Table S1.1 in the supplement to this chapter.

Figure 1.12
The Relation between Market and Security Excess Return

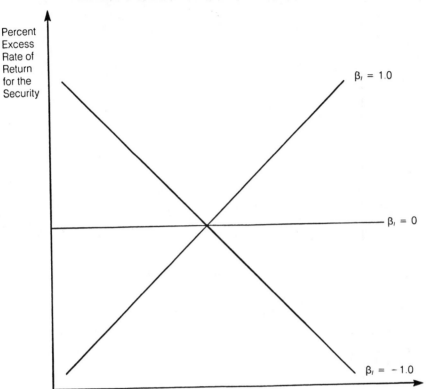

Percent Excess Rate of Return for the Market

where
  ε_i = an error term with zero expected value which captures that component of the security return not related to the market.

To complete this section, let us return to our discussion of the SML. Figure 1.14 shows the most common description of the SML, which is in terms of beta rather than coyariance, as depicted in Figure 1.10. Several points help fix the line on Figure 1.14. Since the market's rate of return relative to itself is obviously 1.0, the beta of the market is unity. The SML meets the vertical axis at the risk-free interest rate, marked as i_F on the diagram. Since the risk-free interest rate is independent of market fluctuations, it is plotted where beta equals zero. These two points thus determine the SML. The line in Figure 1.14 has been drawn upward sloping, indicating the ability to achieve greater expected return by undertaking a greater degree of risk. In fact, the important conclusion to be gleaned from this diagram is how much the expected excess

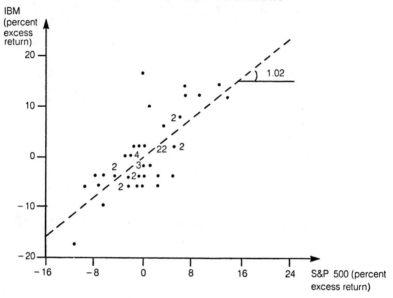

Figure 1.13
Characteristic Lines for IBM and DEC

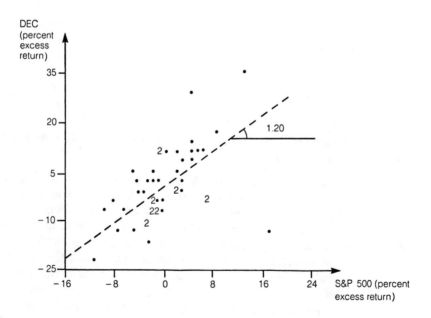

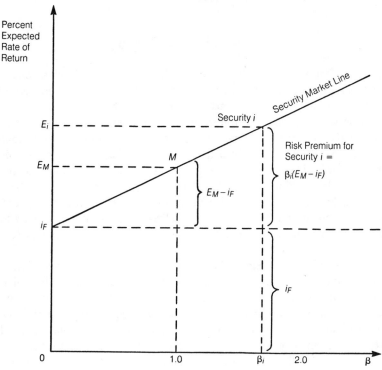

Figure 1.14
The Security Market Line Expressed in Terms of Beta

Risk as Measured by Beta

return increases as beta increases. This difference between the expected return and the risk-free rate is known as the security's risk premium or, alternatively, the expected excess return.

The slope of the SML is given by the market risk premium divided by the beta of the market portfolio, or $E_M - i_F$. Now the expected rate of return on every security i is given by the equation of the SML, namely:

$$E_i - i_F = \beta_i(E_M - i_F).$$

This equation is the fundamental relationship of capital market theory, known as the *capital asset pricing model* (CAPM). It answers the questions stated at the beginning of the section since it provides the relationship between expected return and risk for all securities and portfolios.[18] Moreover, with our discussion

---

[18]Although we have stated the CAPM for securities i, it also holds for all portfolios since they too lie along the SML. For portfolio P, we then have:

$$E_P - i_F = \beta_P(E_M - i_F).$$

above, it shows that the appropriate measure of portfolio risk is beta since this risk alone is compensated in the market.

Modern Portfolio Theory

As we mentioned at the beginning of this chapter, a major assumption of MPT is that portfolio management is performed in a world characterized by uncertainty. Many of the diagrams presented so far have represented expected returns on securities and portfolios. Around these expected returns there will be a "band of uncertainty," indicating that their realization is not guaranteed. For instance, in the SML drawn in Figure 1.14, the expected return for the market portfolio is only an average predicted from a distribution with considerable risk. In addition, the extent of the divergence of the security's return above and below the SML is also uncertain. This is shown in Figure 1.13, where real data are plotted—not every realized return conforms exactly to the simple, predicted linear relationship because of the enormous risk in security returns.

It is convenient to separate the sources of risk into two categories: those related to uncertainty about the market portfolio performance and all other sources. Total security risk can be decomposed into these two sources of uncertainty, defined respectively as *systematic risk* and *residual risk*.[19] Going back to Figure 1.8, all efficient portfolios plot along the capital market line, *AMB*. This means that all efficient portfolios have rates of return that are perfectly correlated with the rate of return on the market portfolio; therefore, the only uncertainty in this relationship is the uncertainty inherent in the market portfolio itself. This then, is systematic risk. Residual risk exists only for inefficient portfolios that do not lie on the CML. Thus, there are three rules for categorizing portfolio risk:

1. Systematic risk is the only source of uncertainty regarding the rate of return for an efficient portfolio.
2. Efficient portfolios have no residual risk.
3. A portfolio or a security with residual risk does not lie on the capital market line.

Since an individual security is unlikely to lie on the CML, it will be inefficient and hence will possess both types of risk. The systematic risk component will remain even when the security becomes part of an efficient portfolio. The residual risk of the security will tend to cancel out against the residual risk of other securities when it is joined with them in an efficient portfolio. In other words, the residual risk can be diversified away.

---

[19]Systematic risk is also referred to as market or undiversifiable risk; residual risk is also referred to as unsystematic or diversifiable risk.

Another way to think about residual risk is to examine its components. For instance, there is the element of risk that is specific to the security itself, without relation to any other security; and there is the element of risk that arises from a "group effect" such as industry risk, which is unrelated to the market as a whole. These two subclasses of residual risk are known as *specific risk* and *extra-market covariance*.[20] Examples of specific risk would be embezzlement and bankruptcy, which is completely unexpected by the market (Penn Central?). Extra-market covariance can be thought of as the risk that arises because the security is part of a certain class of assets, such as growth stocks or the airline industry, and thus is subject to surprises affecting all securities in that class.

The decomposition of total risk into systematic and residual components and the examination of the origins of residual risk lie at the heart of MPT. One method of formalizing this MPT approach is to assume that several *common factors* influence the prices (and therefore the returns) of securities. Each security is exposed to these factors as a function of the fundamental characteristics of the corporation. For instance, there may be factors associated with growth stocks or homogeneous industries (such as the airline industry). In each case, we would expect stocks that are sensitive to a particular factor to perform differently from stocks not sensitive to that factor. Moreover, some stocks would be more exposed to, for instance, the growth factor than others simply because some stocks are more growth oriented than others.

In this approach, we need to isolate a set of factors, plus each security's exposure to the factors, which explain a large fraction of the return of every security. Any component of the return that cannot be identified with one or more factors is specific to the company. In essence, this is the description of a *multiple factor model*.

Economically, we can view the model as follows: A macroeconomic event, such as a monetary crisis, a sudden announcement of a change in fiscal policy, or an energy embargo, will induce changes in the present values of many firms. Consequently, the prices of these firms' securities will change. Moreover, the cause of these price changes will be evident because of the commonality between them. In other words, investors will observe a common factor influencing the returns to a group of securities simply because the performance of the securities in the group will be fairly homogeneous and may be unrelated to the overall performance of the market.

With this multiple factor model and risk classification, we have gone beyond the portfolio theory of the 1960s and early 1970s. In fact, it was as a result of an understanding of the components of risk that the theory became applicable to investment management. This understanding also sets the stage for our fur-

---

[20]This latter term was first used by Barr Rosenberg in "Extra-Market Components of Covariance among Security Prices," *Journal of Financial and Quantitative Analysis,* March 1974, pp. 263–74, to indicate that the risk arises from the covariation of securities, that is, "extra-market," or independent of the market.

ther discussion of MPT since a hallmark of the approach is an explicit acknowledgment that risk exists and that it arises from several sources.

Summary

We have covered the basic concepts that form the body of MPT. The basic building blocks are a concept of reward (expected return), risk (the standard deviation of the return), and preferences regarding how much risk investors are willing to bear in the pursuit of reward. We have also covered the conceptual framework that relates how these variables are interrelated. We have purposely introduced the subject matter with diagrams as opposed to rigorous mathematics in an attempt to foster an intuitive understanding.

We hope that as the reader delves more deeply into the balance of this book, he or she will see the measurements and computer printouts simply as amplification of the concepts presented in this introductory chapter.

Further Reading

There are numerous excellent reviews and expositions of portfolio theory. Below we list a few that will provide valuable supplementary reading for this chapter.

Markowitz, Harry M. *Portfolio Selection: Efficient Diversification of Investment,* John· Wiley & Sons, New York 1959.

————. "Markowitz Revisited." *Financial Analysts Journal,* September–October 1976, pp. 47–52.

Modigliani, Franco, and Gerald Pogue. "An Introduction to Risk and Return." Part 1, *Financial Analysts Journal,* March–April 1974, pp. 68–80. Part 2, *Financial Analysts Journal,* May–June 1974, pp. 69–86.

Rosenberg, Barr. "The Capital Asset Pricing Model and the Market Model." *Journal of Portfolio Management,* Winter 1981, pp. 5–16.

Sharpe, William F. *Portfolio Theory and Capital Markets.* New York: McGraw-Hill, 1970. Particularly chaps. 1 through 5.

————. *Investments.* Englewood Cliffs, N.J.: Prentice-Hall, 1978. Particularly chaps. 5 and 6.

Supplement 1

A Review of Essential Statistics

One of the major impacts of MPT is to reinforce the need for an understanding of statistics, if for no other reason than to point out to a client that past portfolio performance has been not only significant but statistically significant! In one sense, MPT is merely the reflection of a statistician's view of the capital markets. In this supplement we will try to make clear the important statistical concepts, particularly, the concept of risk.

The first definition we need is that of *probability*. For this purpose, it is convenient to use the intuitive notion of frequency, or the proportion of outcomes. When a die is rolled, there are six possible outcomes and (if the die is fair) each outcome is equally likely. If the die is rolled many times and a count is kept of the number of occurrences of each outcome, then the proportion of times a "six," or any other face, is scored will be (approximately) one in six. It is therefore asserted that the probability of a given outcome is $1/6$. Similarly, if we say that the probability of scoring, for instance, a "three" is $1/6$, what we mean is that if the die is rolled many times, the proportion of times that a three is scored equals $1/6$.

Likewise, if a broker predicts that the probability of default on a bond is "small," then in an experiment which repeats the future many times, the bond would default in only a small proportion of these experimental observations. The prediction that the "probability is small" is actually a statement on the frequency of default in a hypothetical experiment in which the future is lived over and over again.

It is convenient to represent probabilities on what is called a *frequency diagram*. Figure S1.1 is a frequency diagram for the distribution of the annual rates of return on a portfolio that has "discrete" outcomes of -28, -8, 12, 32, and 52 percent. This diagram shows that the portfolio will earn a rate of return of 12 percent with probability $1/3$, -8 percent or $+32$ percent with

---

Note: Our purpose in this supplement is to define the most common statistical measures. Readers not familiar with this material may find a more detailed discussion helpful, such as can be found in most elementary statistics texts. See the selected references at the end of the supplement.

35

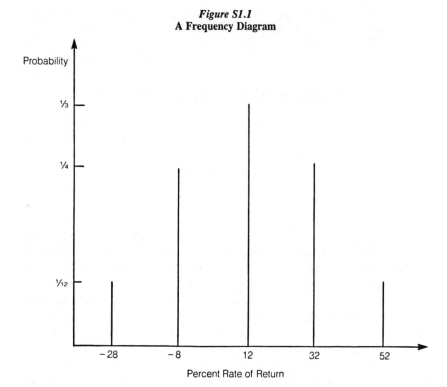

Figure S1.1
A Frequency Diagram

probability $\frac{1}{4}$, and -28 percent or $+52$ percent with probability $\frac{1}{12}$. Notice that the sum of the probabilities of the outcomes is unity, implying that the portfolio is certain to achieve one of these rates of return.

The most likely rate of return is 12 percent since this return is achieved with the highest probability. The statistical term for the most likely outcome is the *mode*. In this example, the mode also represents the "middle" of the distribution—that is, there are an equal number of outcomes above and below 12 percent. The term for the middle of the distribution is the *median*.

Both the mode and the median give an indication of the "typical" outcome, which need not be the same as the average or expected outcome (rate of return). It is the expectation, or *mean*, of a distribution that is the most commonly reported attribute. The mean is defined as the weighted sum of all outcomes where the weights are the probabilities. The algebraic definition is:

$$\text{Mean} = \sum_i p_i x_i, \qquad \text{(S1–1)}$$

where p_i is the probability of outcome i which has value x_i. For the distribution in Figure S1.1, the calculation is:

$$\text{Mean} = (-28/12) + (-8/4) + (12/3) + (32/4) + (52/12)$$
$$= -7/3 - 2 + 4 + 8 + 13/3 = 12\%.$$

In this case, as for all symmetrical distributions, the mean is the same as the median. The values for the mean, the median, and the mode, together with some other attributes to be introduced later, are called *statistics*. The variables which take different values according to some probability law (such as the score from a roll of a die or the rate of return on a portfolio) are called *random variables*.

This discussion has introduced some crucial distinctions—the difference between an outcome of a random variable, the distribution of a random variable, and a statistic of the distribution of a random variable. The discrete distribution of a random variable (in this case the rate of return on a portfolio) is shown in Figure S1.1. This figure shows that the possible outcomes are five rates of return, with the probability of actually achieving a given rate attached to that rate. A statistic is computed from the distribution, is a function of its "shape," and need not coincide with an actual outcome.

This distinction is frequently confused. For instance, some money managers claim that their performance is superb (which it may be), as evidenced by a large extraordinary return, or "alpha," of, say 5 percent per annum as measured over the previous five years. This 5 percent is not the statistician's alpha, and it should not be the investment profession's alpha—rather, the 5 percent is an outcome from a distribution that has a great deal of uncertainty attached to it.

In this situation the important attribute was the mean value or expectation of the extraordinary return distribution five years ago. An outcome or observation such as the figure of 5 percent is just a chance drawing—it may be good, bad, or indifferent. Rolling a die may give us the outcome of scoring a six, but we certainly should not expect to get a six on every throw. A large, positive extraordinary return over the five-year period may have occurred—this is equivalent to scoring a six—but to claim the extraordinary return as an indication of good management in the past and a promise for the future is unwarranted since the 5 percent rate of return was not necessarily the expectation, or mean value, that we would have believed five years ago. Nor, for that matter, is it necessarily the one that we would believe now.

We will return to the important subject of analyzing performance in Chapter 7 after covering some more preliminary material. In particular, we need a more realistic description of probability distributions. This is accomplished by considering continuous, rather than discrete, probability distributions. Figures S1.2 and S1.3 show two such distributions: the first is the *normal* distribution, depicted by the familiar bell-shaped curve, while the second is the related *log-normal* distribution.

Recall that in the discrete case the height of the bar at a certain value gives the probability of achieving that value. In the continuous case it does not make sense to consider the probability of obtaining a specific single value since, at least conceptually, that single value has no "width," so that the probability of exactly obtaining it is zero. Instead, we evaluate the probability of observing outcomes within a certain range, for instance, the probability that positive rates

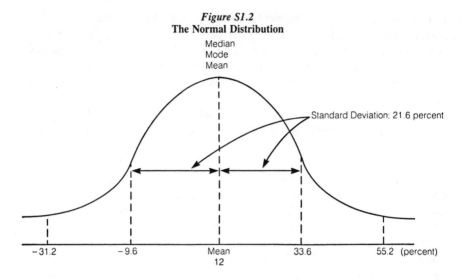

Figure S1.2
The Normal Distribution

of return will be earned or the probability that the rates of return will be between − 10 percent and + 10 percent. The probability of that range is found by calculating the area beneath the curve and between the limits of the range. Therefore, continuous distributions are not nearly so amenable to human manipulation.

However, for the normal distribution it is possible to determine probabilities without raising the specter of the integral calculus to thrombotic heights since many useful areas (and hence probabilities) have been tabulated. One area—and probability—that needs no calculation and holds for every continuous distribution is the area under the entire curve. Because this area corresponds to observing all values for which the distribution is defined, it is also the probability of obtaining at least one of those values, and thus this probability (area) is unity.

Figure S1.3
The Lognormal Distribution

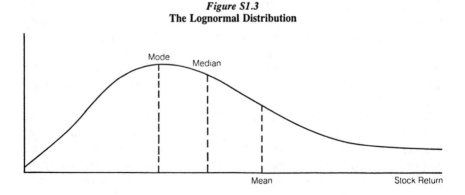

The normal distribution is important for two main reasons: first, it is the distribution which is usually invoked in econometric tests; and second, the natural logarithm of stock returns has been determined empirically to be approximately normally distributed. Since stock returns, which are defined as the ending price plus dividends received divided by the initial price, are necessarily positive due to limited liability, the logarithm of return varies between $-\infty$ and $+\infty$. The lower value corresponds to a stock that plunges to zero (i.e., a return of 0 or a rate of return of -100 percent), while the upper value holds in the fortunate (though unhappily rare) situation of infinite appreciation. If the stock return is one (i.e., a rate of return of 0 percent) then the logarithm of return is zero.

The lognormal distribution is related to the normal distribution by the following rule: If the lognormal distribution is transformed by taking its logarithm, then the normal distribution results. The inverse transformation of the logarithm function is the exponential function, since log $[\exp(x)] = x$ and exp $[\log(x)] = x$. Thus, taking the exponential of the normal distribution gives the lognormal distribution!

Since the logarithm of stock returns is approximately normal, it follows that stock returns are approximately lognormal. The lognormal distribution is shown in Figure S1.3. Note that this distribution is not symmetrical; it stops at the left side at zero (the limited liability of securities) and has an infinite right-hand tail. In this case, the mode and median are to the left of the mean.

Another reason for the introduction of logarithms has to do with the calculation of average rates of return over several periods. The problem of using the arithmetic average rate of return is exemplified with the following rates of return on two stocks:

	Period 1	Period 2
Stock 1	+50%	$-33^1/_3\%$
Stock 2	-50	+100

The arithmetic average rate of return of stock 1 is $8^1/_3$ percent $[(50 - 33^1/_3)/2]$, while that of stock 2 is 25 percent, yet in both cases the initial and terminal values are identical since, for example, stock 1 rose from $100 to $150 before falling back to $100, while stock 2 dropped from $100 to $50, then rallied to $100.

The problem with taking a simple arithmetic average of the within-period rates of return is that these rates of return may be earned on different portfolio values. It should be clear that the fundamental constructs are the beginning and ending values of the portfolio, sometimes described by the *value relative* (= ending value/beginning value). The computation of an average rate is simply a convenience for restating the value relative in terms of a per period rate of return for use in comparisons between portfolios or managers.

One unambiguous method of restating the value relative is to find the constant rate of return which, had it been earned every period and compounded, would have resulted in an equivalent investment. This *equivalent constant return* is a true measure of the average rate of return over several periods and is usually referred to as the average compound rate of return or the geometric mean rate of return. If there are N periods and in the ith period the rate of return is r_i, then the geometric mean rate of return, g, is:

$$g = [(1 + r_1) (1 + r_2) \ldots (1 + r_N)]^{1/N} - 1. \qquad \text{(S1-2)}$$

This equation can be rearranged to demonstrate the interpretation of the geometric mean rate of return as the equivalent constant rate of return. If g is earned every period for N periods, then:

$$(1 + g)^N = (1 + r_1) (1 + r_2) \ldots (1 + r_N).$$

Because it is cumbersome to take Nth roots, this computation is usually written in two steps. The first step is justified since the logarithm of a product is equal to the sum of the logarithms, so that:

$$\log(1 + g) = [{}^1\!/_N \sum_{i=1}^{N} \log(1 + r_i)] = a, \text{ say}, \qquad \text{(S1-3)}$$

where "log" denotes the natural logarithm and "a" is the average of the logarithmic return. This expression can be solved for the geometric mean, g, in the second step to give:

$$1 + g = e^a, \text{ or } g = e^a - 1. \qquad \text{(S1-4)}$$

Expressed in words, the logarithm of one plus the geometric mean rate of return is equal to the mean of the logarithmic returns. In addition, the logarithm of one plus the geometric rate of return is the continuously compounded rate of return over the N periods.

For instance, using the example for stock 1 above:

$$g = \sqrt{(1 + {}^1\!/_2) (1 - {}^1\!/_3)} - 1 = \sqrt{{}^3\!/_2 \cdot {}^2\!/_3} - 1 = 0,$$

which is the correct rate of return (i.e., if the initial and terminal values are identical, then the rate of return *is* zero). If stock 3 has the following returns in each of three periods:

	Period 1	Period 2	Period 3
Stock 3	+50%	−33⅓%	−87½%

then the geometric mean return is:

$$g = ({}^3\!/_2 \cdot {}^2\!/_3 \cdot {}^1\!/_8)^{1/3} - 1 = {}^1\!/_2 - 1 = -{}^1\!/_2.$$

The average loss per period is 50 percent. If 50 percent is lost in each of three periods and then compounded, the terminal value is 12½ percent of the initial value. The continuously compounded rate that results in a loss of $87\frac{1}{2}$ percent of principal value is:

$$\log(1 + g) = \log(1 - 0.5) = \log(0.5) = -0.693.$$

In other words, starting with $100 and continuously compounding at a three-year interest rate of $- 69.3$ percent results in $12.50 at the end of three years. The equivalent annual rate of interest is $- 23.1$ percent, as continuously compounding for three years at this annual rate results in a loss of $87\frac{1}{2}$ percent.

As a final demonstration of the difference between discrete and continuous rates, let us compute the continuous rate which is equivalent to a given discrete rate. Let $1 + r$ be the total return on an investment over some period. Now divide this time interval into n subperiods of equal length and let c/n be the rate of return over each of these subperiods so as to produce a rate of return r over the entire period. Symbolically,

$$1 + r = (1 + c/n)^n.$$

As n gets larger, c tends to the continuously compounded rate of interest and the right-hand side of the equation can be shown to equal, in the limit, e^c; that is

$$1 + r = e^c.$$

Solving for the continuously compounded rate shows $c = \log(1 + r)$.

For these reasons it is much more convenient to work with the logarithm of one plus the security rate of return rather than with proportional rates of return. Figure S1.4 shows the typical distributions of a common stock for the two measures of return, the left being the proportional measure and the right the logarithmic. Because the $\log (1 + x) \sim x$ when x is close to zero, the "middle" of the distribution shows little change between the two measures (although the actual values are different). Large proportional returns tend to shrink toward the center, while small proportional returns tend to expand away from the center, making the logarithmic return virtually symmetrical. For many applications in finance, the subtleties of proportional versus logarithmic return are largely irrelevant. However, for performance measurement and attribution (which we will discuss in Chapter 7), the distinction is vital.

For contrast with the lognormal stock return distribution in Figure S1.3, Figure S1.5 shows the distribution of a short-maturity bond drawn with a mean value equal to that of the stock distribution. The bond distribution has a mode equal to the return which occurs in the absence of default (after all, this *is* usually the most likely outcome). This is simply the return obtained by repayment of principal plus coupon. There is some (however small) probability of default, so the mean is less than the mode.

The distributions shown in Figures S1.3 and S1.5 have the same mean (and the worst outcome), yet they look quite different. The distribution of the stock, for instance, has an infinite right-hand tail, while that of the bond has an ex-

Figure S1.4
Proportional and Logarithmic Rates of Return

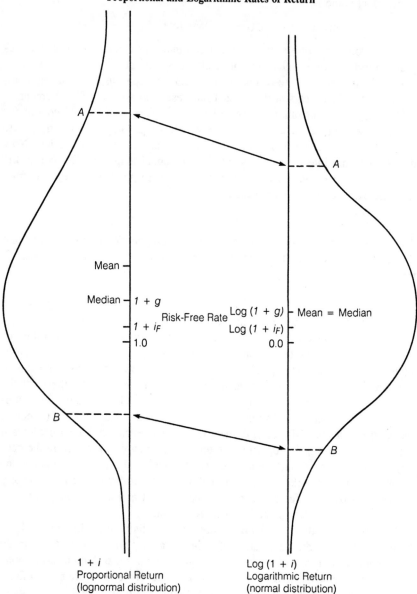

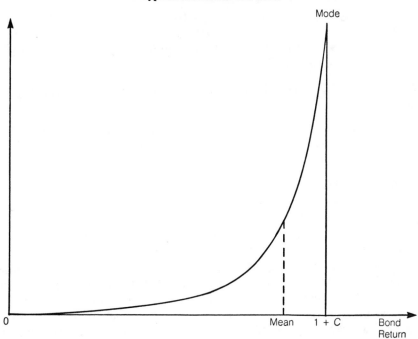

Figure S1.5
Typical Distribution of a Bond

plicit upper bound. How does the statistician differentiate between the two? The answer is, in the same way that the investor separates them—on the basis of risk—although the statistician uses longer and more precise words.

The most common measurement of risk is the *variance* of the distribution. This statistic is calculated in a manner similar to the calculation of the mean; variance is the weighted sum of the squared discrepancies between the values of the individual outcomes and the mean outcome, where the weights are the probabilities. For a discrete distribution the definition is:

$$\text{Variance} = \sum_i p_i(x_i - \text{Mean})^2. \tag{S1-5}$$

If the right-hand side of this expression is expanded, an alternative definition is obtained:

$$\begin{aligned} \text{Variance} &= \sum_i p_i\, x_i^2 - 2\sum_i p_i\, x_i\text{Mean} + \sum_i p_i\, (\text{Mean})^2 \\ &= \sum_i p_i\, x_i^2 - 2(\text{Mean})^2 + (\text{Mean})^2 \\ &= \text{Mean Square} - \text{Squared Mean}, \tag{S1-6} \end{aligned}$$

where, in the intermediate step, we made use of equation (S1–1) and the fact that the sum of the probabilities is one. For the distribution in Figure S1.1, the calculation given by equation (S1–5) is:

$$
\begin{aligned}
\text{Variance} &= (-28 - 12)^2/12 + (-8 - 12)^2/4 + (12 - 12)^2/3 \\
&\quad + (32 - 12)^2/4 + (52 - 12)^2/12 \\
&= (-40)^2/12 + (-20)^2/4 + (0)^2/3 + (20)^2/4 + (40)^2/12 \\
&= 466^2/_3 (\%^2).
\end{aligned}
$$

The calculation using equation (S1–6) is as follows. The mean square is given by:

$$
\begin{aligned}
\text{Mean Square} &= (-28)^2/12 + (-8)^2/4 + (12)^2/3 + (32)^2/4 + (52)^2/12 \\
&= 65^1/_3 + 16 + 48 + 256 + 225^1/_3 \\
&= 610^2/_3 (\%^2),
\end{aligned}
$$

so that the variance is:

$$
\begin{aligned}
\text{Variance} &= 610^2/_3 - (12)^2 \\
&= 466^2/_3 (\%^2),
\end{aligned}
$$

which is the same answer as that obtained above.

Notice two points about this computation: first, variance can never be negative since we are adding nonnegative numbers (if the variance is zero, then we know the outcome for certain, i.e., risky distributions always have positive variance); and second, the units of variance are nonintuitive—in this case, percent squared ($\%^2$). To convert the answer to a more intuitive unit, the square root of variance is taken to form the *standard deviation,* which in this case is 21.6 percent ($21.6 \times 21.6 = 466.6$). (This value is approximately equal to the annual standard deviation of an institutional equity portfolio.) Since the standard deviation is intuitive, it is the natural measure of spread, or degree of variability, in a probability distribution.

The standard deviation plays a crucial role with the normal distribution. A rule of thumb states that two thirds of all observations will fall within one standard deviation of the mean and that $^{19}/_{20}$, or 95 percent, will fall within two standard deviations. Another way of saying this is: If an observation is found which lies more than two standard deviations from the mean, then it is going to be fairly unusual, as this happens on the average only 1 time out of 20.

For instance, if the distribution of a portfolio rate of return is normally distributed with an annual standard deviation of 21.6 percent and a mean of 12 percent, then in two years out of three (because of the inherent risk of the portfolio) it is to be anticipated that annual rates of returns will lie in the range from −9.6 percent to 33.6 percent. In one year out of three more extreme returns should be anticipated; in fact, one year in six a rate of return greater than 33.6 percent or a rate of return less than −9.6 percent would not be surprising. On average, in only 1 year out of 40 will a rate of return of more than 55.2 percent occur or, again in only 1 year in 40, will a rate of return of less than -31.2 percent occur through chance alone, since both these rates of return lie two standard deviations from the mean. This is shown in Figure S1.2.

The ability to quantify the probability of an occurrence is used in estimating the *significance* of an event. From the viewpoint of the experimenter (performance measurer) an experiment corroborates the theory if its results are sufficiently close to expectation. The only question is to decide the meaning of "sufficiently close." It is customary in such cases to construct the 95 percent *confidence interval*, which implies that if the experimental value falls within this region, then the experiment would be considered as corroborating the hypothesis being tested. Alternatively, if the experimental value lies outside the interval, it is said to be significant at the 95 percent level because it signifies that some other theory is needed to explain the outcome.

Consider two simple examples: first, a two-tailed test, and second, a one-tailed test. Suppose a portfolio has normally distributed returns with an annual standard deviation of 20 percent and we hypothesize that the true expected rate of return generated by the manager is zero (the null hypothesis). The alternative hypothesis is that the true expected rate of return is not zero. Over one year the rate of return happens to be 35 percent. Does this cause us to change our hypothesis concerning the manager's ability? Using the rule of thumb that 95 percent of observations fall within two standard deviations of the mean, the confidence interval ranges from -40 percent to $+40$ percent. The 35 percent rate of return is not, therefore, significant (though to the portfolio owner all positive returns, even if not statistically significant, are financially significant). The top diagram of Figure S1.6 shows the nature of this test.

A one-tailed test can be described by changing the alternative hypothesis above. In this case, suppose the alternative is that the manager provides a positive expected rate of return. Note that this specification makes it easier to reject the null hypothesis when positive returns are realized. The 95 percent confidence interval now ranges from $-\infty$ to 32 percent (1.6 times the standard deviation) since there is a 5 percent chance under the null hypothesis of observing a return greater than 32 percent. (See the bottom diagram in Figure S1.6.) In this case the observed 35 percent is significant and will cause us to rethink the original (null) hypothesis concerning the manager's ability.

There are more complex ways of analyzing the width and shape of distributions which are useful for rigorous examination of the statistical properties of an empirical distribution. We will only briefly mention them here, since a full discussion is beyond the scope of this supplement. First, to determine whether the tails are longer in one direction than the other, the *skewness* of the distribution is calculated. Symmetrical distributions (such as the normal in Figure S1.2) have a zero skewness, while the lognormal, for instance, in Figure S1.3, is skewed to the right (positive skewness). Conversely, Figure S1.5 shows a distribution which is skewed to the left (negative skewness). The statistic to determine whether a distribution has long tails and is highly peaked

Figure S1.6
Significance Tests

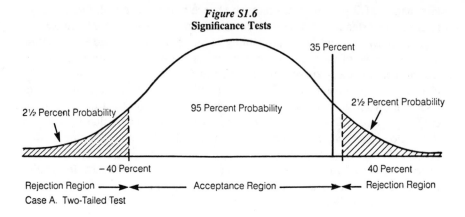

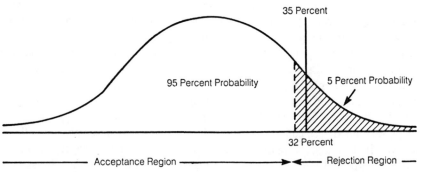

Case B. One-Tailed Test

("tall and fat"), or the opposite, is called *kurtosis*. If portfolio returns were distributed with a high value of kurtosis, we would intuitively expect to observe a large frequency of returns near the mean (this is the tall peak), interspersed with infrequent very large or very small returns (these are the long tails).

We have examined a single distribution in detail, but how are the interrelationships between distributions analyzed? The two most important statistics are the *covariance,* and the *correlation coefficient.* The covariance measures the degree to which two distributions covary, or move together. For instance, is there a tendency for an extreme positive observation from one distribution to be associated with an extreme negative observation from another? This would indicate some (negative) dependency; i.e., the distributions "move" in opposite directions.

The covariance of two distributions is related to both the mean and the variance and is calculated in a manner similar to both. The calculation can be written:

Covariance $[X, Y] = \sum_i \sum_j p_i q_j (x_i - \text{Mean}[X])(y_j - \text{Mean}[Y])$,   (S1–7)

where Covariance$[X, Y]$ denotes the covariance between random variables X and Y; Mean$[X]$ and Mean$[Y]$ are the means of random variables X and Y which have outcomes x_i and y_j with probabilities p_i and q_j; and the summation is over all possible outcomes.

One useful relation that is obvious from the definition is that the covariance between the returns on a risky and a risk-free security (or, equivalently, the covariance between a random variable and a constant) is zero. If security Y is risk-free, then the distribution of Y will contain a single "spike" with unit height (i.e., probability one) at its (constant) rate of return, so that there will just be a single outcome, $y_j = \text{Mean}[Y]$ with $q_j = 1$. Thus, in the case of a risk-free security, $y_j - \text{Mean}[Y]$ is always zero.

If the expression for the covariance is contrasted with that of the variance—equation (S1.5)—it is easily seen that the covariance of a random variable with itself is equal to its variance; i.e., Covariance$[X,X] = \text{Variance}[X]$. Further, the covariance between two random variables is a function of their variances. (In investment terms this indicates that the covariance between two securities is also a function of their individual risks.) In order to obtain a measure of the "co-relation" of the two random variables, which is not dependent upon the two variances, the correlation coefficient is used. The correlation coefficient is defined relative to the covariance as:

Correlation$[X,Y] = \text{Covariance}[X,Y]/\sqrt{\text{Variance}[X] \cdot \text{Variance}[Y]}$.   (S1–8)

This coefficient takes on values between -1 and $+1$. For instance, if the correlation is equal to the lower value, then the covariance is merely the negative product of the standard deviations; if it is zero, then the covariance is zero. Hence, the correlation between the returns on a risky security and a riskless security is always zero.

We are now in a position to derive some useful expressions involving the variance of random variables. First, let a be constant and let X be a random variable. Then:

$$\text{Variance}[aX] = a^2 \text{Variance}[X],$$ (S1–9)

as can be verified from the definition of variance. More important to our future work on portfolios will be the variance of $aX + bY$, where a and b are both constants and X and Y are random variables. If $Z = aX + bY$, then it follows that:

$$\text{Mean}[Z] = a\text{Mean}[X] + b\text{Mean}[Y].$$ (S1–10)

From the definition of variance:

$$\text{Variance}[Z] = \sum_i \sum_j p_i q_j (ax_i + by_j - \text{Mean}[Z])^2,$$

where p_i is the probability of $X = x_i$ and q_j is the probability of $Y = y_j$ and the summation is again over all possible outcomes. Now substituting for Mean[Z] in this expression gives:

$$
\begin{aligned}
\text{Variance}[Z] &= \sum_i \sum_j p_i q_j (ax_i - a\text{Mean}[X] + by_j - b\text{Mean}[Y])^2 \\
&= \sum_i \sum_j p_i q_j \{a^2(x_i - \text{Mean}[X])^2 + b^2(y_j - \text{Mean}[Y])^2 \\
&\quad + 2ab(x_i - \text{Mean}[X])(y_j - \text{Mean}[Y])\} \\
&= a^2 \sum_i p_i(x_i - \text{Mean}[X])^2 (\sum_j q_j) \\
&\quad + b^2 \sum_j q_j(y_j - \text{Mean}[Y])^2 (\sum_i p_i) \\
&\quad + 2ab \sum_i \sum_j p_i q_j (x_i - \text{Mean}[X])(y_j - \text{Mean}[Y]) \\
&= a^2 \text{Variance}[X] + b^2 \text{Variance}[Y] \\
&\quad + 2ab\text{Covariance}[X, Y],
\end{aligned}
\tag{S1-11}
$$

where we have made use of the fact that the probabilities add up to one.

Expressed in words, the variance of two random variables is equal to the sum of the variance of each random variable plus twice the covariance. This result can be extended to more than two random variables; the variance of the sum is equal to the sum of the variances plus twice the sum of all the covariances.

The covariance between random variables $Z = aX + bY$ and W is given by:

$$
\text{Covariance}[W, Z] = a\text{Covariance}[W, X] + b\text{Covariance}[W, Y], \tag{S1-12}
$$

as is readily verified by direct use of the definition. Again, this result can be extended to more than two random variables: the covariance between two sums of random variables is equal to the sum of all possible combinations of covariances between random variables.

One useful application of these general expressions is the determination of the variance of a portfolio over different time horizons. The total return over N periods, TR, is given by:

$$
TR = (1 + r_1)(1 + r_2) \ldots (1 + r_N),
$$

where r_i is the rate of return in period i. The analysis can be simplified by taking the logarithm of this expression, so that the logarithmic total return is:

$$
\log (TR) = \sum_{i=1}^{N} \log (1 + r_i).
$$

It is now straightforward to compute the variance of this expression using the generalization of equation (S1–11). Empirical research has shown that the logarithmic returns are (to a very good approximation) serially independent—i.e., for all periods i, $\log (1 + r_i)$ is independent of $\log (1 + r_{i+1})$—so that the variance of the logarithmic return, Var[log(TR)], can be written in terms of the variance of the period logarithmic returns, Var $[\log(1 + r_i)]$, as:

$$\text{Var}[\log(TR)] = \sum_{i=1}^{N} \text{Var}[\log(1 + r_i)]$$
$$= \bar{\sigma}^2 N \qquad (S1-13)$$

where $\bar{\sigma}^2$ is average variance per period. Thus, the variance of (logarithmic) total return increases in proportion to the number of periods (or, equivalently, time). This result enables us to convert monthly variance into annual variance simply by multiplying by 12. Taking the square root of equation (S1–13) shows that the standard deviation increases by the square root of time, so that the correct method of converting a monthly standard deviation to an annual figure is to multiply by $\sqrt{12}$, or 3.46.

A useful calculation which we will require later is that of the variance of the compound rate of return. From equations (S1–3) and (S1–4) it follows that this variance is given by (using the same notation as was used in those equations):

$$\text{Var}[a] = \text{Var}[\log(1 + g)]$$
$$= (1/N^2) \sum_{i=1}^{N} \text{Var}[\log(1 + r_i)]$$
$$= (1/N^2)(N\bar{\sigma}^2)$$
$$= \frac{\bar{\sigma}^2}{N}. \qquad (S1-14)$$

Here we have made use of the fact that the returns are serially independent. Thus, the variance of the continuously compounded rate varies in inverse proportion to time, so that the standard deviation varies inversely to the square root of time. These two results show that although the variance of the cumulative return increases over longer holding periods, the variance of the compound rate decreases over longer holding periods.

We now complete this supplement with a brief review of the concepts of least squares regression analysis. The simplest regression model has two variables, the dependent variable, Y, and the independent variable, X, related by:

$$Y = \alpha + \beta X,$$

where α and β are constants. If any specific value of X is given, then the corresponding value for Y is also (uniquely) given. In this case the explanatory variable X completely describes the behavior of variable Y.

Suppose now that there is some random influence on the value of Y other than that due to X. For instance, we may be trying to explain the excess return (over the risk-free rate) on a common stock (Y) by its relation to the excess return on the S&P 500 (X), in which case the model could be written as:

$$Y = \alpha + \beta X + \varepsilon. \qquad (S1-15)$$

Here the variability in the common stock is only partially explained by the variability in the S&P 500. The remaining variability is due to the residual factor ε, which cannot be predicted. This relationship is plotted in Figure S1.7, where the effect of the residual factor is to introduce a scatter of points around the line $Y = \alpha + \beta X$.

Estimates of the parameters α and β (the estimates are usually written with "hats," $\hat{\alpha}$ and $\hat{\beta}$) can be calculated by the method of *ordinary least squares*. This involves fitting a line to the scatter of observations of X and Y, such that the sum of the residuals, $\Sigma \varepsilon_i$, is zero and the sum of the squared residuals, $\Sigma \varepsilon^2$, is minimized. Standard formulas exist for obtaining the estimates $\hat{\alpha}$ and $\hat{\beta}$ for the population values α and β. These are given by:

$$\hat{\beta} = \text{Covariance } [X, Y]/\text{Variance } [X]$$
$$\hat{\alpha} = \text{Mean}[Y] - \beta \text{ Mean}[X]. \qquad \textbf{(S1–16)}$$

The regression values of Y, $\hat{Y}_i$, and regression residuals, $\hat{\varepsilon}_i$, are given by:

$$\hat{Y}_i = \alpha + \hat{\beta} X_i$$
$$\hat{\varepsilon}_i = \hat{Y}_i - Y_i.$$

Figure S1.7
Fitting a Line to a Scatter of Observations

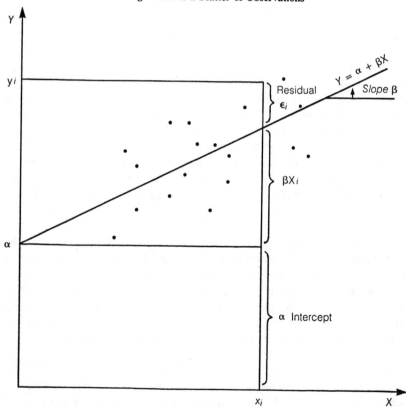

The standard error of the regression, defined as the average sum of the squared residuals $\hat{\epsilon}_i$, provides a measure of the accuracy of the model. For instance, if the standard error is zero, then all regression residuals must be zero, so that X explains all the variability in Y. Another familiar measure of the power of the model, or association among the variables, is the R^2 (*R-squared*). This is also called the *coefficient of determination*, and it measures the proportion of the variance in Y captured by the regression model. Because the R^2 is a proportion, it has a range between zero and one; a value of zero implies that the model explains none of the variability in Y, while a value of one implies that all the variability is captured by X, i.e., the model is a perfect "fit." In symbols, R^2 is defined as:

$$\left.\begin{aligned}
R^2 &= 1 - (\text{Variance}[\hat{\epsilon}]/\text{Variance}[Y]) \\
&= \hat{\beta}^2 \text{Variance}[X]/\text{Variance}[Y] \\
&= (\text{Covariance } [X,Y])^2/(\text{Variance}[X] \cdot \text{Variance}[Y]),
\end{aligned}\right\} \quad \text{(S1–17)}$$

where this last equation follows from the substitution of equation (S1–16). This equation shows that the R^2 is also the square of the correlation coefficient between X and Y (see also equation (S1–8)). Notice that the R^2 is a function of the estimated beta. For this reason, it is a good practice to report the beta and the variance (or standard deviation) of the residual error, rather than the beta and the R^2, when describing the results of a regression. (It is, of course, straightforward to compute the residual variance, given the latter two parameters, from the first form of equation (S1–17) if Variance[Y] is known.)

Obtaining a high R^2 is not sufficient justification for accepting the results from a regression analysis. There are other parameters—such as the signs and significances of the estimated coefficients—that should also be examined carefully. Unfortunately, only a cursory description of the most common test—the t-test—is possible here. This test is used to determine the significance of the coefficients. Under the null hypothesis that the coefficients $\hat{\alpha}$ and $\hat{\beta}$ are zero, the ratios (t-statistics) of $\hat{\alpha}/\hat{s}(\hat{\alpha})$ and $\hat{\beta}/\hat{s}(\hat{\beta})$ are formed where $\hat{s}(\hat{\alpha})$ and $\hat{s}(\hat{\beta})$ are the estimated standard deviations (or standard errors) of $\hat{\alpha}$ and $\hat{\beta}$. Provided that sufficient data points are used in analysis, these ratios are significant at the 95 percent level if they are greater than 2.0 in absolute magnitude. If this is the case, then the null hypothesis would be rejected, leading to the conclusion that a relationship exists between the two variables. The t-statistics are usually reported beneath the estimated coefficients.

These concepts are exemplified in the regression results shown in Table S1.1. This analysis was used to determine the slope of the line for the IBM and DEC plots in Figure 1.13. The dependent variable, Y, is the excess rate of return on IBM or DEC, and the independent variable, X, is the excess rate of return on the S&P 500 over the 60 months ending December 1978.

The estimated beta for IBM, 1.02, is highly significant, with a t-statistic of 11.07; thus, we can reject the null hypothesis that the beta for IBM is zero. On the other hand, the null hypothesis concerning the estimated alpha cannot be

Table S1.1
Regression Analysis of IBM and DEC versus the S&P 500

1. IBM versus the S&P 500

    The regression equation is:

    $$Y = -0.0003 + 1.02X$$
    $$(-0.07) \quad (11.07)$$

    The standard deviation of Y about the regression line is:

    $S = 0.0369$
    R-squared = 67.9%.

2. DEC versus the S&P 500

    The regression equation is:

    $$Y = 0.0035 + 1.20X$$
    $$(0.33) \quad (5.79)$$

    The standard deviation of Y about the regression line is:

    $S = 0.0827$
    R-squared = 36.6%.

---

rejected since its t-statistic of -0.07 is much less than 2.0 in absolute magnitude—that is, we have no reason to believe that the alpha is not zero. The residual standard deviation is 0.0369 per month, or 12.76 percent per year ($0.0369 \times 3.46 \times 100$), which indicates the uncertainty in the IBM return that is not associated with the variability of the S&P 500. The last statistic is the R^2, which indicates that 67.9 percent of the variation in IBM's return can be explained by the S&P 500.

A similar analysis holds for DEC. Again, the estimated alpha is insignificantly different from zero, while the beta is still highly significant. The residual standard deviation is 0.0827 per month, or 28.61 percent per year. DEC is both systematically (the beta is 1.20 compared to 1.02) and residually riskier than IBM.

Finally, it may be that the dependent variable, Y, is hypothesized to be a linear function of several independent variables. For instance:

$$Y = \alpha + \beta_1 X_1 + \beta_2 X_2 + \ldots + \beta_k X_k + \varepsilon,$$

where α and the β_i are constants. Again, least squares regression provides parameter estimates $\hat{\alpha}$ and the $\hat{\beta}_i$, although the formulas are more complicated than in the two-variable model. The measures of association in the multiple regression model are similar to those for the two-variable model. The coefficient of multiple correlation, R^2, measures the proportion of variance in the dependent variable, Y, which is accounted for by the combined influence of the multiple explanatory variables, X_i. The significance of each estimated coefficient can be tested by an appropriate t-test, and the combined significance of the regression coefficients can be determined by the use of an F-statistic derived from the multiple correlation coefficient, R^2.

It is worth noting that the estimates for the parameters in the regression models rely upon some fairly stringent assumptions, most which are not satisfied if stock returns are regressed against portfolio returns. More complex regression models (such as generalized least squares and stochastic parameter regression) can be used, but their description is beyond the scope of this supplement. However, the reader should be warned that naive application of ordinary least squares may be unrewarding.

Case Study 1: The Asset Allocation Decision[1]

Part 1: Computation of the Return
Distribution Statistics

In this example we describe a method that the trust department of a major bank uses to determine the proportion of stocks, bonds, and cash equivalents (90-day Treasury bills) to be held in its discretionary portfolios. This problem is usually referred to as the asset allocation decision.

First, the Investment Policy Committee describes the economic scenarios that it believes may occur during the next four-year period. These scenarios may be referred to as "modest growth," recession," "stagflation," and so on. To each scenario the committee attaches a subjective probability; this is the probability that the scenario will occur. Of course, the sum of these probabilities must be one to indicate the committee's belief that one of the scenarios will in fact happen. Finally, the committee considers each scenario in turn and forecasts the expected rates of return on each asset class over the market cycle, conditional upon the occurrence of the scenario. The outcome of these deliberations is a set of conditional forecasts similar to those shown in Table S1.2.

With this raw data the Investment Policy Committee can determine the risk, reward, and correlation of each of the three asset classes. These calculations are applications of the formulas presented earlier in this supplement. For in-

---

[1]This example is based upon the actual data and procedure used by the trust department of a major New York City bank in its asset allocation decision. We use it simply as a specific example of the methodology discussed in Chapter 1 and the supplement, not as a justification of the approach. We discuss the asset allocation decision in greater detail in Chapter 5.

Further discussion of this approach to the asset allocation decision can be found in Gifford Fong, "Asset Allocation Framework," paper presented at Western Finance Association Meetings, Hawaii, June 1978; and Keith Ambachtsheer, "Investment Scenarios for the 1980's," *Financial Analysts Journal*, November–December 1977, pp. 38–47.

Table S1.2
Forecast Rates of Return (percent)

	Scenarios						
	1	*2*	*3*	*4*	*5*	*6*	*7*
Probability	0.20	0.25	0.10	0.23	0.10	0.10	0.02
Stocks	18.24	14.56	23.70	−0.92	7.55	10.96	−11.95
Bonds	11.15	9.47	11.15	7.20	5.22	6.51	12.32
T-bills	6.18	6.89	6.43	7.70	7.60	7.60	4.50

stance, the expected rate of return on stocks, given by equation (S1–1), is simply:

$$0.2(18.24) + 0.25(14.56) + 0.1(23.7) + 0.23(-0.92) + 0.1(7.55)$$
$$+ 0.1(10.96) + 0.02(-11.95) = 11.05\%.$$

The other expected rates of return are 8.79 percent for bonds and 6.98 percent for Treasury bills. The variance of the return is slightly more complicated. The variances (and hence the standard deviations) of the conditional rates of return are calculated from equation (S1–5). These variances are:

Stocks	74.18 (%²)
Bonds	4.41 (%²)
T-bills	0.48 (%²)

They measure the variability in returns due to the uncertainty concerning which scenario will occur. We must add to this the inherent variability of each asset class.[2] For simplicity, assume that the variance of return is the same in each scenario and given by the following values:

Stocks	29.16 (%²)
Bonds	10.24 (%²)
T-bills	1.69 (%²)

From these values the annual standard deviation can be calculated as:

Stocks	10.17%	$(= \sqrt{74.18 + 29.16})$
Bonds	3.83%	$(= \sqrt{4.41 + 10.24})$
T-bills	1.47%	$(= \sqrt{0.48 + 1.69})$

Frequency diagrams for the three asset classes, together with the means and standard deviations, are given in Figure S1.8.

---

[2] Write $E(R/\text{Scenario}_i)$ and $\text{Var}(R/\text{Scenario}_i)$ as the mean and variance of return conditional on the ith scenario occurring. Then the unconditional variance is given by $\text{Var}[R] = E_i[\text{Var}(R/\text{Scenario}_i)] + \text{Var}_i[E(R/\text{Scenario}_i)]$, where E_i and Var_i indicate that the expectation and variance are calculated with respect to the scenarios.

Figure S1.8
Frequency Diagrams for Stocks, Bonds, and Treasury Bills

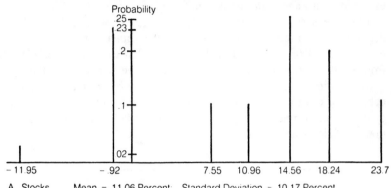

A. Stocks   Mean = 11.06 Percent: Standard Deviation = 10.17 Percent

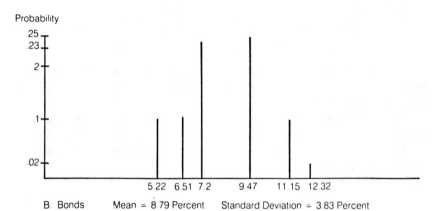

B. Bonds   Mean = 8.79 Percent   Standard Deviation = 3.83 Percent

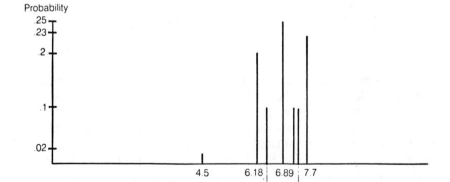

C. Treasury Bills   Mean = 6.98 Percent: Standard Deviation = 1.47 Percent

These statistics provide an indication of the relative merits of investment in each of the individual asset classes. Fortuitously, the stocks provide the greatest expected return and highest risk, the bonds are intermediate on both attributes, and the Treasury bills provide the least expected return and risk. In order to determine the correct proportions of each asset in each investor's optimal portfolio, we need (as explained in the chapter) first to form the efficient frontier from the three (risky) assets. However, before we can calculate the frontier we need an estimate of the covariance or correlation between the three assets. The conditional covariance and correlation coefficients are found from application of the correct formulas above—(S1–7) and (S1–8). The conditional correlation coefficients are as follows:

	Stocks	*Bonds*	*T-bills*
Stocks	1.00	0.61	−0.50
Bonds	0.61	1.00	−0.91
T-bills	−0.50	−0.91	1.00

(We encourage readers unfamiliar with statistics to convince themselves of these values by computing one or two of the off-diagonal elements using the formulas given above.)

To obtain the unconditional correlation matrix we have to make a transformation similar to that made above for the variance. The correlation matrix, as computed by the Trust Department (the historical correlation matrix is required for this computation), was as follows:

	Stocks	*Bonds*	*T-bills*
Stocks	1	0.42	−0.39
Bonds	0.42	1	−0.31
T-bills	−0.39	−0.31	1

Notice that the diagonal elements are all unity because each asset is perfectly correlated with itself, that the stocks and bonds are positively correlated, and that the Treasury bills are negatively correlated with the other two assets.[3]

We now have all the data required to form an efficient frontier. The expected return for an optimal portfolio in the frontier is simply the sum of the weighted expected returns of the individual assets, where the weights are the proportional portfolio holdings, equation (S1–10), and the variance of return is

---

[3]Recall that these statistics are subjective values obtained from hypothesizing various scenarios and are not necessarily indicative of equilibrium or long-term relationships.

given by an equation similar to (S1–11). We defer the actual computation of the efficient frontier to the second part of this case study, which appears at the end of Supplement 2.

Selected References

A lucid exposition of the statistical principles presented in this supplement can be found in:

Dyckman, Thomas, and Joe Thomas. *Fundamental Statistics for Business and Economics*. Englewood Cliffs, N.J.: Prentice-Hall, 1977.

A good reference on least squares regression is:

Johnson, J. *Econometric Methods*. New York: McGraw-Hill, 1972.

A more advanced and complete coverage of the material is:

Fogler, H. Russell, and Sundaram Ganapathy. *Financial Econometrics*. Englewood Cliffs, N.J.: Prentice-Hall, 1982.

Chapter 2

Risk and Reward

In the previous chapter we stressed the fact that the investment environment is characterized by uncertainty and that a logical approach to investment should adequately consider this fact. The aim of this chapter is to more completely analyze the components of risk and reward. The major component of risk, which affects all securities, arises from exposure to the market, or systematic, factor. This realization, in addition to a further decomposition of the risk and reward components beyond the market factor, underlay the refinements which occurred in the MPT approach during the late 70s.

To clarify our explanation of the subject, we begin the chapter with a characterization of the investment process prior to the implementation of the MPT approach. This allows us to outline the gradual introduction of quantitative techniques. While the early attempts of implementing quantitative techniques were not successful, the more thorough breakdowns of risk and reward developed in the early 70s produced techniques that are now being practically applied by many money managers. The chapter supplement, which derives a basic version of the capital asset pricing model, ends with the completion of the asset allocation case study introduced in the supplement to Chapter 1.

The Nonquantitative Approach

In general, portfolio management prior to the introduction of quantitative methods can be described as follows:

Step 1. Select a list of companies judged as possessing management expertise of above-average ability, as being in industries enjoying above-average growth prospects, and as having products which are in the early stages of their growth cycles. These companies can be simply described as being of "good quality."

Step 2. Assign security analysts to study the prospects of the companies and the current price levels of their securities in order to determine the relative valuations of the securities. Such valuations may, for instance, be obtained by comparing estimates of future earnings growth rates with the current price/earnings ratios in order to assess degrees of under- or overvaluation. Some general guidelines may be used. For example, a stock trading at 2.5 times its five-year growth rate may be rated as expensive, while a stock with a 1.2-times ratio may be rated as cheap.

Step 3. Order the securities into a minimum of three categories—buy, hold, and sell—which reflect their relative attractiveness. Naturally, the cheapest or most attractive securities lie at the low end of the spectrum of valuation ratios, while the least attractive lie at the high end.

Step 4. Invest approximately equal proportions of the portfolio in those stocks which are considered most undervalued, or "buys."

A more thoughtful method of portfolio formation than that described in step 4 is frequently encountered. This method forces diversification by ensuring that the portfolio manager compare the portfolio with some benchmark portfolio, for instance the S&P 500. The method can be described as follows:

Step 4a. The weightings of the industry groups in the proposed portfolio are compared to the current weightings of comparable industry groups in the S&P 500. Since the performance of most money managers is measured relative to the S&P 500, the obvious strategy is to outperform the index by overweighting the appraised overperformers and underweighting the underperformers. The degree of under- or overweighting in such cases is highly subjective but seldom extreme. For example, an optimistic energy industry appraisal might trigger a 20 percent portfolio weighting in oil stocks versus an index weight of 15 percent. Seldom are the ratios of the selected weights to the index weights as much as a factor of two times.

This nonquantitative approach obviously emphasizes the valuation of the various securities. However, the amounts owned are highly subjective. For example, the relative ownership of various securities within an industry is usually based on the degree to which management is respected and the relative leadership of companies in their industry. These investment holdings are mainly a matter of what experience allows money managers to be comfortable with. In many cases this leads money managers to be heavily influenced by historical rather than future performance and by the investment behavior of their peers.

The only manner in which risk is controlled is by diversifying the portfolio among a large number of securities, ranging from a minimum of 40 to a maximum of more than 200. The subjective weighting of position sizes often rests as much or more on the "quality" of the company than on its valuation.[1] The underlying reasoning is to stress asset selection, in the belief that portfolio performance will follow directly behind.

Markowitz conducted the first studies of risk in an attempt to treat diversification directly. He pointed out that a complete emphasis on relative undervaluation overlooked the impact of risk. Unless good estimates of both risk and reward were integrated in portfolio design, the superior information held by analysts might not result in superior performance.

Perhaps because the portfolio theory approach was couched in precise mathematics or perhaps because the research at that time concentrated upon the technology rather than the decision process, the attempts to implement portfolio theory in the 1960s were unsuccessful. In any case, just as the nonquantitative approach ignored one part of the decision, the first attempts at applying investment technology tended to belittle security analysis in the race to computerize the portfolio formation process. Inadequate integration of portfolio formation with security analysis was one of the major impediments to useful implementation of portfolio theory.

It should be clear by now that both processes are important for successful portfolio management: security valuation judgments (assessing which companies' securities are superior to those of competitors, i.e., "above average") and the formation of portfolios that reflect those judgments. However, this does not imply that both processes require an equal expenditure of creative effort. As we shall see later, portfolio formation is largely mechanical and easily computerized. On the other hand, valuation is a creative and fragile process which should not—and, in general, cannot—be sacrificed on the altar of computer hardware. In short, security valuation is a profound exercise, while constructing portfolios in response to the information provided by security valuation does not require much human energy since this can be done by applying formal procedures.

---

[1]It is frequently argued that a company of good quality must also be a good investment. This incorrect argument is probably a defensive reaction arising from the manager's quarterly presentations to the sponsor. When the manager invests in "quality" companies, then the sponsor can feel proud of the portfolio and the meeting with the sponsor may be more amicable than it would be if the manager displayed a portfolio of financially risky companies ("dogs"). In this latter situation the sponsor may be apprehensive or embarrassed, even though the manager may believe the "dogs" to be better investments than the "quality" companies. A manager who provides an unusual strategy is more likely to be fired and so bears more business risk than is borne by a manager who "follows the crowd." We shall consider the manager-sponsor relations in more detail in Chapter 6.

Current Perspectives

Conventional wisdom holds that there exist in the capital markets "factors" that affect groups of stocks. For instance, it is frequently observed that small-capitalization companies perform differently than large-capitalization companies, that high-yielding stocks perform differently than growth stocks, that highly levered companies perform differently than companies with low leverage. We can explain such phenomena as consequences of a series of market-wide forces or factors, and we can view every security as having some sensitivity or exposure to the factors, depending on the fundamental characteristics of the company. Further, we can regard the factors as displaying various levels of activity at different points in the business cycle or in the economic environment. This thinking is in keeping with much of today's fundamentally derived investment analysis.

For example, consider the airline industry. If we hypothesize that there is a factor which affects only the airline industry, then airline stocks will be exposed to that factor, while all other stocks will not. Thus, when we observe that airline stocks as a group are performing differently than other stocks, then we may assume that the airline factor is active.

It seems plausible that an energy factor exists. As the cost of energy rises, those companies that use energy will be worse off than those companies that supply it. Whenever energy sources are an important economic consideration (for example, after an OPEC price increase) companies exposed to the energy factor will perform differently than those that are not. Thus, we constantly observe "group effects" as groups of securities in the market are influenced by *common factors*. It should be clear that if we can isolate those factors, calculate each company's exposure to them, and predict each factor's return, then we will have gone a long way toward understanding the economic forces at work in the capital markets. As our discussion unfolds, it will be clear that much of this work has been accomplished.

The simple observation that there is a great deal of commonality in the returns of individual securities has become a building block of the modern approach. Unfortunately, this "simple observation" becomes more complicated mathematically in the process of making it thoroughly rigorous. Nevertheless, that process is the result of the generally accepted observation that stocks respond to the common factors in the marketplace in different, yet predictable ways. This forms the basis for our next discussion.

The Market Model

The casual statement that the differential performance of securities can be attributed to common factors and exposure is too general to be very helpful. The statement leaves several questions unanswered, in particular, exactly what are these factors, and where do we find them? Perhaps the most obvious factor can be called market sentiment or, more precisely, the market factor.

The effect of the market factor is evidenced by the tendency of the market as a whole to rise (or fall) if some stocks rise (or fall) in price over some period. The behavior of the market contains a great deal of information on the behavior of individual stocks. In this general context, we do not have to be too careful about what we mean by the "market" since all broadly based indexes or portfolios are highly covariant. If the Standard & Poor's 500 Stock Average (the S&P 500) increases, then the New York Stock Exchange Composite index will generally increase.

For other purposes, we have to be extremely precise about what we mean by the "market." For these purposes the "market" is the market portfolio, which is the portfolio composed of all securities in proportion to their value. This concept is useful in many contexts. First, notice that the market portfolio is the "average" portfolio, since if all investors' portfolios are aggregated, then the result is the market portfolio. This has important implications for passive management, which we will discuss later in this chapter.

Perhaps more important, in the context of the capital asset pricing model, (CAPM), not only is the market portfolio the average portfolio, but it is also the optimal portfolio. This surprising result arises from some improbable assumptions, but it is sufficiently robust to be an excellent first approximation. The simplest version of the CAPM, as described in the previous chapter, assumes that everybody has identical beliefs concerning future distributions of return (although different preferences) and thus that everybody holds the same optimal risky portfolio, which must therefore be the average portfolio. This one-sentence explanation is exactly what is proved mathematically in the supplement to this chapter.

Unfortunately, the exact market portfolio may be unobtainable, for instance because the shares of some companies do not trade or because obtaining it would require fractional shareholdings. There is also the problem that some companies hold shares in other companies, leading to the "double counting" of this common capitalization. This effect is obvious for American Telephone and Telegraph with respect to the other Bell system companies. In order to make the theory operational, a proxy (most commonly the S&P 500) for the true market portfolio is used. In general, the use of a proxy is acceptable. The weaknesses in the concept occur if investors incorrectly assume that this proxy is their optimal portfolio, or if the proxy is used for performance comparisons of active managers. It should be realized that all proxies (including the S&P 500) for the market portfolio are, to some extent, arbitrary.[2] We will return to

---

[2]The greatest error is produced by the overweighting of large-capitalization, mature companies in the S&P 500 relative to more broadly based indexes. We will argue later that the concept of a "normal portfolio" overcomes many of the difficulties associated with defining the true market portfolio.

these important points later; however, here we will equate the market portfolio with the S&P 500 or some other broadly based index.

With this preamble, the construct of the market return is well defined. If we know the sensitivity or exposure of an individual stock relative to the market, then (theoretically) we can estimate the market component of the return on the stock. In other words, if the market rises (or falls), there is a tendency for individual stocks to rise (or fall), although the rate of response, or sensitivity, of each stock will be different, depending on the stock's fundamental characteristics. This is exactly the construct we discussed in Chapter 1, Figure 1.11, with the security characteristic line. That analysis showed that a security's exposure to the market is measured by its beta.

Let us summarize the discussion thus far. The return on a portfolio, or on a security (which, after all, is a portfolio composed of a single asset), can be expressed as the risk-free return plus an uncertain, or random, return. This random return arises partly from the influence of the market, and thus it comprises a systematic, or market, component. The systematic component is the systematic excess return, that is, beta times the market excess return. Since we cannot expect the market to explain all the variability in all portfolio and security returns, we have to allow for an uncertain residual return, which may be, for instance, the return due to abnormal industry performance. This decomposition is shown in Figure 2.1.

Notice that there are portfolios which have no random residual return. One case is the portfolio composed entirely of the risk-free asset. In this case, the

Figure 2.1
Decomposition of return

In words:

Portfolio or security return (i_P) = Risk-free return + Random return

$$
\begin{aligned}
&= \text{Risk-free return} && (i_F) \\
&\quad + \text{Systematic excess return} && [\beta_P(i_M - i_F)] \\
&\quad + \text{Residual return.} && (\varepsilon_P')
\end{aligned}
$$

In symbols (for portfolio P):

$$i_P = i_F + \beta_P(i_M - i_F) + \varepsilon_P',$$

where

$$
\begin{aligned}
\varepsilon_P' &= \alpha_P + \varepsilon_P; \\
\text{Mean}[\varepsilon_P'] &= \alpha_P; \\
\text{Mean}[\varepsilon_P] &= 0.
\end{aligned}
$$

So

$$i_P - i_F = \alpha_P + \beta_P(i_M - i_F) + \varepsilon_P.$$

---

beta is zero and the return on the portfolio is simply the risk-free rate of interest. A second case is the market portfolio, which has a beta of unity and, by definition, zero residual return. Another way of stating this is that the market portfolio explains all the variability in the market portfolio return.

This simple model, usually referred to as the *market model,* occupies an important place in the theory of finance. It is most frequently written in the form:

$$r_P = \alpha_P + \beta_P r_M + \varepsilon_P, \tag{2-1}$$

where $r_P = i_P - i_F$ and represents the portfolio random rate of return less the risk-free rate of return (the portfolio random excess return), and $r_M = i_M - i_F$ represents the market random rate of return less the risk-free rate of return (the market random excess return).

Equation (2–1) states that the random excess return on the portfolio (r_P) equals the portfolio expected residual rate of return, or alpha (α_P), plus the random systematic excess return ($\beta_P r_M$) plus the random residual rate of return (ε_P), where this last term has an expected value of zero. These relationships are shown graphically in Figure 2.2.

The similarity between the market model, equation (2–1), and the least squares regression equation (S1–15) should be obvious. In fact, the notations alpha and beta for the expected residual rate of return and sensitivity to the market come from their use as the intercept and slope in econometric analysis.

Let us now turn to the decomposition of risk. Taking the variance of equation (2–1) gives:

$$V_P = \beta_P^2 V_M + \omega_P^2, \tag{2-2}$$

where V_P is the variance of the portfolio return, V_M is the variance of the market return, and ω_P^2 is the variance of the residual return. This follows from equation (S1–11), with the constant a equal to the portfolio beta and with b equal to unity. Further, since the residual return has zero correlation with the market return, the covariance term is zero. Equation (2–2) states that portfolio variance is composed of systematic variance and residual variance, where systematic variance is proportional to market variance and portfolio beta squared.[3]

Clearly, if the portfolio is a levered market portfolio, it will have no residual risk (or residual return). Thus, it is only differentiating the portfolio from the market portfolio that induces residual risk (or residual return).

This simple observation has several far-reaching implications. First, recall that systematic risk is market risk; systematic risk is evident in all risky securities simply because there is uncertainty in the economy. There is a unique portfolio of risky securities which is exposed only to systematic risk: this is the market portfolio. Investors who hold the market portfolio are bearing risk in an optimal fashion (i.e., they are not bearing any residual risk) and are providing

---

[3]We will come back to this relation time and again. Notice that it is the sum of the two components of variance that gives total variance.

Figure 2.2
Decomposition of Return in "Up" and "Down" Markets

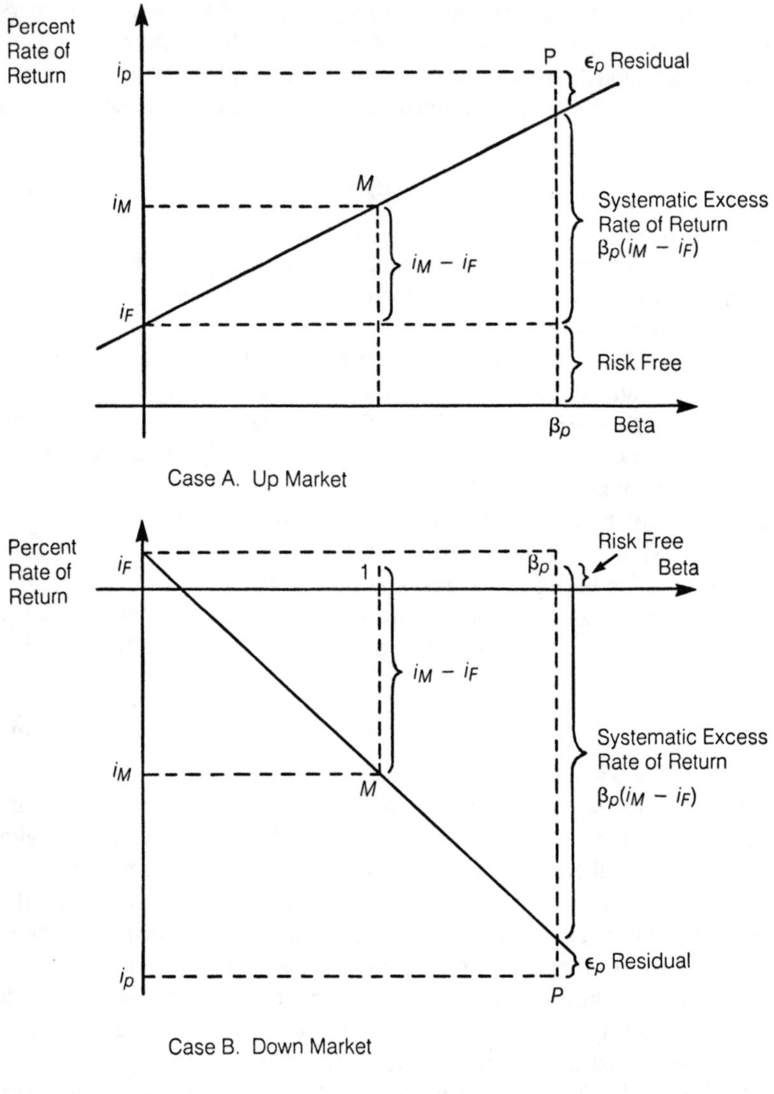

Case A. Up Market

Case B. Down Market

a service to investors who choose not to hold risky assets and therefore do not bear the risk of the economy. We can view this as an insurance contract because investors in risky securities are guaranteeing the returns of other investors by enabling them to hold only risk-free securities. These investors who provide this insurance service are rewarded since they receive as compensation the risk premium offered by risky securities over risk-free securities.

Investors who hold portfolios other than the market portfolio bear both residual and systematic risk. They will be compensated for the systematic risk, as argued above, but will they be compensated for the residual risk? The answer is that there can be no reward in aggregate for bearing residual risk. This follows since residual risk arises only in portfolios which have holdings different from the market portfolio. But if one investor owns a larger (smaller) than market proportion, another investor must own a smaller (larger) than market proportion, since investors in aggregate own the market. Hence, if one investor profits by holding a larger (smaller) proportion, another investor must lose by holding a smaller (larger) proportion. In aggregate, all profits arising from holding positions different from the market portfolio must add to zero. In other words, there can be no reward in aggregate for bearing residual risk.

We justified this concept by arguing from the return dimension. Let us now reinforce the concept by arguing from the risk dimension. Since residual risk occurs only when individual portfolio holdings differ from the market portfolio, it can easily be removed by making those transactions required to make the individual portfolio and the market portfolio identical. This act diversifies away all residual risk. Since residual risk can be diversified away, there can be no compensation in aggregate for bearing it. When investors bear systematic risk, there has been a sharing of risk in the economy; those investors who are unwilling to tolerate risk have transferred it to other investors for a "fee" (the risk premium). When investors bear residual risk, there has been no transference of risk; in fact, there has been an increase in risk because (at least) two investors have engaged in a "side bet" whose expected payoff is zero.[4]

Residual risk, therefore, represents an opportunity for profit to one investor and an opportunity for loss to another. Clearly, such a perverse subject is worthy of further study! However, before we conclude this section, it would be helpful to review the similarities and differences between the CAPM and the market model. These models are among the most prominent constructs in finance, and they are frequently confused since they both demonstrate a particular relationship between every asset and the market portfolio.

The market model simply provides a method of decomposing asset returns into two components: a systematic or market-related component and a residual or nonmarket component. It is a fact that if the market model satisfies certain statistical properties (namely, that the residual, ε_P, is uncorrelated with the market excess return, r_M), then the systematic component is beta times the market excess return. Hence, the market model appeared to early researchers to be a natural framework for estimating beta, as suggested by Figure 1.13.

The simple CAPM is an equilibrium pricing model which suggests that each asset is priced so that its expected reward just compensates for its contribution to market portfolio risk. The asset's expected reward is thus found to be proportional to its beta. For a well-diversified portfolio, an asset's risk contribution will approximate its risk contribution to the market portfolio.

---

[4]Actually negative when transaction and other costs are included.

This version of the CAPM is excessively naive, but space dictates deferring a discussion of the subtleties and "bells and whistles" to another book. There can be no doubt that the model is wrong (for instance, it should be modified to reflect the influence of differential taxation), but it is probably not seriously wrong. Hence, we must treat the model as an excellent "first approximation."

Given that the simple CAPM is only an approximation, does it make sense to spend effort working with the market model? The answer is yes, because the market model can be justified on several grounds besides that of the CAPM. For many applications of MPT, any broadly based portfolio will be as effective as the true (but unobtainable) market portfolio because all broadly based portfolios are highly correlated. Moreover, the existence of low-fee index funds indicates that there is considerable relevance in decomposing return into two components: a component related to the average of investors' holdings and a component unrelated to this average return.

Residual Risk and Return

Since residual risk is easily diversified and has no aggregate benefit, are we to assume that it is of no interest? Emphatically not! Understanding the origins of residual risk is the key to achieving superior relative performance. To achieve a performance record different from that of the market portfolio, one must hold a portfolio different from the market portfolio.[5] But doing so, as we have discussed above, induces residual risk into the portfolio. Hence, the level of residual risk is a measure of the difference between the individual portfolio and the market portfolio as well as an indication of the magnitude of the relative performance of the individual portfolio.

The importance of residual risk in the structuring of a portfolio cannot be overstated. To the extent that the investment manager or the security analyst can identify either under- or overvalued securities, there exists an opportunity for extraordinary return, or *alpha*. If a security is perceived to be overvalued, a rational strategy would be to invest a smaller proportion of the portfolio in that stock relative to its proportion in the market portfolio. Thus, if the appraisal is correct, the portfolio will outperform the market as the security is revalued. Of course, there is the risk that the appraisal is incorrect, and hence, whenever the portfolio differs from the market, the opportunity for making an extraordinary return must be balanced against the exposure to uncertain events that may cause the asset not to perform as expected.

Obviously, it is important to classify these uncertain events. The first type may comprise isolated events that influence only single stocks. Such a specific event for a given company will have no impact on other securities. Second, there may be events that influence a subset of the market, or a group of secu-

---

[5]In the absence of transaction costs, taxes, and other impediments.

rities, such as the airline stocks. These events cannot affect all stocks since events that affect all stocks are market or systematic events, and here we are only concerned with residual effects. This second type of residual effect is therefore called "extra-market" (i.e., unrelated to the market as a whole). The hierarchy of events is as follows: an event is specific if it influences a single company; it is extra-market if it influences a group of companies; and it is systematic if it influences all companies.

We have thus decomposed residual risk into two components: specific risk and extra-market covariance *(XMC)*. Specific risk applies exclusively to a particular asset or company and is independent of all other sources. It is the uncertainty that influences the return of an asset due to events that are related only to that asset. It may, for instance, be associated with an announcement of financial difficulties or the discovery of an unexpected mineral resource, a lawsuit, or the premature retirement of a corporate official.

Extra-market covariance, the other component of residual risk, describes the tendency of similar assets to move together in a manner unrelated to the overall behavior of the market. One example is the strong correlation between the returns of stocks in a cohesive industry, for instance, the airline industry. However, the similarity need not be restricted to industry classification. *XMC* will be induced in the portfolio whenever it has exposure to any common factor of return which is different from the exposure of the market portfolio.

Hence, residual risk is induced by taking positions in the portfolio different from those of the market. Part of this risk arises from taking differential positions on the common factors, which results in *XMC,* and part arises from taking differential positions in the holdings of actual assets, which results in specific risk.

Elements of Risk and Reward

We can now complete the decomposition of risk and return. Let us consider the return dimension first. Residual return is defined as being composed of specific return and the return due to exposure to the common factors. Total return, therefore, comprises the risk-free, systematic excess, the common factor, and specific returns. These are displayed in Figure 2.3.

The components of variance can be defined similarly. Residual risk is composed of *XMC* and specific variance. Hence, the variance of an individual stock (or an unmanaged portfolio) has the following elements: systematic, specific, and *XMC*. If market timing (adjusting the beta of the portfolio to take advantage of perceived abnormal market returns) is a part of the portfolio management strategy, then this induces an additional component of variance.[6] This

---

[6]Market timing as a strategy is discussed in Chapter 5.

Figure 2.3
Components of Return

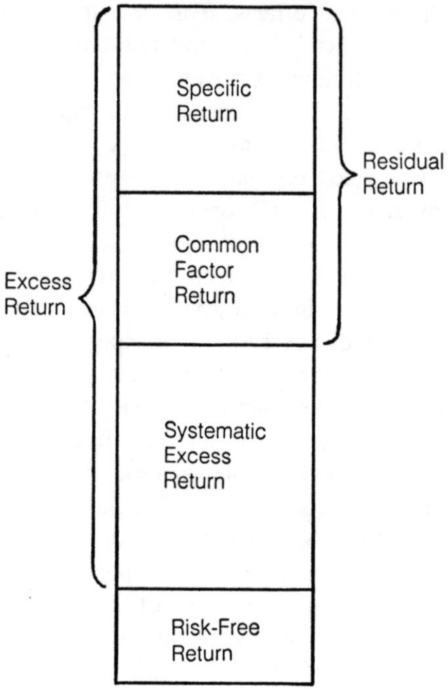

decomposition of variance is displayed in Figure 2.4, together with an indication of the typical relative magnitudes of the components of variance.

These elements of risk and reward are intimately associated with investment strategies which may be classified as follows:

Buy-and-hold (the market). The investor holds a portfolio that is exposed only to systematic risk. In essence, this is an index (or passive) portfolio. This strategy relies on earning the risk premium with a low-level management fee.

Market timing. In its purest form this strategy entails swapping between the risk-free asset and an index portfolio (both zero residual risk assets) in order to earn abnormal expected market returns.

Sectoral emphasis. The portfolio is positioned to earn residual return from exposure to the common factors. We would expect the major proportion of the residual risk to be *XMC*.

Stock selection. This strategy requires the identification of under- and overvalued securities. The portfolio is composed of extreme positions in these assets in order to maximize specific returns. We would expect the major proportion of the residual risk to be specific risk.

Figure 2.4
Components of Variance

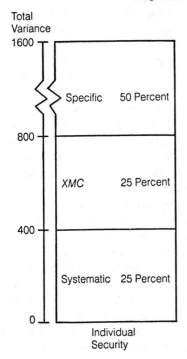

Total
Variance

	Individual Security
Specific	50 Percent
XMC	25 Percent
Systematic	25 Percent

Market Timing	2 Percent
Specific	4 Percent
XMC	4 Percent
Systematic	90 Percent

Single Managed
Portfolio

Three Important Portfolios: Normal, Active, and Systematic

The decomposition of investment returns is useful primarily as a means for understanding portfolio management strategy since it enables portfolio performance to be attributed to investment decisions such as market timing or stock picking. However, to fully analyze portfolio management strategy and portfolio performance we have to know one particular detail of the manager's environment: the manager's *normal portfolio*. The normal portfolio is the one that the manager would hold in the absence of any judgmental information.

Typically, the normal portfolio is specified (at least implicitly) by the manager's client when the account is first awarded. For example, the client may specify that the manager should attempt to beat the S&P 500. In this situation the normal portfolio is the S&P 500 since this is the default position for the manager. Only when the manager has judgments as to over- or undervalued securities should the portfolio differ from the S&P 500.

Alternatively, the client may hire a "boutique" manager with a distinct, permanent sectoral bias, such as a growth stock manager. Implicitly, the client in this case is hiring the manager to beat other growth stock managers and not any broad market index. Here the normal portfolio is represented by the universe of growth stocks, which defines the purchase opportunities for the manager.

If we know both the actual portfolio (the portfolio that the manager is actually holding) and the normal portfolio, then we can infer a great deal about the manager's strategy. In particular, the difference between the actual portfolio and the normal portfolio defines the *active portfolio,* which represents all the transactions that the manager has undertaken in pursuit of active management. In the many cases where the normal portfolio is the S&P 500 and the manager maintains the portfolio beta close to unity, the active portfolio describes all the differences in holdings between the actual portfolio and the S&P 500.

One other variable in the above decomposition about which we should be precise is beta. We have described beta as the exposure of an asset or a portfolio to the market portfolio or, equivalently, as the determinant of an asset's expected return in the context of the CAPM. In estimating betas, some proxy for the market portfolio must be used; this proxy, relative to which an asset's beta or response coefficient is computed, is referred to as the *systematic portfolio.* The construct of the systematic portfolio, as we shall see in later chapters, is useful in getting away from the simple CAPM and toward a more general notion of risk-adjusting portfolio performance relative to a proxy which may be of more concern to a client than is an arbitrary equity index such as the NYSE Composite or the S&P 500.

Now that we have defined these three portfolios, let us continue our discussion of the decomposition of portfolio returns, with particular emphasis on the analysis of investment strategy.

Active and Passive Portfolios[7]

An instructive method of decomposing total return and risk is to view every portfolio as having two components. This breakdown arises from the separation of the investment process into two separate decisions.

---

[7]This distinction and nomenclature were first introduced by Jack Treynor and Fischer Black, "How to Use Security Analysis to Improve Portfolio Selection," *Journal of Business,* January 1973, pp. 66–86. They use the term *passive portfolio* for what we have designated as the normal portfolio. We decided to use the designation normal portfolio since many people have come to use the term *passive portfolio* synonymously with "S&P 500 index fund." We wish to avoid any confusion since, as described in the previous section, a normal (passive) portfolio could be very different from the S&P 500. We will retain the designation passive portfolio for a portfolio that is managed using a passive strategy, as described in Chapter 5.

The first decision results from an analysis of the long-term risks and rewards in the capital markets and leads to the resolution of the portfolio's normal exposure to economic events, as described in the previous section. The second decision is short term; it is the management of the portfolio to take advantage of perceived mispricing and anticipated revaluation in the near future. Note that the second decision is made in response to judgmental information; in the absence of such information there is no reason to change the portfolio from its normal position. Hence, a managed portfolio can be thought of as the sum of two subportfolios. These are the active subportfolio and the normal subportfolio. The normal subportfolio is the core around which the active manager places "bets" by underweighing some stocks and overweighing others.[8]

For example, the owner of funds may decide that the long-term portfolio holding in the international oil industry should be 15 percent. Here the actual method of arriving at this figure is immaterial, but it is important to bear in mind that the 15 percent holding is viewed as a long-term average value, so that it represents the normal portfolio holding. At some particular time, though, the manager may believe that the international oil industry is overvalued and may therefore decrease the portfolio holding to 10 percent. This 5 percent sale is an active decision which the manager expects to reverse later when the international oils are appraised as being correctly valued.

Traditionally, the new international oil holding in this example would be specified as 10 percent. As we shall see later, it is also useful to describe this 10 percent holding as being the sum of a 15 percent normal position and a −5 percent active position. The normal portfolio position is long term and carries no information as to the manager's short-term judgment on valuation. As far as the owner is concerned, the manager's value added is provided by the active portfolio. Thus, the breakdown between active and normal makes clear exactly what benefits the manager is providing.

As we shall argue in Chapter 5, the normal portfolio is likely to be set in accordance with an equilibrium model such as the CAPM, in which case the normal portfolio will be a mixture of the risk-free security and the market portfolio. If this is the case, the the normal portfolio is completely specified by the proportion invested in the market portfolio, which in this situation is exactly the same as the beta of the normal portfolio. For example, if 40 percent of funds are invested in the market (with a beta of 1.0), then 60 percent are invested in the risk-free security (with a beta of zero), so that the combination has a portfolio beta of (0.4)(1.0) + (0.6)(0.0), or 0.4.

In the following example we assume that this is the case, so the holdings in the normal portfolio will be equal to the holdings in an *equal-beta-levered market portfolio,* a market portfolio levered with the risk-free security so as to match the beta of the managed portfolio. The holdings in the active portfolio

---

[8]The normal and active components are sometimes called the *core* and *noncore,* respectively. These latter terms were first introduced by the American National Bank of Chicago.

will be equal to the difference between the managed portfolio holdings and the holdings in the normal portfolio. Hence, we have reduced the portfolio selection problem to the two following decisions.

1. *Selection of the normal portfolio.* In this framework, this decision requires the choice of the normal beta for the portfolio, denoted by β_N. Thus, if the manager has no information, the optimal (normal) portfolio is composed of the risk-free security and the market portfolio, with holdings $1 - \beta_N$ and β_N, respectively. If h_{Mi} is the proportional holding of security i in the market portfolio, then security i is held in the normal portfolio in amount $\beta_N h_{Mi}$. When the normal portfolio is a levered market portfolio, it is exposed only to systematic risk.

2. *Selection of the active portfolio.* This portfolio contains holdings in assets perceived as over- or undervalued and simply exists in order to earn incremental reward from asset selection. Moreover, the active portfolio is responsible for all the residual risk in the managed portfolio. If we denote the holding of the ith asset in this latter portfolio by h_{Pi}, then the active portfolio holding is $h_{Pi} - \beta_N h_{Mi}$.

Let us now consider the investment opportunities for both the active and normal portfolios.[9] Our aim is to decompose the efficient frontier for the managed portfolio into two efficient frontiers, one for the active component and one for the normal component. This will enable us to use the portfolio selection techniques discussed in Chapter 1 to determine the correct exposure to systematic risk (i.e., locate the optimal normal portfolio) and the correct "aggressiveness" for the active portfolio.

The only subtlety concerns total variance, which is the sum of systematic and residual variance, equation (2–2). In decomposing the frontiers, we must work with mean and variance and not mean and standard deviation, as we did in Chapter 1. Unfortunately, while standard deviation is the intuitive measure for risk, variance is the measure we must use in calculations, since variances (and not standard deviations) are additive by definition. The transformation between standard deviation and variance is trivial ($S^2 = V$) but tiresome and necessary. It is also historic, as it is analogous to the Pythagorean theorem for calculating the length of the hypotenuse of a right triangle: "The square of the length of the hypotenuse equals the sum of the squares of the lengths of the other two sides." It is the squares, not the lengths, that add. This is demonstrated in Figure 2.5, which refers to an illustrative portfolio composed of 100 shares of each of the 30 Dow Jones industrial stocks, so that its rate of return is identical to the return on the Dow Jones Industrial Average.

---

[9]The remainder to this section has been drawn heavily from Barr Rosenberg, "How Active Should a Portfolio Be? The Risk-Reward Trade-Off," *Financial Analysts Journal,* January–February 1979, pp. 49–62.

Figure 2.5
The Relation between Systematic, Residual, and Total Risk

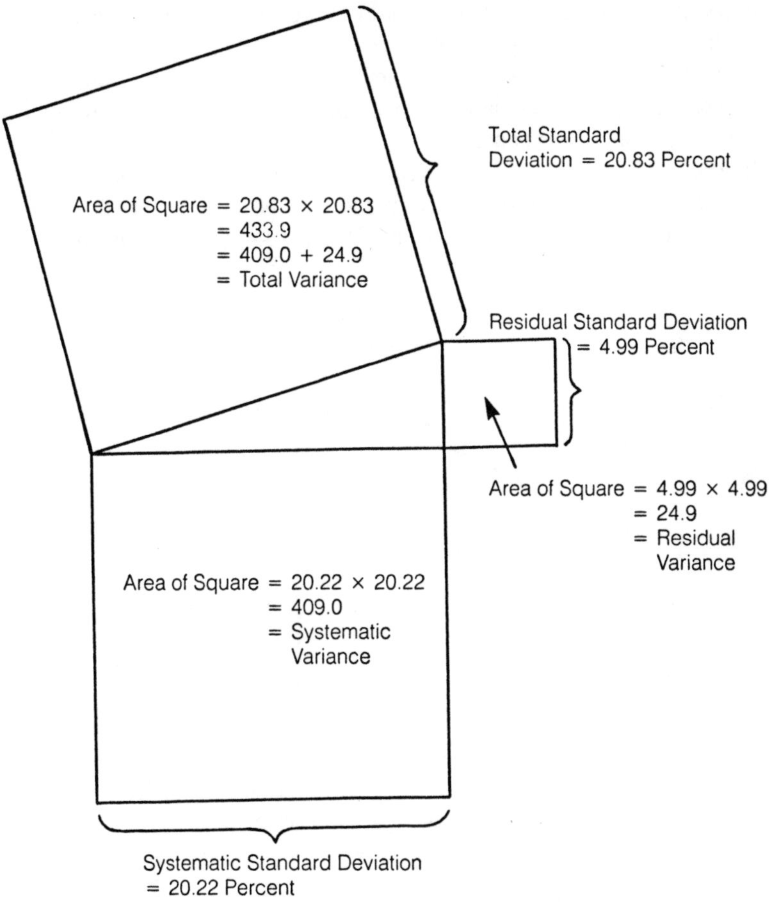

Total Standard
Deviation = 20.83 Percent

Area of Square = 20.83 × 20.83
= 433.9
= 409.0 + 24.9
= Total Variance

Residual Standard Deviation
= 4.99 Percent

Area of Square = 4.99 × 4.99
= 24.9
= Residual
Variance

Area of Square = 20.22 × 20.22
= 409.0
= Systematic
Variance

Systematic Standard Deviation
= 20.22 Percent

Selection of the Normal Portfolio

The simpler case is that of the normal frontier since there is only one variable, the portfolio beta, to manipulate. The expected rate of return on a portfolio on this frontier is given by:

$$E_P = i_F + \beta_P(E_M - i_F), \qquad (2\text{–}3)$$

while the variance of return is:[10]

$$V_P = \beta_P^2 V_M. \qquad (2\text{–}4)$$

---

[10]Taking square roots, the standard deviation of return is given by $S_P = \beta_P S_M$.

Notice that the expected excess return is proportional to beta, as is the standard deviation, while the variance is proportional to beta squared. Therefore, the frontier will plot as a smooth (quadratic) curve on a mean-variance diagram; this is shown in the upper panel of Figure 2.6. For comparison, the frontier in mean-standard-deviation space is plotted in the lower panel. Since both the mean and the standard deviation are proportional to beta, the frontier is a straight line. (This lower panel is similar to that depicted in Figure 1.9.)

The only difference between the two figures is the unit of measurement on the horizontal axis. To go from the lower to the upper we square the horizontal distance, so that the standard deviation of the market (20 percent) in the lower

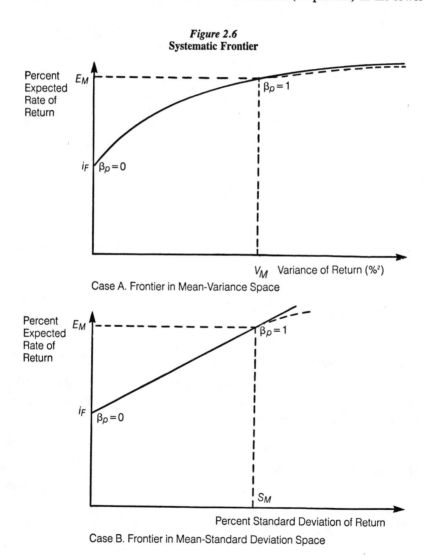

Figure 2.6
Systematic Frontier

Case A. Frontier in Mean-Variance Space

Case B. Frontier in Mean-Standard Deviation Space

diagram gets plotted at 400 ($\%^2$) in the upper. Since the vertical unit is the same, the straight frontier in the lower diagram becomes curved in the upper.

Each point on the frontier represents an optimal combination between the riskless asset and the market portfolio. A real-world constraint prevents the whole frontier from being obtainable and is represented by the dashed line. This shows the situation where it is not possible to lever up the market portfolio by borrowing at the risk-free rate and investing in risky securities. Thus, in order to obtain high-beta portfolios, securities with high betas have to be purchased in greater proportion than their proportion in the market portfolio. This introduces additional risk and so flattens the frontier beyond the market portfolio.

An investor will determine the optimal exposure to risk (or, equivalently, determine the optimal beta) by superimposing indifference curves on the risk/reward region. Since our investor has a utility function that is linear in the mean and the variance of portfolio return, indifference curves will appear as straight lines in mean-variance space. This is exactly the reverse of the situation with the frontiers since the curved indifference curves in mean-standard-deviation space (see Figure 1.4) get straightened in mean-variance space. The equation of a straight line in the mean-variance region is represented by:

$$E_P = \lambda V_P + C,$$

where E_P is the vertical distance (portfolio expected rate of return), V_P is the horizontal distance (portfolio variance of return), λ is the slope of the line (positive since investors are risk averse and demand greater reward for bearing additional risk), and C is the intercept on the vertical axis. Thus, every indifference curve can be written (on rearranging) as:

$$C = E_P - \lambda V_P, \tag{2-5}$$

where C is the level of satisfaction or utility measured as a *certainty equivalent rate of return* (it is in units of rate of return because it represents a distance up the rate of return axis, and it is a certain value because it has zero risk). Thus, the benefit is equal to the portfolio expected rate of return (E_P) less some "cost" which is proportional to the portfolio variance of return. The "cost" is the term λV_P, where λ is the slope of the indifference curve (risk/reward trade-off), which measures the increase in the expected rate of return required to compensate the investor for an increase in one unit of variance. Alternatively, we can argue that as we move out along the indifference curve, both reward and risk increase but cancel out, leaving the benefit level unchanged.

This is shown in Figure 2.7 on the indifference curve with a utility level of C_1. As we move from P_1 to P_2, a decrease in utility resulting from the increase in variance of ΔV is incurred. This disutility has magnitude $(\lambda) \cdot (\Delta V)$, which is exactly offset by the increase in utility resulting from the higher expected return of P_2 relative to P_1, shown as ΔE. Thus, λ represents the disutility to the investor of an added unit of variance.

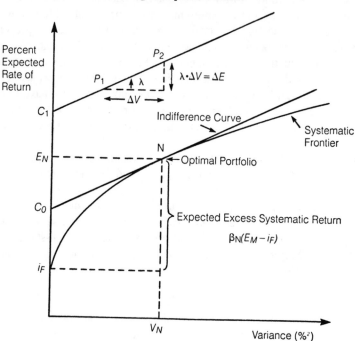

Figure 2.7
Finding the Optimal Portfolio

A lower indifference curve in the figure determines the location of the optimal passive portfolio, N. This represents the normal or default portfolio of the investor and can be thought of as the long-term optimal portfolio. We use *long term* here in the sense that provided the investor's risk aversion remains unchanged (i.e., the slope, λ, of the indifference curve) and the equilibrium values of market variance and expected excess return remain constant, then portfolio N will remain optimal.

Recall that optimality occurs when the indifference curve just touches the frontier. Mathematically, the condition is for the indifference curve to be tangent to the frontier, and hence the slope of the two curves must be the same.[11] Referring to the three phases of portfolio management introduced in Chapter 1, once we have computed the efficient frontier, our only remaining step is to superimpose the indifference curves and so determine the optimal portfolio (the case study in Supplements 1 and 2 shows how the frontier may be

---

[11]If this does not seem obvious, then consider the situation in which the indifference curve has a slope different from that of the frontier. On one side of the optimal portfolio (the point of intersection) the indifference curve must lie underneath the frontier and so contradict the assertion of optimality.

obtained). However, we do require the slope of the indifference curves in order to proceed. We will discuss this aspect in greater detail later, but the point we wish to make here is that the process is reversible. In "one direction" the frontier and the indifference curves are required for determination of the optimal portfolio, but in the "other direction," if we know the optimal portfolio and the frontier, then we can infer the slope of the indifference curves.

In other words, a portfolio manager could question clients as to the slope of their indifference curves (surprisingly, if the inquiry is properly phrased this may not be impossible; see Chapter 5) and so calculate each client's normal beta. Conversely, if a client could determine his/her normal portfolio beta (by alternative methods, for instance, asset allocation procedures), then the portfolio manager could calculate the slope of the client's indifference curve. This slope, the investor's risk/reward trade-off, is useful in establishing the correct level of aggressiveness in active management. For this reason we concentrate for the remainder of the section in pursuing the analysis when an investor can determine the normal beta by a method other than portfolio optimization.

Unfortunately, in order to explain this fully we require some mathematics. From equation (2–5), the level of utility for an arbitrary portfolio, P, is given by $C = E_P - \lambda V_P$. Now, since the optimal portfolio, by definition, offers maximum utility, its beta (the normal beta, β_N) maximizes the value C. The mathematics of this logic is to substitute equations (2–3) and (2–4) into equation (2–5) to obtain:

$$C = i_F + \beta_P(E_M - i_F) - \lambda\beta_P^2 V_M. \qquad (2\text{–}6)$$

The maximum is found by evaluating the first derivative with respect to β_P, i.e.:

$$dC/d\beta_P = E_M - i_F - 2\lambda\beta_P V_M.$$

The optimal level of utility occurs when the first derivative equals zero and, by definition of the optimal normal portfolio, when the beta is β_N. Given these two conditions we can now solve for the slope, λ; i.e.:

$$E_M - i_F - 2\lambda\beta_N V_M = 0,$$

or

$$\lambda = {}^1\!/_2 \, (E_M - i_F)/\beta_N V_M. \qquad (2\text{–}7)$$

This is shown in Figure 2.8, where it is also seen that the slope of the indifference curve is exactly one half of the ratio of the expected excess return to variance of return for an optimal portfolio.[12] The mathematical proof of this is as follows: Denote the optimal mean excess return/variance ratio by the Greek

---

[12]This property follows from the fact that the geometric form of the frontier is a parabola.

letter theta (θ), and recall that the expected excess rate of return of the optimal portfolio is given by $\beta_N(E_M - i_F)$ and variance is $\beta_N^2 V_M$, so that:[13]

$$\begin{aligned}
\theta &= \text{Mean/variance ratio} \\
&= \beta_N(E_M - i_F)/\beta_N^2 V_M \\
&= (E_M - i_F)/\beta_N V_M \\
&= 2\lambda,
\end{aligned} \tag{2-8}$$

from equation (2–7). In other words, all we need in order to infer the investor's risk/reward trade-off is the optimal long-term beta and the mean and variance of the market excess rate of return! In addition, optimal portfolios have the property that the mean/variance ratio is twice the slope of the indifference curve.

We can also determine the value of C_0 in Figure 2.8 from the fact that the

Figure 2.8
Mean/Variance Ratio for Passive Portfolio N

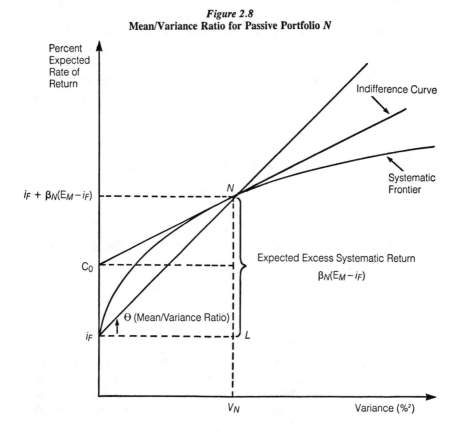

[13]This ratio is usually simply referred to as the mean/variance ratio. Its inverse is frequently referred to as the *risk-acceptance parameter (RAP)*.

slope of the indifference curve is one half the slope of the mean/variance ratio. Since the slope of indifference curve $C_0 N$ is one half the slope of $i_F N$, the distance $C_0 - i_F$ must be one half of the distance between L and N. Now C_0 measures the certainty equivalent systematic rate of return of portfolio N, so that the distance of $C_0 - i_F$ is the systematic *certainty equivalent excess return* (CEER for short) for portfolio N, which, from the figure, is given by $\frac{1}{2}\beta_N(E_M - i_F)$. In other words, when the decision is made to increase the exposure to beta and hence to increase the expected return, only one half of the increase shows up as CEER; the other half is lost as required compensation for the increased risk.

At this point it is worth noting that even if the indifference curves are not linear in mean-variance space, the slope of the indifference curve at the optimal portfolio is still equal to the slope of the frontier. However, in this case we cannot infer the slope of the indifference curve in the whole region but only in the local region about the tangency point.

Selection of the Active Portfolio

Once an optimal level for beta has been determined, the next decision concerns active management. The pursuit of an active strategy can be represented by constructing an active efficient frontier over the systematic frontier. This is shown in Figure 2.9. Again, the optimality of the active strategy is determined at the indifference curve's point of tangency with the frontier.

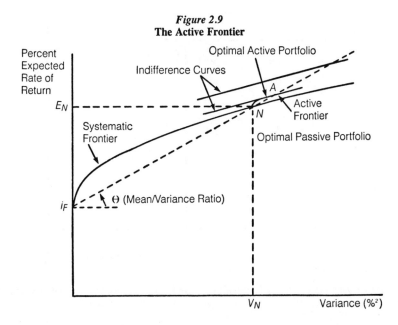

Figure 2.9
The Active Frontier

The first point to be noticed is the small impact of active management on total risk and reward.[14] Since active management fees are fairly substantial, an immediate question arises concerning the economic value of active management to the owner of the portfolio. In order to examine this question thoroughly, we need to explore the region of active management in greater detail.

The location of the optimal active portfolio is at the point of tangency between the active frontier and the indifference curves. Notice that even if the indifference curves are not linear over the entire region, they will be approximately linear over the region of active management. See Figure 2.12 for a geographic display of the relative sizes of the two regions. The optimal active portfolio, A, is shown in Figure 2.9 as the point of tangency between the highest indifference curve and the active frontier. Since the slope of the indifference curve is known, then provided we can measure the residual variance,

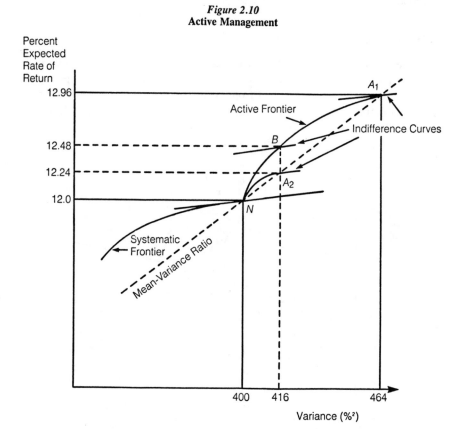

Figure 2.10
Active Management

---

[14]Typical values of the standard deviation of return for managed portfolios would be as follows: systematic, 20 percent; residual, 6 percent; total, 20.88 percent ($= \sqrt{400 + 36}$).

the disutility from residual risk or the "cost" of active management (due to increased risk) can be calculated as simply $\lambda\omega_P^2$.

This is shown in greater detail in Figure 2.10, which displays the active frontier. The optimal active portfolio, A_1, lies not only on the frontier and on the indifference curve but also on the extension of the line of constant mean/variance ratio. The implications of this point are explored in the next section.

Required Alpha and Returns to
Active Management

We are interested in evaluating active management since this is the pursuit that the majority of money managers perform. Here we define active management as taking positions in assets in order to earn superior returns.[15] When this is done the portfolio will also take on added risk, incurring a cost of $\lambda\omega_P^2$. The additional expected return comes from the money manager's "alpha," that is, his or her superior skill relative to the skill of other managers due to any emphasis of industry sectors, market timing, or whatever other strategy the manager uses. In short, active management is not holding an index fund.

In terms of the management style, the active manager can be viewed as "starting" at portfolio N, the normal portfolio, with beta β_N, but delivering that strategy (i.e., that beta) with a portfolio formed by superior active management. The result of this decision can be seen in Figure 2.10 as the move from N up the active frontier to the optimal active portfolio, A_1. Portfolio A_1 is optimal since it is at the point where the indifference curves are tangent to the frontier. It is also at the point where the mean/variance ratio for active management equals that of the normal portfolio.[16] Hence, optimal aggressiveness in the active component is characterized by the achievement of a mean/variance ratio equal to that of the normal portfolio, or in symbols for a portfolio P on the active frontier:

$$\alpha_P/\omega_P^2 = \text{Active mean/variance ratio}$$
$$= (E_M - i_F)/\beta_P V_M$$
$$= \text{normal mean/variance ratio.}$$

Therefore, for the active manager to be optimally aggressive the portfolio alpha must be:

$$\alpha_P^R = (E_M - i_F)\omega_P^2/\beta_P V_M, \qquad (2\text{--}9)$$

---

[15]Superior, that is, to the normal portfolio.

[16]Provided the investor perceives the same disutility to systematic and residual risk. There are occasions, briefly discussed in the next section, when rational investors will exhibit different tolerances to systematic and residual risk.

where the superscript R indicates that this alpha level is required for the present portfolio to be optimal. Now, most portfolios will have a beta close to unity, and for simplicity we will assume that the normal exposure to systematic risk is to have a beta of 1. For this portfolio:

$$\alpha_P^R = (E_M - i_F)\omega_P^2/V_M. \tag{2-10}$$

Since $E_M - i_F$, the mean excess return on the market portfolio, and V_M, the variance of the market portfolio, are long-term values, there is likely to be substantial agreement over their magnitudes. We will assume that $E_M - i_F = 6\%$, $E_M = 12\%$, and $V_M = 400$ ($\%^2$). Hence:

$$\alpha_P^R = 6\omega_P^2/400 = 0.015\ \omega_P^2. \tag{2-11}$$

Thus, whenever the level of portfolio residual risk, ω_P^2, can be measured (and with present methods it can be predicted with substantial accuracy), the required alpha for the portfolio can be calculated.

Notice that this alpha is not the abnormal return the active manager anticipates; rather it is the alpha that must be produced to compensate for the risk exposure of the portfolio. Let us now consider an example of an aggressive portfolio with an annual residual standard deviation of 8 percent.[17] Solving the equation for the required alpha gives a value of a mere 96 basis points. Most managers will breathe a sigh of relief . . . only 96 basis points—that's not much!

Now, turning to Figure 2.10, it can be seen that we have solved the required alpha for portfolio A_1. Further, portfolio A_2, with a residual variance of 16 ($\%^2$), has the same active mean/variance ratio and has a required alpha of only 24 basis points ($0.015 \times 16 \times 100$). Let us suppose that portfolio A_2 represents the current portfolio of a manager who believes that the portfolio alpha is not 24 basis points but 48 basis points (i.e., the manager is confident that a greater expected residual return can be delivered than that required as compensation for the residual risk). In addition, there is agreement that the residual variance of the portfolio is 16 ($\%^2$), so that the manager believes the portfolio to be located at B instead of A_2, i.e., the current portfolio is on a higher active frontier than that required to justify its residual risk. But now B is not an optimal portfolio for the owner since it neither has the correct mean/variance ratio nor does it lie on the tangency point of the frontier and the indifference curve. Thus, if the manager thinks that the portfolio is doing better than is required by the risk level, then the portfolio is not optimal!

In fact, if the manager believes the alpha prediction of 48 basis points, the portfolio should be revised to become twice as aggressive, doubling the alpha to 96 basis points, doubling the residual standard deviation, and quadrupling

---

[17]The median institutional portfolio has an annual residual standard deviation of approximately 6 percent; some mutual and special equity funds may have in the range 10–15 percent; and the residual standard deviations of bank pooled funds are on the order of 3–4 percent. (All figures are relative to the S&P 500).

the residual variance to 64 ($\%^2$), and thus achieving optimality at A_1. We know that A_1 is better because it lies on a higher indifference curve. Alas, the manager and the portfolio are truly hoist by their own petard! By claiming to be better than required, the manager, in fact, claims suboptimality.

In this example, we moved from B to A_1 and increased utility by increasing active reward more than the resulting increase in risk. An easier way to see that B is suboptimal entails increasing reward while keeping the risk constant. This method is shown in Figure 2.11.

The method is to decrease portfolio beta from unity to 0.94 (for instance, by investment in cash) so that systematic variance goes from V_M to $(0.94)^2 V_M$, or from 400 ($\%^2$) to approximately 352 ($\%^2$), a reduction of 48 units of variance. In doing this, we lose some systematic return; that is, instead of $E_M - i_F$ we get 0.94 $(E_M - i_F)$, or a reduction of 36 basis points [$6(1 - 0.94)\%$]. In other words, we have moved down the frontier from N to N_1, where the active frontier now starts. We now take the aggressive position with 64 units of residual variance, taking us back to 416 ($\%^2$), the original level. There is now less

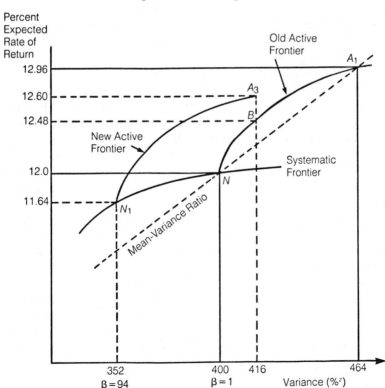

Figure 2.11
Optimal Active Strategies

systematic but more residual risk than before. However, on the expected return dimension we have lost 36 basis points reducing the beta, but we have gained 96 basis from the active management, giving a total increase of 60 basis points, so that the portfolio has an expected rate of return of 12.60 percent as opposed to 12.48 percent. This is shown as portfolio A_3.

What have we achieved? These methods can be used to show the suboptimality of a portfolio when it does not lie on the tangency point between the indifference curve and the active frontier or have the same mean/variance ratio as the normal portfolio. In other words, we have offered a constructive proof of the appropriateness of the required alpha as a device for evaluating the consistency of active management.

Effect of Different Attitudes to Systematic and Residual Risk

The theme of the previous section may be summarized as follows. A rational investor must require that the benefit from active management exceed the cost. The benefit is clearly the expected residual return, or alpha. The cost comprises three components: (1) the increase in the fee for active management over that for passive management (demanded by the money manager to support the valuation and investment process); (2) the increase in transaction costs; and (3) the "cost," or risk, that the reward of active management will not be achieved (that is, the disutility incurred from bearing residual risk).

The previous section described a simple, yet powerful, method for analyzing the consistency of portfolio management. The results of analyses based upon representative institutional portfolios indicate that the management of these assets is far from rational.[18] One reason for this paradoxical situation may be the pension sponsor's (and perhaps the asset manager's) exaggerated aversion to residual risk. If the disutility of residual risk were much greater than that of systematic risk, then the slope of the indifference curve required for finding the optimal active portfolio would be steeper. As can be seen from Figure 2.9, this change in slope would suggest a more cautious approach to active management.

Although this explanation may fit the facts, it is unconvincing because there is little reason to believe that systematic return is any different from residual return (return *is* return, no matter what its origin). One argument that attempts to distinguish between the two returns suggests that expected residual return should be discounted since its existence contradicts efficient markets. However, this reasoning is fallacious since, by definition, expected residual return is expected. Thus, the judgmental information used to determine the reward from active management should, if correctly formulated, already have been adjusted

---

[18]An example of one such analysis appears as a case study in the next section.

for uncertainty.[19] In fact, an argument based on the risk of active management would indicate that there should be *less* aversion to residual risk than to systematic risk. If the portfolio under consideration is part of a large portfolio (as would be the case if a pension sponsor retained several managers, each responsible for one portion of the assets), then the residual risk in any one part of the portfolio is likely to be diversified away relative to the entire portfolio. In this situation, residual risk is less important than systematic risk, suggesting that active management should be even more aggressive than it is.

One rational explanation for the lack of aggressive active management by money managers arises from their relationship with the owners of funds. Increasing the aggressiveness of active management also increases the probability of poor short-term performance. Unless some covenant has been established with the owner of funds, this also increases the likelihood that the manager will be terminated. Hence, the manager increases his or her business risk by becoming more aggressive, although on average this benefits the sponsor. For this reason, there is a great temptation on the manager's part to take minimal residual risk unless the owner of funds understands the manager's dilemma and provides some guarantee of continued employment. We will discuss this problem further in the section, "Conflicts in the Manager-Sponsor Relationship", in Chapter 6.

If, as appears to be common, the inferred benefit of active management is less than the cost, then three possible solutions are suggested: (1) the termination of active management in favor of a passive strategy; (2) the negotiation of lower costs (i.e., lower management fees); or (3) the continuation of active management at a more aggressive level, incurring more residual risk in pursuit of increased expected residual return.

Case Study 2: A Multiply Managed Portfolio[20]

We complete this chapter with a brief case study on a multiply managed portfolio, outlining the use of the portfolio required alpha. A multiply managed portfolio is one in which several managers each invest a portion of the total portfolio. The control and organization of multiply managed portfolios are important problems in investment management and are considered in detail in Chapter 6. For our purposes here, it matters little that the overall portfolio has several managers, but this fact does provide an interesting insight into the different styles that were selected by the sponsor to manage parts of the aggregate portfolio.

The sponsor's aggregate portfolio has eight managers, of whom seven are active managers and one is an index fund manager. In Table 2.1 we show the risk attributes of the overall portfolio and four of the subportfolios. The risk

---

[19]This adjustment for information content is described in Chapter 4.

[20]This case study is based upon an analysis of a pension sponsor's total equity portfolio.

Table 2.1
Aggregate and Components of a Multiply Managed Portfolio

| Portfolio | Beta | Residual Standard Deviation (Percent) | Variance (%²) | | | | α^R (Percent) | CEER (Basis Points) |
			Systematic	Residual	XMC	Specific		
Aggregate	1.05	2.88	473.6	8.3	6.7	1.6	0.125	6.25
Subportfolio 4	1.02	2.98	457.0	8.9	2.1	6.8	0.134	67
Subportfolio 5	1.26	9.26	682.0	85.7	66.9	18.8	1.29	65
Subportfolio 7	1.53	14.68	1,008.5	215.4	162.7	52.7	3.23	161
Index fund	1.00	0.00	430.2	0.0	0.0	0.0	0.00	0

Source: MULMAN analysis. We are grateful to Michel Houglet for performing this analysis. Forecasts of systematic variance are derived from the annual mean and variance of the S&P 500 excess rate of return—6.0 and 429.5, respectively.

predictions in the table are taken from a predictive model of investment risk, which will be discussed in Chapter 3, and are taken relative to the S&P 500 (the proxy for the market portfolio).

The first point to notice is that the aggregate portfolio is very close to being a "slightly levered" index fund since it has a beta of 1.05 (which is only a little different from the S&P 500 beta of unity) and its level of residual risk is very low (less than 3 percent per year), which is riskier than only one of the constituent portfolios, the index fund. The fact that the residual risk in the aggregate portfolio is so small is another example of diversification. The formation of the aggregate portfolio from eight subportfolios is exactly equivalent to forming a portfolio from eight different securities; in both cases "grouping" reduces overall risk to a level lower than that of many of the components.

Second, note that the residual risk arises largely from the *XMC* with only a small fraction due to specific risk (i.e., stock selection). In fact, what has occurred is that the specific component of risk in each of the subportfolios has been diversified away much more than the *XMC* component. This is what we might expect if each manager had a similar style, for instance, a propensity for growth stocks. In this case, exposure to a common factor gets reinforced rather than diversified.

Now, using the definition of required alpha given in equation (2–11), it follows that for the exposure to residual risk in the aggregate portfolio to be justified (at a normal portfolio beta of unity), the expected abnormal return is required to be 12.5 basis points (8.3 × 0.015). Moreover, note that this is an *expected* 12.5 basis points, a number that represents the average performance that would occur if we could repeat the future many times.[21] Hence, this figure is just the mean of a distribution. Fortunately, we have already explained a method of finding the effect of the uncertainty around the required alpha; we called this the certainty equivalent excess return (CEER). Provided that the indifference curves are linear in the entire mean-variance region, the CEER of

---

[21]See the supplement to Chapter 1 for elucidation on this intuition of an expectation.

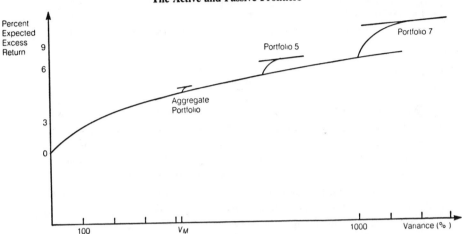

Figure 2.12
The Active and Passive Frontiers

active management is one half of the required alpha (see Figure 2.8). We can explain this as follows. If the government were to introduce a new "risk-free 90-day instrument" which offered a superior return over the current 90-day Treasury bill, how much of an incremental return would be demanded so as to make the sponsor indifferent between this "risk-free instrument" and the active management in the aggregate portfolio?[22] The answer is $6\frac{1}{4}$ basis points, and it is found by measuring the distance above the 90-day Treasury bill rate (i_F) to where the indifference curve cuts the axis. This distance measures the increment in return obtained from active management, and it is in certainty-equivalent form since we are measuring up the vertical axis.

In summary, the active management in the aggregate portfolio is "worth" only $6\frac{1}{4}$ basis points in certain return. Unfortunately, this sponsor portfolio is by no means unusual since the majority of multiply managed sponsor portfolios are close to being index funds. Further, management fees are also paid "in certain" and are usually much more expensive than the $6\frac{1}{4}$ basis points that are required for this risk exposure to be optimal. Hence, if the sponsor believes that the seven active managers are superior (i.e., have a positive alpha), then each manager should be instructed to be more aggressive so as to earn a higher residual return. In this case, the CEER of active management will eventually exceed the management fee. Conversely, if the sponsor believes that the managers are not superior, then the entire fund should be indexed to save active fees (or new managers should be hired).

With this detailed explanation of the aggregate portfolio, the analysis of the component portfolios shown should be clear. Subportfolio 7, the most agressive

[22]This is an expository argument since in the real world arbitrage would prevent the existence of two riskless instruments with different rates but the same maturity.

of the managed portfolios, is a special equity fund. Subportfolios 4 and 5 are relatively typical, institutional portfolios, though the beta of subportfolio 5 perhaps may be higher than usual. Figure 2.12 shows the systematic frontier and the frontiers for the aggregate portfolio, subportfolio 5, and subportfolio 7.

Summary

We have dissected the concepts of risk and reward. By starting with the market as the primitive influence on stock returns, we have begun our description of a comprehensive theory governing the behavior of securities.

We inferred an attitude toward risk and reward from the equity market, and we identified the long-term portfolio as the normal portfolio. This led to a discussion of the active component, from which, provided there is the same aversion to systematic and residual risk, it followed that we could imply the rewards to active management from the risk posture of the portfolio.

Further Reading

Very little of this material has found its way into existing texts. Perhaps the best sources for further reading are the following papers by Barr Rosenberg:

Rosenberg, Barr. "Security Appraisal and Unsystematic Risk in Institutional Investment." *Proceedings of the Seminar on the Analysis of Security Prices.* University of Chicago, November 1976, pp. 171–237.

———"How Active Should a Portfolio Be? The Risk-Reward Trade-off." *Financial Analysts Journal,* January–February 1979, pp. 49–62.

Earlier articles dealing with active and passive strategies include:

Ferguson, Robert. "Active Portfolio Management." *Financial Analysts Journal,* May–June 1975, pp. 63–72.

Treynor, Jack, and Fischer Black. "How to Use Security Analysis to Improve Portfolio Selection." *Journal of Business,* January 1973, pp. 66–86.

Further discussion on the approximation involved in using the CAPM despite an inability to isolate the market portfolio can be found in:

Rudd, Andrew, and Barr Rosenberg. "The 'Market Model' in Investment Management." *Journal of Finance,* May 1980, pp. 597–607.

___ Supplement 2 ___

Diversification and the Capital Asset Pricing Model (CAPM)

In spite of many disbeliever's comments, MPT *is* based upon a solid theory. This theory, the CAPM, is remarkably accurate in its implications for the real world. However, this is not the place for a lengthy discourse on the many versions of the CAPM. Instead, we include here a brief outline of a simple derivation of the most straightforward version of the model.

We begin with some mathematics to describe diversification that will be useful in the subsequent derivation. Then we make some assumptions, use some simple algebra, and derive the basic equilibrium relation. The assumptions are not burdens we must bear—most can be either made innocuous or removed completely at the expense of some high-powered mathematics—but rather a simple foundation on which to build a powerful and realistic model.

That the model contains a great deal of truth seems beyond doubt (though how much and how to unambiguously test for it remains an unanswered and, possibly, unanswerable question). Hopefully, practitioners and decision makers will not wed themselves rigidly to its design. A better point of view would be to approach it as an excellent first approximation in a world where uncertainty is the reason for participation.

The model is framed in terms of expectations. It is a luxury when expectations are realized; this fact is forgotten when appraisers of MPT point to inaccuracies of prediction as a major weakness. In the capital markets it is frequently obvious why anticipation gives way to recrimination; there are powerful forces at work in the economy which cannot be lumped together as market sentiment. These forces are the common factors described in Chapter 2 and referred to by practitioners as "the strength of second-tier stocks," "the weakness of growth companies," and so on.

The explanation of security returns in terms of the response to the common factors is one major change between the early attempts to quantitatively analyze investment management and the present approach. The ability to accurately estimate the factors and every security's response or exposure to each factor is a major breakthrough in our understanding of the capital markets. However, before we can rigorously derive these models, we must further develop the theory of diversification. That is the subject of this supplement.

The notation which we will use is as follows. E, S, and V will denote the expectation, standard deviation, and variance of the random rate of return (remember, $S^2 = V$). Subscripts j and k will refer to assets j and k, and subscript P will refer to a portfolio. The correlation between two random rates of return will be denoted by ρ (the Greek rho), so that the covariance between the random returns on securities j and k is given by $S_j S_k \rho_{jk}$. To save space we will frequently write this covariance as V_{jk}. Recall that the covariance of a random variable with itself is simply the variance; therefore, we make the convention that $V_{jj} = V_j$ for all assets j. Finally, the proportional holding of the jth asset in the portfolio is denoted by h_j.

Recall from Supplement 1 that the expectation and variance of the rate of return of a two-security risky portfolio can be written:

$$E_P = h_1 E_1 + h_2 E_2 = h_1 E_1 + (1 - h_1) E_2 \qquad \text{(S2–1)}$$

and

$$\begin{aligned} V_P &= h_1^2 V_1 + 2 h_1 h_2 V_{12} + h_2^2 V_2 \\ &= h_1^2 V_1 + 2 h_1 (1 - h_1) V_{12} + (1 - h_1)^2 V_2, \qquad \text{(S2–2)} \end{aligned}$$

where we have used the relation that $h_1 + h_2 = 1$.

Notice that if $h_1 = 1$, then $E_P = E_1$ and $V_P = V_1$, and if $h_1 = 0$, then $E_P = E_2$ and $V_P = V_2$. The intriguing situation, and the one we will concentrate upon, occurs when $1 > h_1 > 0$ so that there is positive investment in both securities. In this case, what is the relationship between E_P, E_1, E_2, and V_P, V_1, V_2, the means and variances of return?

The mathematically inclined can eliminate h_1 from the two expressions for E_P and V_P and so be left with a relation between the means and variances of the portfolio and two securities. Other readers will note that the covariance term, V_{12}, is defined as $V_{12} = S_1 S_2 \rho_{12}$, where ρ_{12} is correlation between securities 1 and 2 and S_j is the standard deviation of asset j. What we are interested in is the effect of the correlation coefficient on total risk:

$$\begin{aligned} V_P &= h_1^2 S_1^2 + 2 h_1 (1 - h_1) S_1 S_2 \rho_{12} + (1 - h_1)^2 S_2^2 \\ &= (+) + (+) \rho_{12} + (+), \end{aligned}$$

for $1 > h_1 > 0$, where the $(+)$ denotes that the term is positive. Hence, V_P is a linear function of ρ_{12}, and as ρ_{12} decreases (or increases), so does V_P. Saying this another way, maximum variance occurs when $\rho_{12} = +1$, in which case:

$$\begin{aligned} V_P &= h_1^2 S_1^2 + 2 h_1 (1 - h_1) S_1 S_2 + (1 - h_1)^2 S_2^2 \\ &= (h_1 S_1 + (1 - h_1) S_2)^2. \end{aligned}$$

Taking square roots of both sides gives:

$$S_P = h_1 S_1 + (1 - h_1) S_2. \qquad \text{(S2–3)}$$

That is, when $\rho_{12} = +1$, S_P is just a weighted average of the security standard deviations where the weights are the holdings in the securities.

Finally, since $V_P = S_P^2$, if V_P decreases as ρ_{12} decreases, it follows that S_P also decreases as ρ_{12} decreases; the maximum of S_P (when viewed as a function of ρ_{12}) again occurs when $\rho_{12} = +1$.

This situation is clearer on a diagram. Figure S2.1 shows the two securities and the set of portfolios composed from them on a diagram with E_P plotted on the vertical axis and S_P plotted on the horizontal axis. In this figure security 2 is shown with a higher mean return and variance of return ($E_2 > E_1$, and $S_2 > S_1$). Taking the case of $\rho_{12} = +1$ (since both E_P and S_P are weighted averages of E_1, E_2 and S_1, S_2, respectively), it follows that all portfolios composed of positive amounts of the two securities can be plotted on the straight line between security 1 and security 2.

The other extreme case occurs when the two securities are perfectly negatively correlated; that is, $\rho_{12} = -1$. The expression for portfolio variance is now:[1]

Figure S2.1
The Set of Two-Security Risky Portfolios with Perfect Positive Correlation

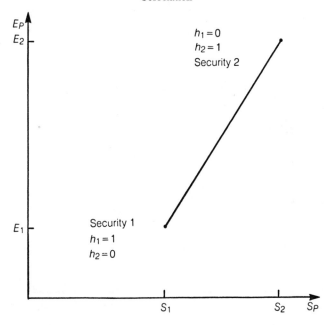

---

[1]The expected portfolio rate of return is still given by equation (S2–1) since it is independent of the correlation coefficient.

$$V_P = h_1^2 S_1^2 - 2h_1(1 - h_1)S_1 S_2 + h_2^2 S_2^2$$
$$= (h_1 S_1 - (1 - h_1)S_2)^2.$$

Taking square roots of both sides gives:[2]

$$S_P = \pm(h_1 S_1 - (1 - h_1)S_2) \qquad \text{(S2–4)}$$

Again, portfolio standard deviation is a weighted average of the security standard deviations, but the weights are now the absolute value of the holdings, with one positive and one negative. One immediate result of this is that it is possible to find a *risk-free* portfolio composed of positive holdings in the two assets. That is, setting $S_P = 0$ in equation (S2–4) and solving for the portfolio proportions gives:

$$h_1 = S_2/(S_1 + S_2); \; h_2 = (1 - h_1) = S_1/(S_1 + S_2).$$

With these weights the two securities are perfectly hedged, resulting in a risk-free portfolio. This is shown in Figure S2.2, where the risk-free portfolios lie along the vertical axis, $S_P = 0$.

We have now analyzed portfolios with the two extreme values for the correlation coefficient. For perfect positive correlation, all portfolios have the av-

Figure S2.2
The Set of Two-Security Risky Portfolios with Perfect Negative Correlation

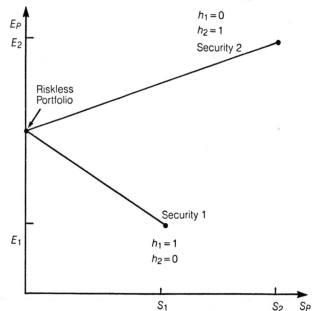

---

[2]We have to take both positive and negative square roots in this case since it is possible for $h_1 S_1 - (1 - h_1)S_2$ to take both signs, although, of course, S_P can only be positive or zero. This implies that the standard deviation will be plotted as two line segments. See Figure S2.2.

erage risk of the constituent securities; while for perfect negative correlation, all portfolios have less than the average risk of the constituent securities. In fact, it is possible to form a risk-free portfolio. For securities which are not perfectly correlated (i.e., have coefficients between −1 and + 1), the set of attainable portfolios will lie between the two limiting attainable frontiers, as shown in Figure S2.3. As the correlation coefficient decreases from + 1 with the asset weights held constant, portfolio standard deviation will also decrease, and it is easily demonstrated that the set of portfolios will follow the smooth curves shown. The startling result is that some portfolios occur on this frontier which have mean returns higher, and standard deviations lower, than security 1.

This is the concept of diversification, or the effect of covariance; by mixing securities which are less than perfectly correlated, we can form portfolios that "dominate" simple securities. For sufficiently small correlation we can always find portfolios with less risk than some component securities.[3]

This raises the interesting question of what happens if we invest in both the risk-free asset and the risky assets. For the sake of simplicity, let security 1 now be the riskless asset, with rate of return i_F. Then, from the equations above we still find that:

Figure S2.3
The Set of Two-Security Risky Portfolios with Correlation between
+1 and −1

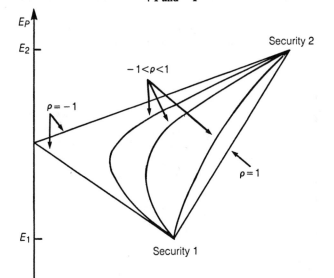

---

[3]For a two-security risky portfolio, the condition for this to hold is that $\rho_{12} < \min(S_1, S_2)/\max(S_1, S_2)$, as can be verified from equation (S2–2).

$$E_P = h_1E_1 + (1 - h_1)E_2 \qquad\qquad\text{(S2–5)}$$
$$= h_1i_F + (1 - h_1)E_2.$$

But now (since $V_1 = 0$ and hence $V_{12} = 0$):

$$V_P = (1 - h_1)^2V_2,$$

so that:

$$S_P = (1 - h_1)S_2. \qquad\qquad\text{(S2–6)}$$

In other words, portfolios composed of risky and riskless assets can be plotted along a straight line between the two securities, as shown in Figure S2.4. This result confirms the linear form of the frontier in Figure 1.1.

It is now a simple step to generalize these results to many assets. First, consider the risky securities where there is less than perfect correlation (in the real world the correlation coefficient between different common stocks is typically on the order of 0.3). The group of risky portfolios will lie in the region shown in Figure S2.5. The set of portfolios which have the greatest mean return for a given level of standard deviation (or, equivalently, the smallest standard deviation for a given level of mean return) will lie along the curved line *LMN*. This is the set of optimal or efficient portfolios, since every rational investor will choose one of these portfolios over the portfolios that lie in the interior. If we now choose one portfolio on this frontier, say, portfolio *L*, and

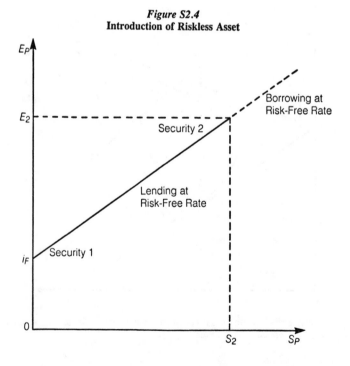

Figure S2.4
Introduction of Riskless Asset

mix it with the risk-free asset, we form portfolios that lie along the line i_FLK. Between i_F and L, assets have positive holdings in both the risk-free security and portfolio L, while beyond L, along LK, investors are "shorting" the risk-free security (i.e., borrowing to lever up portfolio L).

Notice that portfolios along LK are not optimal portfolios for investors since risky portfolios exist along LMN which have the same risk but higher mean return (portfolios LM dominate portfolios LK). To find the set of optimal portfolios we rotate the line i_FLK to i_FMB, where M is the tangent point between line i_FB and risky frontier LMN. It is easily seen that portfolios along i_FMB dominate all other portfolios. In other words, investors will locate risky portfolio M and then mix it with the riskless security to find their optimal portfolio.

This simple model is the rationale for the asset allocation decision. Namely, mix an equity portfolio with bond and cash equivalent holdings to form an overall portfolio that matches the investors' preferences for risk and return. This is equivalent to moving along i_FMB, although the levered equity portfolios MB are usually not obtainable for institutional investors.[4]

With this background, let us move on to the derivation of the CAPM. First, we will need the following assumptions:

Figure S2.5
Attainable Portfolio with Many Assets

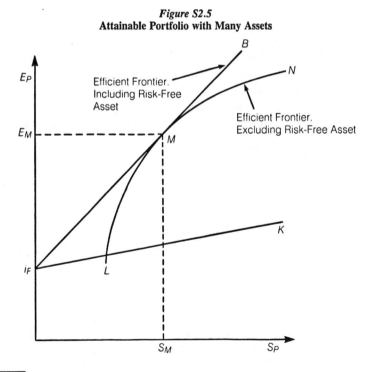

---

[4]Typically, only open-ended mutual funds are legally permitted to lever up and then only to a limit of one third of net assets.

Assumption 1: Each investor makes decisions based upon a prediction of the distribution of security returns; moreover, all investors have identical predictions.

Assumption 2: Each investor measures desirability in terms of the mean and variance of portfolio return.

Assumption 3: Each investor can borrow or lend unlimited amounts at the risk-free rate of interest, which is the same for all investors.

Assumption 4: The capital markets are "perfect"; that is, there are no taxes or transaction costs and no investor is sufficiently large to affect the prices of securities.

Each investor will be faced with a portfolio selection problem. Since every utility function is linear in mean and variance, we can write the selection problem for an individual investor algebraically as:

Problem 1.   Select portfolio holdings so as to maximize U, where:

$$U = E_P - \lambda V_P \qquad \text{(objective function)}$$

such that:

$$\sum_{j=1}^{N} h_j = 1, \qquad \text{(budget equation)}$$

where

E_P = the expected rate of return on the portfolio;
V_P = the variance of return on the portfolio;
h_j = the portfolio proportional holding in the jth security;
$\lambda (> 0)$ = the investor's risk-aversion parameter; and
N = the number of securities from which the portfolio will be chosen.

From Supplement 1, it follows that:

$$E_P = \sum_{j=1}^{N} h_j E_j \qquad (S2-7)$$

and

$$V_P = \sum_{k=1}^{N} \sum_{j=1}^{N} h_k h_j V_{kj}, \qquad (S2-8)$$

where, for notational convenience, we write the covariance between all securities k and j as V_{kj}, so that the covariance of security k with itself (i.e., the variance of security i) is written V_{kk}.

For the sake of simplicity, order the assets so that the risk-free asset is first; that is, $E_1 = i_F$, and h_1 is the holding in the risk-free asset. Recall from Supplement 1 that since the risk-free asset has zero variance:

$$V_{j1} = V_{1j} = 0 \text{ for all securities } j$$

and

$$h_1 = 1 - \sum_{j=2}^{N} h_j,$$

which, when substituted into the equations for the mean and variance of portfolio risk, give:

$$E_P = (1 - \sum_{j=2}^{N} h_j)i_F + \sum_{j=2}^{N} h_j E_j$$

$$= i_F + \sum_{j=2}^{N} h_j(E_j - i_F)$$

and

$$V_P = \sum_{k=2}^{N} \sum_{j=2}^{N} h_k h_j V_{kj}.$$

We may now reexpress the original problem as:

Problem 2.   Select proportional holdings h_j, $j = 2, \ldots, N$ so as to maximize

$$[i_F + \sum_{k=2}^{N} h_k(E_k - i_F)] - \lambda(\sum_{k=2}^{N} \sum_{j=2}^{N} h_k h_j V_{kj}),$$

which is a good deal more tractable than the original form (since the budget constraint has been eliminated), so that there is only the objective function with which to contend. The optimization proceeds by differentiating with respect to each decision variable (the h_j) in turn and then setting the result equal to zero. This gives the following system of $N - 1$ equations:

$$E_2 - i_F - \lambda(2 \sum_{j=2}^{N} h_j V_{2j}) = 0$$

$$E_3 - i_F - \lambda(2 \sum_{j=2}^{N} h_j V_{3j}) = 0$$

$$\cdot$$
$$\cdot$$
$$\cdot$$

$$E_N - i_F - \lambda(2 \sum_{j=2}^{N} h_j V_{Nj}) = 0,$$

where the last parenthesis in each equation follows from (take, for example, the first equation):

$$V_P = \sum_{k=2}^{N} \sum_{j=2}^{N} h_k h_j V_{kj} = h_2^2 V_{22} + h_2 \sum_{j=3}^{N} h_j V_{2j} + h_2 \sum_{k=3}^{N} h_k V_{k2},$$

giving

$$dV_P/dh_2 = 2h_2V_{22} + \sum_{j=3}^{N} h_jV_{2j} + \sum_{k=3}^{N} h_kV_{k2} = 2\sum_{j=2}^{N} h_jV_{2j}.$$

This last summation looks formidable, but recall from Supplement 1 that it simply represents the covariance of security 2 with the portfolio; that is:[5]

$$\sum_{j=1}^{N} h_jV_{2j} = V_{P2}$$

In other words, these equations can be rewritten as:

$$E_j - i_F - 2\lambda V_{Pj} = 0 \text{ for } j = 1, \ldots, N, \qquad \text{(S2–9)}$$

and represent, with the budget equation, the conditions for optimality of portfolio P.[6] If we now multiply the jth equation by h_j and sum over all values of j, it is easy to see that:

$$E_P - i_F - 2\lambda V_P = 0. \qquad \text{(S2–10)}$$

Now eliminating the risk-aversion parameter, λ, between equations (S2–9) and (S2–10), we find:

$$E_j - i_F = V_{Pj}(E_P - i_F)/V_P \text{ for all securities } j. \qquad \text{(S2–11)}$$

This states that optimal portfolios have the property that the expected excess return (over the risk-free rate of return) on all securities is a constant— $(E_P - i_F)/V_P = 2\lambda$—multiple of the covariance of the security with the portfolio.[7]

We now invoke that part of assumption 1 which states that all investors have the same beliefs concerning the future performance of the securities. In other words, all investors face the same Figure S2.5 and all investors will find the same optimal portfolio of risky assets, P, to mix with the riskless asset. Clearly, if all investors purchase only one risky portfolio, then this portfolio has to be pretty special—and it is!

Portfolio P in this equilibrium setting must be the "market portfolio," the portfolio composed of all risky assets with holdings proportional to their capitalization.

We have previously referred to the market portfolio as M. Returning to the last equation and making the substitution:

$$E_j - i_F = V_{Mj}(E_M - i_F)/V_M \text{ for all securities } j, \qquad \text{(S2–12)}$$

---

[5]For convenience we sum over all assets, which is correct since terms involving the first (riskless) asset are all zero.

[6]It is not sufficient just to set the first derivative equal to zero to claim a maximum; we also require the matrix of second derivatives to be negative definite. This condition is satisfied, but for the sake of continuity we omit the proof.

[7]Notice that $\lambda = (E_P - i_F)/2V_P$ for optimal portfolio P, and contrast this result with equation (2–7). When we aggregate all individual portfolio decisions to obtain the CAPM, it is easily seen that both expressions are the same.

which is more frequently written as:

$$E_j - i_F = \beta_j(E_M - i_F) \text{ for all risky securities } j, \qquad \text{(S2–13)}$$

where:

$$\beta_j = V_{Mj}/V_M = \text{Cov}[r_M, r_j]/\text{Var}[r_M], \qquad \text{(S2–14)}$$

and r_M and r_j are the random rates of return on the market portfolio and security j, respectively.

Equation (S2–13) is the familiar CAPM, which states that the expected excess return on all risky assets is linearly related to the expected excess return on the market, where the constant of proportionality is the beta of the asset defined in equation (S2–14). The left quantity, $E_j - i_F$, is the risk premium for the asset j and represents the reward for bearing risk in the form of asset j. The right quantities are composed of a constant for all securities, $E_M - i_F$, which represents the risk premium for the market, and a variable depending upon the particular asset, i.e., β_j. Therefore, if we plot the risk premium of each asset against its beta, we will end up with a straight line—the security market line—as shown in Figure 1.14.

As a final demonstration of the CAPM, let us prove the heuristic argument for the model contained in Chapter 1 and described by Figure 1.9.[8] There the argument was to form a portfolio P composed of fraction h_i of (arbitrary) asset i and fraction $1 - h_i$ of the market portfolio. It follows from equations (S2–1) and (S2–2) that:

$$E_P = h_i E_i + (1 - h_i)E_M \qquad \text{(S2–15)}$$

and

$$V_P = h_i^2 V_i + 2h_i(1 - h_i)V_{Mi} + (1 - h_i)^2 V_M. \qquad \text{(S2–16)}$$

We need to calculate the slope of the frontier between security i and M just as it reaches M in the mean-standard-deviation region; this slope is given by dE_P/dS_P evaluated at $h_i = 0$ (i.e., where there is full investment in the market). We will do this in three steps: first, by calculating dE_P/dS_i; second, by calculating dS_P/dh_i from dV_P/dh_i; and finally, by setting $dE_P/dS_P = (dE_P/dh_i)/(dS_P/dh_i)$.

(1) $dE_P/dh_i = E_i - E_M$

(2) $dV_P/dh_i = 2[h_i V_i + (1 - 2h_i)V_{Mi} - (1 - h_i)V_M].$

Hence, when $h_i = 0$, $dV_P/dh_i = 2(V_{Mi} - V_M)$. Now recall that $S_P^2 = V_P$, so that:

$$dS_P/dh_i = \frac{1}{2}(dV_P/dh_i)/\sqrt{V_P}$$

---

[8]As indicated in Chapter 1, this proof originally appeared in William F. Sharpe, "Capital Asset Prices: A Theory of Market Equilibrium under Conditions of Risk," *Journal of Finance*, September 1964, pp. 425–42.

where V_P is given by equation (S2–16). Now when $h_i = 0$, $V_P = V_M$ and $dS_P/dh_i = (V_{Mi} - V_M)/\sqrt{V_M} = (V_{Mi} - V_M)/S_M$.

$$
\begin{aligned}
(3) \qquad dE_P/dS_P &= (dE_P/dh_i)/(dS_P/dh_i) \\
&= (E_i - E_M)S_M/(V_{Mi} - V_M)
\end{aligned}
$$

when $h_i = 0$. This expression represents the slope of the dashed frontier as it touches the capital market line at M. As indicated in Chapter 1, since the capital market line is a tangent to the frontier, the slopes must be identical. From Figure 1.9, the slope of the capital market line is $(E_M - i_F)/S_M$. Hence:

$$(E_i - E_M)S_M/(V_{Mi} - V_M) = (E_M - i_F)/S_M.$$

Simplifying:

$$E_i - E_M = (E_M - i_F)(V_{Mi}/V_M - 1)$$

or

$$E_i - i_F = \beta_i(E_M - i_F),$$

where we have used equation (S2–14) as the definition for beta.

Case Study 1: The Asset Allocation Decision[9]

Part 2: Derivation of the Efficient Frontier

In the first part of this case study we derived the statistics of the rate of return distribution for the three asset classes of stocks, bonds, and Treasury bills. The results are displayed in Table S2.1.

Our aim in this second part is to derive the efficient frontier of portfolios composed of holdings in these three asset classes. The investment opportunities available from these asset classes are:[10]

1. Each asset class taken individually.
2. Portfolios composed of positive holdings (two asset classes only).
3. Portfolios composed of positive holdings in all three asset classes.

The three portfolios which represent entire holdings in each of the asset classes are shown in the upper diagram in Figure S2.6. If the asset classes are taken in pairs, the three frontiers shown in the upper panel of the figure can also be attained. The formulation of the frontiers is given for the expected rate of return

---

[9]The first part of this case study appeared at the end of the supplement to Chapter 1.

[10]For realism we include the institutional constraint of no short selling.

Table S2.1
Statistics of the Asset Return Distributions

	Mean	Variance	Standard Deviation
Stocks	11.06	103.34	10.17
Bonds	8.79	14.65	3.83
T-bills	6.98	2.17	1.47

Correlation Matrix

	Stocks	Bonds	T-bills
Stocks	1	.42	−.39
Bonds	.42	1	−.31
T-bills	−.39	−.31	1

Covariance Matrix

	Stocks	Bonds	T-bills
Stocks	103.34	16.184	−5.798
Bonds	16.184	14.65	−1.736
T-bills	−5.798	−1.736	2.17

by equation (S2–1) and for the variance by equation (S2–2). We take the square root of this quantity in order to enable the frontier to be plotted in the mean-standard-deviation region. Notice that the two-asset frontiers dominate the single-asset portfolios in several places.

What happens if we include all three assets? In some places nothing changes, but in others the three-asset frontier dominates the two-asset frontiers. The locations where there will be no change are certainly at the end points, i.e., 100 percent invested in Treasury bills and stocks. We simply cannot dominate these portfolios without short-selling one of the other asset classes. In a region close to these single-asset portfolios there will also be no change, since holding only two assets will be better than holding all three. It is in the central region that the most benefit from holding all three assets is obtained, as can be seen from the lower diagram of the figure, which displays the efficient frontiers when all three asset classes are available for purchase.

We can view the computation either algebraically (as discussed above) or geometrically. The main thrust of Chapter 2 and this supplement has been to indicate that the formation of portfolios "averages" the expected returns of the component securities but reduces risk by more than simple "averaging" of the risks of the component securities. In Figure S2.6 this is evident by the curving of the frontier to the left in all of the two-asset portfolios. We can now choose a portfolio on any two-asset frontier, treat it as a single "asset," and form a two-"asset" frontier with the third asset class. In this manner, the three-asset frontier (and, indeed, the n-asset frontier) could be formed as a combination of a series of two-asset frontiers, although direct computation is more convenient.

Figure S2.6
Efficient Frontiers

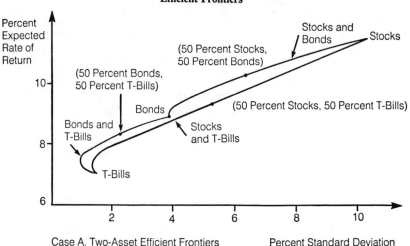

Case A. Two-Asset Efficient Frontiers   Percent Standard Deviation

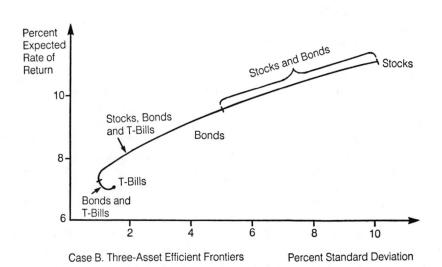

Case B. Three-Asset Efficient Frontiers   Percent Standard Deviation

Selected References

Undoubtedly, the most expository and perceptive description of the material in this supplement can be found in chapters 4 and 5 of Professor William F. Sharpe's text *Portfolio Theory and Capital Markets* (New York: McGraw-Hill, 1970).

Chapter 3

Risk Measurement: First Step toward Portfolio Management

We have now completed a broad overview of MPT, and in the process we have stressed the role of risk. Surprisingly, we have managed to accomplish this without really describing where risk arises or explaining its economic origins. Thus, we begin this chapter by remedying that deficiency and then move on to several related questions. For instance, we need to know which attributes to estimate, what estimation methods are the most efficient, and how to use the resulting estimates to the greatest advantage. We also have to be sure that the procedures are robust (i.e., the estimates contain information), which raises the need for verification.

We illustrate this discussion by analyzing an example portfolio. This portfolio will be familiar to many readers as it is composed of an equal number of shares in the 30 securities comprised by the Dow Jones Industrial Average.

Our portfolio, therefore, has the same rate of return as the DJIA.[1] The S&P 500 is used in this analysis as the proxy for the market portfolio, so the results provide an interesting insight into the performance of these two indexes.[2] Our major aim, however, is to indicate the implications of risk prediction, first for individual securities and then for portfolios.

The supplement to this chapter covers the models of security return in much greater detail. As is shown in the supplement, the model specification directly influences the problem of estimating investment risk.

The Nature of Risk

What is risk? *Risk* is a "technical" measure that indicates the difference between the expected future price of a security and the price that actually occurs. It is important to realize that risk is not "losing money" but a description of uncertain events—both good and bad—which might occur in the future. Risk, therefore, is determined by observing the price of the security and calculating the difference between that price and the price that was expected. The adjective *technical* is used to show that risk depends solely upon the price of the security and upon other variables insofar as they affect that price. Notice that this definition implies that the more distant the investment horizon, the greater the exposure to risk because, as the investment horizon comes closer, the likelihood is that the price will deviate less from its expectation simply through chance.[3]

Although risk is a technical measure, this does not preclude using sources of information in addition to historical price data in the risk estimation procedure. For instance, a bank will not confine a loan officer's inquiries to the record of month-end bank balances when making a commitment on a loan to a prospective client. In a similar manner, sources of company information (other than price) could be used to aid in the prediction of security (and portfolio) risk. The important point here is to recall that common factors influence all securities. In order to understand the variability in security prices, the sensitivities of every security to these factors, in addition to the inherent or specific risk of the company, have to be calculated. But these sensitivities and the specific risk will depend upon the characteristics of the company being studied.

---

[1]The Dow Jones Industrial Average is calculated by first summing the prices of the constituent securities. This total is then divided by a constant (the "divisor") to remove the effect of splits, etc. On December 31, 1978, the value of the divisor was 1.443. After the preparation of this manuscript the composition of the Dow Jones was changed. On June 29, 1979 IBM and Merck were added to the index replacing Chrysler and Esmark. See Andrew Rudd, "The Dow Jones Industrial Average: New Wine in Old Bottles?" *Financial Analysts Journal,* November–December 1979, pp. 57–63, for a detailed description of the effects of these changes.

[2]The choice of the market portfolio proxy as it relates to performance measurement is discussed in Chapter 7.

[3]The mathematics describing this relationship is developed in the supplement to Chapter 1.

Hence, if we are to explain the "technical" price variability, we have to capture the "fundamental" attributes of the company. Thus, we may expect that balance sheet, income statement, and other ratios will help in predicting risk.

However, is it possible to predict reward and risk? Of course, every investor would dearly like to be able to predict returns (or future prices) on all securities very accurately. Unfortunately, for a number of reasons, it seems improbable that even the most talented investor using the most sophisticated computer programs will ever be able to pinpoint future security prices. One reason for this improbability is the large degree of uncertainty associated with security returns. From Figure 2.4 it follows that the total standard deviation of an individual security's rate of return is approximately 40 percent per year. Therefore, one year out of three an annual rate of return greater than 40 percent or less than −40 percent, relative to the mean, would not be surprising. Given this large range of outcomes, accurate point estimates would be unlikely.

The possibility of predicting risk is quite different, since variance remains reasonably constant through time. Of course, the level of risk will change, mainly in response to changes in the uncertainty in the economy; however, there is no reason to believe that the change will not occur slowly and perhaps in harmony with observable changes in the economy.

One conceptual explanation for this is the following. If we were to pronounce that stock A was undervalued, then every investor who believed this information could use it in a rational strategy to earn profits by purchasing stock A. Eventually, this demand for stock A would drive its price up and produce the correct valuation (or even an overvaluation). Thus, security valuation disclosures which contain real information are self-destructive because they will soon be proven wrong.[4] However, a similar pronouncement that stock A is either extremely risky or extremely safe cannot be invalidated because there is no rational way that investors who believe that assessment can specifically use this information in a strategy to earn excess profits. Hence, levels of risk can be disclosed to market participants without causing sudden shifts in portfolio composition which immediately invalidate the risk prediction.

The above also partially explains why MPT products which predict risk levels will not become redundant as the number of users increases. Instead users of these models who understand the concepts will be able to make better decisions by justifying their risk exposure more exactly and will thus make the market more reflective of aggregate judgment. Therefore, risk predictions are used in combination with judgmental information to improve strategic decisions. Of course, as in any competitive market, there will be greater rewards to those investors who synthesize and interpret information better than others. Consequently, there will be rewards to those investors who predict risk better than others, use more accurate models and information sources, and interpret them more successfully.

---

[4]This paradigm has obvious implications for valuation services which are widely disseminated.

One further point needs explanation before we proceed. We have mentioned the words *measurement, estimation,* and *prediction.* The type of analysis that is required depends upon the use to which the attribute is going to be put. In other words, is the requirement for a prediction of risk in the future, or is it an estimation of risk exposure now, or is it the measurement of performance over some historical time period? Too often, these distinctions have been confused; for instance, estimation procedures have been used on historical data to obtain values which are then naively extrapolated to form "predictions" of the future. This has often been done with the estimation of beta. Many purveyors of beta services have run (time series) regressions of an asset's returns versus the market returns (similar to that shown in Figure 1.13 and described in the supplement to Chapter 1) in order to obtain a value of the exposure or sensitivity of that asset relative to the market. This regression coefficient is an average value of the asset beta over the period that was analyzed. Unfortunately, there is no reason to believe that the average value of beta in the past is going to be the best prediction of beta in the future. If beta is to be used to help form judgments on future security returns, then a "predictive beta" and not a "historical beta" is required. It is crucial, therefore, to make sure that the correct statistic is used in each application.

The Prediction of Risk

The subject of risk prediction is extremely complicated; indeed, there are few academicians who would claim to understand the entire subject, and there are even fewer who can agree on both the procedure and the results. Therefore, let us take a somewhat noncontroversial view of the subject.

There are several methods of risk prediction; the first and most obvious is a judgmental procedure. It was this method which Markowitz suggested in his original paper. Unfortunately, the human mind is inadequately prepared for this task. The natural human approach is to concentrate on the most likely value or the average value when faced with uncertain outcomes. For instance, a security analyst is most comfortable when making the best estimate of a future event. Placing uncertainty bounds or confidence intervals around such estimates is, in general, an unnatural human task. For this reason, the approach of judgmental risk prediction is not usually followed. Indeed, judgmental inputs are usually confined to overriding erroneous or obsolete data in order to achieve better estimates in unusual cases.

As mentioned, the most frequent approach for the predication of risk is to use historical price behavior. Due to its simplicity this seems to be the most common of all risk prediction methods. To be explicit, consider the estimation of beta. In Chapter 2 beta was defined as the sensitivity of the expected excess rate of return on the stock to the expected excess rate of return on the market portfolio. Unfortunately, the word *expected* has been used, and no good records of aggregate expectations exist. Thus, a major assumption has to be made to enable average (realized) rates of return to be used in place of expected rates of return, which, in turn, permits us to use the slope of regression line (estimated from realized data) to form the basis for a prediction of beta.

If this assumption, which essentially states that the future is going to be similar to the "average past," is made, then the estimation of historical beta proceeds as follows. Choose a suitable number of periods for which the excess returns of the security and market portfolio proxy are known. There is a subtle trade-off here. When more data points are used, the accuracy of the estimation procedure is improved, provided the relationship being estimated does not change. Usually the relationship does change; therefore, a small number of most recent data points is preferred so that dated information will not obscure the current relationship. It is usually accepted that a happy medium is achieved by using 60 monthly returns.[5] The security series is then regressed against the market portfolio series. This provides an estimate of beta (which is equivalent to the slope of the characteristic line) and the residual variance. (Unfortunately, when this methodology is used, residual variance cannot be decomposed into XMC and specific risk.) This procedure is exactly the one followed in Chapter 1 and its supplement to obtain estimates of risk for IBM and DEC.

It can be shown that if the regression equation is properly specified and certain other conditions are fulfilled, then the beta obtained is an optimal estimate (actually, minimum-variance, unbiased) of the true historical beta averaged over past periods. However, this does not imply that the historical beta is a good predictor of future beta. For instance, one defect is that random events impacting the firm in the past may have coincided with market movements purely by chance, causing the estimated value to differ from the true value. Thus, the beta obtained by this method is an estimate of the true historical beta obscured by measurement error.

An analogy to this problem is the quality control problem of ensuring that a machine which fills 10-pound sacks of potatoes for sale in supermarkets places 10 pounds of potatoes in each sack. The simple solution is to check the weight of sample sacks after filling. However, if the scales used for checking have not been calibrated recently, some random error may be associated with the measurement, so we cannot be certain that the measured weight is the true weight. The best estimate of the weight of each sack after filling, but before checking, is 10 pounds, since this represents the "prior" estimate. Now suppose the weight given by the test scales is 20 pounds. It does not seem reason-

---

[5]We have glossed over a number of econometric subtleties in these few sentences. Those readers who wish to learn more about these estimation difficulties are directed toward the following articles and the references contained there: Merton Miller and Myron Scholes, "Rates of Return in Relation to Risk: A Reexamination of Recent Findings," in *Studies in The Theory of Capital Markets,* ed. Michael Jensen (New York: Praeger Publishers, 1972), pp. 47–78; Lawrence Fisher, "Forecasting Systematic Risk," University of Chicago Working Paper no. 13, May 1978; and Myron Scholes and Joseph Williams, "Estimating Betas from Nonsynchronous Data," *Journal of Financial Economics,* December 1977, pp. 309–27.

able to use this figure as the estimate of the true weight because the 10-pound difference may be due entirely to the random error of the scales. A better estimate of the true weight is obtained by taking an average of the two values in order to compensate for the possible error. This compensation is called the *Bayesian adjustment (BA)*, since the final estimated value (called the "posterior" estimate) of the true weight is adjusted toward the prior estimate. Clearly, the greater the random error in the test scales, the less influence this measurement should have on the posterior estimates, and conversely, if there is no error on the test scales, then the measured weight should be exactly the posterior estimate (i.e., the prior estimate is disregarded). We can write this adjustment as the following equation:

Posterior estimate $= (1 - BA)$ (prior estimate) $+ BA$ (measured value),

where *BA* is a value between zero and one and indicates the degree of reliance that is placed upon the measured value.

The similarity between potatoes and betas must be obvious! In the absence of any information, the best (prior) estimate of a security's beta is unity because this is the (capitalization weighted) average beta. Suppose the measured value from the regression is $H\hat{\beta}$ (the historical beta), then the posterior estimate of beta is $(1 - BA)(1) + (BA)H\hat{\beta} = 1 + BA(H\hat{\beta} - 1)$. In other words, if the beta estimate from the regression is different from one, the posterior estimate of beta will "shrink" toward one because part of the difference is assumed to be measurement error, with the other part being the genuine effect.

The value of *BA* will definitely depend upon the amount of error in the regression. A detailed discussion of the calculation of this parameter is beyond the scope of this book; however, a typical value is about 0.6, so the posterior estimate, $\hat{\beta}$, is given by:[6]

$$\hat{\beta} = 0.4 + 0.6H\hat{\beta}. \tag{3-1}$$

Thus, if we are restricted to the use of historical price information, three possible prediction methods for beta are suggested. These are:

1. *Naive:* $\hat{\beta}_j = 1.0$ for all securities (i.e., every security has the average beta).
2. *Historical:* $\hat{\beta}_j = H\hat{\beta}_j$, the historical beta obtained as the coefficient from an ordinary least squares regression.
3. *Bayesian adjusted beta:* $\hat{\beta}_j = 1.0 + BA(H\hat{\beta}_j - 1)$, where the historical betas are adjusted toward the mean value of 1.0.

---

[6]The value of *BA* may also depend on the particular stock and time. For further discussion see Oldrich Vasicek, "A note on Using Cross-Sectional Information in Bayesian Estimation of Security Betas," *Journal of Finance,* December 1973, pp. 1233–39. A more detailed treatment can be found in Barr Rosenberg and James Guy, "The Prediction of Systematic Risk," Working Paper no. 33, Research Program in Finance (Berkeley: Institute of Business and Economic Research, University of California, February 1975).

In each case, the prediction of residual risk is obtained by subtracting the systematic variance $(\hat{\beta}_j^2 V_M)$ from the total variance of the security. If the historical beta is used, then the residual variance is obtained directly from the regression as described in the IBM and DEC examples in the supplement to Chapter 1.

However, relying simply upon historical price data is unduly restricting in that there are excellent sources of information which may help in improving the prediction of risk. For instance, most analysts would agree that fundamental information is useful in understanding a company's prospects. Thus, we now turn to the *fundamental predictions of risk,* which were pioneered principally by Professor Barr Rosenberg and Vinay Marathe of the University of California at Berkeley.

Fundamental Risk Prediction

The historical beta estimate will be an unbiased predictor of the future value of beta, provided that the expected change between the true value of beta averaged over the past periods and its value in the future is zero.[7] If this expected change is not zero, then the historical beta estimate will be misleading (biased). Thus, if historical betas are used as a prediction of beta, there is an implicit assumption that the future will be similar to the past. Is this assumption reasonable? The answer is, probably not. The investment environment changes so rapidly that it would appear imprudent to use averages of historical (five-year) price data as predictions of the future.

It is a simple exercise to list the possible reasons for the inaccuracy of naive extrapolation. For instance, the company may have acquired a less risky firm, issued debt or undertaken a secondary offering of equity, or sold an underperforming division. In each case, the fundamentals of the company are now different from the historical average, as is the risk exposure. The future beta may also not be equal to the averaged historical beta because the company is exposed to an economic event—for instance, the energy crisis—which is expected to become more pronounced (i.e., the event will have a greater variance) in the future.[8] Alternatively, we can imagine a situation where the economic events are reasonably constant but the company's exposure varies through time. This scenario may describe a growth stock, or a service company whose specialties are changing as it becomes more proficient and experienced.

---

[7]The word *unbiased* is used in its statistical sense, which means that the expected value of the estimate is equal to the true underlying value.

[8]A subtler form of risk prediction occurs when a company's risk profile is estimated, conditional upon a change in the macroeconomic environment (for instance, increased variance of energy events.) Prediction services based on this type of "conditional forcasting" methodology have recently been made available to institutional investors. We will not discuss this approach here, confining ourselves to the more common "unconditional forcasting," which presumes that the future economic variance is similar to, and can be forecast from, the observed historical variance.

In these examples, an accurate prediction of risk will require the evaluation of the company's response to the economic events. In other words, "response coefficients," which are related to the fundamentals of the company, have to be determined.

When an analyst forms a judgement on the likely performance of a company, many sources of information can be synthesized. For instance, an indication of future risk can be found in the balance sheet and the income statement; an idea as to the growth of the company can be found from trends in variables measuring the company's position; the normal business risk of the company can be determined by the historical variability of the income statement; and so on. The approach that Rosenberg and Marathe take is conceptually similar to such an analysis since they attempt to include all sources of relevant information. This set of data includes historical technical and fundamental accounting data. The resulting information is then used to produce, by regression methods, the fundamental predictions of beta, specific risk, and the exposure to the common factors.

The fundamental prediction method starts by describing the company.[9] This entails forming "descriptors," which are ratios that describe the fundamental condition of the company. These descriptors are grouped into six categories to indicate distinct sources of risk. In each case, the category is named so that a higher value is indicative of greater risk.

1. *Market variability.* This category is designed to capture the risk of the company as perceived by the market. If the market was completely efficient, then all information on the state of the company would be reflected in the stock price. Here the historical prices and other market variables are used in an attempt to reconstruct the state of the company. The descriptors include historical measures of beta and residual risk, nonlinear functions of them, and various liquidity measures.

2. *Earnings variability.* This category refers to the unpredictable variation in earnings over time, so descriptors such as the variability of earnings per share and the variability of cash flow are included.

3. *Low valuation and unsuccess.* How successful has the company been, and how is it valued by the market? If investors are optimistic about future prospects and the company has been successful in the past (measured by a low book-to-price ratio and growth in per share earnings), then the implication is that the firm is sound and that future risk is likely to be lower. Conversely, an unsuccessful and lowly valued company is likely to be more risky.

4. *Immaturity and smallness.* A small, young firm is likely to be more risky

---

[9]The remainder of this section is drawn heavily from Barr Rosenberg and Vinay Marathe, "The Prediction of Investment Risk: Systematic and Residual Risk," *Proceedings of the Seminar on the Analysis of Security Prices,* University of Chicago, November 1975, pp. 85–225.

than a large, mature firm. This group of descriptors attempts to capture this difference.

5   *Growth orientation.* To the extent that a company attempts to provide returns to stockholders by an aggressive growth strategy requiring the initiation of new projects with uncertain cash flows rather than the more stable cash flows of existing operations, the company is likely to be more risky. Thus, the growth in total assets, payout and dividend policy, and the earnings/price ratio are used to capture the growth characteristics of the company.

6.   *Financial risk.* The more highly levered the financial structure, the greater is the risk to common stockholders. This risk is captured by measures of leverage and debt to total assets.

Finally, the industry in which the company operates is another important source of information. Certain industries, simply because of the nature of their business, are exposed to greater (or lesser) levels of risk (e.g., compare airlines versus gold stocks). Rosenberg and Marathe used indicator (dummy) variables for 39 industry groups as the method of introducing industry effects. Tables 3.1 and 3.2 give a list of the descriptors used in each category and the set of industry groups.[10]

Unfortunately, the process of going from the descriptors to the final predictions for the three components of risk is lengthy and tedious. For this reason we merely sketch the main steps, though more detail is provided in the supplement to this chapter.

The prediction rules for the systematic risk and residual risk are expressed in terms of the descriptors. The major steps are as follows:

Step 1

For the time period during which the model is to be fitted, obtain common stock returns and company annual reports (for instance, from the COMPUS-TAT data base).[11] The descriptors are then computed from these data. In order to make comparisons across firms meaningful, the descriptors must be normalized so that there is a common origin and unit of measurement.

The normalization takes the following form. First, the "raw" descriptor

---

[10]The exact definitions of these descriptors and industry groups can be found in Rosenberg and Marathe, "Prediction of Investment Risk." The assignment of a company wholly to a single industry is traditional in investment research but quite clearly wrong. A more defensible (and accurate) approach would be to assign a company to industries on the basis of its sales or earnings within those industries. Fortunately, data bases containing the breakdown of corporate sales, assets, and earnings across industries are now becoming available, so the preferred approach is now possible.

[11]The COMPUSTAT data base is one of the data bases collected by Investors Management Sciences, Inc., a subsidiary of Standard & Poor's Corporation.

Table 3.1
Components of the Risk Indices

1. Index of market variability
   Historical beta estimate
   Historical sigma estimate
   Share turnover, quarterly
   Share turnover, 12 months
   Share turnover, five years
   Trading volume/variance
   Common stock price (ln)
   Historical alpha estimate
   Cumulative range, one year

2. Index of earnings variability
   Variance of earnings
   Extraordinary items
   Variance of cash flow
   Earnings covariability
   Earnings/price covariability

3. Index of low valuation and unsuccess
   Growth in earnings/share
   Recent earnings change
   Relative strength
   Indicator of small earnings/price ratio
   Book/price ratio
   Tax/earnings, five years
   Dividend cuts, five years
   Return on equity, five years

4. Index of immaturity and smallness
   Total assets (log)

   Market capitalization (log)
   Market capitalization
   Net plant/gross plant
   Net plant/common equity
   Inflation adjusted plant/equity
   Trading recency
   Indicator of earnings history

5. Index of growth orientation
   Payout, last five years
   Current yield
   Yield, last five years
   Indicator of zero yield
   Growth in total assets
   Capital structure change
   Earnings/price ratio
   Earnings/price, normalized
   Typical earnings/price ratio, five years

6. Index of financial risk
   Leverage at book
   Leverage at market
   Debt/assets
   Uncovered fixed charges
   Cash flow/current liabilities
   Liquid assets/current liabilities
   Potential dilution
   Price-deflated earnings adjustment
   Tax-adjusted monetary debt

values for each company are computed. Next, the capitalization weighted value of each descriptor for all the securities in the S&P 500 is computed and then subtracted from each raw descriptor. The transformed descriptors now have the property that the capitalization weighted value for the S&P 500 stocks is zero. This step unambiguously fixes the "origin" for measurement; however, the unit of "length" is still arbitrary. To standardize the length, the standard deviation of each descriptor is calculated within a universe of large companies (defined as having a capitalization of $50 million or more). The descriptor is now further transformed by setting the value +1 to be one standard deviation above the S&P 500 mean (i.e., one unit of length corresponds to one standard deviation). This procedure is shown diagrammatically in Figure 3.1. Algebraically, we can write:

$$ND = (RD - RD[S\&P])/STDEV[RD],$$

Table 3.2
Industry Groups

1. Nonferrous metals	21. Motor vehicles
2. Energy raw materials	22. Aerospace
3. Construction	23. Electronics
4. Agriculture and food	24. Photographic and optical
5. Liquor	25. Nondurables and entertainment
6. Tobacco	26. Trucking and freight
7. Apparel	27. Railroads and shipping
8. Forest products and paper	28. Air transport
9. Containers	29. Telephone
10. Media	30. Energy utilities
11. Chemicals	31. Retail and general
12. Drugs and medicine	32. Banks
13. Soaps and cosmetics	33. Miscellaneous finance
14. Domestic oil	34. Insurance
15. International oil	35. Real property
16. Tires and rubber goods	36. Business services
17. Steel	37. Travel and outdoor recreation
18. Producer goods	38. Gold mining and securities
19. Business machines	39. Miscellaneous and conglomerates
20. Consumer durables	

Figure 3.1
Standardization of Descriptors

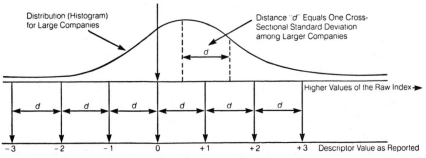

1. The value of the unstandardized descriptor is first computed for every company.
2. The average value for all companies in the S&P 500, weighted by the outstanding value of common equity (capitalization weighting), is then computed. The descriptor is then standardized so that the S&P 500 capitalization weighted mean is zero.
3. Next, the (equal-weighted) standard deviation (d) of the descriptor is computed for the cross section of larger companies (those with capitalization greater than $50 million). There are roughly 1,000 companies in this group. The descriptor is standardized so that the value $+1$ (-1) corresponds to d units above (below) the S&P 500 mean.

where

ND = the normalized descriptor value;
RD = the raw descriptor value as computed from the data;
$RD[S\&P]$ = the raw descriptor value for the (capitalization-weighted) S&P 500; and
$STDEV[RD]$ = the standard deviation of the raw descriptor value calculated from the universe of large companies.

At this stage each company is indentified by a series of descriptors which indicate its fundamental position. If a descriptor value is zero, then the company is "typical" of the S&P 500 (for this characteristic) because the S&P 500 and the company both have the same raw value. Conversely, if the descriptor value is nonzero, then the company is atypical of the S&P 500, and this information may be used to adjust the prior prediction in order to obtain a better posterior prediction of risk. This adjustment is determined in Step 2.

Step 2

Group the monthly data by quarters, and assemble the descriptors of each company as they would have appeared at the beginning of the quarter. The prediction rule is then fitted by linear regression which relates each monthly stock return in that quarter to the previously computed descriptors. (This procedure is described in more detail in the supplement at the end of this chapter.)

Conceptually, the outcome of this step is an additive adjustment for each descriptor. These adjustments are combined as follows.[12] Initially, in the absence of any fundamental information, the beta is set equal to its historical value. Then each descriptor is examined in turn, and if it is atypical, the corresponding adjustment to beta is made. For example, if two companies with the same historical beta are identical except that they have very different capitalizations, then our intuition (which is confirmed by the econometrics) would be to adjust the risk of the large-capitalization company downward, relative to that of the small-capitalization company, because large companies typically have less risk than small companies. Here we have used our fundamental knowledge as additional information to improve the prediction of risk. The econometric prediction rule is similar; the prediction is obtained by adding the adjustments for all descriptors, in addition to the industry effect, to the historical beta estimate. In this manner, all the atypical attributes are simultaneously included in the prediction.

Symbolically, the prediction rule for the beta of security i, in a given month, can be written as follows:[13]

---

[12]The description of the remainder of this step is necessarily simplified; the detailed methodology can be found in Rosenberg and Marathe, "Prediction of Investment Risk."

[13]The prediction rule for residual risk is constructed similarly.

$$\hat{\beta}_i = \hat{b}_0 + \hat{b}_1 \, d_{1i} + \ldots + \hat{b}_J \, d_{Ji} \qquad (3\text{--}2)$$

where

$\hat{\beta}_i$ = the predicted beta;

$\hat{b}_j$ = the estimated response coefficients in the prediction rule;

d_{ji} = the normalized descriptor values for security i; and

J = the total number of descriptors.

In this prediction rule we can think of the first descriptor, d_{1i}, as the historical beta, $H\hat{\beta}$. Thus, if only the first descriptor is used, the prediction rule is similar to the specification of the Bayesian adjustment, equation (3–1). In this case, the linear regression provides estimates for $\hat{b}_0$ and $\hat{b}_1$, which indicate the optimal adjustment to historical beta for predictive purposes. Other descriptors in addition to historical beta are employed and appear in the prediction rule as d_{2i} through d_{ji}. In other words, the fundamental predictions are direct generalizations of the "price only" predictions.

If the company is completely typical of market (i.e., the descriptors other than historical beta are all zero), then there is no further adjustment to the Bayesian-adjusted historical beta. This is intuitive; if the company is in no sense "special," then there is no reason to believe that the averaged true beta in the past will not equal the true beta in the future. However, if the company is atypical, then not all the descriptors (other than historical beta) will be zero. For simplicity, suppose that only the first (historical beta) and second descriptors are nonzero, where the latter has a value of one (i.e., this company is one standard deviation from the S&P 500 value). The prediction rule, equation (3–2), shows that the predicted beta is found by adding the adjustment $\hat{b}_2$ to the Bayesian-adjusted historical beta. In general, the total adjustment is the weighted sum of the coefficients in the prediction rule, where the weights are the normalized descriptor values which indicate the company's degree of deviance from the typical company.

Step 3

Determine the company's exposure to each of the common factors and the prediction of the residual risk components (i.e., *XMC* and specific risk). The first task is to form summary measures or indices of risk to describe all aspects of the company's investment risk. These are obtained by forming the weighted average of the descriptor values in each of the six categories introduced above, where the weights are the estimated coefficients from the prediction rule, equation (3–2), for systematic or residual risk. This provides six summary measures of risk, the risk indices, for each company. Again, these indices are normalized so that the S&P 500 has a value of zero on each index and a value of one corresponds to one standard deviation among all companies with capitalization of $50 million or more.

The prediction of residual risk is now found by performing a regression on the cross section of all security residual returns as the dependent variable where the independent variables are the risk indices.[14] The form of the regression, in a given month, is shown in equation (3–3):

$$r_i - \hat{\beta}_i r_M = c_1 RI_{1i} + \ldots + c_6 RI_{6i} \qquad (3\text{–}3)$$
$$+ c_7 IND_{1i} + \ldots + c_{45} IND_{39,i} + u_i$$

where

r_i = the excess return on security i,

$\hat{\beta}_i$ = the predicted beta, from equation (3–2); and

r_M = the excess return on the market portfolio,

so that $r_i - \hat{\beta}_i r_M$ is the residual return on security i; $RI_{1i}, \ldots, RI_{6i}$ are the six risk indices for security i; $IND_{1i}, \ldots, IND_{39,i}$ are the dummy variables for the 39 industry groups; u_i is the specific return for security i; and $c_1, \ldots, c_{45}$ are the 45 coefficients to be estimated.

The result from this cross-sectional regression is the specific return and specific risk on the security, together with the 45 coefficients. These estimated coefficients represent the returns that can be attributed to the factors in the month of the analysis.

This step is described graphically in Figure 3.2, which shows the modeling of one residual factor, *low valuation and unsuccess (LVU)*, for January 1978. In this month the factor experienced a rate of return of 2.12 percent, which is found as the coefficient of the *LVU* risk index in the prediction rule, equation (3–3). It is shown in the figure by the upward-sloping line passing through the origin.[15] The value of 2.12 percent indicates that a company which has unit exposure to this factor (i.e., the company has an *LVU* risk index of one) will experience a positive return of this magnitude from this source alone. On the average, the return from this residual factor will be zero (if it were nonzero,

[14]See Barr Rosenberg and Vinay Marathe, "Common Factors in Security Returns: Microeconomic Determinants and Macroeconomic Correlates," *Proceedings of the Seminar on the Analysis of Security Prices*, University of Chicago, May 1976, pp. 61–115.

[15]The factor return estimate was obtained from BARRA's Conditional Forecasting Service. The January rate of return for the *LVU* residual factor is almost always positive, suggesting a market inefficiency. One explanation is that companies which have been unsuccessful during the previous year show a positive risk-adjusted performance in January, probably as a rebound from year-end tax selling. See Vinay Marathe's "Elements of Covariance in Security Returns and their Macroeconomic Determinants," Ph.D. dissertation, University of California at Berkeley, 1978; and Michael Rozeff and W. Kinney, "Capital Market Seasonality: The Case of Stock Returns," *Journal of Financial Economics*, Vol. 3, 1976, pp. 379–402. Evidence of this January inefficiency has been reported in the literature over many years. The earliest report which we have been able to find is Sidney Wachtel's "Odds on a December–January Advance," *Barrons*, December 2, 1940, p. 1. Two years later, the same author published a scholarly article entitled "Certain Observations on Seasonal Movements in Stock Prices," *Journal of Business*, 1942, pp. 184–193.

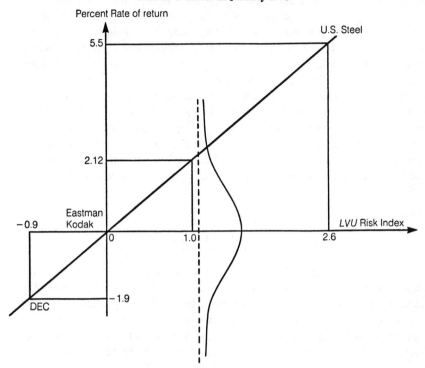

Figure 3.2
THE *LVU* Factor in January 1978

then it would be inconsistent with the simple CAPM, which states that only systematic risk receives compensation) and will be indicated by the probability distribution with a mean at zero rate of return.

The effect of the residual factor on any company is now easy to determine. For instance, in January 1978 U.S. Steel Corporation had an *LVU* risk index of 2.6, so it experienced a rate of return (from this source) of 2.6 × 2.12 = 5.5 percent; Eastman Kodak had an *LVU* risk index of 0.0 and experienced no return; and Digital Equipment had an index value of −0.9 and consequently experienced a rate of return of −1.9 percent. Thus, the effect of the residual factor can be visualized as a teeter-totter or seesaw, where the factor return pivots about the origin (the S&P 500 value). Because the factor shows an average rate of return of zero, there is a large probability of obtaining small (positive and negative) values and a small probability of obtaining large returns. Thus, the teeter-totter is close to horizontal for most time periods, and only in exceptional months does it exhibit extreme upward or downward movements. The amount of "action" depends upon the distance from the origin, that is, the value of the company's risk index; the more atypical a company, the greater is the chance that the company will display extreme returns.

This completes the description of methodology; let us now turn to the results. Rosenberg and Marathe found that by using the technical descriptors (the group which is comprised by the market variability index), a beta could be calculated that would explain 57 percent more of the variance of security return than was explained by the Bayesian-adjusted historical beta.[16] When beta was calculated by simply using fundamental descriptors (in other words, no use whatsoever of price or market-related information) the predictive beta obtained from this calculation explained 45 percent more of the variance than did the Bayesian-adjusted historical beta obtained from price information. The startling result, however, is that when both market and fundamental information were used, the beta obtained was 86 percent better than the Bayesian-adjusted historical beta.

Does Beta Work?

Of course, if a great deal of effort is spent in predicting risk, then it is important that the results contain "information." For instance, if diversified portfolios are ranked from highest predicted beta to lowest predicted beta at the beginning of a year, then the realized excess returns over that year should compare favorably with their beta values. If the market excess return was positive, then the highest beta portfolio should offer the highest return and the lowest beta portfolio should offer the lowest return. Conversely, if the market excess return was negative, the lowest beta portfolio should offer the highest return and the highest beta portfolio should offer the lowest return. Such results are an implication of the CAPM, so it is not surprising that numerous studies have tested the ability of beta to order both security and portfolio returns.[17] The results from these tests are mixed, but overall beta works well. In general, expected return and market risk are related, although, of course, realized returns and expected returns may be quite different.

Naturally, the power of beta to predict portfolio returns will depend upon the accuracy with which beta is estimated. It is important to realize that no one

---

[16]See sec. 7 of Rosenberg and Marathe "Prediction of Investment Risk," particularly table 6, p. 134.

[17]See, for example, William Sharpe and Guy Cooper, "Risk-Return Classes of New York Stock Exchange Common Stocks, 1931–1967," *Financial Analysts Journal*, March–April 1972, pp. 46–54. Unfortunately, a detailed discussion of the various versions and (almost) limitless tests of the CAPM is beyond the scope of this book. For a meticulous study which estimates several specifications, see Barr Rosenberg and Vinay Marathe, "Tests of Capital Asset Pricing Hypotheses," in *Research in Finance*, ed. Haim Levy (Greenwich, Conn.: JAI Press, 1979), pp. 115–223. For a critical analysis of the empirical research on the CAPM, see Richard Roll, "A Critique of the Asset Pricing Theory's Tests—Part 1: On Past and Potential Testability of the Theory," *Journal of Financial Economics*, March 1977, pp. 129–76.

has ever seen the actual beta itself. Therefore, the usefulness of the beta coefficient to predict returns is a function of the accuracy of the beta estimate. "Bad" betas will produce little explanation of the returns from both assets and portfolios. (In part, the mixed results from the studies of the compensation for risk can be attributed to this simple fact.) "Good" betas, on the other hand, have shown remarkable ability at explaining the risk of portfolios.

The distinction between "good" and "bad" betas can be emphasized with the aid of a diagram. Figure 3.3 illustrates the prediction of exposure to systematic risk, beta, in a month when the market rate of return was negative. The vertical axis shows the return on individual securities over the month. The horizontal axis shows the historical beta of these assets at the beginning of the period. If every asset had a return exactly predicted by its historical beta, then every asset would have plotted on the solid, downward-sloping line. This is the theoretically correct line since it passes through the risk-free rate at a beta of zero and through the market return at a beta of unity. However, it is not likely

Figure 3.3
Prediction of Beta and the Explanation of Security Returns

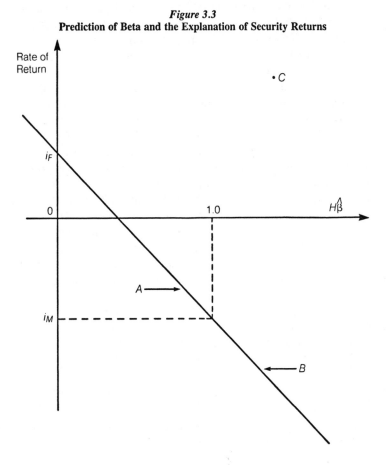

that every asset will have a return exactly as predicted, and so there will be a scatter of points about the downward-sloping line.

A good beta will explain a comparatively large amount of the scatter about the solid line; a bad beta will not explain the scatter. In other words, the good beta's fit to the data will be much better than that of the bad beta. Thus, a better prediction of the beta for stock *A* may have been greater than its historical value, while a better prediction of the beta for stock *B*, may have been smaller than its historical value. In these cases, the scatter of points about the correct line would have been smaller. This "shrinking" is exactly what occurs with the Bayesian adjustment. Thus, if the Bayesian-adjusted historical beta is plotted on the horizontal axis and is a better prediction of beta, then we should expect the points to be less dispersed and to line up more closely with the theoretically correct line. Of course, residual risk will still cause a scatter of points around the line. For instance, stock *C* will still lie far from the line for all reasonable values of beta simply because in this period this company was exposed to a residual factor which had a greater effect than the market. Nevertheless, on the average, the security returns should plot along the line between the risk-free rate at the beta of zero and the market return at a beta of one if the beta predictions contain information. An estimate of the amount of information is found by calculating the dispersion around the line; the measurement of the dispersion is the sum-of-squared stock returns.

One of the better occasions to analyze the information content of beta predictions is when the market displays an extreme return over a short period. At this point, the large systematic component of return can be detected and separated from the "noise" of the residual returns. The month of October 1978 was an unfortunate time for the stock market because in that month the excess return on the S&P 500 was almost − 10 percent. However, it provided an excellent opportunity to evaluate beta predictions.

Figure 3.4 shows the rate of return on the S&P 500 plotted against the fundamental beta prediction for the month of October 1978.[18] The measure of dispersion is the (weighted) sum-of-squared excess returns; that is, for each security the squared difference between the risk-free rate and the security rate of return is computed and then these squared differences are totaled for all securities.[19] The typical squared excess return is shown on the figure as the distance *A*.

The market is the principal factor, and it accounts for much of the variability of return. The naive beta prediction, as explained above, is to assume that all securities have the average beta and so have equal market response. In this case, we would expect security returns to be centered about the S&P 500 return

---

[18]The beta prediction is that derived by Rosenberg and Marathe, "Prediction of Investment Risk," updated to October 1978 by the Fundamental Risk Measurement Service. This example first appeared in the *FRMS Newsletter*, no. 11, November 1978.

[19]The weight for each security is inversely proportional to its specific variance. This is the generalized least squares weighting, which is statistically the most efficient.

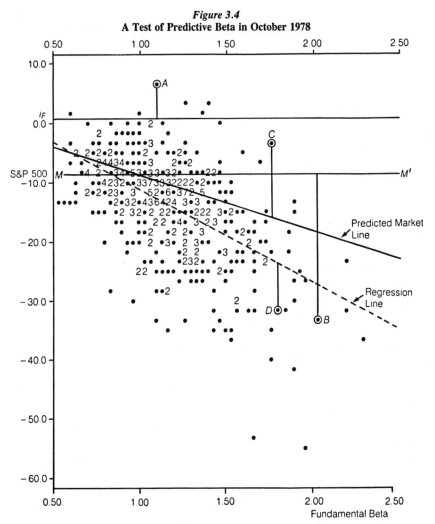

Figure 3.4
A Test of Predictive Beta in October 1978

Source: Fundamental Risk Measurement Service. We thank Vinay Marathe for help in preparing this figure.

(i.e., along the horizontal line MM'). The amount of dispersion accounted for by this prediction is calculated by computing the sum-of-squared differences from this line. (A typical distance is indicated by B on the figure.) This sum-of-squares is usually much smaller than that computed using the risk-free rate. In October 1978 the average squared difference from the S&P 500 return is only 53.7 percent of the average squared difference from the risk-free return. The reduction in the sum-of-squares, $100 - 53.7 = 46.3$ percent, is the "mean square" explained by the market return. This is shown in Table 3.3.

A better prediction for beta is obtained by using the Bayesian-adjusted his-

Table 3.3
Decomposition of Sum-of-Squared Excess Returns for October 1978

	Percentage of Sum-of-Squares
A. Systematic excess return	
Mean square due to S&P 500 return 46.3	
Variance explained by historical beta 3.7	
Variance explained by fundamental beta 9.4	
Subtotal due to predicted systematic return	59.4
B. Residual return	
Variance explained by alignment of residual factors with fundamental beta 7.3	
Balance of residual variance 33.3	
Subtotal due to residual variance	40.6
Total	100.0

torical beta instead of the naive prediction. If Figure 3.4 had been drawn with this beta plotted on the horizontal axis, then the weighted sum-of-squared deviations of the security returns from the correct line would have been exactly 50 percent of the total sum-of-squared excess returns. The difference, 50 − 46.3 = 3.7 percent, shows the improvement obtained by using the Bayesian-adjusted historical beta rather than assuming all betas to be one.

The next step in our evaluation of beta predictions is to find the improvement obtained by using the fundamental beta rather than the historical beta. Again we compute the weighted sum-of-squared returns from the predicted line (distance C in Figure 3.4). When this total is computed, it is found to be only 40.6 percent of the total sum-of-squared excess returns. In other words, the fundamental beta prediction arranges the securities along the horizontal axis so that their returns are much more tightly grouped about the line. The improvement in explanatory power over the Bayesian-adjusted historical betas is 50 − 40.6 = 9.4 percent of the total sum-of-squared excess returns, while the improvement over the naive prediction is 53.7 − 40.6 = 13.1 percent.

The ratio of 13.1 divided by 3.7 measures the relative predictive improvements of fundamental betas and Bayesian-adjusted historical betas. In the previous section we reported that Rosenberg and Marathe found an average improvement of 86 percent (i.e., a ratio of 1.86) in their original study. For October 1978 the ratio was 3.54, so the fundamental prediction performed $3\frac{1}{2}$ times better than the historical beta.

Although beta explained most of the dispersion in security returns in October 1978, there is still substantial residual variability about the line. In fact, the sum-of-squared residual returns (squared distances C) account for 40.6 percent of the total, while the explained sum-of-squares account for 59.4 percent of the total (i.e., R^2 of the market relationship is 0.594). Can we say anything about this residual variability? In fact, we can. The predicted market line is shown in Figure 3.4 as the solid line. However, it need not be the best fit to the realized returns. In other words, if on October 1, 1978, we knew what the market return for the month would be, then the predicted market line would have the form:

$$r_i = 0.0 + 1.0(\hat{\beta}_i r_M), \qquad (3-4)$$

or the excess return on security i is equal to the predicted beta times the market excess return. At the end of October, this relationship can be tested. In particular, was the coefficient of the predicted systematic return exactly one? For this month the best fit was obtained when the coefficient (slope) was 1.9 rather than 1.0. This is drawn as the downward sloping dashed line in Figure 3.4.

Thus, stocks with high (low) betas did much worse (better) than expected. The reason for this is that the residual factors influenced the security returns in the same direction as beta (i.e., the residual factors which were dominant in October tended to reinforce the systematic relationship). When distances D from the line of best fit are squared and then summed, only 33.3 percent of the total sum-of-squared excess returns results. Thus, $40.6 - 33.3 = 7.3$ percent of the sum-of-squared returns were accounted for by the residual factors that "acted like beta," while 33.3 percent of the sum-of-squared returns were truly residual.

To summarize, beta has explained a substantial proportion (on the average approximately 30 percent, rather than 59.4 percent in October 1978) of the variation in individual stock returns. The track record of beta for portfolios is much better than its track record for individual stocks since for portfolios systematic risk accounts for a greater proportion (approximately 90 percent rather than 25 percent) of total risk.[20] We must, therefore, conclude that beta does work, although the historical beta is not necessarily the best beta for predictive purposes. Further, beta tends to work better for portfolios than for individual stocks. We now leave the topic of verification and turn to the benefits of good risk predictions.

Where, Oh Where, Has the Market Portfolio Gone?[21]

The CAPM relates the expected return of each asset to the expected return of the market portfolio. But, alas, the market portfolio is a theoretical construct and is never likely to be found exactly in practice. What were the early researchers to do? Answer: Choose a proxy! In the early days (the 60s), when good data were hard to find, the Dow Jones Average was used. Later the S&P 500 became popular, as did an equal-weighted NYSE index (mainly because

---

[20]See Figure 2.4.

[21]For a further elucidation of this subject, see Barr Rosenberg, "Lament for the Loss of Innocence or the Subtleties of Systematic Return," BARRA Working Paper, September 1980. Also see the references at the end of this chapter.

nobody had collected market weights), until, at the present time, value-weighted proxies for *the* market portfolio can be formed using (essentially) all equity securities. But even this omits many important sectors of the capital markets such as bonds, real estate, and so on. The search for true proximity to the market portfolio appears to be doomed. Does it matter?

The answer depends on the particular application for which the proxy is required. Here, we are concerned with the estimation of systematic risk (beta) and its complement (residual risk) for both single assets and portfolios. (In Chapter 7 we will examine further the case of the market portfolio in performance measurement.) One use of the market portfolio in risk measurement is to represent the principal component of returns within the sector under study. Most markets that have been analyzed, including equities, bonds, and real estate, have a prominent factor which explains most (but not all) of the risk in that sector. Because this factor is so dominant, any broadly based value-weighted portfolio will capture it satisfactorily. This is confirmed by the almost perfect correlation between representative indexes.

The systematic risk coefficient (beta) can be estimated relative to this broadly based sector portfolio and will correctly provide the responsiveness, or sensitivity, of the asset relative to the portfolio, which, as described above, captures the principal element of risk within the sector. Since several practical uses of beta —for instance, its use in attributing performance between stock selection and market timing or in approximating the risk of diversified portfolios—merely require it to be a measure of a security's exposure to this principal component of risk, the exact specification of the market portfolio is unimportant. What is required is a *systematic portfolio* which captures the dominant component of risk within a sector of the entire market. (If we should ever find a sector which did not possess a principal component, this argument would not apply directly.)

Of course, the total risk of an asset should be invariant to the systematic portfolio used to estimate its beta. For example, if the beta of IBM is estimated relative to the S&P 500 (and denoted by $\beta[S\&P]$) or relative to the NYSE (and denoted by $\beta[NYSE]$), then the total risk of IBM, V_{IBM}, should not depend on which proxy for the market portfolio is used. In particular, it follows from the market model, equation (2–2), that:

$$
\begin{aligned}
V_{IBM} &= \text{total risk of IBM} \\
&= \beta^2[S\&P]\, V_{S\&P} + \omega^2[S\&P] \\
&= \beta^2[NYSE]\, V_{NYSE} + \omega^2[NYSE],
\end{aligned}
$$

where

$V_{S\&P}$ = total risk of the S&P 500;

V_{NYSE} = total risk of the NYSE;

$\omega^2[S\&P]$ = residual risk of IBM when the S&P 500 is used as the systematic portfolio; and

$\omega^2[NYSE]$ = residual risk of IBM when the NYSE is used as the systematic portfolio.

The implication of this demonstration is not that the definition of the systematic portfolio is important but rather that the computation of total risk is crucial.

The primary step in risk measurement is to estimate the variance matrix of total returns. The next step is to define the systematic portfolio so that betas can be computed. If the model is specified prior to estimation, there is a danger that the measurement of risk will be incorrect. For instance, if a single-index model is used as the basis to estimate betas, then the computation of risk is influenced by the choice of the index (see the supplement to this chapter for the algebraic proof of this statement). But if a multiple factor model of security returns is correctly specified and estimated and the betas are computed appropriately, then it can be shown that the choice of the systematic portfolio does not affect the computation of total risk.[22]

Benefits of Risk Measurement

Good risk predictions permit the origin and magnitude of risk in a security or a portfolio to be measured. Such an analysis will break down the component of risk that is due to the market (i.e., systematic), the component due to the common factors (i.e., XMC, the risk due to industry emphasis and sectoral emphasis), and the component due to the specific risk of the individual securities.

Let us first consider a single security. As discussed above, the inputs to the prediction process are the descriptors of the company. Thus, the first benefit is some detailed descriptive information on each company. Moreover, this information is statistically "sound" because it forms the basis for the risk predictions; that is, these descriptors have been shown to contain genuine information concerning the status of the firm.

With this background it is possible to discuss Table 3.4. This table contains the descriptors for Allied Chemical Corporation as of December 29, 1978. The first line gives a summary of the company, which we will describe later, while the remainder of the page gives the detailed information which is required to compute the summary values. These are the 48 descriptors used in the risk prediction. The first two descriptors, the historical beta and the historical sigma, are values taken directly from an ordinary least squares regression (i.e., unnormalized) and represent the historical systematic risk coefficient and the historical residual risk. The remaining 46 descriptors are all normalized. The descriptors are organized according to the categories described above and give rise to the indices of risk. To the right of the descriptor names are the normal-

---

[22]For the proof of this, see Rosenberg and Marathe, "Tests of Capital Asset Pricing Hypotheses."

Table 3.4
Descriptors for Allied Chemical Corporation
12/29/78

FUNDAMENTAL RISK MEASUREMENT SERVICE DESCRIPTORS FOR   ALLIED CHEM CORP

						SYSTEMATIC RISK		SPECIFIC RISK	INDICES CHARACTERIZING RISK					
TSYM	CUSIP	SECURITY NAME	SIC CODE	IND GRP	DATA	HISTORICAL ESTIMATE	SHORT & LONG TERM PREDICTIONS	PREDICTION	MARKET VAR	ERNGS VAR · UNSUCCESS ·	SMALLNESS	FINANCIAL GROWTH ·	· INDUSTRY ·	
ACD	01908710	ALLIED CHEM CORP	2800	11	1	1.18	1.35 1.33	26.67%	0.5	-0.2 1.4	0.8	-0.1	0.5 0.3	

DESCRIPTOR	VALUE	CONTRIBUTION TO		
		BETA	SIGMA	RSKINDX
1. HISTORICAL BETA ESTIMATE	1.18	0.067	-0.005	0.25
2. HISTORICAL SIGMA ESTIMATE	22.17	0.000	-0.044	0.00
ALL FOLLOWING DESCRIPTORS ARE NORMALIZED				
3. SHARE TURNOVER, QUARTERLY	0.08	0.001	0.003	0.00
4. SHARE TURNOVER, 12 MONTHS	0.62	0.022	0.005	0.09
5. SHARE TURNOVER, 5 YEARS	0.41	0.003	0.000	0.01
6. TRADING VOLUME/VARIANCE	-0.26	-0.005	-0.003	-0.02
7. COMMON STOCK PRICE {LN}	-0.79	-0.027	0.023	-0.10
8. HISTORICAL ALPHA ESTIMATE	-0.89	0.0	0.0	0.0
9. CUMULATIVE RANGE, 1 YR	0.59	0.064	0.045	0.24
INDEX OF MARKET VARIABILITY				0.48

DESCRIPTOR	VALUE	CONTRIBUTION TO		
		BETA	SIGMA	RSKINDX
23. TOTAL ASSETS {LOG}	-0.43	-0.011	-0.007	0.05
24. MARKET CAPITALIZATION {LN}	-1.48	-0.013	0.017	0.38
25. MARKET CAPITALIZATION	-2.28	-0.095	0.043	0.84
26. NET PLANT/GROSS PLANT	-0.63	0.0	0.0	0.0
27. NET PLANT/COMMON EQUITY	0.86	-0.014	-0.038	-0.49
28. INFLATION ADJUSTED PTEQ	0.62	0.0	0.0	0.0
29. TRADING RECENCY	-0.11	-0.001	-0.001	-0.01
30. INDICATOR OF ERNGS HIST.	0.07	-0.000	-0.000	-0.01
INDEX OF IMMATURITY AND SMALLNESS				0.77

10.	VARIANCE OF EARNINGS	-0.39	-0.001	-0.005	-0.23
11.	EXTRAORDINARY ITEMS	0.30	-0.001	-0.000	0.04
12.	VARIANCE OF CASH FLOW	-0.53	-0.004	-0.001	-0.05
13.	EARNINGS COVARIABILITY	0.50	0.004	0.002	0.04
14.	ERNGS/PRICE COVARIABILITY	0.37	0.009	0.004	0.03
	INDEX OF EARNINGS VARIABILITY				-0.16
15.	GROWTH IN EARNINGS/SHARE	-0.34	0.022	0.008	0.12
16.	RECENT EARNINGS CHANGE	-0.07	0.001	0.001	0.03
17.	RELATIVE STRENGTH	-2.02	0.090	0.065	1.10
18.	INDICATOR OF SMALL E/P	-0.07	0.001	-0.000	0.01
19.	BOOK/PRICE RATIO	0.19	-0.002	-0.002	0.16
20.	TAX/EARNINGS, 5 YEARS	-0.43	-0.014	0.005	-0.05
21.	DIVIDEND CUTS, 5 YEARS	-0.28	-0.003	-0.000	-0.02
22.	RETURN ON EQUITY, 5 YEARS	-0.52	-0.003	-0.006	
	INDEX OF LOW VALUATION, UNSUCCESS				1.35

31.	PAYOUT, LAST 5 YEARS	-0.20	-0.004	0.002	0.07
32.	CURRENT YIELD	0.57	-0.013	-0.016	-0.16
33.	YIELD, LAST 5 YEARS	0.05	-0.001	-0.000	-0.01
34.	INDICATOR OF ZERO YIELD	-0.08	-0.000	-0.000	-0.01
35.	GROWTH IN TOTAL ASSETS	-0.14	-0.006	-0.003	0.04
36.	CAPITAL STRUCTURE CHANGE	-0.51	-0.003	0.002	-0.04
37.	EARNINGS/PRICE RATIO	-0.04	-0.001	-0.000	-0.00
38.	ERNGS/PRICE, NORMALIZED	0.04	-0.0	-0.000	-0.00
39.	TYPICAL E/P RATIO, 5 YRS	0.30	-0.006	-0.009	-0.03
	INDEX OF GROWTH ORIENTATION				-0.13
40.	LEVERAGE AT BOOK	0.34	0.0	0.0	0.0
41.	LEVERAGE AT MARKET	0.29	0.0	0.003	0.06
42.	DEBT/ASSETS	0.65	0.015	0.006	0.39
43.	UNCOVERED FIXED CHARGES	-0.15	-0.001	-0.000	-0.02
44.	CASH FLOW/CURR. LIAB.	-0.17	-0.001	0.001	-0.00
45.	LIQUID ASSETS/CURR. LIAB.	-0.11	-0.001	0.002	-0.05
46.	POTENTIAL DILUTION	-0.30	-0.003	0.001	0.03
47.	PRICE DEFLATED ERNGS. ADJ	-0.88	-0.0	0.0	0.0
48.	TAX ADJ. MONETARY DEBT	-0.27	-0.0	0.0	0.0
	INDEX OF FINANCIAL RISK				0.53

FOOTNOTES : OVERALL CONSTANT TERMS FOR ALL COMPANIES ------- BETA : 0.961 SIGMA : 0.897
           INDUSTRY GROUP ADJUSTMENTS FOR CHEMICALS -- BETA : 0.002 SIGMA : 0.005
           BASE FORECAST FOR SPECIFIC RISK OF ALL COMPANIES : 24.33%
NOTE : CONTRIBUTIONS AS STATED DO NOT APPLY TO COMPANIES WITH DATA CODE NC {NON/COMPUSTAT}

Source: Fundamental Risk Measurement Service.

ized values and contributions to the prediction of systematic risk (beta), specific risk (sigma), and risk index (rskindx).

To explain this table, consider descriptors 10 to 14, the descriptors comprised by the index of earnings variability. The first of these descriptors is the variance of earnings, which has a value of -0.39 for Allied Chemical. The negative sign indicates that the earnings variance of Allied Chemical is less than that for the "typical" company in the S&P 500 (more precisely, the capitalization weighted average of the earnings variance of all the companies in the S&P 500). The magnitude of the value, -0.39, indicates that Allied Chemical lies 0.39 standard deviations below the value for the S&P 500, which is zero. Since the range from minus one to plus one standard deviation includes approximately 67 percent of all observations (with 16.5 percent lying above one standard deviation and 16.5 percent lying below), the value of -0.39 indicates that slightly more than 65 percent of observations have greater earnings variance than Allied Chemical.[23] All other normalized values have analogous interpretations.

The next three columns show the contribution of this descriptor to the predicted beta, the predicted sigma, and the risk index. Because Allied Chemical has less earnings variance than the typical S&P 500 company, it seems intuitive that Allied Chemical would be slightly less risky than the typical S&P 500 company. In other words, if the only information we had about a company was that its earnings stream was more certain than that for the average company, then our natural reaction would be to infer that this company was less risky than the average company. This is indeed the result from the prediction rules: because Allied Chemical has a smaller than average earnings variance, the beta is adjusted downward by 0.001 from the beta value obtained from all other sources. Similarly, the specific risk (sigma) is decreased by 0.005 times the typical specific risk. Thus, if 24.33 percent is the typical specific risk, the forecast for Allied Chemical is decreased by 24.33×0.005 percent $= 0.12$ percent, simply because the company's earnings are more certain than those of the typical company. The total adjustment, ignoring rounding error, from all 48 descriptors gives the systematic (beta) and specific (sigma) risk predictions reported in the summary line.

The last column gives the contributions of the descriptors to the risk index, which are totaled (for this index) beneath descriptor 14. The index of earnings variability for Allied Chemical is -0.16, which again is a normalized value. Therefore, this company is categorized as having less earnings variability than the typical company in the S&P 500, and it lies 0.16 standard deviations below the S&P 500 value of zero. The index of earnings variability, the other five indices, and an industry risk index are reported in the right columns in the summary line at the top of the page. The industry risk index indicates the

---

[23]Provided the distribution of the descriptors is approximately normal, in which case the exact figure can be found from a table of the normal distribution.

degree to which the industry is exposed to uncertain economic events, with a higher value indicating greater exposure. This index is normalized in a manner similar to the normalization of the other indices.

The other important components of the summary line include the historical beta estimate and the short- and long-term predictions of beta. These predictions are optimized for different horizons (three months and five years, respectively), with the short term more dependent upon recent market descriptors and the long term more dependent upon the fundamental structure of the company. The difference between the historical estimate and the short-term beta is the total adjustment, due to the fundamental prediction rule. The next column gives the prediction for the annual standard deviation of specific return, which incorporates the market and fundamental descriptors.

The descriptors for Chrysler Corporation are given in Table 3.5. The interpretation of the Chrysler descriptors parallels that of the Allied Chemical descriptors. Again, consider the index of earnings variability. The first descriptor in this category, variance of earnings, has a value of 5.12. This indicates that Chrysler has such extreme earnings variance that it lies over five standard deviations from the S&P 500 value of zero. This fundamental information indicates that Chrysler is more risky than the typical company and produces a positive adjustment to beta of 0.15 and an adjustment to specific risk of $0.063 \times 24.33 = 0.15$ percent. The contribution to the risk index from the descriptor is 3.01, which is the dominant component of the total risk index value of 3.43. This suggests that Chrysler has a greater earnings variability than the typical company. In addition, since this risk index lies over three standard deviations from the mean, it indicates that Chrysler has a greater exposure to the earnings variability factor than all but a few companies.

The summary lines contain the information found in a " beta book." Table 3.6 gives this information for the 30 stocks in the Dow Jones Industrial Average.

This completes our analysis of a single security, so let us turn to the implications of a portfolio risk analysis. As for a single security, the first benefit from risk measurement for a portfolio is that it provides an indication of the portfolio's descriptor values. These values are shown in Table 3.7 for the portfolio formed from the securities in the Dow Jones Industrial Average on December 29, 1978.

In many respects the values in Table 3.7 are similar to the values in Tables 3.4 and 3.5. The first two descriptors are the (unnormalized) historical beta and the residual risk (sigma), and values are given for the portfolio and the FRMS universe (a capitalization weighted universe of approximately 6,000 securities of interest to institutions) and for the contributions of these descriptors to the short- and long-term beta and the risk index. Descriptors 3 through 48 are the same descriptors as are given in Tables 3.4 and 3.5, and normalized values (so that the S&P 500 has value zero) are given for the portfolio and the FRMS universe, together with their contributions to the beta and the risk index.

Table 3.5
Descriptors for Chrysler Corporation
(12/29/78)

FUNDAMENTAL RISK MEASUREMENT SERVICE DESCRIPTIONS FOR CHRYSLER CORP

TSYM	CUSIP	SECURITY NAME	SIC CODE	IND GRP	DATA	SYSTEMATIC RISK HISTORICAL ESTIMATE	SHORT & LONG TERM PREDICTIONS		SPECIFIC RISK PREDICTION	INDICES CHARACTERIZING RISK: MARKET VAR · ERNGS VAR-UNSUCCESS · FINANCIAL GROWTH · SMALLNESS · INDUSTRY
C	17119610	CHRYSLER CORP	3711	21	1	0.87	1.52	1.51	35.33%	0.5 3.4 3.4 -0.2 -0.1 2.5 0.9

DESCRIPTOR	VALUE	CONTRIBUTION TO BETA	SIGMA	RSKINDX
1. HISTORICAL BETA ESTIMATE	0.87	0.135	-0.069	0.52
2. HISTORICAL SIGMA ESTIMATE	35.68	0.057	0.268	0.22
ALL FOLLOWING DESCRIPTORS ARE NORMALIZED				
3. SHARE TURNOVER, QUARTERLY	0.43	0.004	0.015	0.02
4. SHARE TURNOVER, 12 MONTHS	0.56	0.020	0.005	0.08
5. SHARE TURNOVER, 5 YEARS	0.81	0.006	0.001	0.02
6. TRADING VOLUME/VARIANCE	-1.13	-0.023	-0.012	-0.09
7. COMMON STOCK PRICE {LN}	-2.97	-0.100	0.087	-0.38
8. HISTORICAL ALPHA ESTIMATE	-0.94	0.0	0.0	0.0
9. CUMULATIVE RANGE, 1 YR.	0.26	0.028	0.020	0.11
INDEX OF MARKET VARIABILITY				0.49

DESCRIPTOR	VALUE	CONTRIBUTION TO BETA	SIGMA	RSKINDX
23. TOTAL ASSETS {LOG}	0.40	0.010	0.006	-0.05
24. MARKET CAPITALIZATION {LN}	-1.89	-0.016	0.021	0.48
25. MARKET CAPITALIZATION	-2.53	-0.105	0.048	0.93
26. NET PLANT/GROSS PLANT	-1.54	0.0	0.0	0.0
27. NET PLANT/COMMON EQUITY	2.66	-0.045	-0.116	-1.52
28. INFLATION ADJUSTED PTEQ	2.08	0.0	0.0	0.0
29. TRADING RECENCY	-0.11	-0.001	-0.001	-0.01
30. INDICATOR OF ERNGS HIST.	0.07	-0.000	-0.000	-0.01
INDEX OF IMMATURITY AND SMALLNESS				-0.16

10.	VARIANCE OF EARNINGS	5·12	0·015	0·063	3·01
11.	EXTRAORDINARY ITEMS	1·36	-0·006	0·000	0·17
12.	VARIANCE OF CASH FLOW	3·42	0·029	0·009	0·30
13.	EARNINGS COVARIABILITY	-0·95	-0·008	-0·003	-0·08
14.	ERNGS/PRICE COVARIABILITY	0·16	0·004	0·002	0·01
	INDEX OF EARNINGS VARIABILITY	3·43			3·43
15.	GROWTH IN EARNINGS/SHARE	-0·26	0·016	0·006	0·09
16.	RECENT EARNINGS CHANGE	-2·96	0·038	0·061	1·08
17.	RELATIVE STRENGTH	-1·73	0·077	0·055	0·94
18.	INDICATOR OF SMALL E/P	-0·07	-0·001	-0·000	-0·00
19.	BOOK/PRICE RATIO	5·02	-0·060	0·059	0·31
20.	TAX/EARNINGS, 5 YEARS	-0·12	-0·004	0·001	0·04
21.	DIVIDEND CUTS, 5 YEARS	5·01	0·048	0·003	0·96
22.	RETURN ON EQUITY, 5 YEARS	-1·84	0·009	-0·021	-0·07
	INDEX OF LOW VALUATION, UNSUCCESS	3·37			3·37

31.	PAYOUT, LAST 5 YEARS	-0·99	0·023	0·011	0·33
32.	CURRENT YIELD	-0·31	0·007	0·009	-0·08
33.	YIELD, LAST 5 YEARS	-0·70	0·008	0·003	-0·15
34.	INDICATOR OF ZERO YIELD	-0·08	-0·000	-0·000	-0·01
35.	GROWTH IN TOTAL ASSETS	-0·82	-0·036	-0·017	-0·25
36.	CAPITAL STRUCTURE CHANGE	-0·53	-0·003	-0·002	-0·04
37.	EARNINGS/PRICE RATIO	1·05	0·017	-0·006	0·02
38.	ERNGS/PRICE, NORMALIZED	0·68	0·0	-0·001	-0·05
39.	TYPICAL E/P RATIO, 5 YRS	0·40	-0·008	-0·012	-0·04
	INDEX OF GROWTH ORIENTATION	-0·09			-0·09
40.	LEVERAGE AT BOOK	-0·06	0·0	0·0	0·0
41.	LEVERAGE AT MARKET	1·58	0·0	0·017	0·34
42.	DEBT/ASSETS	0·06	-0·001	0·001	0·04
43.	UNCOVERED FIXED CHARGES	3·11	-0·004	-0·007	0·36
44.	CASH FLOW/CURR. LIAB.	-1·16	-0·009	-0·004	-0·02
45.	LIQUID ASSETS/CURR. LIAB.	-3·40	-0·040	-0·055	1·72
46.	POTENTIAL DILUTION	0·30	-0·003	0·001	0·03
47.	PRICE DEFLATED ERNGS. ADJ	0·28	0·0	0·0	0·0
48.	TAX ADJ. MONETARY DEBT	-1·35	0·0	0·0	0·0
	INDEX OF FINANCIAL RISK	2·52			2·52

FOOTNOTES : OVERALL CONSTANT TERMS FOR ALL COMPANIES ----- BETA : 0.897 SIGMA : 0.961
INDUSTRY GROUP ADJUSTMENTS FOR MOTOR VEHICLES : -- BETA : -0.018 SIGMA : 0.102
BASE FORECAST FOR SPECIFIC RISK OF ALL COMPANIES : 24.33%

NOTE : CONTRIBUTIONS AS STATED DO NOT APPLY TO COMPANIES WITH DATA CODE NC (NON-COMPUSTAT)

Source: Fundamental Risk Measurement Service.

Table 3.6
"Beta Book" Entries for the Dow Jones Industrials
(12/29/78)

SECURITIES FOR: DOW JONES 30 INDUSTRIALS

TSYM	CUSIP	SECURITY NAME	SIC CODE	IND GRP	DATA
ACD	01908710	ALLIED CHEM CORP	2800	11	1
AA	02224910	ALUMINUM CO AMER	3353	1	1
AT	02470310	AMERICAN BRANDS INC	2111	6	1
AC	02484310	AMERICAN CAN CO	3221	9	1
T	03017710	AMERICAN TEL & TELEG CO	4811	29	1
BS	08750910	BETHLEHEM STL CORP	3310	17	1
C	17119610	CHRYSLER CORP	3711	21	1
DD	26353410	DU PONT E I DE NEMOURS	2800	11	1
EK	27746110	EASTMAN KODAK CO	3861	24	1
SWX	29647010	ESMARK INC	2010	4	1
J	30229010	EXXON CORP	1311	15	1
GE	36960410	GENERAL ELEC CO	3634	39	1
GF	36985610	GENERAL FOODS CORP	2000	4	1
GM	37044210	GENERAL MTRS CORP	3711	21	1
GT	38255010	GOODYEAR TIRE & RUBR	3000	16	1
NI	45325840	INCO LTD	1061	1	1
HR	45957810	INTERNATIONAL HARVESTR	3713	21	1
IP	46014610	INTERNATIONAL PAPER CO	2600	8	1
JM	47812410	JOHNS MANVILLE CORP	2950	3	1
MMM	60405910	MINNESOTA MNG & MFG CO	2641	39	1
OI	69076810	OWENS ILL INC	3221	9	1
PG	74271810	PROCTER & GAMBLE CO	2841	13	1
S	81238710	SEARS ROEBUCK & CO	5311	31	1
SD	85368310	STANDARD OIL CO CALIF	2911	15	1
TX	88169410	TEXACO INC	2992	15	1
UK	90558110	UNION CARBIDE CORP	2800	11	1
X	91265610	UNITED STATES STL CORP	3310	17	1
UA	91301710	UNITED TECHNOLOGIES CP	3728	22	1
WX	96040210	WESTINGHOUSE ELEC CORP	3600	18	1
Z	89088110	WOOLWORTH F W CO	5331	31	1

	SYSTEMATIC RISK			INDICES CHARACTERIZING RISK						
HISTOR- ICAL ESTIMATE	SHORT & LONG TERM PREDICTIONS		SPECIFIC RISK PREDIC- TION	MARKET VAR	·ERNGS VAR	·UNSUCCESS	SMALLNESS	GROWTH	· FINANCIAL ·	INDUSTRY
1·18	1·35	1·33	26·67%	0·5	-0·2	1·4	0·8	-0·1	0·5	0·3
0·66	1·00	0·99	25·63%	0·1	0·4	0·1	0·3	0·1	0·5	-0·9
0·71	0·58	0·62	17·32%	-0·8	-0·5	-0·7	1·2	-1·0	0·9	-1·8
0·54	0·72	0·78	17·67%	-1·0	-0·2	0·2	1·0	-1·0	0·0	-0·5
0·53	0·57	0·63	12·12%	-1·1	-0·2	0·0	-2·1	-1·0	0·9	-0·7
1·03	1·21	1·20	33·26%	0·2	4·0	4·4	-0·9	-0·1	1·1	-0·4
0·87	1·52	1·51	35·33%	0·5	3·4	3·4	-0·2	-0·1	2·5	0·9
0·96	1·07	1·04	19·75%	0·4	-0·1	0·4	-1·1	-0·3	-0·0	0·3
1·25	1·06	1·03	22·17%	0·5	-0·7	0·0	-0·8	0·1	-0·8	0·4
0·71	1·00	1·03	24·60%	-0·3	-0·2	1·1	1·3	-0·0	0·6	-0·5
0·82	0·73	0·77	18·01%	-0·6	-0·4	0·1	-1·5	-0·4	-0·2	-0·3
1·37	1·00	1·02	19·40%	-0·2	0·0	0·1	-0·9	0·1	-0·2	0·7
1·02	0·89	0·89	21·82%	-0·1	-0·3	-0·2	1·0	-0·5	-0·1	-0·5
0·74	0·91	0·94	15·59%	-0·5	0·6	0·8	-1·3	-1·7	-0·5	0·9
0·82	0·91	0·97	18·36%	-0·8	-0·3	-0·2	0·3	-0·9	0·8	0·7
0·86	0·92	0·93	25·98%	-0·2	0·2	0·5	0·9	0·1	-0·2	-0·9
1·03	1·35	1·31	24·60%	0·7	0·2	-0·2	0·9	-0·7	1·1	0·9
1·11	1·15	1·16	23·90%	0·0	-0·2	1·0	0·5	0·2	0·5	0·0
0·81	1·26	1·25	26·33%	0·3	0·6	0·2	1·6	-0·5	-0·3	0·8
1·28	1·05	1·02	21·48%	0·5	-0·3	-0·8	-0·6	0·3	-0·3	0·7
0·87	0·93	0·97	22·52%	-0·6	0·0	1·2	0·9	-0·1	0·4	-0·5
0·89	0·75	0·77	17·32%	-0·5	-0·4	-0·3	-0·6	0·5	-0·2	-0·2
1·02	1·20	1·22	24·60%	-0·1	-0·3	1·1	-0·7	-0·0	0·7	1·5
0·86	0·84	0·85	19·40%	-0·2	-0·3	-0·2	-1·3	-0·3	-0·3	-0·3
0·79	0·74	0·79	19·05%	-0·9	0·0	0·9	-1·4	-1·0	0·0	-0·3
0·88	1·05	1·09	21·13%	-0·4	-0·1	1·1	0·1	-0·3	0·4	0·3
0·91	1·21	1·21	28·41%	0·1	0·4	3·1	-0·7	-0·3	0·7	-0·4
0·73	1·11	1·09	25·29%	0·4	0·3	-0·6	0·7	0·5	-0·8	-0·3
1·16	1·30	1·27	27·37%	0·7	0·1	0·2	0·7	-0·5	-0·0	0·7
1·18	1·25	1·26	24·60%	-0·0	-0·3	0·5	1·2	-0·9	0·8	1·5

Table 3.7
Portfolio Descriptors for the Dow Jones Industrials
(12/29/78)

BARR ROSENBERG & ASSOC.
DOW JONES 30 INDUSTRIALS

-- 4. DESCRIPTORS OF THE PORTFOLIO --

ALL FOLLOWING DESCRIPTORS ARE NORMALIZED

DESCRIPTOR	PORTFOLIO	FRMS UNIVERSE	CONTRIBUTION TO PREDICTED BETA SHORT-TERM	LONG-TERM	CONTRIBUTION TO CORRESPONDING RISK INDEX
1. HISTORICAL BETA ESTIMATE	0.9188	0.9575	-0.031	-0.024	-0.1190
2. HISTORICAL SIGMA ESTIMATE	17.8956	24.0810	-0.006	-0.005	-0.0228
3. SHARE TURNOVER, QUARTERLY	-0.0738	0.1076	-0.001	-0.001	-0.0029
4. SHARE TURNOVER, 12 MONTHS	-0.0046	0.1133	-0.000	-0.000	-0.0006
5. SHARE TURNOVER, 5 YEARS	-0.0798	0.0988	-0.001	-0.000	-0.0022
6. TRADING VOLUME/VARIANCE	0.2844	-1.0586	0.006	0.005	0.0224
7. COMMON STOCK PRICE {LN}	0.0897	-0.4331	0.003	0.002	0.0115
8. HISTORICAL ALPHA ESTIMATE	-0.1281	0.1865	0.0	0.0	0.0
9. CUMULATIVE RANGE, 1 YR.	-0.0315	0.2524	-0.003	-0.003	-0.0130
INDEX OF MARKET VARIABILITY					= -0.1280
10. VARIANCE OF EARNINGS	-0.0439	0.3129	-0.000	-0.000	-0.0259
11. EXTRAORDINARY ITEMS	0.0494	0.2319	-0.000	-0.000	0.0063
12. VARIANCE OF CASH FLOW	-0.2898	0.2956	-0.002	-0.003	-0.0258
13. EARNINGS COVARIABILITY	0.0587	-0.0277	0.000	0.000	0.0053
14. ERNGS/PRICE COVARIABILITY	0.1346	0.1119	0.003	0.003	0.0096
INDEX OF EARNINGS VARIABILITY					= -0.0209
15. GROWTH IN EARNINGS/SHARE	-0.3148	-0.0297	0.020	0.021	0.1126
16. RECENT EARNINGS CHANGE	-0.1696	0.0191	0.002	0.002	0.0618
17. RELATIVE STRENGTH	-0.1854	0.2209	0.008	0.009	0.1012
18. INDICATOR OF SMALL E/P	0.1204	0.1800	-0.001	-0.002	-0.0019
19. BOOK/PRICE RATIO	0.2656	0.1584	-0.003	-0.003	0.0165

20	TAX/EARNINGS, 5 YEARS	0.0877	-0.0537	-0.003	-0.003	-0.0314
21	DIVIDEND CUTS, 5 YEARS	0.2831	0.0774	0.003	0.003	0.0543
22	RETURN ON EQUITY, 5 YEARS	-0.3197	-0.1012	0.002	0.002	-0.0126

INDEX OF LOW VALUATION, UNSUCCESS = 0.3113

23	TOTAL ASSETS {LOG}	0.2677	-0.8079	0.007	0.007	-0.0317
24	MARKET CAPITALIZATION {LN}	0.1360	-0.8329	0.001	0.001	-0.0344
25	MARKET CAPITALIZATION	0.3936	-0.7268	-0.016	-0.017	-0.1444
26	NET PLANT/GROSS PLANT	-0.5148	0.1221	0.0	0.0	0.0
27	NET PLANT/COMMON EQUITY	0.1749	0.0696	-0.003	-0.003	-0.0995
28	INFLATION ADJUSTED PTEQ	0.0682	0.0886	0.0	0.0	0.0
29	TRADING RECENCY	-0.1099	-0.2039	-0.001	-0.001	-0.0150
30	INDICATOR OF ERNGS HIST.	0.0743	-0.6212	-0.000	-0.000	-0.0146

INDEX OF IMMATURITY AND SMALLNESS = -0.3139

31	PAYOUT, LAST 5 YEARS	0.2159	-0.2414	-0.005	-0.005	-0.0727
32	CURRENT YIELD	0.2154	-0.1921	-0.005	-0.005	-0.0588
33	YIELD, LAST 5 YEARS	0.2672	-0.0583	0.003	0.003	-0.0579
34	INDICATOR OF ZERO YIELD	-0.0756	0.1376	-0.000	-0.000	-0.0101
35	GROWTH IN TOTAL ASSETS	-0.1952	0.0076	-0.008	-0.009	-0.0588
36	CAPITAL STRUCTURE CHANGE	-0.3541	0.2032	0.002	0.002	-0.0280
37	EARNINGS/PRICE RATIO	0.0240	0.0510	0.000	0.000	0.0005
38	ERNGS/PRICE, NORMALIZED	0.0224	0.0479	0.0	0.0	-0.0015
39	TYPICAL E/P RATIO, 5 YRS	0.1144	0.1538	-0.002	-0.002	-0.0111

INDEX OF GROWTH ORIENTATION = -0.2875

40	LEVERAGE AT BOOK	-0.1076	0.1546	0.0	0.0	0.0
41	LEVERAGE AT MARKET	-0.0182	0.1637	0.0	0.0	-0.0039
42	DEBT/ASSETS	0.0283	0.1489	0.001	0.001	0.0168
43	UNCOVERED FIXED CHARGES	0.0248	0.2460	-0.000	-0.000	0.0029
44	CASH FLOW/CURR. LIAB.	-0.0613	-0.0361	0.000	0.000	0.0010
45	LIQUID ASSETS/CURR. LIAB.	-0.1797	-0.0167	0.002	0.002	0.0913
46	POTENTIAL DILUTION	-0.0380	-0.0333	0.000	0.000	-0.0033
47	PRICE DEFLATED ERNGS. ADJ	-0.2087	-0.1448	0.0	0.0	0.0
48	TAX ADJ. MONETARY DEBT	-0.0243	-0.0812	0.0	0.0	0.0

INDEX OF FINANCIAL RISK = 0.1212

Again, consider descriptor 10 (variance of earnings), which has a value of −0.0439. This indicates that the portfolio is formed in such a way that the earnings variance of its "average" security lies 0.04 standard deviations below the capitalization weighted average of all S&P 500 stocks. In other words, the differences in the variances of the earnings descriptors for the 30 stocks average out to almost zero, so that the S&P 500 and the Dow Jones are almost identical on this characteristic. Interestingly, the next column compares this bias relative to a wider and more representative (of the entire market) universe. The typical security in the FRMS universe has an earnings variance that lies 0.3129 standard deviations above the S&P 500 value. In other words, the earnings variance of the Dow Jones is similar to that of the S&P 500 but is much less than that of the FRMS universe. This is intuitively obvious since the FRMS universe has a predominance of small companies, which tend to have a higher level of earnings variance.

The descriptors permit a simple comparison of the fundamentals of the portfolio relative to both the S&P 500 and the FRMS universe. For instance, the current yield on the Dow Jones (descriptor 32, normalized value 0.2154) is greater than that on the S&P 500 (normalized value zero), which, in turn, is greater than that on the FRMS universe (normalized value −0.1921). Conversely, the growth in total assets (descriptor 35, normalized value −0.1952) on the Dow Jones is less than that on the S&P 500, which, in turn, is less than that on the FRMS universe (normalized value 0.0076).

Only three of the risk indices are much different from the S&P 500 values (of zero): the immaturity and smallness and the growth orientation indices of the Dow Jones are less than those of the S&P 500; the low valuation, unsuccess index is greater than that of the S&P 500. This indicates that the Dow Jones is composed of large, mature, high-yielding securities (relative to the S&P 500) that have been less successful than the typical company in the S&P 500.

We have stated that as the portfolio becomes differentiated from the market portfolio (the S&P 500 in this analysis), it becomes exposed to residual risk. For instance, although the earnings variability index indicates that the Dow Jones is less risky on an absolute basis than the S&P 500, it is clearly more risky on a relative basis. This is logical because of the difference in exposure to a common factor of return. If securities with significant earnings variability do well, the Dow Jones will underperform the S&P 500, and vice versa.

The measurement of residual risk is found from the differential exposure to the common factors (i.e., the degree to which the risk indices are nonzero) and the portfolio specific risk.[24] This information, together with information on the systematic risk of the portfolio, is given in Table 3.8.

This table shows the front page of a PORCH (PORtfolio CHaracteristics) report, which analyzes the Dow Jones Industrial Average relative to the S&P 500. Items A through D show the exposure of the Dow Jones to systematic

---

[24]This computation is described in Supplement 3, equations (S3–17) and (S3–18).

Table 3.8
Summary Statistics Describing Portfolio Risk

```
FUNDAMENTAL RISK MEASUREMENT SERVICE
          PORTFOLIO ANALYSIS
        BARR ROSENBERG & ASSOC.

        DOW JONES 30 INDUSTRIALS
        WEIGHTED AS IN THE INDEX
```

```
PORTFOLIO STATUS AS OF    DECEMBER   29  1978
   ANALYSIS CONDUCTED     JANUARY    29  1979
   FRMS UPDATE AS OF      DECEMBER   29  1978
S&P500    IS THE MARKET PORTFOLIO
```

```
           1.  SUMMARY MEASURES FOR COMMON EQUITY

A.  PREDICTED SYSTEMATIC RISK COEFFICIENT {BETA}—NEXT 3 MONTHS          0.97
B.  PREDICTED SYSTEMATIC RISK COEFFICIENT {BETA}—NEXT 5 YEARS           0.98
C.  ANNUAL STANDARD DEVIATION OF SYSTEMATIC PORTFOLIO RETURN          20.22%
D.  FRMS FORECAST STANDARD DEVIATION OF ANNUAL S&P500 RETURN          20.88%

        PORTFOLIO RISK FORECAST, INCLUDING EXTRA-MARKET COVARIANCE . . .

E.1   STANDARD DEVIATION OF ANNUAL PORTFOLIO RETURN                   20.83%
E.2   STANDARD DEVIATION OF ANNUAL PORTFOLIO RESIDUAL RETURN           4.99%
E.3   COEFFICIENT OF DETERMINATION BY S&P500                  0.943
E.4   REQUIRED ANNUAL PORTFOLIO APPRAISAL PREMIUM {ALPHA}              0.34%
E.5   INFERRED COVENANT INFORMATION RATIO {CIR}              0.069
E.6   INFERRED CEER OF ACTIVE MANAGEMENT                     0.171%

        RISK FORECASTS BASED UPON A SIMULATED 5-YEAR HISTORY OF MONTHLY
        RETURNS FOR THE PORTFOLIO . . .

F.1   STANDARD DEVIATION OF ANNUAL PORTFOLIO RETURN                   19.63%
F.2   STANDARD DEVIATION OF ANNUAL PORTFOLIO RESIDUAL RETURN           4.88%
F.3   COEFFICIENT OF DETERMINATION BY S&P500                  0.938
```

```
        2.  INDICES OF RISK IN THE PORTFOLIO
```

INDEX OF RISK	PORTFOLIO	S&P500	FRMS UNIVERSE	EFFECT OF 0.01 INCREASE ON RESID. STDEV	REQUIRED ALPHA
MARKET VARIABILITY	-0.128	0.0	0.142	-0.0043	-0.03
EARNINGS VARIABILITY	-0.021	0.0	0.226	0.0030	0.02
LOW VALUATION, UNSUCCESS	0.311	0.0	-0.066	0.0099	0.07
IMMATURITY AND SMALLNESS	-0.314	0.0	-0.600	0.0016	0.01
GROWTH ORIENTATION	-0.288	0.0	0.119	-0.0129	-0.09
FINANCIAL RISK	0.121	0.0	0.132	0.0036	0.03

risk. First, the predicted short-term beta is 0.97, indicating that if the S&P 500 exhibits a 10 percent excess rate of return, then we would expect (simply from the exposure of the Dow Jones to systematic risk) that the portfolio will experience an excess rate of return of 9.7 percent. The long-term beta is 0.98, which implies that the prediction (in this instance) is not sensitive to the most recent price action. Item D gives the forecast standard deviation of the annual S&P 500 return, which is used to determine item C. The annual standard deviation of systematic portfolio return, S_{PS}, is given by the formula $S_{PS} = \beta_P S_M$, where S_M is the standard deviation of market return (item D) and β_P is the portfolio beta (item A).[25] Thus, $20.88 \times 0.97 = 20.22$ percent (ignoring rounding errors).

The prediction of residual risk is a very sensitive operation. The method we have discussed above begins by predicting the attributes of all stocks and then extrapolating these results to the portfolio being analyzed. In this explanation, errors could be introduced if the portfolio manager had knowledge of events which radically affected the risk characteristics of the portfolio. To obtain an independent check a historical simulation is performed. This entails constructing returns on the portfolio and the S&P 500, both with current weights, and regressing one against the other. The result of this analysis is given by items F.1, F.2, and F.3. The simulation shows that standard deviation of portfolio return (19.63 percent) is less than that predicted by the risk model for the systematic component, that the residual standard deviation is 4.88 percent, and that the coefficient of determination (R^2) is 0.938.[26] The simulation could be in error because it extrapolates history directly into the future; thus, to form the best prediction, we should average both estimates, the simulation prediction and the risk model prediction.

This combined prediction is given by items E.1 through E.6. The second item, E.2, gives the combined prediction of residual risk, with a value of 4.99 percent. What does this number represent? The risk arises because the Dow Jones is not diversified with respect to the S&P 500, so that the two portfolios have differential exposure to the common factors. The magnitude of the risk is found by averaging the prediction of risk from the model and the forecast from the simulation. We will return to this calculation after describing the remainder of the report.

The total standard deviation, E.1, is found from items C and E.2 (systematic variance plus residual variance = total variance, or $409.0 + 24.9 = 433.9 = 20.83^2$). Notice that the effect of the residual risk upon the total risk is comparatively insignificant. This is because the systematic risk is so much greater than the residual risk. Item E.3, which indicates that 94.3 percent of the portfolio return variability is explained by the market, is an alternative way of specifying the level of residual risk.[27]

Item E.4 is the next important value since it shows the portfolio required alpha. The formula for this computation (assuming that the normal beta is unity) is given in equation (2–10) and repeated below:

$$\alpha_P^R = (E_M - i_F)\omega_P^2/V_M.$$

Assuming that $E_M - i_F = 6$ percent (a reasonable long-term consensus value) and noting from item D that $V_M = 20.88 \times 20.88 = 435.9$ (%^{2}), while from E.2, $\omega_P^2 = 4.99 \times 4.99 = 24.9$ (%^{2}), then:

---

[25]See equation (2–4) and footnote 10 in Chapter 2.

[26]Recall from the supplement to Chapter 1, equation (S1–17), that the $R^2 = (19.63^2 - 4.88^2)/19.63^2 = 361.7/385.5 = 0.938$.

[27]$R^2 = (20.83^2 - 4.99^2)/20.83^2 = 409.0/433.9 = 0.942$.

$$\alpha_P^R = 6 \times 24.9/435.9 = 34.3 \text{ basis points.}$$

Item E.6 is related because it gives the inferred CEER of active management. In Chapter 2 we derived the CEER as one half of the required alpha; i.e., CEER = 34.3/2 = 17.1 basis points.

The only other item in this section is item E.5. This is the inferred *covenant information ratio* (CIR), defined as the required alpha divided by the measured residual standard deviation; that is, E.5 = E.4/E.2. This number represents the inferred "mean/standard deviation" ratio of active management and is related to the mean/variance ratio discussed in Chapter 2. The CIR is useful in the sponsor coordination of managers and will be discussed further in Chapter 6.

This completes the top panel, the summary statistics for the portfolio. The bottom panel gives the risk indices for the portfolio as derived from Table 3.7, the corresponding values for the S&P 500 and the FRMS universe. The extreme exposure of the Dow Jones and the S&P 500, relative to a broader universe, is made clear by these values. In particular, the immaturity and smallness of the Dow Jones lies almost one standard deviation beneath that of the FRMS universe; relative to this broad universe, the 30 Dow Jones stocks are mature and large; or conversely, there are very many small companies in the FRMS universe! Before leaving this panel, notice that the Dow Jones and the FRMS universe have similar financial risk, which is greater than that of the S&P 500.

The two columns on the right give an indication of the sensitivity of the portfolio risk and return to revisions in the holdings. The penultimate column shows the effect on the residual risk if the risk index is changed. For instance, consider the growth orientation index. If the portfolio is revised so that it becomes less deviant with respect to this index, by how much will the residual risk change? The answer is that if the growth orientation index is increased to -0.278 (an increase of 0.01), then the residual risk will be reduced by 0.0129, to 4.977 percent. If the relationship is reasonably linear, revising the portfolio to have a neutral growth orientation will reduce the residual risk to 4.62 percent $(4.99 - 28.8 \times 0.0129)$.

In an actively managed portfolio, a deviant position such as a growth orientation index of -0.288 would only be undertaken if that factor were expected to provide a nonzero return. The last column indicates the amount of expected residual return (alpha) required for the portfolio to be optimal. In this case, the present portfolio is optimal if it is believed that a growth orientation risk index exposure of one will underperform by nine basis points.

Finally, let us return to item E.2 and the combination of the predictions. This computation is shown in Table 3.9, whose three main columns give the results for the FRMS model, the simulation, and the combined prediction. The first line shows that the model estimation of systematic variance is 409.0 units of variance. Statistically, this value has much more information than the simulation, so the value of the 409.0 is used for the prediction. This is not the case with residual risk.

Table 3.9
The Combined Prediction of Portfolio Residual Risk

DECOMPOSITION OF VARIANCE OF ANNUAL PERCENT RETURN				
		FRMS MODEL	SIMULATION	PREDICTION
SYSTEMATIC			409·0	361·7	409·0
SPECIFIC		15·7			
RISK INDICES VARIANCE	2·5				
INDUSTRY VARIANCE	5·5				
R.I.-INDUSTRY COVARIANCE	2·3				

XMC		10·3			

RESIDUAL			26·1	23·8	24·9
			-----	-----	-----
TOTAL			435·0	385·5	433·9

The model permits the decomposition of residual risk into specific risk and *XMC*. Further, *XMC* can be broken down into its components: variance arising from the risk index strategy (risk indices variance), the industry variance, and the covariance between the two. This last component arises because certain industries may naturally have exposure to the common factors (i.e., business machines are growth oriented or utilities are financially risky). In this case, the risk index exposure and the industry exposure are positively correlated, which increases risk above the sum of the variances.[28] The total residual variance predicted by the model is 26.1 units versus 23.8 units for the simulation. Since both sources provide information, the prediction is the average of both values.

So much for the numbers, but what does it all mean?

Interpretation

The Dow Jones Industrial Average has slightly less systematic risk than the S&P 500 and exhibits 4.99 percent annual residual standard deviation. Its systematic risk is close to that of the typical institutional portfolio, while its residual risk is probably greater. The Dow Jones exhibits a more aggressive active strategy than do many institutional portfolios! (Conversely, the typical pension portfolio is a "better" market index, or proxy for the S&P 500, than the Dow Jones.) This level of risk can be justified if the manager believes that the portfolio will exhibit an expected residual return of 34 basis points per year, which is equivalent to 17 basis points of certainty equivalent excess return; i.e., the active management can be justified if it earns 17 basis points in certain return. Those 17 basis points are less than the average active management fee, indicating that the Dow Jones cannot be justified by the sponsor on economic grounds at this point in time and at this level of aggressiveness.

---

[28]The general formula for the variance of the sum of two random variables is given in the supplement to Chapter 1, equation (S1-11).

What is the strategy? A glance at the risk indices in Table 3.8 shows that three indices are important: low valuation and unsuccess, immaturity and smallness, and growth orientation. The portfolio is biased toward high-yielding companies, large and mature companies, and companies which in the past have not been highly regarded by market participants.

Can anything else be said? Yes, from Table 3.9 we can note the breakdown in the components of residual risk. Specific risk is the largest part; this portfolio therefore includes assets with large portfolio proportions and comparatively few stocks; otherwise this component would have been diversified away. This we have called stock picking. Various securities have been "picked" and formed into a portfolio that is substantially exposed to specific risk. This indicates that the portfolio manager has formed judgments concerning the valuation of these securities and has constructed the portfolio to earn the specific return, rather than have it diversified away, possibly because of a perception about its future magnitude.

The exposure to the common factors, *XMC,* is also substantial, and it arises mainly from industry risk. We therefore expect the portfolio to contain some substantial industry holdings.

Thus, without even knowing the stocks or the portfolio holdings, we have been able to deduce the portfolio strategy fairly precisely.

Summary

We have now completed the discussion of the measurement and prediction of the risk of individual securities and portfolios. We have seen that risk can be predicted successfully, though naive estimation methods are frequently unsatisfactory. Risk is a vital and unavoidable characteristic of equity portfolios. If it is to be measured, it seems only reasonable and responsible to measure it in the most accurate and sensitive manner. Knowledge of the level of risk is needed in order to tailor investment strategies to the investor's willingness to bear risk and to provoke portfolio managers to continually justify the risk exposure in terms of anticipated reward. This process of justifying the risk exposure completes the connection between the two crucial dimensions in portfolio management, risk and reward.

The reward dimension that is inferred from the risk analysis is the alpha required to justify taking positions that do not match the market holdings. Residual risk is induced in the portfolio only when the portfolio is differentiated from the market. Similarly, extraordinary return can only be obtained by differentiating the portfolio from the market. Therefore, measuring the residual risk of a portfolio is the first element in determining the aggressiveness of the portfolio manager. If the portfolio displays a low level of residual risk, then the manager is making few "bets" in response to judgment. This may be good or bad, but it is not irrelevant. The portfolio manager has the responsibility to manage. Thus, the degree of management must be continually tracked.

Further Reading

The best articles on the prediction and modeling of security risk belong to the working paper series of the Research Program in Finance of the Graduate School of Business Administration at the University of California at Berkeley. Many of these working papers were published subsequently as articles in finance journals, and these articles are referenced here together with other useful items:

Farrell, James. "Homogeneous Stock Groupings: Implications for Portfolio Management." *Financial Analyst Journal*, May–June 1975, pp. 50–58.

Fouse, William; William Jahnke; and Barr Rosenberg. "Is Beta Phlogiston?" *Financial Analysts Journal*, January–February 1974, pp. 72–82.

Rosenberg, Barr. "Extra-market Components of Covariance in Security Markets." *Journal of Financial and Quantitative Analysis*, March 1974, pp. 263–74.

———, and James Guy. "Prediction of Beta from Investment Fundamentals." *Financial Analysts Journal*, May–June and July–August 1976.

———, and Vinay Marathe. "The Prediction of Investment Risk: Systematic and Residual Risk." *Proceedings of the Seminar on the Analysis of Security Prices*, University of Chicago, November 1975, pp. 85–225.

———, and Vinay Marathe. "Common Factors in Security Returns: Microeconomic Determinants and Macroeconomic Correlates." *Proceedings of the Seminar on the Analysis of Security Prices*, University of Chicago, May 1976, pp. 61–115.

Sharpe, William. *Investments*. Englewood Cliffs, N.J.: Prentice-Hall, 1978, particularly pp. 274–98.

———, and Guy Cooper. "Risk-Return Classes of New York Stock Exchange Common Stocks, 1931–1967." *Financial Analysts Journal*, March–April 1972, pp. 46–54.

For discussion of the importance of the market portfolio; see:

Roll, Richard. "A Critique of the Asset Pricing Theory's Tests—Part 1: On Past and Potential Testability of the Theory." *Journal of Financial Economics*, March 1977, pp. 129–76.

Rudd, Andrew, and Barr Rosenberg. "The 'Market Model' in Investment Management." *Journal of Finance*, May 1980, pp. 596–607.

For a creatively different perspective, see the following article and subsequent correspondence:

Wallace, Anise. "Is Beta Dead?" *Institutional Investor*, July 1980, pp. 23–30.

Supplement 3

Models of Security Prices and the Estimation of Risk

What can be said about the behavior of security prices in the future? This single question has probably absorbed more effort than any other in the theory of finance. Most people are surprised to find that research in this area dates back at least to the last century, is related to several branches of physics, and that an early work on the subject is similar to, but predates, Einstein's work on Brownian motion.[1]

There are two fairly distinct approaches in this research. One is distributional, in that its primary aim is to determine the distribution of stock prices.[2] This approach is intimately connected with market efficiency theories, and it can be considered a descriptive theory of stock returns because its main thrust is to describe the stock process and it makes little effort to understand why one distribution appears to be a better description than another. Thus, the development of this approach has been characterized by the supersession of the models proposed by successive studies using different data or different methods.

The second approach is more inquisitive, in that it attempts to determine the

---

[1]We refer to Bachelier's dissertation *Théorie de la Speculation* (Paris; Gauthier-Villars, 1900); English translation in Paul Cootner ed., *The Random Character of Stock Market Prices* (Cambridge, Mass.: MIT Press, 1964). Professor Samuelson, the Nobel-prizewinning economist at MIT, has written, "Years ago when I compared the two texts, I formed the judgment (which I have not checked back on) that Bachelier's methods dominated Einstein's in every element of the vector." Paul Samuelson, "Mathematics of Speculative Price," in *Mathematical Topics in Economic Theory and Computation* (Philadelphia: SIAM, 1972), p. 6, fn. 2.

[2]See, e.g., M. F. M. Osborne, "Periodic Structure in the Browian Motion of Stock Prices," *Operations Research* 10 (1962): 345–79; Eugene Fama, "The Behavior of Stock Market Prices," *Journal of Business*, January 1965, pp. 34–105; Benoit Mandlebrot and Howard Taylor, "On the Distribution of Stock Price Differences," *Operations Research* 15 (1967): 1057—62; Peter Clark, "A Subordinated Stochastic Process Model with Finite Variance for Speculative Prices," *Econometrica* 41 (1973): 135–56; and Robert Blattberg and Nicholas Gonedes, "A Comparison of the Stable and Student Distribution as Statistical Models of Stock Prices," *Journal of Business*, April 1974, pp. 244–80.

factors which affect the distribution of stock prices.[3] Both approaches are related, because the implications from one impact the other, and both are important to the rational management of investments. However, for our purpose here, results from the second approach are more interesting, so we will merely state our position with regard to the distributional properties without extensive justification.[4]

The starting assumption is that proportional changes in a security's price are "close" to being a random walk. The reason for using proportional changes is that a 10 percent movement is independent of the security's price, so it makes no difference whether the price, for instance, is $100 or $10. In the real world there may be reasons why this is not exactly true, so we include the rider "close."

The random walk statement is a much stronger way of saying that serial correlation in security returns (i.e., the correlation between returns in successive periods) is small. If the correlation were not small, then it would be possible to earn extraordinary profits by forecasting future security price changes from observations of previous price changes. That abnormal returns cannot be earned in this manner is borne out by the majority of empirical research. If these two parts of the assumption held exactly, then it would follow (without making any additional strong assumptions) that stock prices would be lognormally distributed.[5]

This appears to be very close to the distribution actually observed. The only major deficiency in this simple model is that the level of security risk is not constant over time. When allowance is made for the changing level of risk, we can state with a fair degree of confidence that security returns (when observed over weekly or longer time intervals) follow a lognormal distribution with a fluctuating variance.[6]

This is emphasized by Figure S3.1, which, in the top diagram, shows the empirical distribution of monthly logarithm of return for the S&P 500 relative to the normal distribution. Notice that the tails are much longer than predicted by the normal distribution and that there are more observations around the center. (Statistically, the empirical distribution has greater kurtosis than the normal distribution.) The bottom diagram shows the empirical distribution after adjustment for the changing variance. As can be seen, the distribution is more nearly normal, and so the return distribution is close to being lognormal.

---

[3]See, e.g., Benjamin King, "Market and Industry Factors in Stock Price Behavior," *Journal of Business*, January 1966, pp. 139–90; and Barr Rosenberg, "Extra-market Components of Covariance among Security Prices," *Journal of Financial and Quantitative Analysis*, March 1974, pp. 263–74.

[4]Since this is still a fairly contentious area of research, some readers may not agree with our position. For more information, the references in footnote 2 should be consulted.

[5]See the supplement to Chapter 1 (in particular, Figure S1.3) for further discussion on lognormality.

[6]For shorter periods, trading effects may become dominant; see George Oldfield, Jr., Richard Rogalski, and Robert Jarrow, "An Autoregressive Jump Process for Common Stock Returns," *Journal of Financial Economics*, December 1977, pp. 389–418.

Figure S3.1
Empirical Distribution of Security Prices

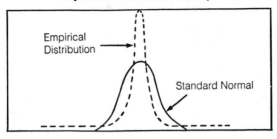

Case A.   Comparison of Standardized Monthly Price Changes to a Standard
Normal Distribution

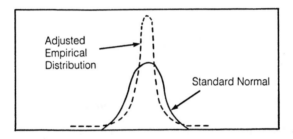

Case B.   Comparison of Standardized Monthly Price Changes Adjusted for Forecast
Variance to a Standard Normal Distribution

Source: Barr Rosenberg, "The Behavior of Random Variables with Nonstationary Variance and the Distribution of Security Prices," Research Program in Finance, Working Paper no. 11 (Berkeley: Institute of Business and Economic Research, University of California, December 1972).

Let us now consider the alternative approach, where the aim is to understand the factors which affect the return distribution. The simplest version of this model is the *single-factor model,* which states that stock returns comprise the return on a single factor plus a random return unrelated to the factor. Algebraically, this can be written:

$$r_j = b_j f + u_j, \tag{S3-1}$$

where r_j is the total excess return (over the risk-free rate) and u_j is the nonfactor return on security j, b_j measures the sensitivity (regression coefficient) of security j to the factor, and f is the rate of return on the factor. It is assumed that u_j and f are uncorrelated, as are u_j and u_k for $j \neq k$.

The mean and variance of the security excess return are then given by:

$$E[r_j] = a_j + b_j E[f], \tag{S3-2}$$

where a_j is the mean of u_j, the nonfactor return, and

$$\text{Var}[r_j] = b_j^2 \text{Var}[f] + \sigma_j^2, \tag{S3-3}$$

where σ_j^2 is the nonfactor variance in security j.

Notice that, as usual, the entire risk of the security arises from two sources: the systematic or factor risk ($b_j^2\text{Var}[f]$), and the nonfactor risk (σ_j^2). In this case, however, the nonfactor risk is completely specific risk since no risk arises from interactions with other securities. In other words, under these assumptions the single factor, f, is responsible for the only commonality among security returns; thus, the random return component that is not related to the factor must be specific to the individual security, j. Hence, industry effects and other forms of *XMC* are not present in this model.

If we form a portfolio, P, with weights $h_{P1}, h_{P2}, \ldots, h_{PN}$, from N stocks, then the random excess return on the portfolio is given by:

$$\begin{aligned} r_P &= \Sigma h_{Pj} r_j = \Sigma h_{Pj} b_j f + \Sigma h_{Pj} u_j \\ &= b_P f + \Sigma h_{Pj} u_j, \end{aligned} \tag{S3-4}$$

where $b_P = \Sigma h_{Pj} b_j$. The mean return and variance are:

$$E[r_P] = a_P + b_P E[f],$$

where $a_p = \Sigma h_{Pj} a_j$, and

$$\text{Var}[r_P] = b_P^2 \text{Var}[f] + \Sigma h_{Pj}^2 \sigma_j^2, \tag{S3-5}$$

where we have made use of the fact that the security-specific risk is *specific*, i.e., independent across securities and independent of the factor return.

The market portfolio is just one particular portfolio. Let the security weights be $h_{M1}, h_{M2}, \ldots, h_{MN}$, and notice that $b_M = \Sigma h_{Mj} b_j$. We can set b_M to any value, and so we choose to set $b_M = 1$.[7] The market return statistics are then:

$$E[r_M] = a_M + E[f]$$

and

$$\text{Var}[r_M] = \text{Var}[f] + \Sigma h_{Mj}^2 \sigma_j^2. \tag{S3-6}$$

The regression coefficient of an individual stock's rate of return onto the market, or beta, is given by:

$$\begin{aligned} \beta_j &= \text{Cov}[r_j, r_M]/\text{Var}[r_M] \\ &= \text{Cov}[b_j f + u_j, f + \Sigma h_{Mk} u_k]/\text{Var}[r_M] \\ &= (b_j \text{Var}[f] + h_{Mj}\sigma_j^2)/\text{Var}[r_M] \\ &= (b_j \text{Var}[f] + h_{Mj}\sigma_j^2)/(\text{Var}[f] + \Sigma h_{M}^2 \sigma_j^2), \end{aligned} \tag{S3-7}$$

so that:

---

[7]This step is equivalent to defining an origin for measurement.

$$\beta_P = (b_P \text{Var}[f] + \Sigma h_{Mj} h_{Pj} \sigma_j^2)/(\text{Var}[f] + \Sigma h_{Mj}^2 \sigma_j^2). \qquad \text{(S3–8)}$$

Notice that the regression coefficient on the market and the regression coefficient on the factor (i.e., b_j and β_j, and b_P and β_P) are close but not identical. The difference lies in the last terms in the numerator and denominator in both cases. Where a single security is concerned, equation (S3–7), the two sensitivities can only be equal when the market portfolio is composed of a single security; however, for a portfolio, the sensitivities will be close whenever the portfolio and market holdings are approximately equal (i.e., whenever $\Sigma h_{Mj} h_{Pj}$ is close to Σh_{Mj}^2). In other words, for well-diversified portfolios (for instance, the majority of institutional portfolios) we may approximate the portfolio beta by its regression coefficient on the factor, and vice versa, that is, $\beta_P \cong b_P$.

This approximation is useful for the analysis of residual return. Recall that the residual return of an individual portfolio (relative to the market portfolio) is equal to the total portfolio excess return less the excess return on an equal-beta-levered market portfolio. That is, the residual return measures the return due to nonmarket strategy:

$$\text{Residual return} = r_P - \beta_P r_M.$$

Thus, the residual variance is given by:

$$
\begin{aligned}
\omega_P^2 &= \text{Var}[r_P - \beta_P r_M] \\
&= \text{Var}[(b_P - \beta_P)f + \Sigma(h_{Pj} - \beta_P h_{Mj})u_j] \\
&= (b_P - \beta_P)^2 \text{Var}[f] + \Sigma(h_{Pj} - \beta_P h_{Mj})^2 \sigma_j^2, \qquad \text{(S3–9)}
\end{aligned}
$$

since the nonfactor return, u_j, is uncorrelated with the factor return. Now, using the approximation that $\beta_P \cong b_P$, it follows that:

$$\omega_P^2 \cong \Sigma(h_{Pj} - \beta_P h_{Mj})^2 \sigma_j^2 = \Sigma \delta_{Pj}^2 \sigma_j^2, \qquad \text{(S3–10)}$$

where $\delta_{Pj} = h_{Pj} - \beta_P h_{Mj}$. In other words, it is the discrepancy between portfolio and the holdings of the (equal-beta-levered) market portfolio that induces residual risk. We have called the portfolio which has these holdings the active portfolio, so we can confirm the statement in Chapter 2 that "the active portfolio contains all portfolio residual risk."

Two variants of the single-factor model are the *single-index model* and the *market model*, equation (2–1).[8] In the market model the single factor is specialized to be the excess rate of return on the market portfolio, while the single-index model identifies the single factor as the excess rate of return on a broad-based index. Essentially, the single-index model is the practical version of the market model since *the* market portfolio is unapproachable in reality.

Equation (S3–1) is restated for the market model as:

$$r_j = \alpha_j + \beta_j r_M + \varepsilon_j. \qquad \text{(S3–11)}$$

---

[8]The single-index model was originally formulated by William F. Sharpe, "A Simplified Model for Portfolio Analysis," *Management Science*, January 1963, pp. 277–93.

In this formulation it is correct to write the sensitivity to the market as β_j since, by definition, a security's beta is the exposure to the market. In addition, to be consistent with Chapter 2, we have already written the nonmarket return as the expectation plus a random term with zero mean; i.e., nonmarket return is $\alpha_j + \varepsilon_j$, where $E[\varepsilon_j] = 0$, and α_j represents the expected abnormal rate of return, or alpha. Again, to conform to the stated assumptions of the single-factor model, the random nonmarket return on security j should be uncorrelated with the market return and similar returns on all other securities. Once again, this implies that ε_j must be a specific return. But now we have the slight problem that the residual return is supposed to be uncorrelated with the market, and yet the market includes security j, so that r_M and ε_j cannot be exactly uncorrelated. A more worrying problem arises from the formula for portfolio variance, equation (S3–5), which is now restated as:

$$\text{Var}[r_P] = \beta_P^2 \text{Var}[r_M] + \Sigma h_{Pj}^2 \sigma_j^2. \tag{S3–12}$$

Again, the market can be viewed as just another portfolio, so that:

$$\text{Var}[r_M] = \text{Var}[r_M] + \Sigma h_{Mj}^2 \sigma_j^2, \tag{S3–13}$$

which states that the market portfolio shows residual variance about itself and thus cannot possibly be true. The problem is that specific variances are counted twice, once in and once out of the market portfolio. This problem is also evident in equation (S3–12), which implies that the minimum residual risk holding occurs where $h_{Pj} = 0$; i.e., there is zero holding in all securities. But this is not true, since by holding nothing, we actually have negative market portfolio positions and are "short" the entire market!

The correct zero residual risk position is given by equation (S3–10) and occurs where $\delta_{Pj} = 0$; i.e., the active portfolio contains no holdings, so that we simply hold the (levered) market portfolio. In this situation, the portfolio performance exactly matches that of the market portfolio, and so no risk is borne in addition to that of the market.

We conclude from this discussion that neither the general single-factor model nor the specific single-index and market models are a realistic description of security behavior. The single-index model has ridiculous implications for portfolios—e.g., equations (S3–12) and (S3–13)—in addition to the problems of the general single-factor model. In this category, the major deficiency is that the existence of *XMC*, or correlations between security residual returns, is denied. To remedy this situation realistically, we use a model which includes several factors. This is the *multiple factor model*, in which security excess rates of return are described by:

$$r_j = \sum_{k=1}^{K} b_{jk} f_k + u_j, \tag{S3–14}$$

where b_{jk} is the exposure, or risk index, of the jth security to the kth factor and u_j is the specific return of the jth security. Now the specific return is genuinely "specific," because the factors can account for all the correlations between assets. There are K factors, and clearly, if $K = 1$, then equation (S3–14) reduces to the single-factor model described earlier.

The mean excess return and variance for security j are given by:

$$E[r_j] = \sum_{k=1}^{K} b_{jk}E[f_k] + E[u_j]$$

and

$$\text{Var}[r_j] = \sum_{k=1}^{K} \sum_{l=1}^{K} b_{jk}b_{jl}\text{Cov}[f_k, f_l] + \sigma_j^2, \qquad (S3–15)$$

where $\text{Cov}[f_k, f_l]$ is the covariance between the factors and equals $\text{Var}[f_l]$ if $k = l$. This multiple factor model is specified by the security factor loadings, b_{jk}, and the factors, f_k.

If we now form a portfolio, P, with weights $h_{P1}, h_{P2}, \ldots, h_{PN}$, from N securities, then the random excess return is given by:

$$\begin{aligned}
r_P &= \sum_{j=1}^{N} h_{Pj}r_j = \sum_{j=1}^{N} h_{Pj} \sum_{k=1}^{K} b_{jk}f_k + \sum_{j=1}^{N} h_{Pj}u_j \\
&= \sum_{k=1}^{K} \sum_{j=1}^{N} h_{Pj}b_{jk}f_k + \sum_{j=1}^{N} h_{Pj}u_j \qquad (S3–16) \\
&= \sum_{k=1}^{K} b_{Pk}f_k + \sum_{j=1}^{N} h_{Pj}u_j,
\end{aligned}$$

where we have written $b_{Pk} = \Sigma h_{Pj}b_{jk}$ as the portfolio loading onto the kth factor. Since the market portfolio is a portfolio, the random excess return on the market is given by equation (S3–16), with M replacing P; i.e.:

$$r_M = \sum_{k=1}^{K} b_{Mk}f_k + \sum_{j=1}^{N} h_{Mj}u_j.$$

Proceeding as before, the beta of the jth asset is given by:

$$\begin{aligned}
\beta_j &= \text{Cov}[r_j, r_M]/\text{Var}[r_M] \\
&= (\sum_{k=1}^{K} \sum_{l=1}^{K} b_{jk}b_{Ml} \, \text{Cov}[f_k, f_l] + h_{Mj}\sigma_j^2)/\text{Var}[r_M].
\end{aligned}$$

It would appear that this complex expression is devoid of meaning; however, this is not the case. Consider the betas of the factors. In particular, for factor k:

$$\begin{aligned}
\beta_{f_k} &= \text{Cov}[f_k, r_M]/\text{Var}[r_M] \\
&= \sum_{l=1}^{K} b_{Ml}\text{Cov}[f_k, f_l]/\text{Var}[r_M],
\end{aligned}$$

and the beta of the specific component of return on the jth asset:

$$\beta_{u_j} = \text{Cov}[u_j, r_M]/\text{Var}[r_M]$$
$$= h_{Mj}\, \sigma_j^2/\text{Var}[r_M].$$

Combining these expressions with that for the beta of the jth asset shows:

$$\beta_j = \sum_{k=1}^{K} b_{jk}\, \beta_{f_k} + \beta_{u_j}.$$

That is, in the multiple factor model the security beta is a weighted average of the factor betas and the beta of the specific return of the security, where the weights are simply the factor loadings for the jth security. Notice that the beta of the security's specific return is nonzero only because the security return is a component of the market return since the security is a part of the market. The intuition with which we wish to leave readers is that, far from being the primitive parameter in finance, the security beta should be regarded as an average of a security's exposures to a large number of factors influencing its return.

Now the residual return, the return due to a nonmarket strategy, on portfolio P is: $r_P - \beta_P r_M$. Hence, the portfolio residual variance, ω_P^2, is given by:

$$\omega_P^2 = \text{Var}[r_P - \beta_P r_M]$$
$$= \text{Var}\left[\left\{\sum_{k=1}^{K} (b_{Pk} - \beta_P b_{Mk}) f_k\right\} + \left\{\sum_{j=1}^{N} (h_{Pj} - \beta_P h_{Mj}) u_j\right\}\right] \quad \text{(S3–17)}$$
$$= \text{Var}\left[\sum_{k=1}^{K} \gamma_{Pk} f_k\right] + \text{Var}\left[\sum_{j=1}^{N} \delta_{Pj} u_j\right],$$

where γ is the Greek letter gamma and $\gamma_{Pk} = b_{Pk} - \beta_P b_{Mk}$ is the discrepancy in the portfolio factor loading and the equal-beta-levered market portfolio factor loading; δ_{Pj} is the discrepancy in the holdings, defined below equation (S3–10), and the last step follows because the specific returns are uncorrelated with the factors. (It is this equation that was used to compute the residual risk for the Dow Jones example in Chapter 3.)

For readers familiar with matrix notation (see also the explanation in "About the Notation in This Book") we can write this last equation succinctly as:

$$\omega_P^2 = \gamma_P' F \gamma_P + \sum_{j=1}^{N} \delta_{Pj}^2 \sigma_j^2, \quad \text{(S3–18)}$$

where F is the factor $(K \times K)$ covariance matrix, γ_P is the K element column vector of discrepant factors loadings, and the prime (') denotes transposition. Equations (S3–17) and (S3–18) are the multiple factor generalizations of equation (S3–9).

The first term on the right side in equations (S3–17) and (S3–18) is the portfolio exposure to the common factors, the XMC. As can be seen, that exposure arises because the portfolio and the market are differentially exposed to the common factors; for instance, if the portfolio is composed of small-capitalization stocks, then the "gamma" for the capitalization factor will be nonzero. Only if all the gammas are zero, so that the portfolio matches the market on the risk indices, will the *XMC* be zero. Notice that *XMC* is completely defined by the risk indices and the covariance matrix, *F*.

The last term in both equations is the specific risk of the portfolio, i.e., the contribution to portfolio risk arising from the specific risk of the component assets. This term has been described above.

Three methods have been used to estimate this model. The first, and earliest approach, was factor analysis.[9] The limitations of this approach are that the factor loadings must be constant over time, the factors lack interpretation, and the number of securities cannot be more than a few hundred. For larger numbers the computational burden soon becomes insurmountable. The second approach assumes that the factors are known. If we can specify all the factors, then the security exposures can be calculated easily by time series regression. Unfortunately, the requirement of specifying the factors is a substantial problem. King identified the factors as the returns on industry indices.[10] However, this ignores other possible factors such as those, for instance, that affect small-capitalization companies versus large-capitalization companies. Further, the industry indices include the specific returns of the constituent securities, which obscures the genuine industry effect. Finally, the specification of industry groups and the assignment of companies to them is not an easy problem to solve. As has been mentioned, it is traditional to assign each company entirely to one industry group. However, only a small fraction of companies clearly belong to a single group.

The final approach is to assume knowledge about the security exposures.[11] In particular, it is assumed that a security's exposure is a linear weighting of the security descriptors, where a descriptor is a measurable characteristic of the company, for instance, a balance sheet ratio. It is this approach that we now describe in more detail.

The starting point is to assume that the probability distribution of logarithmic excess returns for each security, *n*, in each month, *t*, be given by the model:[12]

---

[9]Don Farrar, *The Investment Decision under Uncertainty* (Englewood Cliffs, N.J.: Prentice-Hall, 1962). Recently, Roll and Ross have used a similar approach in their tests of the arbitrage pricing paradigm. Richard Roll and Stephen Ross, "An Empirical Investigation of the Arbitrage Pricing Theory," *UCLA Working Paper no. 15–79, 1979*.

[10]King, "Market and Industry Factors in Stock Price Behavior."

[11]This is the approach taken by Barr Rosenberg et al. The remainder of this supplement is drawn heavily from Barr Rosenberg and Vinay Marathe, "The Prediction of Investment Risk: Systematic and Residual Risk," *Proceedings of the Seminar on the Analysis of Security Prices*, University of Chicago, November 1975, pp. 85–225. However, we have greatly simplified the description in the interest of clarity. For further detail, the original source should be consulted.

[12]The logarithmic excess returns are used (1) to avoid the complications of arithmetic versus geometric averages (see the supplement to Chapter 1) and (2) to improve estimation accuracy, because, with logarithms, the skewness and kurtosis of the residuals are greatly reduced. To keep the notational burden small we have continued to use the same notation, and the reader should be aware that "returns" are logarithmic for the remainder of the supplement.

$$r_{nt} = \alpha + \beta_{nt}r_{Mt} + \varepsilon_{nt}; \text{ for } n = 1, \ldots, N_t, \qquad \text{(S3-19)}$$

where

α = overall average excess return, approximately zero;
β_{nt} = beta coefficient for security n in month t;
ε_{nt} = residual return for security n in month t;
r_{nt} = logarithmic excess return for security n in month t;
r_{Mt} = logarithmic excess return for the S&P 500 in month t; and
N_t = number of securities in month t.

Let the model for beta be given by:

$$\beta_{nt} = b_0 + b_1 d_{1nt} + b_2 d_{2nt} + \ldots + b_J d_{Jnt} \qquad \text{(S3-20)}$$

for all time periods t and securities n, where the b's are coefficients for the systematic risk prediction rule and the d's are the J descriptor values for the nth company at time t. Further, let $E[\varepsilon_{nt}] = 0$ and $Cov[\varepsilon_{nt}, r_{Mt}] = 0$ for all t, and define ω_{nt}^2 to be the residual variance, i.e., $\omega_{nt}^2 = Var[\varepsilon_{nt}]$. The model for residual risk is given by:

$$\omega_{nt} = \overline{\omega}_t(s_0 + s_1 d_{1nt} + s_2 d_{2nt} + \ldots + s_J d_{Jnt}), \qquad \text{(S3-21)}$$

where $\overline{\omega}_t$ is the typical cross-sectional residual standard deviation in month t. This prediction rule is rewritten in terms of the mean absolute residual return, v_{nt}, for security n in month t and the typical mean absolute residual return in month t, $\overline{v}_t$. Therefore, $v_{nt} = E(|\varepsilon_{nt}|)$ and:

$$v_{nt} = \overline{v}_t(s_0 + s_1 d_{1nt} + s_2 d_{2nt} + \ldots + s_J d_{Jnt}). \qquad \text{(S3-22)}$$

The estimation approach proceeds by substituting the beta prediction rule, equation (S3-20), into equation (S3-19) and then performing a "market conditional" regression for beta. The dependent variable is r_{nt}, and the independent variables are $d_{jnt}r_{Mt}$, so the model is:

$$r_{nt} = \alpha + b_0(r_{Mt}) + b_1(d_{1nt}r_{Mt}) + \ldots + b_J(d_{Jnt}r_{Mt}),$$

which provides preliminary estimates, $\hat{b}_0, \ldots, \hat{b}_j$. With these coefficients, the preliminary prediction of residual return is:

$$\hat{\varepsilon}_{nt} = r_{nt} - (\hat{b}_0 + \hat{b}_1 d_{1nt} + \ldots + \hat{b}_J d_{Jnt}) r_{Mt}. \qquad \text{(S3-23)}$$

The next regression is fitted to estimate residual risk. It takes the form:

$$|\hat{\varepsilon}_{nt}| = s_0(\overline{v}_t) + s_1(d_{1nt}\overline{v}_t) + \ldots + s_J(d_{Jnt}\overline{v}_t),$$

where

$$\overline{v}_t = \sum_{n=1}^{N} h_{Mnt} |\hat{\varepsilon}_{nt}|,$$

and h_{Mnt} is the proportion of security n in the market portfolio at time t. This regression provides estimates, $\hat{s}_0, \ldots, \hat{s}_J$.

The final step in this part of the analysis is to obtain prediction of systematic and residual risk by repeating these two regressions, but now using generalized least squares in order to correct for the different levels of residual risk across the securities.[13]

The next task is to decompose the residual return into two components: specific return and the common factor return. This is achieved by a cross-sectional generalized least squares regression where the dependent variable is the residual return in month t, $r_{nt} - \hat{\beta}_{nt}r_{Mt}$, and the independent variables are the risk indices and industry dummy variables. The form of this regression is given in Chapter 3 as equation (3–3), the only difference being that each variable is weighted inversely to the predicted residual risk.

The results from this regression are (1) a cross-sectional pattern of returns on each factor, (2) the factor covariance matrix, and (3) a prediction of specific risk. The last two are important because they permit the evaluation of portfolio residual risk. Referring to equation (S3–18), the factor covariance matrix is represented by F, and the (asset j) specific risk prediction is σ_j^2.

Summary

Unless a portfolio manager constructively and explicitly considers risk, it is difficult to believe that the management process can be anything more than haphazard. For this reason, we have covered the subject in some detail. In this supplement we have considered two approaches to the subject: first, the descriptive theory, which tries to describe the behavior of security prices; and second, the "inquisitive" approach, which attempts to relate the risk exposure to other variables.

Our position with regard to the first approach is that security prices are lognormally distributed, but with a changing variance. It is this changing variance which gives rise to the observed "long tails." In the past, the modeling of the security return distribution was usually achieved by specifying a single-index, or single-factor, model. However, this specification assumes away all XMC and hence is too crude to be useful with present-day econometric methods. The natural extension is the multiple factor model, which is both realistic and sufficiently tractable to be used in conjunction with sophisticated estimation procedures.

We have tried to give a little rigor to some of the bland assertions made in Chapter 3. This material is inherently complicated, but the lack of a commonly accepted theory makes it all the more confusing. Inevitably, there must come a point where the portfolio manager accepts the "black box" presented by the academician or consultant. Our hope is that we have been able to push the

---

[13]This is the statistically efficient approach, and it requires that each observation be weighted inversely to its residual variance.

point of acceptance a little farther away by enhancing awareness of some of the problems, demystifying a little of the jargon, and hence increasing the time available for skepticism and questioning. We believe that patient study of this material will be rewarding because some products are so patently naive that it is too flattering to call them "black boxes."

Selected References

In addition to the references at the end of Chapter 3, the following may be helpful:

Jarrow, Robert, and Andrew Rudd. "A Comparison of the APT and CAPM." Working Paper 81–06. Cornell University, March 1981.

Rosenberg, Barr. "The Behavior of Random Variables with Nonstationary Variance and the Distribution of Security Prices." Research Program in Finance, Working Paper no. 11. Berkeley: Institute of Business and Economic Research, University of California, December 1972.

Ross, Stephen. "The Arbitrage Theory of Capital Asset Pricing." *Journal of Economic Theory,* December 1976, pp. 341–60.

Rudd, Andrew. "Portfolio Efficiency in the Context of a Multiple Factor Model." Paper presented at the Western Finance Association meetings, Hawaii, June 20–26, 1978.

Sharpe, William. F. "The Capital Asset Pricing Model: A Multi-Beta Interpretation." Research Paper no. 183. Graduate School of Business, Stanford University, September 1973.

Chapter 4

The Quest for Alpha

Alpha is the most misunderstood and elusive variable in modern portfolio theory. Part of the confusion arises from the failure to distinguish between an expectation of superior performance over a future time period and the realization of abnormal returns in the past. As discussed in the previous chapters, if one assumes a certain level of risk in order to achieve a potential reward, then the reward received should, in the long run, be commensurate with the risk exposure. If beta properly captures this exposure, then any expected return above the return on assets with similar betas represents positive alpha. In short, alpha is the expected residual rate of return.

By this stage our readers must have realized that we offer no shortcut to amassing stock market wealth. This also holds true for our approach to forecasting alpha. Alpha deduction is a fragile and creative process. It is simply not possible to offer a set of step-by-step instructions for the task of finding undervalued securities; instead, we provide some insights on "how to look" for alpha within the context of designing and organizing a consistent research process.

We start by defining alpha and trying to indicate why it is such a difficult variable to predict. We then discuss market efficiency and the controversy over the random walk, which leads naturally to a description of forming alphas from judgment. The remaining sections cover the dividend discount model, other methods of deducing alpha, and the estimation of the information content of judgments.

The supplement to this chapter describes the implication of alpha generation for portfolio construction and includes a detailed case study of three different management styles.

Definition of Alpha

When we use the word *alpha,* we mean the expected rate of return of a security or portfolio in excess of the risk-adjusted rate of return. In other words, alpha is the average rate of return in excess of that required as fair compensation for the risk incurred. Thus, with respect to a security or a portfolio, the value of alpha shows whether the investment is expected to display a rate of return greater than that of other instruments in the same risk class, and, with respect to a money manager, the value of alpha indicates whether the manager has a talent for providing superior returns. For instance, if we write that a manager has "a positive alpha," then we mean that the portfolios under that manager's control are expected to display returns in excess of the risk-adjusted return. This superior performance is achieved by the manager's talent and ability; thus, the alphas derived from this ability are *judgmental alphas* because the manager's judgment resides in these predictions. In this chapter, when we refer to *alpha,* we mean *judgmental alpha* and not the *required alpha* discussed in the previous chapters.

In the above definition we have implicitly taken the view that the simple CAPM describes the world. In other words, the only expected reward provided in the market is that related to the risk of the market portfolio. In a more complex version of the CAPM, attributes other than systematic risk are compensated. For instance, if capital gains and dividends are taxed at different rates, then there may be an expected reward associated with yield. A more general notion of alpha arises from the distinction between two types of reward: equilibrium reward, which is expected to be earned on average, and abnormal reward, which is obtained by the superiority of the manager's research process or information in comparison with that of other managers. In order to determine the equilibrium reward, a model such as the simple CAPM or one of its generalizations is required.

There are two crucial words in our alpha definition: *expected* and *risk-adjusted*. The word *expected* indicates that alpha is not a single forecast of abnormal return but an expectation or mean of the distribution of abnormal returns. The word *risk-adjusted* indicates that the correct benchmark for measuring alpha is the expected return offered by assets with the same level of systematic risk.

This discussion highlights an important distinction between two problems.

One problem is to construct or deduce the alpha. This estimated alpha represents the input to a portfolio optimization program or some other portfolio formation procedure. The other problem is to determine whether an alpha existed in the past. The first problem is usually called *security analysis*, while the second is called *performance measurement*. The first problem is an application of talent or ability, while the second is an attempt to determine whether talent or ability exists or existed.[1]

Our concern here is with the first problem. However the same difficulties exist in the solution to both problems. One of the difficulties is statistical in nature; another stems from the competitive forces within the market. The first difficulty arises because the risk in common stocks is so enormous, and the ability to forecast alpha so small, that even the most sophisticated statistical tests have a hard time proving alpha's significance.[2] The second difficulty arises because if everybody could agree that one manager or analyst had consistently demonstrated superior information, then that information would soon become devalued as more investors sought and followed his or her advice.

We will demonstrate these difficulties with a simple model. In previous chapters we described how MPT decomposes a security's return into two components as:

Security return = Systematic return + Residual return

The systematic return is perfectly correlated with the market return and is viewed as that component provided by the market as compensation for bearing market risk. This relationship can be expressed algebraically as:

$$r = \beta r_M + \varepsilon', \qquad (4\text{--}1)$$

where

r = the random excess rate of return on an individual security
   or portfolio;
β = the security's beta, an index of market sensitivity;
r_M = the random excess rate of return on the market portfolio; and
ε' = the residual error term capturing that component of return
   not accounted for by the market.

---

[1]We believe it helpful to keep these two concepts distinct. Alpha is used in this book as an expectation, i.e., as one statistic describing the distribution of the *future* returns. Consequently, alphas are used, for instance, in constructing portfolios or selecting managers. If a manager has an alpha, then the performance of the portfolios under his or her management *may* exhibit a realized return in excess of the risk-adjusted return. It is the attempt to draw implications from these returns that is the subject of performance measurement. However, the fact that a realized risk-adjusted return is greater than zero does *not* imply that the manager has or had an alpha.

[2]We will make this statement more precise in Chapter 7. Conceptually, the existence of talent shifts the mean of the distribution without appreciably changing the risk. Thus, reasonable prior beliefs of 1 percent or 2 percent about a manager's alpha are swamped by the typical standard deviation of 20 percent or more. Even ridiculously large hypothesized alpha values of 10 percent or more would take several years to become statistically significant. Of course, even if the manager's talent is not statistically significant, it is still financially significant to the portfolio owner.

In equation (4–1), βr_M measures the systematic excess return. In reality, all estimates have some uncertainty associated with them to allow for inaccuracies in the measurement process or for factors other than the systematic return. This allowance is termed the *residual return* and is denoted by ε'. While it might be tempting to assume that the average value of ε' is zero over time, this may not be the case if inefficiencies exist in the market. To allow for this, ε' is usually expressed as $\varepsilon' = \alpha + \varepsilon$, where ε is random and assumed to average zero over time, and α is a constant which can be a nonzero value. If this $\varepsilon + \alpha$ term is substituted in equation (4–1) for ε', the equation becomes:

$$r = \beta r_M + (\varepsilon + \alpha)$$

or

$$r = \alpha + \beta r_M + \varepsilon, \tag{4–2}$$

our familiar market model equation.

The specification of equation (4–2) is very suggestive of a regression model. We have seen in Chapter 3 that blind application of regression analysis (when attempting to identify beta) is unrewarding. Is the same methodology more helpful in determining alpha? No, actually it is probably even less helpful here because alphas are typically more unstable than betas. In addition, alphas are an expectation for the future, whereas regression analysis is performed on realized returns; therefore, a strong assumption must be made concerning the extrapolation of the past into the future.[3]

Nevertheless, because regression analysis is a common research tool, it is worth exploring the inferences from the results. If the regression model has been correctly specified, beta is the proper measure of risk, and the security is fairly priced, then the regression line should pass through the origin of a graph plotting return versus risk. Figure 4.1 repeats the regression diagrams for IBM and DEC that were shown in Figure 1.13, while Table 4.1 provides the statistical results for IBM and DEC that appeared in Table S1.1.[4]

The results show that the estimated intercept is close to zero in both cases. Digital Equipment has the larger intercept of 0.0035, which indicates that the stock displayed an average monthly abnormal return of 0.35 percent over the 60 months ending December 1978. This does not offer any insight into the possible source of the abnormal return. For instance, did the company report surprisingly good earnings that were not immediately reflected in the stock's price, contrary to the efficient market thesis, which assumes that such events are instantaneously discounted? Or did the abnormal return result from some favorable developments in the computer industry? Or perhaps both reasons were sources of the abnormal return. If we now examine the significance of the

---

[3]This problem, which, as mentioned in Chapter 3, also arises in beta estimation, is the common *"ex-post"* versus *"ex-ante"* distinction found in many finance textbooks.

[4]See the supplement to Chapter 1 for an explanation of regression analysis and an interpretation of the results in this table.

Figure 4.1
Characteristic Lines for IBM and DEC

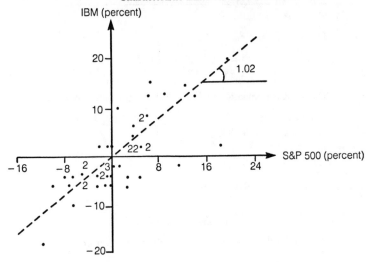

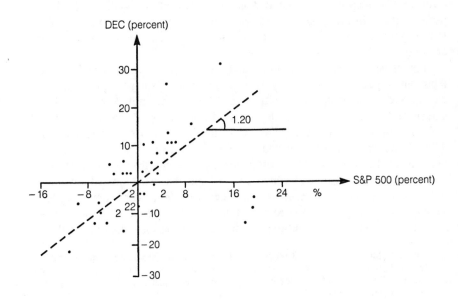

Table 4.1
Statistical Results for IBM and DEC

1. IBM versus the S&P 500

    The regression equation is:

    $$Y = -0.0003 + 1.02X$$
    $$(-0.07) \quad (11.07)$$

    The standard deviation of Y about the regression line is:

    $S = 0.0369$
    R-squared = 67.9%.

2. DEC versus the S&P 500

    The regression equation is:

    $$Y = 0.0035 + 1.20X$$
    $$(0.33) \quad (5.79)$$

    The standard deviation of Y about the regression line is:

    $S = 0.0827$
    R-squared = 36.6%.

estimated intercepts, it is seen that neither intercept is significant at the 95 percent level.[5] In fact, the reported t-statistics are much less than two in absolute magnitude, so we cannot reject the hypothesis that the abnormal returns are zero.

How large are abnormal returns, and are they ever significant? Table 4.2 represents a page from a January 1979 "beta book" listing the predictions for the 30 securities comprised by the Dow Jones Industrial Average.[6] Allied Chemical has an alpha (estimated from the intercept of the regression) of −0.66 with a standard error of 0.83; so the hypothesis of a zero alpha for Allied Chemical cannot be rejected at the 95 percent significance level. In fact, only one of the 30 stocks has an estimated alpha greater than twice its standard error in absolute magnitude. United Technologies has an estimated alpha 2.65 times its standard error; hence, we can reject at the 95 percent confidence level the hypothesis that its alpha is zero. But notice that if the tests are independent of each other, then we would expect one observation (actually, $1/20$ of the 30

---

[5]See the supplement to Chapter 1 for further information on significance tests and t-statistics.

[6]This is the *Market Sensitivity Report* published by Merrill Lynch, Pierce, Fenner & Smith, Inc. We thank Robert Kavee for making it available to us. The estimates are obtained by regressing the security returns, excluding dividends, against the S&P 500 returns, rather than the excess returns, including dividends, used for the analysis of IBM and DEC in this book. The "Adj Beta" column shows a constant Bayesian adjustment to the historical beta of the form $\beta = 0.33743 + 0.66257H\beta$. For more information on the Merrill Lynch procedure, see the Merrill Lynch booklet entitled *Security Risk-Evaluation Service*, March 1972.

Table 4.2
"Beta Book" Entries for the Dow Jones Industrials

MLPF&S MARKET SENSITIVITY REPORT
EDITION I VARIATION I OF DOW JONES 30 INDUSTRIALS
REPORT IS SORTED BY NAME
PORTFOLIO SUMMARY WEIGHTS ADJ BETAS BY MARKET VALUE

TKR SYMB	SHRS HELD	7812 PRICE	MKT VAL (=000$)	PCT. HELD	ADJ BETA	ALPHA	RSQ	RESID ST DV	STD ERR BETA	STD ERR ALPHA	NR. OBS	
ACD	6943	28.25	196.1	2.4	1.13	-0.66	0.47	6.40	0.16	0.83	60	ALLIED CHEMICAL CORP
AA	6943	47.75	331.5	4.1	0.79	0.23	0.17	7.42	0.19	0.96	60	ALUMINUM CO OF AMERI
AT	6943	50.38	349.8	4.3	0.83	0.81	0.49	3.86	0.10	0.50	60	AMERICAN BRANDS
AC	6943	35.88	249.1	3.1	0.68	0.59	0.26	4.30	0.11	0.56	60	AMERICAN CAN CO
T	6943	60.50	420.1	5.2	0.71	0.33	0.52	2.73	0.07	0.35	60	AMERICAN TEL & TELEG C
BS	6943	19.63	136.3	1.7	1.06	-0.57	0.35	7.40	0.19	0.96	60	BETHLEHEM STEEL CORP
C	6943	8.63	59.9	10.7	1.03	-0.42	0.17	11.43	0.29	1.48	60	CHRYSLER CORP
DD	6943	126.00	874.8	0.9	0.98	-0.18	0.37	6.36	0.16	0.82	60	DU PONT DE NEMOURS
EK	6943	58.63	407.0	5.1	1.16	-0.93	0.58	5.38	0.14	0.69	60	EASTMAN KODAK
SwX	6943	24.00	166.6	2.1	0.82	-0.52	0.22	6.70	0.17	0.88	60	ESMARK INC
J	6943	49.13	341.1	4.2	0.89	-0.14	0.55	3.81	0.10	0.49	60	EXXON CORP
GE	6943	47.13	327.2	4.1	1.26	-0.32	0.79	3.64	0.09	0.47	60	GENERAL ELECTRIC CO
GF	6943	32.13	223.0	2.8	1.05	-0.69	0.46	5.81	0.15	0.75	60	GENERAL FOODS CORP
GM	6943	53.75	373.2	4.6	0.84	0.38	0.34	5.26	0.13	0.68	60	GENERAL MOTORS CORP
GT	6943	16.13	112.0	1.4	0.91	0.21	0.43	4.97	0.13	0.64	60	GOODYEAR TIRE & RUBB
N	6943	15.75	109.4	1.4	0.89	-1.07	0.24	7.39	0.19	0.95	60	INCO LTD
HR	6943	36.25	251.7	3.1	1.01	0.84	0.34	7.15	0.18	0.92	60	INTL HARVESTER CO
IP	6943	36.50	253.4	3.1	1.08	-0.39	0.50	5.66	0.14	0.73	60	INTERNATIONAL PAPER
JM	6943	22.63	157.1	2.0	0.87	-0.78	0.24	7.20	0.15	0.93	60	JOHNS MANVILLE CORP
MMM	6943	63.13	438.3	5.4	1.19	-0.13	0.58	5.60	0.14	0.72	60	MINNESOTA MINING & M
OI	6943	17.88	124.1	1.5	0.93	0.37	0.46	4.88	0.12	0.63	60	OWENS-ILLINOIS INC
PG	6943	85.88	617.1	7.7	0.93	0.01	0.62	3.59	0.09	0.46	60	PROCTER & GAMBLE CO
S	6943	19.75	137.1	1.7	1.00	-0.98	0.42	5.88	0.15	0.76	60	SEARS ROEBUCK & CO
SD	6943	46.88	325.5	4.0	0.93	-0.62	0.44	5.10	0.13	0.66	60	STANDARD OIL CO CALI
TX	6943	23.88	165.8	2.1	0.88	-0.25	0.46	4.47	0.11	0.58	60	TEXACO INC
UK	6943	34.00	236.1	2.9	0.98	-0.11	0.51	4.82	0.12	0.62	60	UNION CARBIDE CORP
X	6943	21.25	147.5	1.9	0.99	-0.05	0.35	6.77	0.17	0.87	60	US STEEL CORP
UA	6943	38.88	269.9	3.4	0.84	-2.18	0.26	6.33	0.16	0.82	60	UNITED TECHNOLOGIES
WX	6943	16.63	115.4	1.4	1.11	-0.32	0.33	8.27	0.21	1.07	60	WESTINGHOUSE ELEC
Z	6943	19.38	134.5	1.7	1.13	-0.36	0.43	7.00	0.18	0.90	60	WOOLWORTH F W CO
PORTFOLIO TOTAL			8050.4	ALL	0.96	0.12						

DIVERSIFICATION 43.9

Source: *Market Sensitivity Report*, Merrill Lynch, Pierce, Fenner & Smith, Inc., January 1979.

observations) to be significant at the 95 percent level simply by chance alone. In summary, the lack of statistical significance is a persuasive reason why attempting to deduce alpha, to correlate it with hopefully predictive variables, or, better, to claim and prove that a money manager has an alpha, is such a challenging exercise.

This state of affairs is perhaps the greatest force for change in the world of institutional investing. Unless a money manager can demonstrate an ability to deliver portfolio performance better than that of the market portfolio (proxy), the manager's clients are bound to be skepticial about paying fees for performance when similar results can be purchased from a passive index fund manager for perhaps a 60 percent discount.[7]

How does one attempt to deduce the alpha for a security and then capture it in a portfolio? The methods include attempting to select special situation stocks which may offer excess returns, timing the level of riskiness in the portfolio, optimizing portfolios in order to obtain the most favorable risk/reward trade-off, shifting emphasis among industry groups, or combining any or all of these. But before we can discuss these strategies, we much discover whether it is possible to capture an alpha at all!

Market Efficiency

A security is fairly priced when its expected return is commensurate with the risk incurred. An *efficient market* is one in which all information impacting a security's expected return is reflected in its price. Thus, in such a market a typical investor should expect to earn a fair return (but not a superior or inferior return). The only way to earn a return different from the fair return is to know more about the security than the consensus investor and to use that knowledge advantageously.[8]

Numerous studies have tested market efficiency.[9] These studies can be divided into three groups, depending upon the degree of efficiency tested: the weakly efficient markets hypothesis suggests that historical price and volume

---

[7]The fee structure for the industry is in a state of flux. In general, both taxable and tax-exempt funds incur fees which increase with the total dollar value. As a rough guide, large tax-exempt discretionary funds are charged an annual fee of 0.25 percent of the total dollar value if actively managed and 0.10 percent if passively managed.

[8]One can always obtain an inferior return by paying excessive "transactions" costs such as brokerage commissions or research overhead.

[9]A detailed discussion of market efficiency would take us too far afield. Interested readers should consult either a finance text, such as William F. Sharpe, *Investments* (Englewood Cliffs, N.J.: Prentice-Hall, 1978), particularly chap. 6, or the original articles, for instance, Sidney Alexander, "Price Movements in Speculative Markets: Trends or Random Walks," *Industrial Management Review*, May 1961, pp. 7–26; Fischer Black, "Implications of the Random Walk Hypothesis for Portfolio Management," *Financial Analysts Journal*, March–April 1971, pp. 16–22; Eugene Fama, "Efficient Capital Markets: A Review of Theory and Empirical Work," *Journal of Finance*, May 1970, pp. 383–417; and Jeffrey Jaffe, "Special Information and Insider Trading," *Journal of Business*, July 1974, pp. 410–28.

data contain no information which can be used to earn abnormal profits; the semistrong hypothesis states that markets are so efficient that all public information is immediately reflected in security prices, so that only a few insiders can earn abnormal profits; and the strong form of the efficient markets hypothesis claims that no one can consistently earn abnormal profits since all known information is immediately discounted by the capital markets.

The results of the studies suggest that the first of these three hypotheses should be accepted: there is little or no information to be gained by studying historical technical information. The studies on the semistrong hypothesis typically suggest that prices not only react quickly and rationally to public news, but tend to anticipate it. The last hypothesis, the strong form, is not as well supported. Indeed, some studies on specialists and insiders indicate that the hypothesis can be refuted.

It is important to realize that while this research has not confirmed the efficiency of the market, it has failed to demonstrate that there are consistent violations of market efficiency. For this reason, rather than stress the statistics and discuss in detail the various tests, we feel it more important to develop the intuition that the inefficiency of the market is inherently improbable.

In the United States there are millions of investors and thousands of analysts (over 14,500 analysts are listed in the 1979 Financial Analysts Federation directory alone), all of whom are engaged in a competitive "game." Thus, we can phrase the problem of market efficiency as a personal question (which we will return to later): What makes you think that you can consistently beat millions of other investors? Our feeling is that only a few investors have a competitive edge (either because of their sheer talent or, more likely, because they are exploiting an unconventional strategy) and that once these investors have acted, few "pickings" are left for the remaining investors. This implies that the market is exceedingly efficient in both the weak and the semistrong sense.

The belief that the market is reasonably efficient suggests one of the most important departures of MPT from the traditional investment process. In the past, money managers who did not research a stock, and so had no opinion on its valuation, would not have purchased it. Notice that this "no information position" is effectively translated into a "sell-short the market proportion" decision. By not holding the stock, the manager is taking an active and aggressive position, because anytime that the stock outperforms the market, the managed portfolio will exhibit relatively poor performance (and vice versa). Rationally, a no-information position should imply that the managed portfolio is immune to the performance of the stock. This only occurs when the portfolio proportion and the market proportion are the same.[10]

---

[10]One can feel cynically amused about legal indentures designed to "protect" the investor which prevent the investor from holding the market proportion. For instance, a common constraint is that no more than 5 percent of the portfolio may be in any one asset. Since both IBM and AT&T exceed 5 percent of the capitalization of most bogeys (e.g., the S&P 500), this ruling effectively ensures that these "protected" portfolios will underperform the bogey in the long run.

The MPT approach states that although the manager knows nothing about the stock, other analysts are looking at it, and their research must be such that the stock is, on the average, fairly priced. Thus, the correct approach is to purchase the market proportion or, equivalently, the average holding of all investors who have researched the stock.

The truth of this statement lies in the fact that investment is an unusual competitive game. To be successful at other (professional) competitive sports, such as football, golf and chess, requires a level of talent that mere mortals do not possess. For instance, it is simply not sufficient for an "average" person to watch baseball games for two weeks (or two years) in order to become an "average" major league pitcher or to hit an "average" number of home runs. In other words, an average performance in these sports requires above-average skills. In this sense, the standard of these competitive games has to be measured on an absolute scale, since it is possible for the winning team to be very much better or only a little better than the losing team. Thus, a judgment about one participant carries little information about another.

This is not true with the investment game. Everybody (including the authors and readers of this book) can be an average money manager simply by buying the market proportion (i.e., the average holdings in everything that everybody else purchases). In this way, it is possible to earn the return of the average money manager.[11] The peculiarity in investment is that the average of everybody's strategy is disclosed to all players. By implication, then, all securities are fairly valued until proven misvalued.

Alphas from Judgments[12]

This discussion indicates that in deducing an alpha, the information sources or information processing has to be superior to the average. Exactly how these sources are used depends upon the organization's view of the level of market efficiency. If the organization believes that the market is inefficient, then it would also believe that there is considerable opportunity to earn abnormal profits, and therefore that justifying the investment process in terms of controlling risk or transaction costs is largely irrelevant. Conversely, an organization that believes the market to be almost completely efficient would try to develop a few (but penetrating) insights and to organize an investment process that utilized this information to the best advantage. Such an organization would not tolerate wasted resources in terms of inefficient data handling, increased exposure to residual risk, or unnecessary transaction costs.

We can view the task of security research as one of information processing.

---

[11]Actually, above the return of the average money manager when transaction costs and the costs of research are included: this is the rationale for an index fund.

[12]Helpful discussions on this subject with Hal Arbit of American National Bank are gratefully acknowledged.

Countless sources of information and an endless series of events have implications for investment. The problem is to "massage" this information and to extract only that which is useful in forming relative judgment on the assets which are being followed. Typically, the approach has been to categorize the information along fairly well-defined groups, such as industries and economic sectors. This approach is so traditional as to be almost sacrosanct. However, one can argue that because the approach is so traditional, its likely benefit is small in every case except a reasonably inefficient market.[13] The more efficient the market, the greater are the rewards to unconventional and nontraditional methods.

To summarize thus far: A well designed research effort must express its view on the efficiency of the market because this view will determine the type of personnel, the sources of information, and the processes that will be employed in the attempt to "beat the average manager." In addition, it will dictate the form of the optimal portfolio, for instance, the number and magnitude of the active decisions (i.e., asset holdings different from the asset holdings of the market portfolio). For example, a portfolio manager who believes that the market is totally efficient would disregard all forecasts from the research department on the ground that they will contain no information and will represent complete "noise." Thus, forecasts are of no use unless they include information, as well as an expectation, different from that of the consensus. We will see in the supplement to this chapter that different types of approach to deducing alpha lead to optimal portfolios with utterly different emphases.

The Dividend Discount Model and the Ex-Ante Capital Market Line[14]

The most organized method of generating alpha estimates is from a dividend discount model.[15] This method attempts to estimate a stream of future dividends, which are then used to value the asset. The design of the dividend discount models currently being applied may vary slightly, but in general the assumptions are similar. The basic model assumes that the fair price of a se-

---

[13]As we have indicated above, the classification is also ambiguous and arbitrary; for instance, although the primary industry of companies may be the same, the secondary and tertiary industries of these companies may be quite different. For instance, in which (or how many) industries is General Electric involved?

[14]Some people believe that organizations which use a dividend discount model have embraced MPT, while those that use other valuation models are still in the "dark ages." Neither view is correct. We include a discussion of the dividend discount model simply because it represents a rational method of security valuation. Of course, it should be clear from the discussion that its use is beneficial only if either its specification or its inputs are more realistic than those of other users.

[15]The valuation of common stock by calculating the present value of the dividend stream is usually attributed to John Burr Williams, *The Theory of Investment Value* (Cambridge, Mass.: Harvard University Press, 1938).

curity is the properly discounted value of the future stream of dividends. If psychological or other extraneous market factors have driven a security price below its fair or equilibrium value, the equilibrating forces of the marketplace will, in time, bring the security back in line with its fair value. The security is therefore presumed to possess a positive forecast of return in expectation of its movement back toward its equilibrium value. Naturally, a security estimated to be priced above its fair value would be expected to possess a negative forecast of return until its price has been equilibrated in the marketplace.

The essential assumption of the dividend discount model (i.e., the present value of a security is equal to the discounted value of the expected future dividends) can be written symbolically as:

$$P = \sum_{t=1}^{\infty} \frac{D_t}{(1 + E_t)^{t}}, \tag{4-3}$$

where

P = the present value of the security;
D_t = the dividend expected to be received during period t;
E_t = the expected rate of return, or discount rate to be used in period t; and
t = the index of time.

If it were possible to estimate the (perpetual) stream of dividends and determine the correct discount rates, then equation (4–3) could be used to compute the present value of a security. The resulting investment strategy would then be based upon a comparison of this computed present value with the observed price in the market. This approach presents only two problems: first, the problem of estimating the dividend stream; and second, the problem of determining the discount rates. Let us discuss these problems in turn.

The realistic modeling of the dividend stream depends upon understanding the dividend policy of the corporation and adjusting for the increasing uncertainty that is encountered as one tries to forecast further into the future. The most common modeling method is to divide the future into two or more time intervals and to make different simplifying assumptions concerning the dividend policy of the company in each interval. For instance, the first interval may include the first five years, in which case the analyst may be required to estimate dividends for each year in the interval. There is usually a second interval, which may include years 5 to 20 and for which movement to a long-term equilibrium value is predicted. The last interval may be years 21 to infinity, and the assumption may be that within this interval dividends will grow at a constant rate, which is all that the analyst is required to estimate.

The modeling of the discount rate is no easier since the discount rate depends on the time period and the risk of the corporation. Conceptually, the discount rate is the risk-free spot rate to the time of the dividend, adjusted for the risk of the corporation at the time of the dividend. Two obvious and common assumptions are to ignore the shape of the term structure (i.e., to assume that there is only one short rate, so that the term structure is flat) and to assume a constant risk level for the corporation over time.

The discount rate is now easier to determine because, according to the simple CAPM, only systematic risk is compensated for in aggregate, so that the discount rate should equal the risk-free rate plus a premium that is proportional to the security's systematic risk coefficient, or beta. As an example, securities with a zero beta (so that they are exposed to no systematic risk) are discounted at the risk-free rate, while securities that are exposed to systematic risk are discounted at a higher rate because their dividend stream is less certain. The general formulation for the discount rate for all time periods is, therefore, the familiar equation of the CAPM:

$$E = i_F + \beta(E_M - i_F), \qquad (4\text{--}4)$$

where

i_F = the risk-free rate of interest;
β = the security's beta; and
E_M = the expected rate of return on the market portfolio.

Forecasts of the expected rate of return on the market, E_M, the riskless rate, i_F, and each security's systematic risk are required in order to obtain the discount rate. We may expect, given the previous assumptions, that the forecasts for the last two will be correct on average across the set of securities under analysis. This is not the case for the forecast of the market return, which, if in error, will introduce a systematic basis in the pricing of each stock.

An alternative (and more common) approach is to make the unknown in the divided discount model equation—equation (4–3)—not the present value, P, but the discount rate, E_t. Thus, the dividend stream having been estimated, the current market price is substituted on the left of the equation and the (inferred) discount rate is solved by an iterative computation. Thus, the solution to equation (4–3) is the discount rate that causes the present value of the dividend stream to equal the current price.

At this stage, the CAPM is invoked by, for instance, regressing the discount rates against the predicted beta for each security. The result of this step is an indication of the incremental reward that will be received for an additional unit of systematic risk. The typical method of explaining this procedure is to consider the regression line as an inferred security market line, so that the investment strategy is now based upon whether a particular security plots above, on, or below the line. If the security plots on the line, the natural implication is that its expected return is exactly consistent with its systematic risk, so that the security is fairly priced. If the security plots above (below) the line, then the implication is that it is underpriced (overpriced) relative to its risk level, or that the dividend estimates are too high (low), or that there are other factors—for instance, tax effects—which have not been adequately captured by the model. If the last two explanations can be disregarded, then the degree of mispricing is related to the distance that the security plots from the line. In fact, since that distance represents the difference between the expected rate of return on the security and the expected rate of return on securities with similar betas, the distance is an estimate of the forecast abnormal return.[16] Figure 4.2 shows these latter steps diagrammatically.

When the dividend discount model is used in this last form, the slope of the inferred security market line is computed in the regression and will change through time. This knowledge has a strategic implication (given that the market uses similar risk estimates) because the slope of the line indicates the aggregate risk aversion in the market and so may contain information as to the future market direction.[17] For instance, a flat market line suggests that investors are willing to take risk for little or no expected return, while, conversely, a steep

Figure 4.2
Estimating Forecasts of Abnormal Return from the Dividend Discount Model

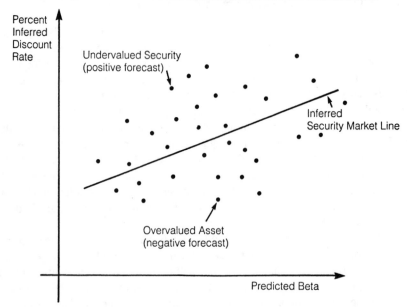

---

[16]These forecasts should not be used directly as alphas but should first be adjusted for information, as described later in this chapter.

[17]This was first suggested by Bill Fouse of the Wells Fargo Bank. See William Fouse, "Risk and Liquidity: The Keys to Stock Price Behavior," *Financial Analysts Journal*, May–June 1976, pp. 35–45.

market line indicates that investors require considerable compensation for assuming risk.

Another strategic use can be made of the dividend discount model by segmenting the securities into different groups prior to the final regression and thus determining the risk/reward relationship within each group. Bill Fouse of the Wells Fargo Bank has suggested using liquidity ratios as the "grouping" variable so as to produce a market line for each liquidity sector (the so-called liquidity fan). Of course, liquidity is not the only interesting variable that can be used in this manner; for instance, current yield or leverage can also be used.

Table 4.3 and Figure 4.3 give one example of such an analysis. These exhibits show the calculation of an ex-ante market plane from the Value Line forecasts for 1,490 companies as of August 1, 1980. The regression takes the forecast return on each asset as the dependent variable and the asset's beta and six risk indices (see the section "Fundamental Risk Prediction" in Chapter 3) as the explanatory variables.

The market plane indicates that an asset with zero exposure to systematic risk and the common factors would be expected to have a return of 10.274 percent. There is an additional return of 6.769 percent at a beta of 1.0; the six risk indices have associated expected returns which can be interpreted similarly. Notice that in the month (August) the prediction is that there will be an incremental return of 1.572 percent for assets which are negatively exposed to growth, i.e., for high-yielding companies. Hence, August promises to be a good month for yield-biased funds (see the supplement to Chapter 5), at least according to these Value Line judgments. This is shown diagrammatically in Figure 4.3.

This completes our general discussion of the dividend discount model as a method of deducing forcasts. We will return to the subject at the end of the chapter, where the practical aspects of implementing the model will be described in detail. Let us now briefly consider alternative approaches to finding alpha.

Table 4.3
Ex-Ante Market Plane, Based on Value Line Data
(8/1/80)

	T-Values
Expected return = 10.274	
+ 6.769 (Beta)	8.328
− 1.873 (Market variability)	−7.494
+ 1.430 (Earnings variability)	11.340
− 0.453 (Low valuation, unsuccess)	−3.303
− 0.176 (Immaturity and smallness)	−1.700
− 1.572 (Growth orientation)	−9.356
− 0.274 (Financial risk)	−2.634
$R^2 = 0.136$.	

Source: Conditional Forecasting Service. We are grateful to Ronald Lanstein and Daniel Beck for performing this analysis.

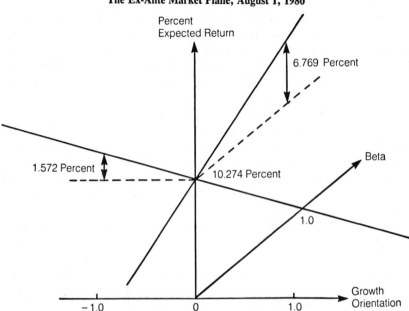

Figure 4.3
The Ex-Ante Market Plane, August 1, 1980

Note: The plane has eight dimensions, one for the expected return and one for each of the seven possible components of return. To simplify the diagram, only three dimensions are shown: those for expected return, beta, and growth orientation.
Source: Conditional Forecasting Service.

Alternative Approaches to Alpha Deduction

Several other means of predicting alpha are commercially available. These will be discussed briefly. All of these techniques have as a common denominator the attempt to capture market inefficiencies, which can also be termed "unique insights." These insights represent predictions by the analyst that are not yet known in the marketplace but that will be realized over time.

Let us start by describing some traditional approaches. One widely known study was conducted by Professors Latane and Jones.[18] They demonstrated that significant deviations of reported earnings from expected earnings produced marked "aftereffects" for at least three months beyond the announcement date. (The expected earnings figure used was the expected 21st-quarter earnings based upon a seasonally adjusted linear projection of the earnings for the pre-

---

[18]Henry A. Latane and Charles P. Jones, "Standardized Unexpected Earnings: A Progress Report," *Journal of Finance*, December 1977, pp. 1457–65. A series of related studies are referenced at the end of this article.

vious 20 quarters.) The greater the deviation when measured in terms of the standard error of the estimating equation, the larger the price aftereffect, both upward and downward. A commercial application based upon this study has been developed. The methodology consists of fitting a regression line through 20 consecutive quarters of 12-month trailing earnings per share in order to project the expected figure for the earnings about to be reported. When an announcement occurs, the latest earnings per share figure is compared with the expected figure and the difference forms the basis for an abnormal return estimate.

Another study, which is also based upon earnings and which attempts to identify market inefficiencies, has recently been published.[19] It indicates that consensus forecasts of earnings per share growth carry little information concerning future price performance. Detecting when consensus earnings forecasts are in error is much more important. Hence, it appears more beneficial to anticipate errors in the consensus than to forecast earnings alone. Again, the study indicates that the effects are not momentary and argues that if at the end of 1975 an analyst was able to correctly identify the degree of error in the consensus earnings forecasts for the year 1976, then a definite discrimination process resulted for that year.

While a one-year sample is too small to document a promising approach, other researchers have independently arrived at the same conclusions. William S. Gray, senior vice president of the Harris Bank, has demonstrated, for the eight years from 1971 through 1978, that a sample of roughly 180 institutional common stocks could be organized into quintiles according to the degree of error between the consensus forecast and the actual earnings results for each year, with the "most positive surprise" quintile always outperforming the "most negative surprise" quintile. This occurred in both rising and falling markets. The obvious research required in order to capitalize in this phenomenon is to determine which analyst's forecasts are the most accurate, so that consensus errors can be anticipated.

Recall from Chapter 2 that residual risk can be meaningfully decomposed into XMC (the risk arising from exposure to the common factors) and specific risk (the risk that is solely related to the security in question). A similar decomposition can be made for the forecast returns; that is, the expected residual return can be expressed as the expected return from the common factors, plus the expected specific return. In fact, this was the idea behind the market plane discussed in Table 4.3 and Figure 4.3. This decomposition is useful because it enables us to suggest and understand strategies for deducing alpha.

One interesting example of deducing an alpha by analyzing a "common element" in corporate financial policy was first described by American Na-

---

[19]Leonard Zacks, "EPS Forecasts—Accuracy Is Not Enough," *Financial Analysts Journal,* March–April 1979, pp. 53–55.

tional Bank.[20] As part of its research effort, the bank noticed that the number of companies repurchasing their own stock (by entering the open market or by a tender offer) varies considerably from year to year. For instance, in 1973 and 1974 there was (relative to the 1960s) a sharp increase in the number of companies that repurchased their own stock; the number declined in 1975 and 1976, however, only to increase again one or two years later. It soon became clear that there were good reasons why companies would find it desirable to repurchase their stock; moreover, these reasons also suggested that the companies which did so might provide superior performance. A careful statistical analysis showed that there were indeed opportunities to be gained by pursuing a strategy based upon isolating particular characteristics of those companies that repurchased their own securities. Thus, the bank obtained a superior performance by exploiting the unconventional strategy of using this common element.

This example indicates the relevance for alpha deduction of understanding unusual behavior which is common to a group of companies. In order to obtain more general results, however, additional structure has to be placed on the description of these "common elements." The natural specification is given in Chapter 3 for the common factors because the factors which explain a significant component of risk will also be those which can be easily identified with components of return. Briefly, the six factors associated with indices of risk are defined in terms of the fundamentals of each firm as follows:

1. *Market variability*. This index is designed to capture an individual security's price volatility. The question to be asked is whether the marketplace, at a given moment in time, is giving an above-average or a below-average reward for price variability.
2. *Earnings variability*. This measure quantifies the uncertainty of earnings.
3. *Low valuation and unsuccess*. This index attempts to capture the characteristics of unsuccessful companies and to determine whether or not a company can be classified as a successful generator of earnings and dividend growth.
4. *Immaturity and smallness*. This index measures the relative size of an organization. For instance, if the marketplace is rewarding small, low-capitalization companies, returns to this factor should be positive.
5. *Growth orientation*. This index distinguishes companies that emphasize dividend payment from those that retain earnings and emphasize growth in company size.

---

[20]This example is taken from a case study presented at the Active/Passive Seminar, May 1978, organized by American National Bank. Stock repurchases have been the subject of several academic studies; for instance, see Theo Vermaelen, "An Analysis of Common Stock Repurchases," Ph.D. dissertation, University of Chicago, 1978. Several articles on stock repurchases have also appeared in the popular press; for instance, see Margaret Yao, "Many Firms Buy Back Their Own Stock, Sometimes at Prices below Book Value," *The Wall Street Journal*, May 3, 1979, p. 46.

6. *Financial risk.* This index measures the appraisal of common equity due to stability (or lack thereof) in the company's capital structure.

In Chapter 3, we described the procedure to estimate the risk associated with the factors, together with their monthly rate of return (see for instance, Figure 3.2, which showed the return on the low valuation and unsuccess factor for January 1978). If the simple CAPM holds, then over the long term the rates of return on each factor should, on the average, be zero (although more complex equilibrium models may predict rewards for one or more of the factors). In addition, if the market is efficient with respect to the factor returns (i.e., if analysts consider the common factors as part of their forecasts so that we cannot describe this area of the capital markets as unresearched or unexploited), then these returns should vibrate randomly about zero. We can check these hypotheses by looking at the cumulative return of the factors over a long period. Of course, we would not expect the realized returns to be identically zero, but we should not be able to "eyeball" clear trends, which would suggest that future factor returns could be forecast from historical returns.[21]

Figures 4.4 through 4.9 show the rates of return on the six factors from January 1974 through December 1981. In each figure, the X indicates the estimated return of the factor in that month (read from the scale at the right). Drawn through this value is a vertical line that represents the one-standard-error band around the estimate. The cumulative rates of return, which are computed by adding the logarithms of the monthly returns for each month, are indicated by the continuous line. The scale for the cumulative return is shown at the left of the graph. (Notice that the scales are different for the six figures.) In general, the monthly rates of return do appear to be fairly random. However, the plots of the cumulative return frequently show that this appearance is wrong, because occasionally they appear to exhibit serial dependence, or a trend.

The cumulative rate of return on the market variability factor shown in Figure 4.4 indicates a rather steady upward drift from mid-1976 through February 1980. Such a drift is exactly what an investor should attempt to determine. It indicates that the marketplace is offering a larger than expected reward for this attribute of a common stock's properties. For this period of time, the more variability in a stock's price behavior, the better. The interpretation of this risk index is akin to the zero-beta portfolio return originally suggested by Fischer Black.[22] In other words, does the predicted capital market line align with the

---

[21]A more analytical discussion of this point can be found in the article by Barr Rosenberg and Andrew Rudd, "Factor-Related and Specific Returns of Common Stock: Serial Correlation and Market Inefficiency," *Journal of Finance,* May 1982.

[22]Fischer Black, "Capital Market Equilibrium with Restricted Borrowing," *Journal of Business,* July 1972, pp. 444–45.

experienced returns of the assets, or do, for instance, high-beta assets perform better or worse than expected? In this latter case, the ex-post capital market line may be steeper or flatter than would be predicted ex-ante, indicating a return to the market variability factor. (See Figure 3.4 and its discussion for an example of this phenomenon.)

Figure 4.4
Rate of Return on the Market Variability Factor

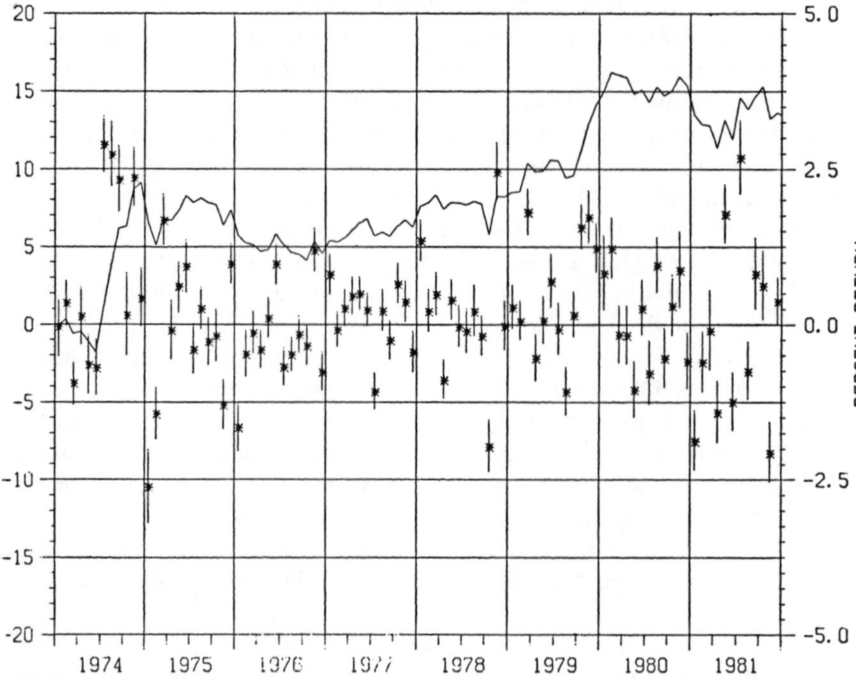

The graph, in Figure 4.5, which shows the rate of return on the earnings variability factor, is a more typical configuration and one more suggestive of an efficient market. Apart from a momentary positive jump in the cumulative rate of return in late 1974, the rate of return is trendless, with low amplitude and seemingly random fluctuations. There is a hint of annual seasonality, with low points reached early in each year's fourth quarter, but this should be considered an illusion—or an accident—in the data until it is more conclusively proven with a better history. A possible explanation is that annual earnings results are not usually known until late in the first quarter, so positive earnings surprises could be anticipated in this period. Tax-loss selling might also account for the low in the fourth quarter. Obviously, these shreds of evidence warrant further investigation.

The rate of return on the low valuation and unsuccess factor is depicted in Figure 4.6. The only exceptional movements seemed to occur during the steep drop of the 1974 bear market, while the sharp rise in late 1974 corresponded with the stock market rally, which celebrated the reversal of tight monetary

Figure 4.5
Rate of Return on the Earnings Variability Factor

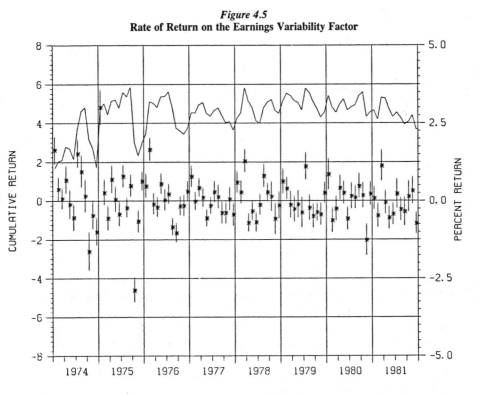

policy and was seen as a precursor to a new upswing in the business cycle. These were periods of extreme and unusual volatility, and while such volatility is easily observable after the fact, it may be considerably more difficult to forecast. Overall there appears to be a downward trend from the beginning of 1975. However, the trend is partially obscured by the "noise" in the monthly returns. Further, the variance of the monthly returns seems to have increased after 1977 as suggested by the larger spread in returns on the diagram.

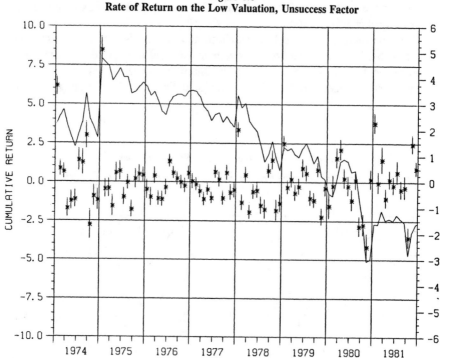

Figure 4.6
Rate of Return on the Low Valuation, Unsuccess Factor

Figure 4.7, the rate of return on the immaturity and smallness factor, presents a different picture. After more than two years of random fluctuation, an upward drift of significance began in late 1976. At the same time, observers of the marketplace could also see a great disparity between the behavior of more heavily capitalized, mature industry securities and that of more dynamic, newer technology issues. This comparison could best be made between a sluggish Dow Jones Industrial Average and the small-stock-dominated Value Line and American Stock Exchange indexes.

The rate of return on the growth orientation factor in Figure 4.8 depicts what many managers suffered from mid-1974 through early 1977—the factor showed a cumulative loss of almost 35 percent! During this period, significant shifts in portfolio structure were taking place. The impact of ERISA was beginning to be felt, and as a result, a large number of portfolio managers were attempting to avoid lawsuits more than they were trying to win the performance derby. "Total return" and "avoidance of risk" became more and more dominant, and many closed-door discussions were held regarding appropriate court testimony to defend investment decisions. Owning a low-dividend-paying stock

with an eye for price appreciation somehow sounded very close to "speculation," and that was obviously the ultimate taboo. To make matters worse,
many "growth" stocks began to produce earnings results that had previously
been associated with "mature growth" companies.

The sixth common factor, financial risk, displayed the rate of return shown

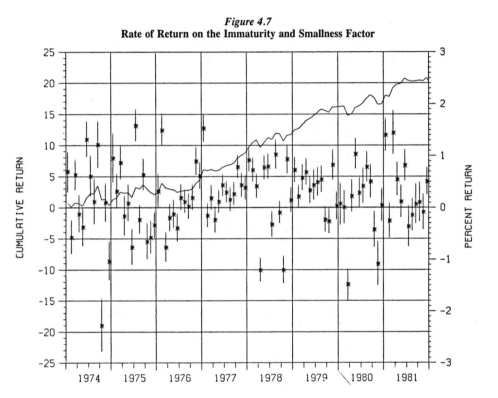

Figure 4.7
Rate of Return on the Immaturity and Smallness Factor

in Figure 4.9. This factor experienced an upward drift from late 1975 through
mid-1979, a period when smaller capitalization, speculative securities were in
an upward trend, while S&P 500 securities lost value. The period was also
characterized by a formal and informal growth in index funds, and, as is characteristic of a competitive market, by a growth in the number of speculators
who decided to play against the index funds. The speculators' reasoning was
that an unusual number of funds would attempt to purchase portfolio positions
in the thinly traded companies of the S&P 500 and that this could offer an
opportunity for price appreciation. In addition, an uptrend market was under

way in noninstitutional equities, where the assumptions of an efficient market-place may be at their weakest. Many private individuals participated in and created this divergence.

Unfortunately, lack of space precludes us from showing the factor return plots for the 39 industry groups in addition to the six factor plots shown above.

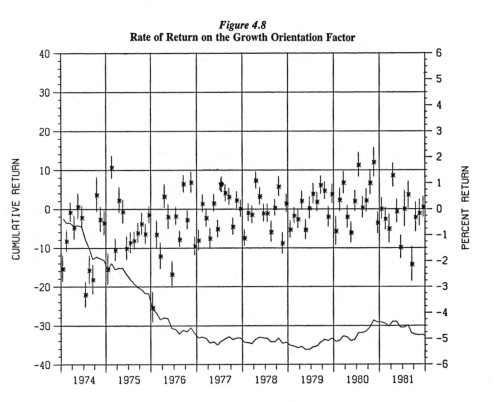

Figure 4.8
Rate of Return on the Growth Orientation Factor

Some of these plots, for instance, those for the international oils and aerospace, are as dramatic as many investors would imagine them to be! However, our emphasis here is on the interpretation of the factor returns—particularly in the context of the simple CAPM—and for this purpose the factor return plots for the 39 industry groups are no different from the six factor return plots already shown.

These graphs of the cumulative rates of return on the factors seem to suggest that there are opportunities to be gained from monitoring the factors. An informal analysis of the plots indicates that they are far from random; perhaps the most obvious plot is that of the growth orientation factor, which lost almost 35 percent in the three years between January 1974 and January 1977 (conversely, high-yield portfolios gained almost 35 percent during this period). The bottom line is that there are clearly benefits to developing expertise at managing money that is highly exposed to one (or more) of the factors.[23] At the same time, it is crucial to continually monitor the portfolio exposure to the factors (i.e., risk indices) and to be ready to take less exposure (slide in toward the center, or

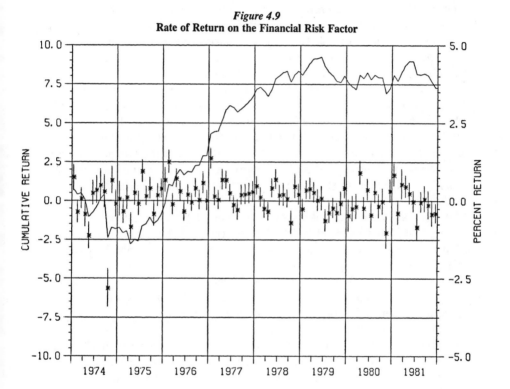

Figure 4.9
Rate of Return on the Financial Risk Factor

even across to the other side, of the teeter-totter) should judgment warrant this. As we shall argue in Chapter 6, the knowledge of the risk indices for a portfolio with multiple managers is most important, because unless the individual managers are carefully controlled, they tend to concentrate on the same factors, which becomes the dominant source of risk in the aggregate portfolio.[24]

---

[23]A portfolio which is managed in this style is one of the examples in the supplement to this chapter.

[24]See also the case study at the end of Chapter 2. Table 2.1 shows that for the particular aggregate portfolio analyzed, *XMC* was the dominant component of residual risk.

Information Content

It would be unreasonable to assume that all forecasts of future performance contain the same level of information. Some analysts may be better (i.e., more accurate) than others. Some analysts may be continually optimistic about the future, while others may be continually pessimistic. Such differences lead to several problems when one is trying to construct consistent alphas from several analysts. Our concern here is not with the method of making a forecast but with what to do with it once it has been made. Thus, we take as given the process which generates forecasts of future performance for a list of securities over a certain time interval. Our task is to take these forecasts and to derive from them the judgmental alphas which provide the best prediction of the residual return that the securities will actually exhibit.

The first problem concerns the form that the forecasts should take. For instance, some money managers require their analysts to simply specify "buy," "hold," or "sell." If these labels pertain to the total return of the stock, then the recommendations will be difficult to interpret since they aggregate the systematic and residual components. In other words, if the analyst is provided the macroeconomic forecast that the market excess return will be positive, then as a first cut all high-beta stocks should be "buys" at the expense of low-beta stocks.

A marginally more defensible rationalization of the three categories would occur if they do indeed reflect residual returns with the assumption that all "buys" ("sells") have the same positive (negative)—but unspecified—alpha and that all "holds" have zero alphas. It seems unreasonable, however, to believe that an analyst can separate stocks into the three categories without being able to differentiate shades of "buys" or "sells." Hence, the three-category recommendation misses the point entirely or wastes a good deal of the analyst's information.

Some organizations increase the "comfort level" of analysts by having five (or more) categories or codings, for instance, A through E, or "strong buy" through "strong sell." With only a small number of categories, the organization is open to the previous criticism. The number of categories could be extended to include all shades of recommendation, limited only by the ability to find descriptive adjectives. However, this ignores the central problem that someone, explicitly or implicitly, will have to interpret the meaning of the category titles and that, as likely as not, different people will interpret them differently.

To us, there is little value in using codings. The forecasts from the analyst are most useful as numerical estimates of the expected residual return. Camouflaging these estimates is a disservice to the analyst and a source of error.

We have three variables to keep track of; these are symbolically defined as:

u = the actual realized residual return on a security;

$\hat{u}$ = the "raw" forecast of the residual return, u, of a security, and

α = the best prediction obtained from the raw forecast, $\hat{u}$, for the actual realized residual return, u.

Clearly, because analysts do vary in their level of optimism/pessimism, the raw forecast may not be the best forecast of residual return. The research process will occasionally work well, and at other times less well. The important property of the process is the average amount of information it contains. Thus, it is convenient to think of the research effort as a probabilistic function which provides forecasts at set points in time. We can think of the forecasts as realizations and or outcomes of a probability distribution which describes the research process.

In order to develop some intuition for the interaction of the various variables, let us describe the derivation of alpha within a Bayesian framework similar to that described in Chapter 3 for the prediction of beta.[25] On the average, the actual residual return is zero (if it were not zero, the residual risk would receive compensation on the average). Hence, the prior prediction for the residual return is zero, which should be used in forming the "best" prediction. The analyst then provides a forecast, $\hat{u}$, for the residual return, which provides an additional item of information and should be combined with the prior prediction. (In Chapter 3 we called this second piece of information the measured value.) Straightforward application of our potato sack analogy gives the following formula for the combined (posterior) forecast:

$$
\begin{aligned}
\text{Posterior estimate} &= \alpha \\
&= (1 - BA)(\text{prior estimate}) \\
&\quad + (BA)(\text{measured value}) \\
&= (1 - BA)(0) + (BA)(\hat{u}) \\
&= BA{\cdot}\hat{u},
\end{aligned}
$$

where BA is the Bayesian adjustment which represents the degree of confidence placed on the measured value relative to the prior estimate. Previously the Bayesian adjustment was a fraction between zero and one, but here it is realistic to let the adjustment be greater than one in order to accommodate analysts who are consistently too pessimistic.

Simply, the analyst's forecast should be shrunk toward, or expanded away from, zero by an amount that captures the information content of the analyst.[26]

---

[25]The prediction of beta has another connection with this subject because we are trying to estimate the expected residual return; without having a good prediction of systematic return, or beta, the whole question of analyzing residual return becomes problematic.

[26]The alphas have to satisfy a further condition, namely, that the market portfolio should have an alpha of zero because the market bears no residual risk. One way to ensure this is to force the capitalization weighted average forecast of all stocks on the followed list to be zero.

In order to derive a simple model that may be used in practice, we need to make one further assumption, namely, that a constant proportion of the residual risk is explained by the forecast. This implies that the analyst's confidence in the forecast is constant through time, so that it is not "easier" to forecast returns at one point in time than at any other point in time. With this assumption we can write the relationship as a simple linear regression, as follows:

$$u = a + b\hat{u} + e,$$

where a and b are coefficients to be estimated by the regression and e is the error term in the regression. Thus, we would use the forecast as the independent variable and the subsequent performance as the dependent variable. This situation is shown diagrammatically in Figure 4.10. The realized residual returns, u, are plotted on the vertical axis, and the forecasts of residual returns, $\hat{u}$, are plotted on the horizontal axis. In the upper diagram, the scatter of points is grouped around the regression line, showing that there is a relationship between what was forecast and what actually occurred. The lower diagram describes the unhappy situation where there is no relationship between the forecast and the realization.

From the theory of least squares regression, we know that the expected value of e is zero (exactly, the sum of the regression residuals is zero), so that:

$$E[u] = \alpha = \hat{a} + \hat{b}\,E[\hat{u}]$$

where $\hat{a}$ and $\hat{b}$ are the estimates of a and b in the regression model. In addition, if the forecasts are correctly adjusted so as to make the market have zero residual return (see footnote 25), then it can be shown that $\hat{a}$ is zero. In other words, to make the forecast of expected residual return unbiased, we need to make the following transformations:

1. Take raw forecast, $\hat{u}$, and scale by multiplying by $\hat{b}$,
2. Add constant $\hat{a}$ to produce an unbiased forecast if the forecasts have not been adjusted.

This procedure corrects the forecast for information content and results in a prediction that represents the "pure information" in the forecast. For instance, if there is no information, then the scatter will be random and $\hat{b}$ will be zero; i.e., absolutely no weight is placed on the forecast to determine the final prediction. Conversely, if the forecast contains complete information and is exactly scaled, then the plot of forecasts and realized residual returns will fall along a straight line with unit slope; i.e., $\hat{b} = 1$, and the forecast will form the judgmental alpha.

The ability of the analyst is measured by the amount of explanatory power in the forecasts. Recall from Supplement 1 that the statistic that measures the explanatory powers is the R^2. Thus, if we say that the R^2 from a regression is 30 percent, then 30 percent of the variability in the realized returns is accounted

Figure 4.10
Using Forecasts to Predict Alpha

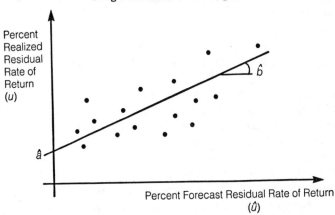

Case A. Forecasts with Information Content

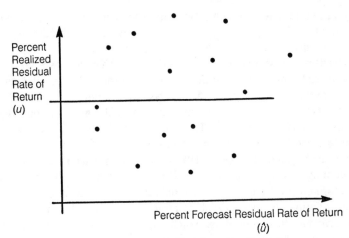

Case B. Forecasts with No Information Content

for by the forecasts. Another, and almost equivalent, index of the analyst's ability is the correlation coefficient (sometimes referred to as the *information coefficient*) between the forecasts and the realized returns. Again, we can appeal to the theory of least squares regression because this correlation coefficient is the square root of the R^2 when the R^2 is reported as a proportion.

It is the judgmental alpha (adjusted forecast) that should be used in the portfolio formation phase and optimization programs. It should now be clear why judgmental alphas (indeed, all alphas) are so small: they have been purged of noise and represent the full knowledge of the analyst concerning the expected residual return.

Case Study 3: The COMVAL System

In this section we describe a practical application of the dividend discount model, with specific reference to the version in use at the Harris Bank. The Harris model will be demonstrated in a complete fashion so that some insights can be gained as to how such a research effort is organized and coordinated, from the initial analyst estimates to the final output of alpha estimates.

The name of the Harris dividend discount model is COMVAL, standing quite naturally for common stock valuation. The essence of the model is to produce a suitably discounted stream of estimated dividends over a 20-year period. In theory, the stream of dividends should be discounted to infinity, since a basic assumption of such a model is that the common stock is assumed to exist in perpetuity. Reality is not quite that convenient, and in the Harris case the 20-year period is assumed to capture the significant portion of the dividend stream. In addition, a 20-year time horizon is consistent with other investment decisions, for instance, the horizon for long-term bonds.

The Harris model segments the time period into three parts over the 20 years; these are years 1 through 3, 4 through 10, and 11 through 20. Specific numerical estimates are generated by a security analyst for earnings per share, dividend payout, equity per share, estimated dividend payment, and return on stockholders' equity for years 1 through 3. The return on equity is computed as earnings per share divided by the equity per share at the end of the previous year. The next time stage (years 4 through 10) is covered by analyst estimates of the secular earnings growth rate, which will be in existence in the 10th year, the secular return on equity, the secular payout ratio, plus an allowance for external factor contributions to these variables produced by such developments as favorable financing. The conditions which apply in the 10th year are described mathematically as follows:.

$$SG = SROE \, (1 - SPO) + EXG, \qquad (4-5)$$

where

SG = the secular growth rate in earnings per share;
$SROE$ = the secular return on equity;
SPO = the secular payout ratio; and
EXG = the contribution to earnings growth from external sources.

This set of conditions is viewed as a target. It is arrived at by trending the conditions estimated to exist at year 3 to the conditions forecast for year 10. In other words, the dividend payout ratio and the return on equity are incremented in equal annual amounts from year 3 to year 10. This process permits the computation of dividends, earnings, and earnings per share estimates for each of years 4 through 10. The following equations are applied for years 4 through 10:

$$E_t = SEQ_{t-1}[(E_3/SEQ_2) + (t-3) \cdot (SROE - E_3/SEQ_2)/7]$$
$$D_t = E_t[(D_3/E_3) + (t-3) \cdot (SPO - D_3/E_3)/7]$$
$$SEQ_t = (SEQ_{t-1})(1 + EXG) + E_t - D_t, \qquad (4\text{--}6)$$

where

$$
\begin{aligned}
E_t &= \text{the earnings per share;} \\
SEQ_t &= \text{the equity per share;} \\
D_t &= \text{the dividends per share;} \\
EXG &= \text{the external growth contribution;} \\
t &= \text{the time index for years 4 through 10;} \\
SROE &= \text{the target return on equity year 10; and} \\
SPO &= \text{the payout ratio at year 10.}
\end{aligned}
$$

If, however, analysts, upon inspection, determine that the trend approach does not adequately reflect reality, specific estimates for these years can be made. This allowance for analyst adjustment is especially important for cyclical, more mature companies in mature industries. The data submission form used by the analysts for each company studied is shown in Figure 4.11.

For years 11 through 20, earnings, dividends, and return data are generated purely by mathematics, with no analysts' estimates. Contributions from external factors are considered nonexistent for this final segment of the 20-year horizon.

In order to treat the final 10 years for the companies analyzed, each company is viewed as trending toward the market's rate of return on equity and its dividend payout, which are assumed to be the same in the 20th year as in the 10th year. The trending of the company's equity return and payout is accomplished in equal increments for years 11 through 20. The starting point for the stock's final 10-year period is the secular return on equity and the secular payout ratio designated by the analyst for year 10. These levels are then trended from the levels at year 10 to the overall market level estimated to exist at year 20. This trending toward the overall market level for the same variables generates the specific earnings, dividends, and returns on equity for each of the final 10 years of the 20-year projection.

The equations used to generate these estimates can be described as follows. Where the stock's secular return on equity is greater than the market's secular return, or the $SROE > SPSROE;$

$$E_t = SEQ_{t-1}[SROE + (t-10) \cdot (SPSROE - SROE)/10]$$
$$D_t = E_t[SPO + (t-10) \cdot (SPSPO - SPO)/10]$$
$$SEQ_t = SEQ_{t-1} + E_t - D_t \qquad (4\text{--}7)$$

Figure 4.11
Data Submission Form

Company Name: _____

Year (Base 1976)	Dividends per Share	Earnings per Share	Shareholders' Equity per Share (1)	Return on Equity	Payout Ratio
1 1977					
2 1978					
3 1979					
4 (2)					
5					
6					
7					
8					
9					
10					

Secular growth rate . . . .   _____

Secular return on equity (assumed to apply
  in year 10) . . . .   _____

Secular payout ratio (assumed to apply
  in year 10) . . . .   _____

External growth (change in shareholders'
  equity per share from a source other than
  retained earnings per share; state as an
  annualized rate) . . . .   _____

Notes:

(1) Return on equity calculated as earnings per share divided by shareholders' equity per share at the end of the previous year.

(2) Specific estimates for years 4 through 10 necessary only if you feel a trendline change in return on equity and payout ratio from year 3 to year 10 does not portray the appropriate pattern of earnings and dividends over this period.

where

$SPSROE$ = the S&P 500 secular return on equity; and
$SPSPO$ = the S&P 500 secular payout.

In the case where the 10th-year secular return on equity for a stock is less than, or equal to, the market's return, the secular return and dividend payout levels are held constant for years 11 through 20. The equations for this case are as follows:

$$E_t = SEQ_{t-1} \cdot SROE$$
$$D_t = E_t \cdot SPO$$
$$SEQ_t = SEQ_{t-1} + E_t - D_t. \qquad (4\text{--}8)$$

Two examples of computer printout of the analyses just presented are contained in Tables 4.4 and 4.5. In Table 4.4 the security is the common stock of Lincoln National Corporation, where the secular return on equity in the 10th year is estimated to be less than that of the market return. As can be seen, the return on equity (R.O.E.) is trended after year 3 to the estimated secular rate at year 10 of 11.0 percent, where it remains for years 11 through 20. The dividend payout rate (PAYOUT) is trended similarly.

Table 4.5 presents the common stock of International Business Machines, a security whose equity return and payout are greater than the market level. The obvious difference between this case and Lincoln National's is that IBM's return on equity and payout are steadily trended downward for the entire 20-year period to the (lower) S&P 500 level.

Several criticisms can be leveled at the assumptions of the dividend-estimating model described so far. Perhaps the most obvious criticism would be that it assumes the trending of an above-average growth company to the market average in 20 years, along with every other such security. While this criticism is valid, an alternative approach would demand a superior means of determining a more appropriate horizon or of maturing the equity return and payout. The criticism suggests the desirability of developing a more involved model; while the development of such a model is a logical avenue for future research, the model presented here is a fair representation of the current state of the art.

The assumption that a uniform trend applies to both cyclical and stable growth companies can also be criticized. In defense against this criticism, the first 10 years of analyst estimates can be made to conform to a more cyclical or trendlike pattern. For years 11 to 20, it would be unrealistic to expect anyone to reasonably estimate a cyclical influence. For a 20-year estimate, it would be unrealistic to expect the analyst to make estimates of anything other than the average level for any of the key variables. In other words, the greatest challenge is to derive reasonable analyst estimates as inputs. When predicting

Table 4.4
Estimated Dividend Stream for Lincoln National Corporation

MARCH 20, 1978 14:09:53

210060020 LNL LINCOLN NATL CORP IND

YEARS 4-10 SOURCE = TRENDED

YEAR	DIVIDEND	EARNINGS	EQUITY	R.O.E.	PAYOUT
1977	1·8000	5·6700	44·800	13·85	31·75
1978	2·1000	6·4000	49·100	14·29	32·81
1979	2·4000	6·8000	53·500	13·85	35·29
1980	2·4530	7·1916	58·239	13·44	34·11
1981	2·4995	7·5915	63·331	13·04	32·92
1982	2·5384	7·9975	68·790	12·63	31·74
1983	2·5687	8·4069	74·628	12·22	30·55
1984	2·5894	8·8166	80·855	11·81	29·37
1985	2·5995	9·2231	87·479	11·41	28·18
1986	2·5981	9·6226	94·503	11·00	27·00
1987	2·8067	10·3953	102·092	11·00	27·00
1988	3·0321	11·2301	110·290	11·00	27·00
1989	3·2756	12·1318	119·146	11·00	27·00
1990	3·5386	13·1060	128·713	11·00	27·00
1991	3·8228	14·1584	139·049	11·00	27·00
1992	4·1297	15·2953	150·215	11·00	27·00
1993	4·4614	16·5236	162·277	11·00	27·00
1994	4·8196	17·8504	175·308	11·00	27·00
1995	5·2066	19·2838	189·385	11·00	27·00
1996	5·6247	20·8323	204·592	11·00	27·00

SECULAR GROWTH RATE   8·03000
SECULAR RETURN ON EQUITY   11·00000
SECULAR PAYOUT RATIO   27·0000
EXTERNAL GROWTH   0·0000

5 YR BETA	780228 PRICE	DISCOUNT RATE	PRESENT VALUE	IMPLIED DISCOUNT
1·3815	33·875	14·584	26·135	12·750

20 years into the future, perhaps the least controversial means of handling inferior performers is to stipulate that they will remain at their subnormal level for the last 10 years of the time period.

The next step in estimating the present value of the securities being analyzed is to determine the discount rate for the overall market, as represented by the S&P 500. The methodology is to generate a 20-year stream of dividends for the S&P 500 in the same fashion as has just been described for individual securities. The first three years of the projection are estimated for earnings, dividends per share, and stockholders' equity. The secular return on equity and

Table 4.5
Estimated Dividend Stream for IBM

MARCH 20, 1978 14:09:53

105080020 IBM INTERNATIONAL BUS MACH

YEARS 4-10 SOURCE = TRENDED

YEAR	DIVIDEND	EARNINGS	EQUITY	R.O.E.	PAYOUT
1977	10·0000	18·3000	85·510	23·70	54·64
1978	11·6000	20·2500	94·160	23·68	57·28
1979	12·6000	22·9400	104·500	24·36	54·93
1980	13·8746	25·2557	116·613	24·17	54·94
1981	15·3610	27·9560	130·024	23·97	54·95
1982	16·9918	30·9180	144·860	23·78	54·96
1983	18·7793	34·1639	161·259	23·58	54·97
1984	20·7366	37·7174	179·369	23·39	54·98
1985	22·8777	41·6039	199·350	23·19	54·99
1986	25·2178	45·8505	221·379	23·00	55·00
1987	26·2725	48·9246	244·031	22·10	53·70
1988	27·1088	51·7344	268·656	21·20	52·40
1989	27·8685	54·5372	295·325	20·30	51·10
1990	28·5319	57·2930	324·086	19·40	49·80
1991	29·0785	59·9558	354·963	18·50	48·50
1992	29·4874	62·4735	387·949	17·60	47·20
1993	29·7374	64·7874	422·999	16·70	45·90
1994	29·8078	66·8338	460·025	15·80	44·60
1995	29·6794	68·5437	498·890	14·90	43·30
1996	29·3346	69·8444	539·399	14·00	42·00

SECULAR GROWTH RATE	10·35000
SECULAR RETURN ON EQUITY	23·00000
SECULAR PAYOUT RATIO	55·0000
EXTERNAL GROWTH	0·7000

5 YR BETA	780228 PRICE	DISCOUNT RATE	PRESENT VALUE	IMPLIED DISCOUNT
0·8675	251·250	11·576	203·044	10·373

dividend payout are then estimated for the 10th year, with the 4th to 10th years of earnings and dividends estimated by applying a similar straight line trending technique to individual stocks. The equations for the trending process are analogous to equation (4–6).

For years 11 through 20, the values are derived by trending the return on equity and the dividend payout in the 10th year to the target values estimated to exist at the 20-year horizon. The equations for accomplishing this final trending are analogous to equation (4–7). Using these data, a computation is made of the discount rate for the market that will equilibrate the 20-year stream of dividends just estimated with the current level of the S&P 500. The equation for accomplishing this is as follows:[27]

$$P = \sum_{t=1}^{20} D_t/(1+MDR)^t + E_{20}/MDR(1+MDR)^{20}, \qquad (4\text{-}9)$$

where

P = the existing S&P 500 level;
MDR = the S&P 500 discount rate; and
E_{20} = the estimated earnings per share at year 20.

The market discount rate is now used as an input to determine the appropriate discount rate for each stock. Each stock's volatility is compared with that of the market through the use of a long-term beta estimate. The equation applied is as follows:

$$SDR = \beta_{STK}(MDR - i_F) + i_F, \qquad (4\text{-}10)$$

where

SDR = the stock discount rate;
i_F = the risk-free rate, defined in this case as the 90-day Treasury bill rate; and
β_{STK} = the individual stock beta.

The stock discount rate can now be combined with the 20-year dividend stream and the earnings per share in year 20 to compute the present value. The computation has been designed to allow for any difference between an individual stock's secular return on equity in year 10 and the secular return on equity of the S&P 500. The differences in discount rates under these conditions are adjusted during years 11 and 20 in order to arrive at a uniform discount rate in year 20.

The equation to compute the present value of an individual security is as follows:

---

[27]The last term represents an attempt to capture the effects of years 21 through infinity and assumes constant annual earnings of amount E_{20} in this period. The present value (in year 20) of this earnings stream is:

$$E_{20}/(1+MDR) + E_{20}/(1+MDR)^2 + \ldots = \sum_t E_{20}/(1 + MDR)^t$$

$$= E_{20}/MDR,$$

which is then discounted back to year 0. The use of earnings, as opposed to dividends, in this period is a compromise made in the attempt to obtain more reliable estimates.

$$PV = [\sum_{t=1}^{10} D_t/(1 + SDR)^t]$$

$$+ \{(1 + SDR)^{-10}(\sum_{t=11}^{20} D_t/ \prod_{j=11}^{t} [1 + SDR - (j - 10)\cdot DIFF])\} \quad (4\text{-}11)$$

$$+ \{[E_{20}/STM\cdot(1 + SDR)^{10}] \prod_{j=11}^{20} [1 + SDR - (j - 10)\cdot DIFF]\},$$

where

PV = the stock present value,

$DIFF$ = 0 for $SROE < SPSROE$, or

$\dfrac{(SDR - MDR)}{10}$ for $SROE \geq SPSROE$;

STM = the stock terminal multiplier, given by

STM = SDR for $SROE < SPSROE$, or

MDR for $SROE \geq SPSROE$; and

Π = the product sign.

The present values for each of the 181 securities on the Harris Bank working list on February 28, 1978, are shown in Table 4.6.

An alternative approach, which was introduced earlier in the chapter, only utilizes the dividends estimated from the preceding equations, the current stock price, and the estimated year 20 earnings per share. These variables are used to derive an implied discount rate according to the following equation:

$$P = \sum_{t=1}^{20} D_t/(1 + IDR)^t + E_{20}/IDR(1 + IDR)^{20} \quad (4\text{-}12)$$

where

P = the present price;

E_{20} = the estimated terminal (year 20) earnings per share;

D_t = the dividends per share;

IDR = the implied discount rate; and

t = the time index for years 1 through 20.

The value of IDR in equation (4-12) is considered the unknown and can be solved for only by means of a "trial and error" search routine, which, in this case, has an error tolerance of plus or minus $0.01. Generating individual implied discount rates enables the construction of a security market line, as discussed in Chapter 1. The security market line can be generated in two ways. One method is to fit a linear regression line through the implied discount rate and beta values for each stock. The other method is to construct the theoretical market line by connecting two points, the risk-free rate at a beta value of zero and the implied discount rate for the market portfolio proxy at a beta value of

Table 4.6
Harris Bank Working List
(2/28/78)

COMPANY		5 YEAR BETA	DISCOUNT RATE	IMPLIED DISCOUNT RATE	2/28/78 PRICE	PRESENT VALUE	PERCENT DEVIATION	RANK OF DEV. FROM PRICE
SN	STANDARD OIL CO IND	0.745	10.86	14.87	44.250	73.988	67.2	1
CNF	CONSOLIDATED FREIGHTWY	1.342	14.36	17.03	22.250	37.047	66.5	2
MOB	MOBIL CORP	0.883	11.67	15.07	58.625	92.621	58.0	3
FM	SECURITY PAC CORP	0.929	11.94	15.06	28.375	44.544	57.0	4
J	EXXON CORP	0.729	10.77	14.56	44.000	68.213	55.0	5
MRO	MARATHON OIL CO	0.965	12.15	15.13	41.500	63.385	52.7	6
RJR	REYNOLDS R J INDS INC	0.608	10.06	13.87	54.125	82.518	52.5	7
ENG	ENGELHARD MINERALS & CHE	1.155	13.26	15.64	23.500	35.756	52.2	8
TX	TEXACO INC	0.824	11.32	14.31	25.500	38.168	49.7	9
AFI	ATLANTIC RICHFIELD CO	0.839	11.41	14.37	44.125	65.623	48.7	10
DE	DEERE & CO	1.240	13.76	15.97	23.125	33.846	46.4	11
MO	PHILIP MORRIS INC	0.764	10.97	13.96	56.625	82.873	46.4	12
SD	STANDARD OIL CO CALIF	0.860	11.54	14.20	37.750	54.870	45.4	13
WFG	WELLS FARGO & CO	1.029	12.52	14.72	24.500	34.897	42.4	14
ITT	INTERNATIONAL TEL & TELE	1.177	13.39	15.50	27.000	37.673	39.5	15
IP	INTERNATIONAL PAPER CO	1.203	14.13	15.97	36.125	50.383	39.0	16
SDC	SEDCO INC	1.261	13.88	14.90	33.125	46.067	38.0	17
BOA	BANKAMERICA CORP	0.939	12.00	14.15	20.750	28.608	37.9	18
TXT	TEXTRON INC	1.019	12.47	14.73	23.005	31.430	36.7	19
PGLN	PEOPLES GAS CO	0.793	11.14	13.99	32.875	43.925	33.6	20
GEN	GENERAL TEL & ELECTRO	0.679	10.48	12.65	28.500	37.904	33.0	21
CIA	COMBINED INS CO AMER	1.496	15.26	16.33	15.125	19.934	31.8	22
FNC	CITICORP	1.099	12.93	14.53	19.875	26.078	31.2	23
SCE	SOUTHERN CALIF EDISON	0.851	11.48	13.64	25.875	33.734	30.4	24
ZB	CROWN ZELLERBACH CORP	1.163	13.31	14.96	29.375	38.176	30.0	25
CK	COLLINS & AIKMAN CORP	1.081	12.83	14.53	10.625	13.768	29.6	26
MIS	MISSOURI PAC CORP	1.301	14.12	15.20	41.000	52.782	28.7	27
PCG	PACIFIC GAS & ELEC CO	0.776	11.04	13.16	41.000	52.708	28.0	28
GM	GENERAL MTRS CORP	1.001	12.36	14.63	58.375	74.643	27.9	29
JPM	MORGAN J P & CO INC	1.013	12.43	13.98	39.750	50.217	26.3	30
SA	SAFEWAY STORES INC	0.988	12.28	14.03	35.500	44.745	26.0	31
INA	INA CORP	1.457	15.03	16.88	34.250	43.026	25.6	32
T	AMERICAN TEL & TELEG CO	0.631	10.20	11.84	60.000	74.496	24.2	33

34	23·9	33·621	27·125	12·87	11·14	0·792	WISCONSIN ELEC PWR CO
35	23·7	33·699	27·250	12·63	10·79	0·733	COMMONWEALTH EDISON CO
36	23·4	51·227	41·505	14·37	13·55	1·204	COOPER INDS INC
37	23·1	23·846	19·375	13·43	11·56	0·864	GENERAL PUB UTILS CP
38	21·5	28·940	23·625	14·28	12·62	1·045	FLORIDA PWR & LT CO
39	20·9	31·933	26·125	14·85	11·25	1·119	NORTHN STS PWR MINN
40	20·7	55·937	46·125	14·38	13·05	1·118	SOUTHERN RY CO
41	20·5	49·507	46·250	14·07	12·65	1·050	XEROX CORP
42	19·5	26·249	41·750	13·73	12·72	1·062	NORTHWEST BANCORPORAT
43	19·3	50·318	21·125	14·00	12·38	1·044	FORD MTR CO DEL
44	18·0	58·752	49·250	13·51	12·75	0·944	CATERPILLAR TRACTOR CO
45	18·0	19·030	42·125	13·50	11·92	0·896	MIDDLE SOUTH UTILS INC
46	17·5	19·324	16·375	13·24	11·75	0·926	PUBLIC SERVICE CO COLO
47	17·2	31·291	26·625	12·94	11·92	0·839	CONTINENTAL OIL CO
48	17·0	17·869	15·250	12·76	11·41	1·034	CENTRAL & SO WEST CORP
49	16·5	39·473	33·750	13·54	12·55	1·157	FIRST BK SYS INC
50	15·4	26·015	26·500	13·93	13·27	1·300	DOW CHEM CO
51	15·0	15·380	32·500	13·45	14·29	1·029	CLARK EQUIPMENT CO
52	14·8	112·388	97·750	13·26	12·52	0·960	DU PONT E I DE NEMOURS
53	14·6	22·394	16·875	13·64	12·34	1·029	TAMPA ELEC CO
54	14·3	33·558	29·375	13·93	13·10	1·168	HOUSTON INDS INC
55	13·4	44·712	38·875	14·00	12·52	1·027	UNION CAMP CORP
56	12·9	19·763	17·375	12·75	13·34	1·041	CINCINNATI MILACRON
57	11·9	21·893	22·500	14·89	13·10	0·927	ANHEUSER BUSCH INC
58	11·0	25·178	46·875	14·96	12·75	1·537	DONNELLEY R R & SONS
59	11·0	511·031	32·875	14·70	11·93	1·502	CONNECTICUT GEN INS CP
60	10·6	36·219	13·875	12·59	15·50	1·270	WARNER COMMUNICATIONS
61	9·6	15·260	20·500	14·70	15·29	0·918	FIRESTONE TIRE & RUBBER
62	9·1	24·056	22·875	12·59	13·93	0·884	TEXAS UTILS CO
63	8·5	14·964	13·625	16·54	11·88	1·599	BEATRICE FOODS CO
64	8·4	14·781	15·875	14·16	15·86	1·322	FEDERAL NATL MTG ASSN
65	8·2	17·205	54·000	14·16	14·24	1·321	GARDNER DENVER CO
66	8·2	58·451	31·125	13·89	14·23	1·259	INGERSOLL RAND CO
67	8·0	26·858	24·875	11·04	13·87	1·259	TRW INC
68	7·9	163·738	151·750	12·04	13·07	0·780	ILLINOIS POWER CO
69	7·5	16·924	15·750	12·85	11·65	0·800	GETTY OIL CO
70	5·5	41·666	39·375	12·66	12·22	0·977	TUCSON GAS & ELEC CO
71	5·5	63·055	59·750	13·43	12·37	0·994	REVLON INC
72	4·9	118·363	117·500	13·15	13·57	1·209	OWENS CORNING FIBERGL
73	4·9	24·119	23·000	12·08	13·10	1·127	NORTON SIMON INC
74					11·42	0·840	STANDARD BRANDS INC

WPC
CWE
CBE
GPU
FPL
NSP
SR
XRX
NOB
F
CTR
MSU
PSR
CLL
CSR
FML
DOW
CKL
DD
TE
HOU
UCC
CHZ
AHU
DNY
CGL
KNS
FIR
TXU
BRY
FNM
GDC
IR
TRW
IPC
GET
TSG
REV
OCF
NSI
SB

Table 4.6 (continued)

	COMPANY	5 YEAR BETA	DISCOUNT RATE	IMPLIED DISCOUNT RATE	2/28/78 PRICE	PRESENT VALUE	PERCENT DEVIATION	RANK OF DEV. FROM PRICE
RAR	REYNOLDS & REYNOLDS CO	1.399	14.69	14.14	18.000	18.849	4.7	75
YTR	YELLOW FGHT SYS INC	1.489	15.22	14.36	25.500	26.650	4.5	76
TMC	TIMES MIRROR CO	1.172	13.36	13.24	22.750	23.645	3.9	77
HPC	HERCULES INC	1.423	14.83	14.29	13.125	13.607	3.7	78
BMY	BRISTOL MYERS CO	0.883	11.67	12.14	28.750	29.760	3.5	79
MGM	METRO GOLDWYN MAYER	1.405	14.72	14.36	25.750	26.550	3.1	80
HTOL	HUGHES TOOL CO	1.380	14.58	13.85	32.250	33.173	2.9	81
CL	COLGATE PALMOLIVE CO	1.010	12.41	12.55	19.625	20.090	2.4	82
WAC	WACHOVIA CORP	1.093	12.90	13.03	16.125	16.506	2.4	83
LKS	LUCKY STORES INC	0.861	11.54	11.94	13.500	13.738	1.8	84
BGH	BURROUGHS CORP	1.206	13.56	13.14	59.625	60.462	1.4	85
GT	GOODYEAR TIRE & RUBR	1.167	13.33	13.42	16.000	16.163	1.0	86
SRG	SCHERING PLOUGH CORP	1.610	13.00	12.78	26.375	26.401	0.1	87
SAP4	S & P INDUSTRIAL AVERAGE	1.000	12.35	12.35	95.375	95.746	0.0	88
TIM	TIDEWATER INC	1.214	13.61	13.07	20.750	20.614	-0.7	89
MIC	MONSANTO CO	1.319	14.22	14.15	45.375	44.962	-0.9	90
GS	GILLETTE COMPANY	1.019	12.47	12.28	25.000	24.496	-2.0	91
PEP	PEPSICO INC	0.926	11.92	11.92	24.625	24.022	-2.5	92
UTX	TRANS UN CORP	0.291	12.04	11.84	34.000	32.570	-4.2	93
WIN	WINN DIXIE STORES INC	0.947	12.06	13.84	34.625	33.070	-4.5	94
HLR	HELLER WALTER E INTL	1.464	15.07	14.70	16.250	15.480	-4.7	95
MNC	MASONITE CORP	1.239	13.75	12.87	15.625	14.763	-5.5	96
BUR	BURLINGTON INDS INC	1.164	13.31	12.85	19.750	18.642	-5.6	97
RAH	ROBINS A H INC	1.098	12.93	12.35	31.125	29.318	-5.8	98
GEB	GERBER PRODS CO	0.966	12.16	11.97	33.750	31.609	-6.3	99
GE	GENERAL ELEC CO	1.019	12.47	11.97	44.750	41.909	-6.3	100
HLT	HILTON HOTELS CORP	1.335	14.32	13.12	27.250	25.304	-7.1	101
CMK	CARNATION CO	0.919	11.88	11.58	27.750	25.735	-7.3	102
CH	CUTLER HAMMER INC	1.228	13.69	12.68	33.750	31.222	-7.5	103
BA	BOEING CO	1.092	12.89	12.67	31.500	29.093	-7.6	104
GIS	GENERAL MLS INC	0.943	12.02	13.55	27.625	25.503	-7.7	105
ACK	ARMSTRONG CORK CO	1.323	14.24	13.55	15.250	14.014	-8.1	106
KO	COCA COLA CO	0.708	10.65	10.55	35.875	32.744	-8.7	107
WY	WEYERHAEUSER CO	1.277	13.98	12.78	20.750	18.890	-9.0	108

109	DEXI	DE LUXE CHECK PRINTERS	0·987	12·28	11·69	24·750	22·442	–	9·3
110	SNO	SNAP ON TOOLS CORP	1·232	13·71	12·59	28·250	25·614	–	9·3
111	SND	SOUTHLAND CORP	1·035	12·56	11·86	24·125	21·683	–	10·1
112	PFE	PFIZER INC	0·986	12·48	11·55	22·000	23·083	–	10·8
113	LDS	LONGS DRUG STORES INC	1·115	13·03	11·91	26·625	19·479	–	11·5
114	NLC	NALCO CHEM CO	0·819	11·30	10·85	76·750	23·334	–	12·5
115	PG	PROCTER & GAMBLE CO	1·456	15·02	14·17	20·750	67·153	–	12·5
116	NLA	NLT CORP	1·501	15·29	14·32	29·500	18·149	–	13·0
117	TIC	TRAVELERS CORP	0·839	14·41	12·01	27·250	23·674	–	13·4
118	SBP	STANDARD BRANDS PAINT	0·997	11·41	11·02	65·375	23·708	–	13·4
119	SLB	SCHLUMBERGER LTD	1·172	12·34	12·34	32·250	56·589	–	13·8
120	TMX	TAMPAX INC	1·433	13·36	13·09	24·250	27·802	–	14·0
121	S	SEARS ROEBUCK & CO	1·000	14·89	10·93	39·000	20·867	–	14·0
122	DEC	DIGITAL EQUIP CORP	1·365	12·38	11·02	29·750	33·525	–	15·0
123	KONS	NATIONAL STL CORP	1·126	14·49	12·32	45·250	35·047	–	16·0
124	AVP	AVON PRODS INC	1·406	13·09	11·52	34·625	38·009	–	18·3
125	FDS	FEDERATED DEPT STORES	1·432	14·73	13·39	23·750	28·274	–	18·4
126	GP	GEORGIA PAC CORP	0·867	14·88	12·73	33·000	19·370	–	18·9
127	ARA	ARA SVCS INC	0·989	11·58	10·37	281·750	26·775	–	19·0
128	RDX	ROADWAY EXPRESS INC	1·322	12·24	12·90	28·250	23·294	–	19·2
129	IBM	INTERNATIONAL BUS MACH	0·924	11·91	10·64	18·125	203·044	–	19·5
130	DNB	DUN & BRADSTREET COS	1·043	12·61	10·80	52·625	22·537	–	19·6
131	CGZ	CAPITAL HLDG CORP DEL	1·203	13·54	11·31	34·000	28·125	–	19·8
132	MRK	MERCK & CO INC	1·125	13·09	11·46	33·625	14·579	–	20·0
133	IAD	INLAND STL CO	1·170	13·35	10·77	32·750	42·206	–	20·0
134	BAX	BAXTER TRAVENOL LABS	1·075	12·79	10·57	29·000	27·204	–	20·7
135	UPJ	UPJOHN CO	1·169	13·34	10·96	53·500	26·892	–	20·5
136	MCLI	MOORE LIMITED	1·001	12·36	10·36	23·000	22·965	251·250	21·0
137	MMC	MARSH & MCLENNAN COS	1·032	12·54	12·75	30·500	41·973	–	21·8
138	AHS	AMERICAN HOSP SUPPLY	1·109	12·99	9·34	37·625	17·979	–	21·8
139	IFF	INTERNATIONAL FLAV & FRA	1·381	14·58	10·58	33·875	16·024	–	22·1
140	EMR	EMERSON ELEC CO	0·731	10·78	12·43	26·750	23·566	–	22·4
141	GWJ	GRAINGER W W INC	1·425	14·84	10·96	44·625	26·135	–	22·8
142	LNL	LINCOLN NATL CORP IND	1·072	12·78	10·64	51·375	20·499	–	23·4
143	AMP	AMERICAN HOME PRODS CP	1·023	12·49	12·03	34·875	34·129	–	23·5
144	MCD	MCDONALDS CORP	1·389	14·63	9·92	24·875	38·897	–	24·3
145	ABT	ABBOTT LABS	0·760	10·95		67·000	26·111	–	25·1
146	LZ	LUBRIZOL CORP					18·603	–	25·2
147	KG	K MART CORP					49·917	–	25·5
148	JNJ	JOHNSON & JOHNSON						–	

Table 4.6 (concluded)

	COMPANY	5 YEAR BETA	DISCOUNT RATE	IMPLIED DISCOUNT RATE	2/28/78 PRICE	PRESENT VALUE	PERCENT DEVIATION	RANK OF DEV. FROM PRICE
LAW	LAWTER CHEMS INC	1.081	12.83	10.58	8.625	6.407	−25.7	149
MMM	MINNESOTA MNG & MFG CO	1.001	12.36	10.28	45.125	33.588	−26.1	150
PBS	PABST BREWING CO	1.122	13.07	10.58	19.750	14.539	−26.4	151
EK	EASTMAN KODAK CO	1.157	13.27	10.64	42.250	31.036	−26.5	152
DAL	DELTA AIR LINES DEL	1.500	15.28	12.44	37.375	27.406	−26.7	153
JCP	PENNEY J C INC	1.408	14.74	12.55	33.375	24.451	−26.7	154
RDS	REVCO D S INC	1.397	14.68	11.94	18.375	13.543	−27.3	155
BOR	BORG WARNER CORP	1.136	13.15	10.80	26.375	19.058	−27.7	156
NIA	NIELSEN A C CO	1.274	13.96	11.41	22.250	15.967	−28.2	157
HBL	HEUBLEIN INC	1.378	14.57	11.37	26.625	18.997	−28.6	158
AA	ALUMINUM CO AMER	1.130	13.11	10.96	39.250	27.352	−29.4	159
LLY	LILLY ELI & CO	1.008	12.40	9.93	38.750	27.133	−30.9	160
TRA	TRANE CO	1.313	14.19	11.72	33.000	22.785	−31.0	161
HJ	HOWARD JOHNSON CO	1.325	14.26	12.09	12.875	8.860	−31.2	162
AMP	AMP INC	1.219	13.64	10.99	24.500	16.825	−31.3	163
AMX	AMAX INC	1.173	13.37	10.64	33.250	22.582	−32.1	164
CRR	CARRIER CORP	1.400	14.70	10.78	15.500	10.341	−33.3	165
AMR	AMERICAN AIRLS INC	1.594	15.83	11.73	9.375	6.230	−33.6	166
TXN	TEXAS INSTRS INC	1.449	14.98	11.61	61.500	40.812	−33.6	167
MOT	MOTOROLA INC	1.540	15.51	11.83	35.000	23.000	−34.3	168
HWP	HEWLETT PACKARD CO	1.300	14.41	11.15	64.000	40.398	−36.9	169
BDK	BLACK & DECKER MFG CO	1.354	14.43	10.64	14.625	9.066	−38.0	170
HON	HONEYWELL INC	1.287	14.03	10.23	43.625	24.547	−43.7	171
GLW	CORNING GLASS WKS	1.341	14.30	10.12	64.125	35.037	−44.5	172
NSC	NATIONAL STARCH & CHEM	1.264	13.90	10.17	11.125	6.230	−44.6	173
BC	BRUNSWICK CORP	1.508	15.32	11.01	14.000	7.708	−44.9	174
NWA	NORTHWEST AIRLS INC	1.636	16.08	12.32	23.625	12.419	−47.4	175
ZE	ZENITH RADIO CORP	1.657	16.20	9.80	12.750	6.643	−47.9	176
MGI	MGIC INVT CORP	1.885	17.53	12.57	15.125	7.239	−52.1	177
SLZ	SCHLITZ JOS BREWING CO	1.285	14.02	7.65	11.125	4.517	−59.4	178
DIS	DISNEY WALT PRODTNS	1.489	15.22	10.17	32.375	11.968	−63.0	179
KN	KENNECOTT COPPER CORP	1.307	14.15	5.61	19.625	4.747	−75.8	180
RAM	RAMADA INNS INC	1.770	16.86	7.67	4.625	0.664	−85.6	181

1.0.[28] Figure 4.12 indicates the upward-sloping "theoretical" market line linking the risk-free rate at 6.5 percent with the market discount rate of 12.185 percent (denoted by the "M") by a series of black dots. The "theoretical" line often has a far different slope than that of the "regression" market line, with

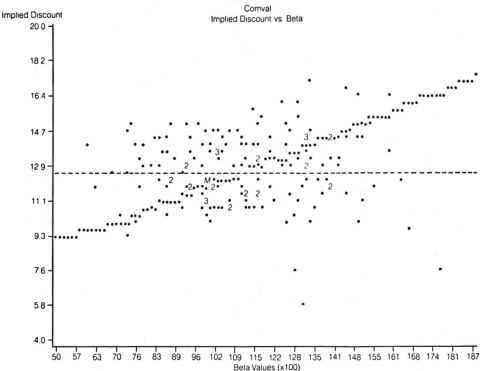

Figure 4.12
Estimated Market Lines
COMVAL
Implied Discount versus Beta

---

[28]There is some controversy regarding what measurement should be used for the risk-free rate. The most widely used rate is that on a 90-day Treasury bill, which is the one used in this case. Others argue that a AAA corporate bond of short-term maturity would be more comparable with common stocks. The 90-day T-bill appears to have the fewest biases attached to its use. There is probably more controversy regarding what should be used in the market portfolio proxy (see Chapter 7 for some discussion of the issues). For a number of applications Harris Bank prefers to use the S&P 400 rather than the S&P 500 as the market proxy. The difference between the indexes is that 20 transportation, 40 utility, and 40 financial companies are included in the 500 which are not in the 400.

the most common case being the one shown, namely where the theoretical slope is steeply upward, while the regression market line (indicated by the dashed line) is relatively flat. A ready comparison can be made between the two equations as follows:

$$IDR_R = 12.185 + 0.460 \cdot \text{Beta} \tag{4-13}$$

$$IDR_T = 6.50 + 5.835 \cdot \text{Beta}, \tag{4-14}$$

where the subscripts R and T indicate the regression and theoretical market lines, respectively.

The coefficient multiplying beta, 0.460 in the regression case, is the slope of the market line, which is far lower than the 5.835 of the theoretical case. The regression market line indicates that a low degree of additional reward can be expected by assuming an incrementally greater degree of risk.

As was mentioned in the paragraph introducing the COMVAL model, the most important result from this form of dividend discount model is the difference of each individual security's present value from either the theoretical or regression market line. Figures 4.13 and 4.14 present examples of both theoretical and regression market line estimates of security excess returns, or alphas, determined by subtracting the discount rate obtained from the appropriate market line, given in equations (4-13) and (4-14), from the implied discount rate provided in equation (4-12). The alpha estimates of Figures 4.13 and 4.14 are organized into beta deciles for comparison purposes. From this, one can readily see the effect of the strong, upward slope of the theoretical market line on the distribution of estimated alpha values, with the major difference being at either end of the beta range. At a beta level of 1.40 or higher, the theoretical market line produces only three stocks with positive alpha estimates, while the regression market line produces 14. At the other end of the beta range, 0.99 or lower, the theoretical market line produces 37 securities with positive values, while the regression market line produces only 28.

It is incorrect, though tempting, to infer from these quite different forecasts that the model is insufficiently robust to be useful. Recall from the previous section that these forecasts should be adjusted for information and further transformed to be comparable. Such a transformation should produce a value of zero for the estimated alpha of the market portfolio. If these steps are taken, then the two sets of alphas (derived from the theoretical and regression market lines) become consistent with each other.

Summary

We have covered a great deal of material in this chapter. The concept of an alpha is difficult to understand: first, it is an expectation for the future; and second, it is not a forecast but a quantum of pure knowledge. Forecasts must be adjusted to remove noise and bias in order to produce this most crucial of

Figure 4.13
Alpha Forecasts from Theoretical Market Line

ALPHA RANK WITHIN RISK CLASS
BASED ON THEORETICAL MARKET LINE

BETA

0.00-0.79		0.80-0.89		0.90-0.99		1.00-1.09		1.10-1.19		1.20-1.29		1.30-1.39		1.40-1.49		1.50-1.59		1.60 & UP	
IDC SYM	ALPHA	IDC SYM	ALPHA	IDC SYM	ALPHA	IDC SYM	ALPHA	IDC SYM	ALPHA	IDC SYM	ALPHA	IDC SYM	ALPHA	IDC SYM	ALPHA	IDC SYM	ALPHA	IDC SYM	ALPHA
SN	4.01	MOB	3.40	MRO	2.98	TXT	2.26	ENG	2.38	DE	2.22	CNF	2.67	INA	1.85	FNM	-0.68	MGI	-4.96
J	3.79	AFI	2.96	FM	3.12	WFG	2.19	ITT	2.11	SDC	1.02	IP	1.08	CIA	1.11	KNS	-0.34	NWA	-3.75
PGLN	2.85	TX	2.99	BOA	1.87	GM	2.27	ZB	1.65	FIR	0.76	MIS	-0.38	HLR	-0.37	CGL	-0.61	ZE	-6.40
MO	2.98	SD	2.66	SA	1.75	CK	1.70	SR	1.33	CBE	0.83	CKL	-0.02	HGM	-0.37	TIC	-0.96	RAM	-9.19
RJR	3.81	SCE	2.15	MSU	1.47	FNC	1.59	XRX	1.02	TRW	0.02	GDC	-0.08	YTR	-0.54	MR	-2.10		
PCG	2.12	GPU	1.87	TE	1.14	FPL	1.66	CMZ	0.90	OCF	-0.14	IR	-0.07	HPC	-0.85	DAL	-2.84		
WPC	1.73	PSR	1.50	CLL	1.02	JPM	1.55	DOW	0.65	BGH	-0.42	MTC	-0.55	NLA	-1.34	MOT	-3.68		
GEN	2.17	NSP	1.61	TSO	0.63	F	1.28	UCC	0.59	UTX	-0.90	HTOL	-0.73	ARA	-1.80	BC	-4.31		
CWE	1.84	CSR	1.34	DNY	0.47	NOB	1.08	GT	0.08	TIM	-0.54	ACK	-0.70	DEC	-2.16				
T	1.65	BRY	0.82	REV	0.35	HOU	1.11	TMC	-0.12	MNC	-0.89	HLT	-1.20	JCP	-2.19				
IPC	-0.69	BMY	0.47	TXU	0.71	FML	0.99	NSI	-0.05	WY	-0.70	CGZ	-1.34	MCD	-2.41				
KO	-0.09	SB	0.66	PEP	-0.00	CTR	1.13	BUR	-0.46	CH	-1.01	LNL	-1.83	CRR	-2.92				
JNJ	-1.03	GET	-0.38	WIN	-0.20	DD	0.63	SHG	-0.22	SNO	-1.20	SBP	-1.57	TXN	-3.37				
AHP	-1.44	LKS	-0.40	GEB	-0.39	AHU	0.66	S	-1.02	BAX	-1.34	FDS	-2.17	DIS	-5.05				
		SLB	-0.45	GIS	-0.35	WAC	0.35	NLC	-1.11	NIA	-1.63	HJ	-2.17						
		PG	-1.20	DEXI	-0.59	CL	0.13	AHS	-1.19	AMP	-1.63	RDS	-2.64						
		IBM	-1.44	CMK	-0.30	SAP4	0.14	GP	-1.57	HON	-2.54	KG	-2.74						
				PFE	-0.72	RAH	-0.00	MCLI	-1.89	NSC	-3.73	TRA	-2.46						
				TMX	-1.32	GS	-0.57	UPJ	-1.77	SLZ	-6.37	HBL	-3.19						
				DNB	-1.53	BA	-0.19	AA	-2.15			HUP	-2.96						
				MRK	-1.27	GE	-0.67	BOR	-2.35			BDK	-3.78						
						SND	-0.70	EK	-2.64			GLW	-4.23						
						LDS	-0.30	AMX	-2.73			KN	-8.54						
						AVP	-0.72	PBS	-2.49										
						IFF	-1.33												
						ABT	-1.40												
						NS	-1.45												
						EMR	-1.64												
						IAD	-1.81												
						MMC	-1.81												
						LZ	-1.85												
						LAW	-2.25												
						MMM	-2.08												
						LLY	-2.47												

Figure 4.14
Alpha Forecasts from Regression Market Line

ALPHA RANK WITHIN RISK CLASS
BASED ON REGRESSION MARKET LINE

BETA

BETA 0.00–0.79

IDC SYM	ALPHA
SN	2.34
J	2.04
PGLN	1.44
MO	1.42
RJR	1.41
PCG	0.62
WPC	0.32
GEN	0.15
CWE	0.11
T	-0.63
IPC	-0.79
KO	-1.96
JNJ	-2.61
AHP	-3.18

BETA 0.80–0.89

IDC SYM	ALPHA
MOB	2.48
AFI	1.80
TX	1.75
SD	1.62
SCE	1.06
GPU	0.85
NSP	0.65
	0.30
BRY	-0.09
BMY	-0.45
SB	-0.49
GET	-0.55
LKS	-0.64
SLB	-1.56
PG	-1.71
IBM	-2.21

BETA 0.90–0.99

IDC SYM	ALPHA
MRO	2.50
FM	2.45
BOA	1.53
SA	1.39
MSU	0.88
TE	0.63
CLL	0.33
TSG	0.22
DNY	0.14
REV	-0.02
TXU	-0.09
PEP	-0.45
WIN	-0.78
GEB	-0.86
GIS	-0.95
DEXI	-1.03
CMK	-1.09
PFE	-1.62
DNB	-1.88
MRK	-1.97

BETA 1.00–1.09

IDC SYM	ALPHA
TXT	2.07
WFG	2.06
GM	1.98
CK	1.84
FNC	1.62
FPL	1.33
JPM	1.32
F	1.06
NOB	0.98
HOU	0.88
FML	0.86
CTR	0.79
DD	0.59
AHU	0.34
WAC	-0.09
CL	-0.29
SAP4	-0.34
RAH	-0.37
GS	-0.46
BA	-0.69
GE	-0.80
SND	-0.89
LDS	
AVP	-1.63
IFF	-1.69
ABT	-1.72
NS	-1.76
EMR	-1.87
IAD	-1.91
MMC	-2.02
LZ	-2.10
LAW	-2.36
MMM	
LLY	-2.72

BETA 1.10–1.19

IDC SYM	ALPHA
ENG	2.93
ITT	2.77
ZR	2.24
SH	1.68
XRX	1.37
CMZ	1.30
DOW	1.21
UCC	1.20
GT	0.69
TMC	0.51
NSI	0.44
BUR	0.34
SRG	0.13
CH	-0.38
NLC	-0.78
AHS	-1.16
GP	-1.18
MCLI	-1.26
GWW	-1.34
UPJ	-1.39
AA	-1.74
BOR	-1.91
EK	-2.08
AMX	-2.09
PBS	-2.12

BETA 1.20–1.29

IDC SYM	ALPHA
DE	3.22
SDC	2.14
FIR	1.63
CUE	1.12
OCF	0.69
BGH	0.40
UTX	0.38
TIM	0.32
MNC	0.11
WY	-0.07
CH	-0.16
SNO	-0.78
BAX	-1.36
NIA	-1.76
AMP	-2.54
HON	-2.60
NSC	
SLZ	-5.13

BETA 1.30–1.39

IDC SYM	ALPHA
CNF	4.23
IP	3.19
MIS	2.42
CKL	1.87
GDC	1.37
IR	1.36
MTC	1.31
RAR	0.76
HTOL	0.32
ACK	-0.07
HLT	-0.07
CGZ	-0.71
LNL	-0.79
SBP	-1.06
FDS	-1.44
HJ	-1.63
KG	
RDS	
TRA	
HBL	
HWP	
BDK	-2.16
GLW	-2.68
KN	-7.17

BETA 1.40–1.49

IDC SYM	ALPHA
INA	4.03
CIA	3.50
HLR	1.84
MGM	1.52
YTR	1.49
HPC	1.45
NLA	1.32
ARA	0.56
DEC	0.24
RDX	-0.12
JCP	-0.28
MCD	-0.41
CRR	-1.05
TXN	-1.24
DIS	-2.70

BETA 1.50–1.59

IDC SYM	ALPHA
FNM	3.62
KNS	2.08
CGL	2.00
TIC	1.45
AMR	-0.43
DAL	-0.81
MOT	-1.06
BC	-1.87

BETA 1.60 & UP

IDC SYM	ALPHA
MGI	-0.48
NWA	-0.61
ZE	-3.14
RAM	-5.33

inputs to the portfolio management process. This last sentence describes an alpha, but how do you find one? We have presented several approaches. These are not offered as final answers since many more methods will undoubtedly be developed as MPT continues to evolve.

At this stage it may be tempting to dismiss the development of alpha forecasts as being too difficult. The methods presented in this chapter may appear unrealistic to some. But if one desires a consistent and systematic approach to investing, then those methods are among the best that are available at this time.

Because the development of alpha forecasts is not easy, there is always a temptation to stay with the old ways and pretend that they were not so bad after all. We hope that the tendency to engage in spontaneous and unspecified strategies or to take refuge in the comfort of quiet, contemplative ruminations justified by "but that is the way we have always done it" will have been altered somewhat by a reading of this chapter, if for no other reason than that active management is the *explicit* pursuit of superior performance—performance that is driven by the input of alphas. Denying explicit judgment as to security valuation is denying active management. And with active management go the fees of active management. There is no middle ground: either judgment is used effectively, or it has no value. The only other aid we can suggest is to show example portfolios, which we do in Supplement 4.

Further Reading

Perhaps the best sources of information on the dividend discount model are Bill Fouse's two *Financial Analysts Journal* articles:
Other useful readings on valuation are:

Bierman, Harold, and Jerome E. Hass. "Normative Stock Price Models." *Journal of Financial and Quantitative Analysis,* September 1971, pp. 1135–41.

Bing, Ralph. "Survey of Practitioners' Stock Evaluation Methods." *Financial Analysts Journal,* May–June 1971, pp. 55–60.

Clendenin, John, and Maurice Van Cleave. "Growth and Common Stock Values." *Journal of Finance,* December 1954, pp. 365–76.

Fouse, William. "Risk and Liquidity: The Keys to Stock Price Behavior." *Financial Analysts Journal,* May–June 1976, pp. 35–45.

————. "Risk and Liquidity Revisited." *Financial Analysts Journal,* January–February 1977, pp. 40–45.

Molodovsky, Nicholas; Catherine May; and Sherman Chottiner. "Common Stock Valuation." *Financial Analysts Journal,* March–April 1965, pp. 104–23.

Few articles have been written on active management and the organization of the research effort. Four readings are suggested below; the last being more a review of the application of capital market theory than a discussion of active management per se:

Arbit, Harold. "Active Management: The Critical Issues." Unpublished paper, American National Bank, May 1978.

————, and James Rhodes. "Performance Goals in a Generally Efficient Market." *Journal of Portfolio Management,* Fall 1976, pp. 57–61.

Lanstein, Ronald, and William Jahnke. "Applying Capital Market Theory to Investing." *Interfaces*, February 1979, pp. 23–38.

Sharpe, William. "Security Codings: Measuring Relative Attractiveness in Perfect and Imperfect Markets." Research Paper no. 486, Graduate School of Business, Stanford University, November 1978.

Finally, the following articles include some treatment of the adjustment of forecasts for information content:

Ambachtsheer, Keith. "Where Are the Customer's Alphas?" *Journal of Portfolio Management*, Fall 1977, pp. 52–56.

Rosenberg, Barr. "Security Appraisal and Unsystematic Risk in Institutional Investment." *Proceedings of the Seminar on the Analysis of Security Prices*, University of Chicago, November 1976, pp. 171–237.

Treynor, Jack, and Fischer Black. "How to Use Security Analysis to Improve Portfolio Selection." *Journal of Business*, January 1973, pp. 66–68.

Supplement 4

Implications of Alpha
Generation for Portfolio
Formation and the Research
Process

In Chapter 4 we argued that alpha is the driving force of active management. Further, we held that the process by which an organization deduces alphas is intimately related to the organization's belief in the extent to which the capital markets are efficient and that this belief, in turn, is related to the manner in which the organization's research effort should be structured. For instance, if the market is almost efficient, then the research effort must be systematized and the portfolio management process carefully controlled because any unnecessary or ill-advised transaction is a "gift" to the competition.[1]

In this supplement we take the argument a step further. The quest for alpha will be directed in well-defined patterns; this does not imply that every research effort will become uniformly conventional, but that the general search methodologies will be easily categorized. Each successful organization will need to retain its individual and proprietary procedure, but once an organization's judgment has been formed, it should be used (and disclosed) in constructing the portfolio. The research process dictates to a large extent the type of portfolio that an organization will manage. (Of course, this in turn influences the type of client that will be interested in the portfolio product.) Therefore, it is useful to concentrate on the end product, the portfolio, in order to understand the implications of alpha generation. It is also useful to analyze the research process in order to determine where the creative effort is best concentrated.

---

[1]The only realistic alternative is that the markets are totally efficient, which appears contrary to the results of academic research and the empiricism of the majority of market participants. The market achieves its level of efficiency by the interaction of the competitive instincts of thousands of investors. It is therefore a human process, of which there are few that can claim 100 percent perfection.

Our starting point is the reiteration of an earlier statement: If the market is reasonably efficient, then traditional analysis (i.e., organizing a research department by industry, performing the inviolable earnings projections, and so on) is likely to be rewarding only to the extent that it is better than everyone else's.[2] If everybody is running in the same race, then only one entrant can win. This argument suggests the desirability of evolving a nontraditional approach or specializing in a particular group of stocks in order to obtain a comparative advantage. We shall describe three approaches that have been developed by professional money managers. These approaches are by no means exhaustive, but they are indicative of the rational and knowledgeable research effort that is now being applied to investment management.

The first approach argues that because the market is reasonably efficient, it will not be possible to easily identify securities which are greatly undervalued. All that can be hoped for is to locate a great many slightly undervalued securities. Moreover, the search for such securities will probably be a good deal less costly than the search for greatly undervalued securities because it may be possible to automate this process to some extent. However, because the search is for a small discrepancy in valuation, it is necessary to be more certain than usual that the promised effect is genuine and not noise. The obvious method is to use several valuation models, and to monitor them constantly for information content, in order to derive a combined prediction with more information content than can be provided by any single model.

The next step is to construct a highly diversified portfolio from the undervalued securities so that the residual risk is very small. If each of the securities is somewhat undervalued, then the claim is that the portfolio will provide an incremental return at virtually no added risk.

The ability to achieve that abnormal return is dependent upon two factors: (1) the identification of sufficient numbers of undervalued companies and (2) explicit control of the residual risk so that the individual asset alphas combine to form a portfolio alpha that is not swamped by the residual risk. However, the magnitude of the incremental return is related to the magnitude of the residual risk incurred, so that this approach can never provide a large incremental return.[3]

Notice that portfolio construction requires the use of an optimization program because the portfolio cannot be exposed to the common factors; i.e., the XMC, must be (close to) zero. If the XMC were substantial, then the portfolio's performance would be subject to the vagaries of the common factor returns. Thus, most of the residual risk must come from specific risk, indicating that the hallmark of this stock-picking approach is portfolios with (1) a large num-

---

[2]"What makes you think that you can consistently beat millions of other investors?" See the section on "Market Efficiency" in Chapter 4.

[3]Of course, this suggests that if the abnormal return is consistently larger than that expected from the level of residual risk, then management ability could be proven statistically in a comparatively short period of time. We will consider this point in more detail in Chapter 7.

ber of names, because the portfolios have to be highly diversified, and (2) virtually no *XMC*. The latter condition suggests that the beta of the equity component must be one.

One disadvantage of the stock-picking approach is that some overvalued assets will have to be held in order to keep the portfolio highly diversified. For instance, even if the valuation judgment suggests that AT&T, IBM, and General Motors have a negative alpha, they will still have to be purchased (to some degree) in order to keep the residual risk of the portfolio small. Would it not be better to exclude these assets and have a portfolio of positive alpha assets at greater risk? For some investors, the answer is yes. If an investor can diversify away, in some other part of the overall portfolio, the increase in risk that arises from not holding these assets (for instance, by using serveral managers in a multiply managed portfolio), then it is clearly beneficial to do so, because the increase in return is achieved at almost no *overall* increase in risk. For investors who cannot diversify this additional risk, the highly diversified portfolio may be a beneficial strategy. As with the other strategies, the optimality of this strategy depends on the management fee as well as the factors mentioned.

A second approach to alpha generation would argue that because so many analysts are trying to find undervalued stocks in a nearly efficient market, it may be beneficial to concentrate on a subset of the market. Specializing in a fairly homogeneous sector of the market could promote the development of a comparative advantage not enjoyed by investors who cannot afford to devote the necessary resources to one area of the market. Notice that the portfolios formed using this strategy will be deliberately undiversified by being exposed to one or more of the factors. In Chapter 4 we showed (Figures 4.4 to 4.9) that in the past the factors have displayed a degree of momentum or serial dependency; this strategy is designed to exploit that effect.

The procedure is to predict the factor returns and then to form portfolios which are deliberately exposed to the factors. In addition, the portfolios may be constructed either to minimize specific risk (so that the portfolio residual return is effectively the factor return) or to include some stock-picking judgment, which will substantially increase the specific risk of the portfolios. Therefore, the ability to achieve abnormal returns in this way is founded, first, upon being able to isolate the factor which will outperform other factors in the future, and second, upon identifying securities which are exposed to this factor.

The disadvantage of this approach is that the managers who favor it tend to become classified as, for instance, "growth stock" or "small-cap" managers. Hence, there is a great temptation to stay exposed to the same factor through thick and thin by staying at one end of the "teeter-totter" rather than changing their exposure in line with the factor forecasts. Meanwhile, the portfolio value is declining.

This is precisely what befell the growth stock managers in 1974–76 when the residual return on their universe was (almost) consistently negative (see Figure 4.8). What are the lessons for funds' owners who are in such a situation?

If a portfolio managed in this way represents the total portfolio of the owner, then perhaps the most realistic solution is to encourage the manager to move into cash rather than remaining exposed to the factor. A better solution for owners who believe that they can also forecast the factors is to reallocate funds among managers in order to obtain the correct exposure. This may be done by firing the manager and hiring a specialist manager with the opposite emphasis.

In a multiply managed portfolio the solution is clearer but possibly more heretical. The managers should be encouraged to announce to the owner when a sector is overvalued. The funds of the manager in that sector should then be transferred to a manager with the opposite emphasis, perhaps with the management fee being retained by the original manager. It may appear that this manager is getting the fee for nothing. This is not true because the manager is providing a valuation of his or her sector ("It is overvalued") which should form part of the manager's performance record and which should make it easier for the owner to sell-short the sector relative to the normal portfolio. We will consider multiple management in greater detail in Chapter 6.

The last approach that will be described here would argue that traditional procedures will not work in an efficient market. What is required is to synthesize sources of unconventional information so as to find insights which have not been exploited previously. Because such insights will be new and unique, there will not be many. Since this is a thoroughly creative and iconoclastic approach, active decisions will be taken slowly and thoughtfully. Thus, the insights can be researched thoroughly, so that when the time comes to act, the portfolio will be totally structured around these insights.

The hallmark of this approach is that the portfolio will have few ideas or bets, perhaps only two or three, and will be exposed to considerable residual risk through exposure to these atypical common characteristics. The common characteristics will change through time, depending on the perceived opportunities. In other words, in contrast to portfolios developed by means of the preceding approach, there is no natural, predefined habitat for such portfolios. These are, by themselves, not typical institutional portfolios. However, when they are used on conjunction with, for example, the active/passive strategy, their overall level of risk need not be excessive. In fact, the mix between active and passive can be designed so as to suit many investor preferences. Moreover, since only a small portion of such a portfolio is managed (extremely) aggressively, the total fee and transaction costs may be less than they would be if the entire aggregate portfolio were less aggressively managed. Finally, the passive component can be designed so as to offset undesirable or unnecessary exposure which may have been induced in the active portfolio as a by-product of the strategy.[4]

The disadvantages of this approach are: (1) it is not clear how much money can be managed in this fashion, because some of the insights may be such that

---

[4]This idea was originated by the American National Bank of Chicago, which called the concept the "compensating core." Compensating core is a trademark of American National Bank. We will discuss this approach further in Chapter 6.

only a small dollar value can be invested; (2) on some occasions the organization may have no insights, in which case there is a temptation to continue with
an aggressive posture when the available information is insufficient to justify
it; and (3) because the portfolio is structured in response to insights, the risk
predictions may understate the true risk by missing the commonality that was
used to construct the portfolio. For instance, if the portfolio is composed of
companies which repurchase their own securities and the risk measurement
does not incorporate this information in the prediction, then the risk level is
likely to be understated by an unknown magnitude.

This completes our overview of the three approaches. Now let us turn to
actual portfolios. We must stress that these portfolios are included only as examples and that we are not suggesting that they have performed or will perform
better or worse than any other portfolios. In addition, the managers may dis-
agree with our comments or with the description of the alpha process that they
have been implicitly ascribed. Our only reason for including portfolios is to
show the range of portfolios that is implied by rational and thoughtful deliber-
ation of the investment process. In the following tables we include an analysis,
in the same form as the Dow Jones Average example in Chapter 3, for portfolios representative of the three approaches.[5]

Example 1

The first example is that of Alpha Plus, a highly diversified portfolio managed by the John Hancock Mutual Life Insurance Company.[6] Table S4.1 shows
the front page of the PORCH analysis. Items A and E.2 show, respectively,
that the beta is exactly one and that the level of residual risk is very small. In
fact, the riskier of the currently marketed index funds have annual residual
standard deviations only a little smaller than that of this portfolio.

The residual risk is composed of *XMC* and specific risk. The former arises
because the risk indices of the portfolio do not match those of the S&P 500.
However, the risk indices, reported at the bottom of the table, are not very
different from those of the S&P 500, with only three—immaturity and smallness, growth orientation, and financial risk—being noticeably deviant. Therefore, we expect the residual risk to be mainly specific risk. This expectation is
confirmed by Table S4.2, which displays the decomposition of the portfolio's
risk; the specific risk is three times as great as *XMC*. The expectation is further
confirmed by the breakdown of industry group investments given in Table

---

[5]Some information has not been reported in order to maintain confidentiality. In addition, the
meaning of some of the data will become clearer after it has been discussed more fully in Chapter
5. Finally, it is somewhat unfair to make direct comparisons between the portfolios, because they
have been designed to satisfy completely different objectives.

[6]John Hancock Mutual Life Insurance Company, John Hancock Place, Post Office Box 111,
Boston, Massachusetts 02117. We thank John Nagorniak for providing the portfolio holdings. For
another description of this strategy, see "Portfolio Strategy—John Hancock Mutual Life Insurance
Co.," *Institutional Investor*, May 1979, p. 87.

Table S4.1
Summary Statistics for Example 1

```
              FUNDAMENTAL RISK MEASUREMENT SERVICE
                       PORTFOLIO ANALYSIS
                    JOHN HANCOCK INSURANCE

PORTFOLIO STATUS AS OF
  ANALYSIS CONDUCTED
  FRMS UPDATE AS OF
S&P500     IS THE MARKET PORTFOLIO


              1. SUMMARY MEASURES FOR COMMON EQUITY

A. PREDICTED SYSTEMATIC RISK COEFFICIENT {BETA}-NEXT 3 MONTHS          1.00
B. PREDICTED SYSTEMATIC RISK COEFFICIENT {BETA}-NEXT 5 YEARS           1.00
C. ANNUAL STANDARD DEVIATION OF SYSTEMATIC PORTFOLIO RETURN           20.83%
D. FRMS FORECAST STANDARD DEVIATION OF ANNUAL S&P500 RETURN           20.80%

        PORTFOLIO RISK FORECAST, INCLUDING EXTRA-MARKET COVARIANCE

E.1    STANDARD DEVIATION OF ANNUAL PORTFOLIO RETURN                  20.92%
E.2    STANDARD DEVIATION OF ANNUAL PORTFOLIO RESIDUAL RETURN          1.96%
E.3    COEFFICIENT OF DETERMINATION BY S&P500              0.991
E.4    REQUIRED ANNUAL PORTFOLIO APPRAISAL PREMIUM {ALPHA}             0.05%
E.5    INFERRED COVENANT INFORMATION RATIO {CIR}          0.027
E.6    INFERRED CEER OF ACTIVE MANAGEMENT                 0.027%

       RISK FORECASTS BASED UPON A SIMULATED 5-YEAR HISTORY OF MONTHLY
       RETURNS FOR THE PORTFOLIO . . .

F.1    STANDARD DEVIATION OF ANNUAL PORTFOLIO RETURN                  21.09%
F.2    STANDARD DEVIATION OF ANNUAL PORTFOLIO RESIDUAL RETURN          2.12%
F.3    COEFFICIENT OF DETERMINATION BY S&P500              0.990

              2. INDICES OF RISK IN THE PORTFOLIO
```

				EFFECT OF 0.01	
			FRMS	INCREASE ON	REQUIRED
INDEX OF RISK	PORTFOLIO	S&P500	UNIVERSE	RESID. STDEV	ALPHA
MARKET VARIABILITY	0.011	0.0	0.187	0.0005	0.00
EARNINGS VARIABILITY	0.028	0.0	0.232	-0.0015	-0.00
LOW VALUATION, UNSUCCESS	-0.054	0.0	-0.031	-0.0027	-0.01
IMMATURITY AND SMALLNESS	0.157	0.0	0.634	0.0003	0.00
GROWTH ORIENTATION	0.122	0.0	0.158	0.0039	0.01
FINANCIAL RISK	-0.107	0.0	0.143	-0.0011	-0.00

Table S4.2
Decomposition of Risk for Example 1

DECOMPOSITION OF VARIANCE OF ANNUAL PERCENT RETURN				
		FRMS MODEL		SIMULATION	PREDICTION
	SYSTEMATIC		433.7	440.5	433.7
	SPECIFIC	2.5			
RISK INDICES VARIANCE		0.4			
INDUSTRY VARIANCE		0.8			
R.I.-INDUSTRY COVARIANCE		-0.5			

	XMC	0.7			

	RESIDUAL		3.2	4.5	3.9
			-----	-----	-----
	TOTAL		437.0	445.0	437.6

S4.3, which shows that the portfolio and the S&P 500 have almost identical holdings.

The actual portfolio holdings are given in Table S4.4. There are 129 common stock holdings, 38 of which are not in the S&P 500, together with a small cash holding which is used as a working balance. Therefore, the portfolio appears to fit our belief as to the type of strategy used.

Table S4.3
Industry Group Investments for Example 1

JOHN HANCOCK INSURANCE

CONTRIBUTIONS OF INDUSTRY GROUP INVESTMENTS TO PORTFOLIO RISK

INDUSTRY	PORT.	PERCENT OF VALUE IN S&P500	FRMSU	AVERAGE BETA OF HOLDINGS IN INDUSTRY
1. NONFERROUS METALS	1.5	2.0	2.4	1.12
2. ENERGY RAW MATERIALS	4.0	2.9	4.5	1.05
3. CONSTRUCTION	3.1	1.5	1.9	1.33
4. AGRICULTURE, FOOD	6.6	4.8	4.2	0.89
5. LIQUOR	0.2	0.7	0.7	1.04
6. TOBACCO	3.3	1.3	0.9	0.66
7. APPAREL	1.0	0.7	0.9	1.25
8. FOREST PRODUCTS, PAPER	2.1	2.7	2.2	1.19
9. CONTAINERS	0.9	0.2	0.2	0.93
10. MEDIA	0.0	2.0	2.1	0.0
11. CHEMICALS	0.5	3.2	3.1	0.92
12. DRUGS, MEDICINE	3.9	5.3	4.0	0.92
13. SOAPS, COSMETICS	1.8	2.8	1.8	1.01
14. DOMESTIC OIL	8.9	6.9	7.1	0.92
15. INTERNATIONAL OIL	3.3	9.4	6.5	0.77
16. TIRES, RUBBER GOODS	1.3	0.3	0.3	0.96
17. STEEL	1.6	0.8	1.1	0.95
18. PRODUCER GOODS	3.4	4.3	4.8	1.05
19. BUSINESS MACHINES	8.6	8.8	5.9	0.97
20. CONSUMER DURABLES	0.3	0.8	1.4	1.34
21. MOTOR VEHICLES	6.5	4.5	3.6	0.92
22. AEROSPACE	2.1	0.9	0.7	1.29
23. ELECTRONICS	1.2	2.5	2.1	1.50
24. PHOTOGRAPHIC, OPTICAL	1.6	1.5	1.0	0.98
25. NONDURBLS, ENTERTNMNT	1.0	0.6	0.7	1.48
26. TRUCKING, FREIGHT	1.6	0.2	0.3	1.32
27. RAILROADS, SHIPPING	2.0	1.7	1.4	1.32
28. AIR TRANSPORT	0.8	0.5	1.6	1.50
29. TELEPHONE	6.6	6.7	5.1	0.59
30. ENERGY, UTILITIES	3.4	5.7	6.7	0.72
31. RETAIL, GENERAL	1.7	2.6	2.4	1.19
32. BANKS	7.0	2.7	3.6	0.95
33. MISCELLANEOUS FINANCE	1.1	1.2	1.3	1.60
34. INSURANCE	3.5	2.4	3.0	1.55
35. REAL PROPERTY	0.4	0.1	0.5	1.93
36. BUSINESS SERVICES	0.6	0.0	0.8	1.03
37. TRAVEL, OUTDR RECREATN	0.0	0.3	0.4	0.0
38. GOLD MNG & SECURITIES	0.0	0.2	0.7	0.0
39. MISC. CONGLOMRTE	2.8	4.3	8.1	0.97

Table S4.4
Asset Holdings for Example 1

JOHN HANCOCK INSURANCE

CONTRIBUTIONS OF INDIVIDUAL ASSETS TO PORTFOLIO RISK

NAME	PERCENT OF PORTFOLIO VALUE	EFFECT OF 1% PURCHASE ON BETA	EFFECT OF 1% PURCHASE ON RESID. STDEV	REQUIRED ALPHA	NUMBER OF SHARES
ABBOTT LABS	0.3	0.0004	0.012	0.03	1200.
AETNA LIFE & CAS CO	0.3	0.0045	0.024	0.06	1200.
ALUMINUM CO AMER	0.7	-0.0002	0.009	0.02	1500.
AMERADA HESS CORP	0.2	0.0034	0.014	0.03	600.
AMERICAN CAN CO	0.9	-0.0007	0.008	0.02	2700.
AMERICAN EXPRESS CO	1.1	0.0060	0.042	0.11	3900.
AMERICAN HOME PRODS CP	0.5	-0.0024	0.006	-0.02	2300.
AMERICAN INTL GROUP	0.4	-0.0068	0.046	-0.12	800.
AMERICAN TEL & TELEG CO	5.0	-0.0044	-0.009	-0.02	10336.
ANHEUSER BUSCH INC	0.2	0.0004	0.012	0.03	1200.
ATLANTIC RICHFIELD CO	2.3	-0.0016	0.029	0.07	4200.
AUTOMATIC DATA PROCESS	0.3	0.0018	0.022	0.06	900.
AVON PRODS INC	0.7	0.0013	0.017	0.04	1800.
BAKER INTL CORP	0.4	0.0019	0.020	0.05	1100.
BANKAMERICA CORP	1.6	-0.0015	0.042	0.11	6900.
BARNETT BANKS FLA INC	0.3	0.0029	0.034	0.09	1600.
BLACK & DECKER MFG CO	0.3	0.0034	0.018	0.05	1600.
BLUE BELL INC	0.7	0.0034	0.036	0.09	3200.
BOEING CO	0.7	0.0036	0.033	0.08	2150.
BORDEN INC	1.2	-0.0026	0.023	0.06	5600.
BURROUGHS CORP	0.8	-0.0012	0.018	0.04	1400.
CARPENTER TECHNOLOGY	0.3	-0.0006	0.013	0.03	1400.
CATERPILLAR TRACTOR CO	1.1	-0.0001	0.009	0.02	2400.
CESSNA AIRCRAFT CO	0.5	0.0018	0.036	0.09	3300.

CHAMPION INTL CORP	0.3	0.0024	0.007	0.02	1400.
CHUBB CORP	0.5	0.0059	0.041	0.10	1500.
CITICORP	1.2	-0.0010	0.038	0.09	6000.
COCA COLA CO	0.7	0.0021	0.007	0.02	2300.
COLONIAL PENN GROUP	0.4	0.0105	0.050	0.12	1800.
CONOCO INC	1.6	-0.0006	0.030	0.08	4800.
CONSOLIDATED FOODS CP	0.7	-0.0017	0.021	0.05	3700.
CONSOLIDATED FREIGHTWY	0.8	0.0038	0.041	0.10	3200.
CONTINENTAL CORP	0.3	0.0023	0.033	0.08	3600.
CONTINENTAL ILL CORP	0.3	0.0015	0.025	0.06	1300.
COOPER INDS INC	0.8	0.0024	0.022	0.06	1600.
CROSS A T CO	0.3	0.0019	0.031	0.08	1200.
DANA CORP	0.4	0.0011	0.015	0.04	1800.
DATA GEN CORP	0.4	0.0050	0.043	0.11	800.
DE LUXE CHECK PRINTERS	0.3	0.0001	0.022	0.05	1300.
DENNYS INC	0.2	0.0081	0.026	0.06	1400.
DIGITAL EQUIP CORP	0.7	0.0039	0.035	0.09	1600.
DOVER CORP	0.3	0.0011	0.013	0.03	6000.
DRAVO CORP	0.4	0.0023	0.023	0.06	1500.
DRESSER INDS INC	0.4	0.0005	0.008	0.02	1000.
DU PONT E I DE NEMOURS	0.5	-0.0008	-0.011	-0.03	1500.
EASTMAN KODAK CO	1.6	-0.0002	0.017	0.04	3600.
EMERY AIR FGHT CORP	0.6	-0.0040	0.051	0.13	3200.
EXXON CORP	2.7	-0.0023	-0.037	-0.09	6000.
FIRST BK SYS INC	0.5	-0.0011	0.031	0.08	1400.
FIRST CITY BANCORP TEX	0.4	-0.0002	0.034	0.08	1400.
FIRST INTL BANCSHARES	0.8	-0.0002	0.031	0.08	1400.
FLORIDA PWR & LT CO	0.6	-0.0031	0.005	0.01	3600.
FLUOR CORP	0.6	-0.0059	0.048	0.12	3600.
FORD MTR CO DEL	2.2	-0.0003	0.022	0.05	6300.

Table S4.4 (continued)

JOHN HANCOCK INSURANCE

CONTRIBUTIONS OF INDIVIDUAL ASSETS TO PORTFOLIO RISK

NAME	PERCENT OF PORTFOLIO VALUE	EFFECT OF 1% PURCHASE ON BETA	EFFECT OF 1% PURCHASE ON RESID. STDEV	REQUIRED ALPHA	NUMBER OF SHARES
GENERAL DYNAMICS CORP	0.7	0.0056	0.037	0.09	2500.
GENERAL ELEC CO	0.8	-0.0004	-0.016	-0.04	1900.
GENERAL FOODS CORP	1.0	-0.0011	0.024	0.06	3800.
GENERAL MTRS CORP	3.9	-0.0013	0.015	0.04	8400.
GENERAL TEL & ELECTRO	0.8	-0.0034	-0.002	-0.00	3500.
GEORGIA PAC CORP	0.7	0.0008	0.016	0.04	3187.
GOODYEAR TIRE & RUBR	1.3	-0.0004	0.018	0.05	9800.
HALLIBURTON CO	0.9	-0.0014	0.023	0.06	1500.
HOUSTON INDS INC	0.4	-0.0015	0.004	0.01	1500.
HUGHES TOOL CO	0.5	-0.0053	0.036	0.09	1100.
INLAND STL CO	0.9	-0.0002	0.016	0.04	3100.
INTEL CORP	0.4	0.0091	0.039	0.10	1050.
INTERNATIONAL BUS MACH	6.2	-0.0015	0.002	0.00	10500.
INTERNATIONAL FLAV & FRA	0.3	-0.0001	0.016	0.04	1700.
JOHNSON & JOHNSON	1.0	-0.0014	0.018	0.05	1600.
K MART CORP	0.4	0.0024	0.011	0.03	1800.
KANSAS CITY PWR & LT CO	0.6	-0.0038	-0.002	-0.01	2600.
KELLOGG CO	0.4	-0.0018	0.011	0.03	2600.
KROGER CO	0.8	-0.0005	0.026	0.06	4200.
LILLY ELI & CO	0.7	-0.0006	0.015	0.04	1500.
M A COM INC	0.3	0.0063	0.030	0.07	1500.
MGIC INVT CORP	0.4	0.0093	0.061	0.15	1900.
MASCO CORP	0.4	0.0037	0.029	0.07	1800.
MCDONALDS CORP	0.5	0.0051	0.031	0.08	1400.
MCDONNELL DOUGLAS CORP	0.4	0.0042	0.024	0.06	1900.

MEAD CORP	0.5	0.0044	0.024	0.06	2400.
MELLON NATL CORP	1.0	-0.0007	0.038	0.09	4100.
MERCK & CO INC	0.7	-0.0008	0.006	0.00	900.
MIDDLE SOUTH UTILS INC	2.0	-0.0033	-0.001	-0.00	5600.
MINNESOTA MNG & MFG CO	2.0	-0.0003	0.024	0.06	4500.
MISSION INS GROUP INC	0.4	0.0072	0.059	0.15	1350.
MORGAN J P & CO INC	0.5	-0.0011	0.031	0.08	1200.
NCNB CORP	0.2	0.0019	0.030	0.00	2000.
NATIONAL STL CORP	0.4	-0.0015	0.012	0.03	1300.
NORTON SIMON INC	0.3	0.0016	0.012	0.03	2152.
OCEAN DRILLING & EXPL	0.3	0.0044	0.021	0.05	800.
OWENS ILL INC	0.9	-0.0007	0.021	0.05	5000.
PARKER HANNIFIN CORP	0.3	0.0015	0.012	0.03	1400.
PENNEY J C INC	0.3	-0.0035	0.007	0.02	1200.
PEPSICO INC	0.5	0.0009	0.010	0.03	2200.
PETRIE STORES CORP	0.3	0.0004	0.018	0.05	1100.
PFIZER INC	0.4	0.0006	0.009	0.02	1400.
PHELPS DODGE CORP	0.2	0.0039	0.007	0.02	1000.
PHILLIP MORRIS INC	2.0	-0.0029	-0.049	0.12	7400.
PHILLIPS PETE CO	2.0	-0.0010	0.032	0.08	6000.
PILLSBURY CO	0.7	0.0005	0.027	0.07	2200.
PROCTER & GAMBLE CO	0.4	-0.0027	0.002	0.08	600.
RAINIER BANCORPORATION	0.3	-0.0002	0.032	0.04	1200.
REVLON INC	0.4	0.0006	0.015	0.05	900.
REYNOLDS R J INDS INC	1.2	-0.0042	0.020	0.05	2400.
REYNOLDS METALS CO	0.7	0.0016	0.016	0.04	2400.
SAFECO CORP	0.2	0.0032	0.032	0.08	800.
ST PAUL COS INC	0.5	0.0057	0.039	0.10	1400.
SANTA FE INDS INC	1.3	0.0019	0.029	0.07	3600.
SCHLUMBERGER LTD	2.3	-0.0014	0.030	0.07	3500.

Table S4.4 (concluded)

JOHN HANCOCK INSURANCE

CONTRIBUTIONS OF INDIVIDUAL ASSETS TO PORTFOLIO RISK

NAME	PERCENT OF PORTFOLIO VALUE	EFFECT OF 1% PURCHASE ON BETA	EFFECT OF 1% PURCHASE ON RESID. STDEV	REQUIRED ALPHA	NUMBER OF SHARES
SEARS ROEBUCK & CO	1.0	0.0011	0.005	0.01	6100.
SERVICE MASTER INDS INC	0.2	0.0004	0.020	0.05	1000.
SPERRY RAND CORP	0.2	0.0013	0.005	0.01	500.
STANDARD BRANDS PAINT	0.3	0.0046	0.029	0.07	1400.
STANDARD OIL CO IND	0.9	-0.0022	-0.010	-0.02	1700.
STANDARD OIL CO OHIO	1.1	0.0008	0.044	0.11	2200.
TEXACO INC	0.6	-0.0022	-0.040	-0.10	2500.
TEXAS UTILS CO	0.9	-0.0021	0.007	0.02	5580.
THOMAS & BETTS CORP	0.5	0.0008	0.018	0.04	1500.
TRANS UN CORP	0.6	0.0014	0.025	0.06	2100.
UAL INC	0.2	0.0081	0.027	0.07	900.
UNION CAMP CORP	0.5	0.0007	0.016	0.04	1400.
UNION OIL CO CALIF	0.7	-0.0001	0.009	0.02	2200.
UNITED TECHNOLOGIES CP	0.5	0.0017	0.018	0.05	1500.
UNITED TELECOMMUN KANS	0.7	-0.0028	0.006	0.01	4500.
WALTER JIM CORP	0.6	0.0041	0.028	0.07	1900.
WARNER LAMBERT CO	0.4	0.0002	0.012	0.03	2200.
WELLS FARGO & CO	0.2	0.0000	0.030	0.08	1000.
WINN DIXIE STORES INC	0.3	-0.0011	0.014	0.04	1200.
YELLOW FGHT SYS INC	0.3	0.0054	0.032	0.08	1900.

Example 2

An example of the second approach is a pension account managed by
T. Rowe Price Associates.[7] Table S4.5 shows the front page of the PORCH
report. This portfolio's beta is substantially greater than that of the S&P 500,
while it has an annual residual standard deviation typical of pension portfolios.
The atypical statistics are the risk indices given at the bottom of the page. Two
indices, the immaturity and smallness index and the growth orientation index,
indicate that this portfolio is highly deviant from the S&P 500. In addition, the

Table S4.5
Summary Statistics for Example 2

```
            FUNDAMENTAL RISK MEASUREMENT SERVICE
                     PORTFOLIO ANALYSIS
                       T. ROWE PRICE

PORTFOLIO STATUS AS OF
  ANALYSIS CONDUCTED
  FRMS UPDATE AS OF
S&P500     IS THE MARKET PORTFOLIO


            1. SUMMARY MEASURES FOR COMMON EQUITY

A. PREDICTED SYSTEMATIC RISK COEFFICIENT {BETA}—NEXT 3 MONTHS      1.18
B. PREDICTED SYSTEMATIC RISK COEFFIEICNT {BETA}—NEXT 5 YEARS       1.15
C. ANNUAL STANDARD DEVIATION OF SYSTEMATIC PORTFOLIO RETURN      24.52%
D. FRMS FORECAST STANDARD DEVIATION OF ANNUAL S&P500 RETURN      20.80%

    PORTFOLIO RISK FORECAST, INCLUDING EXTRA-MARKET COVARIANCE . . .

E.1  STANDARD DEVIATION OF ANNUAL PORTFOLIO RETURN                25.15%
E.2  STANDARD DEVIATION OF ANNUAL PORTFOLIO RESIDUAL RETURN        5.57%
E.3  COEFFICIENT OF DETERMINATION BY S&P500           0.951
E.4  REQUIRED ANNUAL PORTFOLIO APPRAISAL PREMIUM {ALPHA}           0.43%
E.5  INFERRED COVENANT INFORMATION RATIO {CIR}        0.077
E.6  INFERRED CEER OF ACTIVE MANAGEMENT               0.215

    RISK FORECASTS BASED UPON A SIMULATED 5-YEAR HISTORY OF MONTHLY
    RETURNS FOR THE PORTFOLIO . . .

F.1  STANDARD DEVIATION OF ANNUAL PORTFOLIO RETURN                25.63%
F.2  STANDARD DEVIATION OF ANNUAL PORTFOLIO RESIDUAL RETURN        4.82%
F.3  COEFFICIENT OF DETERMINATION BY S&P500           0.965

            2. INDICES OF RISK IN THE PORTFOLIO
```

| | | | FIRMS | EFFECT OF 0.01 INCREASE ON | REQUIRED |
INDEX OF RISK	PORTFOLIO	S&P500	UNIVERSE	RESID. STDEV	ALPHA
MARKET VARIABILITY	0.433	0.0	0.187	0.0094	0.08
EARNINGS VARIABILITY	0.037	0.0	0.232	0.0032	0.03
LOW VALUATION, UNSUCCESS	-0.166	0.0	-0.031	0.0052	0.04
IMMATURITY AND SMALLNESS	1.169	0.0	0.634	0.0224	0.19
GROWTH ORIENTATION	0.868	0.0	0.158	0.0141	0.12
FINANCIAL RISK	-0.266	0.0	0.143	0.0080	0.07

[7]T. Rowe Price Associates, Inc., 100 East Pratt Street, Baltimore, Maryland 21202. Thanks
are due to Jon Greene for providing this example.

market variability and financial risk indices demonstrate that the portfolio is also exposed to these factors. The portfolio is neutral only on the earnings variability index. The actual breakdown of risk, given in Table S4.6, is again in line with our supposition as to the strategy. The variance which arises from the exposure to the factors contributes the major part of the residual risk; a smaller contribution is made by the specific risk. This is due in part to the atypical group of companies which form the portfolio.

The industry variance is insubstantial, which is perhaps a little nonintuitive once the industry group investments are analyzed. The holdings, given in Table S4.7, show that two industries have holdings which greatly exceed the S&P 500 weights, while several other industries have differences in holdings of 2 percent or 3 percent. These holdings do not contribute to a greater amount of industry variance because industry risk is much less severe than most practitioners realize, so that it is possible to take quite extreme positions without increasing the residual risk substantially. Further, the "producer goods" industry is one of the least risky industries, so the holding in this industry contributes less than may be supposed to industry risk.[8]

Table S4.8 shows the asset holdings in the portfolio. There are 56 common stocks, in addition to a holding in the New Horizons Fund, a mutual fund managed by T. Rowe Price Associates.

Table S4.6
Decomposition of Risk for Example 2

	DECOMPOSITION OF VARIANCE OF ANNUAL PERCENT RETURN FRMS MODEL		SIMULATION	PREDICTION
SYSTEMATIC		601·4	633·8	601·4
SPECIFIC		10·2		
RISK INDICES VARIANCE	25·3			
INDUSTRY VARIANCE	4·6			
R.I.-INDUSTRY COVARIANCE	-1·3			
XMC		28·7		
RESIDUAL			38·8	23·3	31·0
TOTAL		640·3	657·1	632·5

---

[8]See Barr Rosenberg and Vinay Marathe, "Common Factors in Security Returns: Microeconomic Determinants and Macroeconomic Correlates," *Proceedings of the Seminar on the Analysis of Security Prices,* University of Chicago, May 1976, pp. 61–115.

Table S4.7
Industry Group Investments for Example 2

T. ROWE PRICE

CONTRIBUTIONS OF INDUSTRY GROUP INVESTMENTS TO PORTFOLIO RISK

INDUSTRY	PORT.	PERCENT OF VALUE IN S&P500	FRMSU	AVERAGE BETA OF HOLDINGS IN INDUSTRY
1. NONFERROUS METALS	2.0	2.0	2.4	1.18
2. ENERGY RAW MATERIALS	11.3	2.9	4.5	1.17
3. CONSTRUCTION	3.7	1.5	1.9	1.28
4. AGRICULTURE, FOOD	8.5	4.8	4.2	1.02
5. LIQUOR	0.0	0.7	0.7	0.0
6. TOBACCO	1.8	1.3	0.9	0.71
7. APPAREL	0.2	0.7	0.9	0.0
8. FOREST PRODUCTS, PAPER	2.5	2.7	2.2	1.05
9. CONTAINERS	0.0	0.2	0.2	0.0
10. MEDIA	0.4	2.0	2.1	0.0
11. CHEMICALS	2.7	3.2	3.1	1.21
12. DRUGS, MEDICINE	9.0	5.3	4.0	1.09
13. SOAPS, COSMETICS	0.0	2.8	1.8	0.0
14. DOMESTIC OIL	4.3	6.9	7.1	0.87
15. INTERNATIONAL OIL	0.0	9.4	6.5	0.0
16. TIRES, RUBBER GOODS	0.1	0.3	0.3	0.0
17. STEEL	0.0	0.8	1.1	0.0
18. PRODUCER GOODS	10.5	4.3	4.8	1.40
19. BUSINESS MACHINES	7.0	8.8	5.9	0.85
20. CONSUMER DURABLES	0.0	0.8	1.4	0.0
21. MOTOR VEHICLES	0.1	4.5	3.6	0.0
22. AEROSPACE	0.0	0.9	0.7	0.0
23. ELECTRONICS	7.2	2.5	2.1	1.29
24. PHOTOGRAPHIC, OPTICAL	0.0	1.5	1.0	0.0
25. NONDURBLS, ENTERTNMNT	0.3	0.6	0.7	0.0
26. TRUCKING, FREIGHT	1.5	0.2	0.3	1.39
27. RAILROADS, SHIPPING	0.0	1.7	1.4	0.0
28. AIR TRANSPORT	0.0	0.5	1.6	0.0
29. TELEPHONE	0.0	6.7	5.1	0.0
30. ENERGY, UTILITIES	0.0	5.7	6.7	0.0
31. RETAIL, GENERAL	6.1	2.6	2.4	1.32
32. BANKS	5.9	2.7	3.6	1.02
33. MISCELLANEOUS FINANCE	0.2	1.2	1.3	0.0
34. INSURANCE	6.2	2.4	3.0	1.54
35. REAL PROPERTY	0.0	0.1	0.5	0.0
36. BUSINESS SERVICES	5.8	0.0	0.8	1.23
37. TRAVEL, OUTDR RECREATN	0.0	0.3	0.4	0.0
38. GOLD MNG & SECURITIES	0.0	0.2	0.7	0.0
39. MISC. CONGLOMRTE	2.5	4.3	8.1	0.97

Table S4.8
Asset Holdings for Example 2

CONTRIBUTIONS OF INDIVIDUAL ASSETS TO PORTFOLIO RISK

NAME	PERCENT OF PORTFOLIO VALUE	EFFECT OF 1% PURCHASE ON BETA	EFFECT OF 1% PURCHASE ON RESID. STDEV	REQUIRED ALPHA	NUMBER OF SHARES
NEW HORIZONS FUND	7.8	0.0016	0.080	0.69	511627.
AMERICAN HOSP SUPPLY	2.0	0.0005	0.062	0.53	46900.
AMERICAN INTL GROUP	1.9	0.0051	0.102	0.88	24500.
AMP INC	1.2	-0.0004	-0.069	-0.60	22600.
ATLANTIC RICHFIELD CO	2.2	-0.0034	-0.066	-0.57	23000.
BAKER INTL CORP	1.5	0.0001	0.039	0.34	25000.
BAXTER TRAVENOL LABS	2.1	0.0007	0.069	0.60	35000.
BEARINGS INC	1.5	0.0019	0.063	0.55	30000.
BLOCK H & R INC	1.6	-0.0009	0.062	0.54	46000.
CITICORP	2.0	-0.0028	-0.079	-0.68	54000.
CITIZENS & SOU N B SAVAN	0.6	0.0012	0.028	0.25	67000.
COCA COLA CO	2.5	-0.0039	-0.033	-0.29	45900.
COMBINED INS CO AMER	1.5	-0.0026	0.074	0.64	50000.
DAYTON HUDSON CORP	1.5	0.0013	0.044	0.38	27000.
DEKALB AGRESEARCH INC	0.9	0.0003	0.043	0.37	21000.
DE LUXE CHECK PRINTERS'	1.2	-0.0016	0.052	0.45	27500.
ECKERD JACK CORP	2.0	-0.0009	0.065	0.56	48000.
ECONOMICS LAB INC	1.1	-0.0008	0.038	0.33	36000.
ELECTRONIC DATA SYS CP	1.5	0.0008	0.061	0.52	42500.
FARMERS GROUP INC	2.1	0.0028	0.099	0.86	60000.
GEARHART OWEN INDS INC	1.8	0.0032	0.085	0.73	30000.
GENERAL REINS CORP DEL	0.7	0.0040	0.089	0.77	6000.
GENERAL SIGNAL CORP	1.5	0.0010	0.083	0.71	33000.
GEORGIA PAC CORP	1.2	-0.0010	-0.008	-0.07	30002.
GRAINGER W W INC	1.0	-0.0014	-0.032	0.28	20000.
HALLIBURTON CO	1.8	-0.0004	0.000	0.00	18500.

HELMERICH & PAYNE INC	1.6	-0.0007	0.044	0.38	20000.
HEWLETT PACKARD CO	1.4	0.0005	0.034	0.29	9900.
INTERNATIONAL BUS MACH	6.0	-0.0033	-0.006	-0.05	56700.
JOHNSON & JOHNSON	1.6	-0.0031	-0.000	0.00	15000.
K MART CORP	2.7	-0.0006	-0.034	-0.29	70000.
LEASEWAY TRANSN CORP	1.2	0.0022	0.007	0.06	40225.
LOWES COS INC	1.0	0.0037	0.088	0.76	41500.
MARLEY CO	1.0	0.0032	0.062	0.53	30000.
MEDTRONIC INC	2.1	0.0044	0.091	0.79	34000.
MERCK & CO INC	1.3	-0.0026	-0.008	-0.07	13200.
MINNESOTA MNG & MFG CO	2.0	-0.0021	-0.011	-0.10	24000.
MORGAN J P & CO INC	1.7	0.0028	0.064	0.55	24700.
MOTOROLA INC	0.9	0.0030	0.072	0.62	136000.
NCNB CORP	1.3	0.0002	0.022	0.19	65200.
NABISCO INC	1.5	0.0035	0.004	0.03	45000.
NALCO CHEM CO	1.2	-0.0001	0.018	0.16	25000.
OCEAN DRILLING & EXPL	1.4	0.0027	0.050	0.43	20300.
PHH GROUP INC	1.2	0.0042	0.126	1.09	46000.
PEPSICO INC	1.6	0.0009	0.006	0.06	45000.
PHILIP MORRIS INC	1.8	-0.0047	-0.013	-0.12	36000.
PHILLIPS PETE CO	2.1	0.0027	0.063	0.55	38000.
RELIANCE ELEC CO	2.2	0.0042	0.050	0.43	25000.
ST JOE MINERALS CORP	2.0	0.0000	0.041	0.36	45000.
SCHLUMBERGER LTD	2.9	-0.0032	-0.032	-0.28	27375.
SOUTHLAND RTY CO	1.3	0.0002	0.049	0.43	24000.
SQUARE D CO	1.6	-0.0011	0.017	0.15	50000.
STANDARD BRANDS PAINT	1.3	0.0028	0.078	0.67	41000.
SUN BKS FLA INC	0.4	-0.0001	-0.010	-0.09	20000.
TEXAS INSTRS INC	1.8	-0.0011	0.061	0.53	14000.
WEYERHAEUSER CO	1.2	0.0018	0.021	0.18	29000.
WILLIAM COS	1.9	0.0015	0.049	0.42	65000.

Example 3

Our final example is the Performance Investment Fund at American National Bank.[9] Table S4.9 shows the first page of the PORCH report, and again the beta is substantially different from one. In this case, the beta is 1.29. However, because the bank views active management as part of the total management of both active and passive portfolios, the active portfolio beta is irrelevant to the construction technique. Item E.2 shows that the residual standard deviation at 11.98 percent is much greater than is typical for institutional portfolios. Where does this incredible amount of risk arise? The risk indices at the bottom of the report show that the portfolio is most exposed to the immaturity and smallness factor, as was the T. Rowe Price portfolio. However, the low valuation and

Table S4.9
Summary Statistics for Example 3

```
FUNDAMENTAL RISK MEASUREMENT SERVICE
           PORTFOLIO ANALYSIS
         AMERICAN NATIONAL BANK
             TOTAL PORTFOLIO
```

```
PORTFOLIO STATUS AS OF    OCTOBER 26 1979
    ANALYSIS CONDUCTED    OCTOBER 29 1979
    FRMS UPDATE AS OF     SEPTEMBER 28 1979
S&P500     IS THE MARKET PORTFOLIO
```

1. SUMMARY MEASURES FOR COMMON EQUITY

A. PREDICTED SYSTEMATIC RISK COEFFICIENT {BETA}—NEXT 3 MONTHS	1.29
B. PREDICTED SYSTEMATIC RISK COEFFICIENT {BETA}—NEXT 5 YEARS	1.27
C. ANNUAL STANDARD DEVIATION OF SYSTEMATIC PORTFOLIO RETURN	27.27%
D. FRMS FORECAST STANDARD DEVIATION OF ANNUAL S&P500 RETURN	21.13%

PORTFOLIO RISK FORECAST, INCLUDING EXTRA-MARKET COVARIANCE . . .

E.1	STANDARD DEVIATION OF ANNUAL PORTFOLIO RETURN		29.78%
E.2	STANDARD DEVIATION OF ANNUAL PORTFOLIO RESIDUAL RETURN		11.98%
E.3	COEFFICIENT OF DETERMINATION BY S&P500	0.838	
E.4	REQUIRED ANNUAL PORTFOLIO APPRAISAL PREMIUM {ALPHA}		1.93%
E.5	INFERRED COVENANT INFORMATION RATIO {CIR}	0.161	
E.6	INFERRED CEER OF ACTIVE MANAGEMENT	0.964%	

2. INDICES OF RISK IN THE PORTFOLIO

INDEX OF RISK	PORTFOLIO	S&P500	FRMS UNIVERSE	EFFECT OF 0.01 INCREASE ON RESID. SIDEV	REQUIRED ALPHA
MARKET VARIABILITY	0.520	0.0	0.185	0.0080	0.13
EARNINGS VARIABILITY	0.501	0.0	0.302	0.0082	0.13
LOW VALUATION, UNSUCCESS	−0.225	0.0	−0.018	0.0182	0.29
IMMATURITY AND SMALLNESS	2.396	0.0	0.619	0.0322	0.52
GROWTH ORIENTATION	0.403	0.0	0.181	0.0033	0.05
FINANCIAL RISK	−0.206	0.0	0.112	0.0123	0.20

---

[9]American National Bank and Trust Company of Chicago, 33 North La Salle Street, Chicago, Illinois 60690. We thank Hal Arbit for letting us use this portfolio as an example.

unsuccess risk index is much less than that of the T. Towe Price portfolio, as is the growth orientation index. Notice that the immaturity and smallness index is almost exactly twice that of the T. Rowe Price portfolio. In other words, this portfolio earns and loses twice as much as the preceding portfolio from exposure to the factor. (See Figure 3.2 for a diagram of this effect.)

The decomposition of risk is given in Table S4.10, which shows that the residual risk arises from *XMC* and specific risk in proportions of almost five to one, while *XMC* arises almost entirely from the risk index exposure. Since the specific risk is large, we may expect to see some substantial active asset holdings in this portfolio.

The industry and asset holdings are given in Tables S4.11 and S4.12. Almost 60 percent of the portfolio is invested in four industries, in which there are substantial positive active holdings. Almost as important, there are some significant negative active holdings in the international oil, business machines, and telephone groups. The list of individual assets is also interesting. The investment weights are 2.0 percent, 2.3 percent, or 5.1 percent of the portfolio; hence, most assets have large active holdings. Only one asset, Ashland Oil, is diversifying, the others being concentrating assets. Since the portfolio is structured in this rather specialized manner, we can be fairly certain that some common elements were used to establish the desired strategy. The asset weights reflect the employment of investment "ideas" or "themes" that cut across the traditional industry lines, in which the individual securities are in fact "interchangeable parts" that are used to gain exposure to the particular strategic factor.

In fact, this portfolio combines three strategies. These are: (*a*) stock-picking, (*b*) a strategy based on advertising expenditures, and (*c*) a strategy based on selecting companies that repurchase their own shares. These three strategies are analyzed in the next nine tables, which show for each strategy the front page of a PORCH analysis, the decomposition of risk, and the list of assets.

As can be seen in Table S4.15, there are four equally weighted issues in the stock-picking strategy. As is to be expected, the portfolio taken by itself is extremely risky, with specific risk being the largest component of residual var-

Table S4.10
Decomposition of Risk for Example 3

		DECOMPOSITION OF VARIANCE OF ANNUAL PERCENT RETURN		
		FRMS MODEL	SIMULATION	PREDICTION
SYSTEMATIC			743·6	743·6
SPECIFIC		25·8		
RISK INDICES VARIANCE	90·7			
INDUSTRY VARIANCE	16·2			
R.I.-INDUSTRY COVARIANCE	10·9			
XMC		117·7		
RESIDUAL			143·5	143·5
TOTAL			887·1	887·1

Table S4.11
Industry Group Investments for Example 3

AMERICAN NATIONAL BANK
TOTAL PORTFOLIO

CONTRIBUTION OF INDUSTRY GROUP INVESTMENTS TO PORTFOLIO RISK

		PERCENT OF VALUE IN			AVERAGE BETA OF HOLDINGS IN
	INDUSTRY	PORT.	S&P500	FRMSU	INDUSTRY
1.	NONFERROUS METALS	0.0	2.0	2.4	0.0
2.	ENERGY RAW MATERIALS	0.0	3.1	4.7	0.0
3.	CONSTRUCTION	2.0	1.5	1.9	1.16
4.	AGRICULTURE, FOOD	4.1	4.7	4.2	0.96
5.	LIQUOR	0.0	0.8	0.7	0.0
6.	TOBACCO	0.0	1.3	0.9	0.0
7.	APPAREL	4.1	0.7	0.9	1.06
8.	FOREST PRODUCTS, PAPER	10.7	2.7	2.2	1.29
9.	CONTAINERS	5.1	0.2	0.2	1.22
10.	MEDIA	22.7	2.2	2.1	1.34
11.	CHEMICALS	0.0	3.6	3.1	0.0
12.	DRUGS, MEDICINE	0.0	5.3	4.0	0.0
13.	SOAPS, COSMETICS	0.0	2.7	1.8	0.0
14.	DOMESTIC OIL	2.0	7.5	7.7	1.19
15.	INTERNATIONAL OIL	0.0	10.1	6.8	0.0
16.	TIRES, RUBBER GOODS	0.0	0.3	0.3	0.0
17.	STEEL	0.0	0.9	1.3	0.0
18.	PRODUCER GOODS	10.2	3.8	4.5	1.24
19.	BUSINESS MACHINES	0.0	7.9	5.3	0.0
20.	CONSUMER DURABLES	2.0	0.7	1.2	1.22
21.	MOTOR VEHICLES	0.0	4.4	3.4	0.0
22.	AEROSPACE	2.0	0.8	0.6	1.12
23.	ELECTRONICS	4.5	2.1	1.9	1.63
24.	PHOTOGRAPHIC, OPTICAL	0.0	1.3	0.9	0.0
25.	NON-DURABLES, ENTERTNMNT	0.0	0.6	0.7	0.0
26.	TRUCKING, FREIGHT	2.0	0.2	0.2	1.45
27.	RAILROADS, SHIPPING	0.0	1.7	1.4	0.0
28.	AIR TRANSPORT	5.1	0.4	1.5	1.57
29.	TELEPHONE	0.0	6.2	4.6	0.0
30.	ENERGY, UTILITIES	0.0	5.4	6.4	0.0
31.	RETAIL, GENERAL	0.0	2.5	2.4	0.0
32.	BANKS	0.0	2.5	3.5	0.0
33.	MISCELLANEOUS FINANCE	0.0	1.1	1.2	0.0
34.	INSURANCE	4.1	2.3	2.9	1.31
35.	REAL PROPERTY	2.0	0.1	0.4	2.00
36.	BUSINESS SERVICES	15.2	0.0	0.9	1.17
37.	TRAVEL, OUTDR RECREATN	0.0	0.3	0.3	0.0
38.	GOLD MNG & SECURITIES	0.0	0.3	0.9	0.0
39.	MISC. CONGLOMRTE	2.0	5.8	9.9	1.32

Table S4.12
Asset Holdings for Example 3

AMERICAN NATIONAL BANK
TOTAL PORTFOLIO

CONTRIBUTIONS OF INDIVIDUAL ASSETS TO PORTFOLIO RISK

	CUSIP	NAME	PERCENT OF PORTFOLIO VALUE	EFFECT OF 1% PURCHASE ON BETA	EFFECT OF 1% PURCHASE ON RESID. SIDEV	REQUIRED ALPHA
1.	02473510	AMERICAN BROADCASTING	2.3	0.0012	0.051	0.82
2.	02608710	AMERICAN FINL CORP OM	2.0	0.0006	0.102	1.65
3.	03208710	AMPEX CORP	2.3	-0.0018	-0.109	1.75
4.	04454010	ASHLAND OIL INC	2.0	-0.0010	-0.037	-0.60
5.	08143710	BEMIS INC	2.0	-0.0026	-0.030	-0.48
6.	09281510	BLAIR JOHN & CO	2.3	0.0018	0.144	2.32
7.	12484510	CBS INC	2.3	-0.0015	0.036	0.58
8.	13986110	CAPITAL CITIES COMMUN	2.3	-0.0006	0.065	1.04
9.	20010110	COMBINED COMMUNICATION				
10.	20975910	CONSOLIDATED PAPERS	2.3	-0.0020	0.030	0.49
11.	22400310	COX BROADCASTING CORP	2.3	0.0002	0.065	1.04
12.	23102110	CUMMINS ENGINE INC	5.1	-0.0001	0.071	1.14
13.	25786710	DONNELLEY R R & SONS	2.3	-0.0028	0.039	0.63
14.	43916100	HOOVER UNVL INC	5.1	-0.0009	0.077	1.24
15.	46069010	INTERPUBLIC GROUP COS	2.3	-0.0018	0.104	1.68
16.	47024510	JAMES FRED S & CO INC	2.0	-0.0002	0.031	0.50
17.	48815210	KELLY SVCS INC	2.0	-0.0001	0.113	1.82
18.	54229010	LONE STAR INDS INC	2.0	-0.0013	0.037	0.60
19.	55430710	MACDONALD E F CO	2.3	-0.0001	0.161	2.58
20.	58943310	MEREDITH CORP	2.3	-0.0002	0.087	1.40

continued

Table S4.12 (concluded)

AMERICAN NATIONAL BANK
TOTAL PORTFOLIO

CONTRIBUTIONS OF INDIVIDUAL ASSETS TO PORTFOLIO RISK

	CUSIP	NAME	PERCENT OF PORTFOLIO VALUE	EFFECT OF 1% PURCHASE ON BETA	EFFECT OF 1% PURCHASE ON RESID. SIDEV	REQUIRED ALPHA
21.	59169010	METROMEDIA INC	2.3	-0.0029	0.091	1.46
22.	63765710	NATIONAL SVC INDS INC	2.0	-0.0026	0.039	0.62
23.	65142710	NEWHALL LD & FARMING	2.0	-0.0023	0.022	0.35
24.	66728110	NORTHWEST AIRLS INC	5.1	-0.0028	0.082	1.31
25.	67660110	OGILVY & MATHER INTL	2.3	-0.0001	0.086	1.39
26.	69882210	PAPERCRAFT CORP	2.0	-0.0014	0.092	1.47
27.	70963110	PENTAIR INC	2.3	-0.0038	0.151	2.42
28.	76168610	REXHAM CORP	5.1	-0.0007	0.160	2.58
29.	77667810	ROPER CORP	2.0	-0.0007	0.100	1.60
30.	81947010	SHAPELL INDS INC	2.0	-0.0071	0.132	2.12
31.	86213110	STORER BROADCASTING CO	2.3	-0.0001	0.056	0.90
32.	87363510	TAFT BROADCASTING CO	2.3	-0.0015	0.077	1.25
33.	88475310	THOMPSON J WALTER CO	2.3	-0.0014	0.104	1.67
34.	88722410	TIME INC	2.3	-0.0001	0.053	0.86
35.	89589510	TRIANGLE PAC CORP	2.0	0.0020	0.136	2.18
36.	91207810	U S INDS INC	2.0	-0.0026	0.053	0.86
37.	91301710	UNITED TECHNOLOGIES CP	2.0	-0.0017	0.052	0.84
38.	92227210	VARO INC	2.0	-0.0051	0.214	3.44
39.	95546510	WEST POINT PEPPERELL	2.0	-0.0020	0.053	0.85
40.	96289820	WHEELABRATOR FRYE INC	2.0	-0.0003	0.087	1.41
41.	97428010	WINN DIXIE STORES INC	2.0	-0.0043	0.018	0.29
42.	98551410	YELLOW FGHT SYS INC	2.0	0.0016	0.069	1.10

Table S4.13
Summary Statistics for Example 3, Strategy A

```
FUNDAMENTAL RISK MEASUREMENT SERVICE
            PORTFOLIO ANALYSIS
          AMERICAN NATIONAL BANK
             INDIVIDUAL ISSUES
```

```
PORTFOLIO STATUS AS OF   OCTOBER 26 1979
  ANALYSIS CONDUCTED     OCTOBER 29 1979
  FRMS UPDATE AS OF    SEPTEMBER 28 1979
S&P500    IS THE MARKET PORTFOLIO
```

1. SUMMARY MEASURES FOR COMMON EQUITY

A.	PREDICTED SYSTEMATIC RISK COEFFICIENT {BETA}—NEXT 3 MONTHS	1·32
B.	PREDICTED SYSTEMATIC RISK COEFFICIENT {BETA}—NEXT 5 YEARS	1·29
C.	ANNUAL STANDARD DEVIATION OF SYSTEMATIC PORTFOLIO RETURN	27·85%
D.	FRMS FORECAST STANDARD DEVIATION OF ANNUAL S&P500 RETURN	21·13%

PORTFOLIO RISK FORECAST, INCLUDING EXTRA-MARKET COVARIANCE · · ·

E·1	STANDARD DEVIATION OF ANNUAL PORTFOLIO RETURN		33·58%
E·2	STANDARD DEVIATION OF ANNUAL PORTFOLIO RESIDUAL RETURN		18·78%
E·3	COEFFICIENT OF DETERMINATION BY S&P500	0·687	
E·4	REQUIRED ANNUAL PORTFOLIO APPRAISAL PREMIUM {ALPHA}		4·74%
E·5	INFERRED COVENANT INFORMATION RATIO {CIR}	0·252	
E·6	INFERRED CEER OF ACTIVE MANAGEMENT	2·368%	

2. INDICES OF RISK IN THE PORTFOLIO

INDEX OF RISK	PORTFOLIO	S&P500	FRMS UNIVERSE	EFFECT OF 0·01 INCREASE ON RESID· STDEV	REQUIRED ALPHA
MARKET VARIABILITY	0·515	0·0	0·185	0·0042	0·11
EARNINGS VARIABILITY	0·513	0·0	0·302	0·0065	0·17
LOW VALUATION, UNSUCCESS	0·288	0·0	−0·018	0·0164	0·41
IMMATURITY AND SMALLNESS	2·186	0·0	0·619	0·0208	0·53
GROWTH ORIENTATION	0·314	0·0	0·181	−0·0025	−0·06
FINANCIAL RISK	−0·124	0·0	0·112	0·0087	0·22

Table S4.14
Decomposition of Risk for Example 3, Strategy A

DECOMPOSITION OF VARIANCE OF ANNUAL PERCENT RETURN	FRMS MODEL		SIMULATION	PREDICTION
SYSTEMATIC			775·4	775·4
SPECIFIC		191·4		
RISK INDICES VARIANCE	100·9			
INDUSTRY VARIANCE	59·5			
R·I·-INDUSTRY COVARIANCE	0·8			

XMC		161·2		

RESIDUAL			352·5	352·5
			------	------
TOTAL			1127·9	1127·9

Table S4.15
Asset Holdings for Example 3, Strategy A

AMERICAN NATIONAL BANK
INDIVIDUAL ISSUES

CONTRIBUTIONS OF INDIVIDUAL ASSETS TO PORTFOLIO RISK

CUSIP	NAME	PERCENT OF PORTFOLIO VALUE	EFFECT OF 1% PURCHASE ON BETA	EFFECT OF 1% PURCHASE ON RESID. STDEV	REQUIRED ALPHA
1. 23102110	CUMMIN ENGINE INC	25.0	-0.0004	0.122	3.09
2. 43931610	HOOVER UNVL INC	25.0	-0.0012	0.123	3.11
3. 66728110	NORTHWEST AIRLS INC	25.0	-0.0025	0.200	5.05
4. 76168610	REXHAM CORP	25.0	-0.0009	0.199	5.03

Table S4.16
Summary Statistics for Example 3, Strategy B

FUNDAMENTAL RISK MEASUREMENT SERVICE
PORTFOLIO ANALYSIS
AMERICAN NATIONAL BANK
ADVERTISING

```
PORTFOLIO STATUS AS OF    OCTOBER 26 1979
   ANALYSIS CONDUCTED     OCTOBER 26 1979
   FRMS UPDATA AS OF    SEPTEMBER 28 1979
S&P500    IS THE MARKET PORTFOLIO
```

1. SUMMARY MEASURES FOR COMMON EQUITY

A.	PREDICTED SYSTEMATIC RISK COEFFICIENT {BETA}—NEXT 3 MONTHS	1.31
B.	PREDICTED SYSTEMATIC RISK COEFFICIENT {BETA}—NEXT 5 YEARS	1.28
C.	ANNUAL STANDARD DEVIATION OF SYSTEMATIC PORTFOLIO RETURN	27.61%
D.	FRMS FORECAST STANDARD DEVIATION OF ANNUAL S&P500 RETURN	21.13%

PORTFOLIO RISK FORECAST, INCLUDING EXTRA-MARKET COVARIANCE . . .

E.1	STANDARD DEVIATION OF ANNUAL PORTFOLIO RETURN		30.74%
E.2	STANDARD DEVIATION OF ANNUAL PORTFOLIO RESIDUAL RETURN		13.51%
E.3	COEFFICIENT OF DETERMINATION BY S&P500	0.807	
E.4	REQUIRED ANNUAL PORTFOLIO APPRAISAL PREMIUM {ALPHA}		2.45%
E.5	INFERRED COVENANT INFORMATION RATIO {CIP}	0.181	
E.6	INFERRED CEER OF ACTIVE MANAGEMENT	1.226%	

2. INDICES OF RISK IN THE PORTFOLIO

INDEX OF RISK	PORTFOLIO	S&P500	FRMS UNIVERSE	EFFECT OF 0.01 INCREASE ON RESID. STDEV	REQUIRED ALPHA
MARKET VARIABILITY	0.556	0.0	0.185	0.0068	0.12
EARNINGS VARIABILITY	0.522	0.0	0.302	0.0061	0.11
LOW VALUATION, UNSUCCESS	−0.630	0.0	−0.018	0.0112	0.20
IMMATURITY AND SMALLNESS	2.388	0.0	0.619	0.0278	0.60
GROWTH ORIENTATION	0.582	0.0	0.181	0.0082	0.15
FINANCIAL RISK	−0.238	0.0	0.112	0.0100	0.18

Table S4.17
Decomposition of Risk for Example 3, Strategy B

DECOMPOSITION OF VARIANCE OF ANNUAL PERCENT RETURN

	FRMS MODEL	SIMULATION	PREDICTION
SYSTEMATIC		762.4	762.4
SPECIFIC	46.7		
RISK INDICES VARIANCE	77.9		
INDUSTRY VARIANCE	28.0		
R.I.–INDUSTRY COVARIANCE	30.0		

XMC	135.9		

RESIDUAL		182.5	182.5
		-----	-----
TOTAL		944.9	944.9

Table S4.18
Asset Holdings for Example 3, Strategy B

AMERICAN NATIONAL BANK
ADVERTISING

CONTRIBUTIONS OF INDIVIDUAL ASSETS TO PORTFOLIO RISK

	CUSIP	NAME	PERCENT OF PORTFOLIO VALUE	EFFECT OF 1% PURCHASE ON BETA	EFFECT OF 1% PURCHASE ON RESID. STDEV	REQUIRED ALPHA
1.	02473510	AMERICAN BROADCASTING	5.9	0.0010	0.084	1.53
2.	03208710	AMPEX CORP	5.9	0.0016	0.129	2.35
3.	09281510	BLAIR JOHN & CO	5.9	0.0016	0.160	2.91
4.	12484510	CBS INC	5.9	-0.0016	0.057	1.04
5.	13986110	CAPITAL CITIES COMMUN	5.9	-0.0007	0.099	1.80
6.	20010110	COMBINED COMMUNICATION	5.9	-0.0022	0.035	0.64
7.	20975910	CONSOLIDATED PAPERS	5.9	-0.0000	0.098	1.78
8.	22400310	COX BROADCASTING CORP	5.9	-0.0030	0.056	1.02
9.	25786710	DONNELLEY R R & SONS	5.9	-0.0020	0.117	2.11
10.	46069010	INTERPUBLIC GROUP COS				
11.	58943310	MEREDITH CORP	5.9	-0.0004	0.105	1.90
12.	59169010	METROMEDIA INC	5.9	-0.0027	0.117	2.12
13.	67660110	OGILVY & MATHER INTL	5.9	-0.0002	0.106	1.92
14.	70963110	PENTAIR INC	5.9	-0.0036	0.160	2.90
15.	86213110	STORER BROADCASTING CO	5.9	-0.0003	0.086	1.55
16.	87363510	TAFT BROADCASTING CO	5.9	0.0013	0.108	1.95
17.	88475310	THOMPSON J WALTER CO	5.9	-0.0015	0.117	2.11
18.	88722410	TIME INC	5.9	-0.0000	0.080	1.45

Table S4.19
Summary Statistics for Example 3, Strategy C

```
              FUNDAMENTAL RISK MEASUREMENT SERVICE
                      PORTFOLIO ANALYSIS
                    AMERICAN NATIONAL BANK
                      BUYBACK STRATEGY


    PORTFOLIO STATUS AS OF   OCTOBER 26 1979
    ANALYSIS CONDUCTED       OCTOBER 26 1979
    FRMS UPDATE AS OF      SEPTEMBER 28 1979
 S&P500    IS THE MARKET PORTFOLIO


           1. SUMMARY MEASURES FOR COMMON EQUITY

 A. PREDICTED SYSTEMATIC RISK COEFFICIENT {BETA}—NEXT 3 MONTHS       1.26
 B. PREDICTED SYSTEMATIC RISK COEFFICIENT {BETA}—NEXT 5 YEARS        1.24
 C. ANNUAL STANDARD DEVIATION OF SYSTEMATIC PORTFOLIO RETURN       26.66%
 D. FRMS FORECAST STANDARD DEVIATION OF ANNUAL S&P500 RETURN       21.13%

      PORTFOLIO RISK FORECAST, INCLUDING EXTRA-MARKET COVARIANCE . . .

 E.1   STANDARD DEVIATION OF ANNUAL PORTFOLIO RETURN                29.54%
 E.2   STANDARD DEVIATION OF ANNUAL PORTFOLIO RESIDUAL RETURN       12.74%
 E.3   COEFFICIENT OF DETERMINATION BY S&P500           0.814
 E.4   REQUIRED ANNUAL PORTFOLIO APPRAISAL PREMIUM {ALPHA}           2.18%
 E.5   INFERRED COVENANT INFORMATION RATIO {CIR}        0.171
 E.6   INFERRED CEER OF ACTIVE MANAGEMENT               1.090%


               2. INDICES OF RISK IN THE PORTFOLIO
```

| | | | | EFFECT OF 0.01 | |
| | | | FRMS | INCREASE ON | REQUIRED |
INDEX OF RISK	PORTFOLIO	S&P500	UNIVERSE	RESID. STDEV	ALPHA
MARKET VARIABILITY	0.490	0.0	0.185	0.0085	0.14
EARNINGS VARIABILITY	0.476	0.0	0.302	0.0078	0.13
LOW VALUATION, UNSUCCESS	−0.098	0.0	−0.018	0.0185	0.32
IMMATURITY AND SMALLNESS	2.509	0.0	0.619	0.0309	0.53
GROWTH ORIENTATION	0.278	0.0	0.181	0.0013	0.02
FINANCIAL RISK	−0.216	0.0	0.112	0.0117	0.20

Table S4.20
Decomposition of Risk for Example 3, Strategy C

| | DECOMPOSITION OF VARIANCE OF ANNUAL PERCENT RETURN | | | |
		FRMS MODEL	SIMULATION	PREDICTION
SYSTEMATIC			710.5	710.5
SPECIFIC		45.1		
RISK INDICES VARIANCE	103.0			
INDUSTRY VARIANCE	12.9			
R.I.-INDUSTRY COVARIANCE	1.3			

XMC		117.2		

RESIDUAL			162.3	162.3
			-----	-----
TOTAL			872.8	872.8

Table S4.21
Asset Holdings for Example 3, Strategy C

AMERICAN NATIONAL BANK
BUYBACK STRATEGY

CONTRIBUTIONS OF INDIVIDUAL ASSETS TO PORTFOLIO RISK

	CUSIP	NAME	PERCENT OF PORTFOLIO VALUE	EFFECT OF 1% PURCHASE ON BETA	EFFECT OF 1% PURCHASE ON RESID. STDEV	REQUIRED ALPHA
1.	02608710	AMERICAN FINL CORP OH	5.0	0.0009	0.127	2.18
2.	04454010	ASHLAND OIL INC	5.0	-0.0007	-0.012	-0.21
3.	08143710	REMIS INC	5.0	-0.0023	-0.047	-0.72
4.	47024510	JAMES FRED S & CO INC	5.0	-0.0001	0.047	0.81
5.	48815210	KELLY SVCS INC	5.0	0.0003	0.123	2.10
6.	54229010	LONE STAR INDS INC.	5.0	-0.0010	0.054	0.92
7.	55430710	MACDONALD E F CO	5.0	-0.0004	0.178	3.05
8.	63765710	NATIONAL SVC INDS INC	5.0	-0.0023	0.047	0.64
9.	65142710	NEWHALL LD & FARMING	5.0	-0.0020	0.037	0.64
10.	69882210	PAPERCRAFT CORP	5.0	-0.0011	0.107	1.82
11.	77667810	ROPER CORP	5.0	-0.0004	0.118	2.01
12.	81947010	SHAPELL INDS INC	5.0	0.0074	0.164	2.81
13.	89589510	TRIANGLE PAC CORP	5.0	0.0023	0.158	2.70
14.	91207810	U S INDS INC	5.0	-0.0023	0.076	1.30
15.	91301710	UNITED TECHNOLOGIES CP	5.0	-0.0014	0.055	0.94
16.	92227210	VARO INC	5.0	0.0054	0.249	4.26
17.	95546510	WEST POINT PEPPERELL	5.0	-0.0017	0.069	1.18
18.	96289820	WHEELABRATOR FRYE INC	5.0	0.0006	0.098	1.68
19.	97428010	WINN DIXIE STORES INC	5.0	-0.0040	0.030	0.50
20.	98551410	YELLOW FGHT SYS INC	5.0	0.0019	0.087	1.49

iance. However, as part of an overall investment strategy of, for instance, a large pension sponsor, the portfolio is far from risky. For instance, forming a portfolio containing 10 percent of this portfolio and 90 percent of a fund which matches the holdings of the S&P 500 will produce a portfolio which is similar to the riskier of the currently marketed index funds which do not use all the securities in the S&P 500.[10] (This combination portfolio would have a beta of 1.132 and an annual residual standard deviation of 1.878 percent.)

The advertising expenditures strategy has a slightly lower residual risk, with most of it now coming from *XMC*. There are 18 stocks, again equally weighted. Finally, the "buyback" strategy has the least residual risk of the three strategies, where again, most of this risk arises from *XMC*. Notice that the proportion of risk arising from industry variance is very different in the last two portfolios; the latter of these portfolios is relatively well diversified with respect to industry risk.

The Examples Compared

The comparison of the portfolios presented in this supplement is intriguing. Table S4.22 shows some summary characteristics of the portfolios and exemplifies several important points. First, and most obvious, a whole range of portfolios can be constructed, each of which may be valuable to an owner of funds. This range cannot (and should not) be specified simply in terms of beta; the level of residual risk is just as important. In order to identify and analyze a strategy, further information is required. The ratio between specific variance and *XMC* is one good indication of the manager's method of going from judgment to the final product. (It is also a good indication of the manager's abilities in the sense that if the strategy is claimed, for instance, to be stock picking and there is only a small fraction of specific risk, then there has surely been some "slippage" in the construction process.)

Table S4.22
Portfolio Statistics

	Example 1	Example 2	Example 3 Total	Example 3 Strategy A	Example 3 Strategy B	Example 3 Strategy C
Beta	1.0	1.18	1.29	1.32	1.31	1.26
Residual standard deviation	1.96	5.57	11.98	18.78	13.51	12.74
Ratio of specific variance to *XMC* . .	3.6/1	1/2.8	1/4.6	1.2/1	1/2.9	1/2.6
Industry variance	0.8	4.6	16.2	59.5	28.0	12.9
XMC	0.7	28.7	117.7	161.2	135.9	117.2
Number of names	129	56 + mutual fund	42	4	18	20

---

[10]Some funds do not buy the whole S&P 500 index. See Chapter 5 for further details.

The last three rows of the table indicate two phenomena associated with diversification. Notice that the industry variance of the total portfolio in Example 3 is only a little greater than the industry variance of the Buyback strategy portfolio (Strategy C), which has the lowest industry variance of the three strategies. Simply forming a portfolio which spreads the industry exposure substantially reduces the risk from this source relative to the average industry risk of the components. Notice that this effect is not so pronounced with total XMC simply because the risk indices on the three subportfolios are similar; that is, they are all extreme on the immaturity and smallness axis. The only diversification effect occurs with the low valuation and unsuccess factor. The proportion of XMC is far greater in the total portfolio than in any of the subportfolios, since specific risk (and industry variance) is diversified but exposure to the risk indices is concentrated. This effect is crucial in multiply managed portfolios where the sponsor may be unaware that the separate managers have a similar exposure to a risk index which is therefore not diversified in the aggregate portfolio.

Finally, a number of articles in the academic literature purport to demonstrate that diversification is synonymous with the number of "names" in the portfolio and that diversification beyond 20 or 30 names is ineffective. It is vital to realize that these results refer to randomly selected, equally weighted portfolios. Institutional portfolios are not randomly selected, nor are they usually equally weighted. Hence, going from 4 to 20 names, as in strategies A and C of Example 3, hardly affects the residual risk; doubling the number, as in the total portfolio in Example 3, still has hardly any effect. All three portfolios of Example 3 show a great deal of commonality in that they are all highly exposed to one factor, even though the actual names, industries, and other characteristics are quite dissimilar.

The lesson from this last discussion, and indeed the entire supplement, is that the method of forming judgment on securities matters a great deal because it "locks in" the type of portfolios that will be presented to clients. Equally as important as the specification of this judgment is the method of integrating it in the portfolio. The chain is only as strong as its weakest link.

Measuring the Effectiveness of the Alpha Generation Process

Let us now turn to the question of how to measure the effectiveness of the alpha generation process. The obvious answer is to take the alphas, form portfolios, and observe how they perform subsequently. Indeed, we shall see later that this is essentially the method to use. However, it is worth noting here that a whole series of portfolios can be formed using the same set of alphas. These portfolios will range from the highly diversified portfolio, an indexlike fund which attaches no importance to the alphas, to the exceedingly aggressive portfolio containing the single stock with the highest alpha. The range between these two end points will include efficient portfolios with differing values of alpha and residual variance. This set of portfolios is, of course, the active frontier depicted in Figure 2.9.

Which of these portfolios should be used in the measurement process? We shall show in Chapter 5 that if investment constraints (e.g., prevention of short-selling, upper bounds on asset holdings) are not binding, then any one of the portfolios can be used. In other words, provided the portfolios are correctly formed and the performance measured correctly, then all portfolios will give identical results as to the information content of the research process. When investment constraints are binding, the measure of benefit or value added from the research process is given by the ratio of alpha to the residual standard deviation (the "alpha-to-omega" ratio, or, to use its correct statistical name, the *information ratio*).

This measure is intuitive; as we move up the active frontier, alpha (the expected abnormal return, measured in percent per year) increases, as does residual variance (measured in percent squared per year—see Supplement 1) and, equivalently, residual standard deviation (measured in percent per year). The best point on this frontier is the point where the benefit per unit cost is maximized; hence, the index (which should be dimensionless) to measure value added is the information ratio.

Our starting point for the following analysis is that the research process should be organized in such a way that the research output increases the research department's information ratio. The aim of the analysis is to determine how the value added from a research process is affected by (1) the length of time the funds are managed and (2) the number of stocks being researched.

The first result is easily obtained because all of the intermediate steps in the calculation have been discussed earlier. Recall from the supplement to Chapter 1, equation (S1–14), that the variance of the compound return decreases in proportion to time. Hence, the standard deviation varies inversely to the square root of time. Let us now consider a manager who continually earns an alpha (in terms of compound return) of 1 percent. Figure S4.1 shows the alpha and the residual standard deviation as a function of time. This manager, therefore, will have an information ratio which will increase in proportion to the square root of time. In other words, we would expect the value added from the (constant) research process over 25 years to be $\sqrt{25} = 5$ times the value added over one year. Intuitively, we would expect the continuation of the investment process over time to result in diversification over a sequence of investments. This is the origin of the idea that the owner of funds must observe a history of the investment strategy in order to evaluate skill at earning abnormal returns. The length of the history depends on how many opportunities there have been to obtain an information advantage; in all highly competitive markets the number of opportunities must be small, and thus the time required to "prove" a manager skillful may be very long.

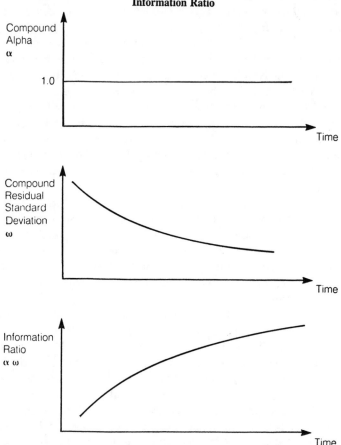

Figure S4.1
Effect of Time on Compound Alpha, Residual Standard Deviation, and Information Ratio

An alternative method of visualizing the effect of the passage of time is shown in Figure S4.2. Time is plotted along the horizontal axis, and the residual returns earned by the manager are plotted along the vertical dimension. One possible sequence of returns is shown by the dotted line. Since the manager's alpha is 1 percent, the returns tend to center about this value in the long run, although the residual risk that is incurred as a result of the active strategy obscures the alpha in any given year.

Suppose the manager bears a constant level of residual risk of 5 percent per year. The one-standard-deviation range is shown by the dashed lines. Since the standard deviation decreases in proportion to the square root of time, the range about the $\alpha = 1$ percent level decreases smoothly until, after 25 years, the range is from zero to $+2$ percent. Indeed, there will a probability of $\frac{1}{6}$ that the manager will have a negative residual return (i.e., be below the market) even though the manager has "delivered every year." The problem is that the

Figure S4.2
Time until Significance

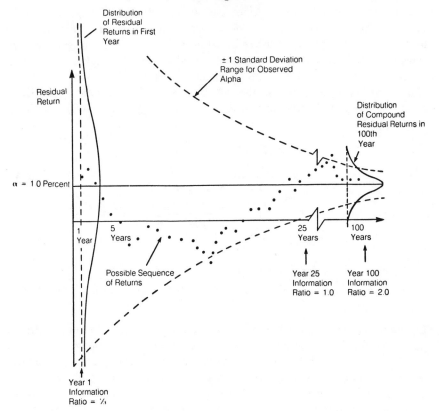

residual risk has obscured the alpha; it is true that the information ratio has gone from $^1/_5$ to 1, or $1/(5/\sqrt{25})$, but the level of risk is still as large as the level of expected abnormal return.

How long must the manager wait before being 95 percent certain that he or she is ahead of the market? This is a straightforward application of the one-tailed significance test introduced in the supplement to Chapter 1. A table of the normal distribution shows that 5 percent of the probability mass for a standard normal distribution lies below -1.6. Hence, the manager has to wait until the compound residual standard deviation, ω, satisfies: $1.6\omega = 1.0$. Now, after T years, the standard deviation has been reduced to $5/\sqrt{T}$; hence, the manager must wait T years, where $(1.6)(5/\sqrt{T}) = 1$, or $\sqrt{T} = 8.0$. In words, after 64 years the manager can be pretty confident that the strategy has been profitable!

The lesson for this supplement comes in two parts: first, residual risk control is crucial to realizing the value added from security analysis; and second, it is unlikely that any analyst will enjoy the luxury (or suffer the ignominy) of having alpha forecasts be proven statistically significant. The implication for Chapter 7 is that using performance measurement to draw unambiguous conclusions concerning the talent of a manager or analyst is wildly unrealistic.

Now let us turn to the effect of the number of stocks being researched. Although the information ratio is the measure of value added, it is easier here to work with the square of the information ratio, $(\alpha/\omega)^2$, or, in general, the square of the expected excess return to standard deviation ratio. This ratio, which is the square of a measure of goodness originally proposed by William Sharpe, has become known in the literature as the *Sharpe ratio*.[11] We shall denote the portfolio Sharpe ratio by Z_P^2, which from equations (2–1) and (2–2) is given by:

$$
\begin{aligned}
Z_P^2 &= (\beta_P E[r_M] + \alpha_P)^2 / (\beta_P^2 V_M + \omega_P^2) \\
&= \frac{\{1 + (\alpha_P/\beta_P E[r_M])\}^2}{V_M/E^2[r_M] + \omega_P^2/\beta_P^2 E^2[r_M]} \\
&= \frac{\{1 + (\alpha_P/\beta_P E[r_M])\}^2}{(1/Z_{PS}^2) + (\alpha_P/\beta_P E[r_M])^2(1/Z_{PR}^2)}
\end{aligned}
\tag{S4-1}
$$

where

$Z_{PS}^2 = E^2[r_M]/V_M$ is the systematic Sharpe ratio; and

$Z_{PR}^2 = \alpha_P^2/\omega_P^2$ is the residual Sharpe ratio, or the square of the information ratio.

Equation (S4–1) shows how the Sharpe ratio for any portfolio can be decomposed into the Sharpe ratio for its systematic and residual components.

We are not so much interested in "any" portfolio as we are in optimal portfolios where the Sharpe ratio is maximized. How is this optimization accomplished? The answer is by allocating funds between the systematic and residual (normal and active) portfolios in the most advantageous manner. If there are no constraints (e.g., upper bounds on holdings) on investment, then the systematic and residual Sharpe ratios are invariant to the wealth in either portfolio. However, the term $\alpha_P/\beta_P E[r_M]$ is not invariant; for instance, if there is zero wealth in the active portfolio, $\alpha_P = 0$, or conversely, if there is zero wealth in the passive portfolio, $\beta_P = 0$. Hence, optimal portfolios are characterized by optimal ratios of $\alpha_P/\beta_P E[r_M]$. Assuming that the investor has an indentical aversion to systematic risk and residual risk, it can be shown that at optimality:[12]

---

[11]The measure of goodness was introduced in William Sharpe, "Mutual Fund Performance," *Journal of Business*, January 1966, pp. 119–38. Jack Treynor and Fischer Black were the first authors to use the term *Sharpe ratio*. The term appeared in their article "How to Use Security Analysis to Improve Portfolio Selection," *Journal of Business*, January 1973, pp. 66–86.

[12]Write equation (S4–1) as $y = (1 + x)^2/(a + bx^2)$; then:

$$
\frac{dy}{dx} = 2[a + (a - b)x - bx^2]/(a + bx^2)^2 = 0,
$$

when $x = -1$ or a/b. Differentiating again shows that these roots are associated with the minimum and maximum, respectively.

$$\alpha_P/\beta_P E[r_M] = Z_{PR}^2/Z_{PS}^2, \tag{S4-2}$$

which on substitution into equation (S4–1) gives:

$$Z_P^2 = Z_{PS}^2 + Z_{PR}^2. \tag{S4-3}$$

In words, at optimality the portfolio Sharpe ratio is equal to the sum of the Sharpe ratios for the passive and active components. Further, from rearranging equation (S4–2), it follows that at optimality:

$$\frac{\alpha_P}{\omega_P^2} = \frac{\beta_P E[r_M]}{\beta_P^2 V_M},$$

or the mean-variance ratio for the active portfolio equals the mean-variance ratio of the normal portfolio. This is a result which we obtained previously in the section, "Active and Passive Portfolios," in Chapter 2.

What implications are there for the analyst's role? It is clear that the analyst has to provide estimates of abnormal return. These together with predictions of risk enable the construction of optimal portfolios. Since the systematic Sharpe ratio is the same for all portfolios, the value added in portfolio performance arises from the active portfolio Sharpe ratio, which should be maximized. Unfortunately, to obtain some simple rules for this maximization we have to make a further simplifying assumption, namely, that the analyst is concerned with forming judgments of specific return only (with the implication that the abnormal return due to common factors is obtained from another source) or that the residual returns between securities are uncorrelated. With this simplification:

$$\alpha_P = \sum_{j=1}^{N} h_j \alpha_j$$

and

$$\omega_P^2 = \sum_{j=1}^{N} h_j^2 \sigma_j^2,$$

so that:

$$Z_{PR}^2 = \left[\sum_{j=1}^{N} h_j \alpha_j \right]^2 / \left[\sum_{j=1}^{N} h_j^2 \sigma_j^2 \right], \tag{S4-4}$$

where

h_j = the proportional holding of the jth security;
α_j = the alpha on the jth security;
σ_j^2 = the specific risk of the jth security; and
N = the number of assets followed.

In order to find the maximum ratio, we differentiate with respect to h_j and set the result equal to zero. The optimal holdings are found to be:

$$h_j = \frac{\alpha_j}{\sigma_j^2} \left(\frac{\omega_P^2}{\alpha_P} \right); j = 1, \dots, N$$

which on substitution into equation (S4–4) gives:[13]

$$Z_{PR}^2 = \sum_{j=1}^{N} (\frac{\alpha_j^2}{\sigma_j^2}) = \sum_{j=1}^{N} Z_j^2, \tag{S4–5}$$

where Z_j^2 is the Sharpe ratio for the residual return on the jth asset. Thus, Sharpe ratios add up to form the portfolio Sharpe ratio:

$$Z_P^2 = Z_{PS}^2 + \sum_{j=1}^{N} Z_j^2.$$

Our general result can be stated in this way: If there are uncorrelated elements of return, then the Sharpe ratio for the portfolio is the sum of the Sharpe ratios for the different elements. Thus, even if each of the different elements has a small Sharpe ratio, the portfolio Sharpe ratio may be very large indeed as long as the research process generates forecasts for the individual elements of return based on independent thinking. If an analyst is equally competent at research-ing all assigned stocks, or more generally, if the departmental research process is equally effective on all stocks, then $Z_{PR}^2 = N\bar{Z}^2$, where $\bar{Z}^2$ is the explanatory power for the typical asset. Finally, taking the square root to obtain the infor-mation ratio, $Z_{PR} = \alpha_P/\omega_P = \sqrt{N}\,\bar{Z}$, so the information ratio increases as the square root of the assets being researched.

We can summarize this analysis as follows. When many different uncorre-lated elements of return (for example, the specific returns on individual secu-rities) are forecast, then the optimal portfolio constructed using all the alphas generated by the research process will have a higher information ratio than that obtained for any one element alone. This is another example of the advantage of diversification and is the essence of effective active research. The effective-ness of the research effort is measured by the sum of the security Sharpe ratios. If market timing is part of the active strategy, then the Sharpe ratio for the systematic component (the normal portfolio) also appears in the summation. Notice that the contribution from the systematic component is equivalent in effect to the contribution from a single asset (i.e., the Sharpe ratios from both sources are simply added). Hence, if the departmental research process achieves the same Sharpe ratio for the systematic component as for a single security, then the amount of resources devoted to both should be the same. Conversely, market timing should only be pursued if it is believed "easy" since it provides the same "payoff" as a single security.

An alternative way of making this point is to appeal to the diversification argument. The expected specific returns on individual assets as forecast by a research process are likely to be tiny. Hence, the information ratio (expected

---

[13]In matrix notation, the general expression for the residual Sharpe ratio is $\alpha' V^{-1} \alpha$, where α is the N-vector of alphas and V^{-1} is the inverse covariance matrix between residual returns. This reduces to equation (S4–5) only when V is diagonal. When V contains some off-diagonal elements, the individual Sharpe ratios do not exactly sum to form the portfolio Sharpe ratio.

return per unit risk) on individual assets will be even smaller. When a portfolio is constructed from these individual assets, the portfolio alpha will simply be the average alpha of the assets, but the specific risk of the portfolio will be *less* than the average specific risk of the assets because of diversification. The portfolio information ratio is now greater than the information ratios of any individual asset. If the research process concentrates on forecasting factor or sector returns, where there are fewer uncorrelated elements of return, the diversification advantage is less. A simple market timing strategy consists of a single forecast where there is no advantage from diversification.

Finally, this idea of diversification can be taken further with the multiple management of portfolios. If each manager has an independent research process, then the Sharpe ratio for the sponsor will be the sum of the Sharpe ratios for the managers. Hence, it is always worthwhile for a sponsor to hire another above-average (i.e., positive after-cost information ratio) money manager. Moreover, since the sponsor's Sharpe ratio, and hence information ratio, is greater than that of any of the managers, we would expect the sponsor to demonstrate skill more rapidly than any of the managers.

For instance, if a sponsor employs nine managers who have independent research processes, and each manager delivers an alpha of 1 percent at a residual standard deviation of 5 percent, then the sponsor's information ratio is 3/5, or $\sqrt{\{\sum_{j=1}^{9} (1/5)^2\}}$. Provided each manager maintains his or her strategy, it will only take 7.1 ($= {}^{64}/_9$) years for the sponsor to be 95 percent certain of showing a positive abnormal return.

Selected References

The three best references for the material in the latter part of this supplement are:

Ferguson, Robert. "Active Portfolio Management." *Financial Analysts Journal,* May–June 1975, pp. 63–72.

Rosenberg, Barr. "Security Appraisal and Unsystematic Risk in Institutional Investment." *Proceedings of the Seminar on the Analysis of Security Prices,* University of Chicago, November 1976, pp. 171–237.

Treynor, Jack, and Fischer Black. "How to Use Security Analysis to Improve Portfolio Selection." *Journal of Business,* January 1973, pp. 66–86.

Chapter 5

Portfolio Management
with MPT

A major tenet of MPT is that a managed portfolio should be constructed so that the holding of each security accurately reflects the manager's judgment ("judgmental alpha") as to its relative valuation. If there is no judgment, i.e., the judgmental alphas are all zero, then the managed portfolio should be the normal portfolio (sometimes called the optimal passive portfolio). When the judgmental alphas deviate from neutral, the optimal portfolio will include an active component and thus will differ from the normal portfolio. This difference reflects the greater weight that has been placed on the individual manager's forecasts for the future, relative to the consensus forecasts.

In this chapter we consider the construction of optimal portfolios within the framework of the active and normal components that were introduced in Chapter 2. Passive investment is designed to replicate the normal portfolio. The most common passive strategy is *indexing,* i.e., holding a portfolio that closely tracks a visible index. The advantage of all passive strategies, including investing in an index, is cost. Passive strategies purchase diversification inexpensively since their transaction cost and management fees are much lower than those for an actively managed portfolio. The most obvious disadvantages of an index fund are that the index may not represent the normal portfolio and superior performance is impossible. Perhaps for this reason, the guarantee (before transaction costs) of average performance is synonymous with tedium (or worse!) to many investors.

Active management, on the other hand, has a better image; it is competitive and exciting—"where the action is." However, active management has its costs. First, the formation of judgmental alphas requires a substantial research effort, which is more expensive than following a passive strategy. In addition, active management entails higher transaction costs and a greater disutility from residual risk than are entailed by passive management. Finally, active management requires superior security analysis since only superior security analysis will result in superior reward; i.e., a portion of all actively managed money must underperform in order to enable the remainder to overperform.[1]

We will develop and discuss management strategies at length, beginning with passive management and then turning to active management. Passive management is introduced via a brief analysis of the asset allocation decision, which is actually a part of the process for selecting the normal portfolio. Our study of active management begins with a simple example which emphasizes the amount by which an optimal portfolio differs from an index fund when the portfolio manager has nonzero judgmental alphas. Intuitively, the larger the judgmental alphas, the greater is the differentiation between the optimal portfolio and the index fund. But by how much? Clearly, one of the inputs to the decision is the set of judgmental alphas on individual securities and the forecast of market return if market timing is part of the strategy. Other inputs include the risk predictions and the utility function, or preference structure, of the investor. Thus, the rational formation of portfolios really does require the synthesis of the various topics covered in previous chapters.

The inputs are specified, but the output—namely the optimal portfolio—is yet to be determined. What is required is a method of "massaging" these inputs to produce the output. This procedure, called *portfolio optimization*, is widely misunderstood. However, it is an important step in portfolio management. We spend considerable time on the various facets of portfolio optimization, including both the selection and revision problems.

We conclude this chapter with two interesting case studies that stress several important points. Perhaps the most important point is that the same judgment can be used to form an entire series of optimal portfolios ranging from the very aggressive to the totally passive. We perform this exercise on an institutional portfolio and determine the set of attainable portfolios. This analysis is very similar to the efficiency analysis that was suggested 30 years ago by Markowitz and described in Chapter 1. However, it differs in one crucial aspect, the efficient frontier appears on the alpha/residual risk diagram and not on the total

---

[1]Here "superior security analysis" means that the forecasts must be both different from and more accurate than the consensus forecast.

risk/total return diagram. Why this difference? In large part it is because some investors may have a different aversion to residual risk than to systematic risk (see the discussion in Chapter 2).

The supplement that follows this chapter gives the mathematical foundations for portfolio optimization and provides some description of the computational problems involved. To demonstrate these points we include an example describing the construction of "yield-biased" passive portfolios.

Setting Up the Sponsor's Problem

In the last few years the use of index funds as one part of a total investment strategy has gained wide acceptance among investors, particularly corporate pension sponsors. An *index fund* is a portfolio that closely tracks a visible index and is designed to be passive. A *passive portfolio* is not managed in the expectation of earning incremental rewards from transient asset or market behavior. It is a comparatively stable portfolio, formed and positioned in response to an analysis of the long-term risk and reward of the capital markets. In general, passive portfolios need not be indexed; they can have quite distinct sectoral or asset emphases, depending upon the investor's attitudes toward risk, the economic environment, and other portfolio holdings.[2]

The basic foundations of finance, as covered in the supplement to Chapter 2, give one justification for the existence of a passive strategy. Under the assumptions described there, every investor's optimal portfolio can, in equilibrium, be separated into a risky and a risk-free component, where the risky component is the same for everybody. Hence, the risky portfolio is the market portfolio. This explanation is a simple restatement of the familiar concept of the capital market line. A generalization of this concept, introduced by Jack Treynor and Fischer Black, extends the argument to the disequilibrium situation.[3] In this case, the investor first solves the equilibrium problem to find the optimal (normal) portfolio (i.e., the mix between the market portfolio proxy and the risk-free security), then superimposes an active strategy to take advantage of the perceived disequilibrium. As discussed in Chapter 2, the normal and active strategies can be conveniently thought of as arising from the separation of the investment process into two subdecisions. The first is an analysis of the long-term risk and rewards in the capital market, which leads to the resolution of the normal exposure of the portfolio. The *normal exposure* is an expression of the natural position for the portfolio and may be stated in terms

---

[2]A good example is the yield-biased passive portfolios currently being marketed. These portfolios are positioned because an analysis of the long-term risk and reward of the capital markets suggests that tax-exempt investors will earn superior returns by shading their portfolios toward higher yielding assets. This point is discussed further in a later section.

[3]Jack Treynor and Fischer Black, "How to Use Security Analysis to Improve Portfolio Performance," *Journal of Business*, January 1973, pp. 66–86.

of an asset mix, or the risk level of the portfolio. In some circumstances, this normal exposure may even be specified in terms of a particular sectoral emphasis, for instance, not holding any airline stocks. The second subdecision is the active management of the portfolio. Active management is the adjustment of the portfolio in response to judgmental information. It takes advantage of the perceived mispricing of assets and their consequent revaluation in the near future. In the absence of judgmental information there is no reason to differentiate the portfolio from its normal position.

In this manner, Treynor and Black thought of a managed portfolio as the sum of two subportfolios: the normal portfolio and the active portfolio. The normal portfolio is the central core around which an active manager places "bets" by underweighting some stocks and overweighting others. Over time the active positions should average out, leaving the normal portfolio. From the investor's point of view this raises two important questions. First, how is the normal portfolio selected. And second, how should the judgmental information be used to provide incremental return that is greater than the increased transaction costs and the management fee?

The second question has implications for performance measurement and the selection of money managers that will be dealt with later in this chapter and in Chapter 7. However, our present task is to finish describing the selection of the normal portfolio, which we introduced graphically in Figure 2.7.

Let us consider the problem facing a pension sponsor attempting to determine the composition of the appropriate normal portfolio. We would argue that the solution to the problem is the result of a long-term equilibrium analysis of the risks and rewards in the capital market. Some sponsors have implicitly based their decision on disequilibrium analysis by hypothesizing some perpetually undervalued sector and concentrating their portfolio in that sector. This reasoning strikes us as erroneous because it implies that other investors are consistently stupid in not taking advantage of the continual mispricing. Instead, we would rather assume that over the long term, on the average, stocks and other investment media are priced fairly. The implication of this reasoning is that, in the absence of special circumstances, the appropriate normal portfolio should be the market portfolio. However, this presents a definitional problem.

To this point we have implicitly (and, on occasion, explicitly) assumed that the market portfolio is composed solely of common stocks. This is completely wrong in theory (although up to this point the error has been rather insignificant and could have been diminished by referring at all times to the "market portfolio of common stocks") because *the* market portfolio is composed of common stocks; corporate, government, and municipal bonds; warrants; and most other financial instruments (with the exception of options and futures contracts).[4] Each of these instruments is held in proportion to its capitalization, so

---

[4]Options and futures are not included because they have a net value of zero; i.e., for every purchaser there is a seller. In both cases, the underlying instruments (i.e., common stock and physical commodity) are included in the market portfolio.

the true market portfolio is the sum of the capitalization weighted portfolios formed from each of the asset sectors (i.e., the "market portfolio of common stocks," etc.). Undoubtedly, common stocks are both the riskiest and the largest part of the true market portfolio, so it makes good sense to concentrate on them first. However, concentrating solely on common stocks brushes aside numerous important decisions: all but one of these can (and, because of space limitations, must) be left to a later book. The decision as to what proportion of an investor's portfolio should be held in common stock (the asset allocation decision) has important implications here.

The Asset Allocation Decision[5]

The theory is all very well, but the notion that the normal portfolio should be, in general, the true market portfolio is impractical. Hence an approximation is required; in practice, institutions allocate funds among (usually) three primary categories of financial assets: cash and equivalents, corporate bonds, and equities. This allocation has two distinct aspects: one refers to the long run; the other refers to an active difference from the norm in the short run. The normal allocation is the allocation believed best for typical circumstances over a long horizon. The second, or active, allocation differs from the normal allocation whenever the investor believes that the short-term prospects differ from the long-run average. This allocation, which is usually described as *market timing*, consists of shifting funds among the asset classes to take advantage of short-term mispricing.

The normal allocation is based on the investor's preferences and on the consensus expectations of investors about the relative performance of the asset classes over a long horizon. This should not be a hurried decision; it should be the result of a slow, deliberate analysis, and it should represent a thoughtful expression of the risks and rewards of the capital markets. When making the allocation decision, the investor is faced with the difficult task of achieving a delicate balance in the trade-off between risk and reward. On the one hand, in accepting the high degree of risk in the equity market, the investor may hope to attain high rates of return. On the other hand, this level of risk may be too great, in which case, as bonds, cash, or their equivalents are added to the portfolio in order to decrease risk, lower expected rates of return must be anticipated. Thus, the optimal allocation depends upon the preference structure of the investor. Determining the optimal allocation of a pension fund, for example, involves understanding both the environment of the fund and the risk and reward opportunities available from various allocations among the asset classes.

---

[5]For this section we include all financial assets, not just common stocks and cash, in the market portfolio. For an analysis of the effect of omitting entire categories of risky assets from the market portfolio, see Andrew Rudd and Barr Rosenberg, "The 'Market Model' in Investment Management," *Journal of Finance*, May 1980, pp. 597–607.

This reasoning indicates that there is nothing confidential about an investor's normal allocation. All that can be inferred by an outsider knowing the allocation is the preference structure of the investor, and this information cannot be used for a strategic advantage.

There are several methods of approaching the allocation problem, depending largely upon the portfolio owner's degree of sophistication. As always, there is a judgmental approach whereby a board of trustees, for instance, will pick an allocation among the asset classes with which it is "comfortable." This is an intuitive method which relies for its justification on the experience and wisdom of the trustees.

An alternative approach, which is more theoretically defensible, is the scenario procedure mentioned in the first two supplements.[6] Here each asset class is considered as a single risky investment opportunity whose return distribution is estimated by specifying an exhaustive set of scenarios. Thus, an investment committee would be charged with the task of describing the complete set of alternative economic scenarios that may occur over the time horizon, together with their respective probability of occurrence.[7] Table 5.1 is an example summary of economic scenarios and the data required for this approach.

The next task is to assume that one scenario will actually occur and to estimate the mean and variance of return of each asset class if that happens. For example, given that "Boom Bust 1" (column 5) occurs, what are the mean and the variance of return of each asset class? This procedure is then repeated for each of the other scenarios. Hence, the estimates required for every scenario are the mean and variance for each asset class, given that the scenario does take place, together with the scenario's probability of occurrence.

From these data, as indicated in the supplement to Chapter 1, the overall mean, variance, and covariances between the asset classes can be calculated. The next step is to form an efficient frontier from the asset classes, as described in the supplement to Chapter 2. The final step, for which there is little guidance, is the hardest.[8] This involves picking a location on the frontier, a task which, theoretically, is accomplished by superimposing the investor's indifference curves on the reward-risk region. In practice, the isolation of the "optimal" portfolio is somewhat arbitrary and involves trying to "second-guess" the preferences of the portfolio's owner from the mean and variance of return on efficient portfolios.

A more sophisticated approach is to simulate the return distribution. An

---

[6]See Supplement 1,fn.1, for references.

[7]This is one of the problems with the approach, since it is probably easier to describe the scenarios for a short horizon (e.g., up to five years) than for the long-term horizon required for the normal decision. Thus, this method may be more useful for the active asset allocation decision than for the normal decision.

[8]For this reason, Jan Mossin criticizes the approach as one of "computing first, and thinking afterward;" Jan Mossin, *Theory of Financial Markets*, (Englewood Cliffs, N.J.: Prentice-Hall, 1973), p. 46.

Table 5.1
Summary of Economic Scenarios

	Modest Growth	Growth Recession	Renewed Growth	Stagflation	Boom Bust 1	Boom Bust 2	Dollar Crisis
Probability	20	25	10	22.5	10	10	2.5
Average growth range . .	3.5	3	4.5	1.5	4.0	3.5	0
Average CPI	5.5	6.5	6	7.5	8	7.5	1
Growth pattern	Declining with some cyclical rebound; growth stabilizes at lower than historical levels	Slowdown developing followed by modest cyclical move upward and then tapering off	Short-term weakness followed by sustained growth longer term	Sluggish growth deteriorating into severe recession	Short-term growth followed by cyclical decline followed by very high unsustainable growth	Short-term growth followed by cyclical decline followed by a less volatile cycle	After modest improvement, deterioration into severe and prolonged decline
Inflation pattern	Secular decline stabilizing at lower than current levels longer term	Fairly flat at relatively high rates	Slowly declining rates fueled by capacity expansion	Persistent high rates with a very slow decline following recession	Increasing rates despite cyclical downturn ultimately peaking in mid 80s.	Increasing rates despite cyclical decline ultimately declining as cycle becomes less volatile	Acceleration followed by extreme weakness with prices falling

example of the simulation approach would be to use a long history of returns on the asset classes to construct distributions of the return on the portfolio under different asset allocations.[9] In its simplest form, this approach makes a strong assumption that "history will repeat itself," in that the distribution estimated from historical data is the same as that from which future returns will be drawn. Alternatively, an analyst could forecast the statistics for the return distribution on each of the asset classes. The advantage of using simulation approach rather than the scenario approach is that in this way the entire distribution (rather than just the mean and variance) of returns to each allocation can be determined, together with an indication of the likely effects of the passage of time. Simulation, therefore, adds information on the time dimension and can aid in answering such questions as, "If we can adequately forecast the distributions of stock, bonds, and Treasury bills, what will be the likely value of the fund at the end of various horizons?"

We can describe this process with the aid of Figure 5.1. For simplicity, assume that there are only two asset classes, stocks and bonds, with probability distributions as shown in the figure. These distributions, together with their correlation, are either estimated from historical data or forecast by an analyst. We now go through the following steps:

1. Select a bond/stock allocation and a time horizon, for example, a 50–50 bond/stock allocation for five years.
2. Select an observation from each of the two distributions according to the laws of probability. For instance, the stock rate of return may be 10 percent and the bond rate of return may be 5 percent.
3. Form the rate of return on the allocation as 0.5(10) + 0.5(5) = 7.5 percent.
4. Repeat steps (2) and (3) four times further, ending with five annual returns for this particular allocation. The series may be: 1.075, 0.932, 0.910, 1.113, 0.872. By applying these rates sequentially, the compound return over the five years is found to be (1.075)(0.932)(0.910)(1.113)(0.872) = 0.885, so that if the initial value of the fund is $10 million, the fund would be worth $8,850,000 at the end of the five years.
5. Repeat steps (2) through (4) several hundred times to produce several hundred values for the compound return. From these observations a probability distribution of the rate of return on the portfolio can be plotted and the statistics of the rate of return, such as its mean and standard deviation, can be calculated.
6. Finally, go back to step (1) and repeat the entire process for alternative allocations and/or investment horizons.

---

[9] E.g., Lawrence Fisher and James Lorie, "Rates of Return on Investments in Common Stock," *Journal of Business,* January 1964, pp. 1–21; and Roger Ibbotson and Rex Sinquefield, "Stocks, Bonds, Bills, and Inflation: Year-by-Year Historical Returns (1926–1974)," *Journal of Business,* January 1976, pp. 11–47.

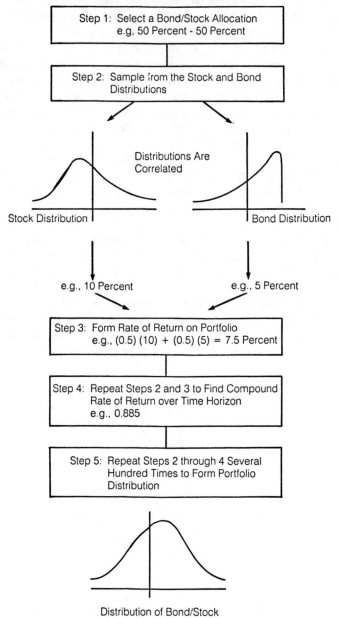

Figure 5.1
The Asset Allocation Simulation Process

Step 1: Select a Bond/Stock Allocation
e.g, 50 Percent - 50 Percent

Step 2: Sample from the Stock and Bond Distributions

Distributions Are Correlated

Stock Distribution

Bond Distribution

e.g., 10 Percent

e.g., 5 Percent

Step 3: Form Rate of Return on Portfolio
e.g., (0.5) (10) + (0.5) (5) = 7.5 Percent

Step 4: Repeat Steps 2 and 3 to Find Compound Rate of Return over Time Horizon
e.g., 0.885

Step 5: Repeat Steps 2 through 4 Several Hundred Times to Form Portfolio Distribution

Distribution of Bond/Stock Allocation

These results can be displayed in several ways. Perhaps one of the better methods (in order to see what is happening) is to plot the mean, and the one- and two-standard-deviation bands for the dollar value of the portfolio over alternative horizons. This type of display is shown in Figure 5.2.

Figure 5.2 shows the growth in the expected value of the portfolio over time. It is upward sloping and increasing at a faster rate, due to the effect of compounding the risk premium. The expected value is, of course, what is anticipated, not what will actually happen. The one- and two-standard-deviation bands indicate the likely range of possible outcomes. The width of the bands increases over time since the standard deviation of the cumulative portfolio value is plotted. (In fact, the standard deviation increases as the square root of time, a result derived mathematically in Supplement 1.) Although the growth in the expected value of the portfolio is reassuring, a run of bad luck could force the portfolio value to zero at the end of, say, five years. Since this point lies outside the negative two-standard-deviation band, it would be an unlikely occurrence (less than 1 chance in 40, or $2^{1}/_{2}\%$). Similarly, there is an almost equal chance of the portfolio being worth $75 million. By considering a diagram such as that shown and interpreting it in this probabilistic sense, the investor or trustees may be able to determine a satisfactory allocation (or rule out unsatisfactory allocations).

A refinement of this approach would be to try to model the interacting factors that determine the distributions of each asset class and their interrelationship. For instance, the first step may be to hypothesize a generating process for the rate of inflation, which is then related to the short-term interest rate, which,

Figure 5.2
Terminal Portfolio Values for Alternative Horizons

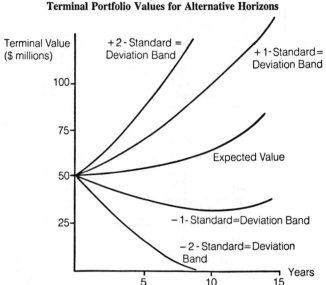

in turn, is related to the return on corporate bonds, and so on. This model-building approach has the advantage of directly integrating the various asset classes, although it is not nearly so straightforward as the previous methods.[10]

Distinction Between Normal and Market Allocations

In each of the approaches described above, the aim is to derive the normal allocation. This allocation is important because whenever the portfolio has an asset mix different from normal, risk is being borne for which there may be no compensation. It is also important to consider the asset allocation decision because there are good reasons why the market portfolio (and particularly its usual proxies) need not be the normal position. In other words, there are good reasons for holding what may appear to an outside observer as "active" positions but are, in fact, long-term passive "biases" relative to the market portfolio.

Certainly, one good reason for not holding the market portfolio is differential taxation on capital gains and dividends. In the United States, income from dividends is taxed at a higher rate than income from capital gains, which leads to a "segmentation" of the market. For instance, consider one investor who is taxable and one who is tax exempt, and consider two securities with the same total expected return, risk level, and capitalization, but with one providing return as dividend income and the other as capital appreciation. Clearly, the two investors are not going to view the securities identically since their aftertax returns from these securities will be different. The proportion of both securities in the market portfolio is the same, and "on the average" the market portfolio will be the optimal passive portfolio for both investors. However, the market portfolio is suboptimal for both investors because the taxable investor will prefer the non-dividend-paying stock (as its return is capital appreciation, which offers the higher aftertax return) and will increase holdings in that stock to the exclusion of the dividend-paying stock. If taxable investors hold more than the average amount of "growth stocks," then tax-exempt investors will hold less than the average amount.

The segmentation due to differential taxation may be even stronger than has been indicated. At first glance, tax-exempt investors do not care what their allocation is because taxation is irrelevant for them (aftertax return is the same as pretax return); it is the taxable investor who really minds whether the security return arises from dividends or capital gains. One can argue that taxable investors will bid up the price of growth stocks in their pursuit of increased aftertax returns and that this will make the total pretax return of growth stocks

---

[10]This type of approach was used to forecast returns on asset classes in the academic study by Roger Ibbotson and Rex Sinquefield, "Stocks, Bonds, Bills, and Inflation: Simulations of the Future (1976–2000)," *Journal of Business*, July 1976, pp. 313–338. It is also the approach taken in the better (i.e., more realistic and useful) commercial asset simulators.

less than that of high-yielding stocks. Therefore, tax-exempt investors can earn an abnormal return by yield-biasing their portfolios. This hypothesis has been the subject of considerable debate among academicians. However, the abnormal return to high-yielding securities has been confirmed by several investigators (and disputed by others), who have estimated the abnormal return to yield to be approximately 30 basis points for every percentage point increase in yield.[11]

This implies that tax-exempt portfolios should be yield biased and that taxable portfolios should be growth biased. In this manner, investors play cooperative game against the Internal Revenue Service. Both investors shade their passive portfolios toward those assets which offer a higher aftertax return. We will see in Supplement 5 that this situation provides an interesting example for portfolio optimization.

A second reason for not holding the market portfolio is that high-beta portfolios may be desirable for certain institutions, principally charitable and endowment funds with a long-term investment horizon and with legal prescriptions governing their spending rules. If these institutions and foundations wish to remain in existence, then they will form portfolios with higher levels of systematic risk and higher levels of systematic return. In doing so, of course, they will also display increased systematic variance of return; however, if they can maintain the intermediate payouts (and provided the investment horizon is long enough), the increased variability will play a lesser role than the increased return, which will become dominant.

Third, there are investors that benefit from integrating the asset and liability sides of their balance sheets. Doing this makes it obvious that the asset side should take on particular attributes. Life insurance companies are one example of this type of investor. These financial intermediaries typically have liabilities that are expressed in nominal terms (i.e., promises to pay stipulated dollar amounts in the future). Clearly, it makes excellent sense for such investors to have portfolios composed of securities with nominal payoffs, for instance, bonds. Although this normal portfolio is dissimilar to the market portfolio, it does provide greater utility. This nonmarket normal portfolio class can be considered under the title of a "liability covariance adjustment" to the normal portfolio. In other words, because the assets and liabilities have a strong covariance, it pays to bear residual risk in the asset portfolio in order to reduce the overall variability between the assets and the liabilities.

Another example of asset and liability covariance may be the investment portfolio held by stockbrokers. The liabilities are the broker's consumption

---

[11]See, e.g., Barr Rosenberg and Vinay Marathe, "Tests of Capital Asset Pricing Hypotheses," in *Research in Finance,* ed. Haim Levy (Greenwich, Conn.: JAI Press, 1979), pp. 115–223; and Robert Litzenberger and Krishna Ramaswami, "The Effects of Personal Taxes and Dividends on Capital Asset Prices: Theory and Empirical Evidence," *Journal of Financial Economics,* June 1979, pp. 163–96. For an opposing theoretical analysis, see Merton Miller and Myron Scholes, "Dividends and Taxes," *Journal of Financial Economics,* December 1978, pp. 333–64.

needs. The assets are represented by human capital and the broker's individual investment portfolio. If that investment portfolio is composed of financial assets, then the income from wages and commissions and the value of the investment portfolio will be very highly correlated (when the market is up, the commission income and portfolio return will increase, and vice versa). Thus, the broker is doubly exposed to financial disaster (and success). Only if the broker has superior forecasting ability should the investment portfolio include major holdings in financial assets. In general, the broker can obtain greater utility by hedging the liabilities, in which case the assets should be invested so as to smooth consumption needs over time, for instance, in real estate and other real assets.

Finally, we have the situation of legal indentures, or social responsibility issues, which may force the exclusion of certain assets. In this case, we can certainly include the case of funds which are prohibited from holding "sin stocks," that is, holdings in the tobacco and alcoholic beverage industries. Another example may be the university endowment funds which have divested themselves of their holdings in South African companies.

In each of the above situations, because certain assets are excluded from the universe of investment opportunities, it is not possible for the appropriate normal portfolio to match the market exactly. However, in all four categories of nonmarket normal portfolios, expected utility is increased by holding a portfolio which is different from the market.

Integrating Assets and Liabilities

The most relevant of these categories for the majority of institutional portfolios is the liability covariance adjustment. The portfolio of assets represents an explicit commitment for the future. For instance, a pension fund's assets represent future payments to the fund's beneficiaries. The management of the assets should be integrated with the liability structure of the fund: to consider the assets in isolation may unnecessarily induce a suboptimal normal asset allocation.

The easiest and most revealing way to consider the assets and liabilities explicitly is to jointly simulate both attributes. The form of the liability structure is dependent upon the nature of the portfolio (i.e., pension fund, endowment fund, etc.) and beyond the scope of this book.[12] Conceptually, the approach is to isolate the important variables determining the liabilities (e.g., for a pension plan these may include mortality, retirement, salary rates, etc.), hypothesize their interrelationship and their impact on the asset side, and then simulate the behavior of the plan through time. The normal allocation is found

---

[12]See Howard Winklevoss, *Pension Mathematics* (Homewood, Ill.: Richard D. Irwin, 1977), and J. Peter Williamson, *Spending Policy for Educational Endowments* (New York: Common Fund, 1976), for a detailed discussion of pension and endowment liabilities, respectively.

from the distribution of plan attributes and may, for instance, be the one min-imizing the probability that the assets will be insufficient to match the liabilities over the long term.[13]

In general, the simulation models applied in practice do not exactly follow this design. The simplification usually made is to simulate the asset side while leaving (mainly for cost considerations) the liability side deterministic. In a deterministic model the effect of random "shocks" (in particular, uncertain inflation) cannot be calculated. Thus, in an economic environment where infla-tion does not exist (!), this may be an acceptable approach. However, if there is inflation, then assets which are excellent inflation hedges (e.g., real estate) and assets which are no hedge (e.g., bonds) are analyzed only with regard to total risk, without taking any account of their ability to hedge inflation.[14] In addition, pension liabilities are becoming increasingly indexed to inflation (ei-ther de jure or de facto), so it is important to incorporate this source of risk. For this reason, it is crucial to jointly simulate the assets and the liabilities in order to determine the correct allocation.

This completes our discussion of the normal allocation decision. We now return to the all-equity environment to analyze the relevance and selection of passive equity strategies.

Passive Investment Strategies[15]

As we indicated earlier, the most common passive strategy at present is the S&P 500 index fund; however, index funds are only a subset of all passive strategies. What, then, delineates a passive portfolio? The definition could be stated as follows: All *passive portfolios* are designed to be stable and to match the long-term performance of one segment of the capital markets rather than being managed with the aim of earning incremental rewards from transient asset or market behavior. We may, for instance, consider a stable portfolio which tracks the performance of a universe of high-yielding securities as pas-sive.

---

[13]For an example of the simulation approach applied to educational endowments, see Rodney Adams, "Endowment Funds Are a Special Case," *Journal of Portfolio Management,* Winter 1977, pp. 37–45; and William F. Sharpe, "The Stanford Investment Simulator," unpublished manu-script.

[14]Are poorly designed models worse than no models at all? It is intriguing to ask whether the relative lack of real assets in U.S. pension portfolios is the result of poorly conceptualizing the asset allocation problem. In contrast, in other countries with historically high inflation rates, for instance, the United Kingdom, real assets comprise a much greater proportion of pension portfo-lios. And well-designed models? Although United Kingdom money managers may have spotted the inflation hedge, in general they missed hedging the decline in national wealth. Performance would have been, and probably will be, better with increased international diversification.

[15]This section is based on Andrew Rudd, "Optimal Passive Portfolio Selection," *Financial Management,* Spring 1980, pp. 57–66. For the remainder of the chapter, the market portfolio refers to the "market portfolio of common stocks."

At this stage it is useful to classify two types of passive strategies:

1. Tracking the performance of an explicit index.
2. Matching a portfolio to a set of attributes where either there is no explicit list of assets (e.g., the yield biased portfolio is a good example where the attributes may include maintaining a beta, β_P, and yield, y_P) or there are constraints on the formation of the fund (e.g., match the S&P 500 without any oil stocks).

The majority of marketed passive portfolios belong to type 1. Type 2 portfolios are more difficult to select and have only recently been endorsed by pension sponsors. Thus, we will concentrate on type 1 portfolios here and will only briefly mention the more difficult strategies at the end of this section.

The actual procedures for selecting passive portfolios are covered in an optimization section later in this chapter. However, it would be helpful to summarize the attributes of passive strategies here. First, a passive strategy is one which meets certain attributes or sectoral goals. These may be specified as a certain beta, for instance, a beta of unity. Second, a passive strategy may require particular weightings in industry or in sectors. Third, there must be minimum residual risk in the passive portfolio relative to the benchmark or bogey. Finally, there must be no transacting in response to judgmental valuation of securities.

An index fund is a special case of this analysis since it requires a portfolio which has minimum residual risk and a beta of unity relative to the specified index. The beta of unity implies that the index and the portfolio exhibit the same exposure to economic events, while the minimal residual risk requires that the portfolio have minimal tracking error about the index. We will consider index fund formation as a special case in one of the case studies described at the end of this chapter.

Leaving aside the rhetoric and the rationalizations, the main advantage of a passive portfolio is that it provides the owner with an "average" performance of one segment of the market at a very low cost. Unfortunately, the purveyors of index funds (and their clients) have become entangled in a competitive situation where it appears vitally important to exactly match the performance of one specific, though arbitrary, "average"—the S&P 500. This has diverted attention from the central benefit of broad and inexpensive participation in the equity markets and has led to the marketing of new, though still arbitrary, indexed products.

The fact that the performance of "the market" can be captured at a low level of residual risk justifies the development of "the theory" (as, for instance, described in Chapter 1) and provides a rational alternative to active management. Of course, it may be advantageous to have the normal portfolio closely approximate the "theoretical" market portfolio; however, the practical difficulties and the resulting costs make this prohibitive.[16] It seems to us that

---

[16]See ibid.

merely because the concept is not exactly attainable is insufficient reason to dismiss the whole subject. Instead, more effort should be directed at providing, first, a vehicle to match the broad performance of the market and, second, vehicles that track the performance of specific segments of the market.[17]

These latter portfolios belong to the type 2 passive strategies mentioned above and should have an important place in the portfolio manager's arsenal. For instance, to take the example of differential taxation again, the market portfolio is not the optimal normal portfolio for both taxable and tax-exempt investors. Leaving the arbitrariness aside, an S&P 500 index fund cannot be the optimal normal portfolio for both types of investor. Instead, the taxable investor has an optimal normal portfolio which is growth biased and the tax-exempt investor has an optimal normal portfolio which is yield biased. On the average, of course, the two portfolios aggregate to the market portfolio. Provided the hypothesis of superior return to high-yielding securities is believed, tax-exempt investors should "index" to a high-yielding universe and taxable investors should "index" to a high-growth universe.

Overview of Active Investment Strategies

MPT has had perhaps its greatest influence in the area of active strategies. After all, it is active portfolio management that most money managers provide, and it is this form of investment strategy that is the most difficult to implement consistently, as is evidenced by the lack of managers who have appeared to outperform the visible indices.

What, then, does MPT have to say about active portfolio management? In order to answer this question, recall the classification of strategies introduced in Chapter 2. The "buy-and-hold" is the passive strategy, which has been adquately dealt with in the earlier sections of this chapter. The active strategies can be classified as market timing, sectoral emphasis, and stock picking. These strategies imply a modification of the normal allocation in response to short-term forecasts for the asset classes, the sectors, and individual stocks, respectively. It is important to realize that special information is required to pursue active management, namely, the expectation that the short-term return will be different from the long-term consensus return. Only if the discrepant forecast is superior to the consensus will the investor profit from the active decision.

Thus, the first implication of MPT is that successful active management requires superior forecasts of the future. Second, portfolio construction must optimally reflect these forecasts. Hence, we must determine the optimal number and magnitude of the active decisions incorporated in the portfolio. In general, the rule is that portfolios must be constructed in such a manner that the contri-

---

[17]Perhaps the most obvious is a fund that matches the performance of small-capitalization stocks. The design of such a fund raises some fascinating technical problems in implementation; these are briefly mentioned in Supplement 5.

bution to portfolio risk is offset, or matched, by the contribution to portfolio reward. We now consider this point in greater detail with reference first to market timing and then to stock selection. Our discussion about sectoral emphasis will be covered as a special case of the analysis of stock selection.

Market Timing[18]

Market timing is the pursuit of an active allocation strategy. To keep a pure focus on this strategy, we will assume that there are only two assets, namely the risk-free asset and the market portfolio, and that the market timer "swaps" between them, depending upon the forecast for future performance. Since both classes bear no residual risk, the overall strategy incurs no residual risk.[19] This strategy is unique among active strategies in that incremental reward can be obtained without the penalty of residual risk. This may sound as if market timers get something for nothing; alas, as we shall shown, this is not the case.

The risk in this strategy is the risk of being wrong, that is, the risk that the consensus will be right and the manager's short-term forecast in error. Hence, the more often the manager shifts, or the larger the shift between cash and the market portfolio, the greater the chances of being wrong and therefore the greater the risk. Equivalently, we can state that the greater the variability in portfolio beta, the greater the risk.

Thus, in terms of the analysis presented in Chapter 2, varying beta induces risk (exactly, the systematic risk per unit time is increased), which can be related to, and must be justified by, a required market return.[20] The entire "loop" would proceed as follows. The portfolio manager forecasts a short-term return on the market. In response to this forecast the beta is modified, which induces increased risk. The more the beta is modified, the greater is the risk and hence the greater is the return that has to be anticipated in order to justify the incremental risk.

---

[18]This section is partly drawn from some unpublished notes by Barr Rosenberg.

[19]This is exactly true if we assume nonnegative holdings in both assets; i.e., the manager cannot act on an extremely favorable market short-term forecast since the highest beta is unity. It is also true (in theory, although unobtainable in practice) if we permit the manager to lever up the market portfolio by borrowing at the risk-free rate and investing in the market portfolio.

[20]It would be convenient to call this the required alpha for the market, and, similarly, to call the judgmental forecast of the short-term rate of return on the market a judgmental alpha. However, alpha is the expected residual return, and neither the market not the risk-free asset are exposed to residual risk; therefore, we retain our pedantry and write "required rate of return" and "forecast rate of return." (Of course, these forecasts should be adjusted for information content and so represent "pure" knowledge, just as the judgmental alphas were purged of noise in the manner described in Chapter 4.) This use of language tends to obscure the real problem, namely, that we are working with the "market portfolio of common stocks" rather than the true market portfolio. In the latter framework, the active allocation (market timing) would certainly induce residual risk about the true market portfolio, and so we could unambiguously talk about an alpha for the common stock sectoral portfolio.

Theory of Market Timing

The key elements required to analyze this decision are the optimal magnitude of the shift in beta in response to a short-term market forecast, and the increase in risk from shifting beta through time. To better understand these topics we have to resort to some simple mathematics.

First, how much should beta be modified in response to a market return forecast? Recall from equation (2–5) that the level of utility (certainty equivalent rate of return), C, of a portfolio can be written as:

$$C = E_P - \lambda V_P, \lambda > 0,$$

where E_P is the portfolio expected rate of return, V_P is its variance, and λ is the amount of expected return demanded as compensation for each unit increase in variance, or the investor's risk-aversion parameter. Since we are working with a levered normal portfolio, we are only concerned with the systematic relationships and so can substitute equations (2–3) and (2–4), i.e.:

$$E_P = i_F + \beta_P(E_M - i_F)$$

and

$$V_P = \beta_P^2 V_M,$$

to give:

$$C_S = i_F + \beta_P(E_M - i_F) - \lambda \beta_P^2 V_M, \tag{5–1}$$

where the subscript S denotes the systematic component and E_M and V_M denote, respectively, the long-term consensus expected rate of return and variance of return on the market. This equation can be rearranged to give:

$$C_S = -\lambda V_M[\beta_P - (E_M - i_F)/2\lambda V_M]^2 + K, \tag{5–2}$$

where K is a constant (independent of beta) given by:

$$K = i_F + (E_M - i_F)^2/4\lambda V_M.$$

Since λV_M is postitive, the optimal value of the portfolio beta occurs when the squared bracket in equation (5–2) is zero. Thus, the long-term, normal value of beta, β_N, which maximizes the certainty equivalent rate of return, is given by:

$$\beta_N = (E_M - i_F)/2\lambda V_M. \tag{5–3}$$

Let us pause for a moment in the development of the mathematics in order to understand what has happened conceptually. Equation (5–1) shows that the utility of the portfolio arises from two sources. First, there is the contribution from the mean return, which is shown in the upper panel of Figure 5.3, and second, there is the disutility from the variance component. The relationship between portfolio (systematic) variance and beta is the familiar quadratic function, $V_P = \beta_P^2 V_M$, which is shown above the horizontal axis in the middle panel of Figure 5.3. However, it is not the total (systematic) variance that represents the disutility, but the product of investor's risk aversion and total (systematic) variance; i.e., the disutility is $\lambda \beta_P^2 V_M$, which is shown beneath the horizontal axis in the same panel.

The bottom panel shows the relationship between portfolio beta and utility and is found by adding the top panel with the bottom half of the middle panel. In short, the bottom panel is the diagrammatic representation of equations (5–1) and (5–2). As beta increases, utility also increases until it reaches a maximum; further increases in beta reduce expected utility. The maximum point is a diagrammatic representation of equation (5–3).

Since E_M, i_F, and V_M are consensus values, they will typically be the same for all investors. The only parameter that depends upon the individual investor is the risk-aversion parameter, λ. For extreme risk averters, λ will be very large and so the disutility from variance will be much greater than it would be for an investor who displays very little risk aversion. This is shown by the lower dashed line in the middle panel, and its effect on the total utility is shown in the bottom panel (again, as the lower dashed line), where it can be seen that the maximum utility for an extreme risk averter occurs at a low level of beta. This is obvious, since an extreme risk averter does not like risk and risk is an increasing function of beta; hence, extreme risk averters choose low betas!

What is perhaps not so obvious is the relationship between the contributions to utility from the mean and variance of return at the optimal beta. The optimal beta occurs where the utility function is flat (recall that the utility function is the sum of the two contributions), so that the slopes of the contribution from the mean and the contribution from the variance at the optimal beta must be exactly offsetting. Only in this case will they result in a flat slope for the utility function at the optimal beta. In other words, beta is increased up to the point where the marginal increase to utility from the expected return is exactly offset by the marginal decrease of utility from the variance of return. That is, we increase beta to the level where we get no more benefit from further increases.

The slope of the contribution to utility from expected return is independent of beta and equals the market expected excess return, $E_M - i_F$. The slope of the contribution to utility from variance is dependent upon beta and equals $-2\lambda \beta_P V_M$.[21] Since one slope is the negative of the other, the optimal beta, β_N, is found by solving the resulting equation, which gives the same answer as equation (5–3).[22]

Now, suppose that the portfolio manager has a short-term discrepant forecast of a_M (where a stands for abnormal return), so that the actual expected rate of return on the market is $E_M + a_M$. In this case, the (systematic) level of utility for a portfolio with beta, β_P, is:

---

[21]Write $y = -\lambda \beta_P^2 V_M$; then the slope is given by the first differential $dy/d\beta_P = -2\lambda \beta_P V_M$.

[22]That is, at optimality $\beta_P = \beta_N$ and $E_M - i_F = -(-2\lambda \beta_N V_M)$, or $\beta_N = (E_M - i_F)/2\lambda V_M$.

Figure 5.3
Finding the Normal Beta

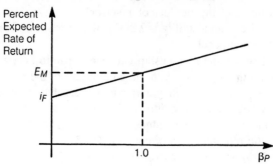

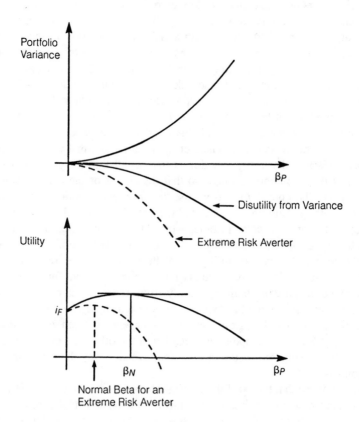

Normal Beta for an
Extreme Risk Averter

$$C'_S = i_F + \beta_P(E_M + a_M - i_F) - \lambda\beta_P^2 V_M$$
$$= -\lambda V_M[\beta_P - (E_M + a_M - i_F)/2\lambda V_M]^2 + K',$$

where K' is another constant. Again, the optimal beta or beta target, β_T, in the presence of a judgmental forecast for the market is found when the squared bracket is zero and given by:

$$\beta_T = (E_M + a_M - i_F)/2\lambda V_M$$
$$= \beta_N + a_M/2\lambda V_M,$$

where we have used equation (5–3) to simplify the last step. Of course, when the short-term discrepant forecast is zero, the beta target is the normal beta. Moreover, the average abnormal return, by definition, is zero (if it were non-zero, then it would be more normal than abnormal), so the average beta target is the normal beta. Hence, on average, the portfolio beta is equal to the normal beta, which again is our definition. It also follows from the last equation that the shift in beta, $\Delta\beta$, is proportional to the market forecast; i.e., $\Delta\beta = \beta_T - \beta_N \propto a_M$. We can substitute equation (5–3) one more time to give:

$$\Delta\beta = a_M\beta_N/(E_M - i_F). \tag{5–4}$$

The effect of the short-term market forecast is shown in Figure 5.4. In the top panel the forecast changes the slope of the contribution to utility from expected return, but it has no effect upon the contribution from variance, so the overall effect is shown in the lower panel. We know that the optimal beta is located where the slope of the contribution to utility from expected return is the negative of the contribution to utility from variance. Since the slope of the variance contribution is proportional to beta, the optimal beta policy is proportional to the market forecast, exactly as was found in equation (5–4).

A consensus investor with a normal beta of unity and a long-term expected excess rate of return on the market of 6 percent would shift beta according to the rule $a_M/6$, so that a short-term market forecast of -3 percent would induce a shift in beta from unity to $1/2$ (i.e., $\Delta\beta = -0.5$). Intuitively, this seems an incredible shift for so small a forecast. It must be emphasized that this -3 percent is adjusted in the manner described in Chapter 4, and thus represents "pure information." A second point is that the beta policy is extremely sensitive to the market forecast. Hence, to make maximal use of the market forecasts, the beta of a portfolio managed by a market timer will have to fluctuate considerably.[23]

This completes the analysis of the beta policy, so now let us consider the risk dimension and, in particular, the magnitude of the increase in risk from market timing. This is a complex subject, and so we will make some simplifying assumptions: first, we will consider only two periods and approximate

---

[23]This is particularly true in the theoretical framework. In practice, transaction costs are an impediment to trading, which causes a damping of the beta fluctuations.

Figure 5.4
Finding the Target Beta

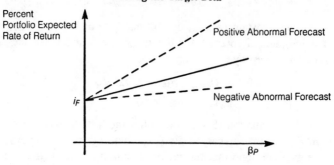

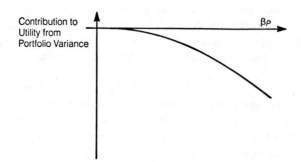

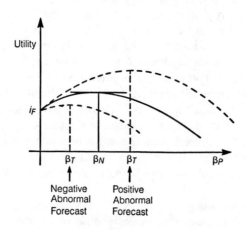

the compound rate of return with the sum of the rates of return in each period. That is, if $(1 + r_1)$ and $(1 + r_2)$ represent the return in periods 1 and 2, then the compound return is approximated by $1 + r_1 + r_2$.[24]

Now the expectation and variance of the compound excess rate of return over the two periods is given by:

$$\text{Expectation} = (\beta_N + \Delta\beta_1)(E_M + a_1 - i_F) + (\beta_N + \Delta\beta_2)(E_M + a_2 - i_F)$$

and

$$\text{Variance} = (\beta_N + \Delta\beta_1)^2 V_M + (\beta_N + \Delta\beta_2)^2 V_M,$$

where a_i represents the abnormal return on the market in the ith ($i = 1,2$) period which is zero on average and uncorrelated between periods, we have assumed that the market variance is the same in both periods, β_N is the long-term beta, and $\Delta\beta_1$ and $\Delta\beta_2$ are the beta shifts in periods 1 and 2. Since β_N is the long-term beta, the beta shifts must average out over time (if they did not, then β_N would not be the long-term beta). Now this last expression for variance can be simplified to:

$$\text{Variance} = 2\beta_N^2 V_M + 2\beta_N(\Delta\beta_1 + \Delta\beta_2)V_M + (\Delta\beta_1^2 + \Delta\beta_2^2)V_M.$$

Notice that the first term represents the normal variance from the long-term beta policy, while the last two terms give the incremental variance due to market timing.

What is the average increase in variance? This is found by taking the expectation of the last two terms. Recall that, on the average, the beta shift is going to be zero, so that the average of $\Delta\beta_1 + \Delta\beta_2$ will be zero. This will not be true of the last term, since we require the average of $\Delta\beta_1^2 + \Delta\beta_2^2$, which is a measure of the variability of beta due to market timing. The expectation of this last term and hence the average increase in systematic variance per period is given by:[25]

$$\text{Average increase in risk from market timing} = \text{Var}[\beta_P]V_M. \qquad \text{(5–5)}$$

Expressed in words, market timing increases the systematic risk per unit time. If the portfolio beta is held constant, the variance of beta is zero, and so there is no increase in risk.

---

[24]The exact compound return is $(1 + r_1)(1 + r_2) = 1 + r_1 + r_2 + r_1 r_2$. Since r_1 and r_2 are likely to be small (e.g., on the order of 0.1), the last term, $r_1 r_2$, is of the order 0.01, or 10 times smaller than the other terms, and so the approximation is reasonable. As was mentioned in Supplement 1, logarithmic returns should be used in multiperiod analyses, in which case this approximation would not be required because the "logarithm of a product is the sum of the logarithms." The cost of using logarithms is a more complicated exposition; hence, we prefer to use the (approximate) arithmetic formulation.

[25]Here we have used the formula $\text{Var}[\Delta\beta] = E[\Delta\beta^2] - E^2[\Delta\beta]$, see equation (S1–6) in Supplement 1, where the last term is zero because the average beta shift is zero, so that $\text{Var}[\Delta\beta] = E[\Delta\beta^2]$. But since the normal beta is a constant through time $\text{Var}[\beta_P] = \text{Var}[\beta_N + \Delta\beta] = \text{Var}[\Delta\beta]$.

Market timing increases the risk of the portfolio, for which the manager anticipates an increase in the mean return. The increase is found from the expression for the expectation of the excess return given above, namely:

Increase in expected return $= (\Delta\beta_1 + \Delta\beta_2)(E_M - i_F) + \Delta\beta_1 a_1 + \Delta\beta_2 a_2.$

On average, how much is gained from the optimal beta policy? At first glance it might seem that the average increase is zero since, on average, $\Delta\beta_1$ and $\Delta\beta_2$ are zero. That this is not the case follows from the fact that under the optimal beta policy the beta shift is a function of the abnormal market return as given in equation (5–4). It is easiest to see the simplification of the formula for the increase in expected return if equation (5–4) is rewritten (using the notation for this example) as:

$$a_1 = \Delta\beta_1(E_M - i_F)/\beta_N$$

and

$$a_2 = \Delta\beta_2(E_M - i_F)/\beta_N.$$

If these expressions are used to substitute for a_1 and a_2 above, we find:

$$\begin{aligned}\text{Increase in expected return} = {}& (\Delta\beta_1 + \Delta\beta_2)(E_M - i_F) \\ & + (\Delta\beta_1^2 + \Delta\beta_2^2)(E_M - i_F)/\beta_N.\end{aligned}$$

As for the variance computation, the first term is zero on average, while the second is a function of the variance of beta; exactly, the average increase in expected return per period is given by:

$$\begin{array}{l}\text{Average increase in} \\ \text{expected return from} \\ \text{market timing}\end{array} = \text{Var}[\beta_P](E_M - i_F)/\beta_N.$$

Finally, it is worth noting that for an optimal beta policy:

$$\begin{array}{l}\text{Average increase in} \\ \text{expected return from} \\ \text{market timing}\end{array} = \theta \cdot \begin{array}{l}\text{Average increase in} \\ \text{risk from market} \\ \text{timing,}\end{array}$$

where

$\theta =$ Mean-variance ratio of the normal portfolio.

In other words, market timing using the optimal policy preserves the risk/reward trade-off of the normal portfolio.

A Numerical Example

This is sufficient algebra. Now let's give a numerical example of these concepts. Suppose there are two portfolios, A and B, with allocations as follows:

	Year 1				Year 2				
	Per-cent Cash	Per-cent Equity	β_P	$\Delta\beta$	Per-cent Cash	Per-cent Equity	β_P	$\Delta\beta$	Average Beta
Portfolio A	25	75	0.75	0	25	75	0.75	0	0.75
Portfolio B	50	50	0.5	−0.25	0	100	1.00	+0.25	0.75

Portfolio A is the stable portfolio with a constant beta of 0.75; portfolio B is managed by a market timer who still maintains the average beta of 0.75. The formula for cumulative variance is given above and calculated as follows, where we have assumed that the market variance is 400 ($\%^2$):

$$\text{Portfolio } A = (0.75)^2 400 + (0.75)^2 400 = 450 \ (\%^2);$$
$$\text{Portfolio } B = (0.50)^2 400 + (1.00)^2 400 = 500 \ (\%^2).$$

The increase in risk for the market timer is 50 units of variance over the two years, or 25 units per year. How does this compare with our expression derived above for the increase in risk? First, the variance of beta for the market timer is calculated as (see equation (S1−5)):

$$\text{Var}[\beta_P] = \tfrac{1}{2}(0.5 - 0.75)^2 + \tfrac{1}{2}(1.0 - 0.75)^2 = (0.25)^2 = \tfrac{1}{16},$$

so that:

$$\text{Var}[\beta_P]V_M = \tfrac{1}{16} \cdot 400 = 25 \ (\%^2),$$

which agrees with our result that the average increase in risk per year, due to market timing, is 25 units of variance.

In other words, active management in the form of market timing has increased the risk of the portfolio. For this increase in risk the manager should expect some reward (why else would the systematic risk exposure be changed?), but how much? In Chapter 2, the required alpha was presented as a method of introducing "quality control" for active management. In particular, it was asserted that given an identical investor's attitude to both systematic and residual risk, the mean-variance ratio of active management should equal the mean-variance ratio of the normal portfolio. Therefore, if we write the required rate of return from market timing as a_{MT}^R, then:[26]

$$\frac{\text{Active required mean return}}{\text{Active variance}} = a_{MT}^R / \text{Var}[\beta_P]V_M$$
$$= \frac{\text{Passive mean return at normal beta}}{\text{Passive variance}}$$
$$= \beta_N(E_M - i_F)/\beta_N^2 V_M.$$

---

[26]Notice that this is the required rate of return that must be achieved for the beta policy to be optimal. It is not the required rate of return for the market. See equations (2−9) and (2−10) for the analogous results for the active portfolio.

We can solve this expression for a_{MT}^R to give:

$$a_{MT}^R = \text{Var}[\beta_P](E_M - i_F)/\beta_N. \tag{5-6}$$

This equation shows the magnitude of the compensation required to justify market timing. If the beta is managed at a constant level (i.e., $\beta_P = \beta_N$), then the variance of beta is zero and no compensation is required. As the beta policy becomes more aggressive, greater reward is required.

For the numerical example above, we have the values $\text{Var}[\beta_P] = \frac{1}{16}$, $(E_M - i_F) = 6\%$, $\beta_N = \frac{3}{4}$, which, when substituted into equation (5-6), gives:

$$a_{MT}^R = 0.5\%, \text{ or 50 basis points per year.}$$

Hence, the manager of portfolio B should believe that the market timing will provide 50 basis points in expected return. Otherwise, the beta policy is not optimal.

To complete this numerical example, let us suppose that the beta policy is optimal and hence given by equation (5-4). Now, solving for the abnormal expected returns on the market that provoked the shifts in beta, given $E_M - i_F = 6\%$, $\beta_N = \frac{3}{4}$, $\Delta\beta_1 = -\frac{1}{4}$, and $\Delta\beta_2 = \frac{1}{4}$, we find that $a_1 = -2\%$ and $a_2 = 2\%$. Hence the increase in expected return from optimal market timing is $\Delta\beta_1 a_1 = (-\frac{1}{4})(-2) = 0.5\%$ in the first year and $\Delta\beta_2 a_2 = (\frac{1}{4})(2) = 0.5\%$ in the second year. We can also use the expression for the average increase in expected return. First, the computation for the mean-variance ratio of the normal portfolio is:

$$\text{Mean-variance ratio} = \frac{\frac{3}{4} \cdot 6}{\frac{3}{4} \cdot \frac{3}{4} \cdot 400} = \frac{1}{50} \, (\%^{-1}).$$

Therefore, the average increase in expected return from market timing is:

$$25 \, (\%^2) \cdot \frac{1}{50} \, (\%^{-1}) = 0.5\%.$$

As we would expect, the rate of return required to compensate for the additional risk is exactly equal to the expected rate of return earned from a beta policy that makes the optimal trade-off between judgment and risk.

These relationships are shown in Figure 5.5. For simplicity, the top panel displays the passive frontier for the case where the expected excess return on the market is the same in both years (i.e., no market forecast, so that the change in beta is either unnoticed or careless). Portfolio A lies on the frontier with a risk level of 225 ($\%^2$), while portfolio B lies on the frontier at location B_1 (variance = 100) one half of the time and at location B_2 (variance = 400) the other half of the time. Thus, on the average, the portfolio lies on the straight line midway between the two locations, at point B, where the variance is 250 ($\%^2$). Notice that this line lies underneath the passive frontier; hence,

Figure 5.5
Market Timing

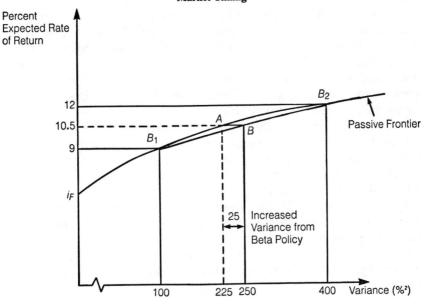

Case A. No Market Forecast

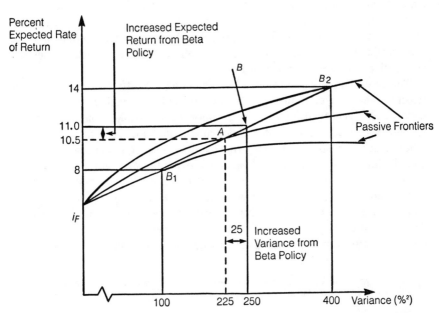

Case B. Market Forecasts of −2 Percent (year 1) and +2 Percent (year 2)

varying beta without explicit forecasts causes the portfolio to become inefficient.

The lower panel shows the case where the forecast of abnormal return is −2 percent in the first year and 2 percent in the second year. Portfolio B now lies above the passive frontier and obtains 0.5 percent more than portfolio A. We can think of portfolio B as lying at one point on the active frontier due to market timing. Other points on the active frontier would be delivered by managers with different forecasts of abnormal return or different aversion to market timing risk relative to systematic risk.

The implication of this section is not that market timing is intrinsically bad but that it adds risk by changing the exposure to market variance. Further, we again have the concept of an attainable frontier from active management—in this case, market timing. If the manager has very little information or a high relative aversion to market timing risk, a conservative strategy might be to go from a 1.0 beta to a 0.95 beta, while an aggressive strategy might be to go from 1.0 to 0.8. Hence, there is an efficient frontier that can be delivered by a market timer and the exact location (specified by its incremental risk and reward) of a portfolio on the market timing frontier depends upon how actively the beta is managed, in terms of both the frequency and the magnitudes of the manager's shifts.

Profits from Market Timing

A market timer has to be very good to break even.[27] A flavor of the mathematics for this unfortunate conclusion was given in the supplement to Chapter 4, where we showed that the Sharpe ratio for the market was only one component of the Sharpe ratio for the portfolio. We will not go further into the mathematics here, because it is rather intricate, but will try instead to develop an intuitive reason for our conclusion.

This intuition can be developed by comparing the difference between stock selection and market timing. With stock selection, investing in a perceived undervalued security results in one addition to a portfolio, and much of the added risk of that security is diversified among the other securities in the portfolio. Hence, the impact of any particular stock selection decision is averaged with the impact of the other decisions. This is not the case with market timing.

With market timing, a single decision is made at a given point in time and thus cannot be diversified with any other market timing decision at the same point in time. In short, in contrast to stock selection decisions, which can be diversified at every point in time, market timing decisions can only be diversified over time. Thus, it is far more obvious when market timing goes astray

---

[27]For an alternative analysis, see William Sharpe, "Likely Gains from Market Timing," *Financial Analysis Journal*, March–April 1975, pp. 2–11.

and one has to be right far more often than wrong in order to benefit from it. The extreme sensitivity of the beta policy to the market forecast means that a market timer has to work very hard to earn an abnormal return.

Between the strategy of market timing and the strategy of stock selection is the strategy of emphasizing the sectors, which may be thought of as *factor timing*. To the extent that several sectors can be emphasized at one time, the decision concerning one sector is diversified by the decisions concerning the others. For this reason, we omit a detailed discussion of sectoral emphasis and proceed with an analysis of stock selection, which incorporates the analysis for factor timing.

Stock Selection

The key to stock selection is that portfolios must optimally reflect the judgmental alphas on the component securities. That is, the return of each individual security holding must contribute to the offsetting of portfolio risk. To take a hypothetical example, suppose we start the week with no information (i.e., we are neutral on every security). The portfolio, then, is the optimal passive portfolio, which for the sake of simplicity we will assume to be the S&P 500 as a proxy for the market portfolio.[28] Now suppose that analysis on Monday indicates that IBM is overvalued and DEC is undervalued. Clearly, we should increase the portfolio holding of DEC at the expense of IBM; thus, relative to the normal portfolio, there is now an overweighting of DEC and an underweighting of IBM.

Because the (now actively managed) portfolio is differentiated from the market portfolio (S&P 500), it is exposed to residual risk. The question now is: To what extent should the holding in DEC be increased and the holding in IBM be decreased? If we completely eliminate the holding in IBM, there will be a negative relative holding of approximately 7 percent in IBM and a positive relative holding of the same amount in Digital Equipment.[29] These relative holdings are referred to as *active holdings* since they are responsible for the residual risk in the portfolio. As these active holdings are increased, in both the negative and positive directions, the residual risk and the portfolio alpha increase.

There is obviously a stage at which the residual risk increases to such a degree that it is no longer beneficial to increase the active holdings. At that stage, the increase in risk is so great that the resulting increase in alpha does not compensate for the additional risk. The most crucial objective in the management of a single portfolio is to maintain asset holdings at a level where the increase in risk can be exactly justified by the increase in reward.

---

[28] This assumption also indicates that the normal beta is unity.

[29] On December 31, 1978, IBM represented 6.97 percent of the S&P 500.

How do we determine this level? Consider an actively managed portfolio with holdings as follows:[30]

	Market Weight	Portfolio Weight	Active Holding	Alpha
IBM	6%	4%	−2%	−$\frac{1}{2}$%
DEC	1	3$\frac{1}{2}$	2$\frac{1}{2}$	3
Burroughs	$\frac{1}{2}$	0	−$\frac{1}{2}$	0

The left-hand column shows the percentage of the assets in the market; the next column shows their percentage in the portfolio. We will assume that the beta of the portfolio is unity and that the asset holdings and attributes other than those indicated above are equal to their market values.

The "Active Holding" column indicates the degree of active management of these assets. The active holding is defined as the difference between the portfolio weight and the market weight and is usually represented by the Greek letter delta, δ.[31] IBM has an active holding of −2 percent, which means that its portfolio holding is 2 percent less than the market holding. Hence, the only difference between this actively managed portfolio and the market portfolio are active holdings of −2, 2$\frac{1}{2}$, and −$\frac{1}{2}$ percent in IBM, DEC, and Burroughs, respectively.

These positions are based upon the analysis of each security's risk-adjusted excess rate of return, or judgmental alpha, which is indicated in the right-hand column. Thus, it is expected that IBM will underperform other stocks in its risk class by $\frac{1}{2}$ percent a year. Recall from Chapter 4 that this is not a point forecast but the mean of the distribution of future abnormal returns adjusted for the information content. Similarly, DEC is expected to outperform other assets in its risk class by 3 percent.

The judgmental alpha on the portfolio is now the weighted sum of the active holdings, where the weights are the alphas. In this portfolio there are 498 stocks with alphas of zero: IBM, which contributed $(−0.02)(−0.5)$ percent, or 1 basis point, and DEC, which contributes $(0.025)(3)$ percent, or 7.5 basis point, for a total of 8.5 basis points of alpha. It is tempting to use the portfolio weights instead of the active weights; in general, however, this is incorrect since the S&P 500 has holdings in IBM and DEC and would have experienced 6 percent and 1 percent of the respective alphas. Only when the alphas are correctly scaled (as they are here) so that the market has zero alpha will these

---

[30]The market weights are only approximately correct; in this context, however, the exact values are immaterial.

[31]The correct definition of the portfolio active holding in the jth security, δ_j, is $\delta_j = h_{Pj} - \beta_P h_{Mj}$, where h_{Pj} and h_{Mj} are the holding of the jth security in the portfolio and the market, respectively, and β_P is the portfolio beta. Since the portfolio beta in the example is unity, the definition in the text is correct. For further discussion, see Supplement 3.

two calculations yield the same result. As has been remarked, the only way to achieve differential performance is to hold a differential portfolio. When a stock performs better than the average, a greater holding than the market must be held in order to achieve a relative benefit, and vice versa.

To determine whether these active holdings are correct, we have to perform the same type of computation as is performed for market timing. However, now there are three dimensions (the three companies) and not one (the portfolio beta). To keep the analysis simple, we will consider the companies in pairs. Thus, we shall be searching for the correct relative weighting between IBM and DEC, given the remainder of the portfolio. In this manner, we need only work with two dimensions.

Figure 5.6 is analogous to the top diagram in Figure 5.3, namely the contribution to utility from expected return, in this case, alpha. The top panel has three axes: the vertical axis is portfolio alpha; the horizontal axis is the holding in IBM; and the axis pointing away from the reader is the holding in DEC. The market portfolio is located at point M with coordinates (6, 1) in the horizontal plane. This point locates the origin for the alpha computation since it is the origin for the active holdings, which are shown as axes meeting at that point. As the active holding in IBM is increased, the portfolio alpha decreases, and so we are moving "downhill" but parallel to the IBM axis. In the other direction, as the active holding in DEC is increased, portfolio alpha also increases, and so we are moving "uphill." The exact value of the portfolio alpha depends upon the location of the portfolio in the alpha plane, which tilts upward to the left and away from the reader. This is shown in another fashion in the lower panel, which graphs the contours of equal alpha. These are straight lines with a slope of $^1/_6$ (i.e., increasing the IBM holding by six units is exactly offset by increasing the DEC holding by one unit).

It is easy to see from the contours that the highest alpha portfolios are obtained by placing as much weight as possible in DEC. However, the more the DEC holding is increased, the greater is the residual risk incurred. We can show the effect of risk in the same two ways. The risk function is drawn in the top panel of Figure 5.7 and looks like one half of an eggshell, with the bottom placed on the market. As active holdings are increased in either direction, residual risk increases at a faster rate. We refer to this as the risk bowl. The bottom panel shows the contours of constant variance, which are approximately concentric ellipses.[32] The ellipses are closer together the farther they are from the market portfolio, indicating that risk is becoming greater at an increasing rate.[33]

---

[32]If the residual returns from IBM and DEC were independent and had the same variance, the contours would be concentric circles centered at the market. Since the residual returns of these companies are unlikely to be independent and with the same variability, the circles become "squashed" and form ellipses.

[33]Mathematically, residual variance increases as the square of the active holding. Thus, an active holding of two units has four times the risk of an active holding of one unit.

Figure 5.6
Effect of Asset Holding on Portfolio Alpha

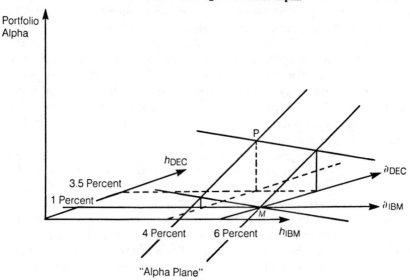

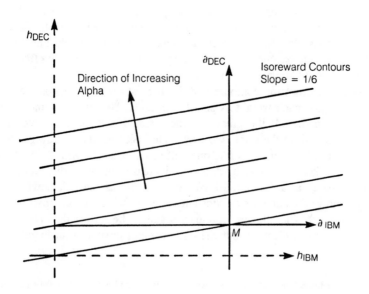

Figure 5.7
Effect of Asset Holding on Residual Risk

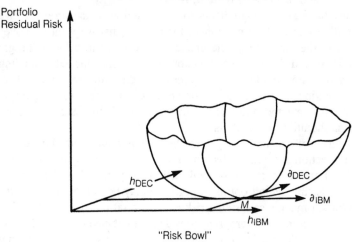

Portfolio
Residual Risk

h_{DEC} ∂_{DEC}

∂_{IBM}

M

h_{IBM}

"Risk Bowl"

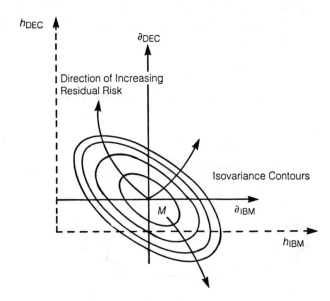

h_{DEC}

∂_{DEC}

Direction of Increasing
Residual Risk

Isovariance Contours

M ∂_{IBM}

h_{IBM}

Moreover, the major axis of each ellipse is upward sloping to the left (in this case), showing that there is less risk in purchasing one asset and selling the other than in purchasing both. The intuition is that IBM and DEC are positively correlated, so that assets are hedged when one is sold short. Finally, when the investor's risk aversion is incorporated (again see the middle panel of Figure 5.3 for the market timing case), the bowl becomes inverted; for different levels of risk aversion, the inverted bowls vary between being wide and shallow and being narrow and deep (see Figure 5.8).

We now have all the ingredients for the solution to the problem. We can argue intuitively from the alpha plane, Figure 5.6, that we want to move from the market in the direction of the greatest slope so as to achieve the greatest incremental reward. This is the direction of increasing the DEC holding and decreasing the IBM holding. As we move in this direction, the risk of the position is pulling the overall utility down, as can be seen from Figure 5.8. In fact, if we become too aggressive, the disutility from residual risk will be greater than the utility from alpha.

Using this method may not get us the best possible portfolio because we chose the direction of travel by looking at the slope of the alpha plane, ignoring the risk bowl and the fact that some directions may have less risk than others. In other words, the overall optimum portfolio may be at a point where there is lower alpha but much less residual risk, so that total utility is improved.

A portfolio optimization program considers simultaneously the effect of both alpha and risk on the portfolio. Doing this prevents misleading the program by looking only at the alpha plane or only at the risk bowl. As we saw from Figures 5.3 and 5.4, if both dimensions are considered simultaneously, then the surface that results has a unique optimum, which is the portfolio sought by the optimization program.

Figure 5.8
Contribution to Utility from Portfolio Residual Risk

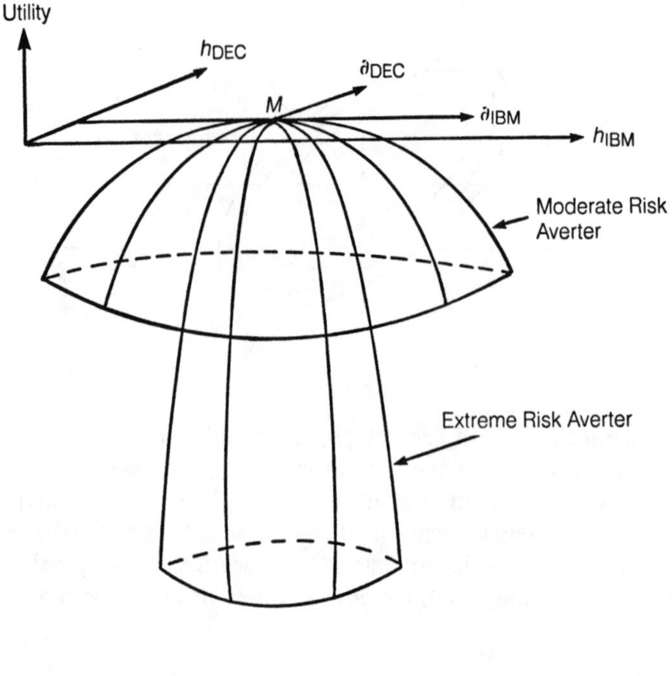

However, it is conceptually easier to work with the contours. In Figure 5.9 we have drawn them in the same diagram. If we now wish to find the best portfolio with an alpha of five basis points, we draw the contour of constant reward (isoreward contour) equal to five basis points. We then look for the portfolios where the contours of constant variance (isovariance contours) cut the isoreward contour.

In the diagram three portfolios, *A*, *B*, and *C*, are shown on the isoreward contour. Which is the optimal portfolio? Portfolio *B* has an alpha of five basis points, but it lies on a contour which has greater variance than that of portfolio *C*. Portfolio *C* is "better"than portfolio *B*. However, portfolio *A* is the optimal portfolio since the isovariance contour is a tangent to the isoreward contour, and hence there can be no other portfolio along the isoreward contour with lower variance. The criterion for optimality is for the isovariance contour to be tangent to the isoreward contour.

We can locate optimal portfolios for all values of alpha. These are shown as points along the "expansion path." Eventually, this path will hit the vertical axis, showing that the IBM holding has been completely sold out. If short sales are prohibited, the expansion path then moves up the axis. The kink in the path indicates that the constraint has prevented the portfolio from achieving the same

Figure 5.9
Solution of the Optimal Portfolio

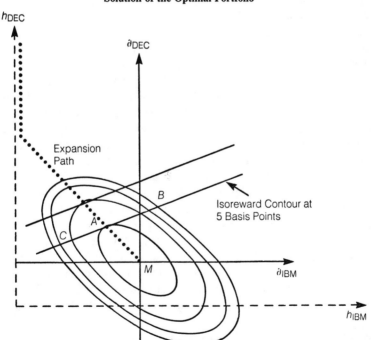

increase of alpha per unit of risk and that another stock, perhaps Burroughs, must be sold to fund the additional purchases of DEC. We will make a more detailed analysis of this kink in the Chapter 6 section "The Information Ratio and Variable Aggressiveness."

This is reasonable as theory, but what are the implications for the real world? Essentially, there are two. First, we can take the risk bowl as given (i.e., use a risk model such as that described in Chapter 3 to determine the isovariance contours) and calculate the tangency point. This is the computation of the required alpha. Or, second, we can proceed directly with judgmental alphas on the assets, the risk model, and compute the optimal portfolio. We refer to these approaches as, first, local optimization, since we are interested in the "local" region around the portfolio, and second, global optimization, since we are interested in finding the overall optimal portfolio.

Local Optimization

In order to calculate the required alphas, we need to determine the risk bowl. Let us start by considering the contribution to portfolio residual risk, measured by the residual standard deviation, from an individual stock. This is displayed in Figure 5.10. Recall that residual risk is composed of specific risk and extra-market covariance. Three curves are displayed in Figure 5.10. One curve, the lowest, is for specific risk. This curve is symmetrical about the market proportion of the stock. When the portfolio holding in the stock exactly matches that of the holding in the market, then the portfolio is immunized against the specific risk of the stock. This follows from the fact that if the stock goes bankrupt (to take the worst example), and hence exhibits a specific return of minus 100 percent, then the market and the portfolio will each display the same relative performance. As the portfolio holding diverges from the market holding, the specific risk of the portfolio increases. For a stock with a low specific risk, such as American Telephone and Telegraph, the slope of this curve at any given point is not steep.[34] For a risky stock, the slope will steepen rapidly as the holding diverges from the market proportion.

The contribution from *XMC* is not quite so straightforward. In the diagram the contribution to *XMC* is shown as a downward-sloping curve over the entire region. However, this need not be true for every stock. In the situation depicted in Figure 5.10, *XMC* decreases as the holding in the stock increases, because this particular stock's exposure to the factors is opposite to the combined exposure of the remainder of the portfolio. In other words, this stock hedges the rest of the portfolio with respect to the common factors of return. One explanation is that the portfolio is biased toward small-capitalization stocks, whereas this is a large-capitalization stock. So, as more and more of the stock is pur-

---

[34]The magnitude of the specific risk prediction for AT&T is shown in Table 3.6 for January 1979. In fact, AT&T has the lowest specific risk of exchange-traded institutional stocks.

Figure 5.10
One Asset's Contribution to Portfolio Residual Risk

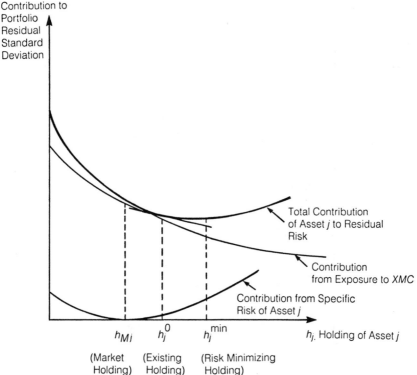

chased, we decrease the exposure to the small-company factor and hence the level of *XMC*. The downward-sloping curve will reach a minimum value at the point where this stock, although hedging the small-company factor, creates additional risk by exposing the portfolio to the other factors.

Residual risk, the sum of specific risk and *XMC*, is shown by the bold curve. Because *XMC* is larger than specific risk, the portfolio residual risk tends to retain its characteristics. It is downward sloping over most of the region and only increases with the larger holdings of the stock. The indication, therefore, is that increasing the existing holding would decrease residual risk. The existing holding is greater than the market proportion, and yet residual risk would be decreased by taking an even larger active holding. To many investment managers this is somewhat counterintuitive.

Figure 5.10 does not represent the only possible case. There are, in fact, five cases to consider, all of which are shown in Figure 5.11. The main point of the five panels is that the relationship between the level of portfolio residual risk and transactions in the stock to minimize residual risk is related to the slope of the risk function at the existing holding. Hence, if we know or can

Figure 5.11
Residual Risk Minimizing Transactions

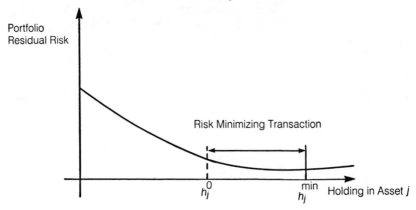

1. A Diversifying Asset

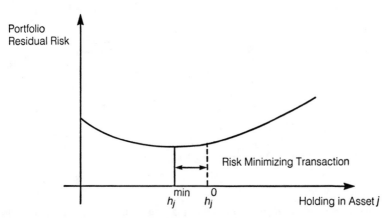

2. A Concentrating Asset (optimal holding is positive)

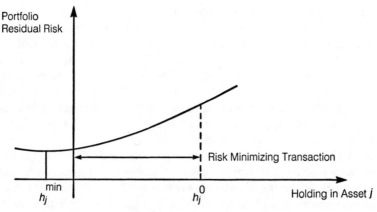

3. A Concentrating Asset (optimal holding is zero)

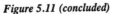

Figure 5.11 (concluded)

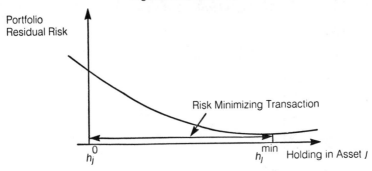

4. A Diversifying Asset (original holding at zero)

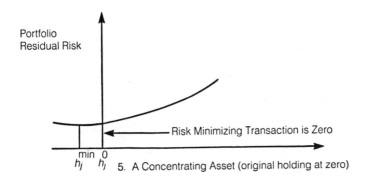

5. A Concentrating Asset (original holding at zero)

calculate the slope, then the transaction that must be made to minimize residual risk can also be found.

How does this help us in analyzing the optimal transaction to be made in response to both risk and return? We can answer this question by reference to Figure 5.12, which shows the trade-off between portfolio alpha and residual risk and is an almost exact replica of Figure 5.3.

The return dimension is described in the top panel: the portfolio alpha is plotted on the vertical axis, while the holding in a particular stock is plotted on the horizontal axis. Since portfolio alpha is linearly related to the holding in the stock, it follows that for the positive alpha asset in the figure an increase in the holding also increases portfolio alpha. The slope of this relationship is the alpha of the stock. The second panel describes the (now familiar) contribution of the stock to portfolio residual risk and is similar to one of the panels shown in Figure 5.11. In this case, we have depicted a concentrating asset since risk increases as the holding increases. By putting these two panels together, we have the situation shown in the bottom panel in Figure 5.12.

Portfolio utility is described by a smooth "hill" whose top represents max-

Figure 5.12
Trading Off Residual Risk and Return

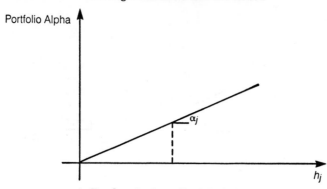

1. The Contribution to Portfolio Alpha

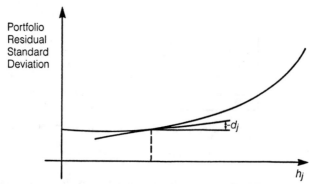

2. The Contribution to Portfolio Residual Standard Deviation

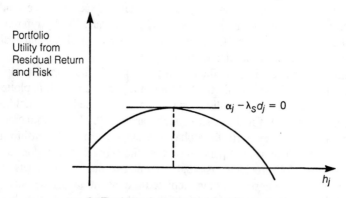

3. The Utility from the Residual Components

Note: λ_s is the investor's aversion to standard deviation, which is different in magnitude to the investor's aversion to variance. See footnote 38.

imum utility. At the very top the increase in portfolio alpha (as shown in the top panel) is exactly offset by the decrease in utility from the increased risk (as shown in the middle panel), adjusted by the investor's risk-aversion parameter.

The next step is extremely powerful. If we can measure the slope of the risk function (the contribution to residual risk from a particular stock) and the risk-aversion parameter, then we have specified one component of the equation that governs optimality. We can then solve this equation and determine the alpha that is required to justify the risk contribution of the stock, or, in other words, the required alpha of that stock.

Figure 5.13 goes through this step in more detail. Case A of Figure 5.13 shows a concentrating holding that has a necessarily positive effect upon residual risk. When the risk contribution is matched against the judgmental alpha, which may be (1) less than the required alpha, (2) equal to the required alpha, or (3) greater than the required alpha, then this results in an optimum holding that is (1) less than the existing holding, (2) equal to the existing holding, or (3) greater than the existing holding. In other words, the comparison of the required alpha with the judgmental alpha indicates whether the portfolio being analyzed is correctly balanced, given the manager's judgment. Case B shows a diversifying holding, which, by definition, has a negative effect upon residual risk. The results of this analysis show that the required transactions are the same as those for a concentrating asset.

This analysis is referred to as local optimization. The risk function is measured from a predictive risk model, and the effect of small changes in the neighborhood of the present portfolio are calculated. This enables the manager to calculate the required alpha of every asset in the portfolio.[35] It then becomes a straightforward matter to screen stocks by comparing the research department's judgments on those assets with their required alphas. This provides a remarkably powerful tool for analyzing whether portfolios accurately reflect the research department's judgments on the individual securities.

To see how this works in practice, let us go back to the example of the Dow Jones Industrial Average.[36] Figure 5.14 shows an example of a report on the stocks in this index viewed as a portfolio. The 30 stocks are listed alphabetically with CUSIP identifiers, percentage of portfolio value, number of shares, and price per share at the end of 1978.[37] It is now obvious why the index displays the amount of specific risk it does; three stocks, Du Pont, Eastman Kodak, and Procter & Gamble, account for almost one quarter (23.7 percent) of the DJIA.

---

[35]In addition, required alphas of assets not held can be calculated. For these assets, the zero portfolio holding or, equivalently, the active holding equal to the negative of the market holding is used to provide an upper bound on the required alpha.

[36]Three additional example portfolios with required alphas can be found in Supplement 4.

[37]CUSIP is a registered trademark of the American Bankers Association's Committee on Uniform Security Identification Procedures. The American Bankers Association identifies many financial instruments with a unique eight-digit identifier.

Figure 5.13
The Required Alpha and the Optimal Transaction

Case A. A "Concentrating" Holding (with positive effect upon residual risk)

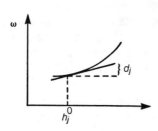

When Traded against an Alpha That Is:

(1) Less than the
Required Alpha

(2) Equal to the
Required Alpha

(3) Greater than the
Required Alpha

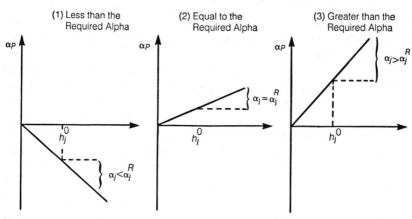

Results in an Optimum That Is:

(1) Less than the
Existing Holding

(2) Equal to the
Existing Holding

(3) Greater than the
Existing Holding

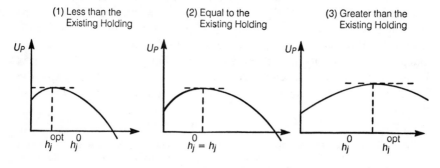

Figure 5.13 (concluded)

Case B: A "Diversifying Holding (with negative effect upon residual risk)

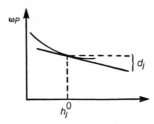

When Traded against an Alpha that Is:

(1) Less than the Required Alpha	(2) Equal to the Required Alpha	(3) Greater than the Required Alpha

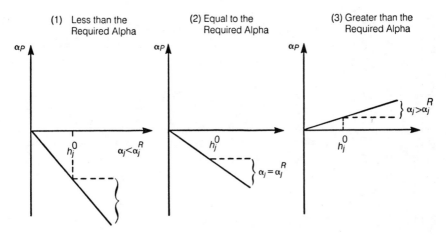

Results in an Optimum that Is:

(1) Less than the Existing Holding	(2) Equal to the Existing Holding	(3) Greater than the Existing Holding

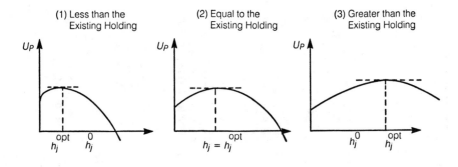

Figure 5.14
Analysis of the Dow Jones Industrial Average (12/29/78)

BARR ROSENBERG & ASSOC.
DOW JONES 30 INDUSTRIALS

CONTRIBUTIONS OF INDIVIDUAL ASSETS TO PORTFOLIO RISK

	CUSIP	NAME	PERCENT OF PORTFOLIO VALUE	EFFECT OF 1% PURCHASE ON BETA	EFFECT OF 1% PURCHASE ON RESID. STDEV	REQUIRED ALPHA	NUMBER OF SHARES	PRICE PER SHARE	ALPHA
1.	01908710	ALLIED CHEM CORP	2.4	0.0038	0.080	0.56	100.	28.25	0.0
2.	02224910	ALUMINUM CO AMER	4.1	-0.0003	0.060	0.42	100.	47.75	0.0
3.	02470310	AMERICAN BRANDS INC	4.3	-0.0039	0.050	0.35	100.	50.38	0.0
4.	02484310	AMERICAN CAN CO	3.1	-0.0025	0.057	0.40	100.	35.88	0.0
5.	03017710	AMERICAN TEL & TELEG CO	5.2	-0.0040	0.004	0.03	100.	60.50	0.0
6.	09750910	BETHLEHEM STL CORP	1.7	0.0024	0.123	0.87	100.	19.63	0.0
7.	17119510	CHRYSLER CORP	10.7	0.0055	0.087	0.61	100.	8.63	0.0
8.	26353410	DU PONT E I DE NEMOURS	10.9	0.0010	0.111	0.78	100.	126.00	0.0
9.	27746110	EASTMAN KODAK CO	5.1	0.0009	0.014	0.10	100.	158.63	0.0
10.	29647010	ESMARK INC	2.1	0.0003	0.045	0.32	100.	24.00	0.0
11.	30229010	EXXON CORP	4.2	-0.0024	-0.011	-0.08	100.	49.13	0.0
12.	36960410	GENERAL ELEC CO	4.1	-0.0004	0.016	0.11	100.	47.13	0.0
13.	36985610	GENERAL FOODS CORP	2.8	-0.0008	0.034	0.24	100.	32.13	0.0
14.	37044210	GENERAL MTRS CORP	4.6	-0.0006	0.060	0.42	100.	53.75	0.0
15.	38255010	GOODYEAR TIRE & RUBR	1.4	-0.0006	0.037	0.26	100.	16.13	0.0
16.	45325820	INCO LTD	1.4	-0.0004	0.038	0.27	100.	15.75	0.0
17.	45957810	INTERNATIONAL HARVESTR	3.1	0.0038	0.064	0.45	100.	36.25	0.0
18.	46014610	INTERNATIONAL PAPER CO	3.1	0.0019	0.059	0.42	100.	36.50	0.0
19.	47812410	JOHNS MANVILLE CORP	2.0	0.0029	0.044	0.31	100.	22.63	0.0
20.	60405910	MINNESOTA MNG & MFG CO	5.4	0.0008	0.021	0.15	100.	63.13	0.0
21.	69076810	OWENS ILL INC	1.5	-0.0004	0.052	0.37	100.	17.88	0.0
22.	74271810	PROCTER & GAMBLE CO	7.7	0.0022	0.009	0.06	100.	88.88	0.0
23.	81238710	SEARS ROEBUCK & CO	1.7	0.0023	0.018	0.12	100.	19.75	0.0
24.	85368310	STANDARD OIL CO CALIF	4.0	-0.0012	-0.000	-0.00	100.	46.88	0.0
25.	88169410	TEXACO INC	2.1	-0.0023	0.011	0.08	100.	23.88	0.0
26.	90558110	UNION CARBIDE CORP	2.9	0.0008	0.071	0.50	100.	34.00	0.0
27.	91265610	UNITED STATES STL CORP	1.8	0.0024	0.093	0.65	100.	21.25	0.0
28.	91301710	UNITED TECHNOLOGIES CP	3.4	0.0014	0.027	0.19	100.	38.88	0.0
29.	96040210	WESTINGHOUSE ELEC CORP	1.4	0.0033	0.041	0.29	100.	16.63	0.0
30.	98088110	WOOLWORTH F W CO	1.7	0.0028	0.036	0.26	100.	19.38	0.0

The three remaining columns indicate the effect of risk upon the portfolio. The first of these, headed "EFFECT OF 1% PURCHASE ON BETA," indicates the change in systematic risk (beta) that would occur if a 1 percent purchase were made in a given asset. For instance, we know from Chapter 3 that the beta of the DJIA, β_A, relative to the S&P 500 is 0.97, that the beta of Chrysler Corporation, β_C, is 1.52, and that the beta of a portfolio is a weighted average of the constituent betas. Thus, for a two-"stock" portfolio composed of Chrysler and the DJIA, the combined beta, β_P, is given by:

$$\beta_P = h\beta_C + (1 - h)\beta_A = \beta_A + h(\beta_C - \beta_A),$$

where h is the weight in Chrysler and $(1 - h)$ is the weight in the DJIA. In this case, $h = 1$ percent, so the change in beta from the purchase of Chrysler is:

$$\beta_P - \beta_A = 0.01(1.52 - 0.97) = 0.0055,$$

which is the value given in Figure 5.14. Hence, purchasing Chrysler, or any of the other assets with positive coefficients in the column under discussion, will increase the systematic risk of the portfolio. Conversely, selling any of these assets or purchasing assets with negative coefficients will decrease risk. In this way the systematic component of risk can be controlled.

Let us now turn to the residual dimension. The numbers in the column headed "EFFECT OF 1% PURCHASE ON RESID. STDEV" indicate the effect upon portfolio residual risk if an asset is purchased; these numbers correspond to the value d_j in Figure 5.12. Only two assets have negative coefficients, Exxon Corporation and Standard Oil Company of California, indicating that these are the only diversifying assets. The effect of Standard Oil is so small that it prints as zero, which suggests that Standard Oil is very close to its minimum residual risk position. Purchasing any of the other 28 stocks will increase residual risk, and hence these are concentrating assets.

We know from our previous discussion that the measurements in this column (i.e., values d_j) give the slope of the surface of the "risk bowl" at the location of the portfolio. We also know that if this portfolio is optimal, the slope of the alpha plane will be related; in fact, the slope of the alpha plane will have the opposite sign to the slope of the risk bowl and will be scaled by the investor's risk-aversion parameter. Since it is possible to measure the slope of the risk bowl by using the risk model, the value of the alpha required to justify holding this position can be inferred. This is exactly what is done in the next column.[38]

---

[38]The formula is $\alpha_j^R = \lambda d\omega_P^2/dh_j$, where $d\omega_P^2/dh_j$ is the slope of the risk (variance) bowl at the holding of the jth security and λ is the investor's risk-aversion parameter. In order to derive the required alpha from the previous column, notice that $d\omega_P^2 dh_j = 2\omega_P(d\omega_P/dh_j)$. This last derivative is 100 times that reported in the "EFFECT of 1% PURCHASE ON RESID. STDEV" column; ω_P (reported in Table 3.8) is 4.99 percent; and $\lambda = 0.0069$ ($\%^{-1}$). We will describe the method for calculating λ in the next section.

The required alpha informs the portfolio manager of the expected rate of return required on each asset for that holding to be optimal. Notice that these numbers are all small; even for Du Pont, with a holding of 10 percent, the required alpha is only 78 basis points. In other words, the portfolio manager must expect Du Pont to outperform its risk class by this amount for the holding to be correct. Intriguingly, Bethlehem Steel Corporation has a required alpha of 87 basis points but is held in the portfolio at a level of only 1.7 percent. This is a classic example of the situation referred to above: if a portfolio manager believed these alphas (or even a scaling of them), then there would be a great (but incorrect!) temptation to infer that because Bethlehem Steel is more undervalued than Du Pont, there should be a greater holding in the steel company. This is wrong (1) because it ignores the risk dimension and (2) because it confuses the portfolio holding with the active holding.

In this case, the S&P 500 holdings in Du Pont and Bethlehem are 0.97 percent and 0.14 percent, respectively, so the active holdings are 9.9 percent and 1.6 percent.[39] The active holding in Du Pont is over five times that in Bethlehem Steel Corporation. This difference is justified since Du Pont, as a company, contributes very little to the *XMC* of the portfolio. Bethlehem, on the other hand, reinforces the portfolio exposure to the factors; it has considerable exposure to the earnings variability factor and the low valuation, unsuccess factor (respectively, 4.0 and 4.4; see Table 3.6). Second, the specific risk of the two companies is very different; Du Pont's specific risk is 19.8 percent, and Bethlehem's is 33.26 percent (see Table 3.6). Thus, with a much larger position than Bethlehem, Du Pont will incur the same residual risk as Bethlehem. Moreover, since we know that the slopes of the risk bowls of the two companies are approximately the same (0.111 for Du Pont and 0.123 for Bethlehem), we can infer the composition of the components (analogous to Figure 5.10), as shown in Figure 5.15.

Finally, it is worth mentioning that the assets in the portfolio can be ranked not only in terms of contribution to residual risk but also in terms of any arbitrary universe. For instance, Figure 5.16 shows the 10 most diversifying stocks in the S&P 500 that are not already in the Dow Jones Industrial Average. They all have negative required alphas for the simple reason that they are diversifying assets, and hence desirable, and yet they are not held in the portfolio. This is because the judgmental expectations of their rate of return are "poor." But how poor? DEC is such a diversifying asset that it has a required alpha of -59 basis points. Thus, if this portfolio optimally reflects the manager's judgment, then it must be believed that DEC has a judgmental alpha of less than -0.59.

At the other end of the spectrum, Figure 5.17 shows the 10 most concentrating stocks. Republic Steel Corporation would increase the residual risk of the DJIA to such a degree that it must offer an alpha of 54 basis points or more in order to be considered for inclusion.

---

[39]E.g., $9.9 = 10.84 - (0.97)(0.97)$. See footnote 31.

Figure 5.15
Decomposition of Risk Contributions for Du Pont and Bethlehem Steel

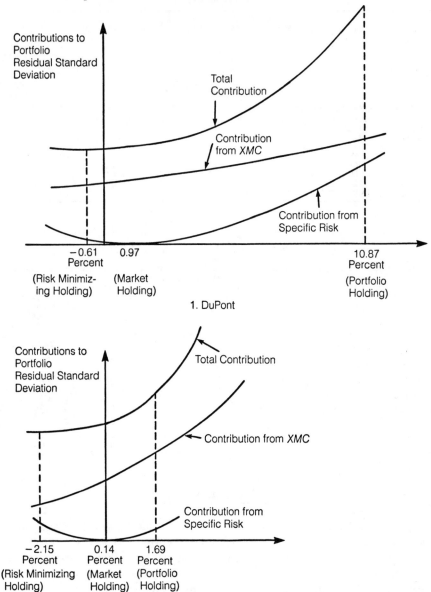

1. DuPont

2. Bethlehem Steel

Figure 5.16
The 10 Most Diversifying Assets in the S&P 500
(12/29/78)

ASSETS LISTED IN INCREASING ORDER OF
MARGINAL CONTRIBUTION TO PORTFOLIO RESIDUAL STD. DEV.

| | | | | | | CHANGES IN PORTFOLIO RISK DUE TO 1% PURCHASE | |
| | | | WEIGHT IN | | REQUIRED | | RESID. |
	CUSIP	NAME	S&P500	PORT	ALPHA	BETA	STDEV.
1.	25384910	DIGITAL EQUIP ...CORP	0.34	0.0	-0.59	0.0043	-0.085
2.	80685710	SCHLUMBERGER LTD	1.29	0.0	-0.55	-0.0007	-0.078
3.	05726410	BAKER INTL CORP	0.15	0.0	-0.50	0.0020	-0.072
4.	45920010	INTERNATIONAL BUS MACH	6.97	0.0	-0.50	-0.0005	-0.071
5.	12611710	CNA FINL CORP	0.05	0.0	-0.48	0.0079	-0.068
6.	45814010	INTEL CORP	0.11	0.0	-0.48	0.0098	-0.068
7.	44449210	HUGHES TOOL CO	0.09	0.0	-0.46	0.0052	-0.066
8.	15231210	CENTEX CORP	0.03	0.0	-0.44	0.0090	-0.063
9.	73190510	POLAROID CORP	0.27	0.0	-0.43	0.0066	-0.061
10.	86827310	SUPERIOR OIL CO	0.21	0.0	-0.41	0.0010	-0.059

Figure 5.17
The 10 Most Concentrating Assets in the S&P 500
(12/29/78)

ASSETS LISTED IN INCREASING ORDER OF
MARGINAL CONTRIBUTION TO PORTFOLIO RESIDUAL STD. DEV.

| | | | | | | CHANGES IN PORTFOLIO RISK DUE TO 1% PURCHASE | |
| | | | WEIGHT IN | | REQUIRED | | RESID. |
	CUSIP	NAME	S&P500	PORT	ALPHA	BETA	STDEV.
461.	45747010	INLAND STL CO	0.12	0.0	0.40	-0.0001	0.057
462.	48931410	KENNECOTT COPPER CORP	0.11	0.0	0.41	0.0066	0.058
463.	54777910	LOWENSTEIN M & SONS	0.01	0.0	0.46	0.0037	0.065
464.	63784410	NATIONAL STL CORP	0.09	0.0	0.48	-0.0008	0.068
465.	04341310	ASARCO INC	0.07	0.0	0.48	0.0036	0.068
466.	96315010	WHEELING PITTS STEEL	0.01	0.0	0.49	0.0040	0.070
467.	45870210	INTERLAKE INC	0.02	0.0	0.50	-0.0010	0.071
468.	02277110	AMALGAMATED SUGAR CO	0.00	0.0	0.50	0.0008	0.071
469.	01020210	AKZONA INC	0.02	0.0	0.51	0.0015	0.073
470.	76077910	REPUBLIC STL CORP	0.06	0.0	0.54	0.0005	0.077

Global Optimization

The method presented in the previous section is ideally suited for analyzing a small number of minor transactions for a portfolio that has been carefully constructed. In other words, local optimization is designed for "fine-tuning" a strategy so as to make certain that the portfolio reflects the most up-to-date judgment. The control mechanism is to compare the required alphas with the judgmental alphas in order to determine whether the portfolio incorporates the correct relative valuation of each asset. The portfolio reflects the current judgment if the two sets of alpha are identical.[40] If they are not identical, then the

---

[40]This is the theoretical condition for optimality. In practice, many managers use weaker conditions—for instance, that the ranking of the two sets of alphas be the same.

portfolio should be revised in order to capture more of the manager's judgment. The optimal revisions are exactly those described in the previous section.

The inputs to the local optimization procedures are: the current portfolio, which is assumed to be optimal (i.e., it accurately reflects the manager's judgment); the predictive model of investment risk; and, the preference structure of the investor (i.e., the risk-aversion parameter, λ). The output is the list of required alphas, that is, the judgment which is genuinely reflected by the composition of the portfolio. Thus, given an (optimal) portfolio, we can calculate the judgment that formed it, but is it possible to take the judgment and form the portfolio directly from it? The answer is, of course, yes—the procedure being portfolio optimization. We use the adjective *global* to refer to the fact that an infinite number of portfolios may have to be searched to find the one which is optimal.

Global optimization is the reverse of local optimization (recall that we introduced this distinction in Chapter 2). The inputs are: the list of judgmental alphas; the predictive model of investment risk; and λ, the preference structure of the investor. The output is the optimal portfolio. The two procedures are shown in Figure 5.18, from which it is clear that if the required alphas are used as the judgmental alphas in the input to the optimization, then the resulting optimal portfolio is exactly the same as the original portfolio which was the subject of the local analysis. In other words, a consistent, although trivial, relationship is established (at considerable cost in terms of computer time) between local and global analysis and between required and judgmental alphas.

Figure 5.18
Comparison of Local and Global Optimization

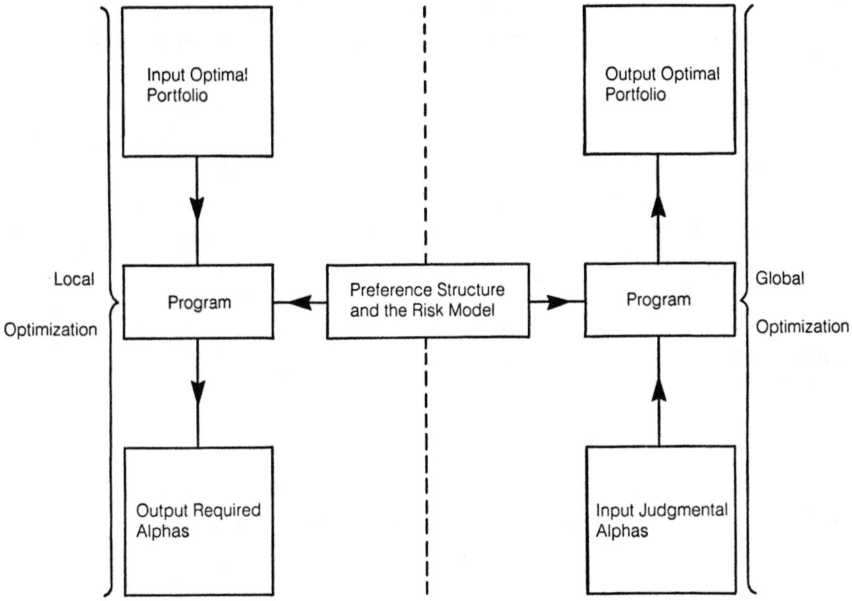

So much for the conceptual foundations of portfolio optimization. But how is it performed? Simply stated, portfolio optimization is the "black box" that achieves many of the goals of portfolio management. In one sentence, the major goal is to obtain, with the lowest possible risk, a high return (which may be specified in terms of cash yield or capital appreciation, or both) after allowance for taxes, transaction costs, and other fees incurred as a result of managing the portfolio. The subtlety is to use this sentence as the basis for fashioning a realistic, quantitative model of the process.

Why, many readers will demand, not leave portfolio construction as a craft—the way it has been for decades—rather than complicate and confuse it in a cloak of mathematical symbolism? The simple answer is that constructing a portfolio to reflect judgment is exceedingly difficult—far too difficult for the human mind to do consistently well—but a machine has the ability to take the judgment and continuously produce portfolios without the emotional biases that are so damaging to performance. We say a machine because the process of going from the judgment to the final portfolio is a mechanical process; there is nothing creative or profound about it, because we can write down the entire procedure as a set of steps which, if followed, will result in the optimal portfolio. In other words, the only ingredient is judgment; the utensils are the predictive risk model and the investor's preference structure; and portfolio optimization is the cookbook. Of course, to get a perfect boiled egg every time, the recipe must include all the important steps. Let us briefly review the recipe for portfolio construction.

We have previously established that a reduction in portfolio risk can be achieved only at a sacrifice in expected return. The greater the importance attached to return, as opposed to risk, the greater will be the level of risk assumed in the portfolio in the pursuit of return. The means by which risk and expected return (plus other portfolio attributes) are made commensurate is the utility function. This function combines the important portfolio attributes into a single objective, which provides an overall measure of desirability.

If we combine this construct with the previous results on risk and expected return, the utility of the portfolio, U_P, can be written as the sum of two components: portfolio utility arising from the market systematic relationships, U_{PS}, and portfolio utility arising from residual or nonmarket relationships, U_{PR}; i.e., $U_P = U_{PS} + U_{PR}$. Let us describe the components in turn.

1. Systematic. The systematic expected excess rate of return on the portfolio is $\beta_P(E_M - i_F)$, while the systematic variance is $\beta_P^2 V_M$, (see, for instance, equations (2–3) and (2–4), so that the level of systematic utility can be written (compare with equation (2–5)):

$$U_{PS} = \beta_P(E_M - i_F) - \lambda\beta_P^2 V_M,$$

where $\lambda(> 0)$ is the investor's risk-aversion parameter. Following the same procedure as in equation (5–2), this expression can be written as:

$$U_{PS} = -\lambda V_M[\beta_P - (E_M - i_F)/2\lambda V_M]^2 + K, \tag{5-7}$$

where $K = (E_M - i_F)^2/4\lambda V_M$ is a constant. To simplify this expression, let us redefine some of the terms. Write $\Lambda_\beta = -\lambda V_M$ and $\beta_T = (E_M - i_F)/2\lambda V_M$. The portfolio utility can now be written:

$$U_{PS} = K + \Lambda_\beta(\beta_P - \beta_T)^2, \tag{5-8}$$

or in words:

Utility = Constant term
+ (Negative coefficient)(Portfolio beta
− Target portfolio beta)^2,

where Λ_β is the negative coefficient. Thus, the systematic relationships reduce to (1) expressing a target beta which is the value deemed most desirable and (2) finding an "aversion parameter," Λ_β, which indicates the dissatisfaction that results from not exactly being on the beta target.[41] This description is the symbolic version of the one shown in Figure 5.3 for market timing. The only differences from that analysis are that here (1) the change is to expected *excess* return and (2) the decision variable is now the short-term beta target as opposed to the long-term normal beta.

2. Residual. The investor's aversion to total risk is measured by λ. This parameter then determines the attitude toward beta through the process described above. It also describes the attitude toward residual variance: the aversion parameter for residual variance, $\Lambda_\omega(< 0)$, equals (in absolute value) that for total variance, λ.[42] What is the benefit received from residual risk? Only alpha, or the expectation of extraordinary return for the portfolio. The contribution to utility from these sources is expressed as follows:

$$U_{PR} = \alpha_P + \Lambda_\omega\omega_P^2,$$

where α_P is the portfolio alpha, ω_P^2 is the portfolio residual variance, and Λ_ω is the (negative) risk-aversion parameter.

We can now combine both components to give:

$$U_P = K + \alpha_P + \Lambda_\beta(\beta_P - \beta_T)^2 + \Lambda_\omega\omega_P^2, \tag{5-9}$$

or

Utility = Constant term
+ Portfolio alpha
+ Λ_β (Portfolio beta − Target portfolio beta)^2
+ Λ_ω (Portfolio residual variance).

If these portfolio attributes completely determine the desirability of the portfolio, then the optimization problem is to maximize the utility given by equation

---

[41]If the beta is on target, then the portfolio utility is just the constant term. If the beta is off target, then the utility is reduced.

[42]We wish to retain two symbols in order to analyze the generalization described in the next section. We have changed the sign of Λ_ω so that all coefficients in the utility function appear with positive signs.

(5–9). Clearly, the constant K is going to play no part in this optimization; it will simply change the absolute values of desirability rather than the relative ranking of the portfolios. Thus, we can omit K from the analysis (and we will do so in subsequent equations). Although equation (5–9) is more complicated than many early optimization specifications, it is still insufficiently realistic for most of the problems encountered in the real world. The single, major deficiency is the omission of transaction costs.

The vast majority of portfolio management decisions take place in the context of the revision of an existing portfolio. If transaction costs (commissions + taxes incurred as a result of sales + losses due to adverse price movements caused by the act of trading) were zero, and if there were no institutional consequences from realizing an asset whose market value differed from its book value, then the existing holdings would be immaterial for the simple reason that it would cost nothing to liquidate the entire portfolio and start from scratch. However, transaction costs do exist and book value considerations do arise, which implies that the portfolio revision problem is crucially influenced by the existing holdings.

The portfolio management goal is to improve the utility of the portfolio risk and return attributes but to do this in such a way that only an appropriate amount of transaction costs and book adjustments are made. This goal is accomplished by an augmented utility function, in which the effects of transactions on utility are included. In general, a different utility coefficient may be attached to the purchase and sale of each individual stock.

For a purchase, the coefficient is determined solely by the transaction costs and will always be negative. For an easily purchased stock, the transaction cost penalty is very small; for a stock that is infrequently traded and difficult to obtain, the transaction cost penalty can be very large.

For a sale of an existing holding, there will again be a transaction cost penalty, typically of the same magnitude as the penalty for a purchase. There may be a modification of this cost (either positive or negative), resulting from the tax effect of a realized capital gain or loss and possible implications of the effect upon book value of such a gain or loss.

The next step is to determine the functional form of the penalty. Little work has been done in this area, but the majority of transaction cost schedules take the following form: $C_0 + C_1 L + C_2 D$, where C_0, C_1, and C_2 are constants, L is the number of shares traded, and D is the dollar value of the trade. In other words, the transaction cost is composed of a setup cost plus an amount proportional to the size of the trade (defined either by shares transacted or dollar value). When the book value and tax considerations are included, this form may become still more complicated. However, the major part of the cost will be proportional to the size of the trade, and so we assume that the form of the penalty for a given asset is of the form:

(Sale penalty on asset) · (Amount of asset sold)
+ (Purchase penalty on asset) · (Amount of asset purchased).

This is shown diagrammatically in Figure 5.19. The total loss in utility from revising the portfolio is the adjusted sum of these terms over all assets transacted. The adjustment required is to amortize the loss in utility over the holding period of the assets. For instance, if one third of the portfolio is "turned over" in one year, then it seems reasonable to allocate one third of the loss to the first year. This adjustment is performed by multiplying the loss by a (negative) amortization factor.

In ideal circumstances, there is no important distinction between the dividend component of portfolio return and the capital appreciation component, so portfolio cash yield is a matter of indifference. However, on some occasions the investment environment is not "ideal." For instance, dividends and capital gains are differentially taxed, so that the distinction between them becomes important in personal trust management; or, in many institutional contexts, yield has important strategic or symbolic consequences (e.g., endowment funds); or legal status may assume significance (e.g., the distinction between income beneficiary or remainderment in a trust portfolio). For these reasons, portfolio yield may be an important goal; in the majority of cases, it can be modeled (1) as a general desire to maximize yield or to achieve a trade-off with some other portfolio attribute or (2) as an important target with respect to cash yield. These two cases are analyzed by adding to the utility function these final terms:

(1) $\Lambda_Y y_P, \Lambda_Y > 0$

   [(Positive coefficient) · (Portfolio yield)],

or

(2) $\Lambda_C(y_P - y_T)^2, \Lambda_C > 0$

   [(Negative coefficient) · (Portfolio yield − target yield)^2].

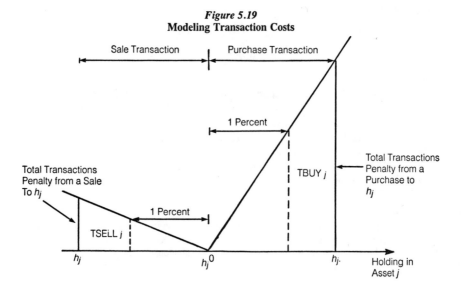

Figure 5.19
Modeling Transaction Costs

Table 5.2 shows the form of the utility function that covers the logic of the major management goals.[43]

Before this formulation can be used, the values for the coefficients Λ_Y, Λ_T, Λ_C, Λ_β, and Λ_ω have to be determined. The crucial parameters are those which set the risk/reward trade-off, namely Λ_β and Λ_ω. The easiest way of obtaining these values is to infer them from the asset allocation decision. For instance, equation (5–3) specifies the long-term, normal value of beta in terms of the expected excess return on the market and the risk-aversion parameter. Recall that $\Lambda_\beta = -\lambda V_M$, so equation (5–3) can be rewritten as equation (5–3'):[44]

$$\Lambda_\beta = -(E_M - i_F)/2\beta_N \qquad (5–3')$$

Thus, given the fairly noncontroversial long-term values (applicable to a typical pension sponsor) of $E_M - i_F = 6\%$ and $\beta_N = 1$, then $\Lambda_\beta = -3\%$, which implies that if the portfolio fails to meet the target beta by one, then the resulting disutility is equivalent to a certain loss of 3 percent. This follows since the

Table 5.2
Utility Function for Portfolio Optimization

In words:

Utility = Portfolio alpha
+ (Positive coefficient) · (Portfolio yield)
+ (Negative amortization factor) · [(Sale penalty)
(Total sales transactions) + (Purchase penalty)
(Total purchase transactions)]
+ (Negative coefficient) · (Portfolio yield - Target yield)²
+ (Negative coefficient) · (Portfolio beta - Target beta)²
+ (Negative coefficient) · (Portfolio residual risk).

In symbols:

$$U_P = \alpha_P + \Lambda_Y y_P + \Lambda_T[\sum_j TSELL_j(h_j^0 - h_j)^+ + \sum_j TBUY_j (h_j - h_j^0)^+]$$
$$+ \Lambda_C(y_P - y_T)^2 + \Lambda_\beta(\beta_P - \beta_T)^2 + \Lambda_\omega \omega_P^2,$$

where
$\Lambda_T(< 0) =$ the transaction cost amortization factor (i.e., the proportion of transaction costs to be applied against this year's return);
$TSELL_j =$ the sale transaction penalty on the jth asset;
$TBUY_j =$ the purchase transaction penalty on the jth asset;
$h_j^0 =$ the original holding in the jth asset;
$h_j =$ the revised holding in the jth asset; and
$(\cdot)^+ =$ maximum $(0,\cdot)$.

[43]For instance, more complicated expressions may include targets for the portfolio risk indices.
[44]This formula is correct for a portfolio which is under the control of a single manager. Some small changes have to be made for the multiple manager situation; see Chapter 6.

contribution to utility from beta, $\Lambda_\beta(\beta_P - \beta_T)^2$, reduces to just Λ_β when $\beta_P - \beta_T = \pm 1$.

The aversion to residual risk is, by our assumption, equal to the aversion to total risk; i.e., $\Lambda_\omega = -\lambda$. From the definition of the systematic risk aversion, Λ_β, it is seen that:

$$\lambda = -\Lambda_\beta/V_M.$$

An approximate value for the market variance is $V_M = 400 \ (\%^2)$. Hence, the residual risk aversion is determined approximately as:[45]

$$\Lambda_\omega = -\lambda = -3/400 = -0.0075 \ (\%^{-1}).$$

The implication of this value is that every increase of one unit of residual variance results in a disutility equivalent to a certain loss of three fourths of a basis point in return.

Another approach for eliciting the investor's risk preferences is to present the investor with a series of risky choices and to have the investor indicate his or her preferences among them. This approach has been used a good deal by experimental psychologists, though (to our knowledge) not by investment consultants.[46]

Finally, the remaining parameters can be found by noting that the units of the utility function are in percentage points of certainty equivalent rate of return. Thus, if the yield of the portfolio is increased by 1 percent, then the increase in utility is Λ_Y percent. Using this type of framework, the values for the coefficients describing the trade-offs can be quantified.

This completes the description of the utility function, which, as indicated earlier, is simply an index of desirability for each portfolio. Some portfolio goals may be not only desirable, but required; for instance, holdings on some assets may be required to be above some minimum or below some maximum. Sometimes such bounds exist to achieve economic objectives (for instance, when a portfolio holding must be maintained above a certain minimum in order to preserve a controlling interest), or to meet legal requirements designed to enforce diversification or to ensure prudence (for instance, the exclusion of short selling), or to reflect preferences (for example, the prohibition of investments in certain industries). Maintaining required minimum or maximum asset holdings is best implemented by means of constraints. Thus, instead of introducing a term into the utility function, absolute restrictions on acceptable portfolios are expressed by upper and lower bounds on holdings.

There is a great temptation to overconstrain the portfolio by using unneces-

---

[45]In footnote 38, the value of λ was computed as 0.0069. The reason for the discrepancy is that this calculation correctly used the predicted market variance. From Table 3.8 (item D), the market standard deviation is 20.88 percent, so the market variance is $(20.88) (20.88) = 435.97$ $(\%^2)$. Hence, $\lambda = 3/435.97 = 0.0069 \ (\%^{-1})$.

[46]See, for instance, Ralph Swalm, "Utility Theory—Insights into Risk Taking," *Harvard Business Review*, November–December 1966, pp. 123–136.

sary restrictions—for instance, to insist that specified proportions of the port-folio be invested in certain industries for no apparent reason. The usual ration-alization for using such constraints is to either force diversification or to prevent the portfolio produced by the optimization program from being "noninstitu-tional" (for example, too concentrated). However, such uses of constraints are counterproductive, for two reasons. First, the constraints are arbitrary and are found by second-guessing the solution. Either the optimal portfolio is known, in which case the use of portfolio optimization is a waste of effort; or it is not known, in which case there is no reason to choose one value rather than another for the constraint (10 percent in business machines sounds reassuring, but why not 11 percent or 9 percent?). Second, the use of the constraints indicates a lack of confidence in one or more of the inputs, most commonly the valuation judgments (alphas) or the risk model. If the inputs are not believed and the output is constrained to conform to some preconceived values so as to produce "vanilla-flavored" portfolios, then the entire exercise seems a little pointless.[47]

For the vast majority of applications the following constraints are all that is necessary:

1.   Upper and lower bounds on assets[48]
2.   A budget constraint to ensure that all wealth is fully allocated
3.   Upper and lower bounds on the portfolio beta
4.   Upper and lower bounds on the portfolio yield

The use of additional constraints, particularly constraints forcing industry hold-ings, should be severely questioned. In general, such constraints will be overly restrictive and will dictate suboptimality. The current sophistication in the pre-dictive modeling of risk suggests that additional constraints are superfluous for enforcing diversification. Table 5.3 shows the mathematical specification of these portfolio restrictions.

Note that the utility function (given in Table 5.2) contains some terms which are linear in the portfolio holdings (for instance, alpha and yield) and some terms which are quadratic in the portfolio holdings (for instance, portfolio re-sidual variance and the contribution from beta), while the portfolio restrictions (given in Table 5.3) include only linear functions of the portfolio holdings. Thus, the portfolio optimization problem, which, descriptively, is the determi-nation of the portfolio that maximizes utility subject to certain restrictions, can be expressed mathematically as the search for asset holdings, h_j, which maxi-mize a quadratic function (utility) subject to several linear constraints.

It is only comparatively recently (the early 1960s) that both the algorithms and the computational power required to solve this type of mathematical prob-lem have become sufficiently developed for portfolio optimization to be realist-

---

[47]Marketing may be a reason: "We use an optimization program!" But what is the response when a client calls the bluff by analyzing the "optimal" portfolio to determine the required alphas?

[48]There may be good reasons why these restrictions should be more complicated than has been suggested here. We will discuss this point at the end of this section.

Table 5.3
Portfolio Restrictions

1. Bounds on asset positions:

$$hmin_j \leq h_j \leq hmax_j$$

for all assets j, where $hmin_j$ and $hmax_j$ are the lower and upper bounds, respectively.

2. Budget constraint:

$$1 = \sum_j h_j.$$

3. Beta constraint:

$$\beta_{min} \leq \sum_j \beta_j h_j = \beta_P \leq \beta_{max},$$

where β_{min} and β_{max} are the lower and upper bounds on portfolio beta, respectively.

4. Yield constraint:

$$y_{min} \leq \sum_j y_j h_j = y_P \leq y_{max},$$

where y_{min} and y_{max} are the lower and upper bounds on portfolio yield, respectively.

ically implemented.[49] This is not a mathematical text, so we will not dwell on the theory and computational complexities of such problems here; it is sufficient to say that the problem is called a quadratic program and that algorithms exist to solve large, realistic problems (several hundred assets) for only a few dollars.[50]

Let us now return to the subject of the bounds on the asset positions (see footnote 48). The realism of the modeling of this aspect is importantly deficient in two regards. The first simplification is that a manager would typically require the following restriction (usually to minimize custodial and accounting expenses): "Either the asset is not held in the portfolio (lower bound of zero), or the holding must be greater than X percent (lower bound of X percent)." Thus, the restriction is an "either/or" constraint. The second simplification is that this model permits the holding to take any value between the upper and lower bounds. In general, the manager will only make transactions in round lots (again for administrative reasons), so the holding should take discrete, rather than continuous, values.

There is no difficulty in modeling these restrictions. The difficulty, perhaps

---

[49]An algorithm is a finite set of logical steps which, when followed, guarantee either that a solution will be obtained or that no solution exists.

[50]The mathematical foundations are covered in greater detail in the supplement to this chapter.

surprisingly, is that their inclusion causes the problem to become computation-ally impossible.[51] Fortunately, it is possible to closely approximate the solution by incorporating these constraints after the simpler problem has been solved. We will describe this generalization to the portfolio optimization model in the supplement to this chapter.

Portfolio optimization is now being used and is proving its value. First, it guarantees the consistent construction of each portfolio; second, it enables each portfolio to genuinely reflect the valuation judgment upon each security; and, third, it frees energy and effort for more important tasks (for instance, the creation of asset alphas). Finally, many problems (for instance, research studies designed to answer "what if" questions) can only be solved with its guidance. Portfolio optimization is truly the recipe for consistent portfolio management. Is this the end of the story? Not quite.

The Residual Frontier

Presented with the solution to a portfolio optimization problem, a portfolio manager may intuitively feel that the computed optimal portfolio is not the correct portfolio for the client.[52] This is not a reason for discarding the portfolio optimization approach but rather an opportunity to examine the foundations and assumptions from which the "optimal" portfolio was constructed. Portfolio optimization is nothing more than a series of logical deductions. If the solution is "wrong," then the specification of the problem or one or more of the inputs must be in error.

Assuming that the problem specification is correct (i.e., incorporates trans-action costs, etc.), then the inputs to the optimization should be checked. Fig-ure 5.18 shows that the inputs include (1) the asset alphas, (2) the risk model, and (3) the investor's preference structure. The most likely candidates for the error are the asset alphas. Again, it is important to stress that the difficulty of arriving at an alpha is not justification for sidestepping the process. As we remarked above, without alphas there is no controlled active management and without active management there is only a passive fee! The fact that the alphas may be incorrect (i.e., suggest a portfolio with which the manager is uncom-fortable) should be a spur to understanding the cause of the error.

It seems reasonable that the risk model is more accurate than the alphas, though some risk models are better than others. This belief can be justified on the grounds that (1) predicting risk is ideally performed by econometric meth-ods and (2) the model can be verified statistically.[53]

---

[51]These constraints change the problem into an integer quadratic program for which there are no general-purpose algorithms.

[52]We assume that the manager's intuition is correct.

[53]It strikes us that any organization which uses any form of investment model bears the respon-sibility of verifying its efficacy.

The final input is the preference structure (risk/reward trade-off) of the investor, and it is this specification that is the topic of this section. Recall from the previous discussion that the systematic trade-off is specified by the coefficient Λ_β. Because this value is obtained from the normal beta, it is unlikely that the optimal portfolio beta will be much different from the value required. The residual trade-off is specified by the coefficient Λ_ω, which is obtained by assuming that the aversion to residual risk is equal to the aversion to systematic risks, i.e., $\Lambda_\omega = -\lambda$. Therefore, one logical reason why the computed optimal portfolio may not appear to be the correct portfolio for the client is that the client's aversion to residual risk may be different from the client's aversion to systematic risk.[54] We can accommodate this structure by first introducing a (nonnegative) parameter, κ (the Greek letter kappa), which measures the aversion toward residual risk relative to systematic risk, and then defining the residual risk aversion as:

$$\Lambda_\omega = -\kappa\lambda. \tag{5-10}$$

If $\kappa = 1$, then residual and systematic risk are to be avoided equally; if κ is greater than one, then residual risk is more disliked than systematic risk; if κ is less than one, then residual risk is less important than systematic risk. Of course, if $\kappa = 0$, then there is no aversion to residual risk.

As indicated in Chapter 2, the normal value for the relative aversion toward these sources of risk should be one (i.e., $\kappa = 1$), provided that the investor's portfolio is controlled entirely by one manager. If there are several managers, then the residual risk in each component becomes diversified when the aggregate portfolio is analyzed. Thus, an individual manager should have less aversion to residual risk than to systematic risk. In addition, the aversion should depend upon the proportion of the investor's fund that is managed. For instance, a manager who has only 1 percent of the investor's total wealth can afford to be extremely aggressive in pursuit of superior performance (i.e., assume a great deal of residual risk) because the impact of that manager's risk upon the aggregate portfolio will be small since most of that risk (but not the return) will be diversified by the remaining 99 percent of the portfolio.

The key concept is that the manager's aversion to residual risk should depend upon the proportion of the investor's wealth that is under his or her management. Thus, money management firms that achieve "consistency" by running one or two model portfolios, which form the target for individual portfolio managers, are pursuing the wrong form of consistency for multiply managed portfolios. The portfolios for different clients should look alike only if the same proportion is under management.

The common elements for every portfolio are the asset valuations, which are reflected with varying intensity depending upon the proportion of the aggre-

---

[54] We briefly introduced the reasons for different attitudes toward these two risk components in Chapter 2. We will touch on the problem again in Chapter 6.

gate portfolio. It should be clear from this discussion that a set of alphas does not generate a single optimal portfolio. Instead, it generates an infinite number of optimal portfolios, each of which is one point on the residual frontier, corresponding to one value of the relative aversion parameter, kappa.[55]

We strongly believe that the utility function should be fully specified prior to the use of portfolio optimization. There is a temptation to calculate the entire frontier (by computing four or five portfolios on it) and then choose one portfolio with which the manager is comfortable. This is the easy approach. It is also suboptimal because the risk/reward trade-off may vary wildly from period to period and thus damage the control of risk. For portfolio decisions it is more productive to think first and compute afterward.[56] However, it is an extremely valuable expository device to compute the residual frontier. For this reason, we include the following case study here and discuss the implementation of variable aggressiveness in the next chapter.

Case Study 4: Varying Portfolio Aggressiveness

The starting portfolio for this exercise is a comparatively aggressive institutional portfolio containing 30 asset holdings. The manager's style is to accent the growth and small-capitalization companies. Figure 5.20, 5.21, and 5.22 show, respectively, the front page of the PORCH analysis, the risk decomposition, and the asset holdings. In Figure 5.22, the assets are ordered by their alpha value.

Figure 5.23 lists the 98 assets that the institution follows (without the 30 assets in the portfolio), again with alpha values. It should be fairly clear from the two asset lists (if only from the scarcity of companies in the S&P 500) that the management style is extreme!

Let us first consider the case of decreasing the aversion to residual risk. The discussion earlier in this chapter suggests that assets with high alphas will be purchased, if less disutility arises from residual risk, and vice versa. The size of the transaction in an asset is related to that asset's contribution to portfolio risk. Figure 5.24 shows the portfolio holdings when the initial portfolio is revised, subject to zero transaction costs and $\kappa = 0.125$; i.e., the aversion to residual risk is one eighth of the aversion to systematic risk.

There are now only 11 assets in the portfolio; each was in the original port-

---

[55]The derivation of kappa for a multiply managed portfolio will be described in Chapter 6.

[56]See footnote 8. Recently parametric quadratic programming algorithms have been developed which compute the frontier fairly inexpensively. At present, their problem specification is not fully general; however, there is no doubt that further advances will be made in the future. See, for example, Jong-shi Pang, "A Parametric Linear Complementarity Technique for Optimal Portfolio Selection with a Risk-Free Asset," *Operations Research*, July–August 1980, pp. 927–41; and Harry Markowitz and André Perold, "Reducing Models of Covariance to Weighted Sums of Squares: A Procedure for the Fast Determination of Efficient Portfolios," paper presented at the Institute for Quantitative Research in Finance, April 1980.

Figure 5.20
PORCH Analysis of Original Portfolio

```
              FUNDAMENTAL RISK MEASUREMENT SERVICE
                      PORTFOLIO ANALYSIS
                    BARR ROSENBERG & ASSOC.


PORTFOLIO STATUS AS OF   OCTOBER 31 1978
  ANALYSIS CONDUCTED    NOVEMBER 12 1978
  FIRMS UPDATE AS OF     OCTOBER 31 1978
S&P500    IS THE MARKET PORTFOLIO
```

1. SUMMARY MEASURES FOR COMMON EQUITY

A. PREDICTED SYSTEMATIC RISK COEFFICIENT {BETA} - NEXT 3 MONTHS   1.21

B. PREDICTED SYSTEMATIC RISK COEFFICIENT {BETA} - NEXT 5 YEARS   1.18

C. ANNUAL STANDARD DEVIATION OF SYSTEMATIC PORTFOLIO RETURN   25.35%

D. FRMS FORECAST STANDARD DEVIATION OF ANNUAL S&P500 RETURN   20.94%

    PORTFOLIO RISK FORECAST, INCLUDING EXTRA-MARKET COVARIANCE . . .

E.1	STANDARD DEVIATION OF ANNUAL PORTFOLIO RETURN	26.31%
E.2	STANDARD DEVIATION OF ANNUAL PORTFOLIO RESIDUAL RETURN	7.04%
E.3	COEFFICIENT OF DETERMINATION BY S&P500	0.928
E.4	REQUIRED ANNUAL PORTFOLIO APPRAISAL PREMIUM {ALPHA}	0.56
E.5	INFERRED COVENANT INFORMATION RATIO {CIR}	0.090
E.6	INFERRED CEER OF ACTIVE MANAGEMENT	0.282%

    RISK FORECASTS BASED UPON A SIMULATED 5-YEAR HISTORY OF MONTHLY
RETURNS FOR THE PORTFOLIO . . .

F.1	STANDARD DEVIATION OF ANNUAL PORTFOLIO RETURN	25.59%
F.2	STANDARD DEVIATION OF ANNUAL PORTFOLIO RESIDUAL RETURN	6.48%
F.3	COEFFICIENT OF DETERMINATION BY S&P500	0.936

2. INDICES OF RISK IN THE PORTFOLIO

INDEX OF RISK	PORTFOLIO	S&P500	FRMS UNIVERSE	EFFECT OF .01 INCREASE ON RESID. STDEV	REQUIRED ALPHA
MARKET VARIABILITY	0.540	0.0	0.150	0.0106	0.09
EARNINGS VARIABILITY	0.191	0.0	0.225	0.0041	0.04
LOW VALUATION, UNSUCCESS	0.077	0.0	-0.090	0.0088	0.08
IMMATURITY AND SMALLNESS	0.974	0.0	0.564	0.0202	0.17
GROWTH ORIENTATION	0.560	0.0	0.112	0.0082	0.07
FINANCIAL RISK	0.081	0.0	0.129	0.0075	0.06

Figure 5.21
Decomposition of Variance

DECOMPOSITION OF VARIANCE OF ANNUAL PERCENT RETURN				
		FRMS MODEL	SIMULATION	PREDICTION
SYSTEMATIC		642.5	613.0	642.6
SPECIFIC	29.7			
RISK INDICES VARIANCE	25.2			
INDUSTRY VARIANCE	4.4			
R.I.--INDUSTRY COVARIANCE	-2.2			

XMC	27.4			

RESIDUAL		57.2	41.9	49.6
		-----	-----	-----
TOTAL		699.8	655.0	692.2

Figure 5.22
Assets in the Original Portfolio

ASSETS IN THE PORTFOLIO LISTED IN INCREASING ORDER OF
MARGINAL CONTRIBUTION TO PORTFOLIO RESIDUAL STD. DEV.

	CUSIP	NAME	INDUSTRY GROUP	WEIGHT IN S&P500	WEIGHT IN PORT	ALPHA	CHANGES IN PORTFOLIO RISK DUE TO 1% PURCHASE BETA	RESID. SIDEV.
1.	74456710	PUBLIC SVC ELEC & GAS	30	0.23	3.27	-0.37	-0.0046	-0.043
2.	71850710	PHILLIPS PETR CO	14	0.76	3.06	-0.35	-0.0031	-0.041
3.	65352210	NIAGARA MOHAWK PWR CP	30	0.14	3.42	-0.25	-0.0048	-0.029
4.	21181310	CONTINENTAL OIL CO	14	0.46	2.95	-0.24	-0.0032	-0.028
5.	45920010	INTERNATIONAL BUS MACH	19	6.39	3.28	-0.22	-0.0031	-0.025
6.	29449710	EQUITABLE GAS CO	30	0.09	3.31	-0.18	-0.0055	-0.021
7.	14912310	CATERPILLAR TRACTOR CO	18	0.79	3.26	-0.16	-0.0018	-0.018
8.	46014610	INTERNATIONAL PAPER CO	8	0.31	3.23	-0.12	-0.0007	-0.014
9.	85313910	STANDARD BRANDS INC	4	0.11	2.92	-0.15	-0.0035	-0.018
10.	261159710	DRESSER INDS INC	2	0.25	3.04	-0.16	-0.0019	-0.018
11.	962166610	WEYERHAEUSER CO	8	0.54	3.69	-0.17	-0.0005	-0.019
12.	76152510	REVLON INC	13	0.25	3.32	-0.33	-0.0013	-0.039
13.	12484510	CBS INC	10	0.24	3.19	-0.34	-0.0003	-0.039
14.	96332010	WHIRLPOOL CORP	20	0.12	2.96	-0.34	-0.0011	-0.055
15.	49904010	KNIGHT RIDDER NEWSPPRS	10	0.12	1.72	-0.47	-0.0006	-0.062
16.	83211010	SMITH INTL INC	2	0.05	3.40	-0.53	-0.0010	-0.062
17.	27646110	EASTERN GAS & FUEL ASSOC	2	0.05	2.67	-0.54	-0.0004	-0.064
18.	91530210	UPJOHN CO	12	0.14	3.72	-0.55	-0.0001	-0.064
19.	08750910	BETHLEHEM STL CORP	17	0.41	2.78	-0.58	-0.0023	-0.068
20.	09702310	BOEING CO	20	0.19	4.04	-0.59	-0.0026	-0.068
21.	25468710	DISNEY WALT PRODTNS	10	0.12	3.03	-0.64	-0.0048	-0.074
22.	58003310	MCDERMUTT J RAY	3	0.08	2.53	-0.68	-0.0014	-0.079
23.	71726510	PHELPS DODGE CORP	1	0.13	2.85	-0.70	-0.0049	-0.081
24.	55265310	MCA PIC	10	0.21	2.24	-0.73	-0.0003	-0.085
25.	07189210	BAXTER TRAVENOL LABS	12	0.06	6.08	-0.76	-0.0019	-0.088
26.	76133810	REVCO D S INC	19	0.25	3.65	-0.77	-0.0003	-0.089
27.	62886210	MCR CORP	12	0.11	3.57	-0.77	0.0019	-0.090
28.	87141610	SYNIFX CORP	12	0.04	3.38	-0.95	0.0036	-0.110
29.	14018610	CAPITAL BLDG COPP DEL	34	0.11	6.84	0.98	0.0020	-0.114
30.	63764010	NATIONAL SEMICONDUCTOR	23	0.04	2.63	1.47	0.0092	0.171

Figure 5.23
Assets in the Followed List

ASSETS IN THE UNIVERSE LISTED IN INCREASING ORDER OF
MARGINAL CONTRIBUTION TO PORTFOLIO RESIDUAL STD. DEV.

	CUSIP	NAME	INDUSTRY GROUP	WEIGHT IN S&P500	WEIGHT IN PORT	ALPHA	CHANGES IN PORTFOLIO RISK DUE TO 1% PURCHASE: BETA	CHANGES IN PORTFOLIO RISK DUE TO 1% PURCHASE: RESID. STDEV.
1.	10550240	BRASCAN LTD	30	0.0	0.0	−0.56	−0.0043	−0.065
2.	54042410	LOEWS CORP	33	0.0	0.0	−0.07	−0.0061	−0.008
3.	38131710	GOLDEN WEST FINL DEL	33	0.0	0.0	−0.00	0.0037	−0.000
4.	20341710	COMMUNICATIONS SATELLI	29	0.0	0.0	0.03	0.0002	0.004
5.	10216910	BOW VALLEY INDS LTD	14	0.0	0.0	0.10	0.0017	0.011
6.	33937610	FLEXI VAN CORP	33	0.0	0.0	0.11	0.0072	0.012
7.	31358610	FEDERAL NATL MTG ASSN	33	0.0	0.0	0.16	0.0041	0.019
8.	21079510	CONTINENTAL AIR LINES	28	0.0	0.0	0.19	0.0052	0.022
9.	10542510	BRANIFF INTL CORP	28	0.0	0.0	0.20	0.0062	0.023
10.	46114310	INTERWAY CORP	33	0.0	0.0	0.21	0.0093	0.024
11.	01724810	ALLEGHENY AIRLS INC	28	0.0	0.0	0.22	0.0081	0.025
12.	27619110	EASTERN AIR LINES INC	28	0.0	0.0	0.22	0.0060	0.025
13.	48309810	KAISER STEEL CORP	17	0.0	0.0	0.23	0.0015	0.026
14.	43751410	HOMESTAKE MNG CO	38	0.07	0.0	0.24	−0.0060	0.028
15.	44449210	HUGHES TOOL CO	2	0.07	0.0	0.25	0.0022	0.029
16.	55284510	MGIC INVT CORP	33	0.0	0.0	0.25	0.0083	0.029
17.	05981510	BANDAG INC	16	0.0	0.0	0.28	0.0015	0.033
18.	01234710	ALBANY INTL CORP	7	0.0	0.0	0.29	0.0027	0.033
19.	34609110	FOREST OIL CORP	2	0.0	0.0	0.29	−0.0001	0.034
20.	20719210	CONGOLEUM CORP	20	0.0	0.0	0.30	0.0037	0.034
21.	54634710	LOUISIANA PAC CORP	8	0.08	0.0	0.31	0.0036	0.036
22.	17784610	CITY INVESTING CO	39	0.0	0.0	0.31	0.0029	0.036
23.	15986110	CHARLES RIV BREEDG LAB	4	0.0	0.0	0.33	−0.0016	0.038
24.	44106510	HOSPITAL CORP AMER	12	0.0	0.0	0.34	0.0020	0.040
25.	35158610	FOX STANLEY PHOTO PROD	36	0.0	0.0	0.35	0.0013	0.041
26.	58016910	MCDONNELL DOUGLAS CORP	22	0.16	0.0	0.37	0.0015	0.043
27.	52077610	LAWSON PRODS INC	3	0.0	0.0	0.39	0.0010	0.045
28.	55479010	MACMILLAN INC	10	0.02	0.0	0.39	0.0011	0.045

(continued)

Figure 5.23 (concluded)

ASSETS IN THE UNIVERSE LISTED IN INCREASING ORDER OF
MARGINAL CONTRIBUTION TO PORTFOLIO RESIDUAL STD. DEV.

	CUSIP	NAME	INDUSTRY GROUP	WEIGHT IN S&P500	WEIGHT IN PORT	ALPHA	CHANGES IN PORTFOLIO RISK DUE TO 1% PURCHASE	
							BETA	RESID. STDEV.
29.	09367110	BLOCK H & R INC	39	0.0	0.0	0.40	-0.0010	0.047
30.	56647210	MAREMONT CORP	21	0.0	0.0	0.40	0.0034	0.047
31.	43509110	HOLIDAY INNS INC	37	0.08	0.0	0.41	0.0057	0.047
32.	11704310	BRUNSWICK CORP	25	0.04	0.0	0.41	0.0032	0.047
33.	25819810	DORCHESTER GAS CORP	2	0.0	0.0	0.41	0.0013	0.048
34.	12327710	BUSINESS MENS ASSURN C	34	0.0	0.0	0.42	0.0026	0.048
35.	29760010	ETHAN ALLEN INC	20	0.0	0.0	0.42	-0.0050	0.049
36.	36955010	GENERAL DYNAMICS CORP	39	0.12	0.0	0.43	0.0054	0.050
37.	40019110	GRUMMAN CORP	22	0.02	0.0	0.43	0.0008	0.050
38.	06714910	BARBER OIL CORP	2	0.0	0.0	0.44	-0.0019	0.051
39.	15231210	CENTEX CORP	35	0.03	0.0	0.44	-0.0019	0.051
40.	49350310	KEYSTONE INTL INC	3	0.0	0.0	0.45	0.0067	0.052
41.	40257810	GULF UTD CORP	34	0.0	0.0	0.45	0.0033	0.052
42.	47989810	JONATHAN LOGAN INC	7	0.01	0.0	0.45	0.0015	0.053
43.	57389010	MARY KAY COSMETICS INC	13	0.0	0.0	0.45	0.0039	0.053
44.	37465810	GIBRALTAR FIN CP CALIF	39	0.0	0.0	0.47	-0.0012	0.054
45.	44175810	HOUSE FABRICS INC	7	0.0	0.0	0.48	0.0048	0.056
46.	52139410	LEAR SIEGLER INC	23	0.0	0.0	0.49	0.0020	0.057
47.	36935210	GENERAL CINEMA CORP	10	0.0	0.0	0.50	0.0026	0.057
48.	29920910	EVANS PRODS CO	8	0.04	0.0	0.51	0.0032	0.058
49.	45662310	INEXCO OIL CO	2	0.0	0.0	0.52	0.0029	0.059
50.	29409810	ENVIROTECH CORP	18	0.01	0.0	0.52	0.0041	0.061
51.	24870310	DENNYS INC	25	0.03	0.0	0.55	0.0039	0.064
52.	12525610	CFS CONTL INC	4	0.0	0.0	0.57	0.0034	0.066
53.	40249610	GULF RFS & CHEM CORP	1	0.01	0.0	0.58	0.0011	0.067
54.	32089110	FIRST MISS CORP	4	0.0	0.0	0.58	0.0031	0.067
55.	30761010	FARINON CORP	18	0.0	0.0	0.59	0.0044	0.068
56.	05380710	AVNET INC	23	0.0	0.0	0.62	0.0037	0.068
57.	26845710	EG & G INC	23	0.0	0.0	0.62	0.0036	0.071
58.	57335010	MARTIN PROCESSING INC	7	0.0	0.0	0.62	0.0039	0.072

#	ID	Company	N					
59.	37011810	GENERAL INSTR CORP	23	0.0	0.000	0.62	0.0058	0.072
60.	44553230	HUNT PHILIP A CHEM CP	24	0.0	0.000	0.63	0.0026	0.073
61.	35849610	FRIENDLY ICE CREAM CP	25	0.008	0.000	0.64	0.0046	0.074
62.	04428110	HOUSTON OIL & MINERALS	14	0.0	0.000	0.65	0.0094	0.075
63.	04341710	ASAMERA OIL LTD	22	0.0	0.000	0.66	0.0072	0.076
64.	12418710	BUTTES GAS & OIL CO	25	0.02	0.000	0.66	0.0038	0.077
65.	57708110	MATTEL INC	4	0.0	0.000	0.67	0.0032	0.077
66.	39006410	GREAT ATL & PAC TEA	39	0.0	0.000	0.67	0.0011	0.078
67.	19584610	COLONIAL PENN GROUP	39	0.0	0.000	0.68	0.0057	0.079
68.	10887340	BIC PEN CORP	32	0.0	0.000	0.68	0.0026	0.079
69.	37935210	GLOBAL MARINE INC	17	0.001	0.000	0.70	0.0079	0.081
70.	55089010	LYKES CORP DEL	19	0.019	0.000	0.73	0.0052	0.085
71.	21236310	CONTROL DATA CORP DEL	2	0.0	0.000	0.73	0.0048	0.085
72.	39013610	GREAT BASINS PETE CO	39	0.0	0.000	0.75	0.0038	0.087
73.	36850110	GELCO CORP	25	0.0	0.000	0.77	0.0053	0.088
74.	34650110	FRANKLIN MINT CORP	35	0.0	0.000	0.77	0.0058	0.090
75.	54153710	LOMAS & NETTLETON MTG	19	0.0	0.000	0.78	0.0052	0.090
76.	25357910	DICTAPHONE CORP	12	0.0	0.000	0.78	0.0012	0.090
77.	23571710	DAMON CORP	35	0.0	0.000	0.78	0.0032	0.090
78.	48617010	KAUFMAN & BROAD INC	39	0.02	0.000	0.81	0.0047	0.092
79.	52621010	LTV CORP	34	0.0	0.000	0.81	0.0083	0.094
80.	12611710	CNA FINL CORP	23	0.05	0.000	0.82	0.0051	0.094
81.	45814010	INTEL CORP	37	0.10	0.000	0.86	0.0075	0.096
82.	30369310	FAIRCHILD CAMERA & INS	19	0.02	0.000	0.90	0.0080	0.105
83.	44856410	WYATT CORP	12	0.0	0.000	0.94	0.0067	0.106
84.	46564010	ITEL CORP	10	0.0	0.000	0.96	0.0034	0.110
85.	23810710	DATAPRODUCTS CORP	39	0.0	0.000	0.97	0.0079	0.111
86.	08264710	BENTLEY LABS INC	23	0.0	0.000	1.09	0.0060	0.112
87.	53276310	LIN BROADCASTING CORP	39	0.0	0.000	1.10	0.0071	0.126
88.	46563210	ITEK CORP	25	0.0	0.000	1.15	0.0101	0.127
89.	00790310	ADVANCED MICRO DEVICES	37	0.0	0.000	1.15	0.0068	0.128
90.	18987310	COACHMEN INDS INC	19	0.0	0.000	1.15	0.0078	0.133
91.	47650210	JERRICO INC	19	0.0	0.000	1.16	0.0049	0.133
92.	15850110	CHAMPION HOME BLDRS CO	39	0.0	0.000	1.28	0.0070	0.133
93.	15640210	CENTRONICS DATA COMPUT	19	0.0	0.000	1.40	0.0070	0.134
94.	23810020	DATAPOINT CORP	39	0.0	0.000		0.0041	0.135
95.	42814610	HESSTON CORP	19	0.0	0.000		0.0064	0.135
96.	10430310	BRADFORD NATL CORP	39	0.0	0.000		0.0071	0.148
97.	30157410	EXECUTIVE INDS INC	39	0.0	0.000		0.0089	0.162
98.	20582610	COMTECH TELECOMMUNICAT	23	0.0	0.000			

Figure 5.24
Assets in the "Aggressive" Portfolio

CONTRIBUTION OF INDIVIDUAL ASSETS TO PORTFOLIO RISK

	CUSIP	NAME	PERCENT OF PORTFOLIO VALUE	EFFECT OF 1% PURCHASE ON BETA	EFFECT OF 1% PURCHASE ON RESID. STDEV	REQUIRED ALPHA	NUMBER OF SHARES	PRICE PER SHARE	ALPHA
1.	07189210	BAXTER TRAVENOL LABS	27.57	-0.0016	0.1656	0.37	235735.	37.63	0.8
2.	08750910	BETHLEHEM STL CORP	7.30	-0.0014	0.0700	0.16	118241.	19.88	0.6
3.	14018610	CAPITAL HLDG CORP DEL	24.02	-0.0007	0.1809	0.41	351351.	22.00	1.0
4.	62886210	NCR CORP	6.93	0.0006	0.0949	0.21	38769.	57.50	0.8
5.	63764010	NATIONAL SEMICONDUCTOR	5.42	0.0079	0.1726	0.39	94010.	19.25	1.5
6.	71726510	PHELPS DODGE CORP	6.07	0.0001	0.0664	0.15	87300.	22.38	0.7
7.	76133810	REVCO D S INC	12.86	-0.0004	0.1271	0.28	165528.	25.38	0.7
8.	83211010	SMITH INTL INC.	10.24	-0.0007	0.0029	0.01	1882.	40.50	0.5
9.	85313910	STANDARD BRANDS INC	1.35	-0.0048	0.0008	0.00	18547.	23.50	0.2
10.	87161610	SYNTEX CORP	3.57	-0.0023	0.0849	0.19	40151.	28.63	0.9
11.	91530210	UPJOHN CO	4.47	-0.0009	0.0539	0.12	31237.	46.00	0.6

Note: The required alphas are computed using the adjusted residual risk aversion given by equation (5–10).

folio. Notice that having a large alpha does not automatically lead to a large portfolio holding—the risk dimension must be taken account of too. For instance, compare the original and revised holdings in Baxter Travenol Laboratories and National Semiconductor.

Let us now take the case of increased aversion to residual risk, relative to systematic risk. In this situation, residual risk is to be avoided to such an extent that a position different from the minimal residual risk position should be taken only for assets with extreme alphas. In effect, the requirement is to form the original portfolio into an indexlike fund; the greater the residual risk aversion, the more indexlike the portfolio will become.

Figure 5.25 shows the holdings in the optimal portfolio obtained by revising the original portfolio, without transaction costs and with $\kappa = 25$. There are now 55 stocks in the portfolio, and there are substantial positions in assets which are diversifying, relative to the characteristics of the other assets.

This problem specification is essentially that required to select an index fund from a universe of assets. As has been mentioned, the key attributes of an index fund are, first, that the fund have a beta of one, relative to the index, and second, that the fund exhibit minimal residual risk, relative to the index. Thus, specification of the index fund problem (in the absence of transaction costs) reduces to:

$$\text{Maximize } U_P = \Lambda_\omega \omega_P^2 \ (\Lambda_\omega < 0),$$
$$\{h_j\}$$

subject to:

$$1 = \sum_j h_j; \ h_j \geqslant 0$$
$$1 = \sum_j \beta_j h_j = \beta_P$$

Notice that all the other terms of the utility function (see Table 5.2) have dropped out of this formulation, either because they are not required (transaction costs, by assumption) or because they have become constants (the contribution to utility from beta).

Figure 5.26 displays the attainable residual frontier obtained from plotting, together with the original portfolio, six revised portfolios with kappa values between 25 and 0.125. Notice that the frontier is curved. At the upper end of this line, the curvature is induced because successively greater amounts of risk must be assumed in order to increase the portfolio alpha. At the lower end, the line terminates at the minimum residual risk portfolio (with no short selling). The curvature here arises from the inability to further reduce risk, because of the short-selling bounds. If the optimization problem were unconstrained—that is, no beta or short-selling constraint—then the frontier would be a straight line.

Between these two extremes lies a portfolio which has the highest alpha for each unit of risk (i.e., the highest information, alpha/residual standard devia-

Figure 5.25
Assets in the "Indexlike" Portfolio

CONTRIBUTION OF INDIVIDUAL ASSETS TO PORTFOLIO RISK

	CUSIP	NAME	PERCENT OF PORTFOLIO VALUE	EFFECT OF 1% PURCHASE ON BETA	EFFECT OF 1% PURCHASE ON RESID. STDEV	REQUIRED ALPHA	NUMBER OF SHARES	PRICE PER SHARE	ALPHA
1.	01234710	ALBANY INTL CORP	1.19	0.0039	0.0363	5.75	15728.	24.25	0.3
2.	01724810	ALLEGHENY AIRLS INC	0.27	0.0097	0.0352	5.57	11465.	7.63	0.2
3.	05981510	BANDAG INC	0.44	0.0033	0.0320	5.05	11022.	12.88	0.3
4.	07189210	BAXTER TRAVENOL LABS	1.64	0.0011	0.0347	5.48	14055.	37.63	0.8
5.	08750910	BETHLEHEM STL CORP	2.46	0.0037	0.0247	3.91	39844.	19.88	0.6
6.	09702310	BOEING CO	1.08	0.0037	0.0282	4.46	5947.	58.50	0.6
7.	10216910	BOW VALLEY INDS LTD	0.83	0.0033	0.0323	5.11	10165.	26.25	0.1
8.	10542510	BRANIFF INTL CORP	0.23	0.0077	0.0310	4.90	6160.	11.88	0.2
9.	10502040	BRASCAN LTD	6.83	-0.0023	0.0342	5.25	159824.	13.75	0.2
10.	11704310	BRUNSWICK CORP	0.88	0.0045	0.0383	6.06	21229.	13.38	-0.6
11.	12327710	BUSINESS MENS ASSURN C	0.93	0.0019	0.0357	5.65	13913.	21.50	0.4
12.	12418710	BUTTES GAS & OIL CO	0.39	0.0028	0.0321	5.07	14708.	8.50	0.7
13.	12484510	CBS INC	2.12	0.0010	0.0304	4.82	13334.	51.25	0.7
14.	14018610	CAPITAL BLDG CORP DEL	1.85	0.0035	0.0472	7.47	27029.	22.00	1.0
15.	14912310	CATERPILLAR TRACTOR CO	6.08	-0.0002	0.0328	5.18	35428.	55.25	-0.2
16.	15986110	CHARLES RIV BREEDG LAB	0.49	0.0007	0.0327	5.17	7039.	22.50	0.3
17.	20341710	COMMUNICATIONS SATELLI	1.47	0.0007	0.0327	5.17	12525.	37.88	0.3
18.	20719210	CONGOLEUM CORP	0.32	0.0060	0.0313	4.96	5857.	17.75	0.3
19.	21181310	CONOCO INC	5.39	-0.0021	0.0332	5.25	67689.	25.63	-0.2
20.	25468710	DISNEY WALT PRODTNS	0.82	0.0039	0.0293	4.64	7298.	36.13	0.6
21.	26159710	DRESSER INDS INC	2.24	-0.0006	0.0290	4.59	18415.	39.13	0.2
22.	27619110	EASTERN AIR LINES INC	0.78	0.0067	0.0326	5.16	29035.	8.63	0.2
23.	27646110	EASTERN GAS & FUEL ASSOC	0.72	0.0011	0.0263	4.16	17839.	13.00	0.5
24.	29449710	EQUITABLE GAS CO	5.54	0.0038	0.0314	4.97	53593.	33.25	0.2
25.	29760010	ETHAN ALLEN INC	0.32	-0.0062	0.0313	4.95	4938.	20.75	-0.4

#	Code	Name							
26.	34609110	FOREST OIL CORP	0.67	-0.0005	0.0330	5.22	17539	12.25	0.3
27.	40257810	GULF UTD CORP	0.52	-0.0031	0.0320	5.06	12794	13.00	0.5
28.	43508110	HOLIDAY INNS INC	0.31	0.0070	0.0311	4.92	5781	17.00	0.4
29.	44106510	HOSPITAL CORP AMER	0.42	-0.0039	0.0318	5.03	4900	27.63	0.3
30.	45920010	INTERNATIONAL BUS MACH	13.03	-0.0015	0.0330	5.23	15869	264.25	-0.2
31.	46014610	INTERNATIONAL PAPER CO	3.11	-0.0004	0.0330	4.14	25030	40.00	0.1
32.	48309810	KAISER STEEL CORP	1.46	0.0006	0.0262	5.09	23051	20.38	0.2
33.	49350310	KEYSTONE INTL INC	0.33	0.0041	0.0322	5.02	5742	18.75	0.5
34.	49904010	KNIGHT RIDDER NEWSPPRS	0.47	0.0032	0.0318	4.15	6487	23.13	0.4
35.	52077610	LAWSON PRODS INC	0.42	0.0023	0.0262	5.07	7335	18.50	0.1
36.	54042410	LOEWS CORP	1.14	0.0081	0.0306	4.84	10022	36.75	-0.1
37.	54634710	LOUISIANA PAC CORP	0.44	0.0053	0.0315	4.98	7885	18.00	0.3
38.	55089010	LYKES CORP DEL	0.25	0.0040	0.0318	5.03	11297	7.13	0.7
39.	55265310	MCA INC	0.60	0.0058	0.0382	6.04	5676	34.25	0.7
40.	55477010	MACMILLAN INC	0.40	0.0025	0.0321	5.08	14327	8.88	0.4
41.	58003310	MCDERMOTT J RAY	0.68	0.0042	0.0235	3.71	9730	52.63	0.7
42.	62686210	NCR CORP	0.97	0.0028	0.0516	8.16	5406	57.50	0.8
43.	63764010	NATIONAL SEMICONDUCTOR	0.71	0.0113	0.0946	14.96	11893	19.25	0.5
44.	65322210	NIAGARA MOHAWK PWR CP	3.73	-0.0028	0.0333	5.27	84935	14.13	-0.3
45.	71726510	PHELPS DODGE CORP	0.77	0.0020	0.0363	5.74	11087	22.38	0.7
46.	71850710	PHILLIPS PETE CO	5.84	-0.0020	0.0332	5.24	62909	29.88	-0.4
47.	74456710	PUBLIC SVC ELEC & GAS	4.80	-0.0025	0.0262	4.15	71836	21.50	-0.4
48.	76133810	REVCO D S INC	0.99	0.0026	0.0413	6.52	12704	25.00	-0.8
49.	76152510	REVLON INC	2.47	0.0000	0.0307	4.85	17124	46.50	0.8
50.	83210010	SMITH INTL INC	0.92	0.0023	0.0379	5.06	7298	40.50	0.5
51.	85313910	STANDARD BRANDS INC	2.80	-0.0020	0.0320	5.06	38346	23.50	0.2
52.	87161610	SYNTEX CORP	0.91	0.0051	0.0543	8.58	10271	28.63	1.0
53.	91530210	UPJOHN CO	1.00	0.0019	0.0272	4.30	7028	46.00	0.6
54.	96216610	WEYERHAEUSER CO	2.80	0.0008	0.0246	3.89	34135	26.38	0.2
55.	96332010	WHIRLPOOL CORP	1.71	0.0020	0.0304	4.81	27213	20.25	0.3

Note: The required alphas are computed using the adjusted residual risk aversion given by equation (5–10).

Figure 5.26
The Residual Frontier

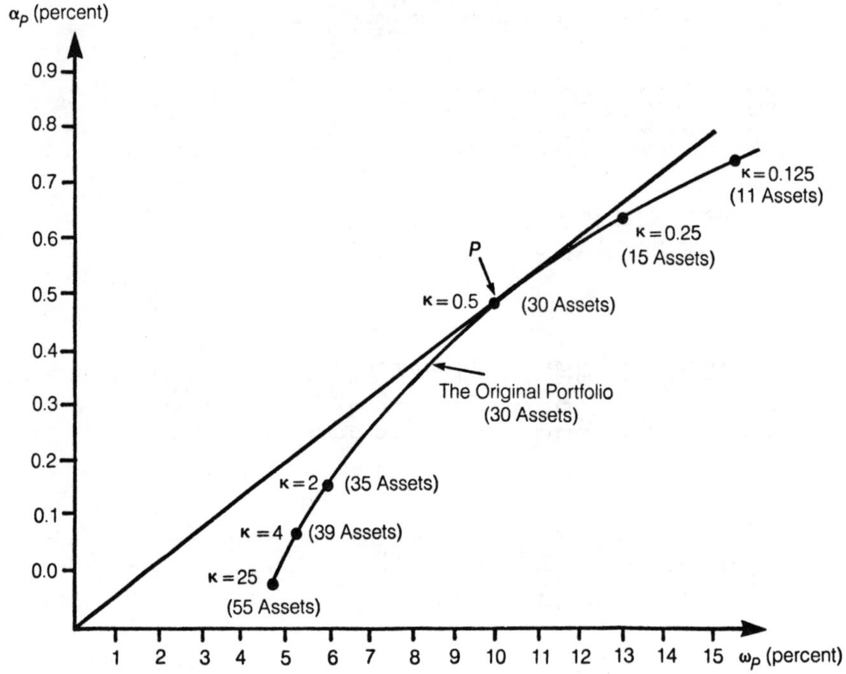

tion, ratio); this is indicated on Figure 5.26 as portfolio *P*. Portfolio *P* is the manager's best portfolio in the sense that it will demonstrate superior valuation judgment before the others because it captures the largest alpha for the risk assumed. Clearly, it is advantageous for all investors to have their portfolios positioned at their manager's highest value of this ratio because at this point they are getting maximum "value added," as discussed in the supplement to Chapter 4. In the context of a fund owner who employs one or more outside managers, the owner must assess the superiority of each. Ideally, the manager and the owner should agree as to how much value added the manager can provide. The owner needs to know this, as we shall show in Chapter 6, so as to correctly allocate the total funds among the managers. The manager needs to reach this understanding with the owner so as to achieve the proper level of aggressiveness (i.e., position the portfolio at *P*). Since this mutual understanding amounts to negotiating a covenant, the information ratio is frequently described as the *covenant information ratio*.[57]

---

[57]See, for instance, Table 3.8, and the accompanying discussion.

Case Study 5: Setting Up a Performance Bogey

Figure 5.27 contains the problem definition for this case study. Notice that there are two parts to the problem. The first problem, and the one most relevant to this chapter, is to determine the composition and attributes of a benchmark portfolio (bogey) that will be used to track the performance of the manager. The second problem, which we will not consider here, is to measure how this strategy would have performed in the past and to analyze its future potential.[58]

Let us briefly review the problem. The first constraint is straight-forward: the current yield on the portfolio should be at least 7 percent. Next, securities must be selected from a defined universe, which is most likely to be the list of approved companies that XYZ has screened (for bankruptcy risk, growth potential, and so on) and permits portfolio managers to hold. We then come to one of the most common, yet least logical, constraints in institutional investment management. The holdings of individual securities are arbitrarily restricted by an upper bound of 5 percent. In this case, the bound was enforced solely to increase the comfort level of senior management (although in some situations insurance companies are legally obliged to conform to a 5 percent upper bound). The 1 percent lower bound can be (partially) justified by accounting, custodial, or other cost considerations.

The last major constraint concerns the risk of the portfolio. Observe that total risk is constrained to (essentially) that of the S&P 500; this constraint, together with the requirement that the fund be fully invested, dictates that the portfolio beta must be no greater than unity. Hence, there is, contrary to the letter, a specific constraint dealing with market risk. Moreover, the more aggressive the manager becomes (i.e., the less diversified, or the greater the level of residual risk), the lower the beta must become. The previous requirement on maximum holding size forces the inclusion of at least 20 stocks in the portfolio. Although it is dangerous (as indicated in Supplement 4) to be dogmatic, it is unlikely that an "institutional" portfolio with 20 stocks will have an annual residual standard deviation of more than 10 percent. Assuming that the S&P 500 has an annual standard deviation of 20 percent, then the maximum beta for the most aggressive portfolio is about 0.87 ($V_P = \beta_P^2 V_M + \omega_P^2$, which implies $400 = \beta_P^2 \cdot 400 + 100$, or $\beta_P^2 = {}^3/_4$).

Moreover, as will be demonstrated in Case Study 6 in the supplement to this chapter, simply by forming a portfolio with a low beta, the manager will have to select a "deviant" set of stocks (for example, low-beta stocks tend to have large capitalization). This exposure, in addition to that required from maintaining a high yield, will induce some residual risk in the portfolio. Hence, the manager is not free to select the "best" 20 stocks since doing so may violate the risk constraint. In fact, as should be obvious from this analysis, the strategy must be highly controlled.

---

[58]See Chapter 7 for a description of performance measurement.

Figure 5.27
Specification of the Performance Bogey

XYZ LIFE INSURANCE COMPANY
Hartford, Connecticut

Thomas L. Smith, Director
Investment Research

April 30, 1979

Professor Andrew Rudd
Cornell University
Ithaca, New York 14853

Dear Andrew:

I have a most particular and pressing challenge at hand, and the purpose of this letter is to acquant you with the task and to ask your advice and assistance in resolving it successfully.

One of our several portfolios is that of our property and casualty subsidiary, the ABC Insurance Company. ABC has, for several years, been invested almost entirely in municipal bonds. We have recently decided to reenter the equity market, with a portfolio size of $100 million in mind, to be accomplished over a period of time.

The portfolio is to be managed to an objective of moderate capital appreciation coupled with a current yield objective of 7 percent or more. The manager will operate within these constraints:

He must select securities from a defined universe of about 250 names.

No single issue may exceed 5 percent or be less than 1 percent of the total.

The standard deviation (cross-sectional) of the portfolio shall not "significantly" exceed that of the S&P 500. There is no specific constraint dealing with market risk or with diversification.

Apart from these constraints, the manager is free to engage in selection or timing strategies (excluding cash—the portfolio must be fully invested) as he wishes. However, his performance objective is that total pretax return (dividends plus appreciation) should exceed that of a "minimum risk bogey" by an annual rate of 1 percent (rates calculated on a time-weighted basis).

My problem is, then: I need to develop a means for determining the composition of the bogey (which presumably will have to be reoptimized periodically when cash is available to invest) and for determining the hypothetical performance of the bogey portfolio. I am also concerned about incorporating transaction costs into the bogey simulation. Finally, the processes to perform these functions should produce output that can be understood by the portfolio manager.

Best regards,

Thomas L. Smith

Thomas L. Smith

TLS:mss

With this preamble, the task of finding the bogey is straightforward. The optimization program has to select a portfolio from the universe with a yield of at least 7 percent, maximum asset bounds of 5 percent, and total risk less than that of the S&P 500.[59] This last requirement can be modeled by setting a beta target of 0.95 and minimizing residual risk. If the optimal portfolio has too much risk, then the beta target is changed and the optimization repeated. Several optimizations may have to be performed with beta targets in the range from 0.90 to 1.00 with the minimal total risk optimal portfolio chosen as the bogey.

Symbolically, the bogey is found by using the following formulation:

$$\text{Minimize } \omega_P^2$$
$$\{h_j\}$$

subject to:

(1) $0 \le h_j \le 5\%$

(2) $1 = \Sigma \, h_j,$

(3) $\beta_T = \Sigma \, h_j \beta_j,$

(4) $7\% \le \Sigma \, h_j y_j,$

where β_T is the target beta, which is less than unity.

This optimization is periodically repeated (perhaps monthly) and forms the bogey for use in a performance measurement program (see Chapter 7).

Summary

We started by considering passive strategies and the normal asset allocation. These complex subjects are rightly being more carefully analyzed by money managers and portfolio owners. Passive strategies deserve to be considered because they are the rational alternative to active management. Our major caveat is that passive strategies arbitrarily tied to the S&P 500 are *arbitrary*. The rational alternative to active management is the passive strategy, which replicates the return on the normal passive portfolio, which, in turn, is identified with the aid of an asset allocation model.

By far the greater part of this chapter is devoted to active management. Although we used a great many words (and not a few Greek symbols), the message is exceedingly simple: actively managed portfolios must optimally reflect the judgmental alphas upon the component securities. This implies that the pursuit of reward is undertaken only up to that point where the "cost" arising from the risk of the strategy offsets the benefit. The measurement of risk and the formation of judgment concerning the valuation of assets must be jointly considered in the responsible management of investment portfolios.

---

[59]The lower asset bounds can be enforced using a method described in Supplement 5.

Further Reading

We list below the two or three major (in our opinion!) articles in each of the main sections of this chapter.

Passive Management

Black, Fischer, and Myron Scholes. "From Theory to a New Financial Product." *Journal of Finance*, May 1974, pp. 309–412.

Good, Walter; Robert Ferguson; and Jack Treynor. "An Investor's Guide to the Index Fund Controversy." *Financial Analysts Journal*, November–December 1976, pp. 27–36.

Rudd, Andrew. "Optimal Selection of Passive Portfolios." *Financial Management*, Spring 1980, pp. 57–66.

Market Timing

Ambachtsheer, Keith. "On the Risks and Rewards of Market Timing" PMS Letter no. 30. Toronto: Canavest House, August 1976.

Grant, Dwight. "Market Timing and Portfolio Management." *Journal of Finance*, September 1978, pp. 1119–32.

Sharpe, William. "Likely Gains from Market Timing." *Financial Analysts Journal*, March–April 1975, pp. 2–11.

Local Optimization

Fisher, Lawrence. "Using Modern Portfolio Theory to Maintain an Efficiently Diversified Portfolio." *Financial Analysts Journal*, May–June 1975, pp. 73–85.

Sharpe, William. "Imputing Expected Security Returns from Portfolio Composition." *Journal of Financial and Quantitative Analysis*, June 1974, pp. 463–72.

Rosenberg, Barr, and Andrew Rudd. "Portfolio Optimization Algorithms: A Progress Report." Research Program in Finance, Working Paper no. 42, sec. 3. Berkeley: Institute of Business and Economic Research, University of California, May 1976.

Global Optimization

Markowitz, Harry, and André Perold. "Reducing Models of Covariance to Weighted Sums of Squares: A Procedure for the Fast Determination of Efficient Portfolios." Paper presented at the Institute for Quantitative Research in Finance, Spring Meeting, Napa, California, April 27–30, 1980.

Rudd, Andrew, and Barr Rosenberg. "Realistic Portfolio Optimization." In *Portfolio Theory—Studies in Management Sciences*, vol. 11, ed. E. J. Elton and M. J. Gruber Amsterdam: North-Holland, 1979.

Sharpe, William. "An Algorithm for Portfolio Improvement." Research Paper no. 475. Graduate School of Business, Stanford University. October 1978.

Residual Frontier

Rosenberg, Barr. "Security Appraisal and Unsystematic Risk in Institutional Investment." *Proceedings of the Seminar on the Analysis of Security Prices*, University of Chicago, November 1976, pp. 171–237.

Supplement 5

Portfolio Optimization

The aim of this supplement is to briefly display the mathematical formulation of the portfolio optimization problem. Initially, we will consider the general problem; then we will turn our attention to the selection and revision of passive portfolios. The final topic of this supplement will be a case study describing the selection of yield-biased portfolios.

As we mentioned in Chapter 5, the key to portfolio optimization is being able to model the decision realistically. At its most basic level, the decision begins with two groups of assets. The first is the current portfolio (which necessarily contains assets with nonzero holdings), and the second is the followed list, which is the list of assets that are available for purchase. In revising the existing portfolio to one which better reflects current judgment or the investor's preferences, several objectives may have to be met. These objectives may include:

1. Controlling the portfolio risk level.
2. Investing additional cash or withdrawing cash from the portfolio.
3. Minimizing transaction costs or controlling turnover.
4. Eliminating an existing holding, maintaining an existing holding (because, for instance, it may represent a controlling interest), or changing an existing holding only if this increases diversification (that is, decreases residual risk) and does not incur excessive transaction costs.

The objectives include many of the features of portfolio revision. Some assets must be sold completely; some assets must not be sold; and some assets should not have their holdings increased but need not be sold. Cash flow may require investing, or the cash holding may have to be increased. The degree of diversification (level of residual risk) may be changed, but throughout all these revisions the transaction costs must be controlled. It should be clear that this problem is far from easy: in order to perform the task of portfolio revision efficiently and effectively, computational assistance is necessary.

In Chapter 5 we described the portfolio optimization problem as the determination of a portfolio which maximizes utility, subject to satisfying several restrictions. We will first express this problem in symbols, so we will need the following notation.

Attributes of Assets

h_j	The portfolio holding of the jth asset
α_j	The alpha of the jth asset, appropriately normalized so that the market (or its proxy) is "alpha neutral"[1]
β_j	The beta of the jth asset
y_j	The yield of the jth asset
h_{Mj}	The holding of the jth asset in the market
$TSELL_j$	The proportional sale transaction cost for asset j
$TBUY_j$	The proportional purchase transaction cost for asset j
h_j^0	The initial portfolio holding in asset j prior to portfolio optimization
$hmin_j$ and $hmax_j$	The minimum and maximum bonds on the holding in the jth asset
f_j	A feasibility adjustment to asset j

Attributes of Portfolios

y_T	The portfolio yield target
β_T	The portfolio beta target
y_{max}, y_{min}	The maximum and minimum acceptable portfolio yields
β_{max}, β_{min}	The maximum and minimum acceptable portfolio betas
ω_P^2	Portfolio residual variance

Utility Coefficient

$\Lambda_Y \, (\geq 0)$	Utility increase from a 1 percent increase in yield
$\Lambda_T \, (\leq 0)$	Transaction cost amortization factor
$\Lambda_C \, (\leq 0)$	Disutility arising from missing yield target by 1 percent
$\Lambda_\beta \, (\leq 0)$	Disutility arising from missing beta target by 1.0
$\Lambda_\omega \, (\leq 0)$	Disutility arising from assuming 1 ($\%^2$) residual variance

---

[1] That is, the alpha of the market (or its proxy) is zero. See also Chapter 4.

The optimization problem can now be expressed mathematically as:

$$\text{Maximize } U_P,$$
$$\{h_j\}$$

subject to:

(1) $h\min_j \leq h_j \leq h\max_j$, for all assets j,

(2) $1 = \sum_j h_j$,

(3) $\beta_{\min} \leq \sum_j \beta_j h_j \leq \beta_{\max}$, and

(4) $y_{\min} \leq \sum_j y_j h_j \leq y_{\max}$,

$$\text{(S5–1)}$$

where

U_P is the measure of portfolio utility, defined by:

$$U_P = \alpha_P + \Lambda_Y y_P + \Lambda_T \left\{ \sum_j TSELL_j(h_j^0 - h_j)^+ + \sum_j TBUY_j(h_j - h_j^0)^+ \right\} \quad \text{(S5–2)}$$

$$+ \Lambda_C(y_P - y_T)^2 + \Lambda_\beta(\beta_P - \beta_T)^2 + \Lambda_\omega \omega_P^2$$

$$\alpha_P = \sum_j h_j \alpha_j, \ y_P = \sum_j h_j y_j, \ \beta_P = \sum_j h_j \beta_j, \quad \text{(S5–3)}$$

and $(\cdot)^+ = \text{maximum } (0,\cdot)$.

Before we continue, it is instructive to compare this formulation with the one suggested by Markowitz. Essentially, Markowitz's problem specification was taken directly from the formulation of mean-variance utility, equation (2–5); that is, maximize $E_P - \lambda V_P$, $\lambda > 0$. The major changes have been the incorporation of transaction cost and the separation of total risk into systematic risk and residual risk to accommodate investors whose aversion to both types of risk may not be the same. This reasoning also suggests the decomposition of total return into systematic and residual components. The final addition of terms involving yield does not alter the problem materially (except to add realism for certain investors). Thus, this formulation is entirely consistent with the original specification; we have merely rearranged the components to make the problem applicable to current institutional practices.

We will restrict attention to the multiple factor model of security returns for the formulation of residual risk. This expression (in matrix notation) was given in Supplement 3, equation (S3–18), and is repeated below (in ordinary notation):

$$\omega_P^2 = \sum_{j=1}^{K} \sum_{l=1}^{K} \gamma_{Pj} \gamma_{Pl} F_{jl} + \sum_{j=1}^{N} \delta_{Pj}^2 \sigma_j^2 \quad \text{(S5–4)}$$

where

$\gamma_{Pj} \equiv b_{Pj} - \beta_P b_{Mj}$ is the jth discrepant factor loading, defined as the difference between the jth factor loading on the

F_{jl} portfolio (b_{Pj}) and the jth factor loading on the levered market portfolio ($\beta_P b_{Mj}$);

is the covariance between the jth and the lth factors;

$\delta_{Pj} = h_j - \beta_P h_{Mj}$ is the jth active portfolio holding, defined as the difference between the portfolio holding in the jth asset (h_j) and the holding in the levered market portfolio ($\beta_P h_{Mj}$);

σ_j^2 is the specific variance of asset j;

K is the number of factors in the multiple factor model; and

N is the number of assets in the market portfolio.

The term $\Sigma\,\Sigma\,\gamma_{Pj}\gamma_{Pl}F_{jl}$ represents the extra-market covariance *(XMC)* in the portfolio, and the term $\Sigma\delta_{Pj}^2\sigma_j^2$ represents the component of portfolio risk arising from the specific risk of individual assets. The sum of these two components is, of course, the portfolio residual variance, ω_P^2, which is a quadratic function of the asset holdings. The optimization problem, therefore, is to maximize a quadratic function, subject to linear constraints, which is called a quadratic programming problem.

Unfortunately, the model is not in a form which can be solved by the majority of general-purpose quadratic programming codes. The difficulty is that the contribution to utility from transaction costs is "piecewise linear" (see Figure 5.19).[2] In other words, the penalty per unit purchase may not be the same as the penalty per unit sale even though the penalty is linear for both purchases and sales. In order to make the problem applicable for quadratic programming codes, the problem has to be transformed.

This transformation associates with each asset, at the most, two new variables, namely, a purchase transaction and a sale transaction. Thus, we write:

$$h_j = h_j^0 + p_k - q_l, \qquad (\text{S5–5})$$

where

h_j = the revised holding;

h_j^0 = the original holding;

p_k = the purchase transaction made to revise the position; and

q_l = the sale transaction made to revise the position.

Clearly, either a purchase or a sale is made so at least one of p_k and q_l is zero; i.e.:

$$p_k \geq 0,\ q_l \geq 0,\ \text{and}\ p_k q_l = 0.$$

---

[2]If there are no transaction costs, then the problem can be solved directly by quadratic programming methods. Some codes can incorporate piecewise linear transaction costs. These are typically based on Lemke's complementary pivot algorithm and, to some extent, suffer from other deficiencies. The development of new algorithms is proceeding very rapidly, and there is no doubt that future codes will be fully general.

Notice that the indexing of the purchase and sale transactions is different from that of the original assets. This is because not all of the original assets will be associated with both a purchase and a sale. For instance, assets in the followed list which are not already in the portfolio can, in general, only be purchased (they cannot be sold because they have zero weight in the portfolio and short sales are generally not permitted).

A second aspect of this transformation stage is to make the problem feasible, that is, to find an initial portfolio which satisfies all the constraints. This is achieved in two stages: first, finding a portfolio which satisifies the asset bounds, and second, finding a portfolio which satisfies the remaining constraints.

The first transformation stage can be described in three steps:

1. $h_j^0 \geq hmax_j$; the initial holding is greater than (or equal to) the bound. Reduce holding by $hmax_j - h_j^0$, and credit the cash account with the proceeds of this feasibility adjustment, $f_j = hmax_j - h_j^0$. Note the transaction penalty of $(TSELL_j)(-f_j)$. Associate sale variable, q_l, with this asset (no purchase variable is necessary because no amount can be purchased), where:

$$0 \leq q_l \leq hmax_j - hmin_j.$$

2. $hmin_j < h_j^0 < hmax_j$; the initial holding is within bounds. Associate both purchase and sale variables, p_k and q_l, with this asset, where:

$$0 \leq p_k \leq hmax_j - h_j^0;$$
$$0 \leq q_l \leq h_j^0 - hmin_j.$$

In this case, there is no feasibility adjustment ($f_j = 0$) and no initial transaction penalty.

3. $h_j^0 \leq hmin_j$; the initial holding is less than (or equal to) the bound. Increase holding by $hmin_j - h_j^0$, and debit the cash account with the cost of this feasibility adjustment, $f_j = hmin_j - h_j^0$. Note the transaction penalty of $(TBUY_j)(f_j)$. Associate purchase variable, p_k, with this asset (no sale variable is necessary because no amount can be sold), where

$$0 \leq p_k \leq hmax_j - hmin_j.$$

Notice that this procedure has split the purchase and sale transaction into two components: first, a component required for initial feasibility, and second, the variable transaction required for optimality. The initial adjustment ensures feasibility, so that asset holdings $h_j^0 + f_j$ satisfy the asset bounds. The purchase and sale transactions from this starting point will be found by the algorithm. Of course, if the initial portfolio satisfies all the asset bounds (step 2 above), then the feasibility adjustments, f_j, are all zero. Therefore, in the presence of asset bounds, equation (S5–5) is written as equation (S5–5'):

$$h_j = (h_j^0 + f_j) + p_k - q_l. \tag{S5–5'}$$

At the completion of these steps the original problem has been transformed into a problem with $P + Q$ variables, each of which has a lower bound of zero and a positive upper bound, where P is the total number of purchase variables and Q is the total number of sale variables. The number of purchases, P, is equal to the number of assets in the portfolio and the followed list that are not at their upper bounds, while the number of sales, Q, is equal to the number of assets in the portfolio and the followed list that are not at their lower bounds. In general, P will be much greater than Q. Notice that it is quite possible for the number of variables in the problem to double. This will occur when only assets in the existing portfolio can be purchased and sold and no asset is at a bound.

The next step is to process the transformed problem to make it feasible with respect to the remaining constraints. This can be expressed as a simple linear program to find, for instance, the minimum transactions required to ensure feasibility with respect to constraints in equations (S5.1).

This entire transformation process can be described more succinctly (in matrix notation, unfortunately) as follows. Let the objective function be $U(h, h^0)$; the constraint matrix, A; and the constraint bounds, b_{min} and b_{max}. (For the budget constraint, the maximum equals the minimum equals one.) The constraint matrix, A, would be composed of three rows: the first containing ones, the second containing asset betas, and the last containing asset yields to correspond to the three constraints in equation (S5.1). Table S5.1 shows the tableau for the untransformed problem.

Table S5.1
Tableau of Untransformed Portfolio

Constraint Number		Activities						Right-Hand Side
		Asset Holdings				Slack Variables		
		h_1	h_2	...	h_N	s_1	s_2	
1.	Budget constraint	1	1		1	0	0	$=$ 1
2.	Beta constraint	β_1	β_2		β_N	1	0	$=$ β_{max}
3.	Cash yield constraint . . .	y_1	y_2		y_N	0	1	$=$ y_{max}
4.	Lower bounds	$h\min_1$	$h\min_2$		$h\min_N$	0	0	
5.	Upper bounds	$h\max_1$	$h\max_2$		$h\max_N$	β_{max} $-\beta_{min}$	y_{max} $-y_{min}$	
6.	Linear terms in objective function . . .	α_1 $+\Lambda_Y y_1$	α_2 $+\Lambda_Y y_2$		α_N $+\Lambda_Y y_N$	0	0	

Note: The objective function also includes nonlinear terms:

$$\Lambda_T \sum_j t_j + \Lambda_\omega \omega_P^2 + \Lambda_\beta \left(\sum_j \beta_j h_j - \beta_T\right)^2 + \Lambda_C \left(\sum_j y_j h_j - y_T\right)^2$$

where

$$t_j = \begin{cases} \text{TBUY}_j(h_j - h_j^0) & \text{if } h_j > h_j^0; \\ \text{TSELL}_j(h_j^0 - h_j) & \text{if } h_j^0 > h_j. \end{cases}$$

Then the initial problem can be expressed using this notation as:

$$\underset{\{h\}}{\text{Maximize}}\, U(h, h^0),$$

subject to:

$$hmin_j \le h_j \le hmax_j, j = 1, \ldots, N$$
$$b_{min} \le Ah \le b_{max}$$

The transformed problem can now be written as:

$$\underset{\Delta h}{\text{Maximize}}\, U(h^0 + f + \Delta h, h^0),$$

subject to:

$$0 \le p_k \le pmax_k; k = 1, \ldots, P$$
$$0 \le q_l \le qmax_l; l = 1, \ldots, Q$$
$$A(\Delta h) + s = b_{max} - A(h^0 + f)$$
$$0 \le s \le b_{max} - b_{min},$$

where Δh is compounded from p and q by reassociating each purchase index k and sale index l with the natural ordering of the assets j; that is, $\Delta h_j = p_k - q_l$. The introduced variables, s, represent the slacks on each of the constraints; for instance, if one slack variable, s_i, is at its lower bound, then the corresponding constraint is at its upper bound, and vice versa. This is made clear in Table S5.2, which shows the tableau of the transformed problem.

All that is required now is to solve the problem! It would be possible to use a standard quadratic programming package to perform this function.[3] However, this turns out to be impossibly expensive because the portfolio problem has several features which makes the use of standard packages very inefficient. The major problem is one of size.

A typical portfolio may have 60 assets, while the average number of assets in a followed list may be 200. This translates into 60 sale variables and 260 purchase variables (provided no asset is at a bound). These 320 variables, however, all have lower bounds of zero and positive upper bounds. For mathematical reasons the lower bounds of zero can be easily handled, but the standard packages usually treat upper bounds by introducing a slack variable and a constraint. For instance, the bounds:

$$0 \le p_1 \le pmax_1$$

would be interpreted as:

$$p_1 + s_1 = pmax_1$$
$$p_1 \ge 0, s_1 \ge 0.$$

---

[3]For instance, IBM supplies a general quadratic programming package.

Table S5.2
Tableau of Transformed Portfolio

Constraint Number	Purchases p_1	p_2	...	p_P	Sales q_1	q_2	...	q_Q	Slack Variables s_1	s_2	Right-Hand Side
1. Budget constraint	-1	-1		-1	1	1		1	0	0	$= 0$
2. Beta constraint	β_{p1}	β_{p2}		β_{pp}	$-\beta_{q1}$	$-\beta_{q2}$		$-\beta_{qQ}$	1	0	$= \beta_{max} - \sum h_j^0 \beta_j$
3. Cash yield constraint	y_{p1}	y_{p2}		y_{pp}	$-y_{q1}$	$-y_{q2}$		$-y_{qQ}$	0	1	$= y_{max} - \sum h_j^0 y_j$
4. Lower bounds	0	0		0	0	0		0	0	0	
5. Upper bounds	$p max_1$	$p max_2$		$p max_P$	$q max_1$	$q max_2$		$q max_Q$	$\beta_{max} - \beta_{min}$	$y_{max} - y_{min}$	
6. Linear terms in objective function	$\alpha_{p1} + \Lambda_y y_{p1} + \Lambda_T t_p p_1$	$\alpha_{p2} + \Lambda_y y_{p2} + \Lambda_T t_p p_2$		$\alpha_{pp} + \Lambda_y y_{pp} + \Lambda_T t_p p_P$	$\alpha_{q1} + \Lambda_y y_{q1} + \Lambda_T t_q q_1$	$\alpha_{q2} + \Lambda_y y_{q2} + \Lambda_T t_q q_2$		$\alpha_{qQ} + \Lambda_y y_{qQ} + \Lambda_T t_q q_Q$	0	0	

Note: The objective function also includes nonlinear terms:

$$\Lambda_\omega \omega_P^2 + \Lambda_\beta (\textstyle\sum h_j \beta_j - \beta_T)^2 + \Lambda_C (\textstyle\sum h_j y_j - y_T)^2,$$

where $h_j = h_j^0 + p_k - q_l$, and t_p, and t_q are abbreviations for $TBUY_j$, and $TSELL_j$, respectively.

This has removed the upper bound but added the variable s_1 (which has a lower bound of zero) and an equality constraint. Suddenly, the portfolio optimization problem has 640 variables and 320 additional constraints. Because the cost of the computation is directly related to the size of the problem, the computational expense has approximately doubled.[4]

What is required is a procedure that exploits the problem structure, namely a small number of linear constraints and a large number of variables which are upper and lower bounded, without having to add slack variables and additional constraints.[5] In addition, because the residual risk can be expressed in the decomposed form of XMC and specific risk, equation (S5–4), it would be useful to be able to retain this specification rather than having to use the full covariance matrix. Finally, portfolio optimization is (in spite of its name) "approximate." For instance, the inputs are probably outdated by the time the solution can be used (for example, the asset prices have changed). Thus, given the choice of getting (1) a good approximation to the true optimal solution inexpensively or (2) the true optimal solution expensively, the former seems more appropriate. This implies the use of "stopping criteria" which would halt the algorithm if, for instance, the improvement in utility becomes negligible at a certain stage in the algorithm.[6] There are only a few algorithms which can take advantage of this structure; one which appears ideally suited to it is the quadratic programming variant of Von Hohenbalken's mathematical programming algorithm. Further details of this approach can be found in the article "Realistic Portfolio Optimization," by Andrew Rudd and Barr Rosenberg.[7]

The solution to the optimization will almost certainly include several small holdings and transactions which are not in multiples of round lots. The easiest way to adjust the holdings and transactions is to use a simple heuristic at the termination of the optimization. For instance, the small holdings can be removed by fictitiously selling them and crediting the cash account with the proceeds. These assets are then taken out of the problem, and the cash is invested in the remaining assets (which have holdings above the minimum) in such a

---

[4]Recall that the cause of this difficulty was the modeling of transaction costs. Hence, early problem formulations "forgot" about transaction costs and made other simplifying assumptions. For instance, the single-index model was used to simplify the residual covariance structure and linear approximations to the quadratic objective function so that less expensive linear programming algorithms could be used. Needless to say, when the backbone of the problem has been assumed away, the solution is both inexpensive and useless.

[5]This ability with the upper bounds is referred to as "implicit upper bounding."

[6]Professor Sharpe has published one approach which could take advantage of this structure (William Sharpe, "An Algorithm for Portfolio Improvement," Research Paper no. 475, Graduate School of Business, Stanford University, October 1978.) This approach can be made more applicable by directly incorporating minimum transaction sizes and the "either/or" type of minimum bound (see Chapter 5). We believe that such hueristic forms (some of which have already been developed by investment consultants) are the way of the future for many applications, rather than "full-blown" optimization.

[7]In E. J. Elton and M. J. Gruber, eds. *Portfolio Theory—Studies in Management Sciences*, vol. 11 (Amsterdam: North-Holland, 1979).

way as to minimize the decrease in utility from the adjustment. Similarly, the transactions which are not in multiples of round lots are revised downward or upwards, to the nearest multiple of round lots. These changes should also be made so as to minimize the decrease in utility. Of course, this derived solution need not be the optimal solution, which would be obtained if the bounds and transaction units were correctly modeled from the start; however, in the vast majority of institutional portfolios the difference is going to be negligible. In fact, the other sources of error (for instance, in the alphas) will dominate the error introduced in adjusting the solution after the optimization.

This formulation differs from the earlier attempts at portfolio optimization only by being more realistic and accurate. Thus, it might be expected that the approach expounded here would present no great surprises to organizations that currently use optimization tools. In general, this is correct; however, for one specialized selection problem the current practice is quite different from our suggested methodology. This is the selection and revision of passive portfolios, in particular, index funds.

Recall that an index fund is a passive portfolio that is designed to track a visible index closely. In general, passive portfolios need not be indexed, but could have distinct sectoral or asset emphases depending upon the investor's attitudes toward risk and the economic environment. However, all passive portfolios, whether indexed or not, are designed to be stable and to match the long-term performance of one segment of the capital markets, rather than to be managed with the aim of earning incremental rewards from transient asset or market behavior.

The method of selecting and revising passive portfolios has received virtually no attention in the literature. In the case of index funds, several authors have briefly commented on the problem without suggesting solutions.[8] Of course, if such a fund were exactly indexed, its composition would duplicate that of the index and, in the absence of cash flows, the selection process would be purely mechanical; the portfolio would require revision only when the index was changed. However, cash flows from dividend income and additional contributions must be invested. It is impractical to allocate this incremental flow perfectly across all assets in the index in order to maintain exact duplication. Instead, larger investments must be made in a smaller number of assets, which are dynamically balanced through time as additional flows are received. Hence, in order to achieve minimal tracking error, the rebalancing of the fund must be as efficient as possible.

As discussed above, the requirements for an index fund are:

1. A beta of unity relative to the index.
2. Minimum *XMC* relative to the index; that is, differences in exposure to the

---

[8]For example, see this supplement's "Selected References," particularly articles by Black and Scholes; Shapiro; and Good, Ferguson, and Treynor.

common factors between the index and the fund portfolio should be minimized.

3. Minimum specific risk.

The last two requirements define the objective of minimizing residual risk. Thus, in this case many of the facilities required for the general optimization problem are irrelevant, so that the problem simplifies considerably, as we shall see below. Surprisingly, the majority of index funds are currently selected and revised by means of heuristic procedure quite different from optimization.

The procedure is to stratify the universe of assets from which the index fund is to be selected (or revised) by dividing that universe into "cells."[9] The portfolio is then selected by investing in assets from the cells. The measure of how closely the portfolio will track the index is approximated by determining the difference between the portfolio holdings and the index cell holdings. If the difference is small, intuition suggests that the portfolio will track the index closely or that the index fund will exhibit little residual risk about the index.

Most of the index fund selection programs currently in use incorporate the following simple heuristic:

1. Assemble the universe of assets from which the fund is to be selected and the index to which the fund will be matched.
2. Specify the dollar value $D, of the index fund.
3. Select the minimum investment size, $h,$ as a proportion of the total value of the fund. The reciprocal of this size, $^1/_h$, determines the number of "units" in the fund. The dollar value of each unit is $hD.
4. Form a capitalization-weighted portfolio with a total value $D from all the assets in the universe, and rank the holdings from largest to smallest. The index fund is formed by purchasing assets that have holdings greater than the minimum position size, $h.$ The size of the transaction is the integer number of units, such that the dollar value of the transaction is closest to the dollar value of the position in the capitalization-weighted portfolio. Purchases start with the asset having the largest capitalization and stop when all units are used. If all purchases are completed and there are still units remaining, continue with step 5.
5. Assign each asset in the universe to one of N mutually exclusive and exhaustive cells. In practice, this amounts to assigning each asset to one industry group. Calculate the investment holdings of the index and the index fund in each of these cells.
6. Rank the cells in order of the difference between the fund holdings and the index holdings, from the most to the least deficient. Starting with the most deficient cell (and with assets in that cell that have not yet been purchased

[9]This description is drawn from Andrew Rudd, "Optimal Passive Portfolio Selection," *Financial Management,* Spring 1980, pp. 57–66.

in step 4), purchase single units until the cell holding of the index fund matches the cell holding of the index to a discrepancy of one unit or less. Continue until all units have been invested.

In summary, the heuristic selects the fund first by matching the fund and the index by company size and then by one other dimension (usually industry groups).

The selection procedure is unsophisticated, in that the only control of tracking error is to minimize the deviations of portfolio holdings from index holdings along the two dimensions of, usually, capitalization and industry groups. Unfortunately, the intuition that keeping the differences in holdings small will cause the tracking error to be small, is frequently erroneous.[10]

The reason is that residual risk is composed of two components, specific risk and *XMC*. Recall that to immunize a portfolio from each company's specific risk, the portfolio holding should equal the index holding. The specific risk contribution of an asset to portfolio risk is proportional to the squared difference between these holdings, see equation (S5–4). Since large differences in holdings are proportionally more serious than small ones, the stratifying heuristic (matching portfolio holdings with the index holdings, starting with the largest companies) probably does a good job of controlling specific risk.

It is with the other component of residual risk, *XMC*, that the problem lies. It is clear from equation (S5–4) that *XMC* is induced into the portfolio whenever the portfolio exposure to the common factors is different from the index exposure, that is, whenever $\gamma_{Pi} \neq 0$. For instance, if the fund has a greater holding in airline stocks than the index does, then whenever the airline stocks perform differently than the index, the fund will display a tracking error. Starting with the large-capitalization stocks may well cause the index fund to be underweighted with small-capitalization stocks. Since the common factors are related (for instance, small stocks tend to be growth oriented), this selection procedure provides considerable opportunity for exposure to several common factors. In other words, stratification makes little attempt to control *XMC*.

Similarly, the procedure does not control the systematic risk level of the index fund. Again, depending upon the position size, *h,* and the actual universe used, the procedure may overweight large-capitalization stocks. These companies tend to have lower systematic risk, causing the index fund and the index to respond with different magnitudes to economic events. Unless the portfolio risk is analyzed subsequent to selection (for instance, from a PORCH analysis), there is no knowledge of the magnitude and direction of this bias.

Finally, there is no indication of the relative benefit or the cost of terms of utility of adding or deleting a stock. This is particularly important when the portfolio is being revised, because the cost of the transaction must be weighed directly against the benefit, which in this case is derived from tracking the

---

[10]See ibid. for examples of these errors.

index more closely. Since there is no quantitative measure of the tracking error, it is not known whether the transaction cost is greater than the disutility arising from the portfolio risk. In other words, there is no indication whether the transactions will be beneficial or not.

Let us now return to the optimization formulation. We indicated above that index fund revision is a simplified version of the general problem. In particular, the alpha and yield terms in the objective function, equation (S5–2), are not used; that is, we can set:

$$\alpha_j = 0, \text{ for } j = 1, \ldots, N,$$

and

$$\Lambda_Y = 0.$$

The beta constraint becomes an equality:

$$\beta_{max} = \beta_{min} = 1,$$

which implies that the contribution to utility from beta becomes a constant—$\Lambda_\beta (1 - \beta_T)^2$—and hence will not affect the selection process (although it will change the level of utility). The yield constraint is inoperative, so we can set:

$$y_{min} = 0\%; \ y_{max} = 100\%.$$

Hence, the optimization formulation for revising an index fund reduces to:

$$\text{Maximize } \Lambda_T \left\{ \sum_j TSELL_j (h_j^0 - h_j)^+ + \sum_j TBUY_j (h_j - h_j^0)^+ \right\} + \Lambda_\omega \omega_P^2,$$
$$\{h_j\}$$

subject to:

$$\left. \begin{array}{l} hmin_j \le h_j \le hmax_j, \text{ for all assets } j; \\ 1 = \sum_j h_j = \sum \beta_j h_j = \beta_P. \end{array} \right\} \quad \text{(S5–6)}$$

In the absence of transaction costs, the objective function can be simplified further to:

$$\text{Minimize } \omega_P^2$$
$$\{h_j\}$$

These are particularly simple problem specifications that can be solved very efficiently, usually at far less cost than that of the stratification procedure. In addition, there are many index fund problems that the stratification procedure fails to solve. This is particularly true if the universe of assets from which the fund is to be selected is not contained within the group of assets comprised by the index.[11] In addition, general passive portfolio selection and revision problems (that is, the type (2) passive strategies defined in Chapter 5) cannot be

---

[11]See ibid. for demonstration of this point.

solved by stratification because the procedure requires matching an existing "index" (that is, a list of assets with their holdings) in step 5 of the heuristic. The optimization approach does not suffer from this problem because the attributes of these general passive strategies are typically expressed in terms of the variables which are already a part of the formulation (for instance, yield).

Interestingly, there are some passive strategies which severely test the abilities of the optimization approach. One example is the passive strategy to match the performance of small-capitalization stocks. Essentially, the difficulty is that the solution from the optimization may not be obtainable because the market for the small-capitalization stocks is so thin. Here the real problem is not so much in the modeling of the risk and return as in allowing for the vagaries of the trading process.

There is a conceptually simple and elegant solution, namely to provide substitutes for every trade. Instead of specifying that 1,000 shares of XYZ Company must be purchased (which may be impossible because at the time the trade is required, the market may be insufficiently liquid or no broker may be willing to "go short" the 1,000 shares to satisfy the client), an "equivalence class" of stocks is given to the trading desk, with instructions to purchase a total of 1,000 shares in that class. The equivalence class is a group of securities, each member of which is considered identical to the others. The trader then "samples" from this class and, depending upon the liquidity of the market in the stocks, may purchase, for instance, 100 shares in one stock, 400 shares in another, and the remaining 500 shares in a third.[12] Thus, the key to the approach is the definition of the equivalence class and the homogeneity of the assets within the class. Although the idea is conceptually simple, the technology required to construct the classes is far from trivial!

This completes our discussion of the formulation of the portfolio optimization problem. We now complete this supplement with a case study describing the techniques used in constructing yield-biased passive strategies.

Case Study 6: Yield-Biased Passive Strategies[13]

The idea that it may be advantageous for tax-exempt investors to hold high-yielding portfolios has recently become popular. The rationale for this belief lies in the differential taxation on capital gains and dividend yield, as described in Chapter 5. In essence, the hypothesis is that an alpha can be associated with each security's yield. The magnitude of this alpha is small—on the order of

---

[12]To our knowledge, the American National bank of Chicago was the first user of this sampling technique and, indeed, the innovator of the small-capitalization stock passive strategy.

[13]This case study is based on Barr Rosenberg and Andrew Rudd, "The Yield/Beta/Residual Risk Trade-off," Research Program in Finance, Working Paper no. 66 (Berkeley: Institute of Business and Economic Research, University of California, January 1978). In this section we only describe the techniques for obtaining the solutions; readers interested in the effects of nonstandard yield and beta strategies on diversifications should refer to the original study.

30 basis points for every 1 percent yield in excess of the market's yield (that is, if the yield on the market is 5 percent, then a stock with a current yield of 6 percent would have an alpha of 0.30 percent. Thus, any strategy aimed at capturing this abnormal return must be carefully designed so that the residual risk incurred does not swamp the alpha.

The study referred to in footnote 13 was designed to determine how aggressive (that is, at what level of yield) optimal tax-exempt portfolios should be. Consequently, a series of optimal portfolios had to be calculated at varying levels of aversion to residual risk.

The first interesting technique concerns the method of "data compression." The universe of assets consisted of approximately 3,600 common stocks. Because this universe was much larger than could be accommodated in an optimization program, it was split into two groups. The first group consisted of the 399 largest firms, which were considered as individual purchase opportunities. The remaining companies were grouped into "composite" assets. In all, 152 composites were constructed. They were based upon the 39 industry groups listed in Table 3.2. For each of these industries the common stocks were divided into four categories: a low-yield, low-beta group; a low-yield, high-beta group; a high-yield, low-beta group; and a high-yield, high-beta group. Of the 156 groups which resulted, one contained a single large asset and was treated as an individual purchase opportunity, and three containing fewer than four companies were merged with another group in the same industry. Within each group, the member companies were weighted in proportion to their capitalization to form a composite asset. Hence, the outcome was 400 individual companies and 152 pooled funds. In this manner, an analysis of (almost) the entire universe of institutional stocks was possible.

The constraints used in the optimization consisted of various yield and beta values corresponding to interesting cases, together with bounds on the asset positions. All analyses used lower bounds on asset holdings of zero. One set of analyses was performed with upper bounds equal to the S&P 500 holding plus 5 percent. For example, the allowable range of holdings for AT&T, which is about 6 percent of the S&P 500, was from 0 to 11 percent of the portfolio. The allowable range for a stock not included in the S&P 500 was from 0 to 5 percent.

These are reasonable restrictions to apply for a small pool of funds that is being invested without arbitrary legal restrictions, and the restrictions may even be conservative in this case. However, a 5 percent portion of a large portfolio may be a dollar value that is an unreasonably large fraction of the outstanding capitalization of a small company. To reflect this limitation, another set of analyses was performed with the more restrictive upper bounds equal to Minimum $\{h_{S\&P} + 5\%, 4h_U\}$, where $h_{S\&P}$ is the S&P 500 holding and h_U is the percentage capitalization of the company in the universe of all 3,600 assets considered in the study. This upper bound results, for example, in a maximum holding of 11 percent for AT&T and of 0.68 percent for a company with $1.5 billion capitalization.

Let us now turn to the objective function. If we knew the level of yield desired (say, y_P), then the optimization formulation would be simply:

Problem 1

$$\text{Minimize } \omega_P^2,$$
$$\{h_j\}$$

subject to:

$$1 = \Sigma h_j, \text{ and } y_P = \Sigma h_j y_j$$

which specifies the minimum residual risk (or the most highly diversified) portfolio with the given yield, y_P. Because high-yielding assets tend to have low betas, a portfolio with a large desired yield, y_P, will have a low beta, which may not be required. Thus, to preserve the portfolio's exposure to systematic risk at a specified level (say, β_P), the following problem could be solved:

Problem 2

$$\text{Minimize } \omega_P^2$$
$$\{h_j\}$$

subject to:

$$1 = \Sigma h_j; \ y_P = \Sigma h_j y_j; \text{ and } \beta_P = \Sigma h_j \beta_j.$$

It should be noted that this formulation makes great demands upon the portfolio manager by requiring y_P and β_P to be specified. ($y_P = 8$ percent is reassuring, but why not $y_P = 8.5$ percent or 7.5 percent? Likewise, setting $y_P =$ market yield (y_M) + 2 percent is convenient, but so are $y_P = y_M + 1$ percent and $y_P = y_M + 3$ percent.) In particular, the formulation requires that the portfolio manager know the solution! It constrains the "return side" and lets the risk be determined from the optimization. If the minimum risk level is unknown before the computations are made, the risk/return trade-off is similarly unknown, so there may be more beneficial strategies than the one specified by y_P and β_P. For example, if the parameters are $y_P = 6\%$ and $\beta_P = 1.0$, then $\omega_P = 5\%$ may be the solution. Depending upon the universe of stocks, however, it may be possible to form a portfolio with $y_P = 6$ percent, $\beta_P = 0.96$, and $\omega_P = 3$ percent or with $y_P = 7$ percent, $\beta_P = 1.0$, and $\omega_P = 5.5$ percent. In other words, completely different (and perhaps more beneficial) portfolios could be obtained by changing the parameters slightly.

The method of avoiding this difficulty is to specify targets and trade-offs for the important portfolio attributes. This formulation may be:

Problem 3

$$\text{Maximize} \qquad \Lambda_C(y_P - y_T)^2 + \Lambda_\beta(\beta_P - \beta_T)^2 + \Lambda_\omega \omega_P^2,$$
$$\{h_j\}$$

subject to:

$$1 = \Sigma h_j$$

where y_T and β_T are the yield and beta targets, respectively, and Λ_C, Λ_β, and Λ_ω are negative coefficients specifying the trade-offs. Now, if $y_T = 6$ percent and $\beta_T = 1.0$ are the most desired levels for these attributes, then this formulation will let the optimization find the best combination of portfolio yield, portfolio beta, and portfolio residual risk, which are closest to the targets and which maximize utility. It may be that the portfolio with $y_P = 7$ percent, $\beta_P = 1.0$, and $\omega_P = 5.5$ percent is preferred to the one obtained by insisting that $y_P = 6$ percent and $\beta_P = 1.0$.

Using these procedures, the residual risk function at different levels of yield and beta was determined. This function, shown in Figure S5.1, represents the penalty in terms of residual variance for requiring nonstandard yield and beta strategies as of April 1977.

Figure S5.1
Contours Describing the Residual Variance Function
(April 1977)

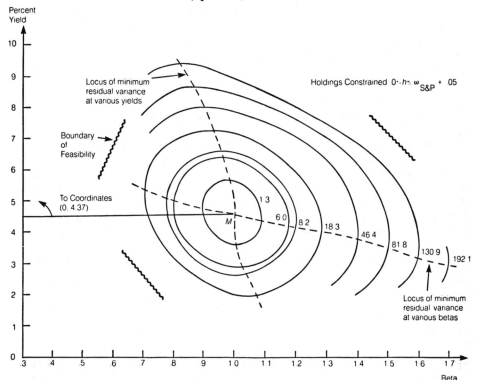

Source: Barr Rosenberg and Andrew Rudd, "The Yield/Beta/Residual Risk Trade-off," Research Program in Finance, Working Paper no. 66 (Berkeley: Institute of Business and Economic Research, University of California, January 1978).

The market (S&P 500) yield was 4.61 percent, and the risk-free rate was 4.37 percent. The almost vertical dashed line represents the locus of portfolios with minimum residual risk at levels of yield (that is, solutions to problem 1). Notice that because this dashed line slopes from the upper left to the lower right, high-yielding (low-yielding) assets tend to have low (high) betas. The other dashed line shows the locus of minimum residual variance portfolios at various levels of beta, and the contours show the level of risk for general yield/ beta strategies. For instance, if the portfolio has a $1\frac{1}{2}$ percent increment in yield over the S&P 500 (to approximately 6 percent), then the portfolio incurs just under six units of variance. The general shape of the residual risk function resembles a (squashed) "bowl," with the lowest point on the S&P 500.[14] Notice that residual variance increases rapidly away from the S&P 500, particularly in the direction of high yield and high beta.

Selected References

Many of the earlier attempts at formulating the optimization problem can be found in the references of standard MBA finance texts. Our feeling is that these are merely of historical interest and are of little value for practical problems. The following references include articles which present the modern approach to optimization and papers relevant to the topics in the supplement.

Black, Fischer, and Myron Scholes. "From Theory to a New Financial Product." *Journal of Finance*, May 1974, pp. 309–412.

Gamlin, Joanne. "Yield Tilt Concept Slides Assets to Wells." *Pensions & Investments*, June 4, 1979, p. 2.

Good, Walter; Robert Ferguson; and Jack Treynor. "An Investor's Guide to the Index Fund Controversy." *Financial Analysts Journal*, November–December 1976, pp. 27–36.

LeBaron, Dean. "The Future of Indexing." Paper presented at the Eighth Annual Meeting, Financial Management Association, Minneapolis, October 12–14, 1978.

Rosenberg, Barr, and Andrew Rudd. "The Yield/Beta/Residual Risk Trade-off." Research Program in Finance, Working Paper no. 66. Berkeley Institute for Business and Economic Research, University of California, 1978.

Rudd, Andrew, and Barr Rosenberg. "Realistic Portfolio Optimization." In *Portfolio Theory—Studies in Management Sciences*, vol. 11, ed. E. J. Elton and M. J. Gruber. Amsterdam: North-Holland, 1979.

Shapiro, Harvey. "How Do You Really Run One of Those Index Funds?" *Institutional Investor*, February 1976, pp. 24–25.

Von Hohenbalken, Balder. "A Finite Algorithm to Maximize Certain Pseudoconcave Functions on Polytopes." *Mathematical Programming*, October 1975, pp. 189–206.

---

[14]The residual risk function drawn in Figure S5.1 is conceptually similar to that depicted in Figure 5.7. The major difference is that the bowl in the earlier figure is a function of the asset holdings, whereas the bowl here is a function of the portfolio beta and yield.

Chapter 6

Master Trusts and the Multiple Management of Portfolios

Some of the most significant practical applications of modern portfolio theory are to be found in the areas of bank master trusts and the multiple investment management of large portfolios. The reason, quite simply, is that MPT allows sponsors to improve their control of the investment management process. The aspects of the investment management process which have come under the closest scrutiny are the selection of money managers, the allocation of funds among managers, the allocation of funds between passive and active strategies, and the direct exchange of securities between portfolios within master trusts.

If the rate of change is the benchmark of distinguishing between evolution and revolution, then MPT is promoting a revolution in the management of large institutional portfolios. Several experienced observers of the institutional investment arena characterize MPT as a cost accounting methodology that helps compare the realized rewards with the incurred costs. Any shortcomings on the reward side are now more obvious and explicable; high-cost active management, regardless of pedigree, is the object of critical examination.

Our initial purpose in this chapter is to describe the operation of a master trust. We then turn from the reporting and security handling problems that arise from retaining several investment managers to the difficulties of controlling the individual managers. The obvious questions are: What are the advantages and what are the disadvantages of having more than one manager? Although obvious, these simple questions appear to have been overlooked by many plan sponsors. We complete this chapter with a case study which provides an analysis of the individual managers and the aggregate portfolio of a plan sponsor.

The supplement to this chapter presents more of the chapter's message. Instead of words, however, we use the language of mathematics and thus attempt to make the arguments both more precise and more robust.

The Master Trust

What is a master trust? It is a management information system that permits a plan sponsor to keep track of, and therefore control, the huge sums of money which have been parceled out to a group of money managers. The master trust has many facets, including reporting tasks, accounting, bookkeeping, and cash management; it provides an overview for the sponsor, who is often inundated with details and unable to obtain a good perspective of the situation; and finally, the master trust has recently become the focus for performance measurement and other forms of portfolio analysis. This last aspect is a logical development because the aggregate portfolio (rather than the individually managed components) is of primary interest to the sponsor and can be fully documented in the computer memory of the master trust.

The growth in the use of master trusts is closely related to the popular trend toward the retention of multiple portfolio managers. Two forces encouraged this trend. The first was the growing pressure from labor for increased retirement benefits. As large business continued to dominate the economic scene, there was a growing tendency to compensate for the absence of the freedom and adventure provided by individual entrepreneurship by offering employees a pension "carrot" after 30 years of dedicated service. As this preference for deferred rather than current compensation grew, so too did pension fund asset values. Moreover, each distinct group of employees typically participated in a plan designed for their particular needs. Large corporations, therefore, usually have several pension plans covering their employees. The distributions shown in Figure 6.1 are indicative of the number of corporate pension plans and the number of managers of corporate pension funds.[1] The second force was more

---

[1]Another distribution of the number of plans can be found in Robert Cirino, "The Master Trust Battle Moves into the Shooting Stage," *Institutional Investor*, June 1978, pp. 104–12. Presumably the dissimilar distributions are a result of sampling differences. Some corporations clearly have larger problems than others; for example, as of September 30, 1980, General Telephone and Electronics employed 35 external managers as well as internal management for its 90 pension plans.

Figure 6.1
Distribution of the Number of Plans and Managers per Corporation

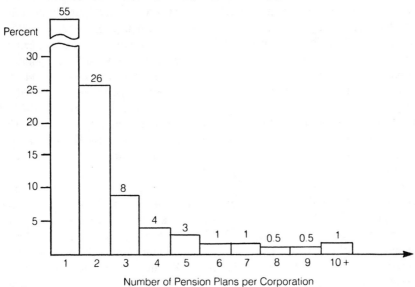

Number of Pension Plans per Corporation

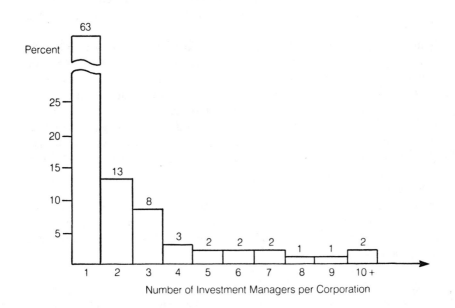

Number of Investment Managers per Corporation

mundane: as the value of the pension assets grew, size constraints and fiduciary considerations dictated multiple management. As the number of managers increased, the organization and control problems also increased, as did the probability of different performance among the various plans. Questions as to why, for instance, the "hourly paid" plan had a lower return than the executive profit-sharing plan (or vice versa) are clearly embarrassing to the corporation. Moreover, ERISA now mandates that the named fiduciary *must* provide the same level of expertise and intensity of investment for all plans. The remedy is to place all the funds in one pool and to allocate units in the pool to each of the different plans, as is done for different investors in a mutual fund. This simple step makes the control and monitoring problems so much more complicated that satisfaction of the ERISA requirements without a master trust is almost impossible for large plan sponsors.

A master trust is a central depository for the employee benefit assets of a corporation. The master trustee acts as both trustee and custodian for all the corporate benefit plans and their investment managers. The benefit plans may cover employees of single plants, divisions, or corporate subsidiaries and may include several different types, such as fixed-benefit plans, salaried plans, non-contributory plans, and profit-sharing plans. By implication, the master trust is beneficial only where multiple asset managers and/or multiple pension plans present the sponsor with a difficult control and communication problem.[2] Since the master trust acts as the center of communication network, its crucial service is to facilitate the information flows among the concerned parties, namely the asset managers, the brokers, the master trustee, the sponsor corporation, perhaps the plan beneficiaries, and the investment consultants, actuaries, and other advisers of the sponsor.

In its present form the master trust offers timely and accurate bookkeeping of asset transactions, a well-designed, consolidated method of reporting to the sponsor, better control of short-term cash (by capturing "float" credits), automatic investment of cash balances, trade date/settlement date/delivery date accounting, with ERISA reporting as a by-product. In some cases, a master trustee will offer additional consulting services, such as assisting a plan sponsor to evaluate the plan's money managers. Of even more importance than management information and control, a master trust, as mentioned earlier, creates a good overview for the sponsor.

Before proceeding to specific MPT applications in the master trust area, we will consider the essential functions of a master trust system. These functions are (1) to monitor and control a pension plan's investments; (2) to generate the necessary government reports; and (3) to provide a management overview of pension assets.

---

[2]Some of the larger corporations find it advisable to have several master trusts, each covering a particular group. For example, there may be two master trusts for pension benefit plans (one for defined benefit plans and one for defined contribution plans) and two master trusts for welfare benefit plans (one for the medical plans and one for the long-term disability plans).

This defines the bare skeleton of the master trust system. However, many additional features are incorporated by various master trustees. One important feature is the timely management of cash generated from dividend income and from the sale of assets on appropriate payable and settlement dates. Float credits created by the purchase of fail-to-deliver securities are properly accounted for and invested in a short-term investment fund (STIF). A good master trust also offers similar cash management flexibility to the investment managers. Ease of administration, which is an obvious benefit of well-organized cash management, offers very real economic advantages. Proper management of the "fail float" can alone generate income which in some cases is as high as 80 percent of the overall master trust fees.

The typical master trust oversees both multiple plans and multiple managers. The typical method of organizing the master trust is shown in Figure 6.2. In this situation, each asset manager is a specialist in either the equity or the fixed-income sectors. In simple variation, shown in Figure 6.3, the sponsor employs balanced managers who manage both equities and bonds. Finally, in another variation, instead of participating through the master trust in the aggregate portfolio, each plan participates directly in each of the managed sectors. This variation, sometimes called a multicomponent plan, is shown in Figure 6.4.

The master trust system's most visible outputs are the reports which provide information to the members of the information network. Clearly, the detail and number of these reports will depend on the sophistication of the sponsor and the master trustee and on the complexity of the pension plan organization. However, the following types of reports are commonly produced by master trusts.

Figure 6.2
Typical Master Trust Organization

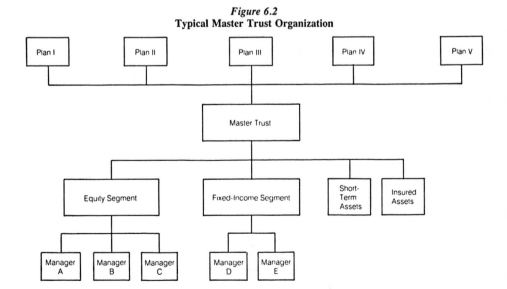

Figure 6.3
Master Trust Organization Using Balanced Funds

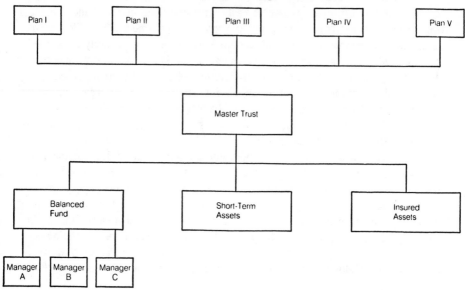

Figure 6.4
Multicomponent Master Trust Organization

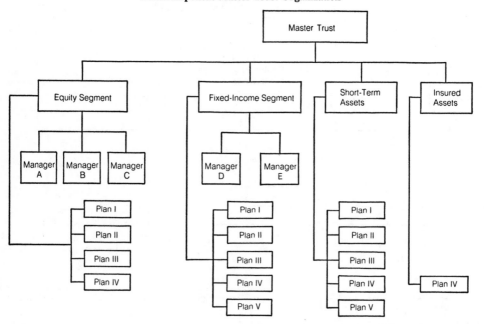

1. *Accounting reports.* These may include a daily ledger detailing activity in the portfolio, monthly transaction statement and statement of property held, quarterly transaction reports showing aggregate security activity, and a certified annual accounting report.
2. *Investment reports.* These include, on a monthly or quarterly basis, reports on the rates of return for each managed portfolio and for the aggregate portfolio; analyses of the equity portfolios, perhaps including a risk analysis for each managed portfolio, and reports on the aggregate portfolio. Similar reports should also be provided for the other asset categories (e.g., bonds and real estate).
3. *Plan accounting reports.* These reports show the financial status of the total pension pool and the inflows and outflows for each plan.
4. *ERISA reports.* These reports provide information necessary to complete and file Form 5500 with the federal government in order to be in compliance with ERISA. The common reports include brokerage fees, custodial and management fees, and the so-called 3 percent transactions.[3]
5. *Other reports.* These may include accrued income schedules, bond maturity schedules, and more specialized performance reports, such as comparisons with similar managed portfolios.

These reports are voluminous, to say the least. Rather than spending a great deal of space describing examples of each type, we show in Figure 6.5 a diagram of the important information flows involved within a master trust. As can be seen, the flows communicate information between three areas, investment decision making, security handling, and plan accounting. As the records of security transactions become increasingly transmitted electronically rather than by shuffling papers, new strategies for managing money become available. For example, one strategy (which we will discuss in more detail later in the chapter) is to centralize all transactions in a single trading facility, possibly at the master trust, by having money managers merely transmit recommended trades to the trustee. The trustee first attempts to clear the trades among other active managers retained by the plan and/or an index fund, and the deal will be completed in the securities market only if the trustee cannot find a manager who is willing to trade.

Figure 6.6 diagrams the flows of security transaction information as they are currently organized. It should be mentioned that this area is already becoming more automated with the advent of such procedures as the Depository Trust Company's Institutional Delivery System.

The challenge facing a plan sponsor is to be able to step back from the

---

[3]There are four categories of reportable transactions which must be filed with the Labor Department. These are: (1) any single transaction representing 3 percent or more of a plan's assets; (2) any series of nonsecurity transactions with the same person totaling 3 percent or more of a plan's assets; (3) any series of transactions in the same security totaling 3 percent or more of a plan's assets; and (4) any series of security transactions with the same person totaling 3 percent or more of a plan's assets.

Figure 6.5
Summary of Master Trust Data Flows

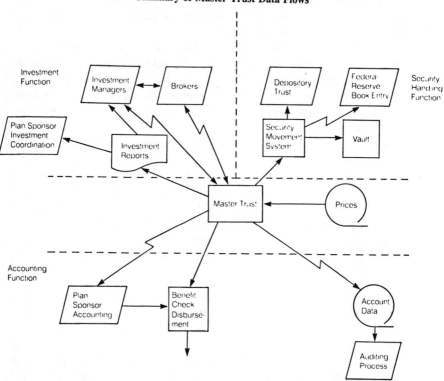

enormous amount of information being generated and to create an overview. When this has been done, an appropriate investment strategy must be decided upon. The monumental task of controlling this intricate system will be addressed in the remainder of the chapter.

Let us briefly outline the decisions that the sponsor faces once the wood has been separated from the trees. The most important question that a pension fund sponsor must answer is, What long-term overall portfolio return must be achieved for the plan to operate successfully? This is the asset allocation decision described in Chapter 5. The question can only be analyzed seriously by considering the pension liabilities and understanding the actuarial assumptions. The outcome of the asset allocation decision is the normal long-term allocation to the important asset categories, commonly specified as a fixed-income/equity mix. Of course, as more asset categories become acceptable for institutional investment, such simple solutions become less realistic.

Let us now assume that the normal portfolio has been decided upon. The next problem is how to assemble a stable of one or more managers to manage the assets. This raises the related questions as to (1) how many managers

Figure 6.6
Transmission of Security Transaction Information

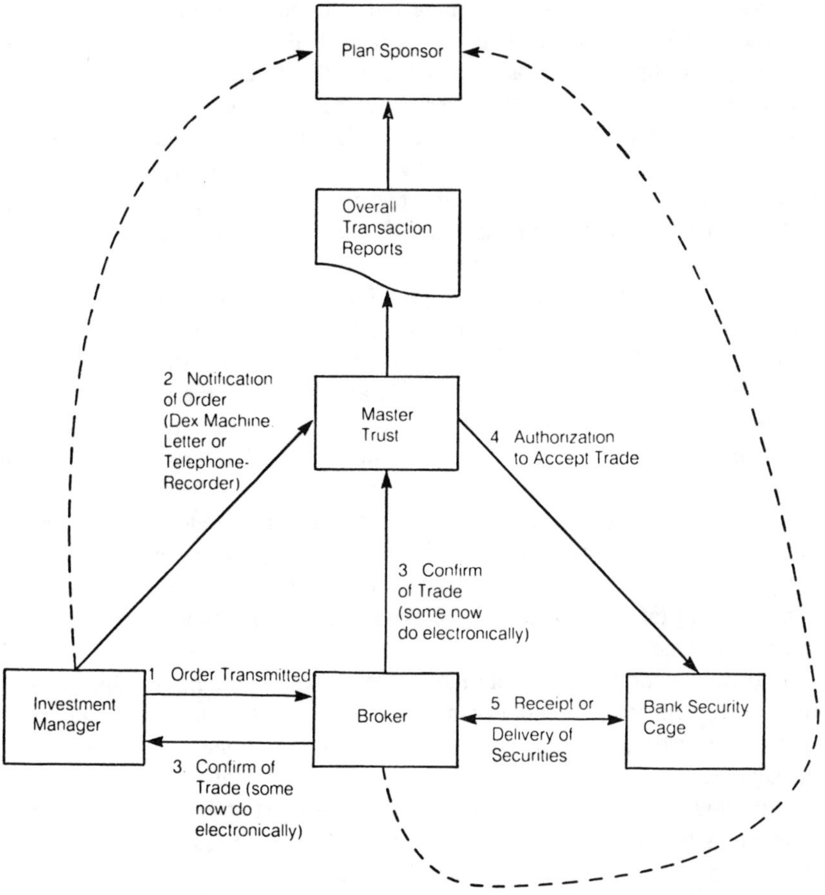

Note: The dashed lines represent recent developments in efficiently organizing the information flows. Some plan sponsors request that investment managers and brokers send them duplicate confirmations of all trades. This helps in the efficient settling of trades and in the arbitration of disputes.

should be hired, (2) what type of investment strategy should be pursued, and (3) how the managers should be coordinated.

Why Have Multiple Managers?

The two main motives for hiring more than one manager appear to have been diversification and specialization. To some extent, underlying both motives has been the recent large increase in the value of pension assets. Many sponsors felt that it was imprudent to have a single manager, who with one error could cause a significant reduction in the value of the assets; rather, hire several managers so that the "errors" (and, notice, the successes if the coordination is inefficient) would average out. Moreover, with a large fund it is possible to hire managers with different specialities (bonds, growth stocks, large-capitalization stocks, and so on) and still place a significant fraction of wealth with each manager. However, since active management fees per dollar managed typically decrease as the assets under management increase, it follows that for a given asset value, increasing the number of managers will increase to some extent both the total fee and the percentage fee paid by the sponsor. Clearly, then, there is a trade-off between the cost and the perceived benefit of the increased diversification obtained by employing multiple managers.

The argument for multiple managers raises some questions. For instance, we mentioned "errors," but whose errors are they? Certainly, the asset manager is responsible for an error in the execution of the investment strategy, but the underlying error lies in the sponsor's assessment of the manager. In other words, if the sponsor could pick "good" managers, then there would be no errors in investment strategy. Further, the abnormal return that the sponsor earns on the aggregate portfolio is the weighted average of the abnormal returns on each of the managed portfolios, but these abnormal returns are a result of the sponsor's selection process. Hence, with multiple management we are very much concerned with the sponsor's skill in selecting managers. Talented sponsors will find talented managers; below-average sponsors will employ below-average managers.

Is diversification a justifiable motive for hiring additional managers? Since (more) efficient diversification can be obtained by shifting funds into a passively managed fund, this motive is apparently irrational. Relative to active management, passive management has the advantages of a lower management fee and lower transaction costs, since the investment strategy of passive management is to buy and hold a diversified, informationless portfolio. As indicated in previous chapters, the simple capital asset pricing model (CAPM) identifies the market portfolio as the normal portfolio for all investors. Of course, this simple model is built upon assumptions that may not hold true for everybody. However, there are generalizations of the CAPM which incorporate more realistic assumptions, such as uncertain inflation, differential taxation, and differential holding periods. This suggests that there are several different "mutual funds," with the optimal normal portfolio for each investor being a weighted average of these funds. The weights will be a function of the investor's circumstances and the investor's exposure to the uncertain inflation and the other factors. In these more complex models, investors will have different normal portfolios, but the fact remains that each investor will have a normal portfolio which is optimal in the absence of appraisal ability.

Of course, an investor who is able to form appraisals of asset returns will hold a portfolio which will be different from the normal portfolio. Forming these appraisals and constructing the differential portfolio are the pursuit of active management, a process which requires an incremental fee to support it.

Clearly, a sponsor should not pay this fee to an active manager unless the sponsor's selection process justifies the belief that the manager will provide an incremental return relative to a defined normal portfolio. Further, this holds irrespective of the number of managers that the sponsor retains. We shall show below that the advantage of multiple management is the increase in alpha which it obtains relative to the alpha obtained by a single manager. We hinted at this conclusion in supplement 4, where we showed that the sponsor's "time until significance" could be a good deal shorter with multiple management than with single portfolio manager.

How large should this incremental active return be? It should certainly be larger than the incremental costs of active management (previously listed in Chapter 2), namely:

1. The incremental fee paid to active managers.
2. The incremental transaction costs resulting from active management.
3. The disutility of the residual risk incurred as a result of active management.

With this preamble in mind, we can now deal with some important questions:

1. If a sponsor does not believe the selection process can identify above average managers, how many managers should be hired and which investment strategy should be followed?
2. If a sponsor does believe that the selection process can identify above-average managers, how many managers should be hired and which investment strategy should be followed?

The answer to the first sponsor's questions is straightforward. This sponsor has no belief that a manager will provide an incremental return, let alone an incremental return after transaction costs. Hence, the correct strategy is to buy and hold the normal portfolio.

Let us now turn to the more interesting case where the sponsor's selection process can identify managers who earn abnormal returns. As we have remarked, the most important measure of skill is the manager's information ratio, the ratio of alpha to residual risk (standard deviation). This ratio is the primary output of the sponsor's selection process, and it should be communicated to the manager, since it expresses the sponsor's belief in the manager's ability. The disclosure of this value indicates an agreement between the sponsor and the manager as to the "performance" which both parties expect, or, more exactly, as to the risk-reward trade-off which the manager is to attain. Because of this agreement, the information ratio in this context is referred to as the *covenant information ratio*.[4]

---

[4]First used in Barr Rosenberg, "Security Appraisal and Unsystematic Risk in Institutional Investment," *Proceedings of the Seminar on the Analysis of Security Prices*, University of Chicago, November 1976, pp. 171–237.

What is the appropriate portfolio management organization for this sponsor? The key point here is that the total portfolio is all that matters to the sponsor. The sponsor is solely concerned with the aggregate return and does not care how it is obtained. The sponsor should monitor the strategy of individual managers to the extent that this improves the aggregate return. The implication is that individual active managers should be hired or fired only if this promises an improvement in the expected aggregate portfolio return. This again indicates the fallacy in the diversification justification for multiple management, since diversification can be purchased less expensively by directing part of the actively managed funds to a passively managed portfolio.[5] Moveover, it is unlikely that, up to the end of the 1970s, many (if any) portfolios of multiply managed sponsors were sufficiently (residually) risky to warrant hiring an additional manager in order to increase diversification. This is shown in Figure 6.7, which is the multiple management version of Figure 2.4.

Figure 6.7
Components of Variance

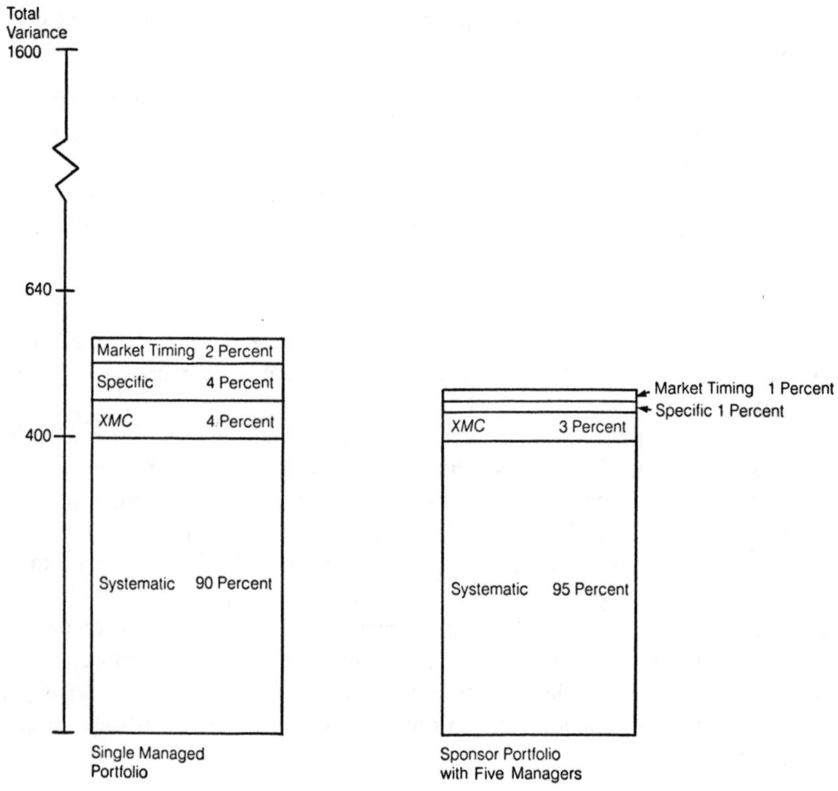

Total
Variance
1600

640

Single Managed Portfolio:
Market Timing	2 Percent
Specific	4 Percent
XMC	4 Percent
Systematic	90 Percent

400

Sponsor Portfolio with Five Managers:
Market Timing	1 Percent
Specific	1 Percent
XMC	3 Percent
Systematic	95 Percent

Single Managed Portfolio   Sponsor Portfolio with Five Managers

[5]We will examine strategies for allocating funds between active and passive portfolios in the next section.

Figure 6.7 repeats the diagram for the components of variance in a typical single-manager portfolio and then shows the components for a typical sponsor portfolio with five managers. Notice that the systematic component is not diversified away, while the other three components are partially diversified. The result is that the systematic component becomes a larger fraction of the total variance. Specific risk is typically reduced the most by diversification since stock selection is likely to be the least correlated among different managers. Market timing and exposure to the common factors are usually more highly correlated and therefore are reduced less.

Sponsor portfolios utilizing multiple management are much less residually risky than portfolios managed by a single manager. For this reason, unless the sponsor knows the investment style of each manager, controls the allocation of funds to the managers, and analyzes the resultant aggregate portfolio, the aggregate is very likely to be a "closet" index fund or worse.[6] Why worse? Well, the component of residual variance which is most likely to remain in the aggregate is XMC. At any given time a large number of managers are likely to have the same relative bias; for instance, in the early 1970s a large number of active managers had a growth-stock bias, while at the end of the 1970s there was a tendency toward small-capitalization stocks. Hence, if the sponsor is unaware of these "biases" in the active managers' styles, several managers in the sponsor's stable may have a similar exposure. This exposure will then become concentrated, rather than diversified, in the aggregate portfolio, as the other elements of variance are diversified away.

This is exactly what happened from 1974 through 1978. Because a large number of active managers had growth-stock-biased portfolios, the aggregate portfolio was also growth stock biased.[7] Sponsors (and many managers) were unaware of this exposure, but they surely observed the asset value decreasing month by month (see Figure 4.8).

This example reinforces our key result, namely, that the total portfolio is what matters. Concentrating too much on the individual managers makes it easy to lose sight of what is happening to the aggregate. The example also provides another guideline for multiple management: the aggregate of the normal holdings of the individual managers must coincide with the sponsor's normal portfolio. If it does not, then there will be some unwanted long-term exposure to a common factor of return. Notice that it is the sponsor's responsibility to see that this is done and that the responsibility cannot be delegated to the individual manager or managers.

---

[6]It is a good bet that the vast majority of large multiply managed funds in the early and middle 70s were closet index funds. One corporation which recognized this is described in Anise Wallace, "Shaking Things Up at General Motors," *Institutional Investor*, February 1980, pp. 89–90.

[7]Even in 1980 this was still very common. "Like other corporate sponsors with big-bank managers, Scanlan admits to discovering that his total portfolio had a definite growth-stock bias." See ibid. See also Case Study 7 at the end of this chapter.

Let us summarize the results so far:

1. Managers should be hired so as to increase aggregate portfolio alpha. They should not be hired to increase diversification since increased diversification can be obtained less expensively by increasing the funds which are passively managed. This is the answer to the question posed by the title of this section.
2. The return on the total portfolio is the sponsor's primary concern. Individual managers are only a means to that end.
3. Beware of undesired exposure to the common factors; the aggregate normal holdings of the individual managers should equal the sponsor's normal portfolio. Undesired exposure should be either hedged or removed by a compensating core or completeness fund.[8]

We have now completed the broad outline of multiple management. Our next task is to fill in some of the finer details: What types of investment strategies should be followed? How aggressive should the managers be? How should the allocation between active and passive management be determined? And, most important, how should the sponsor control the investment managers so as to achieve maximum alpha?

The Design and Control of Multiple Manager Investment Strategies

As an introduction to multiple management investment strategies, we will start by making some gross simplifications (in fact, we will begin with only one manager) before we relax the assumptions. The first strategies will concern the division of funds between passive management and active management. We have demonstrated that this is an important question because passive management is the low-fee alternative to active management. This will lead to some results on how passive management in the multiple manager context should be structured and to ideas on how the strategy can be improved. We will then turn to the subject of active management.

The Active/Passive Strategy with a Single Manager

In Chapters 2 and 5 we discussed at length the active/passive management approach. There are, as has been stressed, considerable benefits to practical implementation of this approach. But how should the implementation be done?

---

[8] Compensating core is a trademark of the American National Bank of Chicago; the Completeness fund originated with the Standard Oil Company of Indiana. See David Tierney, "The Marriage of Judgment and Technology: The Second, The Potent Generation of 'Index' Funds," presentation to the Eighth Annual American Pension Conference, January 11, 1980. We will describe both compensating core and completeness funds in the next section.

What proportion of funds should be allocated to passive management, and what to active? How aggressive should the active fund be?

Before we give solutions to these questions, let us briefly discuss the trade-offs involved in their analysis. First, consider the question as to the correct level of aggressiveness. It should be clear from earlier considerations that aggressiveness does not mean bearing greater total risk or constructing portfolios with higher betas. Instead, it relates to the extent to which active holdings are enlarged in response to the manager's judgment. Low aggressiveness indicates that there is little awareness of any judgment; the active holdings are all close to zero. Extreme aggressiveness indicates that the active holdings are very large. Clearly, one set of judgments is sufficient to produce a whole set of portfolios with varying aggressiveness.[9] It should also be clear that, given an initial active portfolio, doubling the active holdings doubles the alpha and the residual standard deviation and quadruples the residual variance.[10] However, the information ratio—the ratio of alpha to residual standard deviation—remains constant, as we would expect, since it is a measure of the skill residing in the judgments, and both portfolios reflect the same judgment.

What is the trade-off between the level of aggressiveness and the proportion of funds under active management? The sponsor, conscious of the bottom line, wants to maximize aggregate portfolio utility. This initially suggests retaining a skillful manager (one with a positive information ratio) and running all the money actively. However, the fees for passive management are less, as is the disutility of residual risk. For example, suppose the sponsor desires a residual risk level of 5 percent. This can be obtained by actively managing all of the funds at that level or by passively managing one half of the funds and actively managing the other half at a residual standard deviation of 10 percent. With this latter strategy there is a *smaller* total management fee.

Figure 6.8 depicts this situation. The top panel shows the active frontier (in mean-standard-deviation space) as a straight line, with the managed portfolio at $\alpha = 1\%$, $\omega = 5\%$. The sponsor can retain this risk-return posture by indexing half of the portfolio and requesting that the manager become twice as aggressive with the remaining half. The active portfolio will now plot at $\alpha = 2\%$, $\omega = 10\%$.

The middle panel shows the fee structure. Here, the passive fee is 10 basis points (10 cents per $100) and the active fee is an additional 15 basis points (15 cents per $100). The fee schedule (in basis points) can be represented algebraically by the following function:

$$\text{Fee} = 10 + 15w,$$

where w is the proportion of actively managed funds. The relationship between

---

[9]See Case Study 4.

[10]We assume that the alphas in this section are stated net of transaction costs. that there are no nonlinearities in the cost schedule, and that limits on asset holdings are not binding.

Figure 6.8
Trade-off between Total Fee and Aggressiveness

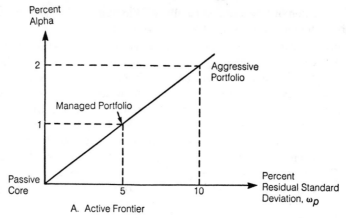

A. Active Frontier

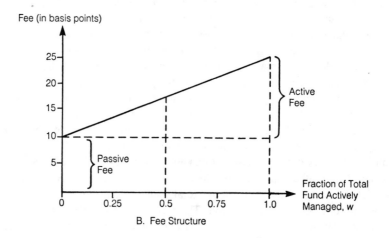

B. Fee Structure

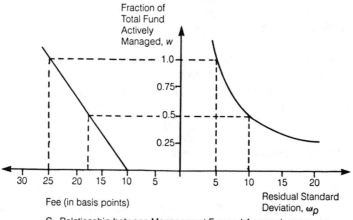

C. Relationship between Management Fee and Aggressiveness

aggregate portfolio residual risk, ω_A (which in this case is 5 percent), and the residual risk of the active portfolio, ω_P, is given by:

$$\omega_A = w\omega_P = 5.$$

The bottom panel of Figure 6.8 combines the fee schedule (in the left quadrant) and the relationship between active portfolio residual risk and the proportion of actively managed funds (in the right quadrant). As can be seen, the plan sponsor clearly benefits from decreased expenses by increasing the amount of passively managed funds and simultaneously increasing the aggressiveness in the active portfolio. Under the assumptions we have made, the optimal, but unrealistic, solution is to passively manage all but an infinitely small fraction of the portfolio, which should be infinitely aggressive.

What are the reasons for arriving at this unrealistic result? Essentially, there are two: we have not considered the costs to the investment manager of becoming more aggressive with a smaller fund, and we have assumed that the manager can deliver a constant (positive) information ratio at all levels of aggressiveness (see footnote 10). Let us examine these two reasons in more detail.

Conflicts in the Manager-Sponsor Relationship

The plan sponsor wants to maximize the value of active management received after transaction costs and fees. The analysis so far suggests that this is accomplished by retaining a skillful active manager and minimizing the amount of actively managed assets. The investment manager, conversely, wants to protect the profits of his or her firm. Since most of the manager's costs are fixed, incremental assets under management are exceedingly profitable, especially if additional labor-intensive client relationships are small. Hence, the two parties have interests which appear contradictory.

The relationship between the plan sponsor and the investment manager is further complicated by the fact that the plan sponsor is typically not represented by a single person. The pension fund administrator has responsibility for day-to-day decisions, but the hiring and firing of investment managers (and, perhaps, the allocation of the aggregate fund to various investment managers) usually rests with the board of directors or some delegated committee. Unfortunately, this committee may be unaware of the consequences of aggressive active management. When periods of bad performance occur—and they inevitably will, even with the most skillful managers—support from the pension administrator may be insufficient to prevent a thorough review and termination of the active manager. This argument reinforces the notion that the best course of action for the investment manager is to bear as little residual risk as possible. As one investment manager stated quite forcibly, "The best way to retain clients is never to be last."

We can show this reasoning more clearly with the following analysis. Suppose the investment manager has the information ratio IR and manages the active portfolio with residual risk ω_P and a beta of unity. A thorough review of the manager—perhaps leading to termination—will probably occur if the portfolio performance consistently falls into the lower quartile of performance by peer institutions. We can model this danger of a review to the investment manager fairly realistically by evaluating the probability that the portfolio performance is, say, 2 percent less than the market for two years running. Equivalently, a review is triggered if the residual return, u_P, is less than -2 percent for consecutive years. If we denote by P the probability of a residual return of less than -2 percent (i.e., $P = \text{Prob}\,[u_P \le -2]$), then the possibility of being subject to termination is represented by P^2. To a close approximation, we can write probability P as follows:[11]

$$P = \text{Prob}\,[Z \le -IR - 2/\omega_P],$$

where Z is the standard normal random variable. Our main concern now is the relationship between the probability of a review, on the one hand, and the level of aggressiveness (ω_P) and the skill (the information ratio, IR), of the manager on the other.

Figure 6.9 shows how the probability of a review is affected by the level of residual risk and the manager's information ratio. Certainly, as the information ratio (manager's skill) increases but keeping the residual risk constant, the probability of a review decreases. However, this decrease is not nearly so dramatic as the increase in the probability of a review as the level of aggressiveness is increased. Notice that although skill is useful, in the precarious world of investment it is by no means the whole story.

A review will not necessarily lead to a termination, but it will certainly be harmful to the relationship between the manager and the plan sponsor. Thus, the manager's strategy is clear: try to take as little residual risk as possible; make the active holdings small enough to permit close tracking of a representative index with, if possible, positive residual return; and leave the aggressive active management to one of the other managers in the plan sponsor's stable. In this way, the manager will rarely (if ever) be last. Unfortunately, while the investment manager's income may be maximized by this strategy, the strategy is not necessarily of any benefit to the plan sponsor or the plan beneficiaries. Let us return to the plan sponsor's interests and their analysis.

The starting point is that the plan sponsor must be convinced that the active manager has a positive information ratio. Next, the plan sponsor knows that the direct costs of trading and management fees are incurred if active investment managers are employed. To overcome these costs, the investment managers must exercise their skill and establish active positions of such magnitude that the rewards obtained from these positions cover their costs, plus the disutility of risk. The investment manager has the desire to do just the opposite and

---

[11]We can approximate the residual return as $u_P = \alpha_P + \omega_P Z = (IR + Z)\omega_P$ after substituting for the information ratio, where Z is the standard normal random variable.

Figure 6.9
The Probability of Review for Managers with Differing Skill and Aggressiveness

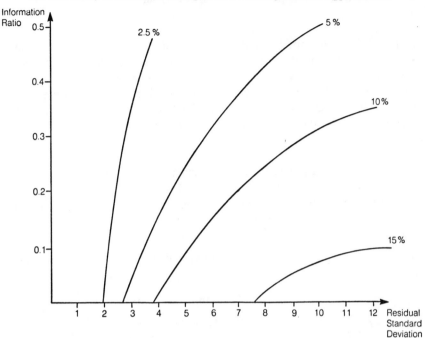

will naturally move toward the index to protect his or her business interests. The only easy way to resolve these conflicting interests is for the plan sponsor to guarantee (in writing) to the investment manager that any adverse impact of aggressive management is understood by the board of directors (or the relevant committee). If the investment manager believes that poor performance as a result of aggressive management will not necessarily lead to a prejudicial review, the sponsor is far more likely to get superior active management.

The next stage is to set the allocation of funds between the active and passive portfolios. As we have seen, there are a continuum of solutions to the problem of choosing the proportion of funds to be actively managed. We can describe this algebraically as follows: Let w be the proportion of actively managed funds, α_A and ω_A^2 the alpha and residual variance of the aggregate portfolio (i.e., the combined active and passive portfolios), and λ the residual variance aversion. The generalization of equation (2–8) shows that at optimality:

Aggregate alpha/residual variance $= 2\lambda$,

or

$$\alpha_A = 2\lambda\omega_A^2.$$

Now $\alpha_A = w\alpha_P$ and $\omega_A^2 = w^2\omega_P^2$, where α_P and ω_P^2 refer to the active portfolio. Hence, when the aggregate portfolio is optimal,

$$\alpha_P = 2\lambda w\omega_P^2 \qquad\qquad (6\text{--}1)$$

is the relationship satisfied by the active portfolio. Further, in the Chapter 2 section, "Active and Passive Portfolios," it was shown that only one half of the expected return shows up as certainty equivalent excess return (CEER) (the other half is lost as compensation for bearing risk). Provided the aggregate portfolio is optimal, we have the result that the certainty equivalent excess return, $CEER_P$, of the active portfolio is given by:

$$CEER_P = \lambda w\omega_P^2. \qquad\qquad (6\text{--}2)$$

Therefore, given the proportion of funds under active management and residual variance, equation (6–2) shows the certain benefit. If the sponsor is rational, this benefit should be greater than the incremental management fee. As a numerical example, let this fee be 15 basis points and let $\lambda = 0.0075$ ($\%^{-1}$). Then equation (6–2) states:[12]

$$CEER_P = \lambda w\omega_P^2 \geq 0.15, \qquad\qquad (6\text{--}3)$$

or

$$w\omega_P^2 \geq (0.15)/(0.0075) = 20.$$

Finally, recall that the active manager's information ratio, *IR*, is given by:

$$IR = \alpha_P/\omega_P = 2\lambda w\omega_P. \qquad\qquad (6\text{--}4)$$

Notice that equation (6–4) is nothing more than a simple restatement of the condition of optimality, equation (6–1), for the active portfolio in terms of the information ratio. Now, combining equations (6–4) and (6–2), we find that:

$$IR\cdot\omega_P = 2\cdot CEER_P. \qquad\qquad (6\text{--}5)$$

Equation (6–5) shows the trade-off (geometrically it is a hyperbola) between the manager's information ratio and the level of residual risk for a given level of certainty equivalent excess return (utility) desired by the plan sponsor. Figure 6.10 shows the shape of this trade-off for representative values of the CEER. Since a rational sponsor will require that the active manager at least provide sufficient value-added to cover the active management fee, the inequality in equation (6–3) applies; namely:

$$IR \cdot \omega_P \geq 0.3.$$

It is clear from the figure, that the plan sponsor's view of residual risk is completely different from that of the manager; the plan sponsor really cannot

---

[12]This value for the residual variance aversion assumed long-term values for the expectation and variance of market excess return, see, e.g., equation (2–11), and a similar aversion between residual and systematic risk, see, e.g., equation (5–10). The value of the coefficient in equation (2–11) is 0.015, which is equal to 2λ. Hence, the values for λ in both places are the same.

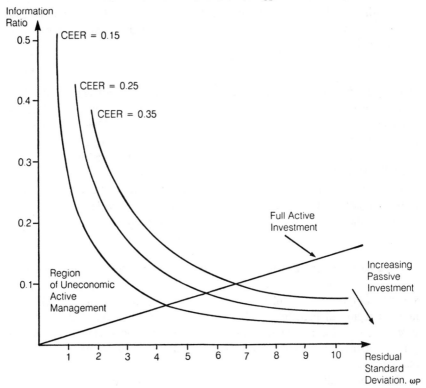

Figure 6.10
The Trade-off between Skill and Aggressiveness

get enough of it! A manager with a low level of skill simply cannot provide sufficient value-added to cover the management fee unless the portfolio residual risk is approximately 5 percent or more. A superior manager will, of course, provide a net benefit at lower levels of risk, but the plan sponsor will benefit substantially as the manager becomes more aggressive.

To some practitioners it appears counterintuitive to insist that a less skillful manager should be more aggressive than a more skillful manager. However, the statement is correct because the proportion of actively managed funds depends on the level of residual risk. In fact, the following three attributes are inextricably linked in setting the optimal strategy:

1. The plan sponsor's estimate of the manager's information ratio.
2. The allocation of funds between the active and passive portfolios.
3. The level of risk in the active portfolio.

Thus, it turns out that the less skillful manager will be managing a smaller proportion of the fund than the more skillful manager.

To demonstrate the interdependence of the three attributes, consider the example of a plan sponsor who believes that a particular manager is only reasonably skillful, with an estimated information ratio of $IR = 0.03$. From equation (6–4), using the numerical value of 0.0075 for the risk-aversion parameter (λ), it follows that:

$$w\omega_P = 2. \tag{6–4a}$$

Hence, one possibility would be for the plan sponsor to allocate all the funds to the manager (i.e., $w = 1$) with the proviso that the portfolio should be only "minimally aggressive" (in fact, the sponsor wants the residual risk level to be 2 percent). Clearly, the sponsor does not want the manager to become too aggressive in this situation; otherwise, the manager, who really does not have the full confidence of the sponsor, may be damaging to the fund.

Unfortunately, this solution is not optimal since the manager is simply not providing sufficient value-added to cover the active fee. Equation (6–2) shows that the certainty equivalent excess return of this strategy is:

$$CEER_P = (0.0075)(1.0)(4) = 0.03,$$

or three basis points. The optimal method for making the manager productive is to require a greater level of aggressiveness in the active portfolio. As can be seen from Figure 6.10, a manager with an information ratio of 0.03 will move into the region of beneficial active management at a residual risk level of 10 percent. Now, from equation (6–4a), we find that the manager has only 20 percent of the funds under management, with the other 80 percent passively managed.

It is worth summarizing this example and the equations into a straightforward statement: The more money passively invested, the more aggressive the active manager has to be and the lower the information ratio the manager has to have. Conversely, if the sponsor has all assets actively managed, the manager has to be skillful, as does the sponsor in locating the manager!

As a final comment on Figure 6.10, we have shown a line which represents portfolios which are 100 percent active. This line is obtained from equation (6–4) by setting $w = 1$, and so measures points which have:

$$IR = 2\lambda\omega_P = 0.015\omega_P.$$

Only below this line will there be holdings in both the active portfolio and the passive portfolio. Points above the line are suboptimal, either because they have far too little residual risk and could become substantially more beneficial to the plan sponsor by being more aggressive or because there is an exaggerated aversion to residual risk. In this latter case, the plan sponsor and the manager are not communicating properly, resulting in the active portfolio not being constructed to the preferences of the sponsor. We will analyze this subject in greater detail later in this chapter.

This completes our discussion of the conflicts between the sponsor and the investment manager. We now turn to the second topic of this section: how the information ratio varies with aggressiveness.

The Information Ratio and Variable Aggressiveness

The situation where the information ratio is not constant at all levels of residual risk, is likely to occur because of constraints on asset holdings. Recall from Figure 5.9 that the expansion path indicates the set of optimal holdings for various levels of reward. It is linear until the worst asset in the portfolio (IBM in Figure 5.9) has been completely sold out. If there is a prohibition against short-selling, then an asset less inferior than IBM must be sold, so that the expansion path "kinks" before moving on linearly. In other words, the prohibition has forced the manager to halt the best strategy in favor of one that is not as good.

This is shown graphically in Figure 6.11. The top panel shows a diagram similar to Figure 5.9, except that portfolio A lies exactly on the kink in the expansion path. Portfolios B and C are more aggressive than portfolio A; portfolio B is the optimal portfolio if short-selling is permitted, and portfolio C is optimal if short-selling is prohibited. Notice that B and C lie on the same isovariance contour but that B lies on a higher isoreward line than C. The difference in reward is the cost of the short-selling constraint. This is shown again in the bottom panel, which shows the active frontier. In the absence of the constraint, the frontier is our familiar straight line (i.e., the alpha-to-omega ratio is constant), but if short-selling is prevented, C lies beneath B and the frontier is curved. The information ratio decreases at higher aggressiveness because successively better ("less worse") stocks are sold off to raise funds to purchase the remaining desirable stocks. Of course, the most aggressive portfolio is invested 100 percent in the highest alpha asset when short-selling is prohibited.

The curvature of the active frontier shows up one limitation of the active-passive strategy. The top panel in Figure 6.12 shows the active frontier that could be delivered by an active manager at differing levels of aggressiveness and the set of active-passive portfolios which lie beneath the frontier. A sponsor desiring a portfolio with residual risk level A would save management fees with the active-passive combination but would give up some active reward in the process. This loss in alpha is the difference between the frontier and the active-passive mixture. One way around this limitation is to manage two or three active portfolios at different levels of risk, instead of just one. This is shown in the bottom panel.

Let us now discuss the plan sponsor's problem when there is more than one manager. Our thrust will be to understand the differences in the implementation of the active-passive strategy as additional managers are added.

Figure 6.11
Cost of Short-Selling Constraints

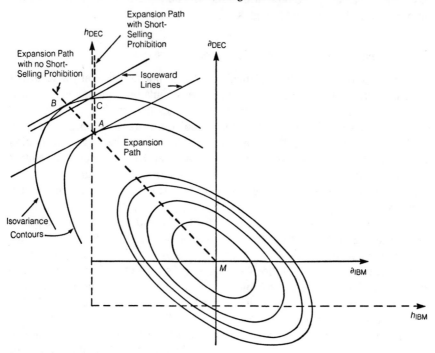

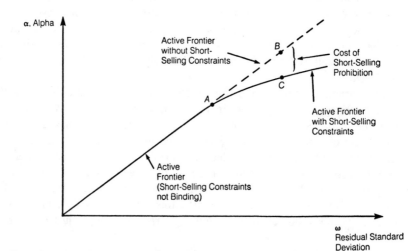

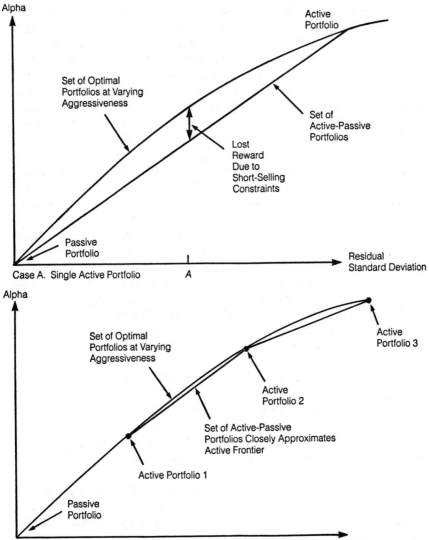

Figure 6.12
Limitation of Active-Passive Strategy due to Short-Selling Constraints

The Active/Passive Strategy with
Multiple Managers

One effect of adding managers, discussed previously, is that the sponsor must ensure that the normal portfolios of the individual managers aggregate to the sponsor's normal portfolio. Is there any more direct effect of multiple management on the active-passive split? Indeed there is.

The elegant device used to explain this is the *centralized* sponsor who pays for judgment rather than for the management of funds.[13] The managers can now be viewed as advisers whose function is to send recommended transactions or alphas to the sponsor, who then decides on the exact trade after the advice from all the "managers" has been considered. The sponsor is now able to combine the alphas and thus form an aggregate prediction with higher information content than is contained in any of the individual alphas. In other words, since the sponsor is in the central position, the redundancy in the managers' (advisers') forecasts can be removed. For this reason, multiple management can be more beneficial than the sum of its parts—or single management.

The implication, which gets us ahead of our story a little, is that the formulas at the beginning of this section apply only to the aggregate or a singly managed portfolio but not to the component portfolios of individual managers in a multiple management organization. The reason, quite simply, is that an alpha constructed by an individual manager in the multiple manager context is interpreted quite differently by the manager than by the sponsor. Without coordination, the manager operates in isolation from the other managers, in contrast to the sponsor, who is primarily concerned with the entire group of managers.[14] For instance, the formula for the inferred covenant information ratio, equation (6–4), does not imply that each manager in the stable should have this level of skill since the redundancy among managers may cause a less skillful manager (in an absolute sense) to become very valuable when he or she is combined with other managers. The sponsor's problem is to find a framework for decentralized management that is as good as the centralized network of advisers.

In a centralized environment it is easy to ensure that the aggregate normal holdings of the individual managers equal the sponsor's normal portfolio. But what if they don't in a decentralized system? For instance, a sponsor may discover that the aggregate portfolio is excessively biased toward growth stocks and may wish to remove the bias without firing one or more managers. An obvious solution would be to hire another active manager with an opposing bias (the specialization motive for multiple management), but this incurs the cost of a search process to find a superior manager with the correct emphasis. A less expensive alternative is to use a passive strategy to remove the unwanted exposures. Currently, two procedures are being used: the completeness fund and the compensating core.

With the completeness fund, the first step in any analysis is for the sponsor

---

[13]First used by Barr Rosenberg in "Institutional Investment with Multiple Portfolio Managers," *Proceedings of the Seminar on the Analysis of Security Prices*, University of Chicago, November 1977, pp. 55–160.

[14]The sponsor will use a procedure similar to the one described in the section "Information Content" in Chapter 4 in order to obtain the information content from a single forecast. The mathematics of the sponsor's problem is developed in the supplement to this chapter.

to define the normal portfolio.[15] Let us suppose that in this case the sponsor decides that the universe is the capitalization-weighted portfolio composed of the approximately 1,750 companies with a market value greater than $50 million. Let us suppose further that the sponsor employs three active managers who operate within the following "habitats" (i.e., these are their normal portfolios):

Manager 1:   The 200 larger capitalization companies

Manager 2:   The S&P 500 universe

Manager 3:   A universe of small-capitalization companies, $200 million and below (i.e., the approximately 750 smaller companies)

Figure 6.13 shows the capitalization-weighted equity market viewed by the sponsor as the normal portfolio, together with the habitat of each manager. Clearly, this sponsor is unrepresented in the universe of medium companies and will be exposed to the differential performance from this group. The completeness fund is designed to fill the gaps and thus ensure that on average the aggregate of the individual managers coincides with the sponsor's normal portfolio.

Notice that each manager specifies his or her own universe and is charged only with outperforming the capitalization-weighted portfolio formed from that

Figure 6.13
Coverage Provided by Active Managers and the Completeness Fund

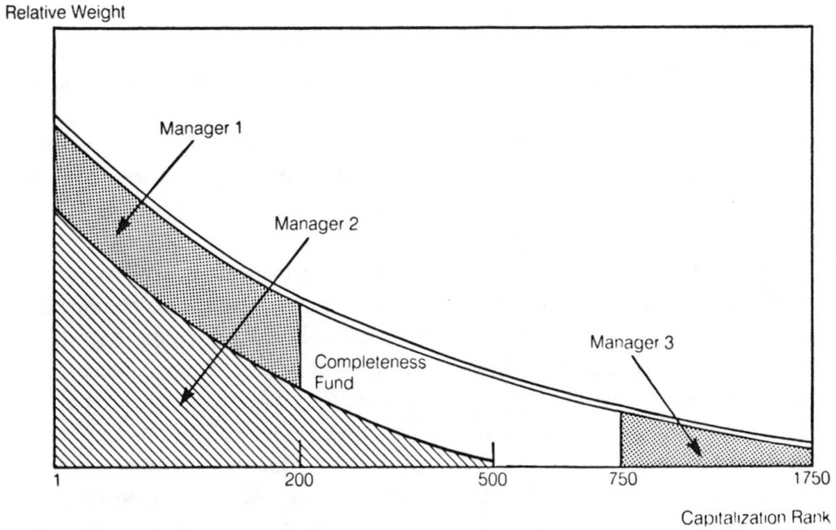

---

[15]This discussion of the completeness fund is adapted from Tierney "Marriage of Judgment and Technology."

universe. Comparison with any other bogey is irrelevant; money managers are judged solely on the basis of their particular declared expertise (as defined by the universe they announce). Thus, each manager selects and explicitly defines his or her performance objective.

It is to the manager's advantage to include in the universe every "dog" (security believed to be perpetually undervalued) that can be found. The universe simply defines the bogey against which the manager is judged; the manager does not have to hold every stock in the universe (however, every stock which the manager holds must be in the universe). Hence, it is to the manager's benefit to make the universe perform as poorly as possible and thus make it easy to beat. The sponsor also benefits since the completeness fund will only include assets which do not appear in any of the managers' universes. Thus, the manager's judgment that an asset will underperform helps the manager and the sponsor. The completeness fund, therefore, is a partial solution to the prohibition against short selling.

With the compensating core, if the sponsor has insufficient funds, it may not be possible to completely fill the voids created because the normal portfolios do not aggregate correctly. The solution is to design a passive core that hedges the undesired exposures. In other words, the core actually counteracts the unwanted active management positions. For instance, suppose a portfolio manager decides that the outlook is better for airline companies than for the overall market (perhaps because of deregulation or because of a forecast extraordinary growth in passenger traffic) and constructs a portfolio by selecting the "best bets" from airline stocks. An analysis of this portfolio may reveal that besides its risk exposure to the airline factor it has a risk exposure to a small-stock factor and an energy factor. The airline bet is desired, but the others are not, and they give rise to casual risk since no explicit bet is associated with their factors.

In contrast to the completeness fund, the compensating core is the result of an optimization program to find a portfolio that minimizes exposure to the unwanted elements of risk. We will discuss this aspect in greater detail in the next section, "Multiple Manager Optimization."

Now let us turn to the coordination of active management. The major difference between multiple manager and single-manager active management is that the abnormal return forecasts by the multiple managers may be related. The dependence between the forecasts suggests that they should not be taken at face value but adjusted to eliminate information that is redundant (i.e., already incorporated into the other managers' forecasts).

How should this be accomplished? In essence, the sponsor must arrive at some estimate as to the amount of nonredundancy in the information that each manager has. This estimate must be communicated to the manager so that the manager can construct portfolios in response to the information he or she possesses that has not already been incorporated into the portfolios of the other managers in the stable. The estimate which the sponsor must provide is called the *dependence-adjustment factor* (DAF). This factor is applied to all of the manager's predictions to adjust them for dependence. For instance, if b is the manager's DAF and α_j is the manager's prediction for the jth stock, then we show in Supplement 6 that in the multiple manager context the manager should use the quantity $b\alpha_j$ as the forecast in his or her individual portfolio construction for this sponsor. (The DAF, b, clearly depends on the other managers in the stable.) If the manager is independent of all the other managers in the stable, then $b = 1$ and the full force of the alpha is employed. If the manager is partially correlated, with the other managers, then b is less than 1.0. If the manager is perfectly correlated with the other managers, then $b = 0$ and the manager provides no information in addition to that of the other managers.

A problem related to the correlation of information among managers, and an obvious disadvantage of multiple management, occurs when one active manager sells a particular stock and another manager purchases it. The overall composition of the fund remains the same, except that there has been a drain of wealth to the brokerage community.

The Inventory Fund

Much effort has been spent in trying to remove this symptom of inefficiency; most notably, an innovative vehicle termed the *inventory index fund* has been created to meet this challenge. The concept is to operate an index fund as an internal clearing operation. The active equity managers responsible for portions of the plan's assets are able (or, in some cases, are required) to interrogate the inventory fund trading desk in order to determine whether the fund can accommodate their orders. If the fund accepts a trade, then the usual transaction price is that of the last trade on a quotation machine, which both parties can view simultaneously. The incentive to utilize the inventory fund is high because this enables the fund manager to avoid the cost of brokerage commissions. In a world where performance is not only stressed but hard to come by, every bit helps.[16]

The challenge to the inventory fund is to determine the degree of accommodation it can offer its equity managers, while also executing the appropriate fund adjustments after the trade, in order to maintain a low tracking error for the index fund. It should be apparent that a smoothly operating portfolio optimization technique is a crucial tool for such an operation. A diagram portraying a model transaction flow for an inventory index fund is presented in Figure 6.14.[17] As the diagram indicates, a potential order generated by active equity manager A is presented to the inventory fund trading desk. If the trade is sim-

---

[16]Jack L. Treynor, "The Institutional Shortfall," *Financial Analysts Journal*, November–December 1976, p. 43.

[17]Adapted from Wayne H. Wagner and Carol A. Zipkin, "Can Inventory Funds Improve Active Equity Performance?" *Financial Analysts Journal*, May–June 1978, pp. 34–36, 68–76.

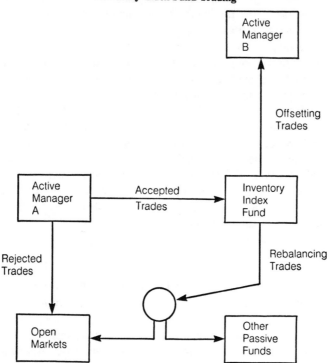

Figure 6.14
Inventory Index Fund Trading

ply rejected, it goes to the open market for execution. If it is accepted, the inventory fund can attempt to execute offsetting trades with another active equity manager, B. If this is not possible, the trade could be absorbed in the inventory fund, or offset with other inventory funds operating for other pension plans, or finally entered in the open market.[18] During this internal clearing process it is, of course, also possible to encounter an additional imbalancing order request.

Given a set of realistic operating cost assumptions, Wagner and Zipkin estimate that simply going to a regular index fund with 20 percent of the assets produced an incremental saving equal to 0.174 percent of managed assets. If, however, the index fund was operated as an inventory fund which accommodated and retained 50 percent of the trades, the potential savings increased to 0.430 percent.

At first glance, the concept seems unambiguously beneficial. However, fur-

---

[18]Quite a stir has been created among members of the brokerage community regarding commission-free trades between various corporate inventory funds. See Nancy Belliveau, "The Fear of Market Inventory Funds," *Institutional Investor*, May 1978, pp. 84–92.

ther consideration shows up several weaknesses. To understand these, let us consider the benefits and costs in turn. The benefit from the inventory fund is decreased transaction costs. In the best of all possible curcumstances, where manager A wishes to purchase/sell n shares of stock x at the same time that manager B wishes to sell/purchase the same stock, then the offset trade saves the commission and prevents the market impact. Where the timing is not identical (or the offsetting trades do not take place in the same stock), the fund must absorb the trade for some length of time.[19] Hence, the operation is not costless, since it exposes the index fund to greater risk (i.e., it has become unbalanced) than would have existed if the trades had taken place in the open markets. Nevertheless, transferring the stock between the managers and the fund, postpones and possibly eliminates transaction costs on the offset trades.

The transaction costs cannot be assumed to have been eliminated completely, because the inventory fund is now unbalanced and some trading may have to take place in order to rebalance it. Let us consider the alternatives: (1) the fund may not be so unbalanced as to require rebalancing immediately, in which case the cost of the increased risk in the inventory fund must be deducted from the saving in transaction costs; (2) the fund may be rebalanced by trading with other passive inventory funds, in which case the cost of rebalancing is likely to be much less than that of a typical active trade; or (3) the fund may be rebalanced by trading in the open market. In this case, the transaction can be viewed as an active decision because it is really the same as the active manager's original trade (manager A's transaction in stock x is accommodated by the fund, and the fund may subsequently trade stock x to rebalance), so the transaction is therefore not really informationless. The transaction cost may be less because economies of scale are achieved by rebalancing the inventory fund rather than having the active manager conduct a "one-off" transaction, but to that cost must be added the cost of the increased risk to the fund between the time of the original accommodated trade and the time of the rebalancing.

In summary, transaction costs are completely eliminated only in the case of a simple contemporaneous swap between two active managers. In the other cases, they are partially eliminated, but at the cost of increased risk to the index fund. How much is the cost? This depends on the degree of accommodation at the inventory fund. Two polar cases can be clearly identified.

In the first case, the inventory fund accommodates all active trades. The net effect is, of course, to nullify all the information of active managers at a saving of all transaction costs. In this situation, the fund is simply taking equal and opposite bets to active managers. In the second case, the fund accommodates

---

[19]Wagner and Zipkin suggest offsetting the trades when the stocks traded by managers A and B are not identical but are in the same industry. This implies that the fund is imbalanced by matching industry weights between the fund and index which, as we have seen in Supplement 5, is a poor criterion. Moreover it assumes that both stocks have similar secondary (and other) industry exposures besides their principal industry. The end result is that there will still be some cost (namely, residual risk exposure) to the trade.

only contemporaneous offsetting trades in the same stock. Here, there is no bet; the fund simply acts as a clearinghouse for the active managers. In cases other than these two polar cases, the benefit derived from the fund is ambiguous. For sponsors who do not have much faith in the appraisal abilities of their active managers, the inventory fund's benefit is a saving in transaction costs, but the fund is second best to a standard passive strategy. Conversely, for sponsors who have some faith in their manager's abilities, the contrariness of the inventory fund obviously detracts from the aggregate alpha in order to achieve a saving of transaction costs by eliminating offsetting trades. However, if the dependence among managers has been correctly computed, we feel that the number of offsetting trades will be small, suggesting that the costs will outweigh the benefits. In short, our view is that the inventory fund concept concentrates too heavily on the negative aspects of individual managers, rather than trying to enhance aggregate performance, with the overall effect of being a second-best strategy.

Multiple Manager Optimization

The sponsor's problem is to maximize the expected reward from active management in excess of the costs borne in pursuing such management. We assume that the sponsor "knows" the managers; that is, the sponsor is aware of each manager's skill, each manager's correlation with the other managers, the manager's fee structure, and the costs associated with hiring and firing managers. The decision variables (i.e., the variables the sponsor can control) are the proportions of the total assets allocated to each manager; the amount devoted to a hedging strategy, if such a strategy is implemented, and the hedging strategy's attributes. How should these proportions be set?

We can specify this problem very simply by using some straightforward mathematics. Assume that the sponsor's optimal passive portfolio is specified by a series of exposures to the factors; i.e., β_N (the normal beta), γ_{Nj} (the normal risk indices), etc. For instance, if the optimal passive portfolio is the S&P 500, then $\beta_N = 1$, $\gamma_{Nj} = 0$. For simplicity, rather than separate beta and the risk indices, let x_{Nk} ($k = 1, \ldots, K$) be the set of values for the K exposures to the factors of the normal portfolio. Again, for the S&P 500, we would have $x_{N1} = 1$, $x_{Nk} = 0$, for $k = 2, \ldots, K$. Also, let x_{jk} ($k = 1, \ldots, K$) be the set of normal values for the K exposures to the factors for the jth individually managed portfolio, where there are J portfolios, not including the hedging portfolio.

Now if the sponsor allocates proportion w_j of total assets to the jth portfolio, then the normal position of the aggregate portfolio (not including the hedging portfolio), x_{Pk}, is the weighted average of the individual normal positions and given by:

$$x_{Pk} = w_1 x_{1k} + w_2 x_{2k} + \ldots + w_J x_{Jk}; k = 1, \ldots, K \quad \text{(6–6)}$$

The sponsor may have some remaining funds available for investing in a hedging portfolio (compensating core or completeness fund). Call this the hedging proportion, w_H, which is given by:

$$w_H = 1 - w_1 - w_2 - \ldots - w_J. \qquad (6\text{--}7)$$

Suppose the normal exposures of the hedging portfolio are given by x_{Hk} ($k = 1, \ldots, K$). Then the normal positions of the aggregate portfolio, x_{Ak}, are simply:

$$x_{Ak} = x_{Pk} + w_H x_{Hk}; k = 1, \ldots, K. \qquad (6\text{--}8)$$

The desired normal positions are x_{Nk} ($k = 1, \ldots, K$), while the current normal positions are x_{Ak} ($k = 1, \ldots, K$). The first task is to find the proportions controlled by the managers, w_j ($j = 1, \ldots, J$), and/or the hedging proportion and the hedging portfolio's normal exposure, w_H and x_{Hk} ($k = 1, \ldots, K$), such that:

$$x_{Ak} = x_{Nk}; \text{ for } k = 1, \ldots, K.$$

One very simple method of solving this problem (although the solution is not always realistic) is to set it up as a linear program (LP). This method always finds the correct hedging portfolio. However, there are occasions when the solution cannot be exactly implemented (e.g., when the hedging beta should be zero), and there is no way in this formulation to find the best implementable solution.

Table 6.1 shows the tableau of the LP, which has $K + 1$ constraints (rows)

Table 6.1
LP Tableau of Multiple Manager Optimization

Constraint number	Manager Proportions			Hedging Proportion	Slack Variables								Right-Hand Side
	w_1	$w_2 \ldots w_J$		w_H	s_{11}	s_{12}	s_{21}	$s_{22} \ldots s_{K1}$	s_{K2}				
1	x_{11}	$x_{12} \ldots x_{J1}$		0	1	-1						=	x_{N1}
2	x_{12}	$x_{22} \ldots x_{J2}$		0			1	-1				=	x_{N2}
.								$\ldots$					
.								$\ldots$					
.								$\ldots$					
K	x_{1K}	$x_{2K} \ldots x_{JK}$		0					1	-1		=	x_{NK}
$K + 1$ .... (budget constraint)	1	1 $\ldots$ 1		1								=	1
Lower bounds ..	0	0 $\ldots$ 0		0	0	0	0	0 $\ldots$ 0	0				
Objective function . (minimize)	0	0 $\ldots$ 0		1	1	-1	1	$-1 \ldots 1$	-1				

and $J + 2K + 1$ activities (columns). One way of specifying the objective function is to require the hedging portfolio to be as small as possible:

Minimize $(s_{11} - s_{12}) + (s_{21} - s_{22}) + \ldots + (s_{K1} - s_{K2}) + w_H.$
{w_j}, w_H

If the objective function value is zero, then the sponsor's normal portfolio can be obtained without the use of the hedging portfolio. The sponsor simply assigns proportion w_j of the total assets to the jth manager. However, if the objective function value is positive, then a hedging portfolio is required. Its attributes are found as follows:

1. Find w_H. This is the proportion of funds assigned to the hedging portfolio. If $w_H = 0$, the solution is not implementable and the more complex procedure outlined below is necessary.
2. If $s_{k1} - s_{k2} = 0$, then $x_{Hk} = 0$.
3. If $s_{k1} - s_{k2} > 0$, then $x_{Hk} = (s_{k1} + s_{k2})/w_H.$

The only way to guarantee realistic solutions is to model the problem more accurately by taking into account the cost of not matching the desired normal portfolio. Since this cost is a function of the portfolio variance, it is also a quadratic function of the holdings. This necessarily implies using a quadratic programming package.

Formally, let the cost of the aggregate normal portfolio deviating from the optimal passive portfolio be approximated by a quadratic function:

$$\sum_{k=1}^{K} \sum_{l=1}^{K} (x_{Ak} - x_{Nk})(x_{Al} - x_{Nl})V_{kl},$$

where V_{kl} represents the disutility of the covariance between the kth and lth elements of risk. For example, if the first element is systematic risk with market variance V_M and disutility λ, and the remaining elements are residual factors (with covariance matrix R and zero covariance with the market) and disutility Λ_ω, then the disutility coefficients V_{kl} are given by:

$$V_{11} = \lambda V_M$$
$$V_{1k} = V_{k1} = 0, \text{ for } k > 1$$
$$V_{kl} = \Lambda_\omega R_{k-1,\ l-1}, \text{ for } k,\ l > 1.$$

The cost component of the sponsor's problem is this case reduces to minimizing:

$$\sum_{k=1}^{K} \sum_{l=1}^{K} (x_{Ak} - x_{Nk})(x_{Al} - x_{Nl})V_{kl}, \qquad (6\text{--}9)$$

subject to equations (6–7) and (6–8). In the most general circumstance, the decision variables will be the individual manager proportions, $w_1, \ldots, w_j$, the hedging proportion, w_H, and the hedging portfolio exposures, x_{Hk} ($k = 1$,

. . . , K). Hence, some variables in the problem are of the form $w_H x_{Hk}$ (i.e., the product of two unknowns) and cause some difficulty. One natural generalization of the multiple manager optimization is to prespecify several passive hedging portfolios, each of which has some unique emphasis. The most intuitive description of these hedging portfolios is as "factor funds," where each factor fund is designed to capture, as much as possible, the effect of only one element of risk.[20]

Suppose there are L factor funds; then we describe their normal exposures with the following (somewhat combersome) notation. Let the lth factor fund be denoted by H_l and its exposures by $x_{H_l k}(k = 1, \ldots, K)$. Let the proportion of funds invested in the lth factor fund be w_{H_l}. Then the budget constraint analogous to equation (6–7) becomes:

$$w_1 + w_2 + \ldots + w_J + w_{H_1} + w_{H_2} + \ldots + w_{H_L} = 1, \quad \text{(6–7a)}$$

and the equation governing the aggregation of the individual portfolios, analogous to equation (6–8) becomes:

$$x_{Ak} = x_{Pk} + w_{H_1} x_{H_1 k} + w_{H_2} x_{H_2 k} + \ldots + w_{H_L} x_{H_L k},$$
$$\text{for } k = 1, \ldots, K, \quad \text{(6–8a)}$$

where x_{Pk} is still given by equation (6–6). The sponsor's problem with regard to the normal portfolio is now specified: minimize the cost given by equation (6–9) subject to equations (6–7a) and 6–8a). Further, there may also be constraints (or bounds) on the permitted investments in the factor funds.

Let us now turn to the active component. The sponsor must estimate the variance due to active management (active variance) of each individual portfolio about its normal position and the correlations between the active components of individual portfolios. Since the factor funds are passively managed, they will display no active variance or correlations with actively managed portfolios. Let ω_j^2 denote the active variance of the jth portfolio, π_{ij} the correlation between active portfolios, and α_j the alpha on the jth portfolio. The sponsor's problem with regard to active management is therefore:

$$\underset{\{w_j\}}{\text{Maximize }} \alpha_A - \Lambda_\omega \omega_A^2, \quad \text{(6–10)}$$

where

$$\alpha_A = w_1 \alpha_1 + w_2 \alpha_2 + \ldots + w_H \alpha_J;$$
$$\omega_A^2 = \sum_{i=1}^{J} \sum_{j=1}^{J} w_i w_j \pi_{ij} \omega_i \omega_j; \text{ and}$$
$$\Lambda_\omega = \text{the disutility to active variance.}$$

---

[20]Interestingly, this approach is used in a slightly different context by State Street Bank and Trust Company, Boston, Massachusetts.

Finally, we need to incorporate management fees and hiring and firing costs. To a good approximation, these can be specified as constant unit costs. The management fees serve to decrease the alpha on the respective portfolio, while the hiring and firing costs are modeled as transaction costs, applicable to the manager's portfolios, in a way similar to that described in Supplement 5.

To summarize, multiple manager optimization attempts to choose the hedging strategy and each manager's proportion of the total funds so as to:

maximize
    active (risk adjusted) reward   —see (6–10)

less
    disutility of deviating from the normal portfolio, the
    management fees, and the hiring and firing costs   —see (6–9)

subject to
    budget constraint,
    hedging policy, and   —see (6–7a)
    other constraints on investment proportions   —see (6–8a)

Selection of Money Managers[21]

Conventional wisdom suggests that a sponsor should choose a manager based upon demonstrated performance. This assumes that "good" performance in the past is indicative of "good" future performance—that is, the environment for investment management will not become more difficult, or staff will leave, and so on. We believe that this assumption is well understood; what we believe is less well understood is that performance in the past may have been due to luck rather than skill. Hence, any significant reliance on historical performance criteria is far from rational.

For instance, in the late 1970s the returns to small companies (i.e., the immaturity and smallness factor, see Figure 4.7) were positive more often than not. Hence, money managers whose normal positions were exposed to immaturity and smallness (i.e., their natural habitat was small companies) would have shown excellent performance whatever their stock selection talent. (One could argue that setting the normal position in favor of small companies indicates talent. However, this would, in general, be incorrect since the normal position is a long-term statement and there is little evidence, despite many academic studies, to suggest that small companies outperform large companies on average over the long term.) It is not surprising to observe in the "Money Mover" columns of *Pensions and Investments* that small-company managers

---

[21]This section draws on some notes by Barr Rosenberg entitled "The Relationship between Investment Advisor and Client: Warranted Residual Risk," handout for a paper delivered at the Seminar on the Analysis of Security Prices, November 5, 1976.

have been gaining clients at the expense of large-company managers. Alas, as more money flows to small-company managers the prices of small companies will be bid up, and the returns to the immaturity and smallness factor are likely to become negative. In short, sponsors may have picked small-company managers at exactly the wrong time. This situation is analogous to the widespread selection of growth-stock managers in the early 1970s.

Finally, to lay to rest the myth that "performance is an unambiguous indicator of talent," recall from Supplement 4 that a useful money manager with an alpha of 1 percent and a residual standard deviation of 5 percent per year requires approximately 64 years in order to demonstrate skill in a statistically significant manner. Certainly performance contains some information, but to choose a manager simply on the basis of two or so years of good performance is (at best!) irresponsible.

Now that we have (at least partially) removed the comforting crutch of performance measurement, how do you select a money manager? The selection process is aimed at one object: to assess the manager's ability to generate alpha or appraisal premium relative to the sponsor's normal portfolio. What sources can be used to assess this ability? There are three:

1. The sponsor's prior belief as to the range of abilities across active managers
2. The sponsor's belief as to the manager's alpha gained from an examination of the procedures used by the manager and all other external evidence *independent* of historical performance
3. The evidence gained by the sponsor from the manager's historical performance

Item 1 sets the basic parameters for the environment: Does the sponsor believe that there are talented managers who can produce superior performance, and what is the range of their abilities? Items 2 and 3 are independent estimates of the manager's abilities; the latter is gained from historical performance, and the former is gained from all other external evidence.

Let $\hat{\alpha}_P$, $\hat{\alpha}_E$, and $\hat{\alpha}_H$ represent prior, external, and historical assessments of the manager's appraisal premium from the three sources. The sponsor now has to combine these three assessments into a combined prediction; this is the familiar process of Bayesian adjustment discussed in Chapter 4 and in the supplement to this chapter. The combined prediction, $\hat{\alpha}_C$, is obtained from the three assessments as follows:

$$\alpha_C = w_P \alpha_P + w_E \alpha_E + w_H \alpha_H, \qquad (6-11)$$

where the weights, w_P, w_E, and w_H, depend on the accuracy of the associated prediction. In other words, the more accurate the prediction, the greater the weight that is placed on it, and, conversely, no weight is placed on a prediction with no information content.

The three assessments can be visualized as each belonging to a different distribution, as shown in Figure 6.15. The sponsor whose conclusions are presented in Figure 6.15 believes that there is a wide range of abilities among managers because the spread of the prior distribution of managerial ability (shown in the top panel) is so wide. (By implication, the sponsor also believes that the market is inefficient. Otherwise, the spread would be extremely narrow.) Here, the standard deviation is 3 percent. Notice that the prior assessment is negative; the sponsor believes that on average before transaction costs active managers perform in line with the market. However, annual turnover is typically 20 percent on average, with round-trip transaction costs of 75 basis points, which implies that the average active manager supports the brokerage industry to the tune of 0.15 percent annually at the sponsor's expense.

The middle panel shows the assessment from external information. After

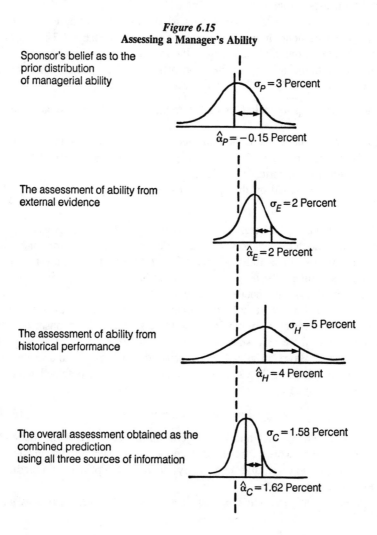

Figure 6.15
Assessing a Manager's Ability

Sponsor's belief as to the
prior distribution
of managerial ability

$\sigma_P = 3$ Percent

$\hat{\alpha}_P = -0.15$ Percent

The assessment of ability from
external evidence

$\sigma_E = 2$ Percent

$\hat{\alpha}_E = 2$ Percent

The assessment of ability from
historical performance

$\sigma_H = 5$ Percent

$\hat{\alpha}_H = 4$ Percent

The overall assessment obtained as the
combined prediction
using all three sources of information

$\sigma_C = 1.58$ Percent

$\hat{\alpha}_C = 1.62$ Percent

examining this source of information, the sponsor believes that the manager under consideration will provide an alpha of 2 percent at a 5 percent annual residual standard deviation. The alpha estimate of 2 percent is unbiased (i.e., on average the sponsor is correct), but it is subject to some error. The uncertainty in the prediction is estimated to have a standard deviation of 2 percent. (This 2 percent figure characterizes the accuracy of the sponsor's selection process based on external information.)

The third panel shows the distribution of assessments from historical information. The sponsor accepts the results from the performance measurement study undertaken by a consultant. These results indicate that the manager had an alpha of 4 percent at an annual residual standard deviation of 5 percent. To summarize, the sponsor's deliberations so far have provided the following information:

	Prediction	Standard Deviation	Variance
Prior belief	$\hat{\alpha}_P = -0.15$	$\sigma_P = 3$	$\sigma_P^2 = 9$
External evidence	$\hat{\alpha}_E = 2.0$	$\sigma_E = 2$	$\sigma_E^2 = 4$
Historical performance	$\hat{\alpha}_H = 4.0$	$\sigma_H = 5$	$\sigma_H^2 = 25$

The general formula for incorporating these three sources of information is given by the two following equations:[22]

$$\sigma_C^2 = \left(\frac{1}{\sigma_P^2} + \frac{1}{\sigma_E^2} + \frac{1}{\sigma_H^2} \right)^{-1} ; \qquad (6\text{–}12)$$

$$\hat{\alpha}_C = \left(\frac{\hat{\alpha}_P}{\sigma_P^2} + \frac{\hat{\alpha}_E}{\sigma_E^2} + \frac{\hat{\alpha}_H}{\sigma_H^2} \right) \sigma_C^2. \qquad (6\text{–}13)$$

Comparing equations (6.13 and (6.11), it follows that:

$$w_P = \sigma_C^2 / \sigma_P^2;$$
$$w_E = \sigma_C^2 / \sigma_E^2; \text{ and}$$
$$w_H = \sigma_C^2 / \sigma_H^2.$$

Now substituting into these equations, we find:

$$\sigma_C^2 = (\text{\textonesuperior}/_9 + \text{\textonesuperior}/_{25} + \text{\textonesuperior}/_4)^{-1}$$
$$= \left(\frac{361}{900} \right)^{-1} = 2.49 \ (\%^2),$$

so that:

$$\sigma_C = 1.58\%.$$

[22]See, e.g., Henri Theil, *Principles of Econometrics* (New York: John Wiley & Sons, 1971).

Our first obvious result, given the previous discussion on the combining of information sources, is that the uncertainty of the combined forecast is less than that of any of the individual forecasts and much less than that of the assessment from historical performance (see bottom panel in Figure 6.15). The expressions for the weights show that:

$$w_P = \sigma_C^2/\sigma_P^2 = 0.28,$$
$$w_E = \sigma_C^2/\sigma_E^2 = 0.63, \text{ and}$$
$$w_H = \sigma_C^2/\sigma_H^2 = 0.10,$$

and hence:

$$\hat{\alpha}_C = 0.28(-0.15) + 0.63(2.0) + 0.10(4.0)$$
$$= -0.04 + 1.26 + 0.40$$
$$= 1.62\%.$$

The statistical (and intuitive) lesson from this analysis is that the greater weights are placed on the more accurate measurements. Historical performance, because of its large associated uncertainty, has a small weight in the final prediction. In this case, because of the greater accuracy of the sponsor's prior belief and the sponsor's assessment from external evidence, greater emphasis is placed on them. Is this a result that may be expected in most cases? Barr Rosenberg reports histograms of survey values for σ_P and σ_E obtained from a group of investment professionals.[23] The values for σ_P ranged from 0 to 2.5 percent (median 1 percent), and the values for σ_E ranged from 0 to 5 percent (median 1.5 percent). Thus, in comparison with our results, the combined variance and weights obtained by the median "investment professional" would be as follows:

$$\sigma_C^2 = \left(1 + \frac{4}{9} + \frac{1}{25}\right)^{-1}$$
$$= \left(\frac{334}{225}\right)^{-1} = 0.67(\%^2),$$

so that

$$\sigma_C = 0.83\%$$

and

$$w_P = 0.67,$$
$$w_E = 0.30, \text{ and}$$
$$w_H = 0.03.$$

The median "investment professional" is clearly unimpressed by historical performance!

---

[23]Rosenberg, "Relationship Between Investment Advisor and Client."

Case Study 7: A Multiply Managed Portfolio,
Part 1—Risk Analysis

In this section, we will discuss a report produced by an investment consultant analyzing a real institutional pension fund.[24] The fund, as of April 30, 1979, had total assets of almost $240 million, divided among four active managers: Behemoth Trust Company, Ortho Growth, Inc., Petite Capital Investors, and Special K Associates. The managers are real, the names have been changed, for obvious reasons.

The format of the initial part of the report follows the PORCH output, described initially in the "Benefits of Risk Measurement" section of Chapter 3. This part, given in Tables 6.2 and 6.3, shows a risk analysis of the aggregate portfolio. The predicted systematic risk coefficient (beta) for the next three months is estimated as 1.03 (item A). The predicted systematic risk coefficient for the next five years is estimated as 1.01 (item B). Item C, the annual standard deviation of systematic portfolio return, is simply the product of the short-term beta estimate, 1.03, and the estimated standard deviation of the S&P 500 index's annual return of 20.84 (item D), which yields a value of 21.48 percent.

The next part of the risk analysis is a forecast of portfolio risk, including the decomposition between residual and systematic risk. The value of 21.91 percent (item E.1) is derived from the decomposition of variance shown in Table 6.3. In column 3, the predicted systematic variance of 461.5 units is added to the estimated total residual risk of 18.6 units, for a total of 480.1. The standard deviation of total risk is the square root of this last number, which yields the 21.91 percent of item E.1 (Table 6.2). Where do the numbers 461.5 and 18.6 come from? The first, 461.5 units of variance, is the predicted level of systematic risk taken directly from the FRMS risk model. The second, 18.6 units of variance, is the predicted level of residual risk, and is found by averaging the prediction from the FRMS model, 25.6, and the value obtained from a historical simulation, 11.5. In the section "Benefits of Risk Measurement" in Chapter 3, we remarked that statistically the simulation provided no information for improving the FRMS beta prediction, but that both sources were valuable for predicting residual risk. Historically, this portfolio has been far less (residually) risky than predicted.

Now what about the 25.6 units of residual risk? As before, we can decompose residual risk into specific risk or variance from stock selection (2.7 units) and XMC (22.9 units). The stock selection in this portfolio is minuscule; active management arises solely from picking certain types of company. Further, from the breakdown of XMC, it is seen that the risk index exposure is the dominant element of risk (12.3 units for XMC versus 4.9 units for industry variance).

The next important measurement is the portfolio residual standard deviation.

---

[24]Interested readers can find an analysis of a more complex multiple manager environment in Rosenberg, "Institutional Investment with Multiple Portfolio Managers," sec. 3.

Table 6.2
Risk Analysis of Aggregate Portfolio

```
FUNDAMENTAL RISK MEASUREMENT SERVICE
     ANALYSIS OF PORTFOLIO AGGREGATE


PORTFOLIO STATUS AS    APRIL 30 1979
ANALYSIS CONDUCTED      JUNE  1 1979
 FRMS UPDATE AS OF     APRIL 30 1979
S&P500    IS THE MARKET PORTFOLIO
```

```
              1. SUMMARY MEASURES FOR COMMON EQUITY
```

A.	PREDICTED SYSTEMATIC RISK COEFFICIENT {BETA}-NEXT 3 MONTHS	1·03
B.	PREDICTED SYSTEMATIC RISK COEFFICIENT {BETA}-NEXT 5 YEARS	1·01
C.	ANNUAL STANDARD DEVIATION OF SYSTEMATIC PORTFOLIO RETURN	21·48%
D.	FRMS FORECAST STANDARD DEVIATION OF ANNUAL S&P500 RETURN	20·84%

```
      PORTFOLIO RISK FORECAST, INCLUDING EXTRA-MARKET COVARIANCE . . .
```

E·1	STANDARD DEVIATION OF ANNUAL PORTFOLIO RETURN		21·91%
E·2	STANDARD DEVIATION OF ANNUAL PORTFOLIO RESIDUAL RETURN		4·31%
E·3	COEFFICIENT OF DETERMINATION BY S&P500	0·961	
E·4	REQUIRED ANNUAL PORTFOLIO APPRAISAL PREMIUM {ALPHA}		0·24%
E·5	INFERRED COVENANT INFORMATION RATIO {CIR}	0·056	
E·6	INFERRED CEER OF ACTIVE MANAGEMENT	0·121%	

```
      RISK FORECASTS BASED UPON A SIMULATED 5-YEAR HISTORY OF MONTHLY
      RETURNS FOR THE PORTFOLIO . . .
```

F·1	STANDARD DEVIATION OF ANNUAL PORTFOLIO RETURN		21·85%
F·2	STANDARD DEVIATION OF ANNUAL PORTFOLIO RESIDUAL RETURN		3·39%
F·3	COEFFICIENT OF DETERMINATION BY S&P500	0·976	

```
                2. INDICES OF RISK IN THE PORTFOLIO
```

| | | | | EFFECT OF 0·01 | |
| | | | FRMS | INCREASE ON | REQUIRED |
INDEX OF RISK	PORTFOLIO	S&P500	UNIVERSE	RESID· STDEV·	ALPHA
MARKET VARIABILITY	0·479	0·0	0·186	0·0123	0·12
EARNINGS VARIABILITY	0·097	0·0	0·254	0·0016	0·02
LOW VALUATION, UNSUCCESS	-0·400	0·0	-0·109	-0·0005	-0·00
IMMATURITY AND SMALLNESS	0·869	0·0	0·624	0·0182	0·18
GROWTH ORIENTATION	0·710	0·0	0·149	0·0185	0·18
FINANCIAL RISK	-0·148	0·0	0·144	0·0064	0·06

Table 6.3
Decomposition of Variance: Aggregate Portfolio

```
        DECOMPOSITION OF VARIANCE OF ANNUAL PERCENT RETURN
```

	FRMS MODEL		SIMULATION	PREDICTION
SYSTEMATIC			461·5	465·8	461·5
SPECIFIC		2·7			
RISK INDICES VARIANCE	12·3				
INDUSTRY VARIANCE	4·9				
R.I.-INDUSTRY COVARIANCE	5·8				

XMC		22·9			

RESIDUAL			25·6	11·5	18·6
			-----	-----	-----
TOTAL			487·2	477·3	480·1

For the aggregate portfolio this number is 4.31 percent (item E.2, Table 6.2), the square root of the 18.6 units of variance shown in Table 6.3. This number hints at the degree of aggressiveness of the active equity managers that is not being offset by their opposing viewpoints, and thus is reflected in the overall portfolio. The 4.31 percent level represents modest overall aggressiveness. If the level had been as low as 2.5 percent, there should have been a justified suspicion that the aggregate portfolio was very close to being an index fund. A level in the area of 6 percent to 8 percent would be strong evidence of aggressiveness on the part of the plan sponsor, even if by accident or default. Another measure of how indexlike the fund is can be found from the coefficient of determination (item E.3, Table 6.2). This indicates how closely the aggregate portfolio is likely to track the fluctuations in value of the S&P 500 index, and, statistically, it is the ratio of the variance explained by the S&P 500 divided by the total variance. From Table 6.3, this computation is seen to be 461.5/480.1 (= 0.961).

The next important measurements are those relating to the risk/reward trade-off implied in the aggregate portfolio's structure. In the vast majority of cases, these are stumbled upon by the plan sponsor. The risk/reward parameters offer a form of feedback which should be useful in cross-checking exactly what the plan sponsor has purchased for the management fees. For this plan, the sponsor specified the normal beta as 1.06, with an expected excess return on the market of 6 percent and a variance of 434.3 units (item D squared, Table 6.2). The mean/variance ratio of systematic return at the normal beta is therefore $6/(1.06)(434.2) = 1/76.7$ percent.

From this risk/reward trade-off, we can calculate the inferred covenant information ratio (CIR) (i.e., the inferred alpha-to-omega ratio) as the predicted residual standard deviation multiplied by the mean-variance ratio, or $4.31/76.7 = 0.056$. The required alpha is now the product of the CIR and the predicted residual standard deviation, or $(0.056)(4.31) = 0.24$ percent. Since only one half of the alpha shows up as increased utility (the other half being compensation for residual risk), the active management fee should not exceed one half of the required appraisal premium (plus the required abnormal expected return from market timing), which is equal to the inferred certainty equivalent excess return (item E.6, Table 6.2), or 12.1 basis points.[25] The active fee, given below in Table 6.5, does exceed this amount and indicates an internal inconsistency in the present aggregate portfolio.

At the bottom of Table 6.2 are shown the risk indices of the aggregate portfolio. It is now clear why the risk index exposure is the largest component of residual variance, since the portfolio demonstrates an undeniable strategy toward stocks with high market variability, immaturity and smallness, and growth orientation, while being underexposed to low valuation and unsuccess relative to the S&P 500.

---

[25]See section "Active and Passive Portfolios" in Chapter 2.

Figure 6.16 indicates that Behemoth Trust manages the largest portion, 49.8 percent, of the aggregate portfolio. Petite Capital Investors and Ortho Growth are both ranked second, with 20.6 percent and 21.8 percent, respectively. Special K assumes a rather small role, with 7.8 percent of the assets. For equity investments the proportions are somewhat different, due to the variations in the degree of commitment to equities. While Behemoth still dominates with 50.8 percent, as shown in Figure 6.17, Petite Capital accounts for 17.8 percent, Ortho Growth for 23.1 percent, and Special K for 8.2 percent. The percentage holdings in cash are nearly equal except for Petite Capital, which has better than twice the average of the other three managers. The exact amounts are shown in Figure 6.18. We now find that of the $240 million, almost 13 percent is in cash. Thus, the equity component has a beta of 1.03/0.87 = 1.18 and a residual standard deviation of 4.31/0.87 = 4.95 percent.

Let us now examine the influence that each manager has on the overall portfolio. One important aspect evolves from the strategies followed by the managers. Figure 6.19 shows the level of risk and its decomposition for the four managers and the aggregate portfolio.[26] This is also shown numerically in Table 6.4. Ortho Growth is assuming the largest amount of risk at 589.9 variance units, followed by the remaining three managers with total variances ranging between 455.7 and 481.9 units. As one might expect, market risk alone is distributed in a similar manner since it is the dominant risk component. Notice that Petite Capital and Ortho Growth are pursuing aggressive strategies with residual risk levels in excess of 6 percent.

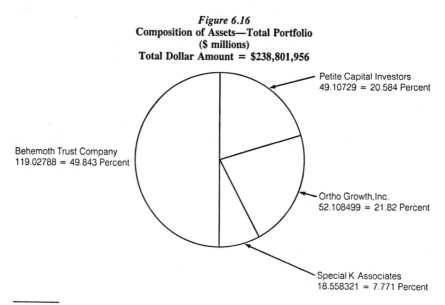

Figure 6.16
Composition of Assets—Total Portfolio
($ millions)
Total Dollar Amount = $238,801,956

Petite Capital Investors
49.10729 = 20.584 Percent

Behemoth Trust Company
119.02788 = 49.843 Percent

Ortho Growth,Inc.
52.108499 = 21.82 Percent

Special K Associates
18.558321 = 7.771 Percent

---

[26]This figure gives a real-world example of Figure 6.7.

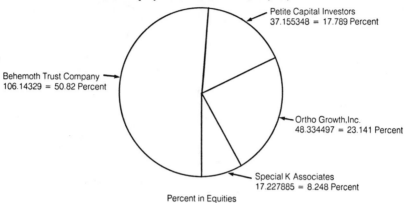

Figure 6.17
Composition of Assets—Equity Investments
($ millions)
Total Equity Dollar Amount = $208,860,788

Petite Capital Investors
37.155348 = 17.789 Percent

Behemoth Trust Company
106.14329 = 50.82 Percent

Ortho Growth,Inc.
48.334497 = 23.141 Percent

Special K Associates
17.227885 = 8.248 Percent

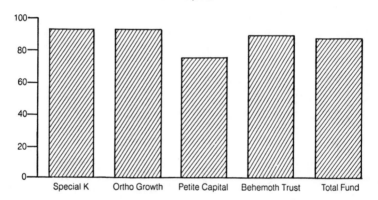

Percent in Equities

Figure 6.20 shows the market risk exposure of the four managers, with Ortho Growth taking the largest amount of market risk, while the other three managers are nearly equal in their exposure. An additional aspect of market risk is portrayed in the same figure; the histogram portrays the normal level of systematic risk for each manager as well as the current level. The normal betas for the managers and the aggregate were set as follows:

Behemoth Trust Company 1.00
Ortho Growth, Inc. 1.19
Petite Capital Investors 1.10
Special K Associates 1.00
             Aggregate portfolio 1.06

The portfolio beta is decidedly less than the normal beta for both Ortho Growth and Petite Capital.

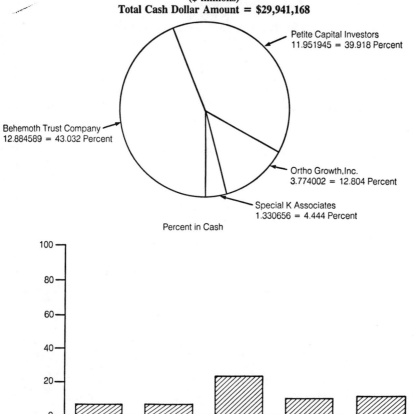

Figure 6.18
Composition of Assets—Cash Investments
($ millions)
Total Cash Dollar Amount = $29,941,168

Petite Capital Investors
11.951945 = 39.918 Percent

Behemoth Trust Company
12.884589 = 43.032 Percent

Ortho Growth,Inc.
3.774002 = 12.804 Percent

Special K Associates
1.330656 = 4.444 Percent

Percent in Cash

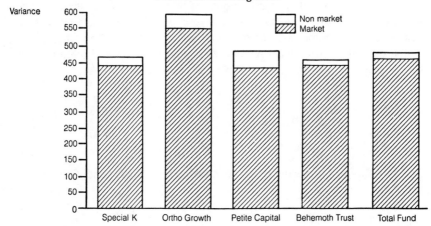

Figure 6.19
Total Fund Risk Magnitude

Variance

Non market
Market

Table 6.4
Total Fund Risk Magnitude

Active Investment Managers	Total Risk		Market Risk			Nonmarket Risk		
	Variance Units	Standard Deviation	Variance Units	Standard Deviation	Percent of Total	Variance Units	Standard Deviation	Percent of Total
Behemoth Trust . . . . . :	455.7	21.35%	440.2	20.98%	96.6%	15.5	3.93%	3.4%
Ortho Growth, Inc. . . . . :	589.9	24.29	550.7	23.47	93.4	39.1	6.26	6.6
Petite Capital Investors . . :	481.9	21.95	433.1	20.81	89.9	48.8	6.99	10.1
Special K Associates . . . :	465.5	21.57	437.3	20.91	94.0	28.1	5.31	6.0
Total fund	480.1	21.91	461.5	21.48	96.1	18.6	4.31	3.9

Table 6.5
Analysis of Nonmarket Risk

Investment Managers	(1) Normal Beta	(2) Current Level Variance (%²)	(3) Standard Deviation (%)	(4) Economic Break-Even Standard Deviation (%)	(5) Risk-Acceptance Parameter (RAP)	(6) Dependence-Adjustment Factor (DAF)	(7) Investment Proportion	(8) RAP Adjusted for DAF and Proportion	(9) Inferred Covenant Information Ratio	(10) Required Alpha (%)	(11) Certainty Equivalent (%)	(12) Management Fee (%)
Behemoth Trust Company . . . :	1.00	15.5	3.93	4.00	72.36	0.37	0.498	53.76	0.073	0.29	0.15	0.15
Ortho Growth, Inc. . . . . . :	1.19	39.1	6.26	6.47	86.12	0.22	0.218	86.91	0.072	0.46	0.23	0.25
Petite Capital Investors . . . :	1.10	48.8	6.99	7.66	79.60	0.25	0.206	97.76	0.072	0.50	0.25	0.30
Special K Associates . . . . :	1.00	28.1	5.31	12.55	72.36	0.28	0.078	259.75	0.021	0.11	0.06	0.30
Total fund	1.06	18.6	4.31	5.67	76.71	1.00	1.00	76.71	0.056	0.24	0.12	0.21

Notes:

1. Column (5) = (1)(Market variance)/(Market expected excess return) = (1)(434.2)/6.
2. Column (6) is predicted by the sponsor.
3. Column (8) = (5)(6)/(7). See the supplement to this chapter for explanation of this adjustment.
4. Column (9) = (3)/(8).
5. Column (10) = (9)(3).
6. Column (11) = (10)/2.
7. Column (4) is that level of nonmarket risk which, when adjusted by the risk/reward trade-off, infers a required alpha equal to twice the management fee.

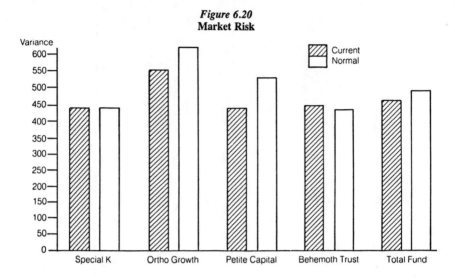

Figure 6.20
Market Risk

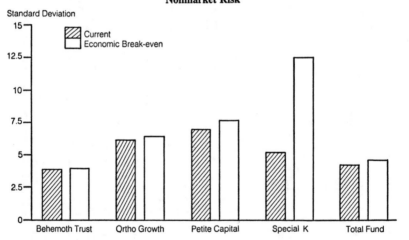

Figure 6.21
Nonmarket Risk

It is in the area of nonmarket risk that active managers can differentiate themselves from market performance by taking risk exposure as a means of generating abnormal return. This is an area where evaluations should be made as to whether the degree of risk taken is at least commensurate with the level of fees charged. If the inferred expected return from the appropriate level of nonmarket risk assumed is not more than twice the management fee, the exercise is not of economic benefit to the plan sponsor.[27] Applying this line of

[27]Since one half of the expected return is lost as compensation for risk, only one half of the expected return results in CEER.

reasoning to the managers in question, each one (as shown in Figure 6.21) is assuming less than an economic level of nonmarket risk. Special K, because of its small investment proportion and its 0.30 percent fee, offers the most uneconomical profile. Details of the specific measurements in each case are given in Table 6.5.

Nonmarket risk, as discussed earlier, can be broken down into variance from risk indices, industry factors, and specific risk due to individual company characteristics. Analyzing each manager in this light offers some clues as to whether the sponsor is receiving diversity in style among the managers. Table 6.6 enumerates some statistics analyzing such risk composition. While all four managers derive nearly the same amount of risk from security selection, the remaining nonmarket risk categories evidence far greater diversity. Ortho Growth and Special K both emphasize risk indices, combined with a small exposure to industry weighting. Behemoth Trust and Petite Capital stress risk indices and industry weightings almost equally.

Table 6.6
Nonmarket Risk

Investment Managers	Risk Indices		Industries		Security Selection	
	Percent of Total	Standard Deviation	Percent of Total	Standard Deviation	Percent of Total	Standard Deviation
Behemoth Trust Company . .	35%	2.7%	44%	3.0%	21%	1.8%
Ortho Growth, Inc.	60	5.6	13	2.6	26	3.2
Petite Capital Investors	37	6.1	34	3.0	29	3.8
Special K Associates	64	4.2	8	1.4	29	3.2
Total fund	62%	3.9%	25%	2.8%	13%	1.6%

Perhaps of greater significance are the correlation coefficients between the nonmarket risk for the four managers. This aspect of the report, shown in Figure 6.22, indicates that Special K is unique, with a low correlation relative to each of the other three managers. As the correlation coefficient matrix demonstrates, the other three managers are very similar. If the plan sponsor was aiming for greater diversity among the managers, some questions should have been raised.

Breaking nonmarket risk into its components, one can find further evidence to support questions about lack of diversity. Figure 6.23 indicates the degree of correlation between the common factors among the four managers. Notice that Special K again stands out as having a unique posture relative to the other three. Among those three, the correlation coefficients are better than 0.9, indicating a high degree of similarity. Table 6.7 goes into greater detail, enumerating the risk indices of the managers. As can clearly be seen, Behemoth, Ortho Growth, and Petite Capital Investors all emphasize market variability, are close to neutral regarding earnings variability, strongly de-emphasize low valuation, place important emphasis on immaturity and smallness, heavily

Figure 6.22
Nonmarket Risk—Correlation Coefficients

	Special K Associates	Ortho Growth, Inc.	Petite Capital Investors	Behemoth Trust Company
Special K Associates	1.000			
Ortho Growth, Inc.	0.108	1.000		
Petite Capital Investors	0.297	0.706	1.000	
Behemoth Trust Company	0.033	0.729	0.611	1.000

Figure 6.23
Common Factor Risk—Correlation Coefficients

	Special K Associates	Ortho Growth, Inc.	Petite Capital Investors	Behemoth Trust Company
Special K Associates	1.000			
Ortho Growth, Inc.	0.196	1.000		
Petite Capital Investors	0.426	0.948	1.000	
Behemoth Trust Company	0.313	0.914	0.919	1.000

Table 6.7
Common Factor Risk—Risk Indices

Active Investment Managers	Market Variability	Earnings Variability	Low Valuation	Immaturity, Smallness	Growth Orientation	Financial Risk
Behemoth Trust Company ..	0.335	0.008	−0.202	0.565	0.499	−0.224
Ortho Growth, Inc.	0.664	0.184	−0.625	0.868	1.149	−0.125
Petite Capital Investors	0.877	0.283	−0.848	1.536	1.071	−0.035
Special K Associates	−0.016	0.006	−0.031	1.309	0.003	0.011
Total fund	0.479	0.097	−0.400	0.869	0.710	−0.148
FRMS universe	0.186	0.254	−0.109	0.624	0.149	0.144

stress growth orientation, and de-emphasize financial risk. Special K, on the other hand is neutral regarding nearly every factor except immaturity and smallness. The picture is quite clear: Special K emphasizes small companies, while the other three uniformly stress higher beta and small companies with strong growth characteristics. A sponsor who desired more than two distinct money management styles would be extremely disappointed.

In the area of industry holdings, Special K also tends to stand alone, whereas the other three managers, with rare exceptions, tend to stress the same areas. As Table 6.8 demonstrates, outside of Petite Capital's strong emphasis on media, many of the other industry areas such as energy materials, drugs, business machines, electronics, insurance, and miscellaneous conglomerates are also stressed. The most notable similarities exist between Behemoth Trust and Ortho Growth; except for these, there are few departures from S&P industry group weightings.

One saving grace for diversification does show up in the area of specific risk, but this is a rather hollow consolation, since specific risk is the least emphasized of the three nonmarket risk areas. As the correlation coefficients for specific risk indicate (see Figure 6.24), there is a low correlation among all of the money managers for the specific returns of the companies they own.

The remaining sections of the consultant's report focus on the specific securities owned in the aggregate portfolio. The final report included here is simply an alphabetical listing of the individual equities in the plan. The major additional feature in the alphabetical list, as shown in Table 6.9, is the detailing of each money manager's holding in each security listed relative to the overall portfolio.

Incredibly, the aggregate portfolio contains over 500 securities.[28] Many of these holdings are so small that they round off to zero in the report. Moreover,

---

[28]Some CUSIP identifiers are not associated with names. These correspond to ncnequity asset categories or to companies not included in the risk model. The large number of assets suggests that one of the managers has included a holding in a pooled or commingled fund in this account.

Table 6.8
Common Factor Risk—Industries

	Portfolio Weightings					
Industries	Behemoth Trust Company	Ortho Growth, Inc.	Petite Capital Investors	Special K Associates	Total	S&P 500
Nonferrous metals	0.7%	0.0%	0.0%	0.0%	0.4%	1.8%
Energy materials	3.2	5.3	3.0	0.0	3.4	2.8
Construction	3.3	0.0	2.7	5.2	2.6	1.5
Agriculture, food	2.9	1.7	0.0	9.0	2.6	4.8
Liquor	0.2	0.0	0.0	0.0	0.1	0.8
Tobacco	1.0	1.5	2.8	1.9	1.5	1.3
Apparel	0.5	1.2	0.0	0.0	0.5	0.5
Forest products, paper	3.4	0.0	0.0	1.8	1.9	2.8
Containers	0.1	0.0	0.0	3.0	0.3	0.5
Media	2.6	3.1	20.6	1.3	5.8	2.0
Chemicals	1.2	3.5	0.0	5.5	1.9	3.3
Drugs	8.4	7.1	7.3	3.2	7.5	5.3
Soaps, cosmetics	5.5	0.0	0.3	1.6	3.0	2.9
Domestic oil	0.7	8.6	5.7	7.8	4.0	6.7
International oil	6.5	3.1	0.0	6.0	4.5	9.4
Tires, rubber	0.2	0.0	0.0	0.0	0.1	0.4
Steel	0.8	0.0	0.0	0.0	0.4	0.9
Producer goods	8.0	5.6	2.3	2.0	5.9	3.5
Business machines	13.8	18.9	9.4	2.9	13.3	9.2
Consumer durables	1.5	0.0	0.0	2.0	0.9	0.8
Motor vehicles	3.2	0.0	0.0	2.7	1.9	4.6
Aerospace	1.2	1.6	2.2	0.0	1.4	0.8
Electronics	4.7	3.2	8.8	1.6	4.8	1.9
Photographic	3.3	3.0	1.6	0.0	2.8	1.7
Nondurables	1.0	1.8	0.0	0.0	0.9	0.6
Trucking	0.6	0.0	0.0	3.0	0.6	0.2
Railroads	0.8	2.3	2.4	1.5	1.5	1.5
Air transport	1.5	2.6	2.7	0.0	1.8	0.4
Telephone	0.1	2.0	0.0	0.0	0.5	6.8
Energy utilities	0.1	0.0	1.8	7.0	1.0	5.5
Retail, general	4.4	3.6	0.0	2.2	3.3	2.7
Banks	1.6	3.8	2.7	6.7	2.7	2.5
Miscellaneous finance	1.2	2.9	0.0	4.5	1.6	1.0
Insurance	4.9	5.2	7.8	6.6	5.6	2.2
Real property	0.3	0.0	0.0	0.0	0.1	0.1
Business services	0.6	4.3	8.4	4.5	3.2	0.0
Travel, outdoor recreation	0.1	0.0	0.0	0.0	0.1	0.3
Gold mining	0.0	0.0	0.0	0.0	0.0	0.2
Miscellaneous, conglomerates	5.8	4.3	7.5	6.6	5.8	5.3

there are few big bets in the portfolio (the largest aggregate holding is IBM at 7.0 percent, which approximately matches the S&P 500 holding).

What can we recommend for this aggregate portfolio? The four managers are very similar; they have each picked a particular group of stocks (identified by their risk index exposure) and invested with little or no stock selection. The

Figure 6.24
Specific Risk—Correlation Coefficients

	Special K Associates	Ortho Growth, Inc.	Petite Capital Investors	Behemoth Trust Company
Special K Associates	1.000			
Ortho Growth, Inc.	0.138	1.000		
Petite Capital Investors	0.151	0.182	1.000	
Behemoth Trust Company	0.111	.0.161	0.118	1.000

risk index emphasis is therefore concentrated in the aggregate portfolio. In short, the aggregate portfolio really has only one bet (represented by any one of the managers) and the four managers provide little diversification. We hope that the sponsor is aware of the exposure, because the portfolio may perform quite unlike the market.

From this risk analysis, Special K, primarily because of its small proportion, adds very little to the portfolio; moreover, all the managers bear so little residual risk that there is virtually no chance that the portfolio will ever cover the management fee. We have two specific recommendations:

1. The sponsor should convince himself or herself that the small-company, growth-stock bias really represents the normal portfolio.
2. The sponsor should consider passively investing part of the portfolio. For instance, terminating the investment management agreement with Behemoth Trust and Special K and then indexing their funds would hardly change the risk posture of the portfolio but would certainly decrease the management fees. At present the portfolio is 50 percent index fund and 50 percent special equity fund. Why not take explicit advantage of this fact?

Table 6.9

Aggregate and Individual Portfolio Listings
(4/30/79)

CONTRIBUTIONS OF INDIVIDUAL ASSETS TO PORTFOLIO RISK

Portfolio code:

1 Special K
2 Ortho Growth
3 Petite Capital
4 Behemoth Trust

#	CUSIP	NAME	PERCENT OF PORTFOLIO VALUE	WEIGHT IN S&P500	BETA	EFFECT OF 1% PURCHASE ON RESID. STDEV	REQUIRED ALPHA	PERCENT OF PORTFOLIO VALUE IN					
								PORT 1	PORT 2	PORT 3	PORT 4	PORT 5	PORT 6
1.	00000000												
2.	00000001												
3.	00000002												
4.	00000003												
5.	00168810	AMF INC	0.2	0.0	1.15	0.029	0.28	0.0	0.0	0.0	0.5		
6.	00244010	AVX CORP	0.0	0.0	1.64	0.160	1.56	0.0	0.0	0.0	0.0		
7.	00282410	ABBOTT LABS	0.5	0.3	0.87	0.029	0.28	0.0	0.0	2.6	0.0		
8.	00790310	ADVANCED MICRO DEVICES	0.6	0.0	1.80	0.181	1.76	0.0	0.0	0.0	0.0		
9.	00814010	AETNA LIFE & CAS CO	0.6	0.4	1.28	0.051	0.50	0.0	0.0	0.0	1.1		
10.	00818210	AFFILIATED BANKSHS COL	0.0	0.0	1.21	0.059	0.57	0.0	0.0	0.0	0.0		
11.	00867710	AMMANSON H F & CO	0.0	0.1	1.38	-0.034	-0.33	0.0	0.0	0.0	0.1		
12.	00915810	AIR PROD & CHEMS INC	0.0	0.0	0.96	0.007	0.07	0.0	0.0	0.0	0.1		
13.	00926610	AIRBORNE FGHT CORP	0.0	0.0	1.07	0.085	0.82	0.0	0.0	0.0	0.0		
14.	01023510	ALABAMA BANCORPORATION	0.0	0.0	0.78	-0.065	-0.63	0.0	0.0	0.0	0.0		
15.	01234710	ALBANY INTL CORP	0.0	0.0	1.21	0.030	0.29	0.0	0.0	0.0	0.0		
16.	01310410	ALBERTSONS INC	0.6	0.0	0.90	0.025	0.24	3.0	1.7	0.0	0.0		
17.	01447610	ALEXANDER & ALEX SVCS	0.9	0.0	1.09	0.085	0.83	0.0	1.4	2.3	0.2		
18.	01849210	ALLERGAN PHARMACEUTIC	0.0	0.0	1.30	-0.110	-1.07	0.0	0.0	0.0	0.0		
19.	01887010	ALLIED BANCSHARES INC	0.0	0.0	0.71	-0.071	-0.69	0.0	0.0	0.0	0.1		
20.	01951910	ALLIED STORES CORP	0.0	0.1	1.11	0.003	0.03	0.0	0.0	0.0	0.1		
21.	01964510	ALLIS CHALMERS CORP	0.1	0.1	1.02	-0.001	-0.01	0.0	0.0	0.0	0.1		
22.	02355110	AMERADA HESS CORP	0.2	0.0	1.13	-0.030	-0.37	0.0	0.0	0.0	0.0		
23.	02377110	AMERICAN AIRLS INC	0.4	0.1	1.31	-0.024	-0.23	0.0	0.0	0.1	0.3		
24.	02390510	AMDAHL CORP	0.5	0.0	1.87	0.216	2.10	0.0	0.0	2.1	0.0		
25.	02473510	AMERICAN BROADCASTING	0.5	0.2	1.27	0.058	0.56	0.0	0.0	2.7	0.1		
26.	02581610	AMERICAN EXPRESS CO	0.7	0.3	1.39	-0.045	-0.43	0.0	2.9	0.0	0.0		
27.	02660910	AMERICAN HOME PRODS CP	0.8	0.6	0.65	-0.018	-0.18	1.2	0.0	0.0	1.3		
28.	02687410	AMERICAN INTL GROUP	0.7	0.0	1.45	0.110	1.07	0.0	0.0	3.0	0.3		
29.	02762710	AMERICAN MTRS CORP	0.0	0.0	1.59	0.070	0.68	0.0	0.0	0.0	0.1		
30.	02938310	AMERICAN SVGS & LN FLA	0.0	0.0	1.50	0.083	0.81	0.0	0.0	0.0	0.0		

(continued)

Portfolio code:

Code	Portfolio
1	Special K
2	Ortho Growth
3	Petite Capital
4	Behemoth Trust

No.	ID	Company			β						α		
31.	03044710	AMERICAN WELDING & MFG	0·0	0·0	1·01	0·081	0·0	0·0	0·0	0·0	0·79	0·0	0·0
32.	03188710	AMP INC	0·8	0·2	1·08	−0·074	0·0	0·0	0·0	0·0	0·72	1·6	1·3
33.	03948310	ARCHER DANIELS MIDLAND	0·3	0·0	0·91	−0·019	0·0	0·0	0·0	0·0	−0·04	0·0	0·0
34.	04232110	ARMSTRONG CORK CO	0·0	0·1	1·02	−0·004	0·0	0·0	0·0	0·0	−0·18	0·0	0·6
35.	04341310	ASARCO INC	0·0	0·1	1·27	−0·019	0·0	0·0	0·0	0·0		0·0	0·1
36.	0445410	ASHLAND OIL INC	0·0	0·0	1·09	−0·059	0·0	0·0	0·0	0·0	−0·57	0·0	0·0
37.	0455710	ASSOCIATED COCA COLA B	0·1	0·0	1·01	−0·051	0·0	0·0	0·0	0·0	−0·07	0·0	0·1
38.	04822210	ATLANTIC BANCORP	0·0	0·0	1·00	−0·051	0·0	0·0	0·0	0·0	−0·50	0·0	0·0
39.	04882510	ATLANTIC RICHFIELD CO	1·0	1·1	0·71	−0·093	4·5	0·0	0·0	0·0	−0·90	0·0	0·0
40.	05275410	AUTO TROL TECHNOLOGY											
41.	05301510	AUTOMATIC DATA PROCESS	0·1	0·0	1·04	0·135	0·0	0·0	0·0	0·0	1·31	0·0	0·1
42.	05350110	AVCO CORP	0·1	0·0	1·60	0·095	0·0	0·0	0·0	0·0	0·92	0·0	0·1
43.	05430310	AVON PRODS INC	1·1	0·4	0·97	0·016	0·0	0·0	0·0	0·0	0·16	0·0	2·1
44.	05634510												
45.	05713310	BAKER BROS INC FLA	0·0	0·0	1·47	0·088	1·5	0·0	0·0	0·0	0·86	0·0	0·0
46.	05849810	BALL CORP	0·1	0·6	0·87	0·021	1·5	0·0	0·0	0·0	0·20	0·0	0·0
47.	06605010	BANKAMERICA CORP	0·5	0·8	0·78	−0·102	1·0	2·7	0·0	0·0	−0·99	0·0	0·0
48.	06714910	BARBER OIL CORP	0·0	0·0	0·98	−0·006	0·0	0·0	0·0	0·0	−0·05	0·0	0·1
49.	06805510	BARNETT BANKS FLA INC	0·0	0·0	1·18	−0·038	0·0	0·0	0·0	0·0	−0·37	0·0	0·0
50.	07189210	BAXTER TRAVENOL LABS	0·2	0·2	1·05	−0·051	0·0	0·0	0·0	0·0	−0·50	0·0	0·4
51.	07379910	BEAR CREEK CORP	0·0	0·0	1·09	0·075	0·0	0·0	0·0	0·0	0·73	0·0	0·1
52.	07741910	BELCO PETE CORP	0·1	0·1	1·06	−0·029	0·4	0·0	0·0	0·0	−0·28	0·0	0·0
53.	08655110	BEST PRODS INC	0·1	0·0	1·60	−0·115	1·4	0·0	0·0	0·0	−1·12	0·0	0·0
54.	08777910	BETZ LABS INC	0·0	0·0	1·11	0·042	0·0	0·0	0·0	0·0	0·21	0·0	0·0
55.	08782410	BEVERAGE CANNERS INC	0·0	0·0	0·99	0·060	0·0	0·0	0·0	0·0	0·58	0·0	0·0
56.	08967110	BIG THREE INDS INC	0·0	0·0	0·95	−0·007	0·0	0·0	0·0	0·0	−0·07	0·0	0·1
57.	09054510	BINNEY & SMITH INC	0·7	0·0	0·96	−0·051	0·0	0·0	0·0	0·0	−0·50	0·0	1·5
58.	09179710	BLACK & DECKER MFG CO	0·7	0·0	1·18	0·042	0·0	0·0	0·0	0·0	0·41	0·0	0·0
59.	09364410	BLOCK DRUG INC	0·0	0·0	1·11	0·057	0·0	0·0	0·0	0·0	0·55	0·0	0·0
60.	09367110	BLOCK H & R INC	0·0	0·0	0·98	0·052	0·0	0·0	0·0	0·0	0·50	0·0	0·0
61.	09702310	BOEING CO	0·8	0·4	1·11	0·052	0·0	0·0	0·0	1·6	0·50	0·0	0·2
62.	09738310	BOISE CASCADE CORP	0·1	0·1	1·06	−0·016	0·7	2·2	0·0	0·0	−0·15	0·0	0·0
63.	09959910	BORDEN INC	0·0	0·0	0·63	−0·044	1·0	0·0	0·0	0·0	−0·43	0·0	0·1
64.	10706110	BRENCO INC	0·7	0·0	1·03	0·026	0·0	0·0	0·0	0·0	0·26	0·0	0·0
65.	11009710	BRISTOL MYERS CO	0·7	0·3	0·86	0·022	0·0	0·0	0·0	0·0	0·21	0·0	1·4
66.	11120510	BRO DART INDS	0·0	0·0	1·12	0·103	0·0	0·0	0·0	0·0	1·00	0·0	0·0
67.	11802510	BUCK ENGR INC	0·0	0·0	0·79	0·104	0·0	0·0	0·0	0·0	1·01	0·0	0·1
68.	12065530	BUNKER RAMO CORP	0·0	0·0	1·51	0·037	0·0	0·0	0·0	0·0	0·36	0·0	0·0
69.	12220510	BURNDY CORP	0·0	0·0	1·11	0·076	0·0	0·0	0·0	0·0	0·74	0·0	0·1
70.	12237510	BURNS INTL SEC SVCS	0·0	0·0	1·05	0·031	0·0	0·0	0·0	0·0	0·31	0·0	0·0

CONTRIBUTIONS OF INDIVIDUAL ASSETS TO PORTFOLIO RISK

	CUSIP	NAME	PERCENT OF PORTFOLIO VALUE	WEIGHT IN S&P500	BETA	EFFECT OF 1% PURCHASE ON RESID. STDEV	REQUIRED ALPHA	PORT 1	PORT 2	PORT 3	PORT 4	PORT 5	PORT 6
71.	12256510	BURNUP & SIMS INC	0.0	0.0	1.70	0.075	0.73	0.0	0.0	0.0	0.0		
72.	12278110	BURROUGHS CORP	0.6	0.4	0.98	0.090	0.88	0.0	0.0	0.0	1.2		
73.	12484510	CBS INC	0.1	0.2	1.01	0.019	0.18	1.3	0.0	0.0	0.0		
74.	12561510	CLC AMER INC	0.0	0.0	1.46	0.007	0.06	0.0	0.0	0.0	0.0		
75.	12650110	CTS CORP	0.0	0.0	1.19	0.069	0.67	0.0	0.0	0.0	0.0		
76.	12879310	CALDOR INC	0.3	0.0	1.15	0.069	0.67	0.0	1.4	0.0	0.0		
77.	13342910	CAMERON IRON WKS INC	0.1	0.0	1.09	0.032	0.31	0.0	0.0	0.0	0.1		
78.	13721910	CANANDAIGUA WINE INC	0.0	0.1	1.22	0.118	1.15	0.0	0.0	0.0	0.0		
79.	13986110	CAPITAL CITIES COMMUN	0.8	0.1	1.12	0.084	0.82	0.0	0.0	3.8	0.1		
80.	14018610	CAPITAL HLDG CORP DEL	0.0	0.1	1.20	0.072	0.70	0.0	0.0	0.0	0.0		
81.	14062710	CAPITOL INTL AWYS INC	0.0	0.0	1.43	0.099	0.96	0.0	0.0	0.0	0.0		
82.	14080710	CARBOLINE CO	0.0	0.0	1.19	0.066	0.64	0.0	0.0	0.0	0.0		
83.	14233910	CARLISLE CORP	0.0	0.0	1.09	-0.014	-0.13	0.0	0.0	0.0	0.1		
84.	14428510	CARPENTER TECHNOLOGY	0.0	0.0	0.78	-0.018	-0.18	0.0	0.0	0.0	0.0		
85.	14841110	CASTLE A M & CO	0.0	0.0	0.72	-0.016	-0.15	0.0	0.0	0.0	0.0		
86.	14912310	CATERPILLAR TRACTOR CO	0.8	0.7	0.88	-0.032	-0.31	0.0	0.0	0.0	1.6		
87.	15687910	CERTAIN TEED CORP	0.0	0.0	1.25	-0.026	-0.26	0.0	0.0	0.0	0.1		
88.	15717710	CESSNA AIRCRAFT CO	0.0	0.0	1.17	0.053	0.51	0.0	0.0	0.0	0.0		
89.	15986010	CHARLES RIV BREEDG LAB	0.0	0.0	0.90	0.045	0.44	0.0	0.0	0.0	0.0		
90.	16161010	CHASE MANHATTAN CORP	0.1	0.2	0.95	-0.094	-0.92	1.8	0.0	0.0	0.0		
91.	16359610	CHEMED CORP	0.0	0.0	1.13	0.054	0.53	0.0	0.0	0.0	0.0		
92.	16533910	CHESEBROUGH PONDS INC	0.0	0.1	0.89	0.033	0.32	0.0	0.0	0.0	0.0		
93.	16789810	CHICAGO PNEUMATIC TOOL	0.0	0.0	1.01	-0.016	-0.16	0.0	0.0	0.0	0.0		
94.	17052010	CHRIS CRAFT INDS INC	0.0	0.0	1.64	0.164	1.59	0.0	0.0	0.0	0.0		
95.	17158310	CHURCHS FRIED CHICKEN	0.4	0.0	1.60	0.097	0.95	0.0	1.8	0.0	0.0		
96.	17303410	CITICORP	0.8	0.4	0.83	-0.093	-0.91	0.0	1.7	0.0	0.8		
97.	17456610	CITIZENS FID CORP	0.2	0.1	0.68	-0.073	-0.71	0.0	0.0	0.0	0.0		
98.	18139610	CLARK EQUIPMENT CO	0.0	0.0	1.09	-0.007	-0.07	2.0	0.0	0.0	0.0		
99.	18148610	CLARK OIL & REFNG CORP	0.1	0.0	1.28	-0.014	-0.14	0.0	0.0	0.0	0.0		
100.	19089310	COBE LABS INC	0.0	0.0	1.31	-0.156	1.52	0.0	0.0	0.0	0.1		

Portfolio code:

1 Special K
2 Ortho Growth
3 Petite Capital
4 Behemoth Trust

No.	Number	Security							1	2	3	4
101.	19109810	COCA COLA BOTTLING CONS	0.0	0.0	1.15	0.0	0.030	0.29	0.0	0.0	0.0	0.0
102.	19114910	COCA COLA BTTLG MIAMI	0.0	0.7	1.49	0.0	-0.076	-0.74	0.0	0.0	0.0	0.0
103.	19121610	COCA COLA CO	1.0	0.0	0.67	0.0	-0.055	-0.53	0.0	0.0	2.0	0.0
104.	19247910	COHERENT INC	0.0	0.0	1.90	0.0	0.187	1.82	0.0	0.0	0.0	0.0
105.	19255510	COLE CONSUMER PRODS	0.0	0.0	1.31	0.0	0.099	0.96	0.0	0.0	0.0	0.1
106.	19328810	COLE NATL CORP	0.0	0.0	1.10	0.0	0.033	0.32	0.0	0.0	0.0	0.0
107.	19355810	COLEMAN INC	0.0	0.0	1.00	0.0	0.046	0.45	0.0	0.0	0.0	0.0
108.	19577420	COLONIAL LIFE & AC INS	0.0	0.0	1.36	0.0	0.074	0.72	0.0	0.0	0.0	0.1
109.	19626710	COLOR TILE INC										
110.	19686410	COLT INDS INC DEL	0.1	0.0	1.12	0.1	0.026	0.25	0.0	0.0	0.0	0.2
111.	20010110	COMBINED COMMUNICATION	0.0	0.0	1.37	0.0	0.106	1.03	0.0	0.0	0.0	0.1
112.	20016510	COMBINED INS CO AMER	0.6	0.0	1.42	0.0	0.057	0.56	0.0	3.4	0.0	0.0
113.	20111110	COMMERCIAL ALLIANCE CP	0.0	0.0	1.42	0.0	-0.013	-0.13	0.0	0.0	0.0	0.1
114.	20341710	COMMUNICATIONS SATELLI	0.0	0.0	0.99	0.0	-0.022	-0.22	0.0	0.0	0.0	0.0
115.	20401510	COMMUNITY PSYCHIATRIC	0.0	0.0	1.09	0.0	-0.105	-1.02	0.0	0.0	0.0	0.1
116.	20582610	COMTECH TELECOMMUNICAT	0.0	0.0	1.89	0.0	0.193	1.87	0.0	0.0	0.0	0.0
117.	20919310	CONSOLIDATED FIBRES	0.0	0.0	1.51	0.0	0.129	1.25	0.0	0.0	0.0	0.0
118.	20923710	CONSOLIDATED FREIGHTWY	0.0	0.0	1.18	0.0	-0.008	-0.08	0.0	0.0	0.0	0.1
119.	21670510	COOPER LABS INC	0.0	0.0	1.19	0.0	-0.097	-0.94	0.0	0.0	0.0	0.0
120.	21701610	COORS ADOLPH CO	0.0	0.1	0.85	0.0	0.061	0.59	0.0	0.0	0.0	0.1
121.	21852510	CORDIS CORP	0.0	0.0	1.89	0.0	0.161	1.56	0.0	0.0	0.0	0.0
122.	22374110	COWLES COMMUNICATIONS	0.0	0.0	1.11	0.0	0.058	0.56	0.0	0.0	0.0	0.0
123.	22400310	COX BROADCASTING CORP	0.0	0.0	1.11	0.0	-0.074	-0.72	0.0	0.0	0.0	0.0
124.	22522410	CRAY RESH INC	0.0	0.0	1.66	0.0	0.215	2.09	0.0	0.0	0.0	0.1
125.	22743010	CROSS & TRECKER CORP	0.0	0.0	1.13	0.0	-0.029	-0.28	0.0	0.0	0.0	0.0
126.	22747810	CROSS A T CO	0.1	0.0	1.04	0.0	0.076	0.74	0.0	0.0	0.0	0.1
127.	22866910	CROWN ZELLERBACH CORP	0.3	0.0	0.94	0.0	-0.033	-0.32	0.0	0.0	0.0	0.5
128.	22879510	CRUM & FORSTER	0.0	0.1	1.32	0.0	-0.057	-0.56	0.0	0.0	0.0	0.0
129.	23571710	DAMON CORP	0.0	0.0	1.52	0.0	-0.085	-0.83	0.0	0.0	0.0	0.1
130.	23581110	DANA CORP	0.1	0.1	0.97	0.0	-0.002	-0.02	0.0	0.0	0.0	0.1
131.	23760610	DATA CARD CORP	0.5	0.0	1.40	0.0	0.198	1.92	0.0	0.0	0.0	0.0
132.	23768810	DATA GEN CORP	0.8	0.0	1.32	0.0	0.195	1.90	0.0	0.0	1.8	0.2
133.	23810020	DATAPOINT CORP	0.0	0.0	1.58	0.0	0.226	2.19	0.0	0.0	1.0	0.0
134.	23820810	DATUM INC	0.0	0.0	1.71	0.0	0.200	1.94	0.0	0.0	0.0	0.0
135.	23913310	DAVIS WTR & WASTE IND	0.0	0.0	1.51	0.0	0.120	1.17	0.0	0.0	0.0	0.1
136.	24344210	DECISION DATA COMPUTER	0.9	0.0	1.46	0.0	0.222	2.15	0.0	0.0	0.0	0.0
137.	24419910	DEERE & CO	0.0	0.3	1.07	0.0	-0.008	-0.08	0.0	0.0	0.0	1.7
138.	24487410	DEKALB AGRESEARCH INC	0.0	0.0	0.96	0.0	-0.025	-0.24	0.0	0.0	0.0	0.0
139.	24788310	DELTONA CORP	0.0	0.0	1.72	0.0	-0.100	-0.97	0.0	0.0	0.0	0.0
140.	24801910	DE LUXE CHECK PRINTERS	0.6	0.0	0.90	0.0	-0.045	-0.44	0.0	2.4	1.5	0.1

(continued)

Table 6.9 (continued)
Aggregate and Individual Portfolio Listings
(4/30/79)

CONTRIBUTIONS OF INDIVIDUAL ASSETS TO PORTFOLIO RISK

Portfolio code:
1 Special K
2 Ortho Growth
3 Petite Capital
4 Behemoth Trust

	CUSIP	NAME	PERCENT OF PORTFOLIO VALUE	WEIGHT IN S&P500	BETA	EFFECT OF 1% PURCHASE ON RESID. STDEV	REQUIRED ALPHA	PORT 1	PORT 2	PORT 3	PORT 4	PORT 5	PORT 6
141.	24836110	DENISON MINES LTD	0.0	0.0	0.73	-0.008	-0.07	0.0	0.0	0.0	0.0		
142.	24870310	DENNYS INC	0.0	0.0	1.41	-0.090	-0.88	0.0	0.0	0.0	0.0		
143.	25274110	DIAMOND SHAMROCK CORP	0.2	0.0	1.16	-0.006	-0.06	1.9	0.0	0.0	0.4		
144.	25384910	DIGITAL EQUIP CORP	1.1	0.3	1.17	-0.197	-1.52	0.0	1.7	0.0	1.4		
145.	25468710	DISNEY WALT PRODTNS	0.6	0.2	1.22	-0.060	-0.58	0.0	0.0	0.0	1.2		
146.	25612910	DR PEPPER CO	0.0	0.0	1.06	-0.016	-0.16	0.0	0.0	0.0	0.0		
147.	25765110	DONALDSON INC	0.1	0.0	1.06	0.041	0.40	0.0	0.0	0.0	0.1		
148.	25786710	DONNELLEY R R & SONS	0.1	0.0	0.87	-0.021	-0.20	0.0	0.0	0.0	0.1		
149.	26000310	DOVER CORP	0.1	0.0	0.94	0.014	0.13	0.0	0.0	0.0	0.1		
150.	26054310	DOW CHEM CO	0.3	0.7	0.89	-0.049	-0.47	0.0	0.0	0.0	0.5		
151.	26353410	DU PONT E I DE NEMOURS	0.4	1.0	0.94	-0.073	-0.71	0.0	1.9	0.0	0.1		
152.	26882910	ERC CORP	0.6	0.0	1.28	0.072	0.70	0.0	0.0	3.1	0.0		
153.	26980310	EAGLE PICHER INDS INC	0.0	0.0	0.96	-0.012	-0.11	0.0	0.0	0.0	0.0		
154.	27746110	EASTMAN KODAK CO	1.7	1.5	0.87	-0.012	-0.02	0.0	0.0	0.0	0.0		
155.	27748810	EASTMET CORP	0.0	0.0	1.00	-0.005	-0.05	0.0	3.0	0.0	2.0		
156.	27805810	EATON CORP	0.1	0.1	0.96	-0.016	-0.15	1.7	0.0	0.0	0.0		
157.	27874910	ECHLIN MFG CO	0.1	0.1	1.03	0.037	0.36	0.0	0.0	0.0	0.1		
158.	27876410	ECKERD JACK CORP	0.0	0.1	0.97	-0.055	-0.53	0.0	0.0	0.0	0.2		
159.	27902910	ECONOMICS LAB INC	0.0	0.0	1.06	0.017	0.17	0.0	0.0	0.0	0.1		
160.	29101110	EMERSON ELEC CO	0.6	0.3	0.90	-0.011	-0.11	0.0	0.0	0.0	1.2		
161.	29121010	EMHART CORP VA	0.1	0.2	1.05	-0.006	-0.06	0.0	0.0	0.0	0.1		
162.	29284810	ENGELHARD MINERALS & CHE	0.1	0.0	1.11	-0.006	-0.06	0.0	0.0	0.0	0.1		
163.	29338910	ENNIS BUSINESS FORMS	0.0	0.0	0.90	-0.066	-0.64	0.0	0.0	0.0	0.0		
164.	29456010	EQUITABLE SVGS & LN ORE	0.0	0.0	1.33	0.068	0.66	0.0	0.0	0.0	1.2		
165.	29909610	EVANS & SUTHERLAND COMPT	0.0	0.0				0.0	0.0	0.0	0.0		
166.	30058710	EX CELL O CORP	0.0	0.0	0.93	-0.013	-0.12	0.0	0.0	0.0	0.1		
167.	30087110	EXCHANGE BANCORP TAMPA	0.0	0.0	1.08	-0.040	-0.39	0.0	0.0	0.0	0.0		
168.	30229010	EXXON CORP	2.7	3.5	1.06	-0.115	-1.12	2.0	3.1	0.0	3.5		
169.	30369310	FAIRCHILD CAMERA & INS	0.0	0.0	1.85	0.112	1.09	0.0	0.0	0.0	0.0		
170.	30700010	FAMILY DLR STORES INC	0.0	0.0	1.42	0.085	0.82	0.0	0.0	0.0	0.0		

(continued)

Portfolio code:

1 Special K
2 Ortho Growth
3 Petite Capital
4 Behemoth Trust

No.	Number	Company			β			1	2	3	4
171.	30959410	FARMERS GROUP INC	0.4	0.0	1.26	0.101	0.99	0.0	0.0	2.1	0.1
172.	31330910	FEDERAL EXPRESS CORP	0.0	0.0	1.73	-0.015	-0.15	0.0	0.0	0.0	0.1
173.	31354910	FEDERAL MOGUL CORP	0.0	0.0	0.92	-0.020	-0.19	1.8	0.0	0.0	0.0
174.	31358610	FEDERAL NATL MTG ASSN	0.5	0.2	1.34	-0.006	-0.05	1.0	0.0	0.0	0.7
175.	31409910	FEDERATED DEPT STORES	0.5	0.0	1.09	—	—	0.0	0.0	0.0	0.9
176.	31540510	FERRO CORP	0.0	0.0	1.43	0.060	0.58	0.0	0.0	0.0	0.1
177.	31644110	FIDELITY UN LIFE INS	0.0	0.0	1.37	-0.087	-0.45	0.0	0.0	0.0	0.0
178.	31846410	FIRST ALA BANCSHARES	0.0	0.0	1.09	-0.046	-0.43	0.0	0.0	0.0	0.0
179.	31868010	FIRST BANCSHARES FLA	0.0	0.0	0.86	-0.044	0.63	0.0	0.0	0.0	0.0
180.	31974710	FIRST COLONY LIFE INS	0.0	0.0	1.24	0.065	—	0.0	0.0	0.0	0.0
181.	32089110	FIRST MISS CORP	0.0	0.0	1.44	-0.060	0.58	0.0	0.0	0.0	0.0
182.	33155410	FIRST NATL BOSTON CORP	0.1	0.0	0.79	-0.090	-0.88	1.6	0.0	0.0	0.0
183.	33765710	FISCHBACH & MOORE INC	0.0	0.0	1.25	-0.022	0.22	0.0	0.0	0.0	0.0
184.	33781910	FISHER FOODS INC	0.0	0.0	1.18	-0.005	0.05	0.0	0.0	0.0	0.0
185.	33841210	FLAGSHIP BKS INC	0.0	0.0	1.37	-0.022	-0.21	0.0	0.0	0.0	0.0
186.	33909910	FLEETWOOD ENTERPRISES	0.0	0.0	1.42	0.097	0.95	0.0	0.0	0.0	0.0
187.	33913010	FLEMING COS INC	0.2	0.1	0.74	-0.005	-0.05	2.1	0.0	0.0	0.0
188.	33942310	FLIGHTSAFETY INTL INC	0.0	0.0	1.29	-0.138	1.34	0.0	0.0	0.0	0.0
189.	33971110	FLINTKOTE CO	0.3	1.1	1.19	-0.009	-0.08	0.0	0.0	0.0	0.0
190.	33973410	FLOATING POINT SYS INC	0.0	0.0	—	—	—	0.0	0.0	0.0	0.0
191.	34060710	FLORIDA COML BKS INC	0.0	0.0	1.05	-0.038	0.37	0.0	0.0	0.0	0.1
192.	34101810	FLORIDA NATL BKS FLA	0.0	0.0	0.92	-0.042	-0.41	0.0	0.0	0.0	0.0
193.	34109910	FLORIDA POWER CORP	0.1	0.8	0.73	-0.084	-0.81	1.7	0.0	0.0	0.0
194.	34537010	FORD MTR CO DEL	0.6	0.0	1.55	-0.072	-0.70	0.0	0.0	0.0	1.2
195.	35039110	FOTOMAT CORP	0.0	0.0	—	-0.102	-0.99	0.0	0.0	0.0	0.0
196.	35158610	FOX STANLEY PHOTO PROD	0.0	0.0	1.08	0.046	0.45	0.0	0.0	0.0	0.1
197.	35160410	FOXBORO CO	0.0	0.0	1.12	-0.081	0.78	0.0	0.0	0.0	0.0
198.	35868510	FRIONA INDS INC	0.0	0.0	1.39	-0.067	0.65	0.0	0.0	0.0	0.0
199.	35906410	FRONTIER AIRLS INC	0.0	0.0	1.00	0.079	0.77	0.0	0.0	0.0	0.0
200.	36110910	FURR S CAFETERIAS INC	0.0	0.0	—	-0.083	0.81	0.0	0.0	0.0	0.0
201.	36223210	G R I CORP	0.0	0.0	1.73	0.088	0.86	0.0	0.0	0.0	0.2
202.	36473010	GANNETT INC	0.1	0.2	0.90	-0.032	-0.31	0.0	0.0	0.0	0.0
203.	36882010	GENERAL AMERN OIL TEX	0.0	0.0	0.93	-0.024	-0.24	0.0	0.0	0.0	0.0
204.	36915410	GENERAL BINDING CORP	0.0	0.0	1.17	-0.044	-0.43	0.0	0.0	1.3	0.0
205.	36935210	GENERAL CINEMA CORP	0.2	0.0	1.18	0.066	0.64	0.0	0.0	0.0	1.3
206.	36950010	GENERAL DYNAMICS CORP	0.1	0.1	1.34	-0.055	0.53	0.0	0.0	0.0	1.3
207.	36960410	GENERAL ELEC CO	1.2	1.7	0.86	-0.025	-0.24	0.0	2.0	0.0	1.5
208.	37044210	GENERAL MTRS CORP	0.8	2.5	0.81	-0.100	-0.97	0.0	2.6	0.0	0.0
209.	37063910	GENERAL REINS CORP DEL	1.3	0.0	1.37	-0.109	1.06	0.0	0.0	0.0	0.0
210.	37083810	GENERAL SIGNAL CORP	0.0	0.1	1.05	0.072	0.70	0.0	0.0	0.0	1.3

Table 6.9 (continued)

Aggregate and Individual Portfolio Listings
(4/30/79)

CONTRIBUTIONS OF INDIVIDUAL ASSETS TO PORTFOLIO RISK

Portfolio code:

1 Special K
2 Ortho Growth
3 Petite Capital
4 Behemoth Trust

	CUSIP	NAME	PERCENT OF PORTFOLIO VALUE	WEIGHT IN S&P500	BETA	EFFECT OF 1% PURCHASE ON RESID. STDEV	REQUIRED ALPHA	PORT 1	PORT 2	PORT 3	PORT 4	PORT 5	PORT 6
211.	37102810	GENERAL TEL & ELECTRO	0.5	0.6	0.58	-0.109	-1.06	0.0	2.0	0.0	0.0		
212.	37244710	GENRAD INC	0.0	0.0	1.02	0.014	0.14	0.0	0.0	0.0	0.0		
213.	37245110	GENSTAR LTD	0.1	0.1	0.94	0.017	0.16	0.0	0.0	0.0	0.2		
214.	37246010	GENUINE PARTS CO	0.0	0.0	1.54	-0.013	-0.13	0.0	0.0	0.0	0.0		
215.	37465810	GIBRALTAR FIN CP CALIF	0.0	0.0				0.0	0.0	0.0	0.0		
216.	37642410	GLADDING CORP	0.0	0.0	1.38	0.124	1.21	0.0	0.0	0.0	0.1		
217.	38121010	GOLDEN ST FOODS CORP	0.0	0.0	1.09	0.087	0.85	0.0	0.0	0.0	0.1		
218.	38274810	GORDON JEWELRY CORP	0.0	0.0	1.12	0.069	0.67	0.0	0.0	0.0	0.0		
219.	38480201	GRAINGER W W INC	0.1	0.0	0.93	0.023	0.22	0.0	0.0	0.0	0.0		
220.	38823510	GRANTREE CORP	0.0	0.0	1.63	-0.001	-0.01	0.0	0.0	0.0	0.1		
221.	39056810	GREAT LAKES CHEM CORP	0.0	0.0	1.17	0.049	0.48	0.0	0.0	0.0	0.1		
222.	40257810	GULF UTD CORP	0.0	0.0	1.17	0.063	0.61	0.0	0.0	0.0	0.1		
223.	40589110	HALL FRANK B & CO INC	0.2	0.0	1.05	0.079	0.76	2.3	0.0	0.0	0.0		
224.	40621610	HALLIBURTON CO	1.4	0.6	0.98	-0.007	0.06	2.0	0.0	2.7	1.7		
225.	41052210	HANNA MINING CO	0.0	0.0	0.82	-0.021	-0.20	0.0	0.0	0.0	0.0		
226.	41170210	HARDEES FOOD SYS INC	0.0	0.0	1.53	0.092	0.89	0.0	0.0	0.0	0.0		
227.	41269310	HARLAND JOHN H CO	0.0	0.0	0.95	0.073	0.71	0.0	0.0	0.0	0.1		
228.	41334210	HARNISCHFEGER CORP	0.0	0.0	1.39	0.032	0.31	0.0	0.0	0.0	0.0		
229.	41387510	HARRIS CORP DEL	0.5	0.0	1.12	0.055	0.54	0.0	0.0	3.1	0.0		
230.	41619410	HARTE HANKS COMMUN INC	0.0	0.0	1.27	0.080	0.77	0.0	0.0	0.0	0.1		
231.	42220010	HELENE CURTIS INDS INC	0.0	0.0	1.32	0.131	1.28	0.0	0.0	0.0	0.1		
232.	42233610	HELMERICH & PAYNE INC	0.4	0.4	0.94	0.004	0.04	0.0	1.3	0.0	1.3		
233.	42345210	HEWLETT PACKARD CO	1.3	0.4	1.11	0.079	0.77	0.0	2.0	1.3	1.3		
234.	42823610	HEXCEL CORP	1.0	0.0	1.16	0.055	0.54	0.0	0.0	0.0	0.0		
235.	42829010												
236.	42887110	HICKORY FARMS OHIO	0.0	0.0	1.48	0.134	1.30	0.0	0.0	0.0	0.1		
237.	43575810	HOLLY CORP	0.0	0.0	1.11	0.065	0.63	0.0	0.0	0.0	0.1		
238.	43705220	HOME BEN CORP	0.0	0.0	1.19	0.043	0.42	0.0	0.0	0.0	0.1		
239.	43850610	HONEYWELL INC	0.5	0.2	1.22	0.088	0.86	0.0	2.3	0.0	0.0		
240.	44106510	HOSPITAL CORP AMER	0.1	0.1	1.14	0.066	0.64	0.0	0.0	0.0	0.2		

#	CUSIP	Company	a	b	c	d	1	2	3	4
241.	44107410	HOST INTL INC	0.0	1.29	0.072	0.70	0.0	0.0	0.0	0.1
242.	44148810	HOUDAILLE INDS INC	0.0	1.07	0.003	0.03	0.0	0.0	0.0	0.1
243.	44156010	HOUGHTON MIFFLIN CO	0.1	1.02	0.048	0.46	0.0	0.0	0.0	0.1
244.	44175810	HOUSE FABRICS INC	0.0	1.29	0.048	0.47	0.0	0.0	0.0	0.1
245.	44485910	HUMANA INC	0.0	1.45	0.083	0.80	0.0	0.0	0.0	0.1
246.	44562810	HUNT INTL RES CORP	0.0	0.79	0.052	0.51	0.0	0.0	0.0	0.1
247.	44851010	HUYCK CORP	0.0	1.06	−0.024	−0.24	0.0	0.0	0.0	0.0
248.	44926810	IC INDS INC	0.1	1.07	−0.065	−0.63	1.5	0.0	0.0	0.0
249.	44974410	INA CORP	0.2	1.32	0.061	0.59	1.9	0.0	0.0	0.1
250.	45230810	ILLINOIS TOOL WKS INC	0.2	0.93	0.007	0.06	1.0	0.0	0.0	0.1
251.	45272210	IMPERIAL CORP AMER	0.1	1.47	−0.025	−0.24	0.0	0.0	0.0	0.1
252.	45400220	INDEPENDENT LF&ACC INS	0.0	1.19	0.048	0.46	0.0	0.0	0.0	0.1
253.	45674010	INFORMATION INTL INC	0.0	1.26	0.099	0.97	0.0	1.2	0.0	0.0
254.	45814010	INTEL CORP	0.3	1.62	0.161	1.56	2.9	7.3	0.0	0.9
255.	45920010	INTERNATIONAL BUS MACH	7.0	0.80	0.025	0.24	10.0	0.0	0.0	9.9
256.	45950610	INTERNATIONAL FLAV & FRA	0.1	0.87	0.041	0.40	0.0	0.0	0.0	0.1
257.	45988410	INTERNATIONAL HIN & CHEM	0.2	0.95	−0.007	−0.07	2.0	0.0	0.0	0.0
258.	46014610	INTERNATIONAL PAPER CO	0.6	1.01	−0.029	−0.28	0.0	0.0	2.9	0.0
259.	46057810	INTERPACE CORP	0.0	1.02	−0.002	−0.02	0.0	0.0	0.0	0.0
260.	46069010	INTERPUBLIC GROUP COS	0.5	0.98	−0.049	−0.48	0.0	0.0	0.0	0.0
261.	46129010	INVESTMENT ANNUITY INC	0.0	1.83	0.209	2.03	0.0	0.0	0.0	0.1
262.	47024510	JAMES FRED S & CO INC	0.3	1.09	0.080	0.78	2.4	0.0	0.0	0.0
263.	47507010	JEFFERSON PILOT CORP	0.1	1.01	0.060	0.58	1.6	0.0	0.0	0.0
264.	47812410	JOHNS MANVILLE CORP	0.1	1.11	−0.009	−0.09	0.0	0.0	1.8	0.0
265.	47816010	JOHNSON & JOHNSON	0.4	0.74	−0.001	−0.01	0.0	0.0	0.0	0.0
266.	47989810	JONATHAN LOGAN INC	0.0	1.35	0.021	0.20	0.0	0.0	0.0	0.1
267.	48082710	JORGENSEN EARLE M DEL	0.0	0.66	−0.018	−0.18	0.0	0.0	0.0	0.0
268.	48119610	JOY MFG CO	0.1	1.11	−0.014	−0.14	0.0	0.0	0.0	0.0
269.	48258410	K MART CORP	0.5	1.10	−0.020	−0.19	0.0	0.0	0.0	1.2
270.	48309810	KAISER STEEL CORP	0.0	1.29	−0.027	−0.27	0.0	0.0	0.0	0.0
271.	48483610	KANSAS CITY LIFE INS	0.1	1.17	0.083	0.81	0.0	0.0	0.0	0.1
272.	48527810	KANSAS NEB NAT GAS CO	0.0	0.62	−0.072	−0.70	1.6	0.0	0.0	0.0
273.	48674610	CROSS & TRECKER CORP	0.0	1.13	−0.029	−0.28	1.0	0.0	0.0	0.0
274.	48917010	KENNAMETAL INC	0.1	0.90	0.012	0.12	0.0	0.0	0.0	0.1
275.	49350310	KEYSTONE INTL INC	0.1	1.24	0.062	0.60	0.0	0.0	0.0	0.0
276.	49765610	KIRSCH CO	0.0	1.31	0.038	0.37	0.0	0.0	0.0	0.0
277.	49904010	KNIGHT RIDDER NEWSPPRS	0.0	1.04	0.046	0.44	0.0	0.0	0.0	0.1
278.	50023010	KOGER PPTYS INC	0.0	1.29	0.044	0.43	0.0	0.0	0.0	0.1
279.	50419510	LA QUINTA MTR INNS INC	0.0	1.52	0.176	1.71	0.0	0.0	0.0	0.0
280.	51460610	LANCE INC	0.1	0.89	0.005	0.05	0.0	0.0	0.0	0.1

(continued)

Table 6.9 (continued)
Aggregate and Individual Portfolio Listings
(4/30/79)

CONTRIBUTIONS OF INDIVIDUAL ASSETS TO PORTFOLIO RISK

Portfolio code:
1 Special K
2 Ortho Growth
3 Petite Capital
4 Behemoth Trust

#	CUSIP	NAME	PERCENT OF PORTFOLIO VALUE	WEIGHT IN S&P500	BETA	EFFECT OF 1% PURCHASE ON RESID. STDEV	REQUIRED ALPHA	PORT 1	PORT 2	PORT 3	PORT 4	PORT 5	PORT 6
281.	52077610	LAWSON PRODS INC	0.0	0.0	1.07	0.058	0.57	0.0	0.0	0.0	0.1		
282.	52206610	LEASEWAY TRANSN CORP	0.0	0.0	1.19	-0.009	-0.09	0.0	0.0	0.0	0.1		
283.	52253410	LEIGH PROD INC	0.0	0.0	1.20	0.053	0.52	0.0	0.0	0.0	0.0		
284.	52540810	LEISURE GROUP INC	0.0	0.0	0.50	0.204	1.98	0.0	0.0	0.0	0.0		
285.	5266410	LENOX INC	0.3	0.0	1.05	0.023	0.22	2.5	0.0	0.0	0.1		
286.	53037010	LIBERTY CORP S C	0.0	0.0	1.24	0.082	0.80	0.0	0.0	0.0	0.0		
287.	53109010	LIBERTY NATL LIFE INS	0.0	0.0	1.15	0.068	0.66	0.0	0.0	0.0	0.0		
288.	53203210	LIFE INS CO GA	0.1	0.0	1.30	0.081	0.79	0.0	0.0	0.0	0.0		
289.	53220210	LIGGETT GROUP INC	0.0	0.0	0.58	0.035	-0.34	0.0	0.0	0.0	0.1		
290.	53245710	LILLY ELI & CO	1.6	0.6	0.81	0.010	-0.10	0.0	0.0	2.2	2.3		
291.	53276310	LIN BROADCASTING CORP	0.4	0.0	1.33	0.140	1.36	0.0	1.4	0.0	0.0		
292.	54302610	LONGS DRUG STORES INC	0.1	0.0	0.82	0.053	0.51	0.0	0.0	0.0	0.1		
293.	54316210	LORAL CORP	0.1	0.0	1.40	0.153	1.49	0.0	0.0	0.0	0.1		
294.	54385910	LOWES COS INC	0.1	0.0	1.36	0.069	0.67	0.8	0.0	0.0	0.0		
295.	54486110												
296.	54927110	LUBRIZOL CORP	0.1	0.0	0.87	0.033	0.32	0.0	0.0	0.0	0.1		
297.	54956210	LUDLOW CORP	0.0	0.0	1.25	0.025	0.24	0.0	0.0	0.0	0.0		
298.	55265310	MCA INC	0.4	0.1	1.42	0.070	0.68	0.0	1.7	0.0	0.0		
299.	56122930	MALLINCKRODT INC	0.0	0.1	1.06	0.020	0.19	0.0	0.0	0.0	0.0		
300.	56480910	MANUFACTURERS HANOVER	0.2	0.2	0.93	-0.083	-0.81	1.8	0.0	0.0	0.1		
301.	56584510	MARATHON OIL CO	0.4	0.0	1.02	-0.050	-0.49	0.0	1.9	0.0	0.0		
302.	57327510	MARTIN MARIETTA CORP	0.2	0.1	0.94	-0.001	-0.01	2.0	0.0	0.0	0.0		
303.	58033310	MCDERMOTT J RAY	0.1	0.1	1.59	0.045	0.44	0.0	0.0	0.0	0.2		
304.	58016910	MCDONNELL DOUGLAS CORP	0.1	0.2	1.12	0.054	0.53	0.0	0.0	0.0	0.1		
305.	58064510	MCGRAW HILL INC	0.1	0.1	0.97	0.028	0.27	0.0	0.0	0.0	0.2		
306.	58210310	MCLEAN TRUCKING CO	0.1	0.0	1.31	0.014	0.14	1.2	0.0	0.0	0.1		
307.	58055510	MEDTRONIC INC	0.1	0.0	1.50	0.070	0.68	0.0	0.0	0.0	0.1		
308.	58574510	MELVILLE CORP	0.1	0.1	1.11	0.018	0.17	0.0	0.0	0.0	0.2		
309.	58754110	MERCANTILE TEX CORP	0.0	0.0	0.99	-0.036	-0.35	0.0	0.0	0.0	0.0		
310.	58860210	MERCHANTS INC	0.0	0.0	0.98	-0.010	-0.10	0.0	0.0	0.0	0.0		

(continued)

Portfolio code:
1 Special K
2 Ortho Growth
3 Petite Capital
4 Behemoth Trust

#	CUSIP			Company		β			1	2	3	4
311.	58933110	1.3	0.0	MERCK & CO INC	0.8	0.79	0.004	0.02	0.0	1.9	0.0	1.6
312.	59018810	0.0	0.0	MERRILL LYNCH & CO INC	0.0	1.67	0.002	0.04	0.0	0.0	0.0	0.1
313.	59159010	0.0	0.1	METPATH INC	0.2	1.47	-0.158	-1.54	1.6	0.0	0.0	0.0
314.	59583210	0.1	0.0	MIDDLE SOUTH UTILS INC	0.0	0.69	-0.106	-1.03	0.0	1.3	0.0	0.1
315.	59771510	0.0	1.6	MIDLAND ROSS CORP	0.0	0.92	-0.011	-0.10	0.0	0.0	2.4	0.1
316.	59848810	0.0	0.3	MIDWESTERN DISTR INC	0.0	1.60	0.092	0.90	0.0	0.2	0.0	0.0
317.	60063310	0.0	0.3	MILLER WOHL INC	0.0	1.37	0.104	1.01	0.0	1.3	0.0	0.0
318.	60107310	0.3	0.1	MILLIPORE CORP	0.0	1.09	0.056	0.54	0.0	0.0	0.0	0.1
319.	60175310	0.1	0.1	MILTON BRADLEY CO	0.0	1.20	0.069	0.67	0.0	0.0	0.0	0.1
320.	60405910	1.6	1.6	MINNESOTA MNG & MFG CO	1.0	0.89	-0.003	-0.03	0.0	0.0	2.4	2.4
321.	60619110	0.4	1.7	MISSOURI PAC CORP	0.1	1.07	-0.017	-0.17	0.1	0.0	2.4	3.0
322.	60705910	1.7	0.0	MOBIL CORP	1.3	0.80	-0.094	-0.92	0.2	0.0	0.0	0.1
323.	60766210	0.0	0.3	MODERN MERCHANDISING	0.0	1.69	-0.135	-1.31	2.0	0.0	0.0	0.0
324.	60855410	0.3	0.1	MOLEX INC	0.0	1.34	-0.091	-0.89	0.0	1.3	0.0	0.0
325.	60902310	0.1	0.5	MONARCH CAP CORP	0.0	1.18	0.068	0.66	0.0	0.0	2.6	0.1
326.	61166210	0.5	0.0	MONSANTO CO	0.3	1.05	-0.035	-0.34	1.7	0.0	0.0	0.0
327.	61578510	0.0	0.5	MOORE LTD	0.0	0.87	-0.018	-0.18	0.0	0.0	0.0	0.2
328.	61680010	0.5	0.0	MORGAN J P & CO INC	0.3	0.79	-0.086	-0.84	0.0	0.0	0.0	0.0
329.	61971110	0.0	0.5	MOSTEK CORP	0.0	0.92	-0.162	-1.57	0.0	2.1	2.6	0.0
330.	62545510	0.5	0.6	MULTIMEDIA INC	0.0	0.99	0.071	0.69	0.0	0.0	0.0	0.0
331.	62671710	0.6	0.2	MURPHY OIL CORP	0.0	1.13	-0.024	-0.23	0.0	0.0	2.8	0.1
332.	62885010	0.2	0.3	NCH CORP	0.1	1.05	-0.067	-0.65	1.6	0.0	0.0	0.1
333.	62916110	0.3	0.0	NLT CORP	0.1	1.30	-0.075	-0.73	0.0	0.0	0.0	0.7
334.	63512810	0.0	0.1	NATIONAL CAN CORP	0.0	0.94	-0.008	-0.07	0.0	0.0	0.0	0.0
335.	63557810	0.1	0.0	NATIONAL CSS INC	0.0	1.57	0.196	1.90	0.0	0.0	0.0	0.1
336.	63562110	0.0	0.0	NATIONAL DATA CORP	0.0	1.26	0.086	0.84	0.0	0.0	0.0	0.0
337.	63565510	0.0	0.0	NATIONAL DISTILL & CHEM	0.1	0.70	-0.015	-0.14	0.0	0.0	0.0	0.0
338.	63690510	0.0	0.0	NATIONAL MINE SVC CO	0.0	1.46	-0.087	-0.84	0.0	0.0	0.0	0.0
339.	63764010	0.0	0.2	NATIONAL SEMICONDUCTOR	0.0	1.83	-0.149	-1.45	0.0	0.0	0.0	0.1
340.	63765710	0.2	0.0	NATIONAL SVC INDS INC	0.0	0.86	-0.009	-0.09	2.0	0.0	0.0	0.0
341.	63789510	0.0	0.0	NATIONAL STUDENT MKTG	0.0	1.64	0.147	1.43	0.0	0.0	0.0	0.0
342.	63862410	0.0	0.0	NATIONWIDE HOMES INC	0.0	1.44	0.148	1.44	0.0	0.0	0.0	0.0
343.	64144010	0.0	0.1	NEVADA SVGS & LN ASSN	0.0	1.41	-0.085	-0.82	0.0	0.0	0.0	0.0
344.	64417110	0.1	0.2	NEW ENGLAND NUCLEAR CP	0.0	1.26	-0.054	-0.52	0.0	0.0	0.0	0.1
345.	65480410	0.2	0.0	NOBLE AFFILIATES INC	0.0	1.22	-0.021	-0.20	0.0	0.0	0.0	0.3
346.	65840810	0.0	0.6	NORTH CENT AIRLS INC	0.0	1.39	-0.049	-0.47	0.0	0.0	0.0	0.0
347.	66728110	0.6	0.0	NORTHWEST AIRLS INC	0.1	1.31	-0.023	-0.23	0.0	1.5	0.0	0.4
348.	66733210	0.0	0.1	NORTHWEST BANCORPORAT	0.1	0.86	-0.061	-0.59	1.4	0.0	0.0	0.0
349.	66752810	0.1	0.0	NORTHWEST INDS INC	0.1	1.20	-0.037	-0.35	1.8	0.0	0.0	0.0
350.	67014820	0.0	0.0	NOXELL CORP	0.0	1.21	-0.085	-0.83	0.0	0.0	0.0	0.0

Table 6.9 (continued)
Aggregate and Individual Portfolio Listings
(4/30/79)

CONTRIBUTIONS OF INDIVIDUAL ASSETS TO PORTFOLIO RISK

	CUSIP	NAME	PERCENT OF PORTFOLIO VALUE	WEIGHT IN S&P500	BETA	EFFECT OF 1% PURCHASE ON RESID. STDEV	REQUIRED ALPHA	PORT 1	PORT 2	PORT 3	PORT 4	PORT 5	PORT 6
351.	67034610	NUCOR CORP	0.1	0.0	1.30	0.049	0.48	0.0	0.0	0.0	0.1		
352.	67034910	NUCORP INC											
353.	67090110	NUCLEAR METALS INC											
354.	67634610	OGDEN CORP	0.1	0.0	0.85	-0.037	-0.36	0.0	0.0	0.0	0.1		
355.	67660110	OGILVY & MATHER INTL	0.2	0.0	1.15	-0.059	-0.57	0.0	1.0	0.0	0.0		
356.	67724010	OHIO CAS CORP	0.3	0.0	1.26	0.087	0.85	0.0	1.2	0.0	0.0		
357.	68626810	ORION CAP CORP	0.0	0.0	1.16	0.051	0.50	0.0	0.0	0.0	0.0		
358.	68826010	OSHMANS SPORTING GOODS	0.0	0.0	1.42	0.094	0.91	0.0	0.0	0.0	0.0		
359.	69032610	OVERNITE TRANSN CO	0.0	0.0	1.02	-0.009	-0.08	1.8	0.0	0.0	0.0		
360.	69076810	OWENS ILL INC	0.2	0.1	0.79	-0.020	-0.20	1.5	0.0	0.0	0.1		
361.	69332010	PHH GROUP INC	0.3	0.0	1.40	0.113	1.10	0.0	1.2	0.0	0.1		
362.	69350610	PPG INDS INC	0.2	0.1	0.89	-0.042	-0.41	1.8	0.0	0.0	0.0		
363.	69371810	PACCAR INC	0.0	0.0	1.18	-0.018	-0.18	0.5	0.0	0.0	0.0		
364.	69452910	PACIFIC LMBR CO	0.1	0.0	0.88	-0.006	-0.06	0.0	0.0	0.0	0.2		
365.	69764310	PAMIDA INC	0.0	0.0	1.53	-0.092	-0.90	0.0	0.0	0.0	0.0		
366.	69846510	PANHANDLE EASTN PIPE L	0.2	0.1	0.90	-0.065	-0.63	2.2	0.0	0.0	0.0		
367.	69911310	PARADYNE CORP											
368.	70108110	PARKER DRILLING CO	0.3	0.0	1.36	0.044	0.43	0.0	1.4	0.0	0.0		
369.	70109410	PARKER HANNIFIN CORP	0.0	0.0	0.96	0.001	0.01	0.0	0.0	0.0	0.0		
370.	70430110	PAY LESS DRUG ST NWEST	0.0	0.0	0.89	0.062	0.60	0.0	0.0	0.0	0.1		
371.	70431810	PAY N SAVE CORP	0.0	0.0	1.00	0.077	0.75	0.0	0.0	0.0	0.0		
372.	70456210	PEABODY INTL CORP	0.5	0.0	1.22	0.044	0.43	0.0	0.3	0.0	0.1		
373.	70816010	PENNEY J C INC	0.5	0.3	1.03	-0.008	-0.08	0.0	0.0	0.0	0.9		
374.	71383910	PERINI CORP	0.0	0.0	1.03	0.029	0.28	0.0	0.0	0.0	0.1		
375.	71461110	PERRY DRUG STORES INC	0.0	0.0	1.36	-0.128	1.24	0.0	0.0	0.0	0.1		
376.	71643410	PETRIE STORES CORP	0.0	0.0	0.85	-0.013	-0.12	0.0	0.0	0.0	0.1		
377.	71726510	PHELPS DODGE CORP	0.0	0.1	1.23	-0.030	-0.30	0.7	0.0	0.0	0.0		
378.	71800910	PHILADELPHIA SUBN CORP	0.2	0.0	1.04	-0.043	-0.42	2.7	0.0	0.0	0.0		
379.	71816710	PHILIP MORRIS INC	1.3	0.6	0.64	-0.020	-0.20	0.0	1.5	2.8	0.0		
380.	71850710	PHILLIPS PETE CO	0.5	0.8	0.78	-0.096	-0.93	0.0	0.0	2.8	0.0		

Portfolio code:

1 Special K
2 Ortho Growth
3 Petite Capital
4 Behemoth Trust

(continued)

Portfolio code:

1 Special K
2 Ortho Growth
3 Petite Capital
4 Behemoth Trust

#	CUSIP	Company	1	2	3	4					
381.	71937210	PIEDMONT AVIATION INC	0.0	0.0	0.00	0.00	0.000	0.49	0.050	1.71	0.0	0.0
382.	72010110	PIER I IMPORTS INC	0.0	0.0	0.00	0.00	0.000	1.08	0.111	1.31	0.0	0.0
383.	72028010	PIONEER HI BRED INTL	0.0	0.0	0.00	0.00	0.000	0.16	0.016	0.89	0.0	0.0
384.	72368610	PITNEY BOWES INC	0.1	0.1	0.01	0.01	0.000	0.84	0.087	0.87	0.1	0.1
385.	72447910	PITTSBURGH D MOINE STL										
386.	72503810	PITTSTON CO	0.0	0.0	0.00	0.00	0.000	0.18	0.019	1.10	0.0	0.7
387.	72570110	PITTSTON CO	0.0	0.0	0.01	0.01	0.000	-0.23	-0.024	1.11	0.0	0.0
388.	72578610	PITTWAY CORP	0.0	0.0	0.00	0.00	0.000	-0.46	-0.047	1.02	0.0	0.0
389.	73019610	PNEUMO CORP	0.0	0.0	0.02	0.02	0.000	-0.28	0.028	1.05	0.0	1.0
390.	73109510	POLAROID CORP	0.9	0.8	1.0	1.6	1.0	0.88	0.091	1.39	1.6	1.3
391.	73282710	POPE & TALBOT INC	0.0	0.0	0.00	0.00	0.000	0.18	0.019	1.17	0.0	0.1
392.	73762810	POTLATCH CORP	0.1	0.1	0.01	0.00	0.000	-0.03	-0.003	1.02	0.0	0.0
393.	74132610	PRESTON TRUCKING INC	0.0	0.0	0.00	0.00	0.000	0.36	0.037	1.38	0.0	0.0
394.	74155510	PRIME COMPUTER INC	0.2	0.2	1.0	1.0	1.0	2.69	0.277	1.96	2.0	1.0
395.	74271810	PROCTER & GAMBLE CO	0.8	1.0	0.8	0.8	1.0	-0.18	-0.019	0.62	1.0	1.7
396.	74339610	PROLER INTL CORP	0.0	0.0	0.0	0.0	0.0	0.38	0.039	1.32	0.0	0.0
397.	74343710	PROPERTY CAP TR										
398.	74366810	PROTECTIVE LIFE INS CO	0.0	0.0	0.00	0.00	0.000	0.78	0.081	1.07	0.0	0.1
399.	74388910	PROVIDENT LIFE&ACC INS	0.0	0.0	0.00	0.00	0.000	0.83	0.086	1.35	0.0	0.0
400.	74531510	PUGET SOUND NATL BK	0.0	0.0	0.00	0.00	0.000	-0.68	-0.070	0.69	0.0	0.0
401.	74603010	PUNTA GORDA ISLES INC	0.0	0.0	0.00	0.00	0.000	0.99	0.102	1.88	0.0	0.1
402.	74629910	PURITAN BENNETT CORP	0.0	0.0	0.10	1.6	0.000	0.77	-0.079	1.14	0.0	0.0
403.	74741910	QUAKER ST OIL REFNG CP	0.1	0.1	0.00	1.0	3.0	-0.39	-0.040	0.91	0.0	0.0
404.	75086310	RAINIER BANCORPORATION	0.0	0.0	0.00	0.0	3.0	-0.47	-0.048	0.87	0.0	0.3
405.	75460310	RAYCHEM CORP	0.8	0.8	0.8	0.8	0.3	0.89	0.091	1.32	0.0	0.0
406.	75468810	RAYMOND CORP	0.0	0.0	0.2	0.0	0.0	0.65	0.067	1.29	3.5	0.0
407.	75511110	RAYTHEON CO	0.6	0.6	0.2	0.6	0.0	0.67	0.069	1.17	3.5	0.0
408.	75726610	REDCOR CORP										
409.	76133810	REVCO D S INC	0.1	0.1	0.1	0.0	0.0	0.68	0.069	1.07	0.0	0.0
410.	76152510	REVLON INC	0.2	0.2	0.2	0.0	0.3	0.37	0.038	0.91	0.0	0.0
411.	76169510	REYNOLDS & REYNOLDS CO	0.4	0.4	1.6	0.9	0.74	0.074	1.30	0.0	0.0	
412.	76175310	REYNOLDS R J INDS INC	0.2	0.2	1.0	10.0	1.9	-0.53	-0.055	0.53	0.0	0.1
413.	76176310	REYNOLDS METALS CO	0.1	0.1	0.10	0.0	0.0	-0.33	-0.034	1.06	0.0	0.1
414.	76775410	RITE AID CORP	0.2	0.2	2.0	2.0	0.66	0.066	1.02	0.0	0.2	
415.	76973910	ROADWAY EXPRESS INC	0.1	0.1	0.0	0.0	0.0	0.14	0.015	1.29	0.0	0.0
416.	77055310	ROBERTSON H H CO	0.0	0.0	0.00	0.00	0.000	-0.04	-0.004	0.93	0.0	0.1
417.	77570710	ROLLINS BURDICK HUNTER	0.0	0.0	0.10	0.00	0.000	0.93	-0.095	1.14	0.0	0.1
418.	77927310	ROUSE CO	0.1	0.1	0.00	0.00	0.000	0.68	-0.070	1.45	0.0	0.1
419.	77938210	ROWAN COS INC	0.0	0.0	0.00	0.00	0.000	-0.47	-0.048	1.38	0.0	0.0
420.	78108810	RUBBERMAID INC	0.0	0.0	0.00	0.00	0.000	0.30	0.031	1.13	0.0	0.1

Table 6.9 (continued)
Aggregate and Individual Portfolio Listings
(4/30/79)

CONTRIBUTIONS OF INDIVIDUAL ASSETS TO PORTFOLIO RISK

#	CUSIP	NAME	PERCENT OF PORTFOLIO VALUE	WEIGHT IN S&P500	BETA	EFFECT OF 1% PURCHASE ON RESID. STDEV	REQUIRED ALPHA	PORT 1	PORT 2	PORT 3	PORT 4	PORT 5	PORT 6
421.	78224220	RUSS TOGS INC	0.0	0.0	0.91	-0.005	-0.05	0.0	0.0	0.0	0.0		
422.	78349810	RYAN HOMES INC	0.1	0.0	1.22	-0.043	-0.42	1.1	0.0	0.0	0.0		
423.	78354910	RYDER SYS INC	0.1	0.0	1.49	0.067	0.65	0.0	0.0	0.0	0.1		
424.	78462610	SPS TECHNOLOGIES INC	0.1	0.0	1.35	0.021	0.21	0.0	0.0	0.0	0.1		
425.	79345310	ST REGIS PAPER CO	0.2	0.1	1.00	-0.026	-0.26	1.8	0.0	0.0	0.1		
426.	79840710	SAN JUAN RACING ASSN	0.0	0.0	1.46	0.122	1.19	0.0	0.0	0.0	0.0		
427.	79985010	SANDERS ASSOC INC	0.0	0.0	1.32	-0.127	-1.23	0.0	0.0	0.0	0.1		
428.	80202010	SANTA FE INDS INC	0.4	0.2	0.98	-0.061	-0.59	0.0	0.0	0.0	0.8		
429.	80203710	SANTA FE INTL CORP	0.0	0.1	1.45	-0.055	-0.53	0.0	0.0	0.0	0.1		
430.	80449810	SAUNDERS LEASING SYS	0.0	0.0	1.33	0.072	0.70	0.0	0.0	0.0	0.0		
431.	80652710	SCHERER R P CORP	0.0	0.0	1.28	0.072	0.70	0.0	0.0	0.0	0.1		
432.	80660510	SCHERING PLOUGH CORP	0.5	0.2	0.95	0.030	0.30	0.0	0.0	0.0	1.0		
433.	80682310	SCHLITZ JOS BREWING CO	0.0	0.0	1.25	0.035	0.34	0.0	0.0	3.0	0.0		
434.	80685710	SCHLUMBERGER LTD	1.8	1.4	0.77	-0.051	-0.49	0.0	2.5	0.0	1.4		
435.	80709310												
436.	80865510	SCIENTIFIC ATLANTA INC	0.0	0.0	1.44	0.132	1.29	0.0	0.0	0.0	0.0		
437.	80936710	SCOTT & FETZER CO	0.2	0.0	1.16	0.033	0.32	2.0	0.0	0.0	0.1		
438.	80974110	SCOTT FORESMAN & CO DEL	0.4	0.1	0.95	0.045	0.44	0.0	0.0	0.0	0.9		
439.	80987710	SCOTT PAPER CO	0.0	0.1	1.07	-0.020	-0.19	0.0	0.0	0.0	0.1		
440.	81185010	SEAGRAM LTD	0.0	0.2	0.84	0.013	0.13	0.0	0.0	0.0	0.1		
441.	81238710	SEARS ROEBUCK & CO	0.4	1.0	1.02	-0.038	-0.37	0.0	0.0	0.0	0.8		
442.	81524610	SEDCO INC	0.1	0.1	1.31	-0.010	-0.09	0.0	0.0	0.0	0.1		
443.	81758710	SERVICE MERCHANDISE	0.0	0.0	1.52	0.125	1.22	0.0	0.0	0.0	0.1		
444.	81761310	SERVICEMASTER INDS INC	0.1	0.0	0.89	0.054	0.52	0.0	0.3	0.0	0.0		
445.	81948610	SHARED MED SYS CORP	0.0	0.0	1.13	0.187	1.82	0.0	0.0	0.0	0.1		

Portfolio code:

1 Special K
2 Ortho Growth
3 Petite Capital
4 Behemoth Trust

No.	CUSIP	Name						1	2	3	4
446.	82503910	SHONEYS INC	0.0	0.4	1.15	0.099	0.96	0.0	0.0	0.0	0.0
447.	82662210	SIGNAL COS INC	0.0	0.0	1.08	0.045	0.44	0.0	2.0	0.0	0.0
448.	82867510	SIMMONDS PRECISION PRO	0.0	0.1	1.43	0.134	1.30	0.0	0.0	0.0	0.0
449.	83083010	SKYLINE CORP	0.5	0.0	0.97	0.090	0.88	0.0	0.0	0.0	0.0
450.	83237710	SMITHKLINE CORP	1.2	0.4		0.031	0.30	2.5	3.5	0.0	0.0
451.	83563610	SONOMA VINEYARDS	0.0	0.0	1.21	0.163	1.59	0.0	0.0	0.0	0.0
452.	83704610	SOUTH CAROLINA NATL CP	0.3	0.1	0.82	-0.055	-0.54	0.0	0.0	1.8	0.0
453.	84345610	SOUTHERN NAT RES INC	0.5	0.0	0.89	-0.043	-0.43	0.0	2.3	0.0	0.0
454.	84367310	SOUTHERN RY CO	0.0	0.0	0.99	-0.052	-0.50	0.0	0.0	0.0	0.0
455.	84484810	SOUTHWEST FLA BKS INC	0.0	0.0		-0.048	-0.46	0.0	0.0	0.0	0.0
456.	84679010	SPARTAN FOOD SYS INC	0.0	0.0	1.46	0.153	1.49	0.0	0.0	0.0	0.0
457.	84756710	SPECTRA PHYSICS INC	0.1	0.1	1.64	0.160	1.55	0.0	0.0	0.0	0.1
458.	85220610	SQUARE D CO	0.1	0.0	0.94	-0.043	-0.12	0.0	0.0	0.0	0.0
459.	85315610	STANDARD BRANDS PAINT	0.0	0.1	1.19	-0.045	-0.43	0.0	0.0	0.0	0.0
460.	85370010	STANDARD OIL CO IND	0.2	1.4	0.65	-0.118	-1.14	2.0	0.0	0.0	0.0
461.	85373410	STANDARD OIL CO OHIO	0.5	0.0	0.96	-0.047	-0.46	0.0	0.0	2.0	0.8
462.	85772110	STAUFFER CHEM CO	0.4	0.2	1.02	-0.011	-0.22	0.0	0.0	0.0	0.0
463.	85926410	STERLING DRUG INC	0.0	0.0	0.90	-0.023	-0.73	0.0	0.0	0.0	0.0
464.	86034210	STEWART & STEVENSON SVCS	0.7	0.0	1.26	-0.075	2.73	0.0	0.0	0.0	0.0
465.	86211110	STORAGE TECHNOLOGY CP	0.7	0.0	1.71	0.212	2.06	0.0	3.8	0.0	0.0
466.	86213110	STORER BROADCASTING CO	0.5	0.0	1.00	0.042	-0.41	0.0	2.9	0.0	0.0
467.	86447310	SUBURBAN PROPANE GAS	0.2	0.0	0.84	-0.051	-0.49	1.9	0.0	0.0	0.0
468.	86663510	SUN BANKS FLA INC	0.0	0.2	1.08	-0.043	-0.42	0.0	0.0	0.0	0.1
469.	86827310	SUPERIOR OIL CO	0.0	0.0	1.00	-0.023	-0.22	0.0	0.0	0.0	0.0
470.	87182910	SYSCO CORP	0.0	0.1	1.07	-0.042	-0.41	0.0	0.0	0.0	0.0
471.	87205610	SYSTRON DONNER CORP	0.0	0.0	1.56	0.149	1.45	0.0	0.0	0.0	0.0
472.	87468710	TALLEY INDS INC	0.0	0.0	0.98	0.025	0.25	0.0	0.0	0.0	0.0
473.	87537010	TANDEM COMPUTERS INC	0.2	0.1	1.66	0.212	2.00	0.0	0.0	1.0	0.0
474.	87913110	TEKTRONIX INC	0.7	0.1	1.17	0.094	0.92	2.0	4.0	0.0	0.0
475.	87943110										
476.	88034510	TENNANT CO	0.0	0.0	0.96	0.026	0.25	0.0	0.0	0.0	0.0
477.	88059310	TENNESSEE VALLEY BNCP	0.0	0.0	0.96	-0.046	-0.45	0.0	0.0	0.0	0.0
478.	88160910	TESORO PETE CORP	0.0	0.1	1.33	-0.010	-0.18	0.0	0.0	1.7	0.0
479.	88169410	TEXACO INC	0.1	1.0	0.69	-0.121	-1.18	0.0	0.0	0.0	0.0
480.	88214710	TEXAS AMERN BANCSHARES	0.0	0.0	0.94	-0.041	-0.40	0.0	0.0	0.0	0.0

(continued)

Table 6.9 (concluded)
Aggregate and Individual Portfolio Listings
(4/30/79)

CONTRIBUTIONS OF INDIVIDUAL ASSETS TO PORTFOLIO RISK

Portfolio code:

1 Special K
2 Ortho Growth
3 Petite Capital
4 Behemoth Trust

	CUSIP	NAME	PERCENT OF PORTFOLIO VALUE	WEIGHT IN S&P500	BETA	EFFECT OF 1% PURCHASE ON RESID. STDEV	REQUIRED ALPHA	PERCENT OF PORTFOLIO VALUE IN					
								PORT 1	PORT 2	PORT 3	PORT 4	PORT 5	PORT 6
481.	88250810	TEXAS INSTRS INC	0.7	0.3	1.15	0.061	0.60	0.0	0.9	0.0	1.3		
482.	88259310	TEXAS OIL & GAS CORP	0.1	0.1	1.20	0.009	0.09	0.0	0.0	0.0	0.1		
483.	88288710	TEXAS GULF INC	0.1	0.1	0.95	-0.025	-0.25	1.6	0.0	0.0	0.0		
484.	88320310	TEXTRON INC	0.1	0.1	1.10	-0.022	-0.22	0.0	0.0	0.0	0.0		
485.	88410210	THIOKOL CORP	0.1	0.0	1.22	-0.057	-0.55	0.0	0.0	0.0	0.1		
486.	88442510	THOMAS INDS INC	0.4	0.0	1.07	0.056	0.55	0.0	0.0	0.0	0.1		
487.	88475310	THOMPSON J WALTER CO	0.5	0.0	1.10	0.047	0.46	0.0	0.0	2.1	0.0		
488.	88673510	TIGER INTL INC	0.5	0.0	1.56	0.044	0.43	0.0	0.0	2.7	0.0		
489.	88736010	TIMES MIRROR CO	0.1	0.1	0.99	0.030	0.29	0.0	0.0	0.0	0.2		
490.	89289210	TRANE CO	0.7	0.0	1.04	0.015	0.15	0.0	0.0	0.0	1.4		
491.	89355310	TRANSCON LINES	0.0	0.0	1.15	-0.012	-0.12	0.0	0.0	0.0	0.0		
492.	89382510	TRANSOCEAN OIL INC	0.0	0.0	0.86	-0.009	-0.09	0.0	0.0	0.0	0.1		
493.	09664810												
494.	90238410	TYMSHARE INC	0.4	0.0	1.40	0.208	2.02	0.0	1.6	0.0	0.6		
495.	90255010	UAL INC	0.6	0.1	1.44	0.018	0.18	0.0	1.1	0.0	0.6		
496.	90342210	UV INDS INC	0.0	0.0	1.59	0.038	0.37	0.0	0.0	0.0	0.1		
497.	90957210	UNITED BANKS COLO INC	0.0	0.0	0.83	-0.063	-0.62	0.0	0.0	0.0	0.0		
498.	90966010	UNITED BRANDS CO	0.0	0.0	1.04	-0.016	-0.16	0.0	0.0	0.0	0.0		
499.	91067110	UNITED INDL CORP	0.0	0.0	1.21	-0.098	-0.95	0.0	0.0	0.0	0.0		
500.	91148510	UNITED SVCS LIFE INS	0.0	0.0	1.17	-0.079	0.77	0.0	0.0	0.0	0.0		
501.	91159610	U S BANCORP	0.0	0.0	0.89	-0.050	-0.49	0.0	0.0	0.0	0.0		
502.	91206110	U S HOME CORP	0.0	0.0	1.68	-0.064	-0.63	0.0	0.0	0.0	0.1		
503.	91212510	UNITED STATES LSG INTL	0.1	0.0	1.51	-0.005	-0.05	0.0	0.0	0.0	0.1		
504.	91265510	UNITED STATES STL CORP	0.3	0.3	1.05	-0.062	-0.60	0.0	0.0	0.0	0.6		
505.	91277510	UNITED STATES TOB CO	0.0	0.0	0.52	-0.012	-0.11	0.0	0.0	0.0	0.1		

#	CUSIP	Name						1	2	3	4
506.	91284310	U S TRUCK LINES DEL	0.5	0.2	0.82	-0.040	-0.39	0.0	0.0	0.0	0.1
507.	91391710	UNITED TECHNOLOGIES CP	0.5	0.0	0.97	-0.040	-0.39	0.0	0.0	0.0	1.0
508.	91326610	UNITOG CO	0.0	0.0	1.02	-0.060	-0.58	0.0	0.0	0.0	0.1
509.	91831410	VSI CORP	0.0	0.0	0.91	-0.005	-0.05	0.0	0.0	0.0	0.1
510.	91979610	VALLEY NB ARIZ PHOENIX	0.0	0.0	0.96	-0.060	-0.58	0.0	0.0	0.0	0.1
511.	92022610	VALLEYLAB INC	0.0	0.0	1.28	0.160	1.56	0.0	0.0	0.0	0.0
512.	92238110	VAUGHAN JACKLIN CORP	0.0	0.0	1.38	0.091	0.89	0.0	0.0	0.0	0.0
513.	92552610	VIACOM INTL INC	0.5	0.0	1.60	0.142	1.38	0.0	0.0	2.9	0.0
514.	92628610	VICTORIA STA INC	0.0	0.0	1.67	0.151	1.46	0.0	0.0	0.0	0.0
515.	93114210	WAL MART STORES INC	0.6	0.0	1.27	0.092	0.89	0.0	2.2	0.0	0.1
516.	93235510	WALLACE MURRAY CORP	0.0	0.0	1.07	-0.003	-0.03	0.0	0.0	0.0	0.0
517.	93339620	WANG LABS INC	0.4	0.0	1.39	0.192	1.87	0.0	1.7	1.3	0.0
518.	93964010	WASHINGTON POST CO	0.2	0.0	0.98	-0.063	-0.61	0.0	0.0	1.0	0.0
519.	94106310	WASTE MGMT INC	0.0	0.0	1.14	0.080	0.78	0.0	0.0	0.0	0.0
520.	94412410	WAXMAN INDS INC	0.0	0.0	1.67	0.113	1.09	0.0	0.0	0.0	0.0
521.	95788610	WESTERN AIR LINES INC	0.0	0.1	1.49	-0.009	0.09	0.0	0.0	0.0	0.1
522.	95768810	WESTERN BANCORPORATION	0.0	0.0	0.87	-0.086	-0.84	0.0	0.0	0.0	0.1
523.	95804310	WESTERN CO NORTH AMER	0.0	0.0	1.40	-0.039	-0.38	0.0	0.0	0.0	0.0
524.	96289820	WHEELABRATOR FRYE INC	0.4	0.0	1.15	0.029	0.28	0.0	2.3	0.0	0.0
525.	96822310	WILEY JOHN & SONS INC	0.0	0.0	0.90	0.074	0.72	0.0	0.0	0.0	0.0
526.	96913310	WILLAMETTE INDS INC	0.0	0.1	1.01	-0.001	-0.01	0.0	0.0	0.0	0.1
527.	97945710	WILLIAMS COS	0.1	0.0	1.07	-0.004	-0.04	0.0	0.0	0.0	0.1
528.	97738510	WITCO CHEM CORP	0.2	0.0	0.79	-0.060	-0.58	0.0	2.3	0.0	0.1
529.	98040010	WOODS PETE CORP	0.0	0.0	1.39	-0.049	-0.47	0.0	0.0	0.0	0.1
530.	98142310	WORLD AWYS INC	0.0	0.0	1.51	0.085	0.83	0.0	0.0	0.0	0.0
531.	98213510	WRATHER CORP	0.0	0.0	1.56	0.186	1.81	0.0	0.0	0.0	0.0
532.	98421410	WYOMING BANCORPORATION	0.3	0.7	1.11	-0.040	0.39	0.0	0.0	0.0	0.0
533.	98412010	XEROX CORP	0.3	0.0	0.95	0.059	0.58	0.0	0.0	0.0	0.0
534.	98515410	YELLOW FGHT SYS INC	0.0	0.0	1.24	0.013	0.12	0.0	0.0	0.5	0.1
535.	98722210	ZIONS UTAH BANCORP	0.0	0.0	1.16	0.052	0.51	0.0	0.0	0.0	0.0

Summary

We began this chapter by describing the development and structure of a modern master trust system. The important information flows in such a system were diagramed, and the attendant reports issued to the parties involved were outlined. Our next area of concern was the reasoning underlying the choice of multiple managers for a pension plan. This discussion led naturally to the analysis of investment strategies with multiple managers and of ways to coordinate such managers. We considered two elements of this coordination process; the selection of a new manager and the assignment of funds among managers. We concluded with an analysis of an actual portfolio plan with four active managers.

We would like to stress that multiple management is not just hiring another manager. It can be extremely costly, but if properly coordinated, it can be highly beneficial. We suggested in the supplement to Chapter 4 and will prove in the supplement to this chapter that multiple active managers acting with independent information can produce an aggregate portfolio performance (Sharpe ratio) better than can be produced by any of the managers acting alone. This is the best justification for multiple management.

It is possible with good-quality measurements to detect many fictions in how a plan is actually being managed. The methods described in the chapter give the plan sponsor a means to evaluate the overall portfolio management process and to make cost-effectiveness judgments regarding the expense incurred to achieve a desired or agreed level of portfolio performance.

While the individual money managers, by owning different securities, may feel strongly that their styles, and therefore their performance results, are independent of one another, it may well be that because of their similar industry emphasis or, even more subtle, their similar common factor emphasis, these managers are not offering the plan sponsor the degree of diversification that was implicitly contracted for when they were hired. As with many other types of human interaction, communication may be the weakest link. The difficulties may arise, not from intentional subterfuge, but from different perceptions of the facts. Better measurement can offer a more uniform understanding of what the facts really are. This is perhaps the greatest contribution of MPT. If the sponsor can better enunciate his aims and money managers can better understand what they are expected to deliver, the resulting more rationalized approach will surely promote better performance by all parties. The key is better coordination.

Further Reading

Very little has been written on the material discussed in this chapter. Two general references which may prove useful are:

Ezra, Don. *Understanding Pension Fund Finance and Investment,* Toronto: Pagurian Press, 1979.

Williams, Arthur. *Managing Your Investment Manager.* Homewood Ill. Dow Jones-Irwin, 1980.

The master trust literature is to be found mainly in practitioner magazines. Although there are a fair-sized number of articles on passive management, to our knowledge there are only two articles, which we list below, on the theory of multiple management.

Catlin, Ephron. "Picking a Master Trustee: A Practical Guide." *Pension World,* September 1978, pp. 35–40.

Cirino, Robert. "The Master Trust Battle Moves into the Shooting Stage." *Institutional Investor,* June 1978, pp. 104–12.

Costa, Michael. *Master Trust: Simplifying Employees Benefit Trust Fund Administration.* New York: American Management Association, 1980.

Willour, David. "Choosing Your Master Trustee . . . ." *Pension World,* September 1978, pp. 56–62.

Passive Management in a Multiple Manager Environment

Belliveau, Nancy. "The Fear of Market Inventory Funds." *Institutional Investor,* May 1978, pp. 84–92.

Ferguson, Robert. "Do Market Inventory Funds Really Make Sense?" *Financial Analysts Journal,* May–June 1978, pp. 38–45.

Tierney, David. "The Marriage of Judgement and Technology: The Second, the Potent Generation of "Index' Funds." Presentation to the Eighth Annual American Pension Conference, January 11, 1980.

Wagner, Wayne, and Carol Zipkin. "Can Inventory Index Funds Improve Active Equity Performance?" *Financial Analysts Journal,* May–June 1978, pp. 34–36, 68–76.

Theory of Multiple Management

Rosenberg, Barr. "Institutional Investment with Multiple Portfolio Managers." *Proceedings of the Seminar on the Analysis of Security Prices,* University of Chicago, November 1977, pp. 55–160.

Sharpe, William F. "Decentralized Investment Management." Presidential address to the American Finance Association Meetings, Denver, Colorado, September 1980.

_S_upplement 6

The Mathematics of Multiple Management[1]

In this supplement we will analyze the problem of multiple management. As indicated in Chapter 6, the task of coordinating multiple managers is a problem in decentralized decision making. The owner of funds has delegated the responsibility for investing the assets to several investment managers, each of whom is individually accountable for some fraction of the aggregate fund. Ostensibly, these managers are totally independent; they have different offices, perhaps in different cities, perhaps even in different countries. Typically, they do not inform one another of investment decisions to buy or sell before the event.[2] Yet the investment community is fairly tight-knit, information conscious, and highly mobile; there is considerable interaction at societies of security analysts, conferences of portfolio managers, and (for some corporations) quarterly meetings with the sponsor. Most managers have access to more or less the same information (though they may process it differently) and are reasonably homogeneous as regards background and training. In short, every investment community has a Harry's Bar, so it is inconceivable that forecasts and actions, alphas and portfolio holdings are independent among the managers.

Consequently, the sponsor is faced with the task of communicating, not with a stable of independent operators, but with a collection of investment managers who are responding fairly uniformly to roughly the same information, but without any direct interaction among themselves. The central problem is: How does

---

[1]This supplement is partly adapted from Barr Rosenberg, "Institutional Investment with Multiple Portfolio Managers," _Proceedings of the Seminar on the Analysis of Security Prices,_ University of Chicago, November 1977, pp. 55–160.

[2]One exception may be the strategy of option overriding, in which manager A writes call options on the equity portfolio of Manager B. Because "naked" short option positions are not permitted, B has to inform A whenever an equity holding is sold. The actual timing of the notification depends on the managers and varies from just before the transacton to the day after the transaction.

the sponsor cajole the various managers to act so that the aggregate of the individual active portfolios is optimal? We can state the problem more forcefully by recalling that an optimal portfolio is one in which the asset holdings optimally reflect the investor's judgment; the input is the judgment, and the output is the portfolio holdings. In the multiple manager context, without the correct coordination, there is no guarantee that the aggregate portfolio optimally reflects any judgment, let alone the combined judgment of the active managers. As far as the sponsor is concerned, the inputs are the portfolio holdings from each of the managers (reflecting each manager's judgment) and the output is the holdings in the aggregate portfolio. Typically, there is no check of whose judgments are consistent with this final portfolio.

A useful paradigm, which indicates the degree of optimality of sponsor coordination, is the equivalent centralized decision-making process. Now the managers simply submit recommended transactions to the sponsor, who aggregates the judgments and trades in response to the combined forecasts. It is clear that as far as utilizing information is concerned this multiple adviser process is far superior to hiring multiple investment managers because the aggregate portfolio always reflects the combined judgment of the advisers. The question is, How can the sponsor coordinate the stable of managers in such a way that they automatically construct portfolios which aggregate to the portfolio that the sponsor would have constructed in the multiple adviser format?

To gain some insight into this problem, we will examine one of the simpler decisions in order to study the form of coordination required to construct optimal aggregate portfolios.

A Demonstration of the Difficulty of Multiple Management

For this demonstration, consider the (comparatively) simple exercise of setting the optimal beta policy.[3] We will make several simplifying assumptions—the implication being that if the coordination is complicated given these assumptions, then sponsors should exercise considerable care in delegating responsibility to multiple managers. The assumptions (in addition to the usual linear mean-variance utility assumptions made throughout) are given below:[4]

1. There are two managers
2. The two managers and the sponsor agree on the long-term expectation and variance of market excess return (i.e., on $E_M - i_F$ and V_M).

---

[3]The determination of the optimal beta policy was discussed in the Chapter 5 section "Market Timing."

[4]Assumption 2 is likely to be approximately true in the real world. Assumptions 3 and 4 require that the manager and sponsor portfolios satisfy equations (5–3) and (5–4). Assumption 1 is genuinely simplifying: more managers will only complicate the form and not the substance of the results.

3. The two managers each act optimally.
4. The aggregate portfolio is optimal.

Our aim is to find the conditions which are implied by assumption 4.

We will use the subscript j to refer to manager j ($j = 1,2$) and the subscript A to refer to the aggregate portfolio. The other notation is as follows:

β_{N_j} and β_{N_A}	The portfolio normal beta
$\Delta\beta_j$ and $\Delta\beta_A$	The difference between the normal beta and the portfolio beta (as a result of the market forecast)
a_j and a_A	The market forecast
λ_j and λ_A	Parameters indicating the disutility from variance (risk-aversion parameters)
w_j	The proportion of the aggregate portfolio value controlled by manager j

Since there are only two managers, their fractions under management must sum to the whole:

$$w_1 + w_2 = 1, \tag{S6-1}$$

and from assumption 3 we know that they act optimally (i.e., in agreement with equations (5–3) and (5–4)); so the normal betas and beta deviation are given by:

$$\beta_{N_j} = (E_M - i_F)/2\lambda_j V_M; j = 1,2 \tag{S6-2}$$

and

$$\Delta\beta_j = a_j\beta_N/(E_M - i_F)$$
$$= a_j/2\lambda_j V_M; j = 1,2. \tag{S6-3}$$

Further, the aggregate normal beta must be the weighted average of the two portfolio normal betas:

$$\beta_{N_A} = w_1\beta_{N_1} + w_2\beta_{N_2} \tag{S6-4a}$$
$$= (w_1/\lambda_1 + w_2/\lambda_2)(E_M - i_F)/2V_M \tag{S6-4b}$$

after substitution of (S6–2). Now we have assumed that the aggregate portfolio is optimal (assumption 4), so the equation for the aggregate normal beta must be of the same form as equation (5–3) or equation (S6–2) that is:

$$\beta_{N_A} = (E_M - i_F)/2\lambda_A V_M, \tag{S6-5}$$

which gives, when compared with equation (S6–4):

$$1/\lambda_A = w_1/\lambda_1 + w_2/\lambda_2. \tag{S6-6}$$

In words, if each of the managed portfolios and the aggregate portfolio are to be optimal, then it is necessary that there be a relationship between the investor's risk-aversion parameters.[5] The obvious form of coordination which satis-fies equation (S6–6) is for the sponsor to inform the managers of λ_A and re-quire them to use it as the risk/reward trade-off in portfolio construction.

We can summarize these initial results as follows. The sponsor, as a result of an asset allocation model, or some other procedure, determines the normal long-term expectation and variance of the market excess return ($E_M - i_F$ and V_M) and, hence, the normal beta for the aggregate portfolio. The sponsor's risk-aversion parameter is then defined by equation (S6–5)). The sponsor now informs each manager of the three parameters $E_M - i_F$, V_M, and λ_A and is guaranteed that no matter how the proportions under management vary, the aggregate normal beta will be correctly set. Alternatively, the sponsor could assign a normal beta to each manager and then continually monitor the aggre-gate portfolio to confirm that its normal beta is correct. In this case, the obvious choice is for the sponsor to assign the aggregate normal beta as the normal beta for each of the components.

Now let us examine the aggregate portfolio's deviation from the normal beta. This is simply the weighted average of the managed portfolio's beta pol-icies; hence, from (S6–3) we find:

$$\Delta\beta_A = w_1\Delta\beta_1 + w_2\Delta\beta_2 \tag{S6–7}$$
$$= (w_1a_1/\lambda_1 + w_2a_2/\lambda_2)/2V_M$$

Again, from assumption 4, it follows that

$$\Delta\beta_A = a_A/2\lambda_A V_M,$$

or:

$$a_A/\lambda_A = w_1a_1/\lambda_1 + w_2a_2/\lambda_2$$

Substitution of equation (S6–6) permits a further simplication, namely:

$$a_A = ba_1 + (1 - b)a_2, \tag{S6–8}$$

where

$$b = w_1\lambda_2/(w_1\lambda_2 + w_2\lambda_1).$$

In words, if the aggregate portfolio is to optimally reflect "sombody's" judg-ment, then this judgment should be a particular weighted average of the market forecasts of the managers. Further, for the particular policy when the sponsor informs the managers of λ_A (so that $\lambda_A = \lambda_1 = \lambda_2$), then:

$$a_A = w_1a_1 + w_2a_2. \tag{S6–9}$$

Again, in words, if the two managers are acting optimally, and the sponsor's port-folio is optimal, one particular coordination policy is followed, then the com-

---

[5]More precisely, the aggregate risk-acceptance parameter is the weighted average of the man-agers risk-acceptance parameters, where the weights are the proportions of the total fund controlled by each manager. See also Chapter 2, fn. 13.

bined forecast for the market must be given by equation (S6–9), which states that the aggregate forecast is the weighted average of the managers' forecasts. Certainly, the *realized* abnormal market returns must obey a similar equation (i.e., the aggregate realized return is, by definition, the weighted average of the managed portfolio's realized returns), but there is no reason why, at optimality, the forecasts must obey this relationship. We shall prove this by showing that the sponsor can construct portfolios with higher forecasts than are suggested by these equations.

Are equations (S6–8) and (S6–9) the best the sponsor can do? The answer is no, which follows clearly when this organization is compared with the multiple adviser organization. Suppose, for example, that manager 1 is a "clone" of manager 2, so that the forecasts of these two managers are always identical; in particular, let the forecasts at one time be $a_1 = a_2 = a$. Equation (S6–9) indicates that multiple management is the same as the multiple adviser case (the sponsor knowing that the managers are clones acts as if there were only one piece of information) and the aggregate forecast is still the quantity a.

Now suppose that the managers are truly independent and (perhaps because of a history of forecasts) that the sponsor knows they are independent. Further, suppose that on one occasion the two managers again have the same forecast, $a_1 = a_2 = a$. The multiple management organization, equation (S6–9), holds irrespective of intercorrelations between the managers, and the aggregate forecast will still be the quantity a. However, the sponsor acting in the multiple adviser framework will do better because if two independent sources predict the same occurrence, this implies that the occurrence is doubly likely. Hence, the multiple adviser framework can adjust for the intercorrelations between manager forecasts.

Succinctly, a manager's forecast when 100 percent of the funds are under management is viewed quite differently from the same forecast when only a fraction of the total funds are under management. In the latter case, we have to determine how much of the forecast is new information and how much is already incorporated in the other manager's forecasts.

Can the sponsor incorporate sufficient instructions in the coordination process so that the managers will adjust for the dependence between forecasts? To answer this, we need to develop the statistics of combining forecasts.

Optimal Combination of Forecasts

In the Chapter 4 section "Information Content," we showed how to adjust a forecast for information content. There, an analyst determined a forecast $\hat{u}$, for the residual return, u, on a stock. By appealing to the theory of least squares regression and provided that the forecasts were normalized so that the market was neutral and a constant proportion of variance was explained, we found that the best prediction, α, was given by:

$$\alpha = \hat{b}\hat{u}, \tag{S6-10}$$

where $\hat{b}$ is the slope coefficient in a regression equation. The formula for $\hat{b}$ was given in Supplement 1, equation (S1-16) as:

$$\hat{b} = \text{Cov}[u,\hat{u}]/\text{Var}[\hat{u}].$$

How is this formula amended if two analysts forecast the residual return? Intuitively, if the second analyst is a clone of (i.e., perfectly correlated with) the first, then that analysts's forecast adds absolutely no new information and there is no substantive change in equation (S6-10). However, if the second analyst is less than perfectly correlated with the first, then that analyst's forecast provides additional information. In this case, rather than using the simple linear regression shown in Figure 4.10, we have to use a multiple regression equation in the form:

$$u = b_1\hat{u}_1 + b_2\hat{u}_2 + e$$

to determine two adjustment factors, $\hat{b}_1$ and $\hat{b}_2$, which are applied to the first and second analysts' forecasts, $\hat{u}_1$ and $\hat{u}_2$, respectively. In this case, we will end up with a combined prediction given by:

$$\alpha = \hat{b}_1\hat{u}_1 + \hat{b}_2\hat{u}_2, \tag{S6-11}$$

and the explanatory power of the resultant alpha will be increased relative to the single analyst's alpha, provided the two analysts are not perfectly positively correlated.

The general formula for $\hat{b}_1$ and $\hat{b}_2$ can be found in most statistics books.[6] To save space, we will simply state a specific theorem on forecasting using the notation and special inforamtion (i.e., that $E(u) = E[\hat{u}] = 0$) that we know pertain to our problem, and leave the general theory to interested readers. Unfortunately, the easiest representation of this material requires matrix algebra.

Theorem

1. Let $\hat{u}$ be a vector of forecasts of returns which are to be employed in constructing an optimal prediction of the actual return vector u. Then this optimal (minimum mean-square error, linear, unbiased) prediction, α, is given by:

$$\alpha = C'D^{-1}\hat{u},$$

where C is the covariance matrix between the forecast returns, $\hat{u}$, and the actual returns, u and D is the variance matrix of the forecast returns, $\hat{u}$.

2. The variance of the optimal prediction, α, denoted by the matrix A, equals its covariance with the actual returns vector, $\hat{u}$. In other words, $A = \text{Var}[\alpha] = \text{Cov}[\alpha,u] = C'D^{-1}C$.

3. The variance, V, of the actual returns, u, equals the sum of the mean-

---

[6]See., e.g., J. Johnson, *Econometric Methods* New York: McGraw-Hill, 1972), chap. 5.

square-error matrix, M, for the optimal prediction, α, and the explained variance matrix, A. That is:

$$\text{Var}[u] = V = M + A,$$

where

$$M = E[(u - \alpha)(u - \hat{\alpha})'].$$

Discussion and Explanation of Theorem

Consider the implications of the theorem for forecasts by two managers for a single asset return. The first result states that:

$$\alpha = \{\text{Cov}[\hat{u}_1, u] \ \text{Cov}[\hat{u}_2, u]\} \begin{bmatrix} \text{Var}[\hat{u}_1] & \text{Cov}[\hat{u}_1, \hat{u}_2] \\ \text{Cov}[\hat{u}_2, \hat{u}_1] & \text{Var}[\hat{u}_2] \end{bmatrix}^{-1} \begin{bmatrix} \hat{u}_1 \\ \hat{u}_2 \end{bmatrix}$$
$$= \hat{b}_1 \hat{u}_1 + \hat{b}_2 \hat{u}_2,$$

where

$$\hat{b}_1 = \frac{\text{Cov}[\hat{u}_1, u] \ \text{Var}[\hat{u}_2] - \text{Cov}[\hat{u}_2, u] \ \text{Cov}[\hat{u}_2, \hat{u}_1]}{\text{Var}[\hat{u}_1] \ \text{Var}[\hat{u}_2] - \text{Cov}[\hat{u}_1, \hat{u}_2] \ \text{Cov}[\hat{u}_2, \hat{u}_1]} \quad (S6\text{--}12)$$

and a similar expression exists for $\hat{b}_2$. The second and third results show that the variance of the optimal prediction takes a particular mathematical form and that the explained variance is equal to the variance of α. The explained variance, as its name suggests, represents the amount of uncertainty in the return, u, explained by the prediction; it is the basic measure of forecast quality. Now if we drop manager 2 (so that a single manager is forecasting one asset return), then the theorem indicates that $\hat{b}_1 = \text{Cov}[\hat{u}_1, u]/\text{Var}[\hat{u}_1]$, which is the same result as was obtained earlier. (This also follows from equation (S6–12) by dividing the top and bottom by $\text{Var}[\hat{u}_2]$ and then setting all terms with a subscript 2 equal to zero.) The second result from the theorem states that the explained variance is given by:

$$\text{Var}[\alpha] = \text{Cov}[\alpha, u] = \text{Cov}^2[\hat{u}_1, u]/\text{Var}[\hat{u}_1]$$
$$= \text{Var}[u]\rho^2,$$

where ρ is the correlation coefficient between the forecast, $\hat{u}_1$, and the subsequent return, u, and we used equation (S1–8) in the last step. The third result shows that the mean-square error of the forecast is $\text{Var}[u](1 - \rho^2)$. The intuition of these last two results is that in the absence of a forecast the investor bears risk $\text{Var}[u]$. However, the forecast explains some variance ($\text{Var}[u]\rho^2$), so that the actual uncertainty faced by the investor is $\text{Var}[u](1 - \rho^2)$, which is less than the risk in the absence of forecasting ability. The investor faces no risk in the unlikely (at least in finance) event that the forecast is perfectly correlated with the actual return, since the investor then knows all the relevant information regarding the future.

With this material as background, we can return to the determination of the optimal beta policy. We will consider this decision initially in the multiple adviser organization and then in the multiple manager organization.

Optimal Beta Policy in a Multiple Adviser Context

As before, let $E_M - i_F$ and V_M be the long-term expectation and variance of market excess return, which both managers and sponsor agree upon. The random market excess return over some period is r_M, so the "residual" or unexpected market return which the managers are attempting to forecast is $u = r_M - (E_M - i_F)$; their forecasts are $\hat{u}_1$ and $\hat{u}_2$. Notice that the mean of the unexpected return is zero and the variance is V_M.[7] Using the procedure outlined in the Chapter 4 section "Information Content," both managers convert their respective forecasts into their optimal predictions, a_1 and a_2, which have the variances $\text{Var}[a_1]$ and $\text{Var}[a_2]$. Since these are optimal predictions, $\text{Var}[a_j] = \text{Cov}[a_j, u] \equiv q_j$ $(j = 1,2)$, where the quantity q_j also represents the explained variance of the predictions; that is, $q_j = V_M \rho_j^2$, where ρ_j is the correlation between the forecast and the subsequent return for manager j. This follows from the second part of the theorem.

We have indicated above that although a_1 and a_2 are constructed without direct collusion between the managers, the information set upon which both are acting and the research methods which they are both likely to be using are highly correlated, implying that a_1 and a_2 are likely to be related. Let c denote the covariance between a_1 and a_2, so that the variance matrix of the manager's optimal predictions is given as follows:

$$\text{Var}\begin{bmatrix} a_1 \\ a_2 \end{bmatrix} = \begin{bmatrix} \text{Var}[a_1] & c \\ c & \text{Var}[a_2] \end{bmatrix}$$

$$= \begin{bmatrix} q_1 & c \\ c & q_2 \end{bmatrix}$$

This matrix was denoted by D in the theorem.

We now have all the data necessary to construct the sponsor's optimal prediction, a_A, using both managers' predictions, a_1 and a_2, in the multiple adviser organization. All that is required is to associate the variables in this example with those used in the theorem. Matrix D has already been computed; the forecast vector u is (a_1, a_2), which, in this case, has elements that are optimal predictions themselves; and matrix C, the covariance between the realization and input predictions, is simply $(q_1\ q_2)$. Hence, the theorem states:

---

[7] $E[u] = E[r_M] - (E_M - i_F) = E_M - i_F - (E_M - i_F) = 0.$ $\text{Var}[u] = \text{Var}[r_M] = V_M.$

$$a_A = (q_1 \; q_2)' \begin{bmatrix} q_1 & c_2 \\ c & q_2 \end{bmatrix}^{-1} \begin{bmatrix} a_1 \\ a_2 \end{bmatrix}$$

$$= (q_1 \; q_2)' \begin{bmatrix} q_2 & -c \\ -c & q_1 \end{bmatrix} \begin{bmatrix} a_1 \\ a_2 \end{bmatrix} /(q_1 q_2 - c^2)$$

$$= b_1 a_1 + b_2 a_2, \tag{S6–13}$$

where

$$b_1 = q_2(q_1 - c)/(q_1 q_2 - c^2)$$

and

$$b_2 = q_1(q_2 - c)/(q_1 q_2 - c^2).$$

Notice that this is in almost exactly the same form as equation (S6–8), but here there is no requirement that $b_1 + b_2 = 1$. This makes intuitive sense. For instance, if the best predictions that the managers can come up with bear absolutely no relation to what subsequently happens (i.e., both managers explain zero variance so that all the uncertainty of the market remains, or, alternatively phrased, the covariance between the prediction and the realization is zero, implying that $q_1 = q_2 = 0$), then the optimal combined prediction has no explanatory power and we would expect both weights to be zero. Setting $q_j = 0$ ($j = 1,2$) into the definition for b_1, b_2 shows that this is the case.

Some other special cases are also interesting. If both managers have the same explanatory power, then $q_1 = q_2 = q$, in which case $b_1 = b_2 = q(q - c)/(q^2 - c^2) = q/(q + c)$, provided $q \neq c$. Again, this confirms the intuition that if the managers are equally accurate, then the same weight should be placed on their predictions. How does the covariance between the manager's forecasts affect the combined prediction? If the managers are truly independent, then $c = 0$ and $b_1 = b_2 = 1$, so that $a_A = a_1 + a_2$. At first glance, this conclusion may seem somewhat worrisome. However, it simply states that the best combined prediction from two independent predictions is their sum. For example, if both managers have predictions that $a_1 = a_2 = 10\%$, then the combined prediction is $a_A = 20\%$. Why not average the two manager predictions? Recall that both predictions are the best that can be formed given the information content of the managers (i.e., the predictions are purged of noise) and that there are two managers, who are acting independently, which serves to reduce the uncertainty further. Thus, the optimal combination is better than the average.

For some readers the theorem may be easier to understand when it is expressed in terms of correlations. We have already expressed the explained variance of the managers as: $\text{Var}[a_j] = q_j = V_M \rho_j^2$, where ρ_j is the correlation between the jth manager's forecast and the subsequent return. The covariance between predictions is: $c = \text{Cov}[a_1, a_2] = \pi_{12}\sqrt{(\text{Var}[a_1] \; \text{Var}[a_2])} = \pi_{12} V_M \rho_1 \rho_2$, where π_{12} is the correlation between the predictions from manager

1 and manager 2. When these values are substituted into equation (S6–13), we find:

$$a_A = b_1 a_1 + b_2 a_2, \qquad \text{(S6–13a)}$$

where

$$b_1 = (\rho_1 - \pi_{12}\rho_2)/\rho_1(1 - \pi_{12}^2)$$

and

$$b_2 = (\rho_2 - \pi_{12}\rho_1)/\rho_2(1 - \pi_{12}^2).$$

This formulation shows quite clearly that the b's depend on how skillful the managers are (i.e., ρ_1 and ρ_2) and on the redundancy between the managers (i.e., π_{12}). Because of this, the weights, b_1 and b_2, are called *dependence-adjustment factors* (DAFs). The intuition is that the sponsor should not treat the prediction from a manager at face value, but rather should adjust it for dependence with the predictions of the other managers. Thus, as far as the sponsor is concerned, the prediction from the jth manager is really $b_j a_j$.

Since both managers have some information content in their forecasts, the uncertainty which they and the sponsor have with regard to the market is less than V_M. How much less? The second part of the theorem provides the answer. Let q_A denote the variance of the combined prediction; i.e., $q_A = \text{Var}[a_A] = \text{Cov}[a_A, u]$. A little algebra shows that:

$$q_A = q_1 b_1 + q_2 b_2, \qquad \text{(S6–14)}$$

or, in terms of correlations,

$$q_A = V_M(\rho_1^2 b_1 + \rho_2^2 b_2). \qquad \text{(S6–14a)}$$

Recall from equation (S1–17) that the R-squared (coefficient of determination) is the ratio of the explained variance to the total variance. Let ρ_A^2 be the R-squared of the combined prediction, then:

$$\rho_A^2 = q_A/V_M = \rho_1^2 b_1 + \rho_2^2 b_2. \qquad \text{(S6–15)}$$

The benefit to the sponsor of multiple advisers is clear. The R-squared of the predictions from managers 1 and 2 is ρ_1^2 and ρ_2^2, respectively. Provided b_1 and b_2 are sufficiently positive, the sponsor is far better off with two managers than with one. Hence, the unexplained variance is given by:

$$\text{Var}[u - a_A] = V_M - q_A \qquad \text{(S6–16)}$$
$$= V_M(1 - \rho_A^2),$$

after substituting equation (S6–15). This is the effective level of systematic variance faced by the sponsor, and it is less than the market variance by the amount of information contained in the combined market forecast. All three parties agree on the long-term variance for the market, V_M. However, none of them actually experience this risk; they only experience the unexplained variance.

With this combined prediction for the market forecast we are now in a position to determine the beta and the beta deviation for the optimal aggregate portfolio in the multiple adviser organization.

Using a generalization of the model in the Chapter 5 section "Market Timing" to account for the experienced variance, we find that the normal beta for the aggregate portfolio, which is the same as the aggregate portfolio beta when $a_A = 0$, is given by:

$$\beta_{N_A} = (E_M - i_F)/2\lambda_A V_M(1 - \rho_A^2) \tag{S6–17}$$

and that the optimal beta policy, given by equation (5–4), is:

$$\Delta\beta_A = a_A\beta_{N_A}/(E_M - i_F) \tag{S6–18a}$$
$$= a_A/2\lambda_A V_M(1 - \rho_A^2), \tag{S6–18b}$$

where a_A is given by equation (S6–13).

Comparison of these results with those obtained previously shows that the only difference is that both the normal beta and the optimal beta policy have been "expanded" by the inverse of $1 - \rho_A^2$. This factor represents the reduction in variance faced by the sponsor because of the information content of the combined prediction.

This analysis adds another dimension to the analysis contained in the "Market Timing" section of Chapter 5. There we assumed that the market forecast, a_M, carried no associated reduction in variance. Which treatment is correct?

The answer is that theoretically we are correct here; we should have used only the unexplained variance in Chapter 5 in the determination of the optimal beta. For a single manager, however, the difference is negligible. There are several ways to demonstrate this, but perhaps the easiest is to recall that the R-squared is equal to the square of the correlation coefficient between the manager's forecast and the subsequent return. The maximum correlation that any single manager is likely to have is, 0.2, which gives a very small R-squared of 0.04. Hence, for the most talented managers, instead of using V_M, we should have used $0.96V_M$. Since this is such a small difference, it is easier, both expositionally and notationally, to omit the correction.

Can we forget the correction here? From equation (S6–14), the variance explained by the combined prediction is the weighted average of the explained variances of the individual managers' predictions where the weights are the dependence-adjustment factors. The general expression for J managers is:

$$q_A = q_1b_1 + q_2b_2 + \cdots + q_jb_J = \sum_{j=1}^{J} q_jb_j,$$

and

$$\rho_A^2 = \rho_1^2b_1 + \rho_2^2b_2 + \cdots + \rho_j^2b_j = \sum_{j=1}^{J} \rho_j^2b_j.$$

If the sponsor could select several almost independent managers, each of whom makes useful forecasts, then the explained variance, and hence the coefficient of determination, could become quite large. In this case, the unexplained variance, $V_M(1 - \rho_A^2)$, may be significantly smaller than the total variance, V_M. In the multiple manager case, the approximation that $q_A \sim 0$ is really only defensible if the managers either are highly correlated or have a low forecasting ability.[8]

Optimal Beta Policy in a Multiple Manager Context

How should the managers be coordinated by the sponsor so that their actions result in the optimal aggregate portfolio? Our problem is to find those parameters which must be communicated to the managers such that equations (S6-17) and (S6-18) hold in addition to equations (S6-4a) and (S6-7).

The first decision pertains to the normal beta and can be separated into two subcases, depending on whether or not the sponsor assigns the aggregate normal beta to each manager.

Case 1: Each manager operates with aggregate normal beta.

Here the sponsor communicates to each manager either (1) β_{N_A} or (2) $E_M - i_F$, $V_M(1 - \rho_A^2)$, and λ_A, and the manager computes β_{N_A} from equation (S6-17).

Case 2: Not all managers operate with the aggregate normal beta.

Here the sponsor communicates β_{N_j} directly to manager j, and the sponsor bears the responsibility of monitoring to ensure that the aggregate normal beta is correct.

The second decision sets the beta deviation. For comparison purposes we maintain the same two subcases for case 1 as above.

Case 1.1: The manager already knows the aggregate normal beta, so the minimum additional information required is $E_M - i_F$, w_j (the proportion of the total assets controlled by manager j), and b_j (the manager's DAF). The manager forms the ratio $\beta_{N_A}/w_j(E_M - i_F)$, adjusts the prediction, a_j, by the DAF to become $a_j b_j$, and finally sets the beta deviation within the funds under management as $\Delta \beta_j = a_j b_j \beta_{N_A}/w_j(E_M - i_F)$.

Case 1.2: In this case, only w_j and b_j are communicated. The manager forms the risk-aversion parameter which should apply to the funds under management from $\lambda_j = \lambda_A w_j$, then adjusts the prediction for dependence to $a_j b_j$. The beta deviation is now set from $\Delta \beta_j = a_j b_j/2\lambda_j V_M(1 - \rho_A^2)$.

Case 2: The most sensible form of coordination here is for the sponsor

---

[8]For the remainder of this supplement we shall continue to use the unexplained variance, $V_M(1 - \rho_A^2)$. Some readers may find it more comfortable to forget about the adjustment for forecasting ability, which, although technically important, in practice causes only a small change in the results.

to communicate w_j, b_j, λ_A, and $V_M(1 - \rho_A^2)$. The application follows as for Case 1.1.

Realistically, it appears that four or more of the following list of parameters must be communicated by the sponsor to the manager if the manager's actions are to result in the optimal aggregate portfolio:

$E_M - i_F$	Market expected excess return
$V_M(1 - \rho_A^2)$	Unexplained variance of market return under the optimal combination of manager forecasts
β_{N_A}	Aggregate portfolio normal beta
λ_A	Aggregate risk-aversion parameter
β_{N_j}	The normal beta for manager j
w_j	The proportion of the total funds controlled by manager j
b_j	Manager j's DAF

This list may appear unduly confusing, but we can summarize the main points very clearly. There are three essential rules for the optimal coordination of multiple managers; one relates to the setting of the normal beta, and two relate to the market timing decisions.

Rule 1: Somebody must take responsibility for making sure that the individual portfolio normal positions aggregate correctly; 99 times out of 100, that "somebody" is the sponsor.

Rule 2: Each individual manager adjusts the risk-aversion parameter (however gotten) for the proportion of the total funds under his or her management. If the sponsor informs the manager of the aggregate parameter, λ_A, then the manager makes the adjustment to $w_j\lambda_A$. This adjustment causes risk aversion to decrease (since $w_j \leq 1$) and the portfolio to become more aggressive. Intuitively, this is the correction for the diversification effect across the multiple managers.

Rule 3: Every manager adjusts his or her forecasts for dependence. Portfolio decisions should be based on pure information; hence, any commonality must be purged. This adjustment serves to shrink forecasts toward zero and hence makes portfolios less aggressive.

It is reassuring to note that a manager's optimal actions depend upon the fraction of total funds under management and upon the degree of redundancy with other managers. Both factors cause the active manager to set the degree of aggressiveness depending on the environment of the total fund. As we have remarked, investment management firms should not attempt to control their portfolio managers by insisting that all portfolios look like a model account.

To do so omits the correction for the redundancy in judgments (which typically will shrink predictions toward zero because the DAFs will be positive but less than one) and the correction for the proportion of funds under management. The latter correction will reduce risk aversion and hence make the portfolio more aggressive. Thus, the two corrections will be in opposite directions but will cancel each other out only when $w_j = b_j$. The correct procedure is to use the variable aggressiveness optimization technique to construct the optimal portfolio for each client specifically.[9]

Optimal Stock Selection in a Multiple Manager Context

The analysis for stock selection (and factor timing) is very similar to that developed above for the beta policy. It is, of course, more complicated because there is now a decision variable for every asset holding rather than a single variable relating to the beta policy. Hence, we will only sketch the important points, partly as a review of the preceding sections and partly to provide an outline of the decentralized decision-making process.

As before, the paradigm of multiple investment advisers is very useful. In this situation, the sponsor can examine the appraisal premiums of the investment managers (advisers) and the information properties of these forecasts. The sponsor's problem is to combine these forecasts into a single optimal prediction for each asset. This is accomplished by use of the prediction theorem, stated earlier in this supplement, which asserts that the optimal combined prediction is of the form:

$$a_A = \sum_{j=1}^{J} b_j a_j,$$

where the weights, b_j, are the dependence-adjustment factors (DAFs). These DAFs purge the manager's predictions of any redundancy of information between the research processes. These weights, which remove any "double counting" of judgment, are a function of the correlations between managers and the accuracy of the managers' forecasts.

This much is straightforward. The difficult task is to communicate within the multiple management organization so that individual managers operating within their own portfolios invest in such a manner that the sum of their portfolios represents the optimal aggregate portfolio. There are two guiding principles to encourage effective coordination. First, each manager should be informed of his or her DAF, which must be used internally to modify predictions. Second, the fraction of the funds under the control of each manager should be known. This is vital because the manager needs this information is order to correctly adjust for the diversification effect of the multiple managers.

[9]See Case Study 4 in Chapter 5.

Summary

Are we in danger of wandering into the world of esoteric mathematics? Some money managers may argue that adjusting RAPs with DAFs is not going to keep sponsors happy, and sponsors will unequivocably state that the trustees will be far from impressed with the jargon. But the present waste of resources is so staggering that sponsors and trustees are becoming impressed with ideas which increase the efficiency of management. Moreover, the ideas enunciated here require no more information than is currently available. They merely require the thoughtful quantification of the solutions to traditional problems.

The sponsor who desires beneficial active management has always had to search for superior managers and to assess their qualifications and skill. Is there likely to be an easy solution? Is there a consultant with access to *the* list of talented managers? No, because if there were a simple rule for locating superior managers, then every sponsor would apply it. The rule would then become self-unfulfilling. For the same reason, if the manager market is efficient, then the publication of performance figures can have no value. In the final analysis, each sponsor subjectively evaluates the potential in a manager's research process and expresses that potential as a single statement.

In the new world, this statement is the covenant information ratio or, equivalently, the correlation coefficient between the appraisal process and the actual returns. Average sponsors will still employ average managers, but they will use them more effectively.

The next parameters which must be determined are the dependence-adjustment factors. Fortunately, given certain assumptions, these can be determined from the manager's portfolios and risk model.[10] Finally, the sponsor must communicate to each manager the fraction of total funds under management so that the manager can correct for diversification across multiple managers. This simple step would help prevent the uneconomic management of small portions of the total fund.[11] It would also be a radical departure from the coordination process for the typical fund.

Selected References

To our knowledge the article by Professor Barr Rosenberg cited in footnote 1 of this supplement and Professor William F. Sharpe's presidential address to the American Finance Association, cited in the references at the end of Chapter 6, are the only previous work in this area.

---

[10]See Rosenberg, "Institutional Investment with Multiple Portfolio Managers."

[11]For a perfect example, notice the risk exposure of Special K given in Table 6.5 of Case Study 7.

Chapter 7

Performance Attribution and Measurement

Perhaps more pages of academic and practitioner journals, and more CPU-seconds of computer time at investment organizations, have been devoted to performance measurement than to any other financial technique. Enthusiastic acceptance of performance statistics has been interspersed with periods of confusion and doubt. The late 1970s and early 1980s seem to be one of the latter periods. It is almost impossible to pick up an investment journal without finding articles critical of performance measurement. These often bear graphic titles, such as "Shortcomings in Performance Evaluation via MPT" or "Performance Measurement Doesn't Make Sense."[1]

In Supplement 4 we demonstrated some limitations to inferring ability from historical performance. Yet there are seemingly limitless services whose offers of performance measurement capabilities are eagerly snapped up by pension sponsors, mutual fund managers, endowment funds, and the like. Are we to

---

[1] Bruce Fielitz and Myron Greene, "Shortcomings in Performance Evaluation via MPT," *Journal of Portfolio Management*, Summer 1980, pp. 13–19; and Robert Ferguson, "Performance Measurement Doesn't Make Sense," *Financial Analysts Journal*, May–June 1980, pp. 59–69.

assume that the majority of investment professionals (those who subscribe to such services) are wasting their (or worse, their clients') money? Or is there some merit to performance measurement? What do subscribers of such services hope to learn from the voluminous (and frequently technicolor) graphs, figures, diagrams, and computer outputs?

In this chapter we will attempt to demonstrate the valid procedures, to discuss the non-valid ones, and to analyze the inferences that can be drawn from the techniques. We do not promise any reassuring answers. We simply attempt to set the record straight.

From the perspective of the fund owner, the aim of performance measurement is partly to monitor investment strategy and partly to identify skill at portfolio management. At the most naive level of the monitor function, many sponsors pay quite substantial fees (for, usually, the most naive performance measurement reports) just to be reassured that their fund is not performing "too far out of line" with other funds. However, from the perspective of the investment manager, performance measurement is more subtle in that it should provide feedback on what actually occurred in comparison with what the manager was trying to achieve. In many respects, this latter usage is more easily reconciled with performance attribution than with performance measurement. As its name suggests, *performance attribution* is concerned with the origins and magnitudes of the fund's components of return rather than with the total return on the fund. Combined with a risk model, attribution can provide statistical evidence of ability in stock selection, market timing, and other strategies.

We start this chapter by describing the current performance measurement procedures, and then we develop the applications of capital market theory, which suggest methods for identifying managerial skill. A discussion of the current criticisms of performance measurement follows, and we state our position. Performance attribution is our next topic. It is followed by a case study showing the performance of the three funds previously analyzed in the supplement to Chapter 4. A brief supplement provides the mathematical derivation for some of the assertions made in the chapter.

Observations on the History and Current Practice of Performance Measurement

A money manager, having been taken to task for lack of aggressiveness at an annual client meeting, decides to change strategy. After selling up the portfolio, the manager places a cashier's check for the entire value of the fund on red at a standard Las Vegas roulette wheel.[2] When the "transaction"

---

[2] No similarity is implied or intended between this and any endowment fund investment strategy, past, present, or future.

has been completed, the manager takes a vacation until the next annual client meeting.[3]

Question: How should performance measurement reflect the abilities of the money manager if red comes up?

Answer: Some years ago the sponsor would have been concerned only with the rate of return demonstrated by the manager. Provided that there is no attempt to imply from this number any level of managerial skill, this is a perfectly acceptable, although limited, approach. The sponsor is happy with a positive return, unhappy with a negative return, and no wiser as to the creative insights of the manager. Unfortunately, human nature makes the erroneous value judgment that the positive return suggests bounteous talent and that the negative return is clear evidence of education at an inferior college.

Nowadays, the concept of adjusting for the risk of the investment is widely accepted as a better foundation for indicating the quality of management. Given two opportunities with the same mean return but different standard deviations, there is a greater probability of obtaining a higher return from the riskier opportunity. In this case, it is clear that a higher realized return is unrelated to the skill of the investor. If the returns are risk adjusted, then managers who operate at different risk levels will not be handicapped. But how should the returns be risk adjusted? The standard procedure is to isolate an unmanaged (informationless) benchmark portfolio, commonly called the *bogey*, having the same risk level as the managed portfolio, and then to compare the two return series. The difference is usually put down to the quality of management, whereas in reality only a fraction of the difference relates to skill, the remainder being noise which obscures the true talent of the manager.

We can rephrase this slightly differently. After the realized returns on the investments have been observed, it is very difficult to establish the level of skill because of the large element of randomness in returns. The true measure of skill is reflected in the ex-ante belief in the investment's abnormal return. If we have a sufficient number of experimental observations, then the hope is that the average value of the ex-post abnormal return will be an unbiased estimate of the ex-ante value.

In the present example, if the money manager has no special information as to the outcome of the investment (i.e., the spin of the roulette wheel), then the return of +100 percent should not be construed as any evidence of talent. From our description, the outcome was obviously pure chance. Indeed, one way to find out whether a manager possesses any forecasting talent would be to compare the returns from the manager's investment with the returns from a roulette wheel that allows no opportunity for forecasting (the bogey). The experimental design would be to compare (by regression, for instance) a long

---

[3]Readers may wish to consider the question of whether this investment strategy is aggressive according to the MPT definition.

series of returns from both. Evidence of forecasting ability or lack of forecasting ability would show up as a nonzero intercept in the regression.

Now let us consider the case where the manager does have some forecasting ability. For instance, before the wheel is spun, the manager may predict that because it is incorrectly balanced, there is a greater probability of red coming up, resulting in a 1 percent abnormal return expected on red.[4] The manager's skill is reflected in this ex-ante value, but again, once the wheel has stopped, the realized return will still be $+100$ percent. Our ex-ante knowledge of the manager's skill has no obvious effect on the outcome. The skill has been obscured by the large risk and will only become evident after repeated observations. Indeed, the manager may have demonstrable skill but because of bad luck may experience a return of -100 percent. However, a continuous series of -100 percent returns would be inconsistent with the hypothesis of superior forecasting ability.

Hence, the performance report on the manager is ambiguous in the sense that the manager and the sponsor can find differing explanations for the source of the performance. The most useful information to the sponsor would be evidence that the manager's favorable performance coincided with skills which were claimed in advance, since such evidence would reinforce the sponsor's judgment of the manager and suggest future favorable performance. Clearly, good performance arising from an area in which it was anticipated by the manager is more predictive of future performance than are excellent results from a source where no ability was claimed. How many sponsors would be willing to rehire the manager for a second year?

So much for Las Vegas. Now let us consider how performance measurement is typically implemented? The portfolio subject to a performance analysis is valued at a series of regularly spaced dates (for instance, monthly or quarterly). Returns are then constructed for the subject portfolio and the bogey (frequently the S&P 500). Total return performance is described by the average and the standard deviation of the return series. Sometimes the subject portfolio is also compared with a population of similarly managed portfolios, by locating its rate of return on a bar chart displaying the highest, first quartile, median, third quartile, and lowest performers from the population. Such a display is shown in Figure 7.1, which indicates the S&P 500 return in relation to the returns of pooled equity accounts.

In order to obtain an indication of managerial skill, the alpha and beta (intercept and coefficient for the bogey) are reported from a regression of the subject portfolio onto the bogey. The regression separates residual return (and risk) from the systematic components, and statistical tests of the alpha are used to indicate any statistical significance.

---

[4]See Edward O. Thorpe, "Optimal Gambling Systems for Favorable Games," *Review of the International Statistical Institute*, 37, no. 3 (1969): 273–93.

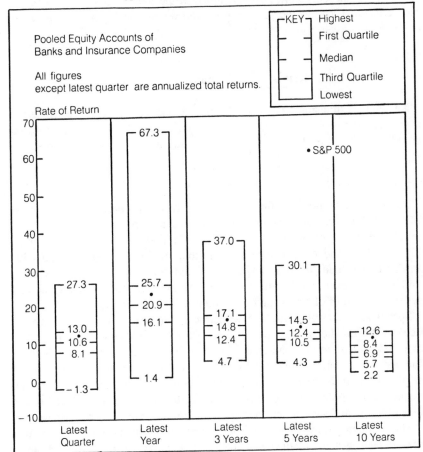

Figure 7.1
Typical Comparative Performance Report

This procedure is a straightforward application of the security market line (SML) discussed in Chapter 2. The major steps in this application are as follows:

1. Compute the subject portfolio return.
2. Choose a bogey and then compute its return.
3. Compute the subject portfolio's beta relative to the bogey.
4. Choose a relation between beta and return, so as to obtain the bogey's return corresponding to the portfolio's beta (equal-beta bogey return).
5. Compute the difference between the portfolio return and the equal-beta bogey return. Identify this return with the skill of the manager.

The majority of criticisms of this approach rest on step 2, although this is by no means the only bone of contention. In the next section we will set out these criticisms, and in the following section we will set up procedures which we think effectively satisfy them.

Criticisms of Performance Measurement

Numerous criticisms have been leveled at the current practice of performance measurement.[5] Our aim in this section is to take up step by step the procedure outlined in the last section, discussing the criticism as we do so.

Step 1: Compute the Subject Portfolio Return

It hardly seems possible that such an obvious step could be the source of criticism. However, there is one major source of error in this computation, namely the timing of payments to and from the portfolio. These payments include dividend and coupon income, contributions by the sponsor, and withdrawals to pay beneficiaries. Payments to and from the portfolio may cause another error because investment transactions are frequently made to accommodate such flows of funds, and these transactions are not costless.

Specifically, contributions and withdrawals are conventionally assumed to occur in the middle of each period.[6] An error occurs whenever contributions (or withdrawals) are not made then, because the correct return on funds is not obtained. The solution, quite naturally, is to correctly account for the timing of the payments. If the flow of funds requires an investment transaction, then this expense (commission plus spread) should not be debited against the manager, since investment flow into and out of the bogey is assumed to be costless.

The problem with dividend and interest payments is that most performance measurement systems assume that income is received on the day it is earned (i.e., the ex-date). In fact, payment is usually received somewhat later, on the payable date (or a day or two after if the security is not held at a depository so that mail delays or procedures to claim dividends from other parties may be involved), which may occur a month or more after the ex-date. Hence, the manager suffers an opportunity loss in not being able to invest the funds which the performance measurement system believes to be on hand. However, since the fund has actually earned the income, it should not be credited on the pay-

---

[5]An excellent summary of the criticisms and suggestions for improvement can be found in Barr Rosenberg, "A Critique of Performance Measurement," paper presented at the spring seminar of the Institute for Quantitative Research in Finance, Napa, California, April 1980.

[6]This convention arose for ease of computation of the rate of return over the period. See *Measuring the Investment Performance of Pension Funds* (Park Ridge, Ill.: Bank Administration Institute, 1968).

able date, because doing this would result in an erroneous portfolio valuation between the ex-date and the payable date. One solution is to credit the discounted value of income on the ex-date, where the discount factor is the risk-free rate from the ex-date to the payable date.[7]

Step 2: Choose a Bogey and Then Compute Its Return

It is this step that has given rise to the major conceptual criticism of the approach.[8] We can state one part of the argument by quoting Professor Roll:[9]

> Individual differences in portfolio selection ability cannot be measured by the Securities Market Line criterion. . . . If the index is ex-ante mean/variance efficient, the criterion will be unable to discriminate between winners and losers. If the index is not ex-ante efficient, the criterion will designate winners and losers; but another index could cause the criterion to designate different winners and losers and there is no objective way to ascertain which index is correct.

Let us take this in two steps. First, if an investor could find an index (which was ex-ante efficient), then the betas of all assets (and, therefore all portfolios) measured relative to that bogey would be related to their expected returns by the same linear function; that is, every asset would lie on the SML. This is a mathematical fact, which was shown graphically in Figure 1.10. Now if every asset's expected return is the same linear function of beta, then there can be no abnormal return associated with active management.

Hence, using an ex-ante efficient bogey means that discrimination between winners and losers is not possible. It also means that there are *no* winners and losers. Why? Because every manager lies on the SML, for the simple reason that mispriced (relative to the bogey) assets do not exist. Thus, the object of performance measurement—to locate superior managers—is completely voided.

We can restate this another way. Suppose that a sponsor attempts to analyze the performance of the stable of managers and that the sponsor is comparing these managers relative to an ex-ante efficient bogey. In order to know that the bogey is ex-ante efficient, the sponsor must specify the expected total returns and variances of returns for all the assets. These are the basic inputs to deter-

---

[7]Suggested by Rosenberg, "Critique of Performance Measurement."

[8]The origin of this criticism is usually attributed to Professor Richard Roll; certainly he is the most forceful proponent of the arguments described here. For example, see his articles "A Critique of the Asset Pricing Theory's Tests," *Journal of Financial Economics,* March 1977, pp. 129–76; "Ambiguity When Performance Is Measured by the Securities Market Line," *Journal of Finance,* September 1978, pp. 1051–69; and "Performance Evaluation and Benchmark Errors," *Journal of Portfolio Management,* Summer 1980, pp. 5–12.

[9]Roll, "Ambiguity When Performance Is Measured by the Securities Market Line," p. 1060.

mine an efficient portfolio, that is, a portfolio with maximum expected return for a given level of variance.

Notice, however, that with these data the sponsor can compute the mean and variance of every portfolio controlled by the managers. There is no need for performance measurement because the sponsor knows, in advance, exactly what the expected reward and risk are.

Performance measurement (and all the other techniques in this book) are not required for another reason—namely, that the sponsor can compute the precise portfolio that optimizes the risk/reward trade-off. Active managers are not needed—beta and risk measurement are irrelevant—since the sponsor has the answer to all investment problems.

Few sponsors are in this enviable situation. Hence, we must assume that the true expected returns and variances are not known. For this reason performance measurement is not vacuous; its aim is to shed a little light on who has the best estimates of the statistics of the return distribution.

Now let us consider the other case—the case which is relevant, since we have argued that nobody can locate an ex-ante efficient bogey. If the bogey is inefficient, then the criterion will designate winners and losers, but another bogey may designate different winners and losers. This is claimed as a criticism, but the best quarter-miler is unlikely to be the best marathon runner. What is required is to define the bogey in advance of the contest, and to make the bogey a sensible benchmark. Our disagreement with the quoted criticism is over the claim that "there is no objective way to ascertain which index is correct." We will devote the next section to the question of setting the bogey.

Step 3: Compute the Subject Portfolio's Beta
Relative to the Bogey

The aim of this step is to obtain the correct parameter value to risk-adjust the bogey. Typically, this is performed as a simple ordinary least squares regression of the subject portfolio's returns versus the bogey's returns. Hence, the "beta" which is computed is an average measure of the historical sensitivity of the subject portfolio to the bogey. Not only is there likely to be estimation error in these measures, but the measures could also be easily biased by the effect of common factors which were active in the time period under consideration.

For example, if low-beta companies do unusually well and high-beta companies perform poorly, then the fitted security market line will be flatter than anticipated. A manager who makes the correct prediction as to this relative outcome will ex-post not be rewarded because the risk adjustment would be along the flatter slope rather than the expected, steeper slope.

Again we come back to the observation that managerial skill is an ex-ante phenomenon, but that ex-post realizations of return, which are frequently used to estimate it, are subject to considerable noise.

Step 4: Choose a Relation between Beta and Return so as to Find the Risk-Adjusted Return on the Bogey

By this step, the process is locked into the acceptance of the simple capital asset pricing model. But it is still worth questioning whether beta is the correct method of risk adjustment. For instance, if there is an expected compensation to dividend yield, then adjusting only for beta will not provide the correct benchmark for performance measurement since high-yielding portfolios will outperform low-yielding portfolios at the same level of beta.

Step 5: Compute Differential Return as an Indication of Managerial Skill

Here the major criticism is one of interpretation. Typically, the intercept from the regression of the subject portfolio return onto the risk-adjusted bogey return is reported as the manager's "alpha," with the presumption that it is a measure of goodness. However, we have repeatedly pointed out that if a manager has a positive alpha, then it is easy to double it simply by doubling the active holdings. Hence, alpha by itself is a meaningless parameter.

The correct parameters to report are the alpha and residual variance, or the alpha and information ratio (the ratio of alpha to residual standard deviation). The measure of skill is the information ratio, which indicates the level of return obtained per unit of risk. The implication is that achieving a low alpha at a high information ratio is more skillful than achieving a high alpha at a low information ratio.

The bottom line for the owner of funds is the amount of utility provided by the manager. If the alpha and residual variance (or functions of these two, so that they can be reconstructed) are provided, then the sponsor can compute the increase in utility obtained from active management. One measure of this value is the *certainty equivalent increase in return* (CEIR) from active management, which is defined as:

$$\hat{\alpha}_P - \Lambda_\omega \hat{\omega}_P^2,$$

where

$\hat{\alpha}_P$ = the estimated historical alpha;

Λ_ω = the disutility from residual variance; and

$\hat{\omega}_P^2$ = the estimated historical residual variance.

It is worth summarizing these criticisms. There are certainly procedural problems with the implementation of the performance measurement process— correctly accounting for the flow of funds, specifying measures of statistical significance, and so on. More important, perhaps, are the conceptual problems which really relate to the choice of the bogey and the method of adjusting risk. Does the bogey have to be efficient? Is beta the correct, or even a good, measure of risk?

A New Framework for Performance Measurement

Much of the confusion which has surrounded performance measurement has been due to the failure to distinguish between two constructs: the normal portfolio and the systematic portfolio.[10] Typically, the current practice of performance measurement confuses the normal and systematic portfolios as a single entity, namely the bogey.

The normal portfolio is really the bogey. It is the rabbit which the manager is attempting to overtake, the comparison portfolio against which the return performance of the active managers is judged. In the current environment, 99 percent of all performance measurement evaluations use the S&P 500 as the normal portfolio. Clearly, this is arbitrary and ambiguous. We have spent considerable space in previous chapters defining the normal portfolio as a construct for applications other than performance measurement. At the expense of repetition, the normal portfolio can be characterized as the set of assets on which the manager is prepared to make a bet. It is the manager's natural habitat.

Operationally, we can define the normal portfolio by a list of assets names (CUSIPs or ticker symbols) and the average or typical weights (or shareholdings) in each asset. An approximation that is quite good for institutional portfolios is to use the capitalization of each asset in the market (broad-based portfolio). From this description, the S&P 500 may be a reasonable normal portfolio for the "vanilla" account. For growth-stock managers, small-company managers, or special equity funds, the S&P 500 may be totally wrong.[11] Moreover, in some situatons the normal portfolio is 100 percent cash, so that the comparison is with the risk-free asset.

How is it decided whether to use a risky normal portfolio or the risk-free asset? This simply depends on the contract under which the sponsor retained the money manager. If the contract explicitly or implicitly indicates that performance will be judged relative to a portfolio, then that portfolio should be used as the normal portfolio in performance measurement.[12] On the other hand,

---

[10]The nomenclature is a little confusing here. The systematic portfolio should not be confused with the passive component of a managed portfolio. The systematic portfolio is sometimes referred to as the sector portfolio. See also footnote 14 below and the section "Where, Oh Where, Has the Market Portfolio Gone" in Chapter 3.

[11]Examine the risk indices of examples 2 and 3 in Supplement 4, or Ortho Growth, Inc., Petite Capital Investors, and Special K Associates in Case Study 7, part 1 (Chapter 6).

[12]The manager should realize that he or she has a vested interest in ensuring that the normal portfolio is reasonable.

if the manager is retained on the understanding that performance will be judged in isolation, and not in comparison with the performance of other managers or of indexes, so that the only indication of "good" performance is the numerical value of the total return, then the normal portfolio should be the risk-free asset. The 100 percent cash normal portfolio is probably reasonable only in personal trust or in-house management or in situations where a single manager controls the total assets of the fund.

Hence, the first step in performance measurement is to determine the return series which arises from the difference between the managed portfolio and the normal portfolio. This difference represents the returns obtained by the manager from making bets on the securities in the universe. It is the result of active management, and therefore it is naturally denoted by the active portfolio.[13] The average reward and risk of this portfolio are clearly interesting statistics, but this is not the end of the story.

On what basis should comparisons among managers be made? Currently, the recipient of performance reports is typically the plan sponsor who is trying to coordinate the stable of managers. From Chapter 6 we know that the parameters of most interest concern the relationship between the actively managed components of the constituent portfolios and the sponsor's aggregate normal portfolio. This usage suggests that the sponsor's equilibrium or normal portfolio be used as the systematic portfolio.

Algebraically, performance measurement is implemented by decomposing active portfolio returns over time in the following manner:

$$r_P - r_N = \alpha^A + \beta^A r_{N_A} + u^A,$$

where

r_P = the actively managed (constituent) portfolio excess return, and
r_N = the normal excess return for this manager,

so that:

$r_P - r_N$ = the active portfolio return,
r_{N_A} = the excess return on the aggregate normal portfolio,
α^A = the active portfolio alpha,
β^A = the active portfolio beta, and
u^A = the active portfolio return unrelated to the aggregate
        normal portfolio.

Notice that the active portfolio beta is likely to be close to zero (for everyone but a market timer) because the managed portfolio beta and the normal portfolio beta will be similar. Hence, the exact specification of the aggregate normal portfolio will be of less importance than the bogey is currently. Further, capri-

---

[13]Again, notice the slight generalization of definition. Previously, when referring to the active portfolio, we implicitly assumed that the market (proxy) is the normal portfolio.

cious bias caused by the common factors is less likely to affect the active portfolio than the managed portfolio. A recent example of such bias occurred at the end of the 1970s, when managers whose natural habitat was small-capitalization companies typically outperformed the S&P 500, not because of skill, but because small companies as a group outperformed large companies at that time.

Ideally, then, a sponsor should concentrate on the active portfolios of the managers being measured. For this approach, every managed portfolio should be associated with a normal portfolio, to form the active portfolio which should be evaluated relative to the sponsor's aggregate normal portfolio. We have been precise in specifying which portfolio should be used where, and consequently we have ended up with three portfolios instead of the usual two. Is there any way of simplifying the process?

There appears to be no way to standardize the manager's normal portfolios, since these vary considerably among managers. The sponsors' aggregate normal portfolios, on the other hand, to the extent that sponsors have thought about the specifications of such portfolios, seem to be reasonably similar to one another and to the value-weighted aggregate of all securities in the sector. Thus, one simplifying step would be to use the (value-weighted) sector portfolio as the systematic portfolio.[14] This does not argue for the use of the S&P 500, but it does suggest that the errors in using the S&P 500 will be small. Better systematic portfolios include the NYSE, Wilshire 5000, and FRMSU.[15]

Let us summarize the discussion thus far. The first element is the construct of the systematic portfolio. For the following reasons (discussed in earlier chapters), managers and/or sponsors separate systematic or sector-wide (i.e., equity or bond) movements from individual or group movements.

1. Sponsors have a different aversion between systematic and nonsystematic risk because of the omitted assets and liabilities.[16]

2. Money managers do not forecast the market in the same way that they perform asset valuation; i.e., the market timing decision is entirely separate from the stock selection decision.

3. The corporate officer responsible for the pension fund is judged quite differently on sector-wide returns than on individual returns—an agency problem. Financial theory suggests that pension assets should be managed with less aversion to residual risk than to systematic risk. However, this exposes the pension officer to performance which may be worse than the sector average in some quarters or years. If everybody suffers (negative systematic return), the

---

[14]Hence, the occasional reference to the systematic portfolio as the sector portfolio, and vice versa.

[15]The NYSE and FRMSU are listed in the glossary. The Wilshire 5000 is a capitalization weighted index formed from 5,000 large corporations by Wilshire Associates, a Los Angeles–based broker. It is occasionally tabulated in *The Wall Street Journal* and *Barrons*.

[16]See Andrew Rudd and Barr Rosenberg, "The "Market Model' in Investment Management," *Journal of Finance*, May 1980, pp. 597–607.

pension officer cannot be made a scapegoat. If only one fund suffers (negative residual return) the pension officer is on the line even if the correct long-term strategy is being followed.

For these reasons, it is important to be alert to the decomposition into systematic and residual returns, for which we need a systematic portfolio. If the use of the systematic portfolio is to attribute sector returns and asset returns (item 2 above), then the S&P 500 is fine because of the existence of a prominent factor in equity returns.[17] However, if the systematic portfolio is to be used in the multiple manager context (items 1 and 3 above), then the systematic portfolio should be the aggregate normal portfolio. At this stage, the argument of standardization suggests that, in the absence of the sponsor's correct optimal passive portfolio, a more broadly based index than the S&P 500 be used, such as the NYSE or the FRMSU.

The optimal passive portfolio is the portfolio that the sponsor desires on average. On average, it is obtained by aggregating the normal portfolios of the individual managers. Hence, as far as actual performance is concerned, the normal portfolios of the managers are irrelevant; the deviations from these normal portfolios which cause the aggregate portfolio to overperform or underperform its normal position are the crucial objects for performance measurement.

Performance Attribution: The Single-Period Analysis[18]

We suggested above that the major aim of performance measurement is to obtain some information about the skill of the manager. Does conventional performance measurement, which measures total performance with, occasionally, a decomposition into systematic and residual components, satisfy this requirement?

Alas not, since there is considerable ambiguity as to the sources of total performance. Most sponsors, and indeed most investors, would feel more comfortable with a manager who states that his or her skill is in, for instance, market timing, and whose statement is subsequently found to be true, than they would be with a manager who claims skill in market timing, but whose superior returns arise from other strategies. Ex-post confirmation of an ex-ante declaration of skill is more indicative of future performance than is a claim to skill based on performance that may have resulted from, for instance, fortuitous exposure to small-capitalization stocks which happened to perform well.

---

[17]See section "Where, Oh Where, Has the Market Portfolio Gone" in Chapter 3.

[18]Professor Eugene Fama appears to have been the first author to examine the sources of performance, in his article "Components of Investment Performance," *Journal of Finance*, June 1972, pp. 551–67. The most modern treatment of the subject which we are aware of is Barr Rosenberg, "Performance Measurement and Performance Attribution," *Proceedings of the Seminar on the Analysis of Security Prices*, University of Chicago, May 1978, pp. 69–119.

Performance attribution systems analyze the components of performance and thus provide an indication of the effectiveness of the research process.[19] The first separation of the components of return is between market (or, more correctly, sector) timing and selectivity. *Market timing* is the strategy whereby a manager alters the portfolio exposure to the sector portfolio in the hope of profiting from forecasts of abnormal sector returns. *Selectivity* is the picking of assets which, for one reason or another, outperform the sector. Performance measurement systems conventionally lump both contributions together as residual or active return.

The second separation decomposes selectivity into its components, i.e., specific returns and the return due to the common factors. At this stage we are able to infer whether the portfolio return was due to a growth-stock, small-capitalization, or oil industry strategy as opposed to a strategy of identifying undervalued assets, irrespective of any commonality.

In the description which follows, we shall assume that the attribution is repeated monthly (i.e., one month is the smallest interval of time); that managed portfolios are only revised at month-end, which is also when dividends and other cash flows are received; and that the comparison portfolio is similarly adjusted so as to be consistent with the managed portfolios.[20] Further, at the beginning of the month we know the attributes of the portfolio (β, ω, risk indices, etc.), and these are representative of the portfolio's attributes for the month as a whole.

The starting point is the normal beta, β_N, for the portfolio, which is the optimal long-term beta chosen in response to the manager's long-term forecasts for the expectation and variance of market excess return, $E_M - i_F$ and V_M, respectively. Hence, the first component of return is:

$$\text{Expected excess return at normal beta} = \beta_N(E_M - i_F).$$

It is unlikely that the market will experience its expected return; the difference is the "surprise" due to market conditions. Let r_M be the realized market excess return, so that the market surprise equals $r_M - (E_M - i_F)$. The portfolio, with normal beta β_N, experiences systematic excess return of $\beta_N r_M$, so that the surprise is given by:

$$\text{Surprise at normal beta} = \beta_N[r_M - (E_M - i_F)].$$

The portfolio beta, β_P, may not equal the normal beta because of a market timing decision. The deviation due to the beta policy is $\beta_P - \beta_N$, which earns

---

[19]Other attribution systems—transaction analyzers—attempt to separate the component of return due to effective trading from the component due to effective security analysis. Their discussion is beyond the scope of this book.

[20]In fact, these assumptions are not far from the truth. The assumptions are for ease of exposition only; clearly, repeating the attribution more frequently (e.g., daily) eliminates the need for these assumptions. Unfortunately, it also introduces statistical problems which arise from asynchronous valuations of thinly traded assets. Discussion of these problems would take us too far afield from our main point.

during the course of the month the difference between the systematic excess return at the chosen beta ($\beta_P r_M$) and the systematic excess return at the normal beta ($\beta_N r_M$). Hence, the return from market timing is:

$$\text{Return from market timing} = (\beta_P - \beta_N)r_M.$$

So much for systematic return. Residual return, the other component of total return, arises from selectivity of assets or groups of assets. Hence, its value is given by:

$$\text{Selectivity} = r_P - \beta_P r_M.$$

Combining these components, we have the relationship:

$$r_P = \text{Portfolio excess return} \qquad\qquad (7\text{–}1)$$

$$= (r_P - \beta_P r_M) + (\beta_P - \beta_N)r_M + \beta_N[r_M - (E_M - i_F)] + \beta_N(E_M - i_F)$$

$$= \text{Selectivity} + \underset{\text{timing}}{\text{Market}} + \underset{\text{normal beta}}{\text{Surprise at}} + \underset{\text{at normal beta.}}{\text{Expectation}}$$

Selectivity can be broken down into its components, by recalling from equation (3–3) that the residual return is given by:

$$r_P - \beta_P r_M = c_1 RI_{P1} + c_2 RI_{P2} + \ldots + c_6 RI_{P6} \qquad\qquad (7\text{–}2)$$

$$+ c_7 IND_{P1} + c_8 IND_{P2} + \ldots + c_{45} IND_{P39} + u_P,$$

where RI_{P1} through RI_{P6} are the portfolio risk index values (i.e., exposures to the risk factors); IND_{P1} through IND_{P39} are the portfolio industry weights (i.e., exposures to the industry factors); u_P is the portfolio specific return; $c_1, \ldots,$ c_6 are the returns to the risk factors; and $c_7, \ldots, c_{45}$ are the returns to the industry factors.

Hence, assuming that there is no normal nonmarket position (i.e., the normal portfolio is a levered market portfolio), we can, knowing the exposures (RI_P and IND_P), compute the return to risk indices and industry groups and the specific returns.[21] Moreover, since individual stocks are broken down in exactly the same way (for example, see the "beta book," Table 3.6), we can decompose portfolio return into the components of return for all the individual securities.

Further, from the risk model there are risk predictions associated with each of the components of return. For instance, our familiar decomposition,

$$V_P = \text{portfolio variance}$$

$$= \omega_P^2 + \beta_P^2 V_M$$

$$= \underset{\text{variance}}{\text{Selectivity}} + \underset{\text{variance,}}{\text{Systematic}}$$

---

[21]If there is a nonmarket normal position, then selectivity is taken relative to all normal positions and not just beta, as in equation (7–1).

shows the risk associated with selectivity. Equation (S3–18) shows the finer decomposition into common factor risk *(XMC)* and specific risk. Systematic variance can be decomposed into the variance of the surprise at the normal beta $(\beta_N^2 V_M)$ and the remainder, which is the net effect of market timing. That is:

$$\beta_P^2 V_M = \text{Systematic variance}$$
$$= (\beta_P^2 - \beta_N^2)V_M + \beta_N^2 V_M$$
$$= \begin{array}{c} \text{Market} \\ \text{timing risk} \end{array} + \begin{array}{c} \text{Normal} \\ \text{variance.} \end{array}$$

Tables 7.1 through 7.3 give an example of attribution analysis for a one-month period (March 1978) of the Performance Investment Fund at American National Bank.[22] Table 7.1 shows the front page of a PERFAT (PERFormance ATtribution) analysis. Item A shows that the risk-free rate for March 1978 was 54 basis points. During the month the excess return (r_M) of the market (proxied by the S&P 500 in this case) was 2.16 percent. The beta of the portfolio (β_P) was 1.36. Hence, the systematic excess return on the portfolio $(\beta_P r_M)$ was 2.93 percent.[23] The beta policy, since the normal beta was specified as unity, was responsible for 77 basis points in return. These entries are shown as items B3, B6, and B7 under the column headed "Percentage Return."

As indicated, predicted standard deviations are associated with these returns. These are given under the column headed "Model Standard Deviation." The final column gives the "Standardized Outcome," obtained by dividing the return by its standard deviation. The standardized outcome, therefore, gives some indication of the statistical significance of the realized return. For instance, if monthly returns were normally distributed, a standardized outcome greater than two in absolute value indicates that there is a 95 percent chance that the return is statistically different from zero. In this month, only item F, the total residual return, suggests managerial skill at a statistically significant level.

Item C1 indicates that the normal policy is for no exposure to the common factors (i.e., taken with B3 and D1, it suggests that the normal portfolio is the S&P 500). However, because the portfolio was exposed to one or more risk indices, there was some selective or residual return.[24] Item C2 shows that the risk index policy provided 2.16 percent in this month, and Item C3 indicates that industry exposure obtained another 1.03 percent, giving a residual return due to the common factors of 3.20 percent. Notice from the next column that the ex-ante risk level associated with this return had a standard deviation almost as large; hence, the standardized outcome is just over 1.0.

---

[22]This portfolio was previously analyzed in Example 3 of Supplement 4. The PORCH analysis there showed the portfolio at another point in time. As before, some data have not been reported in order to maintain confidentiality.

[23]See footnote 2 of Table 7.1.

[24]The active policies will be detailed in Tables 7.2 and 7.3.

Items D1, D4, and D5 refer to the specific returns. Since the market (proxy) is the normal position, there is no specific return at the normal position. The stock selection, designated by Item D4, active policy, contributed 5.32 percent at a monthly standard deviation of 3.81 percent. The total residual return, item F, is found by adding items C6 and D5. The total return due to active management, reported as item J, is item F plus the return due to market timing, item B6. That total is 9.29 percent.

Table 7.2 shows the factor contributions to the monthly residual return. The top six rows show the factors associated with the risk indices, while the bottom 39 rows show the industry group returns. The format is the same in both cases. The first column shows the portfolio exposure to the factor (risk indices and industry group percentage weights) which is contrasted with the market (proxy) exposures in the second column. The third column, which is blank in this case, would specify the normal position if that position were different from the market. The fourth column lists the portfolio active exposures, defined as the difference between the portfolio exposure and the normal exposure, which here is the difference between the portfolio exposure and the market exposure.

Residual return arises from the portfolio active exposures, as shown in equation (7–2). The c's in the equation are listed in the last column under "Factor Value." For instance, the return on the market variability factor (at a risk index value of 1.0) is 0.44 percent (i.e., $c_1 = 0.44$), and the portfolio active exposure to market variability is 0.589 (i.e., $RI_{P1} = 0.589$), so that the contribution to return from exposure to market variability is $c_1 RI_{P1} = (0.44)(0.589) = 0.26$ percent, which is shown in column 5.[25]

The sum of the six risk index contributions to return is the total risk index contribution to return, reported as item C2 of Table 7.1. The sum of the 39 industry group contributions is the total industry policy contribution, reported as item C3.

Associated with this return is risk. The standard deviation of the contribution to return from investment risk is reported in column 6, under the heading "Standard Deviation." Following this, in column 7, is the standard error of that contribution, as estimated from the factor regressions. The standard deviation measures the intrinsic investment risk; the standard error is the degree of uncertainty with which the investment outcome can be estimated. The next column, "Standardized Outcome," gives the ratio of the contribution to return to its total range of uncertainty arising from both investment risk and estimation error.

For example, consider the first risk index, market variability. The portfolio manager's strategy was to have an exposure of 0.589 in this month. The investment risk associated with this market variability exposure was 0.65 percent per month, with an estimation error of 0.33 percent. The total uncertainty from

---

[25]The 0.44 percent value is also shown in Figure 4.4.

Table 7.1
Monthly Attribution of Return

```
        CONDITIONAL FORECASTING SERVICE
MONTHLY PORTFOLIO PERFORMANCE ATTRIBUTION: MARCH  1978    MARKET PORTFOLIO: S&P500

                AS OF 780228

PERFORMANCE REPORTED FOR:    MARCH   1978  FOR EQUITY PORTFOLIO EXCLUDING CASH
{DATE OF ANALYSIS:780816}
```

SOURCES OF RETURN	PERCENTAGE RETURN		MODEL STANDARD DEVIATION	STAN- DARDIZED OUTCOME
A. RISK-FREE		0.54	0.0	
B. SYSTEMATIC EXCESS RETURN				
3. AT NORMAL BETA {=1.00}	2.16		5.95	0.28
6. DUE TO BETA POLICY	0.77		2.13	0.36
7. TOTAL		2.93	8.08	0.28
C. RESIDUAL RETURN: COMMON FACTORS				
1. AT NORMAL POSITION	0.0		0.0	0.0
2. RISK INDEX POLICY	2.16		2.07	1.05
3. INDUSTRY POLICY	1.03		1.71	0.60
6. TOTAL		3.20	3.17	1.01
D. RESIDUAL RETURN: SPECIFIC				
1. AT NORMAL POSITION	0.0		0.0	0.0
4. ACTIVE POLICY	5.32		3.81	1.39
5. TOTAL		5.32	3.81	1.39

F. TOTAL RESIDUAL RETURN	8.51	4.96	1.72

H. TOTAL RETURN	11.98	9.49	1.19
I. TOTAL EXCESS RETURN OF NORMAL POLICY	2.16	5.95	0.28
J. TOTAL RETURN DUE TO ACTIVE MANAGEMENT	9.29	5.40	1.72

FOOTNOTES:

1. INITIAL PORTFOLIO EQUITY VALUE, IN $, IS

2. SYSTEMATIC RETURN = 2.93 = {BETA = 1.36} * {MARKET EXCESS RETURN   = 2.16} = 2.93
   SYSTEM. STD. DEV. = 8.08 = {BETA = 1.36} * {MARKET STD. DEVIATION = 5.95} = 8.08

3. ACTIVE XMC STANDARD DEVIATION = SQUARE ROOT {ACTIVE XMC VARIANCE} = SQUARE ROOT {10.07}
   ACTIVE XMC VARIANCE   =   RISK INDICES VARIANCE = 4.28
                           = 2 * {R.I - INDUSTRY COVARIANCE = 1.43} = 2.86
                                   + INDUSTRY VARIANCE = 2.93 = 10.07

4. POSSIBLE ERROR IN IMPUTING RETURNS TO FACTORS VERSUS SPECIFIC, PRODUCE EXACTLY OFFSETTING
   ERRORS WITH STD ERROR OF 0.99

5. STD. DEV. OF ACTIVE RETURN = SQUARE ROOT {VARIANCE} = SQUARE ROOT {29.17} = 5.40
   VARIANCE OF ACTIVE RETURN =   ACTIVE SYSTEMATIC VARIANCE = 4.56
                                     + ACTIVE XMC VARIANCE = 10.07
                                   + ACTIVE SPECIFIC VARIANCE = 14.55 = 29.17

Table 7.2
Contribution of Factor Returns

ACTIVE PORTFOLIO FACTOR EXPOSURE & FACTOR CONTRIBUTIONS TO MONTHLY RESIDUAL RETURN ON EQUITY & FACTOR VALUE

	EXPOSURE IN EQ. PORT. MKT	NORMAL (IF DIFFT)	ACTIVE EXPOSURE	CONTRIBUTION TO RETURN	STANDARD DEVIATION	STANDARD ERROR	STANDARDIZED OUTCOME	FACTOR VALUE
1. RISK-INDEX FACTORS								
1. MARKET VARIABILITY	0.589	0.0	0.589	0.26	0.65	0.33	0.36	0.44
2. EARNINGS VARIABILITY	0.741	0.0	0.741	0.88	0.38	0.41	1.58	1.19
3. LOW VALUATION, UNSUCCESS	-0.329	0.0	-0.329	-0.05	0.35	0.15	-0.12	0.14
4. IMMATURITY AND SMALLNESS	1.590	0.0	1.590	1.18	1.81	0.53	0.62	0.74
5. GROWTH ORIENTATION	-0.125	0.0	-0.125	0.04	0.11	0.06	0.31	-0.31
6. FINANCIAL RISK	0.228	0.0	0.228	-0.15	0.12	0.11	-0.89	-0.64
2. CONTRIBUTIONS OF INDUSTRY GROUP INVESTMENTS								
1. NONFERROUS METALS	0.0	1.7	-1.7	-0.07	0.07	0.03	-0.94	4.29
2. ENERGY RAW MATERIALS	0.0	2.7	-2.7	0.11	0.13	0.04	0.78	-3.97
3. CONSTRUCTION	0.0	1.1	-1.1	0.01	0.03	0.02	0.42	-1.24
4. AGRICULTURE, FOOD	0.0	5.7	-5.7	0.02	0.13	0.06	0.11	-0.28
5. LIQUOR	0.0	0.7	-0.7	-0.02	0.02	0.01	-0.95	2.87
6. TOBACCO	0.0	1.3	-1.3	-0.03	0.04	0.03	-0.58	2.33
7. APPAREL	0.0	0.6	-0.6	0.00	0.02	0.01	-0.07	-0.23
8. FOREST PRODUCTS, PAPER	5.1	2.6	2.5	0.01	0.08	0.04	-0.13	-0.50
9. CONTAINERS	0.0	0.6	-0.6	-0.00	0.02	0.01	-0.01	0.04
10. MEDIA	14.8	1.7	13.1	0.32	0.29	0.19	0.93	2.47

11. CHEMICALS	0.0	3.3	-3.3	-0.01	0.08	0.05	-0.12	0.32
12. DRUGS, MEDICINE	0.0	5.2	-5.2	-0.05	0.13	0.07	-0.35	0.96
13. SOAPS, COSMETICS	0.0	2.9	-2.9	-0.07	0.07	0.06	-0.79	-2.48
14. DOMESTIC OIL	0.0	5.7	-5.7	-0.05	0.25	0.08	-0.21	0.94
15. INTERNATIONAL OIL	0.0	9.4	-9.4	-0.11	0.40	0.17	-0.24	1.12
16. TIRES, RUBBER GOODS	0.0	0.4	-0.4	-0.00	-0.01	0.02	-0.22	0.82
17. STEEL	0.0	1.0	-1.0	-0.01	0.03	0.04	0.36	-1.32
18. PRODUCER GOODS	0.0	3.5	-3.5	-0.00	0.07	0.23	-0.01	-0.01
19. BUSINESS MACHINES	0.0	8.7	-8.7	0.52	0.25	0.34	1.52	-5.95
20. CONSUMER DURABLES	16.7	0.9	15.8	0.60	0.41	0.02	1.14	-3.82
21. MOTOR VEHICLES	0.0	5.5	-5.5	-0.11	0.12	0.56	-0.66	1.90
22. AEROSPACE	0.0	0.7	-0.7	-0.04	0.02	0.06	-1.59	6.05
23. ELECTRONICS	30.6	1.6	29.0	-0.15	0.74	0.02	-0.16	-0.51
24. PHOTOGRAPHIC, OPTICAL	0.0	1.4	-1.4	-0.03	0.04	0.01	0.46	-2.43
25. NONDURBLS, ENTERTNMNT	0.0	0.7	-0.7	0.00	0.02	0.02	0.07	-0.28
26. TRUCKING, FREIGHT	0.0	0.3	-0.3	-0.01	0.01	0.01	0.96	-4.76
27. RAILROADS, SHIPPING	0.0	1.4	-1.4	0.00	0.05	0.16	0.28	-1.02
28. AIR TRANSPORT	0.0	0.4	-0.4	-0.02	0.03	0.06	-0.55	4.17
29. TELEPHONE	0.0	8.1	-8.1	-0.25	0.26	0.08	-0.84	3.11
30. ENERGY, UTILITIES	0.0	6.6	-6.6	-0.05	0.27	0.04	-0.19	0.79
31. RETAIL, GENERAL	0.0	3.4	-3.4	0.16	0.10	0.02	1.21	-4.62
32. BANKS	0.0	2.6	-2.6	-0.03	0.12	0.03	-0.21	1.04
33. MISC. FINANCE	0.0	1.0	-1.0	-0.01	0.05	0.00	-0.10	0.61
34. INSURANCE	0.0	2.3	-2.3	-0.01	0.11	0.01	-0.12	0.58
35. REAL PROPERTY	0.0	0.1	-0.1	-0.00	0.00	0.01	-0.14	1.01
36. BUSINESS SERVICES	0.0	0.0	-0.0	0.0	0.00	0.00	0.0	0.78
37. TRAVEL, OUTDR RECREATN	0.0	0.2	-0.2	-0.01	0.01	0.00	-1.11	5.08
38. GOLD MNG & SECURITIES	0.0	0.2	-0.02	0.01	0.01	0.00	0.86	-6.20
39. MISC. CONGLOMRTE	32.7	3.6	29.1	0.14	0.0	0.00	0.0	0.47

Table 7.3
Decomposition of Asset Returns

CONTRIBUTIONS OF INDIVIDUAL ASSETS TO EQUITY-PORTFOLIO EXCESS RETURN (MULTIPLIED BY 100)

CUSIP	NAME	HOLDING IN EQ. PORT	MKT	TOTAL RETURN	MKT.	MV	EV	RISK INDICES LVU	IS	GO	FR	INDUSTRY GROUP	SPECIF		RESIDUAL RETURN	STDIZED SPEC RETURN
05380710	AVNET INC	26.7	0.0	375.3	86.1	13.1	5.6	-2.1	45.1	-2.8	7.4	-13.5	236.4	=	289.20	1.0
57325l0	MARTIN MARIETTA CORP	32.7	0.1	587.0	74.5	-4.2	-1.9	-0.2	27.6	10.0	2.0	15.5	463.8	=	512.55	2.3
02473510	AMERICAN BROADCASTING	14.8	0.1	92.9	47.2	6.5	13.4	-3.1	18.5	-2.4	0.1	36.7	-23.9	=	45.78	-0.2
82930210	SINGER CO	16.7	0.1	46.1	62.0	7.5	59.6	1.6	15.4	1.1	-19.3	63.8	-145.6	=	-15.90	-0.9
09738310	BOISE CASCADE CORP	5.1	0.1	32.7	13.1	1.3	6.8	-0.0	4.8	-0.2	-1.0	2.6	5.4	=	19.59	0.1
03208710	AMPEX CORP	4.0	0.0	10.1	10.0	1.8	4.8	-0.7	6.3	-2.0	-3.8	-2.0	-4.3	=	0.09	0.1
	TOTAL FOR PORTFOLIO	100.0	0.4	1144.2	292.9	25.9	88.2	-4.6	117.7	1.9	-14.6	103.1	531.7	=	851.31	

this strategy was $\sqrt{(0.65)(0.65) + (0.33)(0.33)} = \sqrt{0.4225 + 0.1089} = 0.73$. Hence, the standardized outcome is $0.26/0.73 = 0.36$.

In this month, the risk index exposures were correct for market variability, earnings variability, immaturity and smallness, and growth orientation. The strategy with regard to low valuation, unsuccess and financial risk harmed performance. Nevertheless, overall, the risk index policy was beneficial to the tune of 2.16 percent (= $0.26 + 0.88 - 0.05 + 1.18 + 0.04 - 0.15$), which is the figure reported in Table 7.1, item C2. The analysis of the industry group investments proceeds similarly.

Table 7.3 displays the contributions of the individual assets. At this time, there were only six names in the portfolio. Avnet, Inc., comprised 26.7 percent of the portfolio, but it was not included in the S&P 500. Avnet's contribution to the portfolio total excess return (i.e., the product of Avnet's excess return and its portfolio proportion) for the month was 3.753 percent, of which a rate of return of 0.861 percent was systematic or market related.[26] The remaining 2.892 percent was therefore the contribution from residual return which arose from the six risk indices, Avnet's industry group return, and Avnet's specific return. These are shown in the next eight columns in Table 7.3. The final column shows the standardized outcome for the specific component of return and is a measure of the degree of surprise in each asset's specific return. For instance, during the month of March, Martin Marietta Corporation had a specific return which was 2.3 times its predicted specific risk. This was a remarkably favorable return and the most important contribution to portfolio residual return.

Finally, knowing the security exposures to each of the factors, it is possible to decompose the return on individual assets into its components. This is shown for Avnet, Inc., in Table 7.4. Of course, this is simply one example of the multiple factor model, which was described algebraically in equation (S3–14) and is repeated below:

$$r_j = \sum_{k=1}^{K} b_{jk} f_k + u_j$$
$$= b_{j1} f_1 + b_{j2} f_2 + \ldots + b_{j46} f_{46} + u_j,$$

since there are 46 factors (1 systematic and 45 residual). From Table 7.4, we can express the equation numerically as:

$$\begin{aligned}
14.056 = \ &(1.49)(2.16) + (1.12)(0.44) + (0.18)(1.19) \\
&+ (-0.56)(0.14) + (2.28)(0.74) + (0.34)(-0.31) \\
&+ (-0.43)(-0.64) + (1.0)(0.506) \\
&+ (1.0)(8.854),
\end{aligned}$$

where the exposures to industry groups other than number 23 are all zero.

---

[26]Notice that most returns are multiplied by 100 for clarity.

Table 7.4
Elements or Excess Return for Avnet, Inc.

Factor	(1) Security Exposure	(2) Factor Value (%)	(3) Contribution to Security Excess Return	(4) Contribution to Portfolio Excess Return (percent)
The market	1.49 (beta)	2.16	3.225	0.861
Risk indices:				
Market variability	1.12	0.44	0.491	0.131
Earnings variability	0.18	1.19	0.210	0.056
Low val'n, unsuccess	−0.56	0.14	−0.079	−0.021
Immaturity, smallness	2.28	0.74	1.689	0.451
Growth orientation	0.34	−0.31	−0.105	−0.028
Financial risk	−0.43	−0.64	0.277	0.074
Industry group:				
Electronics, no. 23	1.0	−0.506	−0.506	−0.135
Specific return:				
Avnet, Inc.	1.0	8.854	8.854	2.364
Total excess return			14.056	3.753

Notes:
1. Column (3) = Column (2) * Column (1).
2. Column (4) = Column (3) * 0.267.
3. Proportion of Avnet, Inc., in the portfolio = 0.267.

Performance Attribution: The Multiperiod Case

A single monthly period can tell us only so much; to obtain better estimates and more complete information as to the skill of the manager, a longer period needs to be analyzed. However, because investment policy changes periodically, we have to divide up the longer horizon into a series of shorter observation intervals. We again make the assumption that these shorter intervals are months. Now the problem is to aggregate the monthly strategies into the overall (compound) return, which, after all, is the essential statistic.

Unfortunately, this task is not straightforward. To explain this, consider a two-month period where the second subscript, 1 or 2, refers to the period. Further, let the superscript c denote the cumulative value of the variable over both periods. Now the cumulative risk-free return is:

$$1 + i_F^c = (1 + i_{F1})(1 + i_{F2}),$$

and the cumulative return on the normal (systematic) portfolio is:

$$1 + i_N^c = (1 + i_{N1})(1 + i_{N2})$$
$$= [(1 + i_{F1}) + \beta_{N1}r_{M1}][(1 + i_{F2}) + \beta_{N2}r_{M2}],$$

where $r_{Mt} = i_{Mt} - i_{Ft}$ and i_{Nt} is the systematic rate of return at the normal beta (for $t = 1,2$). Multiplying out these two formulas, the cumulative excess return on the normal (systematic) portfolio is:

$$r_N^c = \text{Cumulative normal excess return}$$
$$= (1 + i_N^c) - (1 + i_F^c)$$
$$= (1 + i_{F2})\beta_{N1}r_{M1} + (1 + i_{F1})\beta_{N2}r_{M2} + \beta_{N1}r_{M1}\beta_{N2}r_{M2}$$
$$= \beta_{N1}r_{M1} + \beta_{N2}r_{M2} + i_{F2}\beta_{N1}r_{M1} + i_{F1}\beta_{N2}r_{M2} + \beta_{N1}r_{M1}\beta_{N2}r_{M2}.$$

Now the first two terms in the last equation represent the normal systematic excess returns for periods 1 and 2, but the last three terms arise from the compounding process and confuse the aggregation from monthly intervals to a longer period. In general, none of the performance statistics of interest to us aggregate simply, either additively or multiplicatively. Therefore, we have to resort to more complicated methods.

For our purposes here, it suffices to say that multiperiod analyses require the use of logarithmic rates of return, or continuously compounded rates.[27] Thus, we have to work with proportional rates of return within months and logarithmic rates of return for compounding the monthly results to longer periods. Unfortunately, to add to the complications, there are two subtleties to this transformation. The first is that the risk of the monthly proportional returns affects the monthly logarithmic returns, so that the (logarithmic) return over the entire horizon must be adjusted for the risk of the strategy. The second is that there is a nonlinear interaction between the systematic and residual returns that, again, must be accounted for over the entire horizon.[28] Not surprisingly, it is far easier to do things wrong than right!

With this cursory explanation as background, let us move on to some examples.

Case Study 8: Performance Attribution of
Three Strategies

In Supplement 4 we described the PORCH reports of three very different investment strategies. Here we briefly review selected pages from PERFAN (PERFormance ANalysts) reports for the three portfolios. Readers may find it helpful to review the descriptions of the strategies and the PORCH reports in Supplement 4 before proceeding with this case study.

Example 1

The first strategy is that of the Alpha Plus portfolio managed by the John Hancock Mutual Life Insurance Company. The tables here analyze the predecessor of Alpha Plus, which was managed using the same strategy and methodology. Table 7.5 displays the front page of the PERFAN report, showing the

---

[27] See Supplement 1 for definitions of these constructs.

[28] These mathematical inconveniences are described more fully in the supplement to this chapter.

Table 7.5
Example 1 Decomposition of Investment Return

```
CONDITIONAL FORECASTING SERVICE                 MARKET PORTFOLIO    : S&P500
PORTFOLIO PERFORMANCE ANALYSIS                  ESTIMATION UNIVERSE : A1000
    JOHN HANCOCK INSURANCE                      REGRESSION WEIGHTING: CAP
    ANALYSIS OF PORTFOLIO
```

ANALYSIS PERIOD: JULY 1977 THROUGH DECEMBER 1978
18 MONTHS OF DATA
{DATE OF ANALYSIS: 790115}

1. DECOMPOSITION OF INVESTMENT RETURN, EXPRESSED AS LOGARITHMIC RETURN {*100}

	ANNUAL RATE	CUMULATIVE	MONTHLY RATE
A. RISK-FREE	6.90	10.35	0.57
B. SYSTEMATIC EXCESS RETURN			
1. EXPECTED AT NORMAL BETA	6.00	9.00	0.50
2. SURPRISE AT NORMAL BETA	-10.97	-16.45	-0.91
3. TOTAL EXCESS RETURN AT NORMAL BETA	-4.97	-7.45	-0.41
4. DUE TO CHOSEN AVERAGE BETA	0.04	0.06	0.00
5. DUE TO BETA VARIATION	0.01	0.02	0.00
6. TOTAL REWARD DUE TO BETA POLICY	0.05	0.08	0.00
7. TOTAL EXCESS SYSTEMATIC RETURN	-4.91	-7.37	-0.41

C. RESIDUAL RETURN: COMMON FACTORS

RESIDUAL RETURN: COMMON FACTORS	0.0	0.0	0.0
1. EXPERIENCED AT NORMAL POSITION			
2. DUE TO ACTIVE RISK INDEX POSITIONS	0.98	1.47	0.08
3. DUE TO ACTIVE INDUSTRY POSITIONS	-0.71	-1.06	-0.06
4. DEBIT FOR ACTIVE XMC VARIANCE	-0.01	-0.01	-0.00
5. TOTAL DUE TO ACTIVE FACTOR POSITIONS	0.27	0.40	0.02
6. TOTAL RESIDUAL RETURN DUE TO COMMON FACTORS	0.27	0.40	0.02

D. RESIDUAL RETURN: SPECIFIC RETURN

RESIDUAL RETURN: SPECIFIC RETURN	0.0	0.0	0.0
1. EXPERIENCED AT NORMAL POSITION			
2. DUE TO ACTIVE HOLDINGS	0.98	1.48	0.08
3. DEBIT FOR SPECIFIC VARIANCE	-0.01	-0.01	-0.00
4. TOTAL SPECIFIC RETURN DUE TO ACTIVE POSITIONS	0.98	1.47	0.08
5. TOTAL RESIDUAL RETURN DUE TO SPECIFIC RETURNS	0.98	1.47	0.08

E. ADJUSTMENT FOR NONLINEAR INTERACTION	-0.05	-0.08	-0.00
F. TOTAL RESIDUAL RETURN	1.19	1.79	0.10
H. TOTAL RETURN	3.18	4.77	0.26
I. TOTAL EXCESS RETURN OF NORMAL POLICY	-4.97	-7.45	-0.41
J. TOTAL RETURN DUE TO ACTIVE MANAGEMENT	1.25	1.87	0.10

decomposition of logarithmic return for the 18-month period from July 1977 through December 1978. The format is very similar to the PERFAT analysis shown in Table 7.1.

Item A is the risk-free rate of return; items B, C, and D relate to the systematic components, the common factor components, and the specific return, respectively; item E is the nonlinear interaction between the systematic and residual components described in the previous sections; and items F, H, I, and J are self-explanatory. The normal portfolio is specified as the market portfolio (proxy), which is the S&P 500 in this case. Throughout, we will refer to the column headed "Annual Rate."

It was expected that the market would display a 6 percent excess rate of return over the long term (item B1). However, over this 18-month period the S&P 500 was down, giving rise to the surprise of -10.97 percent (item B2). The portfolio average beta over the 18-month period was less than 1.0, so the portfolio picked up 4 basis points (item B4) relative to the normal beta. Moreover, the portfolio beta was not constant during the entire period; it varied slightly, and when it did, it was, on average, the correct strategy (i.e., the manager increased beta prior to the S&P 500 showing positive abnormal returns, and vice versa). This variation in beta was responsible for 1 basis point (item B5), leading to the total reward due to beta policy of 5 basis points (item B6).

The portfolio was beneficially exposed to the risk indices to the tune of almost 1 percent per year (item C2), but industry positions decreased return by 71 basis points (item C3). Item C4 is one of the adjustment factors arising from the variance of the strategy; however, because the active XMC is so small, the adjustment is also small. In total, the common factor position of the strategy produced 27 basis points (item C6).

Items D2 and D3 show the return due to stock selection and the adjustment due to specific variance.[29] The overall residual return was 1.19 percent (item F), and the return due to active management was 1.25 percent (item J).

Table 7.6 shows the decomposition of model variance over the 18-month period. Item B3 is the S&P 500 variance at an annual rate; however, because the average beta is less than 1.0, the portfolio is exposed to 6.12 units of variance less than the index (item B4). The variation in beta causes a small increase in risk.[30]

Items C2, C3, C4, C5, and D4, and D5 are self-explanatory and similar to the decomposition shown in the PORCH reports. Table S4.2 shows the decomposition for the portfolio residual risk at one point in time; qualitatively, the style is very similar, the only major difference being that the variance levels at the time of the PORCH analysis were almost 50 percent of the averages listed in the PERFAN.

---

[29]Compare the split between common factor return and specific return with their variance components shown in Table S4.2.

[30]See "Market Timing" section in Chapter 5.

Table 7.6
Example 1 Decomposition of Variance

II. DECOMPOSITION OF MODEL VARIANCE {LOGARITHMIC * 100}

	ANNUAL RATE		CUMULATIVE		MONTHLY RATE	
A. RISK-FREE		0.0		0.0		0.0
B. SYSTEMATIC EXCESS RETURN						
3. AT NORMAL BETA		433.48		650.23		36.12
4. DUE TO CHOSEN AVERAGE BETA	-6.12		-9.19		-0.51	
5. DUE TO BETA VARIATION	0.02		0.04		-0.00	
6. INCREMENT DUE TO BETA POLICY		-6.10		-9.15		-0.51
7. TOTAL EXCESS SYSTEMATIC RETURN		427.38		641.08		35.62
C. RESIDUAL RETURN: COMMON FACTORS						
1. AT NORMAL POSITION		0.0		0.0		0.0
2. DUE TO ACTIVE RISK INDEX POSITIONS	0.89		1.33		0.07	
3. DUE TO ACTIVE INDUSTRY POSITIONS	0.85		1.28		0.07	
4. DUE TO {R.I. - IND.} COVARIANCE	-0.53		-0.80		-0.04	
5. TOTAL DUE TO ACTIVE FACTOR POSITIONS	1.21	1.21	1.81	1.81	0.10	0.10
6. TOTAL DUE TO COMMON FACTORS						
D. RESIDUAL RETURN: SPECIFIC RETURN						
1. AT NORMAL POSITION	0.0		0.0		0.0	
4. DUE TO ACTIVE POSITIONS	4.49	4.49	6.74	6.74	0.37	0.37
5. TOTAL DUE TO SPECIFIC RETURN						
F. TOTAL RESIDUAL RETURN		5.70		8.55		0.48
H. TOTAL RETURN		443.09		649.63		36.09
I. TOTAL EXCESS RETURN OF NORMAL POLICY		443.48		650.23		36.12
J. TOTAL RETURN DUE TO ACTIVE MANAGEMENT		-0.40		-0.60		-0.03

Table 7.7
Example 1 History of Standardized Active Outcomes

V. TIME SERIES OF STANDARDIZED ACTIVE OUTCOMES

	SYSTEMATIC	RISK INDEX	INDUSTRY	TOTAL XMC	SPECIFIC	TOTAL RESIDUAL	TOTAL
MIMIMUM VALUE	-1.57	-0.77	-1.99	-1.63	-0.56	-1.19	-1.20
MEAN VALUE	-0.06	-0.32	-0.19	-0.09	-0.14	-0.17	-0.17
MEDIAN VALUE	-0.22	-0.24	-0.32	-0.14	-0.17	-0.06	-0.09
MAXIMUM VALUE	1.38	1.36	1.93	1.62	1.24	1.42	1.40
STANDARD DEVIATION	0.69	0.63	1.05	1.07	0.54	0.72	0.69
1. JULY 1977	-0.33	0.27	-1.50	-1.02	0.39	-0.15	-0.16
2. AUGUST 1977	-0.29	0.21	-1.99	-1.63	-0.47	-1.19	-1.20
3. SEPTEMBER 1977	0.15	0.43	-1.22	-0.04	-0.67	-0.61	-0.62
4. OCTOBER 1977	-0.78	-0.12	0.47	0.29	-0.35	-0.17	-0.15
5. NOVEMBER 1977	-0.53	0.84	0.87	1.54	0.20	-0.90	-0.87
6. DECEMBER 1977	-0.01	0.10	-0.59	-0.33	-0.28	-0.40	-0.40
7. JANUARY 1978	1.09	-0.18	-1.60	-1.53	0.14	-0.49	-0.38
8. FEBRUARY 1978	-0.36	0.61	-0.54	0.16	-0.23	-0.14	-0.16
9. MARCH 1978	-0.36	0.99	0.94	1.62	0.80	1.42	1.40
10. APRIL 1978	1.38	-0.77	1.93	0.52	-0.19	0.11	0.17
11. MAY 1978	0.13	1.32	-0.44	0.90	-0.46	0.84	0.84
12. JUNE 1978	0.36	0.89	-0.42	0.34	-0.43	-0.24	-0.04
13. JULY 1978	-0.83	0.17	0.00	0.12	0.90	0.88	0.77
14. AUGUST 1978	-0.45	1.36	0.54	1.57	-0.56	0.14	0.13
15. SEPTEMBER 1978	0.19	-0.28	-0.66	-0.91	-0.43	0.02	0.04
16. OCTOBER 1978	-1.57	-0.75	-0.41	-0.41	1.24	-0.90	0.84
17. NOVEMBER 1978	-0.29	-0.04	-1.48	-1.21	-0.41	-0.94	-0.96
18. DECEMBER 1978	-0.14	0.76	0.95	1.52	0.26	0.95	0.89

Table 7.7 shows the time series of monthly standardized outcomes of active management. As discussed above, the standardized outcome is a measure of skill; if there were no skill, we would expect the time series to be distributed randomly about zero, like the standard normal distribution.[31] When there is skill, the standardized outcome should be distributed about the information ratio. Each outcome is an estimate of the ratio, with the mean of the series being the best estimator.

The top five lines in the table show the statistics of the return series. In each case the spread between the minimum and maximum values is wide showing that the statistical information in any one month's results is small. With the exception of the mean of the industry information ratios (-0.32), the mean values are positive. For some reason, the research process tends to pick overvalued industries. However, when the industries are taken with the risk indices, the forecasting of the common factors displays skill (at least as far as this test shows). The mean total residual (0.17) and total active outcomes (0.17) are both positive and greater than the median values (0.06 and 0.09, respectively), indicating that the underlying distribution of information ratios may be positively skewed.

Example 2

The second example is a pension account managed by T. Rowe Price Associates. In this example the period of analysis is 15 months, from January 1978 through March 1979. The normal portfolio was specified as the S&P 500 for January through September 1978; for October 1978 through March 1979 it was specified as a levered market portfolio with a beta of 1.08.[32]

Table 7.8 shows the front page of the PERFAN report. The expected excess return on the S&P 500 was 6 percent; however, item B1 is greater than 6.0 because the normal beta was greater than unity for part of the period. The main implication of this page is that the majority of the active return came from the risk index policy. In fact, 2.33 percent of the 3.61 percent active return came from the immaturity and smallness exposure.[33] Other pages in the report (not shown here) indicate that the exposure to this factor varied between 0.92 and 1.18; hence, it appears that this strategy is more a long-term normal exposure than an active management device. The remainder of the active return not accounted for by common factors arises almost equally from beta policy and stock selection.

---

[31]The standard normal distribution is a normal distribution with a mean of zero and a variance of one. See Supplement 1.

[32]These sample reports are taken from an investment consultant's performance measurement service. Our belief is that it would be more realistic for a growth-oriented, small-company normal portfolio to be specified in this situation.

[33]The 2.33 percent figure comes from a page of the report that is not shown here. Item J in Table 7.8 gives the total active return. See Figure 4.7 for the risk index exposures of this portfolio.

Table 7.8
Example 2 Decomposition of Investment Return

CONDITIONAL FORECASTING SERVICE
PORTFOLIO PERFORMANCE ANALYSIS

MARKET PORTFOLIO : S&P500
ESTIMATION UNIVERSE : A100
REGRESSION WEIGHTING: CAP

ANALYSIS PERIOD: JANUARY 1978 THROUGH MARCH 1979
15 MONTHS OF DATA
{DATE OF ANALYSIS: 798426}

I. DECOMPOSITION OF INVESTMENT RETURN, EXPRESSED AS LOGARITHMIC RETURN {*100}

	ANNUAL RATE	CUMULATIVE	MONTHLY RATE
A. RISK-FREE	7.82	9.78	0.66
B. SYSTEMATIC EXCESS RETURN			
1. EXPECTED AT NORMAL BETA	6.10	7.62	0.51
2. SURPRISE AT NORMAL BETA	-3.74	-4.70	0.51
	----	----	----
3. TOTAL EXCESS RETURN AT NORMAL BETA	2.34	2.93	0.20
4. DUE TO CHOSEN AVERAGE BETA	0.31	0.39	0.03
5. DUE TO BETA VARIATION	-0.07	-0.08	-0.01
	----	----	----
6. TOTAL REWARD DUE TO BETA POLICY	0.24	0.30	0.02
	----	----	----
7. TOTAL EXCESS SYSTEMATIC RETURN	2.58	3.23	0.22

C. RESIDUAL RETURN: COMMON FACTORS						
1. EXPERIENCED AT NORMAL POSITION	3.13	0.0	3.92	0.0	0.26	0.0
2. DUE TO ACTIVE RISK INDEX POSITIONS	0.10		0.13		0.01	
3. DUE TO ACTIVE INDUSTRY POSITIONS	-0.03		-0.04		-0.00	
4. DEBIT FOR ACTIVE XMC VARIANCE	-----		-----		-----	
5. TOTAL DUE TO ACTIVE FACTOR POSITIONS	3.20	3.20	4.00	4.00	0.27	0.27
6. TOTAL RESIDUAL RETURN DUE TO COMMON FACTORS		3.20		4.00		0.27
D. RESIDUAL RETURN: SPECIFIC RETURN						
1. EXPERIENCED AT NORMAL POSITION		0.0		0.0		0.0
2. DUE TO ACTIVE HOLDINGS	0.30		0.38		0.03	
3. DEBIT FOR SPECIFIC VARIANCE	-0.01		-0.02		-0.00	
4. TOTAL SPECIFIC RETURN DUE TO ACTIVE POSITIONS	0.29	0.29	0.36	0.36	0.02	0.02
5. TOTAL RESIDUAL RETURN DUE TO SPECIFIC RETURNS		0.29		0.36		0.02
E. ADJUSTMENT FOR NONLINEAR INTERACTION		-0.12		-0.15		-0.01
F. TOTAL RESIDUAL RETURN		3.37		4.21		0.28
H. TOTAL RETURN		13.78		17.22		1.16
I. TOTAL EXCESS RETURN OF NORMAL POLICY		2.34		2.93		0.20
J. TOTAL RETURN DUE TO ACTIVE MANAGEMENT		3.61		4.52		0.30

Table 7.9
Example 2 Decomposition of Variance

II. DECOMPOSITION OF MODEL VARIANCE {LOGARITHMIC * 100}

	ANNUAL RATE		CUMULATIVE		MONTHLY RATE	
A. RISK-FREE		0.0		0.0		0.0
B. SYSTEMATIC EXCESS RETURN						
3. AT NORMAL BETA		464.45		680.56		38.70
4. DUE TO CHOSEN AVERAGE BETA	18.51		23.13		1.54	
5. DUE TO BETA VARIATION	0.36		0.45		0.03	
6. INCREMENT DUE TO BETA POLICY		18.87		23.59		1.57
7. TOTAL EXCESS SYSTEMATIC RETURN		483.32		604.15		40.28
C. RESIDUAL RETURN: COMMON FACTORS						
1. AT NORMAL POSITION		0.0		0.0		0.0
2. DUE TO ACTIVE RISK INDEX POSITIONS	19.41		24.26		1.62	
3. DUE TO ACTIVE INDUSTRY POSITIONS	4.26		5.33		0.36	
4. DUE TO {R.I. - IND.} COVARIANCE	2.95		3.68		0.25	
5. TOTAL DUE TO ACTIVE FACTOR POSITIONS		26.62		33.28		2.22
6. TOTAL DUE TO COMMON FACTORS		26.63		33.28		2.22
D. RESIDUAL RETURN: SPECIFIC RETURN						
1. AT NORMAL POSITION		0.0		0.0		0.0
4. DUE TO ACTIVE POSITIONS	8.10		10.13		0.68	
5. TOTAL DUE TO SPECIFIC RETURN		8.10		10.13		0.68
F. TOTAL RESIDUAL RETURN		34.73		43.41		2.89
H. TOTAL RETURN		518.05		647.56		43.17
I. TOTAL EXCESS RETURN OF NORMAL POLICY		464.45		580.56		38.70
J. TOTAL RETURN DUE TO ACTIVE MANAGEMENT		53.60		67.00		4.47

Table 7.10
Example 2 History of Standardized Active Outcomes

V. TIME SERIES OF STANDARDIZED ACTIVE OUTCOMES

	RISK INDEX	INDUSTRY	TOTAL XMC	SPECIFIC	TOTAL RESIDUAL	TOTAL
MINIMUM VALUE	-1.09	-1.26	-1.82	-0.61	-0.91	-0.98	-1.00
MEAN VALUE	0.20	0.21	0.02	0.17	0.03	0.17	0.17
MEDIAN VALUE	0.14	0.34	0.24	0.14	0.19	0.24	0.30
MAXIMUM VALUE	1.57	1.16	2.05	1.06	1.48	0.82	0.84
STANDARD DEVIATION	0.74	0.62	1.25	0.51	0.63	0.56	0.58
1. JANUARY 1978	-1.09	0.10	0.80	-0.43	0.31	0.53	0.30
2. FEBRUARY 1978	-0.36	0.34	-1.56	-0.43	0.06	-0.35	-0.38
3. MARCH 1978	-0.36	-0.66	-1.28	-0.04	0.56	-0.24	-0.32
4. APRIL 1978	1.38	-0.44	2.05	0.45	0.45	0.60	0.84
5. MAY 1978	-0.13	1.16	0.24	1.06	-0.60	0.66	0.68
6. JUNE 1978	-0.36	0.45	1.01	0.77	0.29	0.82	0.74
7. JULY 1978	0.83	-0.09	0.90	0.29	0.19	0.35	0.48
8. AUGUST 1978	-0.45	-0.78	-1.51	0.07	1.48	0.75	0.83
9. SEPTEMBER 1978	-0.19	-0.20	-1.15	-0.41	-0.91	-0.98	-1.00
10. OCTOBER 1978	-1.57	-1.26	-1.58	-0.48	0.44	-0.20	-0.07
11. NOVEMBER 1978	-0.29	-0.85	-1.82	-0.02	-0.35	-0.15	-0.17
12. DECEMBER 1978	-0.14	0.37	1.05	0.75	0.21	0.75	0.75
13. JANUARY 1979	0.57	-0.30	-0.42	-0.43	-0.79	-0.75	-0.72
14. FEBRUARY 1979	0.60	-0.06	0.52	0.14	-0.29	-0.03	0.08
15. MARCH 1979	-0.81	0.78	-0.19	0.63	-0.60	0.24	-0.07

Table 7.11

Example 3 Decomposition of Investment Returns

```
CONDITIONAL FORECASTING SERVICE        MARKET PORTFOLIO    : S&P500
PORTFOLIO PERFORMANCE ANALYSIS         ESTIMATION UNIVERSE : A1000
                                       REGRESSION WEIGHTING: CAP
AMERICAN NATIONAL BANK
ANALYSIS OF PORTFOLIO
```

ANALYSIS PERIOD: MAY 1976 THROUGH APRIL 1978
48 MONTHS OF DATA
{DATE OF ANALYSIS: 8005213}

I. DECOMPOSITION OF INVESTMENT RETURN, EXPRESSED AS LOGARITHMIC RETURN {*100}

	ANNUAL RATE	CUMULATIVE	MONTHLY RATE
A. RISK-FREE	7.56	30.24	0.63
B. SYSTEMATIC EXCESS RETURN			
1. EXPECTED AT NORMAL BETA	6.00	24.00	0.50
2. SURPRISE AT NORMAL BETA	-7.60	-30.41	-0.63
3. TOTAL EXCESS RETURN AT NORMAL BETA	-1.60	-6.41	-0.13
4. DUE TO CHOSEN AVERAGE BETA	-0.54	-2.18	-0.05
5. DUE TO BETA VARIATION	-1.21	-4.85	-0.10
6. TOTAL REWARD DUE TO BETA POLICY	-1.76	-7.02	-0.15
7. TOTAL EXCESS SYSTEMATIC RETURN	-3.36	-13.44	-0.28

C. RESIDUAL RETURN: COMMON FACTORS						
1. EXPERIENCED AT NORMAL POSITION	5.15		20.62		0.43	
2. DUE TO ACTIVE RISK INDEX POSITIONS	-1.69		-6.75		-0.14	
3. DUE TO ACTIVE INDUSTRY POSITIONS	-0.18		-0.72		-0.01	
4. DEBIT FOR ACTIVE XMC VARIANCE		0.0		0.0		0.0
5. TOTAL DUE TO ACTIVE FACTOR POSITIONS	3.29		13.18		0.27	
6. TOTAL RESIDUAL RETURN DUE TO COMMON FACTORS		3.29		13.18		0.27
D. RESIDUAL RETURN: SPECIFIC RETURN						
1. EXPERIENCED AT NORMAL POSITION	7.37		29.48		0.61	
2. DUE TO ACTIVE HOLDINGS	-0.43		-1.71		-0.04	
3. DEBIT FOR SPECIFIC VARIANCE		0.0		0.0		0.0
4. TOTAL SPECIFIC RETURN DUE TO ACTIVE POSITIONS	6.94		27.77		0.58	
5. TOTAL RESIDUAL RETURN DUE TO SPECIFIC RETURNS		6.94		27.77		0.58
E. ADJUSTMENT FOR NONLINEAR INTERACTION		0.38		1.52		0.03
F. TOTAL RESIDUAL RETURN		10.62		42.46		0.00
H. TOTAL RETURN		14.82		59.27		1.23
I. TOTAL EXCESS RETURN OF NORMAL POLICY		-1.60		-6.41		-0.13
J. TOTAL RETURN DUE TO ACTIVE MANAGEMENT		8.86		35.44		0.74

Table 7.12
Example 3 Decomposition of Variance

II. DECOMPOSITION OF MODEL VARIANCE (LOGARITHMIC* 100)

	ANNUAL RATE	CUMULATIVE	MONTHLY RATE
A. RISK-FREE	0.0	0.0	0.0
B. SYSTEMATIC EXCESS RETURN			
3. AT NORMAL BETA	436.32	1745.30	36.36
4. DUE TO CHOSEN AVERAGE BETA	190.87	763.49	15.91
5. DUE TO BETA VARIATION	13.89	58.55	1.16
6. INCREMENT DUE TO BETA POLICY	204.76	819.04	17.06
7. TOTAL EXCESS SYSTEMATIC RETURN	641.08	2564.34	53.42
C. RESIDUAL RETURN: COMMON FACTORS			
1. AT NORMAL POSITION	0.0	0.0	0.0
2. DUE TO ACTIVE RISK INDEX POSITIONS	37.90	151.60	3.16
3. DUE TO ACTIVE INDUSTRY POSITIONS	20.60	82.41	1.72
4. DUE TO (R.I. - IND.) COVARIANCE	13.28	53.13	1.11
5. TOTAL DUE TO ACTIVE FACTOR POSITIONS	71.79	287.14	5.98
6. TOTAL DUE TO COMMON FACTORS	71.71	286.85	5.98
D. RESIDUAL RETURN: SPECIFIC RETURN			
1. AT NORMAL POSITION	0.0	0.0	0.0
4. DUE TO ACTIVE POSITIONS	111.60	446.41	9.30
5. TOTAL DUE TO SPECIFIC RETURN	111.60	446.41	9.30
F. TOTAL RESIDUAL RETURN	183.31	733.26	15.28
H. TOTAL RETURN	824.40	3297.60	68.70
I. TOTAL EXCESS RETURN OF NORMAL POLICY	436.32	1745.30	36.36
J. TOTAL RETURN DUE TO ACTIVE MANAGEMENT	338.07	1552.30	32.34

Table 7.9, which shows the decomposition of risk, is analogous to the PORCH "snapshot" given in Table S4.6. For this portfolio, the PORCH and PERFAN decompositions are very similar.

Table 7.10 shows the time series of standardized outcomes. Again, the dominant features are the statistics and outcomes pertaining to the risk index forecasts.

Example 3

This example refers to the Performance Investment Fund at American National Bank. Again, the normal portfolio is the S&P 500 (and again, this does not appear to be very realistic), but now we are fortunate in having four years of data, from May 1976 through April 1980.

Table 7.11 is the front page of the PERFAN report. This shows, for the first time in these examples, some degree of beta variation. However, even here, the effect of that variation is tiny compared to the effect of the other strategies, which are (1) stock selection and (2) risk index exposure. Table 7.12 shows the decomposition of risk. In this case, the comparison with PORCH (Table S4.10) shows quite distinct differences. In fact, from a history of the investment policy (not shown here), it is possible to see at least three quite distinct strategies within the four-year time span. This is quite in keeping with the organization's views on active management, described in Supplement 4.

Table 7.13 lists the time series of standardized outcomes. Here the spread between minimum and maximum values is wider than before, perhaps indicating that the underlying distribution of information ratios may have changed with the changes in strategy. The mean and median values of the risk index and specific return strategies are both positive and (relatively) large. The industry forecasting seems perverse, with a negative mean outcome. This leads to an overall *XMC* forecast with a small information ratio. The string of eight predominantly negative values for the residual return standardized outcome from September 1979 through April 1980 might also be noted. These negative outcomes indicate that several consecutive monthly outcomes provide little information as to the overall benefit of a strategy. As we have remarked before (e.g., supplement 4), "time until significance" can be very long.

Table 7.13
Example 3 History of Standardized Active Outcomes

V. TIME SERIES OF STANDARDIZED ACTIVE OUTCOMES

		SYSTEMATIC	RISK INDEX	INDUSTRY	TOTAL XMC	SPECIFIC	TOTAL RESIDUAL	TOTAL
MINIMUM VALUE		-1.84	-2.04	-2.55	-1.48	-1.78	-1.90	-1.90
MEAN VALUE		-0.11	-0.22	-0.28	-0.03	-0.20	-0.17	-0.13
MEDIAN VALUE		-0.14	0.21	-0.31	0.06	0.27	0.14	0.03
MAXIMUM VALUE		1.38	2.28	2.86	1.67	2.19	2.38	1.92
STANDARD DEVIATION		0.65	0.77	1.14	0.75	0.89	0.83	0.81
1.	MAY 1976	-0.20	-0.64	0.86	1.03	-0.70	-0.17	-0.23
2.	JUNE 1976	-0.64	0.57	2.26	1.67	0.42	1.14	1.29
3.	JULY 1976	-0.19	-0.48	-0.18	-0.48	0.11	-0.14	-0.21
4.	AUGUST 1976	-0.05	-0.14	-2.11	-1.02	1.31	0.49	0.45
5.	SEPTEMBER 1976	-0.33	-0.57	-1.02	-0.40	-0.14	-0.13	-0.00
6.	OCTOBER 1976	-0.40	-0.53	-1.04	-0.84	1.32	0.54	0.34
7.	NOVEMBER 1976	-0.08	1.84	-0.65	0.91	-0.43	0.21	0.16
8.	DECEMBER 1976	0.84	0.50	-0.15	0.27	0.85	0.84	1.10
9.	JANUARY 1977	-0.87	2.28	0.36	1.10	2.19	2.38	1.92
10.	FEBRUARY 1977	-0.32	0.20	-0.45	-0.01	0.81	0.61	0.45
11.	MARCH 1977	-0.27	1.26	-1.25	1.52	-1.78	-0.37	-0.44
12.	APRIL 1977	-0.04	0.03	-0.55	0.36	1.86	1.62	1.49
13.	MAY 1977	-0.32	0.52	-0.47	0.60	0.65	0.89	0.70
14.	JUNE 1977	0.72	0.09	-0.51	-0.24	0.58	0.28	0.55
15.	JULY 1977	-0.33	-0.06	0.09	0.01	0.07	0.06	-0.08
16.	AUGUST 1977	-0.29	0.11	0.45	0.31	-0.93	-0.53	-0.60
17.	SEPTEMBER 1977	-0.15	-0.09	-0.27	-0.19	-0.22	-0.04	-0.02
18.	OCTOBER 1977	-0.78	-0.35	-0.23	-0.37	-0.33	-0.49	-0.10
19.	NOVEMBER 1977	-0.53	-0.63	-0.81	-0.08	-0.39	-0.27	-0.01
20.	DECEMBER 1977	0.01	-0.14	-0.12	-0.04	-0.39	-0.28	0.26

21.	JANUARY	1978	-0·06	0·48	-0·10	0·96	-0·12	1·36	-1·09
22.	FEBRUARY	1978	-0·21	0·39	-0·29	0·26	-0·36	0·63	-0·36
23.	MARCH	1978	-1·72	-1·72	-1·39	-1·01	-0·60	-1·05	-0·36
24.	APRIL	1978	-1·45	-1·14	-1·02	-0·56	-1·45	-2·04	-1·38
25.	MAY	1978	-1·10	-1·14	-0·50	-1·37	-1·09	-0·66	-0·13
26.	JUNE	1978	-0·56	-0·53	-0·24	-0·61	-0·29	-0·44	-0·36
27.	JULY	1978	1·13	1·08	1·12	0·27	0·31	0·07	0·83
28.	AUGUST	1978	-1·15	-1·21	-0·67	-1·24	-0·41	-1·05	0·45
29.	SEPTEMBER	1978	-0·47	-0·55	-0·86	-0·51	-0·39	-0·54	-1·19
30.	OCTOBER	1978	-1·01	-0·40	-0·54	-0·04	-1·99	-1·16	-1·57
31.	NOVEMBER	1978	-0·38	-0·51	-0·32	-0·42	-1·92	-0·69	-0·29
32.	DECEMBER	1978	-0·06	-0·07	-0·44	-0·48	-0·95	-0·01	-0·14
33.	JANUARY	1979	0·85	0·63	0·95	0·14	-0·38	0·34	0·57
34.	FEBRUARY	1979	-0·82	-0·83	-0·99	-0·05	-0·33	0·29	-0·60
35.	MARCH	1979	-0·76	-0·71	-0·46	-0·55	-0·66	1·05	-0·81
36.	APRIL	1979	-0·14	-0·19	-0·70	-0·57	-0·24	0·81	-0·06
37.	MAY	1979	-1·11	-1·05	-0·98	-0·47	-0·27	-0·39	-0·40
38.	JUNE	1979	-0·21	-0·31	-0·34	-0·08	-1·18	0·62	-0·55
39.	JULY	1979	0·85	0·86	0·52	0·70	-0·49	0·99	-0·06
40.	AUGUST	1979	-0·09	-0·06	-0·15	-0·06	-0·82	0·36	-0·86
41.	SEPTEMBER	1979	-1·11	-1·11	-0·85	-0·73	-1·87	-0·17	-1·03
42.	OCTOBER	1979	-0·93	-0·49	-0·05	-0·67	-1·14	-0·26	-1·23
43.	NOVEMBER	1979	-0·01	-0·15	-0·25	-0·38	-2·55	-0·86	-0·70
44.	DECEMBER	1979	-0·06	-0·13	-1·73	-1·14	-0·72	0·54	0·14
45.	JANUARY	1980	-0·12	-0·08	1·67	1·29	-2·19	0·06	-0·83
46.	FEBRUARY	1980	-1·97	-1·90	-1·19	-1·48	-2·54	-0·08	-0·13
47.	MARCH	1980	-0·97	-1·06	-0·68	-0·82	-2·86	-0·81	-1·84
48.	APRIL	1980	-1·09	-1·04	-0·91	-0·64	-1·39	0·21	-0·57

Case Study 7: A Multiply Managed Portfolio,
Part 2—Performance Measurement[34]

Here we reproduce a section of the performance summary of an investment consultant's report on a real institution fund. While the names have obviously been changed, the performance results are those of four well-known money management firms. The period analyzed is from the beginning of January 1978 through March 1979, except for Special K Associates, which was hired in June 1978. The returns have been broken down into their four sources: market timing, common factors (extra-market covariance and industry group factors), and security selection. Two of the managers, Behemoth Trust Company and Petite Capital Investors, were measured against normal portfolios which were not equal to the market proxy (S&P 500). The normal portfolios had nonunit betas and exposure to the risk indices as specified by the managers' prestated investment style; i.e., if growth orientation was a stated objective, then this was taken into account and reflected in the return to risk indices row included under "Normal excess return," in the following tables. Unfortunately, the exact specifications of the normal portfolios are not stated.[35]

For Behemoth Trust Company and Ortho Growth, Inc., the time-weighted total return for the period analyzed was 10.65 percent and 18.77 percent, respectively (see Table 7.14). The risk-free rate of return was 8.14 percent for the period, the normal excess return was 2.88 percent for Behemoth and 2.22 percent for Ortho Growth. The normal portfolio of Behemoth was exposed to one or more of the common factors and thus received a 1.99 percent return, which indicates that Behemoth's style earned a return in the period studied independent of any active management skill. Ortho Growth, whose normal portfolio was the S&P 500, had zero return for the risk indices.

This investment consultant indicates the significance of the return by a probability assessment. An assessment of P percent indicates that there is a P percent probability that the return is drawn from a distribution whose mean is different from zero. Conceptually, this is similar to the calculations of the probable significance of the standardized outcome in the PERFAT and PERFAN reports.

The first row in the next category, "Active management," is "Market timing," which is defined in this case as the sum of the gain from a different average beta plus the variation in portfolio beta. Market timing yielded an overall negative return of -0.74 percent for Behemoth and -0.11 percent for Ortho Growth. The fact that portfolio betas for the period were different from their predefined normal position gave Behemoth a positive 0.06 percent return, while Ortho did even better at 0.81 percent. Both managers were penalized for

---

[34]The first part of this case study dealing with the risk analysis of the fund appeared at the end of Chapter 6.

[35]Consultants, please note!

Table 7.14
Performance Summary for Behemoth Trust Company and Ortho Growth, Inc.
(cumulative time period: 1/78–3/79)

	Behemoth Trust Company		Ortho Growth, Inc.	
	Return	Probability Assessment	Return	Probability Assessment
Actual rate of return				
Time-weighted	10.65%		18.77%	
Dollar-weighted	10.65		18.77	
Performance analysis				
Risk-free rate	8.14		8.14	
Normal excess return				
Market risk	2.88	43%	2.22	42%
Risk indices	1.99		0.0	
Active management				
Market timing	0.74	29	−0.11	48
Average Beta	0.06		0.81	
Beta variation	−0.80		−0.92	
Risk indices	−0.56	31	4.16	80
Industry	−1.49	20	0.84	64
Security selection	−0.70	66	−4.57	88
Active management subtotal	−2.02	25	9.19	89
Total analytical return	10.8	58	20.46	70
Difference (actual analysis)	−0.15		−1.69	

Cumulative returns have been annualized.

varying beta as a market timing device: Behemoth encountered a −0.80 percent return, and Ortho Growth fared even more poorly, with a −0.92 percent return.

Emphasis on the various risk indices cost Behemoth a −0.56 percent return, while Ortho Growth produced a large 4.16 percent return. Industry group emphasis cost Behemoth −1.49 percent in return, while Ortho Growth produced a positive 0.84 percent. Security selection, the fourth and final category for evaluating active management, gave Behemoth a modest 0.70 percent return compared with Ortho Growth's 4.57 percent. Behemoth's active management subtotal was −2.02 percent, while Ortho's Growth's 9.19 percent return was large enough to warrant a probability assessment of 89 percent, indicating a high probability of skill (or an 11 percent probability that this return was due entirely to random fluctuation). The low 25 percent probability assessment for Behemoth's active management subtotal reflects the high degree of randomness in the result. The difference between the actual return and the total analytical return of −0.15 percent for Behemoth and −1.69 percent for Ortho Growth occurred due to (1) the nonlinear interactions and risk adjustments from compounding, and (2) trading during the month (some of the columns may not add correctly to the printed subtotals for the same reasons).

Table 7.15 presents the performance statistics for the second pair of money

Table 7.15
Performance Summary for Petite Capital Investors and Special K Associates
(cumulative time period: 1/78–3/79)

	Petite Capital Investors		Special K Associates	
	Return	Probability Assessment	Return	Probability Assessment
Actual rate of return				
Time-weighted	10.24%		12.05%	
Dollar-weighted	10.24		12.05	
Performance analysis				
Risk-free rate	8.14		9.06	
Normal excess return				
Market risk	3.02	43%	5.08	48%
Risk indices	6.38		0.0	
Active management				
Market timing	−4.10	11	−0.31	58
Average Beta	0.0		0.13	
Beta Variation	−4.10		−0.18	
Risk indices	−0.85	29	2.05	61
Industry	−1.00	32	−5.43	1
Security selection	−1.46	35	1.76	64
Active management subtotal	−6.97	11	−2.19	39
Total analytical return	9.68	55	11.75	57
Difference (actual analysis)	0.56		0.30	

The cumulative time period for Special K Associates is June 1978 through March 1979. Cumulative returns have been annualized.

managers studied, Petite Capital Investors and Special K Associates. Since Special K's performance was only measured from June 1978 through March 1979, the results are not perfectly comparable, but the important differences will be noted in the following discussion.

For Petite Capital, the total return for the entire period, spanning January 1978 through March 1979, was 10.24 percent. The risk-free rate for this period was 8.14 percent. The returns from the market, based on Petite's Capital prestated normal beta and exposure to the common factors (i.e., its "style"), were 3.02 percent and 6.38 percent, respectively. Special K, on the other hand, earned a total return of 12.05 percent for its abbreviated period, while experiencing a risk-free rate of 9.06 percent during this time span. The normal portfolio for Special K was the S&P 500.

The active management analysis in this case shows that both Petite Capital and Special K were unable to produce positive returns during the periods studied. Petite Capital's average beta corresponded with its prestated policy; therefore, its average beta recorded a 0.0 return. But varying beta produced a substantial negative return of −4.10 percent. Here is significant evidence of a market timing strategy, and according to the analysis, that strategy was unfortunate. Special K's average beta for the period produced a positive 0.13 percent return, but its beta variation produced a small negative return of -0.18 percent.

Strategy with regard to the risk indices produced a negative result of -0.85 percent for Petite Capital but a positive 2.05 percent for Special K. Industry group emphasis produced negative results in both cases: -1.00 for Petite Capital and a large -5.43 percent for Special K. Security selection penalized Petite Capital with a negative -1.46 percent return but rewarded Special K with a positive 1.76 percent return. In both cases, the returns from total active management were negative, with a -6.97 percent return for Petite Capital and a -2.19 percent return for Special K. The total analytical returns were less than the actual returns in both cases, indicating that some return, 0.56 for Petite Capital and 0.30 for Special K, could be attributed to within-month trading or other causes.

If one is to accept these numbers at face value, Ortho Growth would win the performance contest. Its strategy with regard to the risk indices and security selection shows a high probability of skill. However, is this really skill or an incorrect normal portfolio? Security selection is less affected by the normal portfolio than return due to the risk index policy, so perhaps even with a normal portfolio that is more in tune with Ortho Growth's (fictitious) name and risk indices, security selection skill may still be in evidence.[36] Behemoth is a prime candidate for passive management (with a yield bias, perhaps, to hedge the growth exposure of the other managers), since it shows little evidence of providing any value-added.

Petite Capital is worthy of further inspection. It lost all along the line: market timing, risk index and industry strategy, and stock selection. Is Petite Capital a market timer? Or are these results (as the authors suspect) an indication of poor discipline in controlling the portfolio construction process? Certainly, there is little evidence in the assessments that future rewards will be commensurate with the risks taken.[37] Special K shows some evidence of risk index and security selection skill, but the (lack of a realistic) normal portfolio may account for much of this.

Figures 7.2, 7.3, and 7.4 are typical of the graphical performance reports put out by consultants to offer some assistance in summarizing the performance of money managers. In terms of total return, without any further analysis, Ortho Growth appears to dominate the other three managers (see Figure 7.2). Returns due to normal policy, which are not perfectly comparable due to Ortho Growth's and Special K's unspecified policies, are given in Figure 7.3. The difference between the two figures is the sum of the risk-free rate and active

---

[36]See Table 6.7 in part 1 of this case study.

[37]However, given the risk exposure of Petite Capital and the performance of the immaturity index subsequent to this period (Figure 4.7), Petite Capital's performance numbers and client accounts seem likely to have grown.

Figure 7.2
Quarterly Total Returns

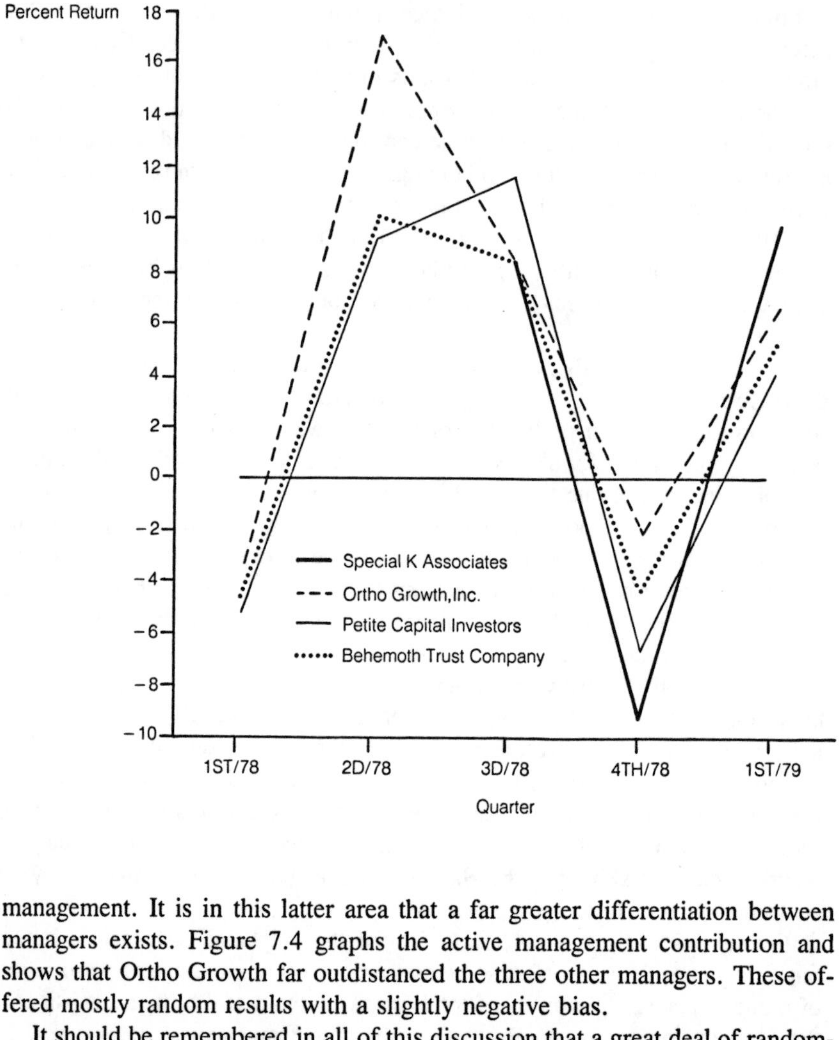

management. It is in this latter area that a far greater differentiation between managers exists. Figure 7.4 graphs the active management contribution and shows that Ortho Growth far outdistanced the three other managers. These offered mostly random results with a slightly negative bias.

It should be remembered in all of this discussion that a great deal of randomness is involved in the measurement of an ever-changing market and that a style which brings handsome returns in one phase of the market may well do exactly the opposite in another phase irrespective of any skill of the manager. The period covered for the evaluation must always be stressed. In this study, the five quarterly observations are too few to make any firm conclusions.

Our major purpose in presenting these performance measurement statistics was to portray a sample of the types of analyses that investment consultants are producing for their clients. There are many unanswered questions in the part of

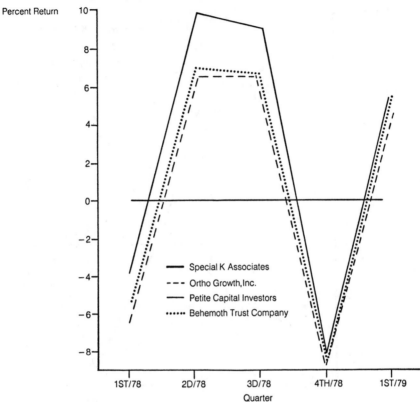

Figure 7.3
Quarterly Excess Normal Policy Return Contributions

Percent Return

—— Special K Associates
--- Ortho Growth, Inc.
— Petite Capital Investors
••••• Behemoth Trust Company

Quarter

the report shown here; however, never before in the history of money management has such careful scrutiny been given to investment results as at present. The current tendency is to increase the scrutiny, which is perhaps the major reason for acquiring an understanding of the techniques applied, and their limitations.

Summary

We have covered a lot of material in this chapter. Much of the current methodology on performance measurement and fund evaluation is naive, as is its purpose—namely, to reassure the pension fund trustees and managers. There is little of external value in such common statements as "Our perfor-

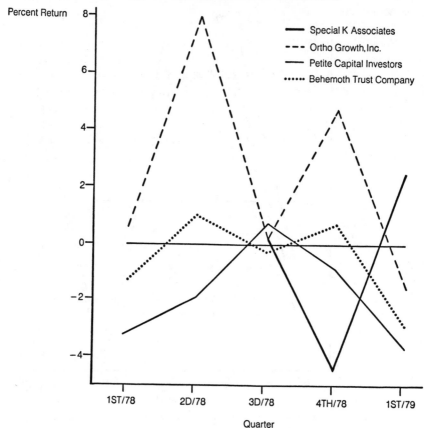

Figure 7.4
Quarterly Active Management Return Contributions

mance last quarter was in the first decile'' or ''Our returns last year were lower than the S&P 500 but higher than the Dow Jones Average, but we hope for better performance in the future.'' Sometimes the search for a worse-performing index is harder, but common factor exposure almost guarantees that at least one of the indexes—S&P 500, S&P 400, NYSE, AMEX, NASDAQ, Dow Jones Industrials, and so on—will make even the worst-performing fund look good.

It is worth remembering that performance measurement and attribution is only one side of a coin whose other side is risk measurement. And one fund's risk may be another fund's profit opportunity. Thus, there are no absolutes; there are only relative measures of benefit which must be evaluated in the context of the sponsor. The illusory quest for the ultimate, uniquely efficient portfolio is destructive to the pursuit of active management. Given the existence of abnormal returns and active management, we need to learn all that can be learned about an investment manager's research process and expertise; one source of this information is the measurement of historical performance and inferences based on the results.

The steps are reasonably straightforward. The manager has to provide active returns relative to the sponsor's normal portfolio. Since part of the manager's portfolio—the part which we have called the manager's normal portfolio—is a constant part of the sponsor's normal portfolio, it can provide no active benefit. Hence, we have to separate out the manager's bets from the manager's normal portfolio and to benchmark those bets relative to the sponsor's normal portfolio. The first task of the investment consultant is clear: specify the normal portfolio of each manager. In the master trust context, where there are good data, this task is easily accomplished.

Further Reading

The literature on performance measurement is simply enormous. Below we list our favorites.

Early articles

Fama, E. "Components of Investment Performance." *Journal of Finance*, June 1972, pp. 551–67.

Jensen, M. "The Performance of Mutual Funds in the Period 1954–1964." *Journal of Finance*, May 1968, pp. 389–416.

Measuring the Investment Performance of Pension Funds. Park Ridge, Ill.: Bank Administration Institute, 1968.

Sharpe, W. F. "Mutual Fund Performance." *Journal of Business*, January 1966, pp. 119–38.

Treynor, J. "How to Rate the Management of Investment Funds." *Harvard Business Review*, January–February 1965, pp. 63–76.

Recent Articles

Cornell, Bradford. "Asymmetric Information and Portfolio Performance Measurement." *Journal of Financial Economics*, 1979, pp. 381–90.

Mayers, D., and E. M. Rice. "Measuring Portfolio Performance and the Empirical Content of Asset Pricing Models." *Journal of Financial Economics*, March 1979, pp. 3–28.

Roll, Richard. "A Critique of the Asset Pricing Theory's Tests." *Journal of Financial Economics*, March 1977, pp. 129–76.

————. "Ambiguity When Performance Is Measured by the Securities Market Line." *Journal of Finance*, September 1978, pp. 1051–69.

————. "A Reply to Mayers and Rice." *Journal of Financial Economics*, December 1979, pp. 391–400.

————. "Testing a Portfolio for Ex-Ante Mean/Variance Efficiency." In: *Portfolio Theory—Studies in the Management Sciences*, vol. II, ed. E. Elton and M. Gruber. Amsterdam: North-Holland, 1979.

Rosenberg, Barr. "Performance Measurement and Attribution." *Proceedings of the*

Seminar on the Analysis of Security Prices, University of Chicago, May 1978, pp. 69–119.

————. "A Critique of Performance Measurement." Paper presented at the spring seminar of the Institute for Quantitative Research in Finance, Napa, California, April 1980.

————, and Andrew Rudd. "Option Performance Analysis." *Proceedings of the Seminar on the Analysis of Security Prices,* University of Chicago, November 1981, pp. 37–74.

Rudd, Andrew, and Barr Rosenberg. "The 'Market Model' in Investment Management." *Journal of Finance,* May 1980, pp. 597–607.

Wallace, Anise. "Is Beta Dead?" *Institutional Investor,* July 1980, pp. 23–30.

Supplement 7

The Statistics of Performance

In this supplement our aim is to explain mathematically some of the intricacies of proportional and logarithmic return over single and multiple periods. This explanation provides the justification for our bland assertions in the chapter concerning the variance adjustments and nonlinear interactions. We then turn to the problem of estimation and consider the statistical properties of the attributes being analyzed.

The conventional performance measurement procedure is to compare the portfolio rate of return for each of a series of intervals with the return series from the bogey portfolio over the same intervals. Almost without exception, the rate of return on the two portfolios is defined as the arithmetic or proportional rate of return:

$$i_P = \frac{\text{Capital appreciation and dividend yield}}{\text{Value at beginning of period}}.$$

This proportional return is also conventionally applied in the single-period capital asset pricing model; namely:

$$E[r_P] = \beta_P E[r_M],$$

where $r_P = i_P - i_F$ and $r_M = i_M - i_F$ are the excess rates of return. Hence, one justification for specifying proportional returns in performance measurement is their use in the premier model in finance.

A difficulty with proportional rates of return lies in extending the analysis over more than one period. We demonstrated this in Supplement 1 with the familiar example of an investor who doubles the value of a portfolio in one period and halves it in the next. Mathematically, the arithmetic average return is an increasing function of portfolio risk. In Chapter 7 we gave another example where we tried to decompose the two-period normal portfolio rate of return into the risk-free rate of return and the normal portfolio excess rate of

471

return. Unhappily, this decomposition is confused because of the compounding between the two periods.

The conclusion which we drew in Chapter 7 was to remain with proportional returns within the single period but to use the logarithmic transformation when aggregating over several periods. Here we want to describe and justify that transformation more completely. Suppose that in a two-period model we decompose total portfolio returns, i_{P1} and i_{P2}, into their risk-free components, i_{F1} and i_{F2}, their systematic excess components, $\beta_1 r_{M1}$ and $\beta_2 r_{M2}$, and their residual components, u_1 and u_2; that is:

$$i_{P1} = i_{F1} + \beta_1 r_{M1} + u_1, \tag{S7-1}$$

and

$$i_{P2} = i_{F2} + \beta_2 r_{M2} + u_2. \tag{S7-2}$$

These two equations represent the basic single-period decomposition shown in Table 7.1.

Now over the longer interval composed of the two periods, the total return is: $(1 + i_{P1})(1 + i_{P2}) = 1 + i_{P1} + i_{P2} + i_{P1}i_{P2}$, so that the cumulative rate of return is:

$$i_P^c = i_{P1} + i_{P2} + i_{P1}i_{P2},$$

where the superscript c denotes the cumulative value. Similarly, the risk-free cumulative rate of return is:

$$i_F^c = i_{F1} + i_{F2} + i_{F1}i_{F2},$$

which suggests that the excess rate of return is:

$$i_P^c - i_F^c = (i_{P1} - i_{F1}) + (i_{P2} - i_{F2}) + i_{P1}i_{P2} - i_{F1}i_{F2}$$
$$\neq [1 + (i_{P1} - i_{F1})][1 + (i_{P2} - i_{F2})] - 1.$$

This is another demonstration that the proportional model breaks down under compounding (i.e., the compounded excess returns do not equal the compounded total returns less the compounded risk-free returns).

Worse still, what happens to the risk decomposition, of equations (S7–1) and (S7–2)? The compound excess return on the portfolio is:

$$r_P^c = \text{Compound excess return}$$
$$= (1 + i_{P1})(1 + i_{P1}) - (i + i_{F1})(1 + i_{F2})$$
$$= \beta_1 r_{M1}(1 + i_{F2} + u_2) + \beta_2 r_M (1 + i_{F1} + u_1)$$
$$+ \beta_1 \beta_2 r_{M1} r_{M2} + u_1(1 + i_{F2}) + u_2(1 + i_{F1}) + u_1 u_2. \tag{S7-3}$$

At first glance, since this equation splits into terms involving beta only and residual returns only, it may be thought that a sensible decomposition into systematic and residual components results. Alas, this is not so. The easiest way to see this is to note that if we set $u_1 = u_2 = 0$ in equations (S7–1) and

(S7–2), then the period excess returns are entirely systematic (i.e., $\beta_1 r_{M1}$ and $\beta_2 r_{M2}$). Using this device with equation (S7–3), we note that the systematic component of the compound excess return, r_{PS}^c, is:

$$r_{PS}^c = \beta_1 r_{M1} (1 + r_{F2}) + \beta_2 r_{M2} (1 + i_{F1}) + \beta_1 \beta_2 r_{M1} r_{M2}. \quad (S7–4)$$

Similarly, setting $\beta_1 r_{M1} = \beta_2 r_{M2} = 0$ in equation (S7–3) to obtain the residual component, r_{PR}^c, we find:

$$r_{PR}^c = u_1(1 + i_{F2}) + u_2(1 + i_{F1}) + u_1 u_2. \quad (S7–5)$$

Finally, comparing equations (S7–3), (S7–4), and (S7–5), we find:

$$r_P^c \neq r_{PS}^c + r_{PR}^c,$$

or the systematic and residual components do not add to form the total. The error is:

$$r_P^c - (r_{PS}^c + r_{PR}^c) = \beta_1 r_{M1} u_2 + \beta_2 r_{M2} u_1, \quad (S7–6)$$

or cross-product terms arising from an interaction between the residual and systematic components in different periods. Moreover, the greater in number the components of return (i.e., factors) and the periods, the greater in number these cross-product terms become. In essence, equation (S7–6) is the origin of the nonlinear interaction adjustments.

One way out of this problem is to work with logarithmic returns. In Supplement 1 we showed that the logarithm of the compound return was the sum of the logarithms of the periodic returns and that the logarithmic return was equal to the continuously compounded rate of return. The logarithmic return uses the natural logarithm, denoted by $ln(\cdot)$ or by the superscript star when the context is clear, and defined as: $ln(1 + i_P) \equiv i_P^*$. A Taylor series expansion of the logarithm shows:

$$i_P^* = ln(1 + i_P) = i_P - \frac{1}{2} i_P^2 + \frac{1}{3} i_P^3$$
$$- \ldots \text{(Terms of higher order).} \quad (S7–7)$$

Since i_P is small (so that the squared and higher order terms are even smaller) for monthly data, the logarithmic return is approximately equal to the arithmetic rate of return.

We are now faced with the logarithmic representations of the decompositions, equations (S7–1) and (S7–2). The natural form for these is the so-called linear logarithmic model, namely:

$$ln(1 + i_{P1}) = ln(1 + i_{F1}) + \beta_1[ln(1 + i_{M1})$$
$$- ln(1 + i_{F1})] + ln(1 + u_1), \quad (S7–8)$$

and

$$ln(1 + i_{P2}) = ln(1 + i_{F2}) + \beta_2[ln(1 + i_{M2})$$
$$- ln(1 + i_{F2})] + ln(1 + u_2). \quad (S7–9)$$

For notational convenience, denote the logarithmic excess return by:

$$r_p^* \equiv ln(1 + i_P) - ln(1 + i_F)$$
$$= i_P^* - i_F^*,$$

Equations (S7–8) and (S7–9) can then be written succinctly as:

$$r_{P1}^* = \beta_1 r_{M1}^* + u_1^* \tag{S7–8a}$$

and

$$r_{P2}^* + \beta_2 r_{M2}^* + u_2^*. \tag{S7–9a}$$

Recall that the logarithm of the compound return is the sum of the logarithms,[1] so that the logarithmic compound excess return, $ln(1 + r_P^c)$ is given by:

$$ln(1 + r_P^c) = r_{P1}^* + r_{P2}^* = \beta_1 r_{M1}^* + \beta_2 r_{M2}^* + u_1^* + u_2^*. \tag{S7–10}$$

In this case, the model is preserved under compounding; i.e.:

$$ln(1 + r_P^c) = ln(1 + r_{PS}^c) + ln(1 + r_{PR}^c),$$

where

$$ln(1 + r_{PS}^c) = \beta_1 r_{M1}^* + \beta_2 r_{M2}^*$$

and

$$ln(1 + r_{PR}^c) = u_1^* + u_2^*.$$

Moreover, any further decomposition of the logarithmic residual return will be additive in its logarithmic components.[2]

The linear logarithmic model seems to be the answer to all our problems. Are there no drawbacks to it? Unfortunately, there are. In short, the linear logarithmic model is not the way the world works. The easiest way to see this is to note that, by definition, e.g., equation (S7–8a), the linear logarithmic model specified a *linear* relationship between the asset j logarithmic excess return, r_j^*, and the market logarithmic excess return, r_M^*. Also, by definition:

$$r_M^* = ln(1 + i_M) - ln(i + i_F),$$

and

$$r_j^* = ln(1 + i_j) - ln(1 + i_F).$$

Therefore, exponentiating:

$$(1 + i_F) \exp(r_M^*) = 1 + i_M, \tag{S7–11}$$

and

---

[1] See equation (S1–3).

[2] See e.g., Barr Rosenberg, "Performance Measurement and Attribution," *Proceedings of the Seminar on the Analysis of Security Prices*, University of Chicago, May 1978, pp. 69–119.

$$(1 + i_F) \exp(r_j^\star) = 1 + i_j, \qquad \text{(S7–12)}$$

where $\exp(\cdot)$ is the exponential function. But the market rate of return is simply the weighted average of the asset rates of return; i.e.:

$$1 + i_M = \sum_j h_{Mj}(1 + i_j), \qquad \text{(S7–13)}$$

where h_{Mj} is the holding of the jth asset in the market. Combining equations (S7–13), (S7–12), and (S7–11) gives:

$$\exp(r_M^\star) = \sum_j h_{Mj} \exp(r_j^\star),$$

or

$$r_M^\star = ln[\sum_j h_{Mj} \exp(r_j^\star)]. \qquad \text{(S7–14)}$$

But now $r_j^\star$ is a *nonlinear* function of $r_M^\star$. The only way to remove this discrepancy is to work in continuous time and to require continuous rebalancing of the portfolio and the market.[3] However, in the context of performance measurement, this makes the comparison portfolio an infeasible investment strategy and hence an unfair benchmark.

We are therefore forced to accept single-period proportional returns, that is, equations (S7–1) and (S7–2), but then to convert them to logarithmic returns before aggregating according to equation (S7–10). To make these results easier to follow, we will work through two examples. The first will be considerably simplified in that the subject portfolio will be a levered market portfolio. The second will introduce active management and its consequent complications.

Example 1

The portfolio is a levered market portfolio with the following data:

$$i_{F1} = 1\%; \quad i_{M1} = 11\%; \quad \beta_1 = 1.0;$$
$$i_{F2} = 2\%; \quad i_{M2} = 3\%; \quad \beta_2 = 2.0.$$

Hence, the within-period rates of returns, i.e., equations (S7–1) and (S7–2) appear as:

$$i_{P1} = 1 + (1)(11 - 1) = 11\%;$$
$$i_{P2} = 2 + (2)(-3 - 2) = -8\%.$$

The next step is to convert to logarithmic returns:

---

[3]This appeal to continuous time to remove nonlinearities is analogous to the argument used to prove the Black-Scholes option pricing formula. It was also the approach taken in Michael Jensen "Risk, the Pricing of Capital Assets, and the Evaluation of Investment Portfolios," *Journal of Business,* April 1969, pp. 167–247.

$$i^\star_{P1} = ln(1.11); \quad r^\star_{P1} = ln(1.11) - ln(1.01); \quad i^\star_{F1} = ln(1.01);$$
$$i^\star_{P2} = ln(0.92); \quad r^\star_{P2} = ln(0.92) - ln(1.02); \quad i^\star_{F2} = ln(1.02).$$

The cumulative returns then follow as:

$$ln(1 + i^c_P) = ln(1.11) + ln(0.92) = ln(1.0212) = 0.021;$$
$$ln(1 + i^c_F) = ln(1.01) + ln(1.02) = ln(1.0302) = 0.030;$$
$$ln(1 + r^c_P) = ln(1.11) - ln(1.01) + ln(0.92) - ln(1.02)$$
$$= ln(1.0212) - ln(1.0302) = ln(0.991263) = -0.009.$$

Hence, the cumulative performance in logarithmic and proportional returns appear as shown in Table S7.1. The proportional return is computed by two methods. Method 1 computes the risk-free return as $(1.01)(1.02) - 1.0$, and the total return as $(1.11)(0.92) - 1.0$, with the difference being attributed to systematic excess return. Method 2 computes the systematic return as the product of the periodic systematic returns (namely, $(1.10)(0.90) - 1.0$), keeping the risk-free return and total return computations as method 1. Notice a "fudge factor" appears if the systematic excess returns are incorrectly compounded directly (method 2) rather than the result of subtracting compounded risk-free returns from the compounded total returns (method 1), since the total return must be the sum of the parts. In this case, it is truly a "fudge factor" because the value attributed to the cumulative systematic excess return is not the complete amount. In certain instances (see Example 2 below), we cannot exactly compute the complete contribution from a particular source, in which case the difference is attributed to the nonlinear interactions between the components.

Let us now move on to the case of active management. Within-period returns will be given by equations (S7–1) and (S7–2), and as remarked above, the proportional returns will be converted to logarithmic returns. In particular, proportional return u_1 will be converted to logarithmic return $u^\star_1$. Now u_1 is an outcome from some distribution with mean α and variance ω^2. We will assume that the variance is constant over the measurement interval.[4] From equation (S7–7), it follows that:

Table S7.1
Decomposition of Investment Return, Example 1

	Logarithmic Return ($\times$ 100)	Proportional Return (percent)	
		Method 1	Method 2
Risk-free return	3.0	3.02	3.02
Systematic excess return	−0.9	−0.90	−0.01
"Fudge factor"			−0.89
Total return	2.1	2.12	2.12

---

[4]This assumption is made here simply for convenience of exposition and will be dropped in the discussion of estimation later in the supplement.

$$u_1^\star = \ln(1 + u_1) = u_1 - \tfrac{1}{2}u_1^2 + . . . \qquad \text{(S7-14)}$$

Therefore, taking expectations:

$$
\begin{aligned}
E[u_1^\star] &= E[u_1] - \tfrac{1}{2}E[u_1^2] + . . . \\
&= \alpha - \tfrac{1}{2}(\text{Var}[u_1] + E^2[u_1]) + . . . \\
&= \alpha - \tfrac{1}{2}(\alpha^2 + \omega^2) + . . . ,
\end{aligned}
$$

where we have used equation (S1-6). Typically, the mean, α, is small, so that α^2 is even smaller. Hence, α^2 and terms in u_1 of higher order than quadratic can be safely ignored, giving:

$$E[u_1^\star] \sim \alpha - \tfrac{1}{2}\omega^2. \qquad \text{(S7-15)}$$

Moreover, taking variances of equation (S7-14) shows:

$$\text{Var}[u_1^\star] \sim \text{Var}[u_1] = \omega^2.$$

Thus, the logarithmic return has (approximately) the same variance but a smaller mean. If we simply took logarithms of the residual return, we would, over time, bias the mean upwards by an amount equal to one half of the variance. Hence, the transformation to logarithms should include an adjustment (debit) for active variance. With this preamble, let us consider Example 2.

Example 2

In addition to the data presented in Example 1, we also admit active management as follows:

$$
\begin{aligned}
u_1 &= -1\%; \\
u_2 &= +2\%; \\
\omega^2 &= 25 \ (\%^2) \text{ per period.}
\end{aligned}
$$

Hence, the within-period rates of returns appear as:

$$
\begin{aligned}
i_{P1} &= 1 + (1)(11 - 1) + (-1) = +10\%; \\
i_{P2} &= 2 + (2)(-3 - 2) + (2) = -6\%.
\end{aligned}
$$

The total portfolio returns have now changed to:

$$
\begin{aligned}
i_{P1}^\star &= \ln(1.10) = 0.095; \\
i_{P2}^\star &= \ln(0.94) = -0.062; \\
\text{and } \ln(1 + i_P^c) &= \ln(1.10) + \ln(0.94) = \ln(1.034) = 0.033,
\end{aligned}
$$

but $r_{P1}^\star$, $r_{P2}^\star$, $i_{F1}^\star$, and $i_{F2}^\star$ are the same as in Example 1. Part of the residual return calculation is as follows:

$$
\begin{aligned}
u_1^\star &= \ln(0.99) = -0.01; \\
u_2^\star &= \ln(1.02) = 0.020.
\end{aligned}
$$

Hence, the contribution to return attributable to active management is:

$$ln(1 + u^c) = ln(0.99) + ln(1.02) = ln(1.0098) = 0.01,$$

less the debit for active variance, which is 0.0025/2 per period, or 0.0025. However, this is not the complete contribution since we are directly compounding within-period residual returns and the nonlinear interaction with the other components of return has been omitted. The magnitude of the interaction is simply that required to bring the residual return up to its correct value.[5] The decomposition of investment returns appears as shown in Table S7.2

Table S7.2
Decomposition of Investment Return, Example 2

	Logarithmic Return ($\times$ 100)	Proportional Return (percent)
Risk-free return	3.0	3.02
Systematic excess risk	−0.9	−0.90
Residual return	1.0	0.98
Debit for active variance	−0.0025	
Nonlinear interaction	0.2025	0.30
Total return	3.3	3.4

With this basic framework it is a simple generalization to include additional residual common factors of return. Each is handled analogously to the total residual return in Example 2 and provides a basis for attribution, as shown, for example, in Table 7.5.

The next step is to aggregate the monthly risk contributions. Under the assumption that returns are serially uncorrelated (for which there is considerable evidence in the real world), the variance contributions add over time.[6] Thus, it is possible to associate each cumulative return with a cumulative variance, with the end product being a time series of standardized outcomes and an overall estimate of the information ratio.

The only subtlety with these estimators is to model how changes in the mean active return are related to the variance of the active return (i.e., the relation of α_t to ω_t^2, or in logarithmic returns, of α_t^* to ω_t^{*2}) over time.[7] There are two realistic methods of modeling this process, which suggest different estimators of the information ratio. One evolves from the assumptions that the disutility coefficient, λ, is constant over time. In this case, as explained in Chapter 2, it is optimal for the manager to maintain a constant mean/variance ratio. In other

---

[5]To repeat a previous result, the nonlinear interaction will only vanish when within-period factor returns are given by a linear logarithmic model.

[6]See e.g., equation (S1–13).

[7]This discusion is adapted from Rosenberg, "Performance Measurement and Attribution," which should be consulted by readers interested in further details.

words, opportunities with greater alphas are undertaken only with proportionally higher variances. This implies that there is, in every period, some constant k, such that:

$$\alpha_t^* = k\omega_t^{*2},$$

which specifies the constant mean/variance ratio ($= k$) assumption. In this case, k is a primary parameter to be estimated. This is, perhaps the more powerful approach of the two because it takes account of the changes in aggressiveness due to strategy as well as the actual "bets" at various points in time.

The other approach is to assume that changes in risk may be unrelated to changes in the information ratio. The presumption is that the information ratio or level of skill remains constant over time, while the level of risk will change, for instance, because of the scarcity or otherwise of profitable opportunities found by the research process. In this case, the assumption is of a fixed information ratio; i.e.,

$$\alpha_t^* = z\omega_t^*.$$

Here the constant of proportionality, which is equal to the information ratio, is the essential parameter to be estimated.

Chapter 8

The Implementation of MPT and Its Future Prospects

We have discussed a good deal of theory in the first seven chapters of this book, but although we have presented various case studies which gave some application of the material to the real world, we have not written much about implementation. We want to remedy that situation in this chapter by indicating how MPT is being used in the early 1980s—in short, to do a performance measurement study on MPT.

Having done that, we will look to the future. What are the likely applications of quantitative methods in the next decade or so, and what is the future of MPT?

The Implementation of MPT

At its current stage of development, modern portfolio theory has made the greatest inroads by far in the areas of risk measurement and performance measurement. These inroads have stemmed partly from the strong pressure of pension fund consultants upon their clients to use more sophisticated methods to monitor and measure their plan money managers. The most vocal complaint, as we indicated in Chapter 6, has been that too much fee money is being paid for too little performance. One reason for this complaint is too low an assumption of risk on the part of the active managers. Hence, it is natural for pension fund consultants to stress risk and performance measurement. Frequently, these consultants are part of the new breed of salespeople from bank master trusts. Clearly, promoting their own measurement services not only enlightens their clients but may also enlarge their client base. MPT capability is fast becoming the deciding factor in attracting new master trust business.[1]

An additional impetus to the better servicing of pension plans is being provided by the growing visibility of pension liabilities in corporate accounts. These numbers are no longer easily hidden in the footnotes, and for some corporations, especially older concerns in mature industries, the numbers are truly staggering.[2] Pension fund liabilities which reflect a negative net worth are not unusual. There is a great need for better accounting, closer monitoring, and greater control of both pension liabilities and pension assets; there is even a strong case for coordinating pension planning and corporate planning.[3]

As was briefly touched upon in Chapter 5, the basic investment decision of the pension plan relates to setting the asset allocation. Sophisticated simulation routines are now available which project the viability of fund performance based on a series of possible scenarios relative to inflation, asset returns, and plan obligations. Rather than depending on single-point forecasts, plan sponsors use Monte Carlo simulation techniques to generate a range of probable outcomes for possibly 20 years into the future. The beauty of such techniques is that they examine a broad range of scenarios in order to portray in very practical terms the implications of that investment decision for the corporation. In short, plan sponsors are now in a position to preexperience the future.

There are numerous commercial models available from consulting actuaries and investment consultants. Typically, the complexity of these models is so great that the consultant designs and then performs the analysis.[4] Since this

---

[1]See, e.g., "Getting Choosy about Master Trusts," *Institutional Investor*, March 1980, pp. 77–80.

[2]See, e.g., Paul Wilson, "Danger Ahead for CFOs—Pension Fund Assets Are Fast Catching Up to Corporate Net Worth," *Financial Executive*, August 1979, pp. 11–17.

[3]The Financial Accounting Standards Board has recently announced revised guidelines for the accounting of pension plans. One difficulty with analyzing the pension plan is that it is sandwiched between the interest of various professional groups—lawyers, actuaries, accountants, corporate executives and investment managers and consultants. Historically, each group has examined or been responsible for a single aspect; what is really required is an integrated approach to the whole plan. This is happening, but slowly.

[4]Caveat emptor! *Complicated* does not necessarily mean *realistic*, just as *simple* is not always synonymous with *worthwhile*.

exercise is intended to determine the long-term allocation, the simulations are not repeated frequently. Clearly, such projects are fairly expensive.

So much for the long-term decision. The short-term decisions fall much more into our purview since they are easier to relate to the bottom line: Is the pension sponsor getting value for the management fees? Two principal aspects of this question concern us: first, the selection of the money managers, and second, the monitoring of the active managers.

Few of the consultants (or of the corporations which do not use outside help in the selection process) use anything close to the procedures outlined in Chapter 6. In general, most of the selection processes for money managers are based on historical performance.[5] Unfortunately, either sponsors are unwilling (or unable) to understand the dearth of real information in performance figures or their fears of an ERISA lawsuit prevent them from disregarding such information. Private discussions with several consultants specializing in manager selection indicate that the frequently used criteria, other than historical performance, are largely irrelevant for predicting investment ability. Occasionally, the style or habitat of the manager plays some role, as does a corporate or professional relationship between the manager and the plan sponsor or perceptions of integrity and honesty.

As far as the monitoring of managers is concerned, the implementation of MPT is far more advanced. Risk measurement is an important tool in analyzing the aggregate portfolio and determining its level of aggressiveness. Although risk analysis of the aggregate portfolio only dates from 1976 or so, it is quite common now. Again, the competitive urges of master trusts have ensured this, and monthly or quarterly analyses are becoming the widely accepted norm. Less common is the monitoring of intermanager correlations and the dependence-adjustment factors, but the technology is being disseminated to sponsors with astonishing rapidity.

The design of hedging funds is another technique that has come into use, partly because master trusts have emphasized this technique. The next stage is to integrate multiple manager optimization and performance attribution. For instance, performance can be attributed relative to the money manager's "style." If especially good or poor results occur, statistical tests can suggest whether the results were merely an accident or whether they may have been due to skill. The new dominance of better measurement has forced most money managers to hire quantitatively oriented MBAs or security analysts not just to improve their marketing image but to act as "translators." It is not unusual for the head of a money management firm to bring along his translator at client meetings to discuss the prior quarter's performance, where the translation takes

---

[5]At the time of writing, the majority of new money managers retained by corporations were small-compnay specialists who would have displayed good historical performance (see Figure 4.7). If corporations fired managers as readily as they hire them using the performance yardstick, we would quickly see changes in the management of many funds.

place out in the open before the client. While the procedure is somewhat strange, it is evidence of the change that has been taking place.

Alpha generation is the largest gray area in the entire MPT arsenal. Doctrinaire academics feel that the high efficiency of the capital markets makes alpha forecasting a worthless effort. On the other hand, many practitioners believe that there is sufficient inefficiency in the capital markets and a sufficient availability of unique insights to make alpha forecasting a worthwhile endeavor. The initial efforts in forecasting alpha where the design of dividend discount models similar in nature to the model presented in Chapter 4. Most large investment managers use or experiment with such an approach. Because of the widespread use of such models, any advantage rests with superior inputs. The empiricists of the MPT world, armed with larger and better data bases and comparatively inexpensive computer time, have begun to develop multivariate regression models. The idea underlying this approach is that a combined prediction with improved overall forecasting ability can be found by assembling a group of individually marginal forecasting techniques. To our knowledge, approximately a dozen money managers are working in this direction.

Security valuation is one ingredient in portfolio construction. While it might be tempting to think that applying a rule of thumb (or experience) to estimated risk and return values could produce optimal portfolios, the interrelationships are simply too complex. A small, but growing, percentage of institutional portfolios are managed using optimization techniques which balance risk against expected reward. This type of effort is still very much in the experimental stage, with most money managers unwilling to make a total commitment to these techniques. The main reasons for this unwillingness are a lack of understanding and the substantial change that such a commitment might force the people side of the organization to undergo. Many current roles are threatened by these developments.

The lack of faith in optimization is invariably demonstrated by the example of an optimistic alpha forecast. The usual experience is that an optimistic alpha forecast of 5 percent will cause an optimized portfolio to hold 15 percent or more of the stock in a portfolio. Because absolutely nobody (!) holds 15 percent of one stock in a portfolio, optimization is discarded.[6] In reality, it is the alpha that should be questioned first, but few egos are happy with such a conclusion. Since many money managers are inexperienced in mathematical techniques and the forecasts suffer from little faith, few money managers are willing to risk their reputations on them. While this is changing as more managers progress up the learning curve, widespread use of optimization still lies in the future.

---

[6]Most large portfolios are multiply managed, but people consistently examine the minutiae of the individual portfolios rather than the aggregate portfolio. Hence the exaggerated aversion to residual risk. To show the error in this approach, we could have rearranged the holdings of the four managers in Case Study 7 (Chapters 6 and 7) so that the total portfolio remained the same but Behemoth Trust held only one stock (Investment Annuity, Inc.?). Our bet is that everybody would have concentrated on the foolhardiness of Behemoth's (one-stock) portfolio to the exclusion of the big picture.

Perhaps the greatest tragedy of MPT takes place when an organization wantonly embraces the new techniques. Too many mathematicians approach the securities market as if it were a neatly controlled physical problem, rather than the complex human problem it truly is. The art of the challenge is dismissed as trivial and irrelevant. Most experienced security analysts and portfolio managers are intimidated by mathematics and computers and are stubbornly unwilling to learn. Rather than growing and adapting, they leave the organization. If an organization rigidly adheres to simply demanding number inputs for its MPT forecasting models, it will end up with recently graduated MBAs who will gladly provide the numbers, which are probably meaningless because the recent graduates have had no practical experience with the businesses being forecast. Eventually, the GIGO ("garbage in, garbage out") phenomenon manifests itself.

The more successful organizations seem to approach the new techniques as a laboratory experiment. Forecasting techniques are tested; paper portfolios are created; and in-house MPT specialists develop practical techniques which can interface with the existing organization. If the results are good, natural curiosity is the teacher and the organization gradually sharpens its skills. Being induced rather than forced, the organization avoids the natural resistance to change. The guiding principle seems to be the avoidance of extremes.

Much thinking about organizing a research effort seems to be built upon the implicit assumption that there must be an optimal or universal solution to the problem of money management.[7] This attitude overlooks the most basic element of the situation—the people performing the research. Their skills, experience, and temperaments are just a few of the important variables that define a unique situation. A heavily quantitative approach may even lessen forecasting ability. There are examples of analysts whose understanding of an industry, thorough knowledge of company strategies, and recognition that market bearishness is an error enable them to demonstrate above-average and nonrandom results. Such analysts usually despise attempts to quantify the techniques employed. In their minds, forecasting is an art and therefore beyond quantification.

It is possible to define the goals of the research effort. Is discovering special situations a goal? Analyzing the major components of the S&P 500? The more clearly stated the goals, the better the solution. Once the goals have been defined, a logical structure of necessary skills should be enumerated. Then research projects and responsibilities should follow, so that the feedback process provided by the framework of MPT can be organized. In this manner a realistic answer to the problem at hand can be created. This does not mean that the process is now finished. Quite the contrary. Ideally, a thorough examination of research procedures should be conducted on a regular basis, perhaps annually, in order to check for weaknesses and errors as well as strengths and successes. The world and its markets are constantly changing. How can the research effort

---

[7]If there were a universal solution, there would be no superior money managers.

adapt? What new areas, if any, should be investigated? Are there new strategies to be tested? Such questions should always be asked.

One of the main reasons for adopting at least some of the elements of MPT is to provide a disciplined framework for the research effort. Change of personnel is a serious problem and can introduce a great deal of instability into performance results. It is also possible to get swept up in the fads of the investment community as various industry groups or investment styles produce a period of profitability. The temptations to imitate success are all too strong, while success is highly transient. Experience teaches that such chasing of rainbows usually matches adoption with defeat. Again, there are no universal answers. But good planning and defining goals can help avoid these pitfalls. Whether a dividend discount model or some other valuation model is the chosen form of forecasting, the important point is to run a thread of consistency through the analyst's efforts.

How do money managers get to embrace MPT? There are usually two routes: either there is an individual or a group of individuals who actively promote the use of MPT or, more commonly at present, there is client pressure. Pension plan sponsors exposed to MPT through master trustees, consultants, or one of their managers learn the advantages of greater control and exert considerable influence on all of their managers to become similarly involved.

The advantages of MPT as it is currently implemented are discipline and control. MPT encourages portfolio managers to follow consistent procedures, and thus the style of the firm becomes more explicit and the results across portfolio managers become far more uniform and predictable. The major advantage that we have stressed in this book, namely better allocation of creative resources, is only just beginning to be accepted. The perceived disadvantage of MPT (at least before implementation) is mainly its effect on people.

The process of assimilating MPT is reasonably uniform. The MPT champion (or the MPT designate if client pressure dictates the use of MPT) starts by performing a risk analysis of a typical account. This is the stage of learning the jargon and capabilities of the technology. The next stage is to begin analyzing the risk in several accounts, with the aim of comparing them and interpreting their aggressiveness and required alphas. At this level of use, MPT is employed as a feedback device to provide some unbiased support to the managers. The majority of MPT users perform risk analyses on all their (major) accounts at month-end.

Concurrently, these organizations may use portfolio optimization for research projects, special studies, and specific strategies (i.e., index funds). However, to integrate optimization directly into the management process requires a greater commitment, since quantitative valuation judgments on the followed securities are required. The level of development is such that at this time the major bank trust departments and investment advisers are proceeding in this mode. Optimization is run monthly or more frequently when judgments are changing rapidly. The portfolio manager responsible for the account checks and confirms the trades, which are then passed to the trading desk.

Performance measurement and attribution tools tend to remain the province of the consultants at bank master trusts and are only infrequently the province of the research directors at money management firms. This is unfortunate since attribution provides revealing insights into the research capacity. Nevertheless, attribution analyses are becoming more widely used by portfolio managers.

So much for the advantages; what are the disadvantages? The major stumbling block to greater implementation is fear: fear that the decision process is being subjugated by a "black box" that is only understood by a few academics and fast-talking consultants and fear that organizational disruption will become rife. In reality, a cavernous black hole exists in the traditional process, in contrast to the perceived black box of MPT; as we have argued throughout this book, the traditional method of money management contains no rationale for going from judgment to portfolio. Hence, the fear is of exchanging comfortable, but ambiguous, tradition for an explicit and analytic recipe.

The fear of organizational disruption is more realistic. Portfolio managers fear loss of autonomy, increased management oversight, and reduced job status. Older managers are intimidated by unfamiliar concepts and by recent MBAs who think statistically and lack real-world (investment) sophistication.

But most organizations who have adopted MPT feel that its disadvantages have been wildly exaggerated. Where MPT has been introduced, portfolio managers have usually been interested and have been encouraged to use the system at their own pace. There have been very few resignations or job terminations because of the introduction of quantitative methods. But, conversely, familiarity with MPT has been a prime consideration in hiring new portfolio managers.

Finally, it is worth examining why institutions have discontinued the use of MPT methods. Essentially, there have been two reasons: (1) the MPT champion was ineffective in getting support or went to another organization; or (2) the characteristics—usually the budget—of the institution did not warrant MPT usage. Investment professionals who understand MPT and can communicate with portfolio managers are in great demand, and hence command high salaries. It is sometimes a difficult problem for organizations to retain such employees at high salaries relative to those of equally senior but less sought after positions in the hierarchy.

The Applications of MPT to Nonequity Assets

There are two directions for financial research on which we should comment. The first may be loosely termed the future of the capital asset pricing model; the second is the application of quantitative techniques to financial instruments other than U.S. equities. Since the development of equilibrium pricing models (of which the CAPM is one example) is intimately related to the future of MPT, we will defer discussion of this aspect until the next section. Here we will briefly concentrate on "other" applications.

Bonds

The development in bonds has been to depart from the yield curve toward a term structure of interest rates. Work has also been done to integrate such key variables as call features and firm liquidity in the prediction of the fair value for a bond. These applications have been directed to both the government and the corporate markets. It becomes clear, especially when dealing with low-quality ("junk") and convertible corporate bonds, that the corporation as a whole and the equity in particular have a large influence on the value of corporate bonds. With this in mind, the natural analytical mode for the evaluation of all corporate financial instruments is to consider the corporation as *the* entity and to analyze all its securities as a package.

For a number of reasons, the U.S. bond markets have not been as well scrutinized historically as the U.S. equity markets. The major reason is that machine-readable data bases of prices, terms, and conditions did not become available until the late 1970s.[8] Moreover, bonds, particularly corporate bonds, are very complex instruments.

In order to briefly sketch the direction of MPT applications to bonds, we will first consider the "simple" government market. Then we will turn to the more complex fixed-income markets. The initial reaction is that government bonds are easy because they are all very similar and because they are default-free. Unfortunately, this is not strictly true. There are at least three differentiating elements of value to government bonds, namely:

1. The current yield (taxation considerations and coupon preferences combine to determine the value attached to different coupon levels).
2. The flower bond privilege (certain bonds can be redeemed at par to pay estate taxes).
3. The call feature.

Moreover, Treasury bills as a group, because they are used as reserve requirements and have no coupons (which removes the inconvenience of redeeming coupons), may be priced differently than are notes and bonds. Finally, when one considers government agency and guaranteed bonds (e.g., FNMA, World Bank, and TVA), a host of additonal features complicate the analytical process. Thus, even the default-free market is far from homogeneous. For this reason, the historical approach of drawing a yield-curve fails (as does the traditional approach of pricing by analogy) because the distinguishing features cause the curve to become a "cloud."

---

[8]Data on call features, sinking funds, and so on.

The first step to rigorous analysis is to estimate the present value of the stream of payments. There are three equivalent procedures for discounting a riskless stream; these are to use:

1. The spot interest rates.
2. Discount factors.
3. The term structure of forward interest rates.

Consider a pure discount bond that matures at time T with a principal repayment of F. Its present price, P_0, is simply the discounted value of F; that is:

$$P_0 = F/(1 + R_T)^T, \tag{8–1}$$

where R_T is the (annualized) *spot rate* of interest between now and time T. We can also write equation (8–1) as:

$$P_0 = Fd_T,$$

where $d_T = 1/(1 + R_T)^T$ and represents the *discount factor* to be applied to a payment that will be made at time T. In other words, the value of receiving $1 at time T is $$d_T$ today.

Of course, not every bond is a simple discount bond, but most bonds which do not have complicating characteristics can be represented as a package of discount bonds. Let C_t represent the coupon paid by a bond at time t. Then its present value is:

$$\begin{aligned} P_0 &= C_1/(1 + R_1) + C_2/(1 + R_2)^2 + \ldots + (C_T + F)/(1 + R_T)^T \\ &= C_1d_1 + C_2d_2 + \ldots + (C_T + F)d_T, \end{aligned} \tag{8–2}$$

where R_t is the (annualized) spot rate of interest between now and time t and d_t is the discount factor applied to payments at time t (i.e., $$d_t$ is the cost today for receiving $1 at time t).

Now consider the relationship to forward rates of interest. For example, consider a bond with two coupons remaining. From equation (8–2) we find:

$$P_0 = C_1/(1 + R_1) + (C_2 + F)/(1 + R_2)^2. \tag{8–3}$$

What do we expect the bond's price to be one period from now, after the coupon C_1 has been paid? We do not know its exact price, but we can specify its dependence on interest rates, namely:

$$P_1 = (C_2 + F)/(1 + r_{1,2}), \tag{8–4}$$

where $r_{1,2}$ is the one-period spot rate at time 1 over the period from time 1 to time 2. (In order to specify the beginning and ending times, we have to add two subscripts to r.) But now we can view the price of the two-period bond in equation (8–3) as the discounted value of its price one period in the future, i.e., the price given in equation (8–4);

$$\begin{aligned} P_0 &= (C_1 + P_1)/(1 + R_1) \\ &= C_1/(1 + R_1) + (C_2 + F)/(1 + R_1)(1 + r_{1,2}). \end{aligned}$$

The current price depends on the known spot rate for the first period, R_1, and the implied interest rate that holds over the second period, $r_{1,2}$, i.e., $r_{1,2}$ is the one-period rate of interest one period forward in time, or the *one-period forward rate*. In general, we can write equation (8–2) as:

$$P_0 = C_1/(1 + R_1) + C_2/(1 + R_1)(1 + r_{1,2}) + \ldots$$
$$+ (C_T + F)/(1 + R_1)(1 + r_{1,2}) \ldots (1 + r_{T-1, T}),$$

where $r_{t,t+1}$ is the rate for t periods forward or the t period forward rate. Comparision of this equation with equation (8–2) shows that $1 + r_{1,2} = (1 + R_2)^2/(1 + R_1)$, or, in general, $1 + r_{t,t+1} = (1 + R_{t+1})^{t+1}/(1 + R_t)^t$.

The forward rate structure is the most natural of these three representations, because the t period forward rate is the cost of moving funds from time t to time $t + 1$. This type of interaction is missing with the yield curve because the yield to maturity is a strange function of several attributes of the bond. By definition, the *yield to maturity*, Y, satisfies:

$$P_0 = C_1/(1 + Y) + C_2/(1 + Y)^2 + \ldots + (C_T + F)/(1 + Y)^T,$$

or

$$P_0(1 + Y)^T - C_1(1 + Y)^{T-1} - C_2(1 + Y)^{T-2}$$
$$- \ldots - (C_T + F) = 0. \tag{8–5}$$

Hence, Y is a function of the current price, the face value, all coupons and their payment dates, and the maturity of the bond. If the set of Y's are plotted versus maturity for a set of bonds, then the curve fitted to these points is called a *yield curve*. The major problem with the yield curve, besides the errors introduced by heterogeneity, is that it implies that intermediate cash flows are reinvested at the yield to maturity. Only when there is a single cash flow, as with a pure discount bond, does the yield to maturity have economic meaning; namely, it is equal to the spot rate, as comparison of equations (8–5) and (8–1) shows. The better way of describing the relationship between interest rates and time is the *term structure of forward rates*, which plots forward rates $r_{t,t+1}$ versus time.

Our task is to estimate the discount factors, given the coupon stream and the principal payments.[9] Unfortunately, because of the heterogeneity of the instruments, the use of equation (8–2) as the estimation framework leads to incorrect results. One straightforward method of accounting for the heterogeneity, which is in the spirit of the equity estimation methods introduced in Chapter 3, is to assume a constant adjustment per unit time to the discount factors, where the adjustment is determined from the bond's differentiating characteristics.

We can rewrite equation (8–2) as follows:

---

[9]Since there is a unique relationship between discount factors, spot rates, and forward rates, we can choose which one of the three to estimate.

$$P_0 = C_1 d_1/(1 + \kappa) + C_2 d_2/(1 + \kappa)^2$$
$$+ \ldots + (C_T + F)d_T/(1 + \kappa)^T, \tag{8-6}$$

where the Greek letter kappa (κ) represents the adjustment to the discount factors for this particular bond. (Of course, if the bond has no differentiating characteristics, $\kappa = 0$.) A good assumption for the form of the kappas is that they are linear in the differentiating characteristics. For instance, let x_1, x_2, x_3, x_4, and x_5 be *descriptors* of a bond that indicate its likelihood of differential valuation because of the current yield effect, the flower bond privilege, the call provisions, the Treasury bill convenience premium, and special characteristics of agency bonds. Then suppose:

$$1 + \kappa = b_1 x_1 + b_2 x_2 + b_3 x_3 + b_4 x_4 + b_5 x_5, \tag{8-7}$$

where the b's are coefficients to be estimated. Estimates of the b coefficients indicate the market's appraisal of these differential characteristics. The complete estimation problem is to find the d's and b's using equations (8-6) and (8-7), over all bonds which are currently accurately priced.

Modeling corporate bond prices proceeds analogously, the only difference being that there are more differentiating characteristics. In addition to those metioned above for default-free instruments, a corporate model must take into account the following:

1. Default premium.
2. Sinking fund effects.
3. Convertibility.

It is interesting to note that these three characteristics, as well as the call provision, are options.[10] For instance, common equity can be viewed as a call option on the value of the firm, with the exercise price equal to the face value of the outstanding bonds. This relationship suggests that a bond subject to default can be viewed as a default-free bond and a written put, since the equity holders can "put" the firm to the bondholders if times get hard. Hence, the default premium can be valued by option theory as the price of a put. The sinking fund option takes many forms, but at its simplest it gives the corporation the right to sink a certain fraction of the bonds at the lower of the market price or the sinking fund price. Convertibility is simply the option of the bondholders to exchange one asset of the corporation for another asset.[11] The call provision gives the corporation the right to retire the bond issue at a certain (the call) price. The default and conversion options have values that depend

---

[10]For an excellent introduction to option contracts, see Mark Rubinstein and John Cox, *Option Markets*, (Englewood Cliffs, N.J.: Prentice-Hall, in press). The following description is only intended to give a "flavor" of the analytical process; interested readers should consult the references for more details.

[11]Not necessarily an asset of the same corporation. For instance, in 1980 Textron issued debt which was convertible into Allied Chemical equity.

mainly on the value of the firm (i.e., the stochastic process of firm asset values), while the sinking fund option and the call provision are valued from the stochastic process of interest rates.

Considerable effort has been spent modeling these options in the process of valuing corporate bonds. The future direction of research into valuing bonds will almost certainly continue along these lines. The developments that take place will surely have profound impacts not only on secondary trading in the bond market, but also on the issuance of debt and private placements.

The next step after valuation is the prediction of risk. The valuation approach naturally lends itself to the development of a risk model since risk in the bond market arises primarily from changes in the discount factors (i.e., changes in the term structure) and secondarily from changes in the market's assessments of bond characteristics. All of the applications arising from a risk model, which we have discussed in this book in terms of common stock, apply to bonds as well. Bond performance measurement and attribution, bond optimization, and the coordination of multiple managers naturally follow. In some sense the bond equivalent of index funds is the strategy of *immunization*, which is the "indexing" to a prespecified set of cash flows. With a risk model the capability of accurate immunization is achieved.

This approach can be extended to Eurodollar and municipal bonds. The latter are fascinating because of both the operational (there are in excess of 1.5 million municipal bond issues) and the theoretical (i.e., tax consequences) problems involved. Unfortunately, lack of space prevents us from developing the models that are likely to be used, but we are confident that by the mid-1980s all three categories of bonds, which are generally regarded as inefficient (i.e., containing opportunities for abnormal return) by practitioners, will become more liquid and efficient by reason of the growth in the application of analytical methods to them.

Real Estate

Real estate is probably the third most important category of assets for institutional investors, after equities and fixed-income assets. Thus, it is somewhat surprising to find an almost complete absence of empirical knowledge regarding real estate returns. There appear to be no realistic indices which attempt to measure price appreciation, cash flow, or return from real estate.[12]

The main reasons for the lack of risk and reward estimates for real estate is that there are no easily observable transaction prices. Real estate is not standardized and homogeneous; there is no central real estate market; investors' holding periods are diverse, and they are frequently longer than the holding periods for other assets; and transaction costs (commissions and information

---

[12]Research aimed at producing useful indices has started; see James Hoag, "Toward Indices of Real Estate Value and Return," *Journal of Finance*, May 1980, pp. 569–80.

costs) are large. In short, the analysis of real estate seems to confront every difficult issue in asset pricing.

Yet real estate pooled funds must be valued quarterly so as to provide investors with quarterly rates of return. The solution that these funds use is to hire an appraiser who provides a subjective estimate of the value of their holdings at a given point in time. The appraiser obtains the estimate by assimilating the fundamental characteristics of the property and the macroeconomic conditions and, through mental gyrations, computes the answer. This process gives us an inkling of the correct approach for objectively valuing real assets.

The process is essentially no different from the application of multiple factor models to equities and fixed-income securities.[13] The idea is to develop a valuation function composed of the fundamental characteristics of the assets. This valuation function is then fitted to transaction prices. Once the valuation function has been estimated, the value of nontransacting property at any point in time can be found by simply substituting the property's fundamental characteristics.

Since we can do this at one point in time, we can also do it at various points in time and so obtain the asset's compound rates of return. Moreover, a time series of valuations provides the opportunity for the estimation of a risk model based on the changing assessments made by the market for the fundamental characteristics used in the valuation function.

The only difficulty with this approach is obtaining the fundamental characteristics.[14] Because of the heterogeneity of real estate and the vast numbers of real estate properties, it is likely that analysis will be confined to only the most important homogeneous subclasses of real estate. Nevertheless, real estate promises to be one of the most successful applications of MPT in the coming decade.

Foreign Securities

Since the mid-1970s, pension sponsors have shown considerable energy in investing some of their assets in foreign securities. The primary reason for doing so has been the low correlation between the foreign markets and the U.S. markets. Hence, the effect of diversification has been to considerably reduce overall levels of risk. This is not the place for a deep analysis of international investment. Suffice it to say here that to be weighed against the advantage of increased diversification are several problems associated with the move overseas. Much has been written about the advantages of international investment;

---

[13]For equities, the multiple factor model is typically fitted to the return. However, for infrequently traded assets (both equity and fixed income), the model is fitted to the price.

[14]This seems to be the major problem with all asset categories. The COMPUSTAT data base for equities has been available for almost 20 years; the terms and conditions data base (see footnote 8) has been available for less than 5 years; the equivalent real estate data base is being collected only now.

little has been written about the disadvantages. Among the latter we note the following two.

First, although investment in foreign securities may reduce the total risk of the fund, any such gain may be made at the expense of greatly increasing the exposure of the fund to "new" common factors. For instance, consider an excessively simple example where the objective of the fund is to be worth $L (the value of the liabilities) at some future time. Let A_d be the value of the assets at that same future time when the initial investment was in domestic securities. The risk to the fund can then be expressed as:

$$\text{Var}[A_d - L] = \text{Var}[A_d] + \text{Var}[L] - 2\,\text{Cov}[A_d, L],$$

where we have used equation (S1–11). Suppose that instead of being invested entirely in domestic securities, some fraction of the assets is invested in foreign securities. As is well known, diversification causes the total risk of the asset portfolio to decrease; for instance, let $\text{Var}[A_f] = a^2\,\text{Var}[A_d]$, where A_f is the value of the assets when part of the fund is invested in foreign securities, and a (less than one) is the fraction of risk (standard deviation) reduced by foreign investment. Now the risk to the fund, after foreign investment, is:

$$\begin{aligned}\text{Var}[A_f - L] &= \text{Var}[A_f] + \text{Var}[L] - 2\,\text{Cov}[A_f, L] \\ &= a^2\,\text{Var}[A_d] + \text{Var}[L] - 2a\,\text{Cov}[A_d, L],\end{aligned}$$

after application of equation (S1–12) and substitution for A_f. Hence, the change in risk is:

$$\text{Var}[A_d - L] - \text{Var}[A_f - L] = (1 - a^2)\text{Var}[A_d] - 2(1 - a)\,\text{Cov}[A_d, L].$$

Some simple algebra shows that foreign investment will *increase* risk if the correlation, ρ, between the assets and the liabilities is large. In particular, risk to the fund will increase if:

$$\rho > (1 + a)\,\text{Std}[A_d]/2\,\text{Std}[L],$$

where Std [·] denotes the standard deviation.

Second, the costs of foreign investment may be substantially greater than the costs of domestic investment. These costs include custodial, informational, transaction, and liquidity premiums. Table 8.1 shows representative costs for domestic and international investment as estimated by major U.S. plan sponsors that were in the process of deciding whether to invest internationally.

Concentrating on the assets of the pension fund may make the decision to invest abroad seem unambiguously beneficial. But if the liabilities and the domestic assets are sufficiently correlated (as they might be if the liabilities are largely denominated in the domestic currency and an important common factor—for instance, inflation—affects both categories), then investing abroad may be harmful to corporate health. Even if benefits exist, they must be substantial to overcome the costs.

The state of the art of MPT abroad is generally a few years behind that of

Table 8.1
Representative Costs of Domestic and International Investment

	International Portfolio		U.S. Portfolio		Difference	
	Passive	Active	Passive	Active	Passive	Active
Commissions	0.10%	0.59%	0.05%	0.27%	0.05%	0.32%
Withholding taxes	0.40	0.61	—	—	0.40	0.61
Management fees	0.17	0.65	0.10	0.25	0.07	0.40
Custodial fees	0.15	0.15	0.05	0.08	0.10	0.07
	0.82%	2.00%	0.20%	0.60%	0.62%	1.40%

Note: Based on U.S. $20 million account.

the United States. Risk measurement services similar to those developed in the United States in the mid-60s are available for equities in the United Kingdom, France, Australia, and some Far Eastern markets. The lack of accounting sophistication and/or disclosure mechanisms suggests that risk measurement models will be less explanatory for foreign equities than for the U.S. equities.

The early foreign ventures of U.S. funds appear to have been split evenly between active and passive ventures. Several foreign security index funds have been created, and these appear to be well funded. Active management is becoming more widespread as U.S. bank trust departments and investment counselors set up operations abroad and as foreign managers become better known in the United States.

The lack of sophisticated risk models for foreign markets has usually meant that foreign passive strategies are based on the simple stratification heuristic discussed in Supplement 5. For instance, a fund may buy the 10 largest companies in a given country in proportion to their weight in a visible index.

Personal Trust

To date MPT has been concentrated on large pension fund applications, but there are good reasons why at least parts of the methodology will gradually be implemented in the management of other types of portfolios. One prime target is the taxable portfolios in personal trust departments. The personal trust business of many eastern banks, easily outstrips their pension business. Unfortunately, the problems of personal trust management are not only exceedingly complicated, being bound up in the legal machinations of estate law, but are steeped in the tradition of personal service and the family retainer. It is, therefore, highly labor intensive and costly for the banks to perform personal trust business properly. The personal trust is also a natural target for efficient information processing.

In essence, the problem is as follows. The trust department may have responsibility for several thousand portfolios, each of which may have particular legal constraints and conflicting beneficiaries. For instance, a common trust deed stipulates that the income from the portfolio is to go to one beneficiary (the income beneficiary) during his or her lifetime and that afterward the principal is to pass to another beneficiary (the remainder person). Clearly, there are conflicting considerations with regard to how the fund should be managed during the lifetime of the income beneficiary. For instance, depending on the tax status of the income beneficiary, certain strategies (e.g., investing in municipal bonds for individuals in high tax brackets) may be preferred over others.

As a consequence of all the constraints surrounding the individual trust, such trusts have historically been handled by a single person who has responsibility for up to 100 or more of them which are dealt with in rotation once every three or four months. Naturally, the need to deal with all of the noninvestment considerations leaves hardly any time to pay much attention to the subtleties of investment.

The natural solution is to use an optimization program capable of handling taxation constraints. Every portfolio could then be automatically analyzed using the latest investment judgment. The portfolio manager would then have far more time to spend in advising beneficiaries on matters relating to taxation, the setting of goals, and so on. Again, the key to MPT is the efficient allocation of scarce resources.

The Acceptance of MPT by the Investment Community

A common subject of discussion in today's investment community is whether or not MPT is a passing fad. If MPT is a fad, then it would have to be appraised as contributing nothing to the construction of portfolios or the measurement of portfolio performance. The point being missed in such discussions is that a major change is taking place, namely the rationalization of the institutional investment process. This process is in harmony with the better measurement and control procedures that have entered all business management processes in the United States with the advent and acceptance of computer technology. And as computer time becomes ever less expensive and information processing becomes a more and more accepted standard for measuring the quality of management, the investment community will not be bypassed.

Even the severest critics of MPT must admit that the implications of the theory, which suggest how terribly difficult it is to design portfolios that consistently beat the market averages, are all too true. The fact that diversification makes achieving abnormal portfolio performance exceedingly difficult can be easily demonstrated and explained by the theory. Any decision-making process can benefit from better measurement, and that is precisely what MPT provides.

Perhaps the greatest resistance to the application of MPT comes from its being an agent of change. In a world of continuous change, there is a desire to keep doing the same old thing, but to survive and prosper one must adapt to the new conditions.

What are these new conditions, where is MPT today, and why has it come this far? To go back to the beginning, MPT describes the selection of portfolios by investors who wish to maximize the expected reward consistent with their individual willingness to bear risk. The first part of the MPT puzzle to be solved successfully was in the area of risk measurement. The early attempts to measure risk focused on the variability of a security's price relative to some broad average, typified by the S&P 500. This relative measure was named beta.

With the advent of better data bases and better statistical tools, the ingredients for more accurate measurements were falling into place. One final prerequisite was necessary before the number crunching could begin—namely, the development of a model or theory to explain the forces affecting stock returns. In this theory, systematic or market risk and residual or nonmarket risk were seen as containing further dimensions. Both sources of risk were the result of common factors operating in the economy. This multiple factor model, as it has become known, provided a framework that permitted better predictions of beta. In addition, residual risk could be broken down into two components, one relating to the company itself, or specific risk, and the other comprising residual factors relating to the industry in which the company operated and other classes or groups of securities with common attributes, such as atypical growth orientation or financial risk. This latter component of residual risk was called extra-market covariance *(XMC)*.

This explanation of stock price variability, in which the multiple factors account for some 40 percent of the variability in a *single* asset, made possible the correlation of risk exposure with the associated rewards.[15] While the rewards generally could not be forecast well, at least portfolio performance measurement and attribution could be analyzed in a far more thorough and effective manner than had been possible previously. This was therefore the first important area for the practical application of MPT.

Perhaps the weakest link in the developmental chain for MPT has been the area of forecasting abnormal reward, or alpha. Even in this area great changes have taken place. A decade ago, exceedingly few academicians denied the strong efficiency of the equity markets. Now, it is more common to hear that the case for efficiency is weaker than had been believed. Commercial products are available, whether dividend discount models or multivariate models, which demonstrate at least some degree of forecasting ability. Alpha forecasting is the new area of focus, and it has many faces. Some conceptual purists tend to feel that a dividend discount approach is the road to better forecasts. Others favor

---

[15]The multiple factors account for considerably more than 40 percent of the variability in a portfolio context. Second-generation multiple factor models can now explain some 60 percent of individual stock price variability. The theoretical limit depends on the amount of risk which is truly specific and, empirically, on the extent of the data bases and the veracity of the model.

the development of a multivariate model which may use a dividend discount model as one of its input sources.

In attempting to forecast returns, one needs to know the forecasting ability of the in-house research staff or the commercial model. This analysis is beginning in earnest. Even the conclusions of a nonquantitatively oriented analyst regarding a company's business outlook or management ability can be graded on a scale of 1 to 10. Such inputs can be tested for their information content with regard to future realized returns. Progressive research departments are doing this kind of testing at present and more rather than less of it seems likely in the future.

As the firm appraises its abilities, it will define where improvement is needed and it will work to upgrade its forecasting skills. Various market sectors or themes might be tested, such as small companies versus large companies, so that a unique and marketable style may emerge. Even now, some analysts are evaluated on their ability to forecast future earnings for the companies they follow and the salary increments of these analysts are scaled to the information content of their forecasts over a certain test period.[16]

The product of this effort aimed at implementing MPT is the increasing amounts of capital that are being managed by optimization techniques. The most important reason for adopting portfolio optimization is that this results in the better allocation of scarce resources. Other reasons are that portfolio optimization removes emotion from the decision-making process and permits the better control (or justification) of residual risk.

Using portfolio optimization eliminates emotion and conteracts the prime weakness of most portfolio managers—falling in love with a security or an industry that has performed well. Given a valid forecasting methodology, an optimization program will undergo regular weeding and upgrading of the portfolio based on the current outlook for a security, irrespective of whether the security's historical performance has been good or poor. The program does not rest on its laurels or drop its guard; it simply continues to process information in an unbiased and consistent manner. And aside from the manager's emotional quirks, there are also the foibles of the guidance committee that refuses to ever sell IBM or some other security because of misplaced nationalism, past performance, or the confusion of quality with value. Change occurs in the future, and that is exactly where portfolio optimization, fed with return forecasts, focuses its attention.

A most challenging problem for MPT was that of aiding pension fund sponsors in overseeing their multiply managed portfolios. What appeared to be a cost accounting problem turned out to be a problem in optimal decentralized management. Investment management is a $250 billion industry, and if the average management fee is 0.5 percent, then $1.25 billion in fees are generated

---

[16]We are not advocating this approach, but merely stating one current practice. As we have remarked earlier, security analysis is an art that demands subtlety and creativity. The reward structure should be defined to encourage these traits.

annually, which is obviously not a trivial amount. Are sponsors (and pensioners) getting their money's worth? What was discovered in the early analysis of multiply managed funds was that most pension plans were essentially large index funds, with most of the individual money managers canceling out each other's performance through excessive diversification. Was there an alternative? Yes, in the form of low-cost passive strategies which could achieve the same results willingly. And so the index fund revolution began to grow.

Sponsors also began doing a better job of selecting and controlling their stable of money managers. The result is that it has become less easy to sell oneself as a growth manager if a risk analysis demonstrates the model portfolio to be yield oriented or, worse yet, a closet index fund. This trend is still gaining in force. More and more money managers, out of self-defense, are having to develop measurement expertise in order to compete effectively.

Just from the improved measurement techniques for risk and performance, pension plan sponsors at major corporations have changed their attitudes toward selecting and monitoring their money managers. They are tending to work with fewer money managers and with more precise strategies for the ones they do select. In addition, the corporations that are dissatisfied with the quality or cost of the investment service they are being offered are more and more beginning to manage their own plans—in-house management is no longer the exception. Closely involved in many of these changes are bank master trusts, which offer the data processing, security handling, and consulting services to assist pension plans in upgrading their own measurement skills. There is internal joking in the industry about token "quants," young MPT-oriented MBAs who are hired by money managers to create the illusion of cutting-edge sophistication at sales and client meetings. The irony is that the number of quants is not only increasing but that their ideas and analytical approach to problem solving are being incorporated into the money management process.

An obvious outgrowth of these trends is the increasing numbers of consultants and computer specialists who act as translators and advisers for those who are attempting to adopt MPT techniques. This new service industry is not only interpreting MPT but is also aiding the interface of MPT with the accounting, auditing, actuarial, legal, and data processing staff. The impact of computer technology is crucial; new applications programs are run in a time-sharing mode and (perhaps more common in the future) with on-site miniprocessors. This will offer greater efficiency, shorter turnaround time on analyses, and lower cost. In the next decade portfolio managers will undoubtedly be able to sit down at a desktop computer terminal, input the new return forecasts from the research department, create a new optimized portfolio for a customer, approve the changes, and then electronically transmit the necessary order forms to the trading room or to other supervisory or fiduciary authorities. Farfetched? This is simply a matter of good systems design and programming. In fact, an obvious part of the program will be feedback from the trading desk, with automatic updating of the account to reflect the changes made.

Among what types of institutions are the changes being made, and at what level? As one might guess, the greatest amount of change is taking place at the large banks, insurance companies, and corporations that have the research staffs and one or more quantitative specialists to test the application of some of the new investment techniques. Several of these large institutions have their own return forecasting models and are running optimized portfolios. Several are also offering forecasting models and other services to the investment community at large.

A half dozen of the larger institutionally oriented Wall Street brokerage firms are offering a range of products which include dividend discount model output, performance measurement services to test forecasting ability, optimization programs to design portfolios, historical beta files, and special consulting services. Most of the customers for these services are medium-size banks, insurance companies, and corporations that do not have their own staffs and are willing to use someone else's product. It is doubtful, however, given the structure of the brokerage business, whether brokerage firms can be serious purveyors of analytical investment services. In all probability, this "second tier" of customers will be served by independent consultants, under the aegis of consultant actuaries, master trusts, data suppliers, or software companies.

In the meantime, the use of quantitative tools will become more widespread. The investment profession is exceedingly mobile and competitive, so that its adoption of new ideas is rapid. Sophisticated sponsors will demand that the new quantitative tools be considered and understood. If the implementation of these methods is rejected, then the rejection will have to be articulate and logical.

This naturally suggests that the future models will be more complex. Is there not a danger that they will become too complex and intricate to be useful? In answer, let us repeat a well-known analogy: a Ph.D. in aeronautical engineering is not needed in order to feel comfortable flying in an aircraft; the benefits of airplane technology are available to the aerodynamically uninformed. MPT can be implemented successfully by nonmathematicians. However, the intricacies of MPT applications, will result in an enormous reliance on computational efficiencies, such as optimization techniques.

The acceptance of computer technology will accelerate a trend which has just begun. The job responsibilities of portfolio managers and security analysts will change. Currently, in most money management firms, the portfolio manager is the client contact, an "assembler" of judgments from several analysts, and the portfolio constructor. We feel that the analysts will become more dominant in their role of undertaking research and forming judgments, although the research process will probably be organized along different lines than at present. The output from the research process will be a number stating the relative valuation of the security in question. The portfolio manager will lose some responsibility for portfolio construction but will become more involved with clients. The portfolio manager's job definition will lay much more stress on setting objectives, understanding the environment (i.e., specifying the covenant information ratio and so on), and conferring with the fund owner on overall economic and investment strategy. We envisage the portfolio managers of today taking on more of the role of investment consultants tomorrow.

The existing organizations for the management of pension funds will be the catalysts for these changes. Institutional investment is a highly competitive business, so that money managers and sponsors depend on attracting the best junior personnel. Typically, these will be graduates from business schools who have been exposed to analytical methods and financial theory. The "token quants" will probably not be token for long.

The need to adapt to rapid developments in investment technology and financial instruments has added excitement to the investment profession. Once one considers the changes that are now taking place, rather than viewing MPT as a fad, one might better ask what part of the investment profession MPT will affect next.

The Future of MPT

MPT, the scientific approach to investing, is likely to become more widespread in the future. There are numerous reasons for this, but the most persuasive for us is the widespread view that the capital markets are (at a minimum) reasonably efficient. It is not easy to form insights that are immensely and consistently profitable. The implication, which is slowly dawning, is that research resources should be allocated for maximum effect.

The sources of information and the quantity and quality of data concerning the financial status of corporations and the vitality of national and regional economies are simply enormous. Regulators are forcing more and more disclosure of accounting and economic activity. All of these data are, at least partially, relevant to the search for superior performance, but this means that the investment process must be efficiently organized to assimilate, analyze, and act on the available information. To us, MPT is the methodology that is required to perform these tasks. It seems inconceivable that unspecified, back-of-the-mind approaches can consistently supply the skills required for the management of large pools of assets, given the complexity of financial instruments and the investment environment.

It also seems inconceivable that the capital asset pricing model will remain preeminent. Risk and return will still be the two main driving forces that affect investors when they select portfolios, but the underlying equilibrium relationship between these forces is unlikely to remain specified in terms of the simple CAPM.

The simple CAPM indicates that a single component of risk is compensated, namely exposure to the market portfolio of all risky assets. All other components of risk are perfectly diversifiable and uncompensated. However, alternative equilibrium models, or capital asset pricing hypotheses, suggest that there may be several factors of risk that deserve compensation. The search for these factors and their rewards promises to be theoretically exciting. However, the end result of this research will be crucial for practitioners since it suggests that the equilibrium values of the various asset classes are functions of their exposures to these risky factors. Hence, the appropriate (equilibrium) portfolio for a given investor will be determined after noting any special investor characteristics, such as tax status, risk aversion, liability distribution, and so on, from the equilibrium rewards to the factors. Since these rewards set the framework for the valuation of assets, they also describe the opportunities for abnormal return.

We feel that this further development of financial theory will increase the need for MPT. The specification of the equilibrium rewards is the framework for effective research and for the design of the normal portfolios. Unfortunately, the CAPM and MPT are synonymous in many people's minds, even though the CAPM taken literally rules out active management. MPT has evolved from adherence to the simple CAPM in the 1960s to its present advanced state, and more intricate and realistic descriptions of equilibrium will add further refinements to our understanding of return and risk and their interaction.

Finally, there will be the impetus from the cheaper processing costs and the increasing availability of mini- and microcomputers. The economics of data processing are such that distributed data processing using client-based minicomputers is the most likely way of the future. With the use of uniform system programs, the main memory of these computers is generally more efficiently utilized. Simpler user languages will allow many practitioners, including practitioners who are not steeped in MPT or quantitative method, to design and monitor portfolios. The disadvantages of time-sharing systems, namely, greater running cost, sluggish or interrupted transmission, and overnight processing to reduce costs, are avoided with the minicomputer system. Such a hands-on system, offering instant feedback to input data, will allow more and smaller portfolios to be optimized. With good systems design, the bookkeeping aspects of the problem could also be handled in a way that should free the portfolio manager's time further.

Summary

At present, the investment community is split among the adherents of MPT, vocal but still in the minority; a camp comprising practitioners who oppose, discredit, and otherwise fight the new methodology as they would any change; and the ubiquitous silent majority. Perhaps the greatest resistance to MPT comes from nonmathematicians who feel intimidated by the mathematical techniques and the Greek letters spouted by MPT promotors—alphas, betas, lambdas, and so on. The need for translation into ordinary financial jargon is still great and largely unmet. But, over time, this will gradually change. Risk and reward are still there, as they always will be.

Not everything can be quantified, but some things can now be measured which previously were not properly measured or were not measured at all. Perhaps the greatest improvement for the financial community as a whole would be realization that investing is by no means a sure thing. If this seems obvious, why, then, do most analysts make point earnings forecasts? Despite the tremendously volatile world that they inhabit, many first-, second-, and lower-team analysts pretend they have a sure thing until they have to account for a demonstrably wrong forecast. Then it's "bad luck," or "everybody else ruined it," or . . . .

Many critics of MPT refuse to apply it on the ground that many of the capital asset pricing assumptions are wrong. Typical are "The markets are not completely efficient." "The S&P 500 is not the market portfolio." "What is alpha anyway?" "I can't explain it in common terms!" "Covariance is too unstable for me to rely on it for optimization!" "The world is changing too fast!" "MPT just doesn't capture enough of the real world!" "At least my approach is based on some relationships I've seen work over time!"

MPT does not pretend to explain or measure everything, but it is a starting point toward defining what can be measured. Beta does provide excellent estimates of the riskiness of a security. Rather than having nothing to define risk, here is at least something with a degree of reliability. This does not mean that better measurements are not possible. In fact, new risk models are now being developed.

When it comes to models, there are well-designed models and poorly designed models, just as in life there are good and poor characterizations of reality. A model is nothing more than a logical rule which attempts to capture the behavior of a phenomenon.

Further Reading

To get some feel for the current level of MPT implementation, we direct interested readers toward *Pensions and Investments* and *Institutional Investor* with the warning that all information in these publications should be subjected to a Bayesian adjustment! References on some of the other material in this chapter include the following.

Directions for Investment Research

Rosenberg, Barr. "The Present State and Future of Investment Research." Address to the 11th Congress of the European Federation of Financial Analysts Societies, The Hague, Netherlands, October 1980. A shortened version of this address appeared as "The Current State and Future of Investment Research," in the *Financial Analysts Journal*, January—February 1982, pp. 43–50.

Bonds and the Analysis of Interest Rates

Houglet, Michel. "The 'Yield Effect' in Government Bonds." *Proceedings of the Seminar on the Analysis of Security Prices,* University of Chicago, May 1980, pp. 267–90.

Rudd, Andrew. "The Application of Modern Portfolio Theory in Bonds." Presented at the Fixed Income Seminar, New York Society of Security Analysts, April 1980.

Senior Liabilities as Options

Rudd, Andrew. "The Valuation of Corporate Liabilities as Options." Presentation at the Berkeley Program in Finance, Silverado, Napa, May 1980.

Read Estate

Hoag, James. "Toward Indices of Real Estate Value and Return." *Journal of Finance,* May 1980, pp. 569–80.

Foreign Securities

Lessard, Donald. "World, Country, and Industry Relationships in Equity Returns: Implications for Risk Reduction through International Diversification." *Financial Analysts Journal,* January–February 1976, pp. 31–38.

Personal Trust

Rosenberg, Barr, and Richard Grinold. "Optimal Investment Decisions for a Simple Trust." BARRA working paper, 1980.

Glossary

Active fee. The portion of the management fee that is in excess of the sum likely to be charged for passive management.

Active frontier. The set of optimal increments to expected return that are obtainable from active management. It is a path, in the shape of a quadratic curve, rising upward from the optimal passive portfolio to higher levels of reward at higher levels of risk.

Active holding. The difference between the total holding in a portfolio and the normal holding in a portfolio. Where the normal holding is not clearly defined, so that the comparison portfolio is the market portfolio, the base from which the active holding is computed is a levered market portfolio with a beta equal to that of the portfolio in question ("equal beta, levered market portfolio").

Active management. The pursuit of transactions with the objective of profiting from competitive information—that is, information which would lose its value if it were in the hands of all market participants. Active management is characterized by a process of continued research to generate superior judgment, which is then reflected in the portfolio by transactions that are held in order to profit from the judgment and that are liquidated when the profit has been earned.

Active reward. The increment in portfolio expected return due to active management. In general, active reward can be earned in four distinct ways: transaction effectiveness, market timing, active positioning with regard to common factors, and specific returns. In each case the reward results from an active position differing from the normal position.

Active risk. The risk arising from active management in excess of the risk that would be incurred at the normal position. The main sources of active risk are market timing, common factor positioning, and specific risk associated with stock selection.

505

Aggressiveness. For a given set of judgments, take larger positive positions in stocks believed to be undervalued and sell off a larger amount of stocks believed to be overvalued. The extent to which active holdings are enlarged to respond to judgment.

Alpha. The "risk-adjusted expected return" or the return in excess of what would be expected from a diversified portfolio with the same systematic risk. When applied to stocks, alpha is essentially synonymous with misvaluation: a stock with a positive alpha is viewed as undervalued relative to other stocks with the same systematic risk, and a stock with a negative alpha is viewed as overvalued relative to other stocks with the same systematic risk. When applied to portfolios, alpha is a description of extraordinary reward obtainable through the portfolio strategy. Here it is synonymous with good active management: a better active manager will have a more positive alpha at a given level of risk.

For expository purposes, alpha is usually expressed as percentage annual return—e.g., 1 percent per annum. For mathematical purposes, alpha is expressed as an adjustment to proportional return (or logarithmic return), again expressed as an annual rate—e.g., 0.01.

Alpha, historical. The difference between the historical performance for a period and what would have been earned with a diversified market portfolio at the same level of systematic risk over that period. Under the simplest procedures, historical alpha is estimated as the constant term in a time series regression of the asset or portfolio return upon the market return.

Alpha, judgmental. The final output of a research process, embodying in a single quantitative measure the degree of under- or overvaluation of stocks. Judgmental alpha is a product of investment research and unique to the individual or organization that produces it. It is derived from a "forecast" of extraordinary return, but it has been adjusted to be the expected value of subsequent extraordinary return. For example, among those stocks that are assigned judgmental alphas of 2 percent, the average performance (when compared to other stocks of the same systematic risk with alphas of zero) should be 2 percent per annum. Thus, the average experienced performance for any category of judgmental alpha should equal the alpha itself. A judgmental alpha is a prediction, not retrospective experience.

Alpha, required. The risk-adjusted expected return required to cause the portfolio holding to be optimal, in view of the risk/reward trade-off. The required alpha is found by solving for the contribution of the holding to portfolio risk and by applying a risk/reward trade-off to find the corresponding alpha. It can be viewed as a translation of portfolio risk exposure into the judgment which warrants that exposure.

Asset allocation. The process of assigning investments across broad categories or sectors of assets. The sectors typically considered include equities, bonds, real estate, and international investments. The output of asset allocation is a set of normal investment proportions in the various sectors. The decision as to individual assets within the sectors is ordinarily not considered in asset allocation, although broad characteristics, such as the normal beta or the normal yield, in sectoral portfolios can be treated as part of asset allocation.

Basis point. A basis point is $1/100$ of 1 percent.

Bayes' law. The rule whereby various independent sources of evidence are combined to obtain an optimal combined estimate or prediction. The rule states that each element of evidence should be weighted inversely to its error variance.

Bayesian adjustment. Named after the Reverend Thomas Bayes, this refers to a statistical procedure in which judgmental data are combined with empirical data. The optimal Bayes estimator is that combination of the individual's prior judgment and the evidence from observations of the process (measurement) which has the smallest mean square error (or error variability) in prediction. A security's judgmental alpha can be viewed as a Bayesian adjustment of the analyst's forecast, and the pension sponsor's forecast of the alpha obtained from a money manager is a Bayesian adjustment of the historical performance of that money manager, with adjustment for other evidence on that money manager which feeds into the judgmental process.

Beta. The systematic risk coefficient which expresses the expected response of asset or portfolio excess return to excess return on a market portfolio. For example, a beta of 1.5 implies that if the excess return on the market portfolio is positive, 1.5 times this positive return can be expected, while if the excess return on the market portfolio is negative, 1.5 times this negative return can be expected. The concept of a beta coefficient can be applied to an asset, to a portfolio, or even to one "market portfolio" when compared to another. Various surrogates for the market portfolio can be used when computing the beta coefficient, and it is now the general practice to use the S&P 500 as a surrogate. For strictly correct definition, the beta coefficient would have to be computed relative to the true portfolio of all assets (both financial and nonfinancial).

The beta coefficient can also be viewed as the regression coefficient of the security return upon the market return.

Beta, fundamental. Predicted systematic risk coefficients (predictive of subsequent response to market return) that are derived, in whole or in part, from the fundamental operating characteristics of a company.

Beta, historical. Historical measure of the response of a company's return to the market return, ordinarily computed as the slope coefficient in a 60-month historical regression.

Beta, long-term. Prediction of the response of a company's return to the market return over a long horizon (five years).

Beta, short-term. Prediction of a systematic risk coefficient in the near future (a horizon of three months, applying to market response over this brief horizon).

Bogey. An unmanaged (informationless) portfolio used as the benchmark in performance measurement. *See also* Comparison portfolio.

Capital asset pricing hypotheses. Relationships between asset characteristics and asset values which can be expected to obtain over the long term in capital markets. The most prominent hypotheses are derived from features of competitive equilibrium in capital markets that can be expected to persist over the very long term. The most important among these are hypotheses that expected security returns will be increasing functions of security features such as systematic risk, taxable yield, smallness of total risk, or negative skewness.

Capital asset pricing model (CAPM). The simplest version states that the expected excess return on securities will be exactly in proportion to their systematic risk coefficient, or beta. The CAPM implies that the total return on any security is equal to the risk-free return, plus the security's beta, times the expected market excess return. Extensions of the capital asset pricing model admit other capital asset pricing hypotheses (*see* Capital asset pricing hypotheses).

Certain equivalent increase in reward (CEIR).   The difference in expected rewards which measures, in units of certain expected reward, the improvement of a superior portfolio over an inferior one. The construct can be extended to take two portfolios of similar but not identical risk and to apply an adjustment for disutility of variance, to convert the portfolio with higher risk to an equivalent portfolio at the lower risk, and then to compute the CEIR as the difference between the expected reward of the equivalent portfolio and the expected reward of the inferior portfolio.

Certainty equivalent excess return (CEER).   The total utility of a risky investment, expressed in terms of units of certain reward. The CEER is the expected reward, which, if it were known with certainty, would give the same satisfaction to the investor as the risky investment in question. The CEER can be viewed as equal to the expected reward on the risky investment, less a deduction for the disutility of the variance of that investment.

Coefficient of determination (R^2).   A statistical term describing the fraction of variance in the dependent variable that can be explained by the independent or explanatory variable(s). The coefficient of determination is a pure number ranging from 0 to 1, with 1 giving perfect explanation. It is often used to describe the fraction of investment risk in portfolios that can be associated with market risk. R^2's for singly managed portfolios typically range from 0.8 up to 1, with a median at about 0.95. For multiply managed pension sponsor portfolios, R^2's presently range from about 0.96 to 1, with a median at about 0.98.

Commingled fund.   An investment fund in which the manager pools the assets of several trust accounts to permit more efficient management and to reduce administrative costs. Also called a *collective investment fund* or a *common fund*.

Common factor.   An element of return that influences many securities and hence is a "common factor" in the returns on those securities. Common factors can be associated with relevant features of stocks that cause them to be exposed. Important features that acquire associated common factors are industry groupings and risk indices. By virtue of their common influence on many stocks, common factors are ingredients in the market return as well as ingredients in the residual returns of the stocks that they influence most.

Common factor, residual.   The residual common factor is equal to the "risk-adjusted" common factor, which is obtained by subtracting from the common factor the expected response of that factor to the market portfolio. It is also the contribution to securities' residual return from the common factor, with the common factor's contribution to the systematic return of securities having been deducted. It is the element of securities' residual return that is in common across securities.

Comparison portfolio.   The portfolio used to define the return against which another portfolio is to be evaluated. Most commonly, it is now the S&P 500. Present developments are leading toward the substitution of better surrogates for the market return and in some cases toward a replacement of the market return by the normal universe or portfolio for the manager.

Confidence region.   A statistical term defining a range of values within which we have a certain degree of confidence that a random variable will fall. The most commonly used region is the 95 percent confidence region, which is such that we can expect 95 percent of values to fall within it. This region approximately spans ±2 standard deviations centered on the mean.

Constraints on holdings.   Accepted restrictions on the magnitude of investment holdings that can be admitted into the portfolio. The most common constraint is the limitation against short-selling, which constrains all holdings to be greater than or equal to zero. For many investors, there are also upper bounds on investment holdings. Occasionally, constraints also apply to minimum and maximum positions in industry groups.

Continuous return (continously compounded return). Another name for the logarithmic return (*see* Logarithmic return).

Core/noncore. Partitioning of funds between a (core) passively managed portfolio which is like an index fund and an actively managed portfolio (noncore). Different clients have different mixtures of these two portfolios, and hence experience combined portfolios with different aggressiveness.

Correlation. A statistical term giving the strength of linear relationship between two random variables. It is a pure number, ranging from -1 to $+1$: $+1$ is a perfect positive linear relationship; -1 is a perfect negative linear relationship; 0 is no linear relationship. For jointly distributed random variables, correlation is often used as a measure of strength of relationship, but it fails when a nonlinear relationship is present.

Covariance. The tendency of different investment returns to have similar outcomes, or to "covary." When two uncertain outcomes are positively related, covariance is positive, and conversely. The magnitude of covariance measures the strength of the common movement. For the special case of a return's covariance with itself, the simplified name of *variance* is used. Covariance can be scaled to obtain the pure number, correlation, that measures the closeness of the relationship without its magnitude.

Covenant information ratio. An agreement between money manager and client as to the expected information ratio (*see* Information ratio) to be produced by the manager. The agreement is intended as a guideline for appropriate behavior on the part of the manager and for appropriate evaluation practice on the part of the client, and in this sense it represents a "covenant."

Cumulative return. The investment return cumulated over a number of periods, ordinarily expressed as a proportional return.

Custodian. A depository of securities for purposes of safekeeping. The custodian may collect income and dividends and do simple reporting on the assets. The custodian does not have fiduciary responsibility.

Dependence-adjustment factor (DAF). A multiplicative factor applied to the expected reward from a money manager to correct for dependence between his own judgmental process and the judgmental processes of other money managers in the client's multiply managed portfolio. If one money manager's judgmental process is entirely independent of the judgmental processes of the others, the adjustment factor will be 1 and no change will occur. Typically, when money managers' judgments are positively interdependent, the dependence-adjustment factor will be less than 1 and will have the effect of scaling down information content. However, peculiar patterns of interdependence can give rise to adjustment factors that are greater than 1 or negative.

Descriptor. A variable describing the individual firm which is computed by a prespecified formula. Approximately 50 descriptors of individual companies are used as a basis for the risk indices and risk predictions in the Fundamental Risk Measurement Service, from which many of the analytical reports in this book were drawn.

Directed trust.   A custodian with the added capability of fiduciary responsibility. The directed trustee typically has investment responsibility for short-term cash reserves.

Discretionary trust.   A trust for whose assets the trustee has investment responsibility.

Distribution, lognormal.   A probability distribution for which the logarithm of the variable is normally distributed (*see* Distribution, normal). The distribution arises when a number of independent random factors are multiplied together, and consequently it is to be expected from a compounding of a series of independent returns.

Distribution, normal.   The familiar bell-shaped curve, which is called the "normal" distribution because it is the distribution that occurs when large numbers of independent factors are added together. It is a symmetrical distribution, with approximately two thirds of all outcomes falling with ±1 standard deviation and approximately 95 percent of all outcomes falling within ±2 standard deviations.

Disutility of variance.   A debit against the desirability or "utility" of an investment which arises from the variability in investment outcomes. Thus, the utility of an investment is reduced by the disutility of its variance.

Disutility-of-variance coefficient.   The coefficient which, when multiplied by the variance of an investment, produces the disutility of that variance. The form of this coefficient is the ratio of the unit of return to a certain number of units of variance. When these units are computed for percentage return, a typical magnitude for the coefficient would be the range of $1/100$—that is, the disutility of 100 units of variance is one unit of expected return.

Diversification.   The reduction in risk that is obtained by investing (positive) wealth in assets which are not perfectly positively correlated. Diversification is the spreading of risk among a number of different investment opportunities. Since the assets are not perfectly correlated, losses of any one asset tend to be offset by gains on other assets. In this manner, the risk of a portfolio may well be less than the average risk of its constituent assets. The measure of diversification is either the R^2 or the residual standard deviation. *See also* Hedging.

Earnings variability.   A risk index. Earnings variability is a weighted average of earnings-per-share variability over time, cash flow variability over time, the dependence of corporate earnings on the economy or "earnings beta," and measures of the unpredictability of earnings, such as the proportion of extraordinary items.

Efficient frontier.   A general term for the set of optimal portfolios at differing levels of reward and variance. Each portfolio on the frontier offers the highest possible expected reward at its level of variance and the lowest possible variance at its level of expected reward. The term is also used for total investment results, the source of which can be decomposed into the efficient frontier from passive management and the active efficient frontier. The total efficient frontier is the "envelope" of combinations of passive and active frontiers. *See also* Passive frontier and Active frontier.

Employee benefit trust.   A trust that holds the assets of a pension, profit-sharing, stock bonus, or thrift plan operated for the benefit of a corporation's employees or a labor union's members.

Equity.   A general term applied to common stock and to other instruments that are highly sensitive to the total value of the firm and hence behave like common stock. The latter category includes warrants and, usually, all convertible senior liabilities, such as preferred stock and convertible bonds. Nonconvertible preferred stock, although technically equity, is sometimes excluded from this group and lumped along with bonds.

ERISA. An acronym for the Employee Retirement Income Security Act of 1974. which set up the Pension Benefit Guaranty Corporation (PBGC) to assure workers that they would receive pension benefits. The act also established federal fiduciary standards to regulate private pension and welfare benefit plans.

Excess return. The return in excess of a risk-free rate. The excess return is computed by subtracting the promised risk-free rate from a security's return.

Expansion path. A series of investment strategies, each of which is optimal according to an external criterion but which differ along some axis, such as aggressiveness or systematic risk. No point on the expansion path is dominated by any other, so that a separate external criterion must be applied to select the optimal point for any particular investor.

Expected return. The average investment return. Expected return is the mean of the probability distribution of investment return.

Expected value. A statistical term, also called the *mean* (*see* Mean).

External information. Information on a process other than observation of the process itself. When applied to the problem of predicting investment performance, external information refers to all information about the skills of the money manager, except the historical performance, which is the direct observation of the past output of the management process. External information is used to supplement historical performance as a basis for predicting future performance.

Extra-market covariance (*XMC*). The element of risk in investment returns arising from common factors net of the market or, in brief, from extra-market factors. *XMC* is one of the four elements of portfolio risk, along with systematic risk, risk from market timing, and specific risk.

Fail float. The cash balance arising when security (particularly purchase) transactions are not completed on the settlement date by the delivery of securities. After a transaction has been made, it must be settled in five business days. Master trusts make the cash available on the fifth day, but if the securities are not delivered, the cash can be invested in a short-term investment fund for at least one day.

Fiduciary. A person who, by acting for another's benefit, holds a legally enforceable position of trust. Defined for legal purposes in Section 3(21)(A) of ERISA.

Financial risk. A risk index. Financial risk measures leverage in the financial structure of a firm, both in terms of the long-term capitalization and in terms of the excess of short-term liabilities over assets. It is a weighted average of descriptors that measure leverage, coverage of fixed charges, the ratio of debt to total assets, current liquidity, and net monetary debt.

FRMSU. An acronym for the Fundamental Risk Measurement Service universe, the aggregate of all companies in the Compustat data base and those other companies in the Interactive Data Corporation (IDC) data base that are of interest to institutional investors. In total, there are about 7,000 companies in the universe. On December 31, 1979, the market value of the FRMSU was $1,247 billion.

Generalized least squares (GLS). Regression method used to obtain the most efficient estimates of model parameters. Conceptually, the weighting can be understood as inverse to the disturbance, or error variance: the greater the error variance, the smaller the weight given to an observation or to a dimension within the observations.

Growth orientation. A risk index. Growth orientation measures the extent to which a company pursues a strategy oriented toward growth (and thus attempts to provide returns to stockholders through the uncertain receipts of future projects rather than the immediate returns of existing operations). The greater the growth orientation of a company, the longer is the duration of the schedule of future payments to stockholders. The growth orientation index is a weighted average of descriptors of the growth rate in total assets, payout, and dividend policy and of the earnings/price ratio, which is an expression by the market of expected earnings growth.

Hedging. The process whereby the risks of several opportunities are largely or completely ("perfect hedge") offset. Hedging requires either that the two opportunities be negatively correlated (gold stocks and brokerage firm stocks or a put option and its underlying security), in which case positive amounts are invested in both opportunities, or that the two opportunities be positively correlated (a call option and its underlying security or two very similar securities), in which case one opportunity is short-sold. Hedging is the offsetting of risk; diversification (*see* Diversification) is the spreading of risk.

Historical performance. A record of past returns on a managed portfolio usually monthly or quarterly, which is usually analyzed in connection with a comparison portfolio. Performance is analyzed for accomplishment (measurement of total return) and evidence of ability (attribution of performance to its causes).

Holdings, investment. The fraction of a portfolio or index in a given asset. For example, a holding of 0.03 corresponds to the investment of 3 percent of the value of the portfolio in that asset. Holdings are usually expressed as percentages for expository purposes. The sum of the holdings in a portfolio is always 1. *See also* Investment proportion.

Immaturity and smallness. A risk index. Immaturity and smallness is primarily a measure of a firm's small size and of its youth. A higher value on the index indicates a smaller and typically younger firm. The index is a weighted average of various measures of size (total assets, capitalization, and market value), the maturity of capital structure (ratios of net to gross plant and of plant to equity), and the age of the firm.

Index fund. A particular passive strategy which attempts to match the return on a market index, usually the S&P 500.

Indifference curve. A line joining all of the situations which are equally satisfying to the investor. An investor's preferences can be described by a collection of indifference curves varying from lower to higher, such that movement from one curve to a higher curve is desirable and movement along a curve is a matter of indifference. One use of the curves is to represent the characteristics of a complicated risky portfolio by the riskless portfolio that is indifferent to it. Another key application is that the slope of the indifference curve, when plotted in mean/variance space, yields the risk/reward trade-off.

Industry grouping. A homogeneous collection of business endeavors. Each company is either assigned to a single principal industry or apportioned across industries according to its activities in various industry segments. Common factors associated with industry groups are an important element in multiple factor risk models. A portfolio's exposure to an industry group, arising from the companies in that group which are held in the portfolio, is a source of common factor exposure. Industry factors are associated with each of the industry groups.

Information coefficient. A measure of the precision in an analyst's forecast. Imprecisely defined in current practice as the coefficient of determination (*see* Coefficient of determination), or its square root, between forecasts and subsequent performance.

Information ratio. The ratio of the expected excess reward for an activity to the standard deviation of that activity. The more positive the ratio is, the more desirable is the activity. Since it is the ratio of a mean to a standard deviation, the information ratio is conceptually related to a t-statistic. An information ratio may also be called a *reward-to-variability ratio*. For active management, the information ratio equals alpha/omega. For passive investment, the information ratio equals (Excess return on the market)/(Standard deviation of market return).

Investment proportion (or **weight** or **holding**). The ratio of the total invested value in an activity to the total value of the portfolio. Such proportions are usually represented as percentages for exposition, but for mathematical applications they are represented by decimal fractions.

Isoreward line (or **contour**). A line joining all portfolios that offer equal total reward. Since the expected return function is linear in portfolio holdings, the isoreward contours are straight lines; hence, they are called isoreward lines. Just as the contours on a topographical map represent lines of equal altitude, and thus represent a three-dimensional surface in two dimensions, isoreward lines can be used to represent a three-dimensional reward surface in two dimensions.

Isovariance contour. Lines that represent the collection of portfolios with constant variance. Since variance is a quadratic function of investment holdings, the variance surface is a conic section and isovariance contours are ellipses. When investment is constrained, the isovariance contour is more complex but retains an elliptical quality.

Levered market portfolio. Any mixture of the risk-free asset and the market portfolio of all risky assets. In fact, when the investment in the market portfolio is between 0 and 100 percent, it is a mixture of the market portfolio and of lending at the risk-free rate. When the investment in the market portfolio is greater than 100 percent, there is true leverage, in the sense that funds borrowed at the risk-free rate are invested in the market portfolio. The beta of the levered market portfolio is equal to the investment fraction in the market portfolio. Hence, a perfectly diversified portfolio at a given level of beta, "the equal-beta levered market portfolio," is obtained as the mixture of the risk-free asset and the market portfolio, with the investment fraction in the market portfolio equal to that beta.

Logarithmic return. The logarithm of the porportional return, or of 1 + the rate of return. Since returns are compounded over time by multiplication, and since multiplication corresponds to addition to logarithms, logarithmic returns are added over time to obtain the cumulative logarithmic return. Where the return is relatively small in magnitude, 100 times the logarithmic return approximates the rate of return on the security. The logarithmic return is also called the *continuously compounded rate of return*.

Long position. An investment holding which is positive. *See also* Short position.

Low valuation and unsuccess. A risk index. This index is a measure of the extent to which the firm has failed to be successful in the past or is now pessimistically valued (low valuation), suggesting expectations of poor success in the future. The index is a weighted average of past growth and earnings per share, recent earnings growth, relative strength, the effective past tax rate, the past return on equity, the book/price ratio, and indicators of very low current earnings and of past dividend cuts.

Management fee.   The fee charged by the money manager for supervision of investment, as distinct from the custodial or trustee fee. The lowest management fee is generally charged for passive management, with higher fees for active management. Each manager's fee schedule generally encourages large pools of money, with a declining fee for each increment of funds added. Aside from the distinction between passive and active management, few, if any, fee schedules now include an increase in cost for greater aggressiveness. However, money managers who charge higher fees are typically more aggressive.

Market capitalization.   The market value of all outstanding shares, whatever their ownership. Thus, a company's closely held shares are included in this count. Market capitalization represents the value of a company's equity to all investors and consequently the portion of a company's value in the total market portfolio.

The difficulty with this definition arises where a company's shares are held by another company whose equities are also included in the market portfolio. If the value of the first company's shares contributes to the value of the second company's shares, the first company's shares will be double-counted. Consequently, for correct definition, market capitalization should exclude shares held by other companies whose common stock is included in the computation of the market portfolio, or equivalently, the value of the shares held by the other companies should be deducted from their market capitalization. From a computational point of view, the latter procedure is simpler.

Market inventory fund.   A method of using the assets of an index fund to save transaction costs in a multiply managed portfolio. Each of the managers is required to offer a trade to the inventory fund before dealing with outside brokers. The inventory fund is rebalanced periodically in the attempt to track the index.

Market portfolio.   The portfolio of all assets other than the risk-free asset. For practical purposes, it seems to be impossible to extend this portfolio far beyond the market portfolio of financial assets, and even here, surrogates that include only a fraction of all financial assets are generally used. Since the market portfolio contains all assets, the weight of each asset in the portfolio is in proportion to its outstanding value, or its market capitalization.

Market variability.   A risk index. Market variability measures the extent to which a security's behavior in the market is indicative of risk. It is a weighted average of descriptors of the variance and covariance of the security with the market portfolio, of market price, and of the extent of share turnover. Another observation of market variability is by way of the implicit option variance, which is solved by analysis of the market price of the option on the security.

Master trust.   A pooling of one sponsor's assets, which may include multiple managers and multiple plans, into a single-trust entity through which the sponsor can fund all of its employee benefit plans and thereby simplify their administration.

Mean.   The value that is to be expected, on average. Among many repetitions or trials of a random process, this will be the average value.

Mean/variance ratio.   The ratio of the mean expected excess return on an element of investment to the variance of return. The conditions for optimization of a portfolio across several investment opportunities take the form that mean/variance ratios be equal, or strongly related.

Median.   A statistical term denoting the value of a random variable, such that 50 percent of all possible values lie above this value and 50 percent lie below.

Mode.   A statistical term denoting the most likely value of a random variable. For the normal distribution, the mean, median, and mode coincide; for asymmetric distributions, they may differ.

Modern portfolio theory.   The theory of portfolio optimization which accepts the risk/reward trade-off for total portfolio return as the crucial criterion. Derived from Markowitz's pioneering application of statistical decision theory to portfolio problems, optimization techniques and related analysis have been increasingly applied to investments.

Multiple factor model.   A specification for the return process for securities. This model states that the rate of return on any security is equal to the weighted sum of the rates of return on a set of common factors, plus the specific return on the security, where the weights measure the exposures (or sensitivity) of the security to the factors. These exposures are identified with the microeconomic characteristics, or descriptors (*see* Descriptor), of the firms.

Several simplifications of this model have been used historically. If there is only one factor, it becomes a *single-factor model;* if this one factor is identified with an index, it is called a *single-index model;* if the single factor is identified with the market factor, it becomes the *market model.* Depending on the statistical specification, some of these could become a *diagonal model,* which simply indicates that the covariance matrix between security returns is (or can easily be transformed into) a diagonal matrix.

Multiple management.   The common practice among pension sponsors with larger portfolios of apportioning the funds among several managers, each responsible for one component. Multiple management is a form of decentralized decision making whereby the sponsor provides certain central guidelines and each manager then has decentralized responsibility for acting within them.

Normal aggregate portfolio.   The aggregate portfolio that a pension sponsor determines would be optimal over the long run in the absence of special information. Timely, superior information generated in the course of active management would cause holdings to deviate from this normal position, and as the nature of special information averages out over time, these deviations can be expected to average to zero. Hence, the central tendency of actively managed portfolios over the long run should equal the normal aggregate. The normal aggregate is established with long-run considerations in mind as a portfolio that would be ideal in view of equilibrium rewards in the capital markets that are consistent with capital asset pricing hypotheses accepted by the investor. The extent to which risk is taken in the normal aggregate portfolio reflects the risk/reward trade-off of the investor.

Normal portfolio (normal universe).   The average position or portfolio to be expected from a given manager over a long horizon. A managed portfolio differs from the normal portfolio as a consequence of active present positions based on special information. The normal portfolio can often be approximated by taking the capitalization-weighted universe of common stocks followed by the manager (the normal universe). Sometimes, however, the manager will follow this universe but establish normal targets with respect to industries and risk indices that differ from the capitalization-weighted average characteristics of the universe. In this case, it is best to establish the normal portfolio by averages of these target values.

NYSE. An abbreviation for the universe of all common stocks listed on the New York Stock Exchange. The NYSE contains more than 1,500 securities, weighted in proportion to market capitalization. On December 31, 1979, the market value of all companies in the NYSE was $963 billion.

Omega. The last letter in the Greek alphabet, symbolized by what looks like a curly w, is used as a symbol for the residual standard deviation of portfolio return, or, more generally, the standard deviation of active return.

Optimal passive portfolio. This is the equilibrium passive investment vehicle. Also called the *normal portfolio* or the *normal aggregate portfolio* (*see* Normal aggregate portfolios, Normal portfolio).

Optimization. The best solution among all the solutions available for consideration. Constraints on the investment problem limit the region of solutions that are considered, and the objective function for the problem, by capturing the investor's goals correctly, provides a criterion for comparing solutions to find the better ones. The optimal solution is that solution among those admissible for consideration which has the highest value of the objective function.

The first-order conditions for optimality express the trade-offs between alternative portfolio characteristics, the trade-offs that obtain at the optimum solution.

Ordinary least squares (OLS). The most common regression method, used to compute parameter values such that the squared differences between data values and fitted values are minimized. *See also* Generalized least squares.

Passive frontier. The efficient frontier composed solely from passive (information-less) management. In the case where the optimal passive portfolio is a levered market portfolio, the passive frontier is composed of different mixtures of the risk-free asset and the market portfolio.

Passive management. Any investment practice that achieves a stated investment goal, on the assumption that security returns are at equilibrium levels, so that disclosure of the assumption will not change expected security returns. In its narrow usage, the term *passive management* refers to the maintenance of index funds whose goal is to closely match the return on a fixed index. In this connection, asset management involves the control of portfolio holdings and effective transaction procedures so as to assure that the portfolio return will be near to the index return. In a more general sense, passive management can be applied to any management procedure that does not generate superior information (information that is, by nature, competitive and that would lose its value if it were possessed by others), so that disclosure of the investment procedure in no way reduces its validity. An example of the wider definition of passive management would be a yield-tilted portfolio with an unchanging objective.

Performance attribution. The process of attributing portfolio returns to causes. Among the causes are the normal position for the portfolio, as established by the owner of funds or the manager, as well as various active strategies, including market timing, common factor exposure, and asset selection. Performance attribution serves as a function ancillary to the prediction of future performance, inasmuch as it decomposes past performance into separate components that can be analyzed and compared with the claims of the manager.

Performance measurement. The process of computing experienced performance in a portfolio in order to measure the manager's contribution. The computation of portfolio return should allow for adjustments reflecting contributions and withdrawals by the owner of funds, and for a procedure to compute the time-weighted rate of return in view of these portfolio flows. In addition, the treatment of dividends and coupons should account for appropriate reinvestment.

Prior judgment. A term (from Bayesian statistics) referring to the expectations of the analyst before confronting the data on the case in question. In the context of performance prediction, prior judgment is drawn from the recognition that the money management business is competitive, so that the average money manager, by an accounting identity, earns the average return to all managed portfolios, less the average management fee. Prior judgment is further implemented by the analyst's belief, as to the range of skills across the population of money managers. Each money manager subsequently encountered is viewed at first from this prior perspective, and Bayesian modification leads to a posterior appraisal of abilities which uses subsequent evidence.

R^2. The square of the multiple correlation coefficient. Another name for the *coefficient of determination* (*see* Coefficient of determination).

Rate of return. The change in value of the investment, which includes capital appreciation (or loss) plus cash yield, divided by the initial value. Rate of return is usually expressed, for expository purposes, as a percentage annual rate, but for mathematical purposes it is expressed as a decimal fraction (e.g., 0.07 for a 7 percent return).

Regression. *See* Generalized least squares and Ordinary least squares.

Residual common factor. *See* Common factors, residual.

Residual return. The component of return that is uncorrelated with the return on the market portfolio (or the comparison portfolio). Residual return is also called *unsystematic* or *diversifiable* return. All components of active management, except market timing, contribute to residual return at one point in time.

Residual risk. The component of risk associated with residual return. Residual risk is composed of extra-market covariance and specific risk.

Return. The ratio of the value of an investment at the end of a period, plus any payouts during the period, divided by the initial value. Return is (depending on the length of the period) a number close to 1.0 and represents one plus the rate of return. *See* Rate of return.

Reward-to-variability ratio (RVR). Another name for the information ratio (*see* Information ratio).

Reward/variance. Another name for the mean/variance ratio (*see* Mean-variance ratio), equal to the ratio of expected excess return to variance of return.

Risk. The uncertainty of investment outcomes. Technically, the term *risk* is used to define all uncertainty about the mean outcome, including both upside and downside possibilities. Thus, in contrast to the layperson, who would think of the downside outcome as risk and of the upside outcome as potential, a measure of total variability in both directions is typically used to summarize risk. The more intuitive concept for risk measurement is the standard deviation of the distribution, a natural measure of spread. Variance, the square of the standard deviation, must be used in comparing independent elements of risk.

Risk-acceptance parameter (RAP). The extent to which an investor is ready to accept risk in pursuit of expected reward, also called the risk-tolerance parameter. A larger value for the parameter implies an investor who will take greater risks in pursuit of the same opportunity. Thus, an investor with a higher risk-acceptance parameter will ordinarily invest a larger fraction of the portfolio in equities, as opposed to less risky alternatives such as bonds, than will an investor with a lower risk-acceptance parameter.

Risk-free return (risk-free rate).   The certain return promised on the purely "risk-free" investment. Conceptually, such an investment should have guaranteed purchasing power at its termination. In practice, the construct is usually defined by the rate of return on U.S. Treasury securities for the investment period. These securities have no risk in nominal returns but substantial risk in real purchasing power.

Risk index.   A variable computed for each asset, such that the variable determines the asset's exposure to a common factor. Risk indices include market variability, earnings variability, low valuation and unsuccess, immaturity and smallness, growth orientation, and financial risk. In each case, a higher value of the index implies a company that is more strongly exposed to the common factor.

Risk/reward trade-off.   The point where the added benefit from a larger position is just offset by the increased risk. Thus, at the optimum position, a trade-off between the contribution to reward and the contribution to risk from increased pursuit applies. At optimum, the same trade-off will apply for all investment opportunities, unless other investment objectives intervene.

S&P 500.   An index of 500 common stocks, maintained by Standard & Poor's Corporation, which is commonly used as a comparison portfolio. The securities in the index are changed from time to time so as to maintain an emphasis on large and successful companies and to keep appropriate representation of a number of industry groups. On December 31, 1979, the market value of the 500 stocks was $716 billion.

Sector portfolio.   A representative portfolio for a group of assets that combine to make up a sector. For example, the S&P 500, or some other equity universe, might be a representative portfolio for the equity sector. Thus, the term *sector* is a more precise definition of the misnomer *market,* which is often used to define the sector portfolio for equities as the market portfolio. Sector portfolios can also be defined for other asset categories such as bonds and real estate.

Security depository.   A specialized custodian where securities certificates are deposited and transferred by bookkeeping entry.

Selectivity (stock selection).   The pursuit of active holdings in individual stocks, as distinct from market timing. Under this definition, selectivity would include both common factor positioning and positioning with regard to individual specific returns. We generally tend to use selectivity, under the name *stock selection* or *stock picking,* as an intuitively clear reference to positioning with regard to specific returns only, reserving the term *common factor positioning* for exposure to common factors.

Sharpe ratio.   The square of the information ratio, equal to the squared mean excess return divided by the variance of return. When an investment portfolio is constructed over a wide range of independent opportunities, the Sharpe ratio for the optimum total portfolio is the sum of the Sharpe ratios for the separate opportunities. Thus, the Sharpe ratio, although much less intuitive than the information ratio, is used in determining the benefit obtained from combining separate opportunities.

Short position (short-sell).   A negative investment holding. Institutional investors (with the exception of certain mutual funds) are prevented from taking short positions. Typically, the closest these investors can get to a short position is to write call options.

Short-term investment fund (STIF).   A cash management tool designed to maximize income to a master trust. Its principal use is in the daily investment of dividends and fail float.

Significance (statistical significance).   A statistical term used to suggest that a hypothesis is importantly confirmed (or, more properly, that the opposite hypothesis is importantly denied) by data. The usual criterion for statistical significance is that there is only a 5 percent (or 1 percent) chance that the result could have arisen by chance if the opposite hypothesis were true. For example, abnormal performance is said to be significant when there is only this very small probability that the performance could have arisen by chance if the true hypothesis were that no skill was present.

Simulation.   The procedure in which a model of a process is built and then operated, so that the characteristics of the true process can be described by the characteristics of the operating model.

Simulation, stochastic.   The special form of simulation required when some of the variables in the model are random (stochastic). In this case, simulation usually requires (particularly when the model is nonlinear) that the model be operated many times, each time using one realization of the possible values of the random variables. The frequency distribution of the model outcomes is then used to approximate the true probability distribution of the process.

Specific returns.   Returns that are specific to a company and are uncorrelated (or negligibly correlated) with the specific returns on other companies. Specific returns are also called "unique," "idiosyncratic" or "independent" returns. The risk and reward arising from these specific company factors are also called *specific risk* and *specific reward.*

Standard deviation.   A statistical term which measures the spread or variability of a probability distribution. The standard deviation is the square root of variance. Its intuitive meaning is best seen in a simple, symmetrical distribution, such as the normal distribution, where approximately two thirds of all outcomes fall within ±1 standard deviation of the mean, approximately 95 percent of all outcomes fall within ±2 standard deviations, and approximately 99 percent of all outcomes fall within ±2.5 standard deviations. The standard deviation of return—or, more properly, of the logarithm of return, which is approximately symmetrically distributed—is very widely used as a measure of risk for portfolio investments.

Standard error.   A statistical term defined as the standard deviation of error in an estimate. The error in the estimate arises from disturbances in the data unrelated to the true process. The standard error measures the degree of uncertainty in the estimate of the true process that is caused by the presence of these disturbances. It can be computed, knowing the nature of the data and inferring the amount of uncertainty from the scatter of actual data about the fitted model. One of the important principles of statistical estimation is that attached to every estimate should be a standard error that gives the accuracy of the estimate. When comparing alternative modes of estimation, the one with the lower standard error is the more statistically efficient and is preferred.

Standardization.   The scaling of descriptors and risk indices. Standardization involves setting the zero point and the scale of measurement for the variable. An example might be taken from temperature, where the centigrade scale is standardized by setting zero at the freezing point of water and establishing the scale (the centigrade degree) so that there are 100 units between the freezing point of water and the boiling point of water. Standardization for risk indices and descriptors sets the zero value at the capitalization-weighted mean of the companies in the universe and sets the scale so that one unit equals one cross-sectional standard deviation of that variable among the 1,000 largest firms.

Systematic.   The component of return that is associated with the broad-based market or sector portfolio. Also, the reward expected from the market portfolio and the risk of that reward are referred to as *systematic reward* and *systematic risk*. More generally, the risk and reward of any asset that can be associated with that asset's exposure to the market are termed *systematic*. Systematic reward generally refers to the excess return, rather than the total return, associated with the market.

Systematic frontier.   The reward/risk opportunities from investment in the market portfolio. When unlimited borrowing at the risk-free rate is available, the systematic frontier is a simple quadratic curve, beginning with zero risk at the risk-free asset. When borrowing is precluded, it is a simple quadratic curve through to the market portfolio and tails off thereafter, as the higher-beta strategies can only be obtained by imperfectly diversified portfolios that add residual risk. *See also* Passive frontier.

Systematic portfolio.   The portfolio which defines systematic risk and relative to which betas are estimated. *See also* Sector portfolio.

Transaction costs.   The costs incurred for a portfolio when securities are changed for other securities. Transaction costs are deducted from the value of the portfolio directly, rather than paid as fees to the money manager. These costs arise from three sources: (1) commissions and taxes paid directly in cash; (2) the typical "dealer's spread" (or one half of this amount) earned by a dealer, if any, who acts as an intermediary between buyer and seller; and (3) the net advantage or disadvantage earned by giving or receiving accommodation to the person on the other side of the trade. The third component averages out to zero across all trades, but it may be positive or negative, depending on the extent to which a trader, acting urgently, moves the market against himself.

Trust.   A fiduciary relationship in which the owner of property transfers legal title to a trustee that keeps or uses the property for the benefit of another person, the beneficiary. The creator of the trust may or may not be the beneficiary or trustee. Moreover, the beneficiaries may be of several classes—for instance, those who receive the income from the property ("income beneficiaries") or those who receive the proceeds from the final distribution of the trust ("remaindermen").

Trust instrument.   A written document setting forth the terms of the trust.

Trustee.   An individual or institution (corporate trustee) that holds legal title to a property and administers it for the beneficiary. ERISA provides that every employee benefit plan shall be managed consistent with a trust instrument which specifies a "named fiduciary" who has the ultimate authority for the plan. Plan trustees, who have exclusive authority and discretion over the management of the fund's assets, are named in the trust instrument or appointed by the named fiduciary.

t-statistic.   A statistical term for the difference between a random variable and its mean, divided by the standard deviation of the random variable. When the random variable is estimated from a population of n observations and the standard deviation is estimated from the residual variability of that population, the resulting ratio has a well-known distribution called the t-distribution. Consequently, the t-statistic can be used to do a test of whether the random variable differs significantly from the hypothesized mean. Where the number of observations, n, is greater than 30, the distribution is quite close to the normal distribution. When using a t-statistic for skill or information content, we are looking for large positive values of the statistic which urge us to reject the null hypothesis that no skill or information is present (that the mean is zero).

Universe. The list of all assets eligible for consideration for inclusion in a portfolio. At any time, some assets in the universe may be temporarily ruled out because they are currently viewed as overvalued. However, the universe should contain all of those securities that might be considered for inclusion in the near term if their prices move to such an extent that they become undervalued. Sometimes the term *universe* is also used to define the normal position of a money manager, equating his normal holding with the capitalization-weighted average of the securities in his universe or followed list.

Unsystematic return. An alternative name for residual return, that part of return which is not associated with the market.

Utility. A measure of the overall desirability or goodness of a person's situation. In the theory of finance, the term *utility* is used to define the desirability of a risky series of outcomes. The utility (or expected utility) of a set of risky outcomes is assumed to measure its goodness, so that a package with higher utility is always perferred to one with lower utility. In portfolio theory, utility is almost always defined by a function of the mean and variance of portfolio outcomes, which is then called a mean/variance utility function. The further assumption that the utility function is linear in its two arguments (mean and variance) results in a linear mean/variance utility function, LMVU.

Value relative. The ratio of ending value to the beginning value. Sometimes also called a *wealth-relative*.

Variable aggressiveness. *See* Aggressiveness.

Variance. A statistical term for the variability of a random variable about its mean. The variance is defined as the expected squared deviation of the random variable from its mean—that is, the average squared distance between the mean value and the actually observed value of the random variable. When a portfolio includes several independent elements of risk, the variance of the total arises as a summation of the variances of the separate components.

Yield. The return on a security or portfolio in the form of cash payments. Most yield comes from dividends on equities, coupons on bonds, or interest on mortgages. In general, yield is defined in terms of the component of return that is taxable as ordinary income. Consequently, since the capital gain on a Treasury bill or other discount note is viewed for tax purposes as a form of interest, it is also included in the definition of yield. Yield is usually described, for expository purposes, in percentage terms (e.g., 7 percent per annum), but for mathematical purposes it is expressed as a decimal fraction (e.g., 0.07).

Index